Public Opinion

Third Edition

To my parents, Dale and Janice Clawson, for all their love, laughter, and babysitting.

To my mother, Rachel Oxley, whose encouragement and optimism never wavered, and to my entire family for supporting my endeavors.

Public Opinion
Democratic Ideals, Democratic Practice

Third Edition

Rosalee A. Clawson
Purdue University

Zoe M. Oxley
Union College

 |

For information:

CQ Press
2455 Teller Road
Thousand Oaks, California 91320
E-mail: order@sagepub.com

SAGE Publications Ltd.
1 Oliver's Yard
55 City Road
London, EC1Y 1SP
United Kingdom

SAGE Publications India Pvt. Ltd.
B 1/I 1 Mohan Cooperative Industrial Area
Mathura Road, New Delhi 110 044
India

SAGE Publications Asia-Pacific Pte. Ltd.
3 Church Street
#10-04 Samsung Hub
Singapore 049483

Printed in the United States of America

Library of Congress Cataloging-in-Publication Data

Names: Clawson, Rosalee A. | Oxley, Zoe M.

Title: Public opinion: democratic ideals, democratic practice / Rosalee A. Clawson, Zoe M. Oxley.

Description: Third edition. | Washington, D.C. : CQ Press, 2016. | Includes bibliographical references and index.

Identifiers: LCCN 2015051476 | ISBN 9781506323312 (pbk. : alk. paper)

Subjects: LCSH: Democracy. | Public opinion. | Political socialization. | Mass media and public opinion.

Classification: LCC JC423 .C598 2016 | DDC 321.8—dc23
LC record available at http://lccn.loc.gov/2015051476

This book is printed on acid-free paper.

Acquisitions Editor: Michael Kerns
Editorial Assistant: Zachary Hoskins
Production Editor: Kelly DeRosa
Copy Editor: Mark Bast
Typesetter: Hurix Systems Pvt. Ltd
Proofreader: Sarah J. Duffy
Indexer: Mary Mortensen
Cover Designer: Anupama Krishnan
Marketing Manager: Amy Whitaker

Certified Chain of Custody
Promoting Sustainable Forestry
www.sfiprogram.org
SFI-01268

SFI label applies to text stock

17 18 19 20 10 9 8 7 6 5 4 3 2

Brief Contents

Contents

Tables, Figures, and Features

Tables

Figures

Boxes

Public Opinion in Comparative Perspective

Preface

As we write this preface in the fall of 2015, campaigning for the 2016 Democratic and Republican presidential nominations is well underway. Candidates are highlighting a range of issues, including immigration, inequality, health care, combating ISIS, same-sex marriage, and abortion. Unlike the 2012 contest, which saw the reelection of President Barack Obama, the economy is not dominating but rather is competing with other issues for the candidates' focus. Two women are running for president—one from each party—and their presence has at times brought gender dynamics to the fore. Race has not been a frequent topic of discussion on the campaign trail, despite the fact that, by effective use of social media to draw public attention to the issue, race relations and tensions were recently thrust into the spotlight in the wake of police shootings of unarmed black men and women. Ethnicity, on the other hand, has been a highly charged campaign issue, at least on the Republican side as candidates have used the phrase "anchor babies" and referred to Latino immigrants as rapists and criminals. Public dissatisfaction with politics as usual, although nothing new, is fueling support for outsider candidates, such as Republicans Donald Trump, Carly Fiorina, and Ben Carson. Indeed, in the face of deeper elite partisan polarization, legislative gridlock, and antagonistic rhetoric on the airwaves and online, public trust in government and support for political institutions have reached record lows in recent years.

These trends reflect and have implications for U.S. public opinion. As a result, we have tried to capture the importance and effects of developments such as these in this third edition. This edition also contains new or expanded sections on the topics of partisanship, polarization, the Millennial generation, social media, same-sex marriage, and civil liberties in the post-9/11 era. We have incorporated exciting and important new scholarship on media effects, the opinion-policy relationship, personality, and race-coded political issues. All the while, we maintain a focus on enduring questions in the study of public opinion.

Our pedagogical goals for this edition remain the same. We want students to grasp how fascinating and important it is to study politics generally and public opinion more specifically. What better way is there to attain that goal, we think, than to discuss public opinion in the context of democratic thought? After all, it is the particular salience of public opinion within a democracy that makes its study so vital and interesting. To that end, we situate the field's empirical research within a normative framework, specifically theories of democracy, and focus on especially important and revealing studies rather than tediously summarizing every available piece of research. We organize the text into sections, each of which poses a normative question that is significant for democratic theory: What should be the relationship between citizens and their government? What should be the role of citizens in a democracy? Are citizens' opinions pliable? Do citizens organize their political thinking? Do they demonstrate an understanding of and commitment to the democratic "basics"—that is, are they knowledgeable? Interested? Attentive? Do they support civil rights and civil liberties? The chapters in each section present evidence to help students answer the question at hand, giving them both the content and context of public opinion. This organization encourages students to understand and interpret the empirical evidence in light of normative democratic theories, thus enhancing their critical analysis skills.

We want students to appreciate the thrill of conducting research and producing knowledge and to learn that conclusions about public opinion emerge from original scholarship on the topic. Yet we also want them to understand that no one piece of research is perfect and that the ability to evaluate the strengths and weaknesses of a piece of research is a vital skill. So we devote attention to explaining specific studies in some depth throughout the text. Rather than presenting only the conclusions that are drawn from a study, this approach lets students see how those conclusions were reached, exposes them in a fairly organic way to the range of research methods used in the study of public opinion, and illustrates how the choice of method influences the conclusions that researchers draw. We thus use an "embedded" research methods approach throughout the book rather than consigning methods to one stand-alone chapter. In addition, we provide an Appendix to Chapter 1 that encapsulates the basic information students need about key public opinion methods.

This book includes other important pedagogical features. We focus heavily on American public opinion, but Chapters 2–12 contain feature boxes called "Public Opinion in Comparative Perspective" that highlight public opinion issues in a variety of countries and serve to deepen students' understandings of American public opinion. A wealth of data is presented in more than eighty tables and figures throughout the book to help students grasp important research findings. Key concepts appear in bold in each chapter and are listed at the end of each chapter. The key concepts are also defined in the Glossary at the end of the book. Each chapter also contains a list of suggested sources for further reading. Brief explanatory annotations are provided with each suggested source to guide students as they delve deeper into a topic.

ACKNOWLEDGMENTS

With each edition of this book, we find we require assistance from fewer people as we revise. Having said this, the help we did receive was extremely valuable. Rosie's Human Basis of Politics students and Zoe's Public Opinion students provided useful feedback on the book, most especially pointing out when material was not crystal clear or organized well enough. For thoughtfully reviewing chapters for this edition, often on short notice, we thank Bas van Doorn, Walter Schostak, and Ryan Whelpley. Since the publication of the first edition, we have been approached by many professors who have used the textbook in their classes. We were heartened to hear their (mostly!) positive comments, were happy to learn we were on the right track with our approach, and welcomed their suggestions for areas in need of improvement.

Everyone we worked with at CQ Press was supportive, professional, and friendly, as had been the case with our previous books. We especially thank Sarah Calabi for her enthusiasm for the project and guidance. Elise Frasier and Zachary Hoskins carefully and efficiently managed the submission of our chapters as well as the preparation of material for publication. It was a joy to work with Elise again. She was supportive and cheerful throughout, even as we kept missing our deadlines. She even drafted a particularly challenging figure for us, freeing us up to concentrate on writing. For the care and professionalism with which he copyedited this edition, we thank Mark Bast. As our production editor, Kelly DeRosa shepherded the book through the final prepublication stages with ease. We also thank Elaine Dunn for her diligent and speedy copyediting on the first edition. Her initial feedback continues to shape our work. We worked closely with others at CQ on earlier editions of the book. For their never-ending encouragement and wonderful advice, we thank Brenda Carter, James Headley, and, most especially, Charisse Kiino.

We also thank the professors that CQ Press commissioned to review the book as we were preparing to revise it for the third edition. Their feedback was extremely helpful. They include Gar Culbert, Cal State–Los Angeles; Mike Schmierbach, Penn State University; Andrea M. Quenette, University of Kansas; Adam Schiffer, Texas Christian University; and Erin Cassese, West Virginia University. We would be remiss if we did not acknowledge the invaluable guidance provided by the faculty who reviewed the manuscript for our first and second editions, including Scott Basinger, Stony Brook University; Mark Brewer, University of Maine; John Bruce, University of Mississippi; Johanna Dunaway, Louisiana State University; Howard Gold, Smith College; Paul Goren, University of Minnesota; Richard Hofstetter, San Diego State University; Ted Jelen, University of Nevada–Las Vegas; Mary Fran T. Malone, University of New Hampshire; James Monogan, University of Georgia; Kimberley Nalder, CSU-Sacramento; Tom Nelson, Ohio State University; Shayla Nunnally, University of Connecticut; Kurt Pyle,

Michigan State University; Robert Y. Shapiro, Columbia University; and Matt Wilson, Southern Methodist University.

Along with these CQ-commissioned reviewers, many others provided valuable and specific feedback on material for prior editions. Their suggestions then continued to shape this third edition of the book. For that, we thank Ben Bauer, George Bizer, Richard Fox, Cary Funk, Ewa Golebiowska, Mike Grady, Jennifer Jerit, Suzanne Parker, Evan Reid, Keith Shimko, Jeremy Zilber, John Zumbrunnen, and, most especially, Janice Clawson. For prior editions, we also received all manner of help from many others, including Carol Cichy, Michelle Conwell, David Hayes, Lisa Howell, Katsuo Nishikawa, Andrea Olive, Bill Shaffer, and Helen Willis. We must also mention our many Ohio State friends, who have supported and encouraged us throughout. John Clark, Larry Baum, and Staci Rhine, in particular, have shared their suggestions and wisdom along the way. Finally, we will always owe a debt of gratitude to our graduate school advisers—Paul Allen Beck, Thomas Nelson, and Katherine Tate—and to our undergraduate mentors—Janet Martin and Bruce Stinebrickner. Bruce Stinebrickner also gave us helpful feedback on Chapter 1, which strengthened that chapter.

Although it does not quite take a village to raise our children, we have needed help from many to care for our sons. Knowing that they were in the hands of loving and responsible caregivers and friends enabled us to write without worry. For this, Zoe thanks Anna Ott, Samantha Couture, Heather Hutchison, and a long list of former and current Union College students. Rosie thanks Pauline Wein, the wonderful staff at the Patty Jischke Early Care and Education Center, the dedicated teachers at New Community School, numerous coaches, and most especially her parents, Dale and Janice Clawson, who are always willing to keep their grandson for days on end. Rosie also thanks Lori Norris and Sharon Phillips for their assistance with household matters.

Finally, we owe special thanks to our families. We were both raised by parents who placed priority on education and who encouraged us to pursue whatever channels most interested us. Their faith that we would succeed in our chosen career paths provided us with the confidence to try to do just that. Sadly, Zoe's mother passed away before this book was first completed. She was very pleased to learn that we were writing a book, and we know that she would have been proud to read it. When writing the first edition, Rosie's husband was deployed much of the time. He was around for most of the second and third revisions, although Rosie is quite sure there were times he would have preferred Iraq or Afghanistan to yet another conversation about public opinion. When he's not around (and even when he is), Rosie depends heavily on her family—a big thanks to Dale and Janice Clawson; Tammy, Mike, Troy, and Jared Harter; Jill, Scott, Liv, and Sadie Castleman; and her Cleveland cousins. Our sons Alonzo and Owen bring us tremendous joy. Over the years, they have developed many of their own opinions, most of which we welcome. We are thrilled to say they enjoy watching the presidential debates with us. We are fortunate to have very supportive husbands. Des and Dale not only enjoy talking about politics and have useful computer skills that we have put to good use, but they also do a disproportionate share of the household and parenting duties when we are immersed in writing. We don't know how we got to be so lucky.

CQ Press, an imprint of SAGE, is the leading publisher of books, periodicals, and electronic products on American government and international affairs. CQ Press consistently ranks among the top commercial publishers in terms of quality, as evidenced by the numerous awards its products have won over the years. CQ Press owes its existence to Nelson Poynter, former publisher of the *St. Petersburg Times,* and his wife Henrietta, with whom he founded Congressional Quarterly in 1945. Poynter established CQ with the mission of promoting democracy through education and in 1975 founded the Modern Media Institute, renamed The Poynter Institute for Media Studies after his death. The Poynter Institute (*www.poynter .org*) is a nonprofit organization dedicated to training journalists and media leaders.

In 2008, CQ Press was acquired by SAGE, a leading international publisher of journals, books, and electronic media for academic, educational, and professional markets. Since 1965, SAGE has helped inform and educate a global community of scholars, practitioners, researchers, and students spanning a wide range of subject areas, including business, humanities, social sciences, and science, technology, and medicine. A privately owned corporation, SAGE has offices in Los Angeles, London, New Delhi, and Singapore, in addition to the Washington DC office of CQ Press.

PART I

What Should the Role of Citizens Be in a Democratic Society?

CHAPTER 1

Public Opinion in a Democracy

BETWEEN THE MEMORIAL DAY and July 4th holidays in 2015, President Barack Obama made a number of speeches that referenced American public opinion. On the morning that the Supreme Court's decision legalizing same-sex marriage was released, he stated that that decision "affirms what millions of Americans already believe in their hearts: When all Americans are treated as equal we are all more free."[1] While acknowledging in these remarks that some Americans oppose marriage equality, he also emphasized that, overall, the public had shifted toward supporting same-sex marriage in a relatively short period of time. Two days earlier, at an event commemorating LGBT Pride Month, President Obama went a bit further, not only labeling the change in Americans' opinions as "incredible" but also implying that the public's change of view had encouraged officials to change as well. "A decade ago, politicians ran against LGBT rights. Today, they're running towards them," he said, to applause from the audience.[2]

Over and over again, the president's comments that summer suggested that public opinion matters, that what the public thinks about political and social issues is important. He, for example, encouraged the public to express their views to policymakers, even stating during a discussion about health care in Tennessee "that elected officials respond to public opinion."[3] At other times, President Obama implored officials to heed the public's views, such as when he called on members of Congress to "listen to the American people['s]" support for further engagement with Cuba and lift the Cuban embargo.[4] His most detailed comments about the potential of public opinion were delivered two days after nine African Americans were shot and killed in the Emanuel African Methodist Episcopal Church in Charleston, South Carolina. While acknowledging the difficulty of passing gun control legislation in Congress, even in the face of other recent mass shootings, President Obama nonetheless outlined a path toward changing the national gun laws, one focused squarely on the public:

> We need a change in attitudes among everybody—lawful gun owners, those who are unfamiliar with guns. We have to have a conversation about it and fix this. And ultimately, Congress acts when the public insists on

action. . . . We've got to shift how we think about this issue. And we have the capacity to change, but we have to feel a sense of urgency about it. We, as a people, have got to change. That's how we honor those families. That's how we honor the families in Newtown. That's how we honor the families in Aurora.[5]

As these examples illustrate, in a democracy, such as the United States, we expect the public to have a role in governmental decision making. Yet the precise role that citizens should play in a democracy has been argued about for centuries. Whether the public actually can and really does live up to democratic expectations is also a debatable topic. In the pages that follow, we explore the normative issues related to how the public ought to function in a democracy. Throughout this book, we review empirical studies of public opinion that describe how the public does function in America. We then link these studies back to the normative theories of how citizens should behave in a democracy. Focusing on public opinion from these two angles will, we hope, provide you with a broad understanding of this important topic.

THEORIES OF DEMOCRACY

A simple definition of *democracy* is "rule by the people." What exactly, however, does rule by the people mean? Answering this and related questions about democracy is neither easy nor straightforward. In fact, many people across many centuries have devoted their lives to examining democracy and delineating the proper characteristics of a democracy. **Democratic theory** is "the branch of scholarship that specializes in elucidating, developing, and defining the meaning of democracy."[6] Among other topics, democratic theorists deliberate over how the people should rule in a democracy (by voting directly on all laws or by electing representatives for this task) as well as who should qualify as a democratic citizen (all adults, only those who are educated, or some other group). Democratic theorists also focus on citizens' ruling capabilities and the role of the public in a democracy, as indicated by the following overview of major democratic theories.

Classical Democratic Theory

The earliest Western democratic societies emerged in the city-states of ancient Greece. In Athens's direct democracy, for example, governing decisions were made by the citizens, defined as all nonslave men of Athenian descent. All citizens were eligible to participate in the Assembly, which met at least forty times per year. Assembly members debated all public issues, often at great length, before making any final decisions. The Assembly tried to reach a consensus on all matters, and unanimous decisions were preferred, under the belief that the common interest would only be realized when everyone agreed.[7] When unanimity was not possible, votes were held to resolve differences of opinion. The implementation of the

Assembly's decisions was conducted by smaller groups of men, who had been selected by lot or directly elected by the Assembly. These officials served for short periods of time and were not allowed to serve multiple terms in a row. These procedures ensured that many different men would serve in this executive capacity and that all citizens would have an equal chance of fulfilling these roles.[8]

One of the few surviving descriptions of Athenian citizens and their democratic participation is contained in Pericles's oration at a funeral for fallen soldiers:

> It is true that our government is called a democracy, because its administration is in the hands, not of the few, but of the many; yet while as regards the law all men are on an equality for the settlement of their private disputes, as regards the value set on them it is as each man is in any way distinguished that he is preferred to public honors, not because he belongs to a particular class, but because of personal merits; nor, again, on the ground of poverty is a man barred from a public career by obscurity of rank if he but has it in him to do the state a service. . . . And you will find united in the same persons an interest at once in private and in public affairs, and in others of us who give attention chiefly to business, you will find no lack of insight into political matters. For we alone regard the man who takes no part in public affairs, not as one who minds his own business, but as good for nothing; and we Athenians decide public questions for ourselves or at least endeavor to arrive at a sound understanding of them, in the belief that it is not debate that is a hindrance to action, but rather not to be instructed by debates before the time comes for actions. For in truth we have this point also of superiority over other men, to be most daring in action and yet at the same time most given to reflection upon the ventures we mean to undertake; with other men, on the contrary, boldness means ignorance and reflection brings hesitation.[9]

As Pericles portrays, Athenian democracy was characterized by the active participation of public-spirited men. In fact, he labeled "good for nothing" those men not taking part in public affairs. This passage also alludes to other key characteristics of democratic citizenship that appear in **classical models of democracy**, such as high levels of attention to and interest in political matters and the capability of deciding matters in favor of the general interest rather than only to advance one's own selfish interests.

Writing centuries later, Jean-Jacques Rousseau proposed a theory of democracy that has much in common with the classical model. Rousseau strongly advocated **popular sovereignty**, the principle that citizens hold the ultimate power in a democracy. He argued in *The Social Contract* that "sovereignty [is] nothing other than the exercise of the general will" and "since the laws are nothing other than authentic acts of the general will, the sovereign can act only when the people is assembled."[10] Rousseau also distinguished the "general will" from the "will of all": "the general will studies only the common interest while the will of all studies private interest, and is indeed no more than the sum of individual desires."[11] In other words, the general will is not determined by simply adding up every person's individual opinions but, rather, reflects what is in the best interest of the entire society. Procedurally, Rousseau favored a **direct democracy** in which all citizens (restricted to property-owning free men) were to meet, discuss, and decide on the content of the laws. As in the Athenian Assembly, Rousseau envisaged vigorous legislative debate with a preference for unanimous decisions. Active political participation by the citizenry served multiple purposes for Rousseau. It was the only method by which the general will could be reached and enshrined in law. Active participation was also beneficial for the individual participants; in other words, political participation had "intrinsic value . . . for the development of citizens as human beings."[12]

Rousseau's theory did depart from classical democratic theory in two important ways. First, Rousseau preferred that the citizens not be as involved in implementing the laws as they were in crafting legislation. He placed less faith in the public's ability to execute laws and proposed that a body of administrators be selected for this duty.[13] The administrators would be selected by the citizens and would be expected to follow the general will but would be distinct from the citizen assembly. Second, Rousseau's vision of democracy relied on relative economic equality among citizens, as enshrined by all free men having only a limited right to property. This does not mean that Rousseau favored *strict* equality of property but, rather, that he opposed *unlimited* accumulation of wealth. Short of this, some inequality was acceptable. Further, according to Rousseau, a citizen would not be able to make decisions for the benefit of all if he were motivated by fear of losing his economic independence. The right to enough property to make each citizen economically free from other citizens would prevent the formation of groups motivated by economic self-interest. Rousseau feared that the existence of such groups would undermine the creation of laws benefiting the common good.[14]

Later democratic theorists and practitioners have criticized classical democratic theory as unworkable for most societies. First, the city of Athens and Rousseau restricted citizenship rights to a degree that has become unacceptable for many democracies. In both cases, only free men were citizens; women and slaves were not given political rights. Further, the existence of a slave economy in Athens and the reliance on women for unpaid domestic labor created much leisure time for the free men to participate in government.[15] The amount of time necessary to participate in the Assembly debates (forty times per year!) is simply not feasible for most contemporary working adults. Second, most democratic polities are larger than were the Greek city-states or the eighteenth-century towns of Rousseau's Europe. In fact, both the Greeks and Rousseau assumed that "[only] in a small state, where people could meet together in the relative intimacy of a single assembly and where a similarity of culture and interests united them, could individuals discuss and find the public good."[16] One of the primary reasons more modern democratic theories, including those that follow, departed from the classical variants was to accommodate popular rule in large, diverse, and populous nation-states. In fact, and as will become clear as you proceed through the chapters of this book, democratic theory has very much evolved away from classical democracy in an attempt to speak to actual conditions in present-day societies. Nevertheless, classical democracy was the first historical variant of democracy, so understanding it is important for understanding more recent democratic theories.

Theories of Democratic Elitism and Pluralism

In contrast to classical democracy, theories of democratic elitism and pluralism do not allocate to citizens direct involvement in governmental decision making. Rather, the citizenry exerts indirect control by electing officials to represent their views and make decisions. This, of course, is the defining characteristic of a **representative democracy**. **Democratic elitists** view frequent competitive elections as the primary mechanism by which citizen preferences are expressed. Voters select their preferred candidates, and the elected officials deliberate over and vote on the nation's laws. These officials (or political elites) are accountable to the public in that they must periodically run for reelection. Thus, the elites have an incentive to represent the wishes of the public, and the will of the public will be reflected, to some degree, in governmental decisions. Yet the daily decisions are made by the elites, who, by their knowledge and expertise, are better able to make these decisions. Joseph Schumpeter outlines his theory of democratic elitism as follows:

> Suppose we reverse the roles of these two elements [the selection of representatives and the decision-making power of the voters] and make the deciding of issues by the electorate secondary to the election of the men who are to do the deciding. To put it differently, we now take the view that the role of the people is to produce a government. . . . And we define: the democratic method is that institutional arrangement for arriving at political decisions in which individuals acquire the power to decide by means of a competitive struggle for the people's vote.[17]

Pluralists also view competitive elections as one important mechanism by which citizens hold elected leaders accountable. Unlike democratic elitists, however, pluralists emphasize the essential role performed by groups in representative democracies. **Interest groups** are collections of like-minded individuals that attempt to influence elected officials and other governmental decision makers regarding issues of concern to them. As intermediaries between the public and the elites, such groups are especially important for transmitting the wishes of the citizenry to government officials in between elections. According to pluralists, when many groups are actively engaged in debating public issues, bargaining ensues among the groups and the public policies that result are compromises among the various groups' preferences.[18] Because interest group leaders have the desire and knowledge to lobby government officials, members of the public do not need to be actively involved to have their views represented in lawmaking. For example, citizens who care about human rights do not need to write letters to their elected officials but can, instead, have their concerns vocalized by an interest group such as Amnesty International or Human Rights Watch. Leader responsiveness to public concerns should result, argue pluralists.

Why have democratic elitists and pluralists proposed a more minor role for citizens in democratic politics? Simply put, "the individual voter was not all that the theory of democracy requires of him."[19] In practice, much evidence suggests that not all citizens are interested in or knowledgeable about politics, that levels of citizen apathy run high, and that many do not participate in politics. This evidence, collected by social scientists beginning in the 1940s, contributed to the development of democratic elitism and pluralism.[20] Indeed, it was the disconnect between dominant democratic theories and the reality of life in existing democracies that focused theorists' attention on actual democratic practices.[21] Put another way, the theories of democratic elitism and pluralism were constructed by examining contemporary democracies to determine what features they shared, particularly the levels of political involvement and interest among the citizenry.[22] Note that deriving a democratic theory based on observations from existing democracies results in a very different theory than that which emerged from ancient Athens.

Contemporary democratic elitism and pluralism can trace their intellectual roots to earlier theorists of representative democracy, such as the English philosophers Jeremy Bentham and James Mill and the American James Madison.[23] These earlier theorists, especially Madison, advocated that most people are not capable of democratic citizenship in the classical sense. In *Federalist* No. 10, written in 1787, Madison argues that humans are self-interested and will pursue what benefits themselves rather than the nation as a whole. In societies where the liberty of individuals to form their own opinions and pursue their own goals is ensured, groups of similarly interested people will form. By Madison's definition, such groups, or **factions**, consist of citizens "who are united and actuated by some common impulse of passion, or of interest, adverse to the rights of other citizens, or to the permanent and aggregate interests of the community."[24] To overcome the negative effects of such factions, the causes of which are "sown in the nature of man," Madison proposes a republic in which a few citizens are elected by the rest of the public to serve in the national government.[25] In his own words,

The effect of [a representative democracy] is . . . to refine and enlarge the public views by passing them through the medium of a chosen body of citizens, whose wisdom may best discern the true interest of their country and whose patriotism and love of justice will be least likely to sacrifice it to temporary or partial considerations. Under such a regulation it may well happen that the public voice, pronounced by the representatives of the people, will be more consonant to the public good than if pronounced by the people themselves, convened for the purpose.[26]

Similar beliefs in the decision-making superiority of elite officials are reflected in the writings of contemporary democratic elitists and pluralists. In an especially uncharitable view of the public, Joseph Schumpeter states as fact "that the electoral mass is incapable of action other than a stampede."[27] More broadly, he argues that the public is capable of voting but little else and that therefore the elites should be allowed to make decisions in between elections without public interference. Elite control over decision making should also result in more stable governments, with fewer changes in policy due to public impulses. Some theorists also emphasize that elites are more supportive of democratic norms and values, especially the civil rights and liberties of marginalized and/or unpopular groups, than are members of the public. In general, they suggest, this support for rights and liberties is beneficial to a democracy where decision making is in the hands of the elite.[28] The elites are not immune from public pressures to restrict individual liberties but will typically sort out such issues among themselves, with a preference toward maintaining such liberties.

Critiques of democratic elitism and pluralism have come from many quarters. Participatory democrats, as we describe in the next section, interpret the empirical evidence related to citizen participation vastly differently than do democratic elitists and pluralists. Others have contradicted the pluralist assumptions that interest groups will represent all points of view and that governmental officials are responsive to these groups. Government officials can choose to ignore a group's demands, especially when they believe the group lacks widespread public support. For example, Amnesty International's pleas in 2003 to the U.S. military to stop the abuse of Iraqi prisoners in Abu Ghraib prison went largely unheeded until the news media became aware that photographs of the abuse existed, photographs that were eventually released to the American public in 2004.[29] More recently, public outcry in favor of the principle of net neutrality contributed to decision making at the Federal Communications Commission. In the spring of 2014, the FCC proposed rules changes that would have permitted the content on some websites to be transmitted more quickly than on other sites. Initially, a few interest groups and Internet companies were active in opposing the proposed rules. Once word of these possible changes spread more broadly, thanks in part to coverage on John Oliver's HBO show *Last Week Tonight*, the FCC received millions of public comments. Most people advocated for an open, neutral web whereby

Internet service providers cannot speed up or slow down the delivery of a website's content. The FCC changed course. In February 2015, they dropped their original proposal and instead voted in favor of new regulations that promote net neutrality.[30]

Further, some groups possess more resources than others and thus have more influence over policymaking. As well stated by political scientist E. E. Schattschneider decades ago, "The flaw in the pluralist heaven is that the heavenly chorus sings with a strong upper-class accent."[31] This fact did not go unnoticed by pluralists. Some accepted the inequality of political resources and argued that the inequalities did not accumulate within certain types of people but, rather, were dispersed throughout society. In other words, "individuals best off in their access to one kind of resource are often badly off with respect to many other resources. . . . Virtually no one, and certainly no group of more than a few individuals, is entirely lacking in some influence resources."[32] Pluralists, however, did not fully develop the implications of group inequalities, an oversight that has been somewhat rectified by more recent theorists in this area.[33] Assumptions about noncumulative inequalities have also been challenged. Business groups, these critics contend, occupy a privileged position in U.S. politics due to their wide array of resources.[34]

Finally, Jack Walker's assessment of democratic elitism takes quite a different form. He charges the democratic elitists with changing "the principal orienting values of democracy."[35] Earlier democratic theorists stressed the importance of citizen participation and the personal benefits that accrue to individuals from this participation. In contrast, under democratic elitism, "emphasis has shifted to the needs and functions of the system as a whole; there is no longer a direct concern with human development. . . . [Elitists] have substituted stability and efficiency as the prime goals of democracy."[36] Participatory democracy, the final democratic theory we examine, represents a shift back toward the developmental functions of democracy that Walker supports.

Participatory Democracy

As its name suggests, **participatory democracy** emphasizes the importance of political participation by the public. Whereas participatory democrats recognize the need for representative democracy in nations as large as the United States, they also see the possibility and benefits of more political involvement by the public than is currently practiced.[37] Because participation is linked to social class and wealth today, participatory democrats advocate greater political involvement of all citizens as a means to redress inequality. "This is not to say that a more participatory system would of itself remove all the inequities of our society," writes one theorist. "It is only to say that low participation and social inequity are so bound up with each other that a more equitable and humane society requires a more participatory political system."[38]

BOX 1.1 WHAT ABOUT THE WOMEN?

". . . factions, the causes of which are 'sown in the nature of man . . .'"
                                                    James Madison, 1787

". . . make the deciding of issues by the electorate secondary to the election of the men who are to do the deciding."
                              Joseph Schumpeter, 1976 (originally published in 1943)

"The individual voter was not all that the theory of democracy requires of him."
                    Bernard Berelson, Paul Lazarsfeld, and William McPhee, 1954

When you read these quotations in this text, did they sound unusual to you? Did you stop and wonder whether the original writers really meant their statements to refer only to men? Or are women implicitly included as well? Would these statements have taken on a different meaning if a female noun or pronoun had been used? What if Madison had stated that the causes of factions are "sown in the nature of woman"? Would you have paused and wondered about that statement? Today, writers often substitute "him or her" for "him" or even alternate using "him" and "her" or "man" and "woman" when their statements apply equally to men or women. This was not always the case, however, and certainly was not the norm in the 1700s or even as recently as the 1950s. One way to determine whether the authors did mean to refer only to men when they wrote these sentences would be to read more writings by these authors to try to determine their opinions regarding the political roles and rights of women. It is useful to bear in mind, however, that women's increasing involvement in politics has been accompanied by changes in language use (not coincidentally). Early theorists might not have made their views toward women's role in politics known because this role was minimal, by law and by custom. Furthermore, when women did engage in political activities, they were not viewed as political actors and could more easily be overlooked. Thus, in some instances, it can be difficult to sort out whether these writers really meant to refer to men only or whether by "man" they really meant "human." We encourage you not to just assume that using "man" implies women as well but, rather, to consider the time period in which the author was writing and the nature of his or her conclusions regarding women and men in politics. In other words, do stop and think when you encounter "him" or "man" rather than merely breezing over these words.

Our approach in this book is to alternate using male and female nouns and pronouns when our statements are meant to apply to both women and men. So, unless otherwise specified, when we say "her" or "woman" we could have also said "him" or "man."

This theory of democracy originated during the protest movements of the 1960s and also represented dissatisfaction with the democratic elitist and pluralist models that were dominant at that time.[39] Participatory democrats agreed with these other theorists that levels of disinterest and apathy ran quite high among the American public, but they disagreed over the reason for these attitudes. Rather than citizens being politically disinterested by nature or simply preferring to spend their time on other pursuits, such as family, work, and leisure, participatory democrats argue that the political system, with its relatively few opportunities for meaningful citizen influence, breeds apathy. To political scientist Benjamin Barber, people "are apathetic because they are powerless, not powerless because they are apathetic. There is no evidence to suggest that once empowered, a people will refuse to participate. The historical evidence of New England towns, community school boards, neighborhood associations, and other local bodies is that participation fosters more participation."[40] **Citizen apathy** is thus a problem to be examined and solved rather than an accepted fact of political life in modern democracies.[41]

Participation in democratic decision making provides many personal benefits to those who engage in this activity, according to participatory democrats. On this point, they agree with democratic theorists of earlier eras, especially the nineteenth century's John Stuart Mill.[42] Citizens become more politically and socially educated and can develop their intellect and character through political participation. By communicating with and learning from other members of the public, individuals can look beyond their own self-interest and come to know what is best for the community or nation as a whole. In short, participation, in and of itself, can produce better democratic citizens.[43] Peter Bachrach, in articulating his vision of democracy as fostering individual self-development, states, "The majority of individuals stand to gain in self-esteem and growth toward a fuller affirmation of their personalities by participating more actively in meaningful community decisions."[44]

According to some participatory democrats, a fully participatory society necessitates more citizen involvement in decision making in governmental as well as nongovernmental institutions, such as the workplace or school. As Bachrach asks, why should people be excluded from decision making by private organizations when these decisions strongly affect their own lives and livelihoods?[45] Further, engaging in decision making at work and in other nongovernmental venues could increase governmental participation. Engagement in workplace decision making fosters civic skills, provides valuable experience, and, if effective, could create more confidence in an individual's ability to influence governmental decisions.[46] The flip side of this argument is that the lack of involvement in decision making in daily life will probably translate into disengagement from political participation, as the following clearly demonstrates: "After spending the day following orders without question at the factory, a worker cannot be expected to return home in the evening to act like the civics textbook's inquiring, skeptical, self-actualizing citizen. Students who are taught primarily to obey authority in school are not likely to grow into effective democratic citizens."[47]

Skeptics of participatory democracy argue that the public does not respond to participatory opportunities as the theorists contend they will. When barriers to political participation are eliminated or reduced, citizens have not necessarily become more politically active. For example, the National Voter Registration Act of 1993, more commonly known as the motor-voter bill, made voter registration easier and, supporters alleged, would increase voter turnout once enacted. Even though registration rates did increase in the wake of this reform, the levels of voter turnout did not substantially increase because of motor-voter.[48] More broadly, some scholars conclude that participatory democrats' assumptions about the public are unrealistic.[49] Rather than desiring to become more involved in politics, many citizens actually dislike politics and wish to avoid the type of conflict that typically emerges during decision making. In other words, although citizens might in fact learn from one another, as participatory democrats suggest, the more likely response of citizens, others argue, is to bypass any opportunity for deliberation, especially if the chance of disagreement is high.

Democratic Theory and Public Opinion

As you can see, these theories of democracy are quite broad, addressing many features of democratic governance. In our overview in this first section of the book, we have highlighted aspects of the theories that are most relevant for the study of public opinion. In particular, we have discussed how the different theoretical perspectives answer this question: What should the role of citizens be in a democratic society? This is a key issue that democratic theorists have long debated. In fact, we have organized this textbook around fundamental questions that speak to democratic theory debates about the public.

The second section of the book addresses an important question about the capabilities and competence of citizens: Are citizens pliable? Classical democratic theorists and participatory democratic theorists envision citizens who hold informed, stable opinions based on reason and concern for the general will. At the same time, these theorists believe democratic citizens should be open to persuasion from others but not so open that their brains fall out. In other words, citizens should change their attitudes based on information and evidence, not simply change their minds willy-nilly. As we have discussed, elite democrats and pluralists have lower expectations for the public. They presume that many citizens' opinions are ill-informed and that citizens are often influenced by political leaders, the media, and reference groups in society. By examining the role of socialization in shaping political views, the effects of the mass media on opinion, and the stability and instability of political attitudes, the upcoming section addresses the pliability of the public.

Do citizens organize their political thinking? This critical question, addressed in the third section of the book, speaks directly to the quality of public opinion. Classical democratic theorists and participatory democratic theorists expect citizens to hold a wide range of political attitudes that are organized in a meaningful fashion. For participatory democrats, it is crucial that citizens have a sophisticated understanding of politics so they can voice their views and influence elected officials. Elite democrats envision a citizenry that is much less proficient, although they still want citizens to be competent enough to hold officials accountable at election time.

The fourth section examines citizens' appreciation for essential aspects of democratic citizenship and governance by asking this question: Do citizens endorse and demonstrate democratic basics? The democratic basics we focus on are knowledge of, interest in, and attention to politics; support for civil liberties; and support for civil rights. Whether the public is knowledgeable and interested enough for democratic governance has long divided democratic theorists. Theorists also disagree on what level of citizen support for civil liberties and civil rights is needed for a healthy democracy. Classical and participatory democratic theorists, of course, want citizens to value these democratic basics. Elite democrats and pluralists worry much less about such matters, primarily because they view elites as the key actors in a democracy.

The fifth section of the book addresses a pivotal question about the nature of citizenship in a democratic society: What is the relationship between citizens and their government? Classical and participatory theorists want citizens to be actively involved in politics. Participatory democrats expect leaders to take public opinion into consideration as they make decisions, which would lead citizens to trust their government. Elite democratic theorists, in contrast, value trust in government for the stability it brings to the political system, not because it is a function of citizens being pleased with the responsiveness of their government. Further, elite democrats prefer that the public's influence on government is largely limited to voting in elections.

In the final section of the book, we pull it all together with this question: What do we make of public opinion in a democracy? We review the theoretical debates and summarize the empirical evidence, but ultimately we leave it to you to make sense of the role of citizens in a democratic society.

WHAT IS PUBLIC OPINION?

Public opinion is, on the one hand, a term that is familiar to most people and, on the other hand, rather difficult to define. Popular conceptions of public opinion might include phrases such as "the voice of the people." For most of us, public opinion is probably best represented by the results from opinion polls, such as those reported on the evening news or in the newspaper. Among public opinion observers and scholars, many different definitions have been proposed. Although researchers do not agree on one single definition of public opinion, some commonalities exist across specific definitions. First, most emphasize that public opinion refers to opinions on governmental and policy matters rather than on private matters (such as one's favorite flavor of ice cream or favorite movie). This characteristic is implied by a description of public opinion as "those opinions held by private persons which governments find it prudent to heed."[50] Of course, what constitutes a private matter might be in dispute. For centuries, the problems of domestic violence and rape within marriage were considered to be private affairs best left to a married or intimate couple to resolve. Societal views on this topic have changed, however, so that now people assume governments have to be involved in addressing these serious problems.

Second, in recent decades a consensus definition of public opinion has emerged. As one example, *public opinion* has been defined as "simply the sum or aggregation of private opinions on any particular issue or set of issues."[51] In this view, public opinion refers to the preferences of individuals, tallied such that each person's opinion counts equally. Following the consensus, this is the definition that we use in this book.

However, despite the consensus, some have raised important objections to defining public opinion as a "one person, one vote" aggregation. One of the earliest critiques came from sociologist Herbert Blumer. Society, according to Blumer, is organized hierarchically and "is not a mere aggregation of disparate individuals."[52] Certain individuals have more influence over the formation and expression of people's opinions, and treating each person's opinion as equal ignores this simple fact. For example, the leaders of labor unions not only attempt to influence the opinions of their members but also present their members' views to government policymakers. Simply tallying up individuals' opinions on a specific issue also overlooks the dynamic opinion formation processes among groups and among people. In Blumer's words, public opinion "is a function of a structured society, differentiated into a network of different kinds of groups and individuals having differential weight and influence and occupying different strategic positions."[53] Blumer further attacks the "one person, one vote" accounting of opinions by arguing that not all opinions are treated equally by government policymakers, in part because not all opinions of the public actually reach these policymakers. Opinions that do not come to the attention of decision makers will not influence their decisions.

Blumer directs his criticisms toward the public opinion polling industry, arguing that polls are incapable of capturing public opinion as he understands the concept. By reporting the opinions from a random selection of individuals, polls epitomize the "one person, one vote" aggregation of people's preferences. Not only are polls an unnatural forum for expressing one's opinions, argues Blumer, but they also are unable to capture the opinion formation process that he identifies. Opinion polls do not report, for example, whether a poll respondent "belongs to a powerful group taking a vigorous stand on the issue or whether he is a detached recluse with no membership in a functional group; whether he is bringing his opinion to bear in some fashion at strategic points in the operation of society or whether it is isolated and socially impotent."[54]

Blumer wrote in 1948, at a time when public opinion polling was in its infancy. Opinion polls have grown in use and influence since then, becoming the dominant method by which public opinion is assessed. Further, as this one method has become dominant, there has been a narrowing in our understanding of public opinion—a narrowing around the consensus definition previously described.[55] Despite this, Blumer's insights are spot-on today, argues Susan Herbst.[56] Herbst, a public opinion scholar, encourages us to reconsider what public opinion means in our digital age. Citizens engage in political conversations through a variety of means these days: the Internet, cell phones (talking and texting), and social media, to name a few. It is in these (often digital) exchanges where public opinion is to be found and understood. Herbst labels these communication patterns "textured talk" and finds them "so superior to the aggregation of anonymous individuals gathered in our artificial 'publics' produced by polls."[57] In addition to providing more convenient outlets for political expression, new communication technologies have also created audience segmentation. Should they choose to, citizens can rely on digital sources that convey information on specific topics or that present information from only one political viewpoint. For instance, political blogs are ubiquitous on the Internet, and many of them are very narrowly focused by issue or by ideology. As technology has led to a rise in public segmentation, should public opinion continue to be defined as the aggregation of each individual's opinion? Perhaps, as one communication scholar and pollster recently stated, rather than an aggregate public, "multiple publics have become the defining characteristic of public opinion."[58]

In contrast, Robert Weissberg is not much bothered by the manner in which the concept of public opinion is defined.[59] Rather, he is worried when the public's policy opinions *as measured by polls* too strongly influence the decisions of elected officials, particularly in the domain of social welfare. Compared to the complex choices officials confront, poll respondents are often faced with simple options, such as whether social welfare spending should be increased, be decreased, or remain at current levels. When responding to such a poll question, an individual might consider what the trade-offs to increased spending would be, such as whether taxes would increase or other areas of government spending would decrease, or she might not consider these trade-offs at all. Knowing that a majority of the public supports increased spending not only does not provide specific enough policy advice to policymakers but might also result in representatives rushing to follow the wishes of the public without considering the budgetary implications of doing so. "Governance via public opinion polling," concludes Weissberg, "does not fortify democracy."[60]

Others have also emphasized the poor quality of public opinion as assessed by polls, arguing that survey respondents often provide snap, top-of-the-head judgments. Contrast this with **public judgment**, a state that exists when "people have engaged an issue, considered it from all sides, understood the choices it leads to, and accepted the full consequences of the choices they make."[61] Encouraging and cultivating thoughtful public judgment, according to this view, is necessary if we want the public—and not only those people with specialized knowledge and expertise—to govern in a democracy.

We mention these criticisms not because we find them superior to the consensus definition of public opinion. Instead, we are sympathetic to these concerns because we find the "public opinion as aggregation of individual views" definition too limiting. In addition to the concerns already outlined, we are troubled that this consensus approach draws our attention only to one feature of public opinion: the content of people's political opinions. Although it is important to know how the public feels about an issue, focusing only on the content of people's opinions overlooks many equally important features of public opinion. Understanding public opinion requires us to explore other topics, such as the sources of those opinions, the processes by which opinions are formed and altered, the organization of an individual's opinions, and the impact of public opinion on public policy. In the chapters that follow, we describe studies that illustrate a variety of definitions of public opinion. Along the way, therefore, we touch on the many facets of public opinion. But, as will become evident, most scholars of public opinion do rely on the consensus definition of public opinion, whether implicitly or explicitly.

DEFINING KEY CONCEPTS

Each of the chapters in this book addresses a specific aspect of public opinion in America. In these chapters, you will repeatedly encounter a few of the same concepts and terms. We define those concepts here, so that you will understand the later chapters more thoroughly.

Attitude and Opinion

Two terms that we use frequently in this book are *attitude* and *opinion*. These words are undoubtedly familiar to you, and you will probably agree that they are similar to each other. They both have sparked considerable attention to their meanings, however, and numerous definitions have been proposed for each, especially for attitude. The term *attitude* is one of the most important concepts in psychology and has been for many years. Over seventy-five years ago, a prominent social psychologist presented a "representative selection" of sixteen definitions of attitude and then proposed his own comprehensive definition.[62] In the many decades since, still more scholars have discussed and debated the meaning of attitude. Of the many possible definitions of **attitude**, we prefer this one: "Attitude is a psychological tendency that is expressed by evaluating a particular entity with some degree of favor or disfavor."[63] A similar approach defines an attitude as "a general and enduring positive or negative feeling about some person, object or issue."[64]

These two definitions highlight some key features of an attitude. First, people hold attitudes toward targets ("entity" or "person, object or issue"). In the realm of political attitudes, possible types of objects for which we have attitudes are policy issues, political candidates or politicians, groups (such as the National Rifle Association [NRA] or feminists), and institutions of government. Second, attitudes represent an evaluation of an object, generally articulated as favorable or unfavorable, as liking or disliking, or as positive or negative. So, in terms of specific political attitudes, your friend might favor school prayer, dislike President Barack Obama, support the NRA, dislike feminists, and disapprove of Congress. It is also possible to have a neutral (neither favorable nor unfavorable) attitude toward a target. Neutral attitudes might result from not being informed enough about an object to evaluate it positively or negatively. Alternatively, you might assess certain features of an object positively and other features negatively. If these cancel each other out and prevent you from an overall positive or negative evaluation of the object, you might conclude that your attitude is neutral.

So, now, what is an **opinion**? Similar to an attitude, an opinion refers to a specific object and expresses a preference, such as support or opposition, toward that object. As with attitudes, opinions vary in that not everyone holds the same opinion toward an object. Though acknowledging these similarities, many scholars distinguish between these two concepts by stating that an opinion is an expression of a latent attitude. That is, whereas an attitude is not observable, an opinion is a verbal or written expression of that attitude. Distinctions such as these are more common in the field of psychology than in political science. In political science, you are not only likely to see the two terms used synonymously but are also more likely to encounter the concept of opinion than attitude. We view these two terms as much more similar than dissimilar and thus use them interchangeably in this book. This no doubt reflects our training as political scientists, but it also reflects common use of the terms. In fact, in most thesauruses, *opinion* and *attitude* are presented as synonyms of each other.

When thinking about a specific attitude or opinion, it is obviously important to consider its *direction* (support versus oppose, favorable versus unfavorable, and so on). For the study of public opinion, we also need to bear in mind two other characteristics of attitudes and opinions: extremity and importance. The **extremity** of an opinion refers to whether support (or opposition) for the opinion object is slight or strong. You might, for example, *slightly* favor U.S. intervention in foreign military conflicts but *strongly* favor laws that prohibit testing cosmetics on animals. **Attitude importance**, in contrast, focuses on how meaningful a specific attitude is to you or how passionately you care about the attitude. Although we may have attitudes toward a wide range of political and social objects, not all of these attitudes will be of equal importance, at least for most of us. The more important an attitude is, the less likely it is to change over time and the more likely it will direct certain behaviors, such as thinking about the attitude object or influencing our vote preferences for political candidates.[65] Also, even though it is often the case that more extreme attitudes are also more important, this does not necessarily have to occur.[66] Take the two examples presented here. You might have a more extreme opinion toward animal testing than U.S. military intervention, but the latter opinion might be more important to you, especially when it comes to evaluating national politics, such as the performance of political leaders.

Opinion Ingredients: Beliefs, Values, and Emotions

Specific political opinions do not stand alone in people's minds. Instead, they are often related to, even guided by, other mental constructs, most especially beliefs, values, and emotions. These three often have evaluative content—content that can help to determine an individual's specific opinion toward a related entity. **Beliefs** are thoughts or information a person has regarding an attitude object, often regarding what the person thinks to be true about the object. A person might, for example, believe that the possibility of a very severe punishment, such as the death penalty, will not deter most people from committing a serious crime. Someone possessing this belief would be more likely to oppose capital punishment than would someone who believes in the deterrent power of death penalty laws. Beliefs about the characteristics of members of social groups, such as blacks or Christian fundamentalists, have a specific name, **stereotypes**. Stereotypes can be positive or negative, and people can hold both positive and negative stereotypes toward the same group. Examples of positive and negative stereotypes include blacks as athletic or lazy and Christian fundamentalists as charitable or intolerant. Believing certain stereotypes is often related to support for public policies that affect the group in question. White Americans who believe most blacks are lazy, for instance, are unlikely to support social welfare policies, especially compared with people who do not believe this stereotype.[67]

Values are specific types of beliefs. According to a prominent values researcher, "a value is an enduring belief that a specific mode of conduct [instrumental value] or end-state of existence [terminal value] is personally or socially preferable to an opposite or converse mode of conduct or end-state of existence."[68] Examples of instrumental values include independence, responsibility, and self-control, whereas examples of terminal values include a peaceful world, family security, and freedom. Unlike other types of beliefs, values refer to ideals.

Values are also assumed to be quite stable over time for individuals, as highlighted by this definition: "By values we mean general and enduring standards."[69]

Whereas value change can and does occur, stability is more common. Some have even argued that values are central to people's political belief systems, certainly more central than are attitudes.[70] Further, much public opinion research demonstrates that values are quite important in influencing people's specific political attitudes. For instance, opposition to social welfare spending is more likely among those who value responsibility, a sense of accomplishment, and economic individualism and less likely among those who value equality.[71] Finally, certain values are more salient in American political culture than others in that they guide political opinions more strongly. These include individualism, egalitarianism, and limited government.[72] Not all Americans value these three, to be sure, but whether a person values or does not value each is related to opinions on many specific political matters.

Whereas beliefs are considered to be the cognitive components of attitudes, **emotions** make up the affective component. Emotions are feelings that a person has toward the attitude object and are oftentimes more consequential than beliefs in attitude formation.[73] Emotions are especially common when it comes to evaluating political individuals or groups. You might feel warmly toward a politician and thus evaluate her (and even her job performance) highly. In contrast, fearing a politician would probably lead to poor assessments of her but also might transfer into not supporting the issues that she supports. Negative affect that is felt toward a specific group is commonly referred to as **prejudice** and can influence attitudes toward politicians who are members of that group as well as policies designed to benefit the group. Emotional reactions can also influence opinions toward political issues or public policies. Anxiety that a foreign leader could detonate a nuclear weapon somewhere on U.S. soil could lead a person to support a strong national defense and a preemptive foreign policy. Finally, people can feel positively toward an attitude object but also hold negative beliefs about the object. For example, someone could admire Latinos for their work ethic while at the same time hold negative stereotypes about their intelligence or abilities.

Party Identification

Throughout this book, we present examples of many different political opinions. One opinion that we refer to often, because it is a core opinion for many Americans and crucial to understanding the nature of public opinion in the United States, is party identification. **Party identification** refers to a person's allegiance to a political party (typically the Democratic or Republican Party) or identification as independent of a party. It is a self-classification rather than a description of the person's behavior, as the following excerpt from *The American Voter*, a classic study about voting first published in 1960, highlights:

> Only in the exceptional case does the sense of individual attachment to party reflect a formal membership or an active connection with a party

apparatus. Nor does it simply denote a voting record, although the influence of party allegiance on electoral behavior is strong. Generally this tie is a psychological identification, which can persist without legal recognition or evidence of formal membership and even without a consistent record of party support. Most Americans have this sense of attachment with one party or the other. And for the individual who does, the strength and direction of party identification are facts of central importance in accounting for attitude and behavior.[74]

In other words, a person could consider himself to be a Republican without ever formally registering as such or without always voting for Republican candidates. Party identification is, instead, an attitude one has about his attachment to a political party. Typically, then, to determine someone's party identification, a survey taker would not ask whom she voted for most recently but, rather, ask her whether she identifies with a particular party, emphasizing the self-identification component of this attitude. To illustrate, two examples of questions used by national survey organizations to assess the party identification of the American public follow:

Generally speaking, do you usually think of yourself as a Republican, a Democrat, an Independent, or what? [If Republican or Democrat:] Would you call yourself a strong (Republican, Democrat) or a not very strong (Republican, Democrat)? [If Independent, Other or No Preference:] Do you think of yourself as closer to the Republican or Democratic Party?[75]

No matter how you voted today, do you usually think of yourself as a Democrat, Republican, Independent, [or] Something else?[76]

We highlight party identification here because it is important in American political culture for a number of reasons. First, for an individual, party identification is quite stable over time, certainly more stable than other political attitudes.[77] When a change does occur, it is most likely to consist of people switching from identification with one of the two major parties to considering themselves to be Independent or vice versa. That is, switching from identifying with one of the parties to the other does not occur very often. Second, party identification is a global attitude that is related to many specific political attitudes (such as policy opinions or evaluations of political leaders). Third, people's party identification can influence the interpretation of newly encountered information. When learning of damaging information about a Democratic president, for example, a Democrat is likely to interpret this information quite differently than a Republican. Related to this, party identification can help a person to make sense of political issues and topics, especially those that are unfamiliar. We elaborate on these and other aspects of party identification throughout this book.

In Figure 1.1, we present the breakdown of Americans' party identifications (as Democratic, Republican, or Independent) in every presidential election year since 1952. Focus first on the **partisans**, those who identify as Democratic or Republican (the solid lines). We see that American adults are much less likely to identify with the Democratic Party now than they were in the 1950s and 1960s. Whereas one-half of the population considered themselves Democrats in those decades, since 1988 less than 40 percent have. This does not necessarily mean, however, that Americans are now identifying as Republicans in much larger numbers. Republican self-identification was slightly less common in 2008 than the early 1950s. Perhaps more noteworthy, the percentage of the public identifying as Republican has not varied much (between 23 and 30 percent) over this time period.

The most significant change in party identification over the past fifty years is the switch from partisans to **partisan independence**. In fact, beginning in 1988, Independents have been more common than either Democrats or Republicans in all but two presidential election years (1996 and 2012; refer to the top dotted line in Figure 1.1). There was a substantial increase in Independents during the 1960s; only about 23 percent of the population considered themselves to be Independent in 1960, but 35 percent did so in 1972. These percentages, however, include people who lean toward supporting one of the major parties. That is, when initially asked whether they consider themselves to be Democratic, Republican, or Independent, they claim to be Independents. Yet, when then asked if they are closer to one of the parties, most of these Independents do indicate closeness to one party.

Figure 1.1   Party Identification, 1952–2012

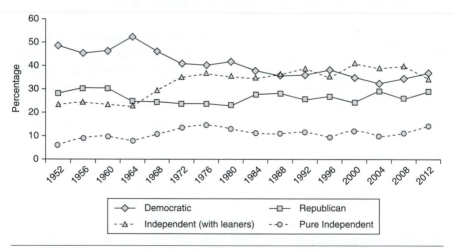

Source: Analysis of American National Election Studies Cumulative (1948–2004), American National Election Studies 2008, and American National Election Studies 2012 data files.

Removing these **leaners** from the analysis presents a very different picture (see the dotted line at the bottom of the figure). Although there are more pure Independents now than there were in the 1950s, the increase has not been very large (from 6 percent in 1952 to 14 percent in 2012). Most of the increase in Independents, thus, seems to have been among the leaners, people whose initial identity is as Independent but who ultimately lean toward a party. Finally, in 2012 leaners were nearly equally likely to feel close to the Democratic as to the Republican Party. Among the pure Independents that year, 32 percent indicated that they felt closer to the Republican Party, whereas 31 percent leaned toward the Democrats.

EMPIRICAL ASSESSMENTS OF PUBLIC OPINION

As should have been clear from the democratic theory section earlier in this chapter, the main goal of these theories is to present **normative** conclusions. That is, most theorists outline how a democratic government and society *ought* to be structured, including what ought to be the role of the citizenry. Democratic theories are not entirely normative, however. According to one view, the best models of democracy "have been both explanatory and justificatory or advocatory. They are, in different proportions, statements about what a political system or a political society is, how it does work or could work, and statements of why it is a good thing, or why it would be a good thing to have it or to have more of it."[78]

To rephrase, theories of democracy can contain normative and empirical components. The empirical features are statements about how a society actually *is*, based on observations of democratic societies. These observations of reality can be important components of democratic theories and can complement or contribute to a theory's normative conclusions, as we have discussed with the theories of democratic elitism and pluralism. In contrast to the normative focus of democratic theories, **empirical analyses** of public opinion place primacy on accurately describing and explaining real-life phenomena. Any broader conclusions, whether normative or otherwise, are of secondary importance for fields of empirical study.

Most public opinion scholars, and nearly all that we feature in this book, are empiricists. Examining public opinion empirically requires, of course, that this phenomenon be measured in some way. Measuring public opinion is not an easy or obvious task, however. What if, for example, you wanted to know whether the public supports same-sex marriage. How would you determine public opinion on this issue? You could stop people on the street, ask them if they agree gays and lesbians should be allowed to marry their partners, and tally up the responses. You could read letters to the editor in the newspaper to gauge public sentiment on same-sex marriage. You could look to elected officials' statements about the public to determine how citizens feel about this issue or assume that most people do support same-sex marriage because the U.S. Supreme Court ruled in favor of such marriages. These are just a few possibilities, and although each has its advantages (and disadvantages), none can be ruled out as clearly inappropriate. In fact, all are examples of approaches that have been used, at one time or another, to measure public opinion. The Appendix to this chapter discusses a variety of public opinion research methods, methods that we will illuminate throughout the chapters of this book.

THEMES OF THE BOOK

By reading this book, you will learn a lot about public opinion in the United States. One way that we try to fulfill this goal is by linking normative democratic theories with findings from empirical studies of public opinion. Rather than only considering what researchers have concluded about public opinion, throughout this book we discuss the democratic theory implications of a study or a body of research. We hope this approach will encourage you to evaluate the public opinion research through the lenses of the democratic theories outlined earlier and also to evaluate the democratic theories in light of the empirical studies. This will deepen your assessments of these democratic theories and provide you with a broad understanding of public opinion.

There are many, many empirical studies on public opinion. Summarizing all of these would be a daunting task for us and would produce a book that would be tedious for you to read. Thus, we have not attempted to discuss every relevant study on each topic. Instead, in each chapter, we focus on prototypical and especially influential studies that bring the fundamental questions into sharp focus. Our discussions of these prototypical studies are detailed and are meant to illustrate the strengths and weaknesses of each study. To evaluate well the conclusions from a study, you need to know what is good about the research and what its limits are. Using this approach will, we hope, encourage you to consider how public opinion is studied as well as better understand how a choice of methodology can influence the conclusions that researchers draw. We also anticipate that this feature of our text—what we call "embedded methods"—will teach you about specific research methods better than if the topics were presented in a separate chapter devoted only to methodology. If at any point you want to have more information about a method you are reading about, however, you can always refer back to the Chapter 1 Appendix for details about the specific method.

Finally, as we discussed earlier, the book is organized into sections. Each section poses a question that is important for democratic theory, and the chapters in the section present evidence and arguments to help you answer that question. We will not answer these questions, however. In fact, these questions do not have "correct" answers. Instead, we present evidence and tools to help you think through the material critically and challenge you to make your own judgment regarding the capacity of citizens to function effectively in a democracy.

In the next section we address this question: Are citizens pliable? We explore this question through specific chapters devoted to the topics of political socialization, how the mass media shape public opinion, and attitude stability. Chapters in the section that follows address this question: Do citizens organize their political thinking? We begin by examining whether individuals' opinions are organized along a liberal-conservative dimension or by partisanship. We also focus on other factors that might organize opinions, including reference groups, personality, self-interest calculations, values, and historical events. The book then moves on to this question: Do citizens endorse and demonstrate democratic basics? We focus on how knowledgeable, interested, and attentive citizens are, and we investigate public support for civil liberties and civil rights. Next, we ask, what is the relationship between citizens and their government? Specifically, we take up the topics of citizen trust in government and support for the institutions of government. We also examine the relationship between public opinion and public policy. In the final section, we take a broad assessment of the role of public opinion in the United States, asking, what do we make of public opinion in a democracy? The concluding chapter reviews normative debates over the role of citizens in a democracy and summarizes the empirical evidence that speaks to these debates.

KEY CONCEPTS

attitude / 18	normative / 23
attitude importance / 19	opinion / 18
beliefs / 19	participatory democracy / 10
citizen apathy / 12	partisan independence / 22
classical models of democracy / 5	partisans / 22
democratic elitists / 7	party identification / 20
democratic theory / 4	pluralists / 7
direct democracy / 6	popular sovereignty / 5
emotions / 20	prejudice / 20
empirical analyses / 23	public judgment / 17
extremity / 18	public opinion / 14
factions / 8	representative democracy / 7
interest groups / 7	stereotypes / 19
leaners / 23	values / 19

SUGGESTED SOURCES FOR FURTHER READING

Each chapter in this book ends with a list of readings and websites. If you wish to investigate any of a chapter's topics further, perusing these lists of suggested sources will be a good step to begin your exploration.

Bachrach, Peter. *The Theory of Democratic Elitism: A Critique*. Washington, DC: University Press of America, 1980.

Pateman, Carole. *Participation and Democratic Theory*. Cambridge, UK: Cambridge University Press, 1970.

Pateman, Carole. "Participatory Democracy Revisited." *Perspectives on Politics* 10 (2012): 7–19.
Walker, Jack L. "A Critique of the Elitist Theory of Democracy." *American Political Science Review* 60 (1966): 285–295.

These authors are proponents of participatory democracy. In these works, they present reasons for supporting this theory and explain why democratic elitism is problematic. In her 2012 article, Pateman contrasts participatory democracy with deliberative democracy.

Bryan, Frank M. *Real Democracy: The New England Town Meeting and How It Works*. Chicago: University of Chicago Press, 2004.

Bryan presents an in-depth and illuminating analysis of the New England town meeting. Unlike representative democracies, these meetings involve all eligible citizens coming together to debate and vote on town matters. For this reason, Bryan labels the town meeting "real democracy."

Dahl, Robert A. *Who Governs? Democracy and Power in an American City*. New Haven, CT: Yale University Press, 1961.
Schumpeter, Joseph A. *Capitalism, Socialism and Democracy*. 5th ed. London: Allen and Unwin, 1976.

The theories of democratic elitism and pluralism are discussed in these works.

Goidel, Kirby, ed. *Political Polling in the Digital Age: The Challenge of Measuring and Understanding Public Opinion*. Baton Rouge: Louisiana State University Press, 2011.

The intriguing essays in this volume discuss how changes in communication technology are influencing both opinion polling and our thoughts about what public opinion is.

Held, David. *Models of Democracy*. 2nd ed. Stanford, CA: Stanford University Press, 1996.
Macpherson, C. B. *The Life and Times of Liberal Democracy*. Oxford: Oxford University Press, 1977.

Macpherson and Held have organized the numerous variants of democratic theory into a manageable number of models (four for Macpherson and nine for Held), some of which we have presented in this chapter. For a description of similarities and differences among theories of democracy or an introduction to specific theorists, these books are recommended.

Shapiro, Robert Y., and Lawrence R. Jacobs, eds. *The Oxford Handbook of American Public Opinion and the Media*. Oxford: Oxford University Press, 2011.

The chapters in this edited volume summarize recent scholarship on a wide variety of public opinion topics. Discussions of both normative and empirical issues are included.

American Association for Public Opinion Research, www.aapor.org

AAPOR is the professional organization for public opinion researchers. This website contains information about the organization, statements regarding the misuse of polls and poll results, guidelines for journalists who write about polls, and a helpful list titled "Fifty Books That Have Significantly Shaped Public Opinion Research."

Appendix
Studying Public Opinion Empirically

IN THIS APPENDIX, we describe a variety of methods for empirically studying public opinion. As you will see, each method has strengths and weaknesses. Further, some methods are better than others at answering particular public opinion questions. As we proceed, we refer to studies examining death penalty attitudes to illustrate how each method works in practice.

PUBLIC OPINION SURVEYS

Today, the most common method for assessing public opinion is via a **survey** or **public opinion poll**. Most of us are familiar with polls or, at the very least, the results of polls. The survey results that we frequently encounter (in the news media, on the Internet, and so on) are based on the responses provided by a **sample** of people to the same list of questions. In scientific surveys, respondents are *selected randomly* to represent a specific **population** (such as students at the University of Kansas, residents of New Mexico, or citizens of the United States). Survey respondents answer a series of questions, often by selecting one response from a list of options provided by the survey interviewer. For example, to gauge public sentiment on the issue of capital punishment, a survey might include the following question: "Are you in favor of the death penalty for a person convicted of murder?" Those being surveyed would respond by selecting "favor" or "oppose" or, in some cases, "no opinion" or "I don't know." These types of questions, with a limited set of response options, are called **closed-ended questions**.

Questions can be worded in a variety of ways, and the choice of which words to include can have important, sometimes even dramatic, effects. To illustrate **question wording effects**, let's examine two ways the Gallup Organization has asked people about their death penalty attitudes. In October 2014, Gallup polled a random sample of 1,017 adults living in the United States. Respondents were asked whether they support the death penalty for convicted murderers (see Table A.1). Almost two-thirds of respondents supported the death penalty. Just one month earlier, in September 2014, Gallup polled a random sample of 1,252 U.S. adults but this time asked respondents to indicate which they favor more,

Table A.1   Question Wording and Response Options Matter

Response options	Question wording
	October 2014: "Are you in favor of the death penalty for a person convicted of murder?"
Favor	63%
Oppose	33
No opinion	4
Response options (rotated)	September 2014: "If you could choose between the following two approaches, which do you think is the better penalty for murder: the death penalty or life imprisonment with absolutely no possibility of parole?"
Death penalty	50%
Life in prison	45
No opinion	5

Source: Data from Jeffrey M. Jones, *Americans' Support for Death Penalty Stable*, Gallup, Washington, DC, http://www.gallup.com/poll/178790/americans-support-death-penalty-stable.aspx?utm_source=position4&utm_medium=related&utm_campaign=tiles

the death penalty or life in prison. Support for the death penalty dropped to 50 percent when respondents had a choice of punishments for convicted murderers.[1] This is a substantial difference, and very different conclusions would be drawn about public support for the death penalty depending on which survey question was used.

It is also important to pay attention to what response options are presented to respondents as well as the order in which those options are provided. Take Gallup's September 2014 question, for example. When citizens were asked to choose between the two approaches, one-half of the respondents were read the death penalty option first and the life in prison option second. The other half were read the choices in the reverse order. The choices are rotated because of concerns about **response order effects**.[2] Quite simply, citizens' opinions can be influenced by the order in which responses are presented to them. In addition, note that no middle or undecided categories were provided to respondents. As a result, citizens who were ambivalent or indifferent on the topic were unable to express their views.

To illuminate another concern about question wording and response options, let's discuss a question used by the National Race and Crime Survey to assess opinion toward the death penalty. The wording is, "Do you strongly oppose, somewhat oppose, somewhat favor, or strongly favor the death penalty for persons convicted of murder?"[3] Notice that response options from both points of view are provided in the stem of the question, which is what survey researchers call a **balanced question**. In contrast, Gallup's October 2014 question refers only to the pro–death penalty position, which may encourage respondents to answer in that fashion. As a result, balanced questions are considered superior to questions that may lead respondents in one direction or another.

So, when you come across poll results, it is important to know the question wording, the response options, and the order in which those options were presented. Similarly, if you ever report the results of an opinion poll, you also need to provide all that information. Otherwise, it is very easy to mislead, whether intentionally or not, those who are reading your summary of the results.

In a perfect world it is also important to know the order in which survey questions are asked. For instance, in the October 2014 Gallup survey, respondents were also asked whether they "believe the death penalty is applied fairly or unfairly in this country today." This was asked *after* respondents provided their opinion on the death penalty. But what if this question had been asked *before*? Respondents would have been primed to think about the fairness of the death penalty, which could have influenced their support for the policy. Specifically, respondents concerned about the fairness of the death penalty might be less likely to say they favored the policy when that concern was fresh in their minds, and vice versa. Therefore, when you analyze a public opinion survey, it is best to examine not only the question you are interested in but also the context in which that question is situated. Unfortunately, researchers and especially journalists do not always provide the text of the entire survey, so it is often difficult to evaluate whether **question order effects** are influencing the results.

Public opinion polls have a number of advantages. Randomly sampling people from a specified population allows us to draw conclusions about the opinions of the entire population. Why is that the case? Because a **random sample** is one in which chance alone determines which elements of the population make it into the sample. For example, let's say you want to draw a sample of twenty-five students from a class (or population) of one hundred students, and you want the opinions of the twenty-five students to reflect the opinions of all one hundred students. How would you draw that sample? You could have each student write his or her name on a slip of paper, collect the one hundred names in a hat, give it a good shake to make sure the names are all mixed up, and then draw out twenty-five names. Consequently, it would be chance alone that would determine which twenty-five students ended up in your sample. When respondents are selected in this manner, and *not* on the basis of their specific characteristics (such as race or political views), we can generalize the results from the sample to the larger population from which the sample was drawn. The ability to draw such conclusions is known as **external validity**. For polls that include only respondents who *opt* to participate, the results are applicable *only* to those people who answered the survey questions. Because such poll results are based on what is called a **convenience sample**, not a random sample, they cannot provide information about a larger population.

Another advantage of surveys is that answering a closed-ended question is not very time-consuming, so each respondent can answer many questions without being overly burdened. Also, many individuals can be asked the same questions, again because the time commitment per person is not great. Providing survey respondents the same questions with the same response options facilitates the tallying of results (such as 63 percent of Americans support the death penalty) and also allows for a comparison of public opinion over time, provided, of course, that the same questions are asked at different times. For instance, as shown in Figure A.1, public support for the death penalty has fluctuated since 1991. In the early 1990s, three-quarters (or more) of the public favored the death penalty, but by 2000 only two-thirds did. After 2001, perhaps because of the 9/11 terrorist attacks, support for the death penalty increased somewhat to 72 percent, but since the mid-2000s, support has settled at around two-thirds of the public in favor of the policy.[4]

Surveys also have many uses. News media organizations use polls to measure the public's political and social opinions, and candidates conduct polls to

Figure A.1   Public Opinion toward the Death Penalty, 1991–2014

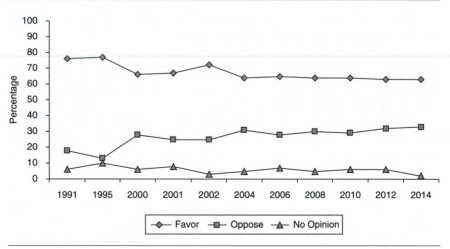

Source: Data from Jeffrey M. Jones, *Americans' Support for Death Penalty Stable*, Gallup, Washington, DC, http://www.gallup.com/poll/178790/americans-support-death-penalty-stable.aspx?utm_source=position4&utm_medium=related&utm_campaign=tiles

Note: Here is the question wording: "Are you in favor of the death penalty for a person convicted of murder?"

determine which voters support them and why. Public opinion scholars find surveys useful for assessing the content of the public's opinions as well as describing how people's opinions differ. In particular, it is often interesting to examine whether different groups have different attitudes on important issues of the day. Because Gallup surveys record respondents' gender in addition to their death penalty attitudes, it is possible to investigate whether men and women hold different attitudes on this issue. Indeed they do. In 2012, for example, 67 percent of men favored the death penalty, whereas only 59 percent of women supported capital punishment for convicted murderers. The gap in attitudes is even greater when you examine differences by education. Sixty-eight percent of people who have not gone to college support the death penalty compared with 50 percent of people who have a postgraduate education.[5]

A specific type of survey, called a **panel study** or **longitudinal survey**, allows scholars to determine whether people's opinions have stayed the same over time. In a panel study, the *same* people are asked their opinions on the same issues more than once. A study conducted by Robert Bohm and Brenda Vogel illustrates the use of this type of survey to track people's death penalty attitudes across more than a decade.[6] In the late 1980s, Bohm and Vogel surveyed college students at the beginning of the semester during which they were taking a class on the death penalty. They resurveyed the students at the end of the semester and then again a couple of years later. In 1999, Bohm and Vogel surveyed these (now former) students for the fourth time. The researchers were interested in whether students' attitudes changed after becoming more informed about the death penalty during the class and whether that attitude change was lasting. They found that students were less supportive of the death penalty immediately after taking the class, but over time the students reverted to their initial levels of support for the policy. They concluded that information about the death penalty can influence citizens in the short run but that views on the policy are largely driven by personality traits and values, which trump knowledge in the long run.

Panel studies are ideal for tracking changes in opinion across time, but it is important to note that **attrition** is a potential weakness of such studies. Attrition refers to the drop-off in the number of respondents over time. In the Bohm and Vogel study, for example, 120 college students were initially administered the survey, but only 69 were still participating in the study by the fourth wave. If the students who stopped participating were systematically different from the students who continued to participate, we would need to be cautious about drawing conclusions from the study. Further, this particular panel study did not use a random sample, which limits the external validity of the results; however, many panel studies do rely on random samples, so their results can be generalized to the broader population.

Public opinion data can be collected using a **survey mode**, such as phone, Internet, mail, or face-to-face. Each of these modes has strengths and weaknesses.

Researchers should consider the topic, population of interest, and survey context to determine which mode to use.[7] For example, it is typically better to ask sensitive questions over the Internet or via mail rather than face-to-face. Complex, long questions are generally not appropriate for phone surveys. The Internet is particularly useful for surveys of specific, narrow populations, such as college students or members of an interest group. In some cases the best approach is to combine modes, which is called a **mixed-mode approach**. A survey researcher might contact respondents via mail with a postcard to inform them they have been chosen to participate in a study to be conducted by phone. Another mixed-mode approach is when respondents are asked via e-mail whether they prefer to receive a survey via the Internet, mail, or phone. The researcher will then deliver the survey according to each respondent's preference.

The Gallup survey of death penalty attitudes mentioned earlier was conducted over the phone with 50 percent of the respondents contacted on landlines and 50 percent on cell phones. Obviously it is critical to include cell phone numbers in the sample given their widespread use in society today and given that young adults are more likely to *only* have cell phones. Do keep in mind that regardless of the particular survey mode, a random sample is necessary to generalize the results of the sample to the population. Gallup, for example, uses a standard technique, **random digit dial**, in which chance alone determines which phone numbers are called in their surveys. This ensures that all phone numbers have the potential to be called rather than just those numbers on a phone list. As a result, Gallup's surveys are generalizable to the population.

EXPERIMENTS

Another common method used by public opinion researchers is experimentation. Although there are many types of public opinion **experiments**, in the most common form, the researcher manipulates a feature of the study and then assesses individual or group responses. Imagine you wanted to know how individuals respond to different types of news stories on the death penalty. You could assess this experimentally by providing one type of news story to one group of participants in your study and another type of news story to another group. After reading the news stories, these **subjects**, as participants in an experiment are called, would be asked whether they support the death penalty.

Many news media studies use experimental designs just like that to see whether citizens' opinions are influenced by different news content. For example, Frank Dardis et al. created newspaper stories to frame the death penalty in different ways.[8] One story constructed the death penalty as an affront to moral values (the morality frame), whereas another story emphasized that the policy was fundamentally flawed because innocent people might be executed (the innocence frame).[9] Some subjects read the story with the morality frame, and others read the one with the innocence frame. Subjects then completed a questionnaire that asked them to list the important factors they considered when determining their opinion on the death penalty. Dardis et al. found that subjects exposed to the innocence frame were more likely to mention innocence-related considerations as important factors in determining their attitudes toward the death penalty than subjects presented with the morality frame. Thus, the news frames shaped the ingredients of the subjects' death penalty attitudes.

The two key features of experiments that distinguish them from other methods and that allow for powerful causal conclusions to be drawn are manipulation and random assignment.[10] **Manipulation** involves the researcher varying access to information, events, or whatever is the focus of the research among experimental participants. In the example we have been discussing, the researchers manipulated exposure to news frames. **Random assignment** refers to the process by which people are assigned to experimental groups. With random assignment, it is chance alone that determines which subjects get in which condition. For instance, in the Dardis et al. experiment, subjects were randomly assigned to read a story framed in terms of either innocence or morality. Individuals are randomly assigned to groups, perhaps by flipping a coin to establish the person's assignment, in the expectation that individual characteristics that might be related to the study's goals are equally likely to appear in all groups. Because men are more supportive of capital punishment than women, for example, it is important that not all men be assigned to the same group in an experiment designed to assess the impact of news stories on how citizens think about capital punishment. Random assignment ensures that chance, rather than a person's characteristics, determines experimental group assignment.

With successful random assignment, a researcher can be very certain that any differences in opinions or behaviors found across experimental groups are due to their exposure to the original stimulus (that is, due to the experimenter's manipulated feature). Experiments thus allow researchers to conclude that one factor causes another—a feature of research designs called **internal validity**. The ability to draw such causal conclusions is the primary advantage of experiments over other research methods. For example, you could conduct a survey and ask people if they have read news articles framing the death penalty in terms of innocence and whether they support the death penalty. If those who have read these stories are less likely to favor capital punishment, it would be tempting to conclude that the innocence frame influenced individuals' opinions. But you could not rule out the possibility that those who opposed capital punishment *before* exposure to the news stories were more likely to search out and read such stories. So a person's political opinions might have influenced her news habits rather than the other way around. If, however, you expose some people to the innocence news story and others to a story framed in a different way, and you still find that those exposed to the innocence frame are less supportive of the death penalty, you can be much more certain that the news frame influenced their opinions.

Although experiments possess internal validity, they often have less external validity. That is, by using convenience samples (such as college students enrolled in introductory mass communications courses, as Dardis et al. did in their study) rather than random samples, experimenters cannot claim their sample is representative of the broader population. One way to address this weakness is to include an experimental design within a nationally representative survey. This method, called a **survey-based experiment**, entails randomly assigning survey respondents to experimental conditions. This approach "combine[s] the causal power of the randomized experiment with the representativeness of the general population survey."[11]

Mark Peffley and Jon Hurwitz used this approach in their national survey of race and death penalty attitudes.[12] They embedded an experiment in their survey by randomly assigning respondents to receive one of three versions of a question about the death penalty (see Table A.2). In the baseline condition, respondents received a death penalty question with no additional information. In the other

Table A.2   Support for the Death Penalty in a Survey-Based Experiment

	Baseline with no argument	Racial argument	Innocent argument
	"Do you strongly oppose, somewhat oppose, somewhat favor, or strongly favor the death penalty for persons convicted of murder?"	"Some people say that the death penalty is unfair because most of the people who are executed are African Americans. Do you strongly oppose, somewhat oppose, somewhat favor, or strongly favor the death penalty for persons convicted of murder?"	"Some people say that the death penalty is unfair because too many innocent people are being executed. Do you strongly oppose, somewhat oppose, somewhat favor, or strongly favor the death penalty for persons convicted of murder?"
White respondents	65%	77%	64%
Black respondents	50	38	34

Source: Adapted from Table 5.1 of Mark Peffley and Jon Hurwitz, *Justice in America: The Separate Realities of Blacks and Whites* (Cambridge, UK: Cambridge University Press, 2010), 158–159.

Note: Figures are the percentage of each group that somewhat or strongly favors the death penalty.

two conditions, respondents received information either about racial disparities and the death penalty or about innocence and the death penalty. Peffley and Hurwitz's results are fascinating. First, whites were substantially more supportive of the death penalty than blacks across all three conditions. Second, whites and blacks did not respond in the same way to the different arguments. Support for the death penalty fell significantly among blacks when they were exposed to either the racial or the innocence argument. In contrast, whites were not moved by the innocence argument, and they actually became *more* favorable toward the policy when presented with the racial argument. Because respondents were randomly assigned to the conditions, we can conclude with great confidence that the different arguments influence opinion on the death penalty. Moreover, because the respondents were selected randomly from the U.S. population, the results of this study apply to the American public in general.[13] In other words, this study has both internal and external validity.

INTERVIEWS

Asking people about their political views is also accomplished by **in-depth interviewing**. Unlike surveys in which hundreds (or thousands) of people are asked a series of closed-ended questions, interviewers ask their respondents much broader, often **open-ended questions**. That is, interviewers typically do not provide their respondents with a list of response options and ask them to select one but, rather, allow the interviewees to answer a question however they want. An interviewer interested in public opinion toward the death penalty might ask the following question: "What do you think about the death penalty?" This question encourages respondents to not just assess their overall opinion on the issue but consider the roots of their opinion and perhaps even grapple with any contradictory thoughts they might have about the policy. Topics such as racial disparities in the application of the death penalty, the deterrent effect of the death penalty, or popular culture references to the death penalty might emerge in response to this question. Note that the question does not provide response options, thus allowing the respondent to answer in multiple ways. The question prompts respondents to explain *why* they hold their opinions, and if respondents do not volunteer such information, interviewers can follow up and ask them directly to explain their perspectives. Such *why* questions, because they are open-ended, do not appear frequently on opinion surveys, yet they can provide very useful information about public opinion.

Allowing respondents to decide what is most appropriate when answering questions results in responses that are more likely to reflect their actual thinking (no matter how organized or how messy) on the topic. By forcing respondents to select a preconceived option, surveys might not measure real opinions on an issue. To take an obvious example, survey respondents confronted with the "favor" or "oppose" option to a death penalty question will typically select one of these options even if their real attitude is "I support the death penalty when I am certain that the person convicted of murder did, without a doubt, commit the murder, but often one cannot be certain, beyond a doubt, that the person actually did commit the murder and there are now many examples coming to light when incorrect decisions were made by juries." An in-depth interview is very likely to capture the nuances of this person's view, whereas a public opinion survey with closed-ended questions simply cannot.

In-depth interviews can be especially useful when researchers are interested in understanding the views of a particular group of people. For example, Sandra Jones conducted in-depth interviews with forty-nine people active in the anti–death penalty movement to understand what mobilized them to get involved.[14] Jones found that many activists were motivated by moral outrage but that their outrage was complex and nuanced. To illustrate, an African American male leader of the movement had this to say about the death penalty:

> Not only is it dehumanizing, but everything else that wraps around it is immoral. It's immoral to have another human being strapped down for the purpose of killing them. It is immoral to put the warden in such a conflict. The one thing I've learned from doing this work is when I came to it I had such a clear sense of who was good and who was evil. All that got blurred very quickly. You can't hate a guard who cries over an execution. You can't hate a warden who is shaking during an execution.[15]

It would be difficult, if not impossible, to capture the detailed richness of this person's views about the death penalty using a survey, but in-depth interviewing allowed the researcher to assess the fullness of this activist's perspective.

Because open-ended questions typically take longer to answer, the number of individuals participating in an interview is usually much smaller than the number who respond to a survey. With a smaller number of participants in a study, who have not been randomly selected to participate, it is inappropriate to draw conclusions that can apply to a larger population. Thus, studies using interview respondents are often criticized for not being representative of a larger population, a weakness that does not apply to surveys of randomly selected individuals.

FOCUS GROUPS

Focus groups resemble interviews in a number of ways, including that they both are used by researchers to examine how people think about political issues and that they use open-ended questions. The primary differences are that focus group research is conducted on multiple people at once and consists of a group discussion that is moderated and guided by a trained individual. Focus group researchers are often interested in learning how individuals construct political issues in their mind, how people communicate about a particular issue, and how an individual's discussion of a topic responds to communication from others in a group. In this way, focus groups are "a way to observe interaction among people that is important in understanding political behavior that is not possible to observe using more traditional empirical methodology."[16] To examine public opinion on capital punishment, for example, a focus group could be used to assess how people discuss this issue, including which features of it are especially compelling or relevant. Focus group participants could also be asked to read news articles or view movies about capital punishment and then discuss their reactions to determine how a group constructs meaning from such stories.

With the goal of understanding the complexity of citizens' death penalty opinions, Diana Falco and Tina Freiburger conducted six focus groups with twenty participants from Indiana County, Pennsylvania.[17] The researchers asked the participants to brainstorm about their positive and negative beliefs about the death penalty and to indicate their general opinion on the policy. Participants were also asked to read various crime scenarios and evaluate whether they would support the death penalty in each situation. Falco and Freiburger found that many citizens held both positive and negative views of the death penalty and that almost all citizens took characteristics of the offender or the victim into account as they responded to the crime scenarios. The researchers concluded that the twenty citizens in these focus groups have views on the death penalty that are much more complicated than suggested by "favor" or "oppose" responses to a survey question. Because the focus group participants do not constitute a random sample, the results cannot be generalized to the public as a whole. Nevertheless, these results are still very important because they help scholars think more carefully about how to design survey questions to more adequately measure the complexity of citizens' subtle, and sometimes tangled, views on the death penalty.

CONTENT ANALYSIS

The final method we profile here is content analysis. As its name indicates, **content analysis** is a technique used to analyze the content of communication. More specifically, it has been defined as "a research technique for the objective, systematic and quantitative description of the manifest content of communication."[18] Content analysis can be applied to any type of communication, such as a news media story, a speech by a politician, a popular television show, a blog, or a novel. The primary object of content analysis is to systematically summarize the content of the selected source or item. This is done by selecting specific criteria of the communication to analyze and then carefully coding a selection (such as stories or speeches) along these criteria. For example, a speech could be analyzed for the number of times a specific word is used, the number of times a topic is mentioned, and whether the speaker uses any examples from his or her personal life.

In terms of public opinion research, many topics can be examined using content analysis. If a researcher wishes to know how the news media present public opinion on an issue, such as capital punishment, the content of news stories can be analyzed. Is public opinion represented as opinion survey results or as quotations from individual people? Or are elected officials asked what they think the public thinks about this issue?

In studies that seek to determine whether news media coverage is related to public opinion, content analysis is also used to examine this coverage. Recall the Dardis et al. experiment we discussed earlier. In that study, subjects were exposed to news stories about the death penalty framed in terms of either morality or innocence. Dardis et al. did not simply pull those media frames out of thin air; instead, they content analyzed abstracts of capital punishment news articles in the *New York Times Index* between 1960 and 2003 to identify frames. By systematically analyzing what types of arguments were used in these abstracts, the researchers were able to examine common frames used in the *New York Times* coverage. The morality frame, for instance, included arguments about retribution, such as the "eye for an eye" rationale for the death penalty. The innocence frame, in contrast, included arguments about the possibility that a person on death row might be innocent due to a tainted or racist criminal justice system.[19] Dardis et al. found that the innocence frame received little attention prior to the 1980s but that it became a prominent frame in the 2000s. The morality frame received significant attention in the 1970s but has been less prevalent since then, although it continues to receive meaningful attention in the *New York Times*.

CONCLUSION

These five methods—surveys, experiments, interviews, focus groups, and content analysis—are the most common approaches used to assess public opinion. Surveys are by far the most frequently used approach, whereas focus groups and content analysis are the least common. Each method has advantages and disadvantages, and some methods are more appropriate than others for addressing particular types of public opinion questions, as the chapters in this book further illustrate.

Last, most of these research methods require human participation. Conducting research on people involves a host of ethical considerations. Chief among these concerns are that participants should voluntarily agree to participate, they should offer their informed consent before the study begins, and they should not suffer undue physical or psychological harm while participating in the study or afterward. For a detailed discussion of these and other ethical matters involved when using people as research participants, refer to The Belmont Report (listed in the Suggested Sources for Further Reading).

Key Concepts

attrition / 33

balanced question / 31

closed-ended questions / 29

content analysis / 39

convenience sample / 32

experiments / 34

external validity / 31

focus groups / 38

in-depth interviewing / 37

internal validity / 35

manipulation / 35

mixed-mode approach / 34

open-ended questions / 37

panel study or longitudinal survey / 33

population / 29

public opinion poll / 29

question order effects / 31

question wording effects / 29

random assignment / 35

random digit dial / 34

random sample / 31

response order effects / 30

sample / 29

subjects / 34

survey / 29

survey-based experiment / 36

survey mode / 33

Suggested Sources for Further Reading

Aronson, Elliot, Phoebe C. Ellsworth, James Merrill Carlsmith, and Marti Hope Gonzales. *Methods of Research in Social Psychology*. 2nd ed. Boston: McGraw-Hill, 1989.

Gilens, Martin. "An Anatomy of Survey-Based Experiments." In *Navigating Public Opinion: Polls, Policy, and the Future of American Democracy*, ed. Jeff Manza, Fay Lomax Cook, and Benjamin I. Page. Oxford: Oxford University Press, 2002.

Krueger, Richard A., and Mary Anne Casey. *Focus Groups: A Practical Guide for Applied Research.* 5th ed. Thousand Oaks, CA: Sage, 2015.

Rubin, Herbert J., and Irene S. Rubin. *Qualitative Interviewing: The Art of Hearing Data.* 3rd ed. Thousand Oaks, CA: Sage, 2011.

Weber, Robert Philip. *Basic Content Analysis.* 2nd ed. Thousand Oaks, CA: Sage, 1990.

Each of these sources provides a detailed overview of one specific research method: experiments, survey-based experiments, focus groups, interviewing, and content analysis.

Asher, Herbert. *Polling and the Public: What Every Citizen Should Know.* 8th ed. Washington, DC: CQ Press, 2010.

Dillman, Don A., Jolene D. Smyth, and Leah Melani Christian. *Internet, Mail, and Mixed-Mode Surveys: The Tailored Design Method.* 4th ed. Hoboken, NJ: Wiley, 2014.

The most common method for measuring public opinion is the opinion poll or survey. Asher's book is an informative and readable introduction to all aspects of survey research. If you are planning to conduct a survey yourself, the Dillman, Smyth, and Christian book is a must-read. It provides practical advice and detailed examples of best practices.

Lepore, Jill. "Politics and the New Machine." *New Yorker*, November 16, 2015. http:// www.newyorker.com/magazine/2015/11/16/politics-and-the-new-machine
"Does Polling Undermine Democracy?" *New York Times*, November 30, 2015. http://www.nytimes.com/roomfordebate/2015/11/30/does-polling-undermine-democracy

The Lepore article provides a historically grounded analysis of public opinion polling in modern times. "Does Polling Undermine Democracy?" appears on the opinion pages of the *New York Times* and provides several different perspectives on the contemporary role of polling in a democratic society.

"Ethical Principles and Guidelines for the Protection of Human Subjects of Research" (also known as The Belmont Report), http://ohsr.od.nih.gov/ guidelines/belmont.html
"Standards and Ethics," American Association for Public Opinion Research, https://www.aapor.org/AAPORKentico/Standards-Ethics.aspx

The Belmont Report was produced by the National Commission for the Protection of Human Subjects of Biomedical and Behavioral Research in 1979. This influential report established basic ethical principles that should be followed by scholars conducting research on human participants. This report is a must-read for anyone who collects data from human participants. The American Association for Public Opinion Research has developed standards, identified best practices, and articulated a code of ethics for people conducting survey research and using survey data for policymaking.

PART II

Are Citizens Pliable?

DO U.S. CITIZENS hold stable political attitudes? Or are many people pliable, with their attitudes frequently changing? These questions highlight a core difference among the democratic theories we profile in this book—beliefs regarding the political capabilities of the public. Which view suggests a more capable public? Is it best for people to hold opinions that stay the same over years or for people to be open to new perspectives? Put another way, do citizens need to be open to new ideas, fresh leaders, and policy innovations? Is it possible to guarantee that without having citizens susceptible to a politician's every whim?

These are important questions for any student of the democratic public to consider. Before reaching any firm answers, however, it is important to know where people's opinions originate, when and under what conditions they are likely to change, for whom opinions are likely to be stable versus changeable, and what role external communication sources play in influencing opinions. These topics are addressed in this section in specific chapters on the topics of political socialization, the mass media, and attitude stability and change.

CHAPTER 2

Political Socialization

IN 1987, an eight-year-old girl named Betsy wrote a letter to her mayor soliciting some advice. Journalists at National Public Radio learned of this letter, leading one of them (Noah Adams) to interview her.

Noah:	You wrote a letter to the mayor of New York, Mayor Koch.
Betsy:	Right.
Noah:	Tell me about that please.
Betsy:	Well I wrote to him because my parents are getting divorced and I really don't know who to turn to. I just told him that my parents are getting divorced and my dad is with somebody else and I was just getting used to something and now this and it's really kind of hard on me and I'd like an opinion.
Noah:	Why did you write to Mayor Koch?
Betsy:	'Cause he's somebody who I thought he's very good to us I guess because he's the mayor and he knows a lot of things and I thought he would know about this too.
Noah:	Did you get an answer back?
Betsy:	Yes.
Noah:	What did he say?
Betsy:	He . . . um . . . it's very short. "Thank you for the letter. I was saddened to learn of the difficult times you are experiencing now. It is important for you to share your feelings and thoughts with someone during this time. I wish there was an easy solution to these problems but there is not. Please remember that you are loved and that people care about you. All the best. Sincerely, Edward Koch."
Noah:	That's nice. Was that reassuring to you in a way?
Betsy:	No.[1]

Young Betsy had already developed views toward political leaders. Befitting her age, her image of Mayor Koch was largely favorable, although subject to revision based on her encounter with him. In other words, her political opinions were forming. The manner by which we all learn about politics and develop political opinions is called **political socialization**. Put another way, "political socialization is the process by which people acquire relatively enduring orientations toward politics in general and toward their own particular political systems."[2] As we elaborate on in the next section, this process begins in childhood.

There are many sources of people's political opinions. Important **socialization agents** include schools, peers, and the news media. Primary among these, however, is the family. In fact, among early socialization researchers, parents were thought to play the most influential socializing role.[3] In the pages that follow, we review the research supporting this conclusion, as well as discuss how the broader political context influences developing political opinions. Recently, scholars have focused on an alternative way that political attitudes are acquired—genetics. We review this hot, and somewhat controversial, area of research near the end of the chapter.

Another way to think of political socialization is as the transmission of key political values and norms from one generation to the next. This view of socialization focuses on how societies "inculcate appropriate norms and practices in citizens, residents or members."[4] David Easton and Jack Dennis were proponents of this approach, linking socialization to the maintenance of a democratic political system.[5] In particular, Easton and Dennis described the main goal of early socialization as fostering confidence and trust in as well as positive affect toward the political system. They further argued that the widespread holding of these attitudes is important for the persistence of a nation's government. Failure to transmit these norms to new generations of children could threaten a nation's stability.

Consistent with Easton and Dennis's view, successful socialization would result in citizens who support the nation's system of government and who respect political authority. Such outcomes would please democratic elitists. First, socializing citizens in such a way could lead them to defer to political leaders and the leaders' expertise. This would preserve the dominance of elite decision making with lesser involvement from the citizens, as democratic elitists prefer. Second, this type of socialization emphasizes system support over individual development, a goal that democratic elitists support but one that other democratic theorists, most especially participatory democrats, find worrisome.

In contrast, pluralists hope that socialization develops strong political identities and a clear sense of how individuals' interests are best represented in the political system. Especially with a clear sense of their own similarities to the political parties, citizens can more easily pursue their interests and hold elected officials accountable for representing them.[6] Thus, pluralists would favor a socialization process that results in strong partisan identification. To what degree does socialization accomplish the goals of these democratic theorists? We return to this question at the end of the chapter.

CHILDHOOD SOCIALIZATION

Childhood socialization typically begins during the elementary school years, when children learn about the political world and develop political orientations. From the fourth grade, "children move from near—but not complete—ignorance of adult politics to awareness of most of the conspicuous features of the adult political world" by the eighth grade.[7] One of the earliest political attitudes formed is a highly positive evaluation of the nation. Children believe that the United States is better than other nations and at an early age develop a strong emotional attachment to the nation.[8]

Benevolent Leader Images

Another notable political orientation of elementary school children is their ideal-ization of leaders, especially the president. In one of the classic studies of child-hood socialization, Fred Greenstein asked fourth through eighth graders in New Haven, Connecticut, to rate specific political executives in 1958.[9] Substantial majorities of children who knew these leaders rated them as "very good," whereas barely any children (less than 1 percent) rated the leaders as "bad." For example, 71 percent of the children evaluated the president's job performance as very good, with a further 21 percent feeling that the president was doing a "fairly good" job. These evaluations were higher than adult assessments of the president. During the time of Greenstein's study, 58 percent of the adult public approved of Dwight Eisenhower's performance. Similar positive assessments emerged in a study of second through eighth graders living in a Chicago suburb.[10] These children were asked to compare the president to "most men" on a number of characteristics. Large majorities of children felt that the president is more honest, is more knowl-edgeable, and works harder. When asked to evaluate the president as a person, nearly all (over 90 percent for most grades) students said the president is "the best person in the world" or a "good person."

The words children use to describe political leaders and their duties are quite interesting and further demonstrate the positive attitudes children hold.[11] Green-stein asked the children in his study, "What kinds of things do you think the Mayor [President, etc.] does?"[12] Some of their responses appear in Table 2.1. These children generally described the leaders doing good deeds and providing for people's basic needs. Further, this **benevolent leader imagery** exists for most children in the absence of factual information about the leaders. As the examples in the table demonstrate, some children do not describe the leaders' duties accu-rately, for example, assuming that the mayor pays workers or makes swings. Yet this does not prevent them from possessing positive attitudes about the leaders.

Table 2.1   Children's Descriptions of Political Leaders

Leader	Description
The president . . .	"gives us freedom" (8th grader)
	"[does] good work" (6th grader)
	"has the right to stop bad things before they start" (5th grader)
	"is doing a very good job of making people be safe" (4th grader)
	"deals with foreign countries and takes care of the U.S." (8th grader)
The mayor . . .	"makes parks and swings" (5th grader)
	"sees that schools have what they need and stores and other places too" (5th grader)
	"pays working people like banks" (5th grader)
	"helps everyone to have nice homes and jobs" (4th grader)
	"sends men to build parks for us and make our city be a good one" (4th grader)

Source: Fred I. Greenstein, "The Benevolent Leader: Children's Images of Political Authority," *American Political Science Review* 54 (1960), 939.

In 2000, Amy Carter and Ryan Teten asked Nashville school children the same questions that Greenstein had asked New Haven children in 1958.[13] The results from 2000 were similar to the earlier results in one important respect: fourth- through eighth-grade children continued to hold idealized and benevolent images of the *office of the presidency.* Compared to earlier decades, however, children of today are much more likely to evaluate the *president himself* negatively. Recall that 71 percent of Greenstein's children felt that the president was doing a "very good" job and another 21 percent evaluated the president's performance as "fairly good." The results from Carter and Teten's study were 14 and 28 percent, respectively. Furthermore, 28 percent of the children in 2000 assessed the president as "bad," whereas only 1 percent of the 1958 children held this attitude.

Children come to have political attitudes from a number of different sources. In terms of their idealized images of leaders, children transfer their generally positive feelings toward authority figures they personally know (such as parents) to political leaders.[14] That is, although children might not know exactly what the president does, they understand that the president is a person of authority and deserves respect. In addition, parents serve as agents of socialization by sharing information and assessments of leaders with children. Although these adults may hold negative attitudes toward specific leaders, they probably (although as we note later, not always) temper or sugarcoat their feelings when discussing politics with their children, thus explaining why children's attitudes toward leaders are generally more positive than adults' attitudes.[15]

Another important agent of childhood socialization is the school. Elementary school rituals, such as reciting the pledge of allegiance and singing patriotic songs, foster patriotism and loyalty to the nation among children. In school, children also learn to follow rules and obey authority figures, behaviors that they pursue in nonschool settings as well.[16] Elementary school curricula and teachers generally do not directly inculcate children to hold specific political attitudes, such as support for a specific public policy.[17] By high school, civics curricula have been shown to influence students' levels of political knowledge and trust in government, but curricular effects on political attitudes of elementary school children are uncommon.[18]

Features of the political context, such as current events, also influence children's attitudes. One study assessed the opinions of Detroit-area children in grades four, six, and eight in 1966 and again in 1968.[19] In 1968 children were less likely than in 1966 to believe the president is responsive to the people or that the government is helpful to their families. Why? Children became more critical in part because of the events that transpired during these two years, specifically riots in Detroit, the assassination of Martin Luther King Jr., and the escalating war in Vietnam.

The Watergate scandal also had immediate and lingering effects on children's images of the president. In 1972, a burglary occurred in the Democratic National Committee headquarters in the Watergate complex in Washington, DC. Amid allegations that he tried to cover up his involvement in this burglary, President Richard Nixon resigned from office two years later. To examine the effects of this scandal while events were still unfolding, Greenstein compared the attitudes of children in 1969–1970 with those held in June 1973.[20] Although these children viewed the president somewhat less positively in the second time period, assessments of the president did not become significantly more negative during the early 1970s. In a very specific domain, however, children's attitudes toward the president did change. Compared with four years earlier, in 1973 children were much more likely to believe that the president is above the law (31 versus 58 percent, respectively, expressed this view). Finally, Carter and Teten's finding that children's evaluations of the president were more negative in 2000 can probably be traced to Watergate.[21] The Watergate era ushered in a sustained period of increasingly negative views of government and politicians among the American public, including children.

Age, Class, Ethnic, and Racial Differences

Although positive images of political leaders are fairly common among children, there are important exceptions to this trend. Older children were substantially less likely to view leaders in an idealized fashion.[22] Further, children's assessments of a president's personal qualities (such as honesty) became more negative as the children got older, but their evaluations of the president's governing-related characteristics (such as working hard and being knowledgeable) remained positive. The president is thus "increasingly seen as a person whose abilities are appropriate to the demands of the office."[23] In other words, largely because of cognitive development, children are better able with age to distinguish between the role of president and the person who is the president, with their view of the person becoming somewhat more negative.

Significant class and racial differences also exist in children's evaluations of political leaders. In 1967, Dean Jaros, Herbert Hirsch, and Frederic Fleron surveyed children from Appalachia (specifically eastern Kentucky).[24] They selected this region because its higher-than-average levels of poverty and relative isolation distinguish it from most middle- and upper-class regions of the United States. Jaros, Hirsch, and Fleron's results are strikingly different from those obtained by Greenstein and others. Appalachian children demonstrated much less positive attitudes toward leaders and the political system. Whereas 77 percent of the fifth to eighth graders in the Chicago area, for example, believed that the president works harder than "most men,"[25] only 35 percent of the Kentucky children held this view. Also, 26 percent of the children in Appalachia believed that the president is "not a good person" compared with only 8 percent of Chicago-area children. Rather than Greenstein's benevolent leader, Jaros et al. conclude that **malevolent leader imagery** is more common in eastern Kentucky. Their results are important not only for what they demonstrate about political socialization in Appalachia, a region that is not often studied, but also because they caution us against concluding that positive images of political authority are universally held among American children.

Compared with white children, idealized images of the president are less common among black children. In a 1969–1970 study of children's attitudes, 32 percent of black children possessed positive or idealized assessments compared with 55 percent of white children.[26] These racial differences generally exist at all grade levels but are especially notable as children become older. For example, whereas attitudes toward the president and police officers were similar for black and white second graders, by eighth grade black children held significantly more negative images than their white peers.[27]

Racial differences also exist when we consider other political attitudes. White school children tend to have considerably higher levels of political trust and efficacy compared with black school children. **Trust** assesses the degree to which individuals agree that political leaders are honest and act in the public's interest. **Efficacy** refers to the belief that one can influence the decisions of government officials and the belief that these officials are responsive to public wishes. When levels of trust and efficacy by children's race were compared in the 1960s, black children had consistently lower levels of efficacy than did their white peers. Racial differences in trust, however, only emerged in research conducted after summer 1967, at which point levels of trust were lower among blacks. Before then, white and black children had similar levels of trust. That year marked a time when the black community as a whole became less trusting of the government, in part because urban riots were occurring in the United States and the policy gains achieved during the civil rights movement had seemingly ended.[28]

Ethnic and racial differences in children's political attitudes have persisted. In 2003 and 2004, Kim Fridkin, Patrick Kenney, and Jack Crittenden surveyed white, African American, Latino, and Native American eighth graders in and around Phoenix, Arizona.[29] Compared with the minority students, white students displayed more trust in government and higher levels of political efficacy. Native Americans had the lowest levels of both trust and efficacy.

In one of the few recent examinations of younger children's political attitudes, Christia Spears Brown, Rashmita Mistry, and Rebecca Bigler conducted a small survey of African American children in the aftermath of Hurricane Katrina.[30] Katrina, a powerful hurricane, landed on the Gulf Coast in late August 2005, with devastating consequences. Massive flooding and property damage occurred, notably in New Orleans. Governmental response to the hurricane was widely considered to be too slow and inadequate. Meanwhile, Americans throughout the nation witnessed the crisis unfold on their television sets. The New Orleans victims were disproportionately black and poor, leading Brown and her colleagues to explore black children's attitudes toward the government response and attributions of responsibility for the inadequate relief efforts. Their sample was drawn from schools in one city—Los Angeles—and contained only African Americans. Thus, their results cannot speak to racial differences in relevant attitudes or to nationwide attitudes. Yet Brown, Mistry, and Bigler report a number of interesting findings, particularly regarding age differences. Their youngest participants (second graders) were more likely to evaluate President George W. Bush's performance favorably than were the older respondents (eighth graders). In terms of what was responsible for the delay in relief reaching the victims, the younger children were most likely to credit logistical challenges (such as the difficulty in rescuing thousands of people). The eighth graders, on the other hand, were more likely to believe racial discrimination was a factor.

What might account for class, ethnic, and racial differences in children's attitudes? According to one approach, ethnic and racial minorities have less power than whites in the political system and less reason to believe that political leaders will respond to their wishes. Furthermore, past ethnic and racial discrimination at the hands of government (such as school segregation, police violence, and voter disenfranchisement) has generated mistrust toward the government among affected group members. Black, Latino, and Native American children are aware of these current and past realities, which contributes to their having different attitudes from white children.[31] In other words, this **political reality explanation** posits that political attitudes respond to actual political events and phenomena.

Parental communication is also an important factor. Jaros, Hirsch, and Fleron attribute the Appalachian children's less favorable assessments of leaders and the political system to their parents' views. Among Appalachian adults, "there is a great deal of overt, anti-government sentiment. . . . Rejection of and hostility toward political authority, especially federal authority, has long characterized the region."[32] Attempts to explain racial and ethnic differences in trust and efficacy also posit a role for parents. Fridkin and her colleagues found that children who discussed politics with their parents had more positive attitudes toward government but also that political discussions were more common in the homes of middle-class white children than black, Latino, Native American, or working-class white children.[33] Fridkin, Kenney, and Crittenden also wonder about the nature of political discussions in the homes. Negative views toward government (particularly the government's past and present interactions with minorities) might be shared between minority parents and children, they argue, more so than in white households. Unfortunately, these researchers did not assess the *content* of family political discussions. Their work, as well as that of Jaros, Hirsch, and Fleron, suggests that future studies of childhood socialization should examine family conversations more fully.

PARENTAL TRANSMISSION OF POLITICAL ATTITUDES

As they move into adolescence, children begin to acquire specific political opinions to add to the more general orientations toward government and political leaders gained during early childhood. Parents are thought to be a key source of these political attitudes, perhaps even the most important source, as the following quotation illustrates: "Whether the child is conscious or unaware of the impact, whether the process is role-modelling or overt transmission, whether the values are political and directly usable or 'nonpolitical' but transferable, and whether what is passed on lies in the cognitive or affective realm, it has been argued that the family is of paramount importance."[34]

In 1965, Kent Jennings and Richard Niemi began a study to examine directly the similarity between adolescents' political attitudes and those of their parents.[35] Their research—one of the most influential political socialization studies conducted in the United States—improved on prior socialization studies in important ways. Thus, we profile their study in this section. We begin with the socializing role played by parents during their children's adolescence and then explore whether attitudes acquired by the children remain stable during their adult years. For both **adolescent socialization** and **adult socialization**, we focus heavily on the acquisition of one important attitude—party identification.

Parental Transmission during Adolescence

Empirically, one could assess the influence of parents' attitudes on their children by using a number of approaches. One method involves surveying the children, asking them their political attitudes and also asking them to report their parents' attitudes. (Similarly, one could survey parents, querying them about their and their children's attitudes.) This approach is limited, however, because of the possibility that the children either do not know their parents' attitudes or assume that their parents' attitudes are the same as theirs. If the latter occurs, this projection could lead to the parents' and children's attitudes appearing to be more similar than they really are. To avoid these problems, Jennings and Niemi surveyed children and their parents separately, with members of each group completing their own questionnaires. In total, 1,669 high school seniors took part in the first (1965) wave of their study. For approximately one-third of these students, their father was randomly selected to complete a questionnaire. The mother was randomly selected for another third, and both parents were selected to be surveyed for the final third.

Another advantage of Jennings and Niemi's study is that their research participants were selected to represent the entire nation. Rather than studying parents and children from one city or one geographical area, these researchers used a national sample. High schools across the nation were randomly selected, with steps taken to ensure that this sample accurately represented the entire population of high schools in the United States. Thus, the ninety-seven selected high schools included those from cities, suburbs, and rural areas; those with varying numbers of students; those from every geographical region of the nation; and both public and private schools. Within each selected school, fifteen to twenty-one seniors (depending on the size of the school) were randomly selected to participate in the study. This approach to selecting study participants, known as a **national probability sample**, allowed Jennings and Niemi to make inferences from their participants to the entire nation of high school seniors and their parents. With other methods, researchers must be more cautious in their conclusions. Selecting participants from one's local area, for example, does not allow a researcher to draw conclusions about the entire nation. Further, if participants volunteer to participate instead of being randomly selected, we cannot be certain that these self-selected participants' attitudes mirror those of the greater population. In fact, these people very likely may have more intense attitudes or be more politically aware, factors that increase the likelihood that an individual will voluntarily participate in a political survey.

To assess how thoroughly parents transmit their political attitudes to their offspring, Jennings and Niemi compared a variety of political attitudes between parents and their children. One of their most significant conclusions is that children are more likely to share their parents' **party identification** than other political attitudes (see Table 2.2). The figures presented in Table 2.2 are tau-bs, which measure how closely associated two items are. The possible range of tau-b is from 0 to 1.0. In Jennings and Niemi's study, the higher the value of tau-b, the more children shared the same attitudes as their parents. Smaller values, then, indicate that offspring and parents had dissimilar attitudes.

With a tau-b of .47, the correlation between parental and offspring party identification is stronger than for the other political attitudes studied by Jennings and Niemi. Analyzing this relationship in another way, the researchers found that 59 percent of high school seniors had the same general partisanship as their parents

Table 2.2   Similarity of Political Attitudes between Parents and Offspring

Political attitude	Correlation between parents and offspring (tau-b)
Party identification	.47
Political issues/civil liberties:	
School integration	.34
School prayer	.29
Communist should be allowed to hold office	.13
Speeches against churches and religion should be allowed	.05
Evaluations of groups:	
Catholics	.28
Southerners	.22
Labor unions	.22
Negroes	.20
Whites	.19
Jews	.18
Protestants	.13
Big business	.08
Political cynicism	.12

Source: Data from M. Kent Jennings and Richard G. Niemi, "The Transmission of Political Values from Parent to Child," *American Political Science Review* 62 (1968): 173, 175, 176, 178.

(for example, if the child was a strong Democrat, the parent was either a strong, weak, or Independent-leaning Democrat). In only 7 percent of the parent-child pairs was one person a Democrat and the other a Republican, or vice versa. This result led Jennings and Niemi to conclude that the "transmission of party preferences from one generation to the next is carried out rather successfully in the American context."[36] One significant difference in partisanship did emerge from their analysis: the children were more likely to be politically independent than their parents (35.7 versus 23.9 percent identified as Independent, respectively). Unbeknownst to them at the time, Jennings and Niemi's data capture a snapshot of a decades-long trend of Americans becoming more weakly attached to the political parties, a topic we return to shortly.

Political attitudes other than partisanship appear to be passed from parent to child less often, as demonstrated in Table 2.2. Among political issue opinions, parents and children were more likely to hold the same attitudes regarding school integration and school prayer compared to civil liberties items, such as allowing individuals with unpopular views to hold office or give public speeches. Parent-child agreement on evaluations of political groups, such as "Catholics" or "Negroes," falls in between their similarity on attitudes toward policy issues and civil liberties. Finally, there is little agreement between parents and offspring on their degree of cynicism toward politicians and the political system. Overall, seniors are much less likely to be cynical than their parents, a result that coincides with the childhood socialization research presented earlier. Jennings and Niemi attribute this finding to the fact that schools serve as powerful socializing agents, inculcating positive views of the nation (through rituals and curricula) while avoiding much critical analysis of the U.S. government.

These results tell us something about adolescent socialization in the 1960s, but what about in more recent decades? Fortunately, Jennings and Niemi were not done exploring political socialization in 1965. The high school seniors they first interviewed in 1965 were reinterviewed three more times, the last time in 1997. The children of the former high school seniors were also interviewed in 1997. This research design permits an exploration of parent-child transmission for two different time periods, which is exactly what Kent Jennings, Laura Stoker, and Jake Bowers did.[37] In other words, they compared the correspondence between the attitudes of the 1965 high school seniors and their parents (in 1965) with the correspondence between these former seniors and their children (in 1997).

Jennings, Stoker, and Bowers found that, across a variety of political issues, the likelihood that a child in his late teens will hold the same attitudes as his parents was largely the same in 1997 as it had been in 1965. Furthermore, parent-child correspondence was higher for party identification in 1997 than almost all other issues. In a departure from 1965, however, parental transmission of two attitudes—toward gay rights and abortion—was higher than for party affiliation. The authors attribute this to the high salience and moral basis for both of these issues. In the end, they conclude that "the patterns of political reproduction do not differ appreciably across the generations."[38] Jennings and Niemi's initial results were thus not timebound; that is, they were not a product of the political times of the 1960s.

Taking this work a step further, Jennings, Stoker, and Bowers explored when the transmission of party identification from parents to their children would be enhanced. In particular, they identified family characteristics that should result in parents providing frequent and clear cues regarding their political views to their offspring. Two seem to be especially important: **family politicization** (the degree to which parents are politically active and politics is discussed in the household) and parental **attitude stability**. As demonstrated in Figure 2.1, the correspondence of party identification between parents and children was indeed higher in more politically active and conversant families than low-politicization families. Also, the more stable a parent's party affiliation was, the more likely a child identified with the same party as her parent. These two results held for both time

Figure 2.1 Parent-Child Correspondence of Party Identification by Family Politicization and Parental Attitude Stability

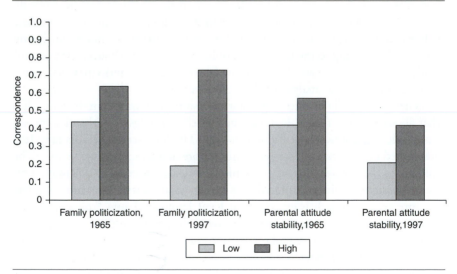

Source: Data from M. Kent Jennings, Laura Stoker, and Jake Bowers, "Politics across Generations: Family Transmission Reexamined," *Journal of Politics* 71 (2009), 789.

Note: Bars represent the correspondence of the parent's and children's party identification, derived from multivariate regression analyses. Correspondence is measured on a scale of 0 to 1, with 1 indicating parents and children shared the same party identification within every pair. A score of 0 would mean that parent and child party identification is not the same for any of the pairs.

periods, but the effect of both family characteristics was stronger in 1997 than in 1965, as demonstrated by the larger gap between the light- and dark-colored bars for 1997 than for the earlier time.

Do Preadult Attitudes Persist into Adulthood?

Once children leave adolescence and enter adulthood, do their political attitudes remain the same? If not, do they change in predictable ways? There are a number of methods to study adult socialization. One of the most effective ways is to survey the same group of people when they are adolescents and then again when they are adults. This method, called a **panel** or **longitudinal study**, is the approach taken by Jennings and Niemi. As already mentioned, they interviewed their sample of high school seniors four times: in 1965, 1973, 1982, and 1997. Although they were not able to reinterview all of the 1,669 seniors who had participated in the original study, they did reinterview nearly 1,000 of the participants in all four waves of the study. This study design allows a comparison of the attitudes of these individuals at various points in their life—as high school seniors, at twenty-six years old, at thirty-five years old, and again at fifty years old—to directly assess whether their late-adolescent political attitudes persisted into and throughout adulthood. This panel study has resulted in a rich array of information and has produced a number of interesting insights into adult socialization.

In particular, we have learned a lot about the stability of party identification over time from analyses of this panel study. Figure 2.2 demonstrates how stable the high school seniors' party affiliation was from the year of their high school graduation (1965) to their midtwenties (1973) to two other time periods: 1973–1982 (when the former seniors aged from twenty-six to thirty-five) and 1982–1997 (when they aged from thirty-five to fifty). For now, focus your attention on the white bars for each time period. The bar is shorter for the 1965–1973 time span than for the other two. This means that these respondents' party identification was most likely to change between the ages of eighteen and twenty-six. After passing through their midtwenties, their party affiliation remained more stable. In fact, the level of stability was the same between the ages of twenty-six and thirty-five as between thirty-five and fifty.[39] Finally, similar findings exist for opinions toward political issues such as racial policies, school prayer, and political tolerance. Attitudes shifted around a fair bit when the members of the high school class of 1965 were in their early twenties but did not change as much throughout their later adulthoods.[40]

This pattern supports an **impressionable years model** of attitude stability. The impressionable years, typically late adolescence and early adulthood, can be a time of personal growth and development. As an individual goes through her impressionable years, personal experiences (such as moving away from the childhood home, beginning a career, or getting married) can have political ramifications. In particular, her political views may fluctuate. According to this

Figure 2.2   Stability of Party Identification over Time, Overall and by Preadult Parent-Child Correspondence

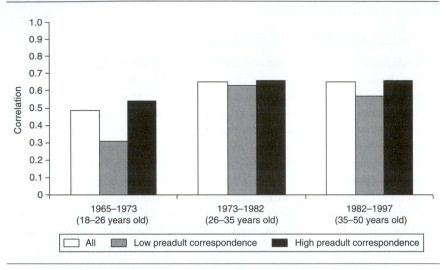

Source: Data for "All" bars from Laura Stoker and M. Kent Jennings, "Of Time and the Development of Partisan Polarization," *American Journal of Political Science* 52 (2008), 623; data for other bars from M. Kent Jennings, Laura Stoker, and Jake Bowers, "Politics across Generations: Family Transmission Reexamined," *Journal of Politics* 71 (2009), 794.

Note: Bars represent the stability of party identification across each time period, as measured by continuity correlations.

understanding, those in their early twenties lack the experience to have consistent political opinions. As young adults grow older, they experience fewer genuinely new events that influence their political opinions. Their political views then become more firmly grounded in their past experiences and are thus more resistant to change.[41] The impressionable years model is a specific type of a broader class of socialization dynamics—**life cycle effects**. The life cycle explanation presumes that people's political attitudes are influenced by their age (by their place in the life cycle). Theoretically, these effects could occur at many different stages in a person's life. Yet the most consistent effects of age on political attitudes are the ones we have already mentioned: attitude volatility during the impressionable years followed by relative stability later in adulthood.[42]

From the Jennings-Niemi panel data, we have learned that political opinions of many people undergo changes as they enter adulthood. Now, let's bring parents back into our discussion, particularly the degree of parent-child attitude similarity at the end of adolescence. Return your attention to Figure 2.2, focusing now on the colored bars. Recall that this figure presents the over-time stability of party identification for Jennings and Niemi's panel respondents for three different time periods. The gray bars represent stability over time among those whose party affiliation did not correspond closely to that of their parents' party affiliation when they were eighteen years old. The black bars represent over-time stability among preadults who had a high correspondence with their parents.

This analysis, which was conducted by Jennings, Stoker, and Bowers, uncovered two interesting findings.[43] First, from ages eighteen to twenty-six, people who possessed a party affiliation similar to their parents experienced less volatility in their partisanship compared to those whose partisanship was dissimilar from their parents. As Jennings and his colleagues explain, "Those young adults entering [adulthood] more securely attached to the political 'apron strings' of their parents were more likely to withstand the novelties they were to encounter. Those less anchored in that way proved to be far more vulnerable, and thus more apt to change."[44] Second, between ages twenty-six and thirty-five and again between thirty-five and fifty, the stability of the party identification of these individuals over time was much less dependent on whether they had shared their parents' partisanship when they had been eighteen. The story here is much more about increases in stability over time as an individual leaves the impressionable years (the gray and black bars for both of the later two periods are taller than for the first period). In contrast, the gap between the gray and black bars is much smaller for either of the final two time periods compared to the first.

In another example of the lingering effects of parental socialization, Niemi and Jennings compared the parents' party affiliation and their offspring's affiliation separately for those offspring who held consistently conservative versus consistently liberal opinions toward specific political issues (such as school integration, support for American involvement in Vietnam, and the proper role of government in providing jobs).[45] We might expect that individuals with strong and consistent conservative opinions would identify as Republicans. Yet for offspring with such conservative opinions who were raised in a home of strong Democrats, the typical party identification at age eighteen was weak Democrat. Eight years later, these individuals identified more often as political independents, albeit leaning somewhat toward the Democratic Party. Nine years after this, these offspring (now about thirty-five years old) were quite clearly Independent in their political affiliation. So, although the partisanship of these individuals moved away from the Democratic Party and became more in line with their ideological leanings, the pull of their preadult socialization (particularly their parents' partisanship) prevented them from identifying as Republicans, even though they held conservative issue opinions.

Finally, recent work by Elias Dinas demonstrates that the degree of family politicization during adolescence influences attitude stability in adulthood.[46] The findings from this work might surprise you. Recall that in more politically active and conversant families, children are more likely to share their parents' partisanship than in less political families. As children enter adulthood and leave the family home, however, it is actually the children of the more politicized families that are most likely to move away from their parents' party identification. How might this be? Young adults from more politically engaged families carry this political interest with them as they embark on their new lives. They are more likely to discuss politics and be aware of political happenings than their peers who were raised in less politically tuned-in households. Exposure to new ideas and information results in some offspring from politicized families revising their partisanship, most especially during their young-adult years. In contrast, because children from less politicized households "end up less politically engaged as adults, their partisanship is not as subject to the social and political forces that prompt partisanship changes."[47]

GENERATIONAL AND PERIOD EFFECTS

So far, we have primarily discussed the role that individuals and institutions play in shaping the political attitudes of children and adolescents. The development of political opinions is also influenced by the political context, such as specific political events and broader political trends.

When changes in the political context influence the political socialization of an entire age cohort, a **generational effect** on political attitudes occurs. In other words, the opinions of an entire generation of people can be influenced by the nature of the times. This is especially likely for those who are in their impressionable years. Take, for instance, the formation of party affiliation among those who came of age during the post–World War II period.[48] They were socialized at a time when the political parties were weakening on the national stage. Beginning in the 1950s, national politicians began to build personal campaign organizations rather than tying themselves clearly to the national parties. Television coverage of campaigns tended to focus on the candidates rather than the parties, and the candidates could bypass the parties and their grassroots campaign organizations by using television to disseminate their messages directly to the voters. These changes in the broader context influenced the partisanship of individuals whose formative socialization occurred during this period. In particular, they were less likely to identify strongly with either the Democratic or Republican Party than were cohorts who had been socialized earlier, when parties had been more dominant.

As the political parties were changing nationally, regional developments were also afoot. Notably, white voters in the southern United States began to shift their allegiance to the Republican Party in the 1960s. During the decades immediately prior to this, Democratic support among whites in the South had been strong, so strong that the region was known as the Solid South. Much to the chagrin of Southern Democratic whites, however, the national Democratic Party championed civil rights legislation in the 1960s. The partisan context in the region thus changed, with the Democratic Party becoming much less popular over time. Following a generational effects model, this changed context produced effects on partisanship in the region among those who were leaving adolescence. Southern whites who were in their formative years during or after the 1960s were less likely than older whites in the region to adopt a Democratic Party identification. Successive generations became less and less Democratic as they entered adulthood.[49] In fact, by 1984, Southern whites who were just then becoming eligible to vote were more likely to be Republicans than Democrats.

A **period effect** occurs when salient features of the political period influence the political attitudes of many, *regardless of age*. Note that period effects differ from generational effects in one important way: generational effects result when aspects of the political context shape the political attitudes only of people who are similar in age (such as those who are in their impressionable years). A few examples should serve to illustrate this difference. In fact, the studies we used to demonstrate generational effects in the two previous paragraphs also uncovered period effects. Recall the first example. It demonstrated that Americans were less likely to hold strong partisan attitudes after World War II because generations of citizens were socialized in an era when the national political parties had weakened. At the same time, across many age cohorts, the percentage of people identifying as Independents increased. This turn away from the parties and toward partisan independence happened among younger citizens who were just entering adulthood as well as among older adults.[50] In other words, citizens of all ages were somewhat influenced by the decline of parties on the national political stage, a period effect.

Similarly, a changed political context produced period effects in the South. Not only have new generations of white Southerners displayed lower levels of identification with the Democratic Party than prior generations, but also Southern whites *across many generations* have been less likely to identify as Democratic over time.[51] For example, the average party identification of white Southerners who entered adulthood in the 1960s was between Independent-leaning Democrat and weak Democrat. By 2004, the average party affiliation of this cohort was between Independent and Independent-leaning Republican. In other words, the partisanship of this group continued to change as they aged, even when they were well past their formative years. The drift toward Republican Party identification occurred among other generations of Southern white adults as well. Key features of the 1960s help to explain why. That decade was "a time of considerable political strife that would have been difficult—if not impossible—to avoid. Civil rights protests, government action to promote civil rights without precedent since Reconstruction, the assassination of high-ranking leaders, ghetto riots, and the like all went beyond normal headline news. . . . The seemingly uniform change in partisan attitudes found in all of our cohorts may reflect this uniquely powerful barrage of information."[52]

The Millennial Generation

Generational differences abound in our society, in musical tastes, use of technology, clothing preferences, and communication patterns, to name a few. Age cohorts can also differ from others in terms of political outlooks and behaviors. More specifically, a **political generation** "refers to a group that is [politically] distinctive in any number of respects by virtue of having experienced a specific set of social, economic, technological, and/or political circumstances at a formative period in their lives."[53] In other words, a generation of people—such as the Baby Boomers (born between 1946 and 1964) or Generation Xers (1965–1980)—pass through their impressionable years around the same time and thus are exposed to the same political and social context during this crucial time in their lives. If this exposure results in a set of distinctive political views for the generation, a political generation exists.

What about today's youngest generation, those born after 1980? Do **Millennials** differ politically from earlier generations? In terms of a variety of political views, yes. They are much more likely to consider themselves political independents than are members of previous generations (50% versus 39% for Generation X and 37% for Baby Boomers).[54] Ideologically, they are more liberal. Compared to older cohorts, Millennials are more supportive of LGBT rights, racial and gender equality, a path to citizenship for undocumented immigrants, and government involvement to address societal ills.[55] Data from the 2014 General Social Survey demonstrate some opinion differences among Millennials, Generation Xers, and Baby Boomers (see Figure 2.3). For the first six topics displayed in the figure, Millennials' attitudes are clearly distinct from the other two generations, in the more liberal direction for all. For the two issues of abortion and gun control, however, generational differences do not emerge.[56]

Cataloging differences among generations is relatively straightforward, although explaining why such differences exist is tricky.[57] For one, at a given point in time, generations differ by when they went through their impressionable years as well as their current age. Put another way, today's Millennials' attitudes might differ from Baby Boomers' simply because they are younger rather than because they were socialized in a different historical setting. Furthermore, generations differ in a myriad of politically relevant ways, making it challenging to sort out which factors might contribute to generational distinctiveness. Bearing this complexity in mind, a few possible explanations for the Millennial generation's distinctiveness have been proposed, although all would benefit from more rigorous empirical testing. Coming of political age during a time of political polarization and government stalemate has likely contributed to the Millennials' weaker ties to the political party system. White Millennials' more liberal racial attitudes have been attributed to one key political event that happened as many were entering

Figure 2.3   Generational Differences in Attitudes, 2014

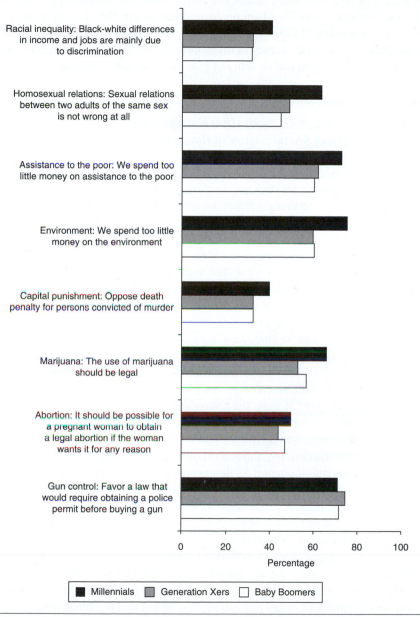

Source: Analysis of the General Social Survey Cumulative Data File, 1972–2014.

Note: The bars represent the percentage of respondents who agreed with each position.

adulthood: the election of Barack Obama as president.[58] The fact that the Millennial generation is more racially and ethnically diverse than other generations likely contributes to its liberalism on issues such as equality, immigration, and government activism.[59] Other societal factors are probably relevant as well, such as the greater presence of women in the workforce, the increase in nontraditional families, and the heightened visibility of gays and lesbians in popular culture.

Public Opinion in Comparative Perspective
BOX 2.1 POLITICAL SOCIALIZATION IN NIGERIA AND IRAN

In many nations around the world, the primary agents and processes of political socialization are the same as those in the United States. This is especially the case in firmly established democracies. Among nondemocratic nations or those that recently transitioned to democracy, however, the socialization process can look quite different.

Take Nigeria, for example. Since breaking away from British colonial rule in 1960, Nigerians have witnessed multiple military coups and thus a long period of military rule. Civilian, democratically elected leaders have ruled Nigeria since 1999. Not surprisingly, such political instability contributed to Nigerians' views of politics, notably increasing cynicism toward the government. At the same time, there are also strains of faith in democratic procedures among the public.[1]

The Nigerian government might have played a role in socializing such support for democratic procedures. In the years before a new Nigerian constitution was adopted in 1999, the nation's military leaders developed programs to prepare the public for a transition to democracy. This attempt at government socialization is typically not found in the United States or in European democracies. Yet, although state-sponsored programs seem to have promoted public support for democracy in the abstract, cynicism toward officials and the day-to-day functioning of the Nigerian government persists. These attitudes result from citizens' "everyday contact with the state," such as direct interaction with local officials as well as media portrayals of government corruption.[2]

In most authoritarian or totalitarian nations, schools play a key role in transmitting values and beliefs. Such is the case in the Islamic Republic of Iran, where the schools attempt to create "good Islamic citizens out of young Iranians."[3] Iran has a mixed political system. The nation is a theocracy, with Islamic law dominant over other laws and with the supreme leader appointed by religious clerics. At the same time, citizens do elect officials into key positions, such as the president and members of parliament.

The Iranian government attempts to socialize school children in a variety of ways. Students are required to study Islam, are taught that the nation's rulers before the 1979 Islamic Revolution were immoral, and learn poems criticizing Western nations (most notably the United States). The images in textbooks reinforce national laws, such as by always portraying women wearing veils.

The schools in Iran do not control all political socialization, however. Inside the home, families discuss contemporary politics and historical events, often in ways that counter the government's presentation. Some parents and grandparents, for instance, hold memories of Iran's prerevolutionary leaders and politics that diverge from what the textbooks portray, memories that are passed on to younger generations of Iranians. Thus, the government's messages are being contradicted by other agents of socialization. Whether this will influence Iranian politics in the future is very much an open question. As two scholars of Iranian politics conclude, "The challenge today for the regime is either to accommodate and represent pluralistic discourse or to impose the single voice of unity. Their decision and capacity in this regard will determine whether Iran will move toward more democratic politics or authoritarianism."[4]

1. A. Carl LeVan and Oladimeji Aborisade, "Politics in Nigeria," in *Comparative Politics Today: A World View*, 11th ed., ed. G. Bingham Powell Jr., Russell J. Dalton, and Kaare Strøm (New York: Pearson, 2015), 646, 650.
2. Ibid., 650.
3. H. E. Chehabi and Arang Keshavarzian, "Politics in Iran," in *Comparative Politics Today: A World View*, 11th ed., ed. G. Bingham Powell Jr., Russell J. Dalton, and Kaare Strøm (New York: Pearson, 2015), 557.
4. Ibid., 561.

GENETIC INHERITANCE OF POLITICAL ATTITUDES

From our parents, we inherit, among other things, our hair color, eye color, and height. Could some of our political attitudes also result from **genetic inheritance**? Yes, according to research conducted by John Alford, Carolyn Funk, and John Hibbing.[60] Not surprisingly, it is not at all easy to sort out what portion of a person's political attitudes might be genetically inherited, influenced by family during early socialization, or influenced by other agents of socialization. After all, we cannot ask a newborn baby whether she is a Republican or a Democrat at the moment of her birth, before her postnatal political socialization begins. Alford, Funk, and Hibbing necessarily took a very different approach in examining the relationship between genetics and politics by borrowing research approaches from scientists who specialize in genetics.

Specifically, Alford et al. compared the similarity in political opinions of monozygotic twins (typically known as identical twins) to the similarity of dizygotic twins (fraternal twins). The genetic material of monozygotic twins is the same because the conception of these twins involved the fertilization of one egg by one sperm. In contrast, dizygotic twins are conceived when two eggs are fertilized by two separate sperm at the same time. Thus, these twins' genetic makeup is only 50 percent identical (which is the same for any pair of siblings). This fact regarding known differences in genetic makeup between monozygotic and dizygotic twins is an important foundation of Alford et al.'s research. They also assume, as do all who conduct research on twins, that the influence of environmental factors (parental socialization, outside influences on attitudes, and so on) is roughly the same for each type of twin. This does not mean that every twin's attitudes are influenced precisely the same amount and in the same way. Rather, the assumption is that the impact of environment on attitudes is the same, on average, for monozygotic twins as it is for dizygotic twins.[61]

With this foundation in place, Alford, Funk, and Hibbing examined how similar the political opinions of twins are separately for monozygotic versus dizygotic twin pairs. Unlike other studies of socialization within families (such as Jennings and Niemi's), Alford et al. do not need to compare parents' attitudes with their children's; comparing twins' attitudes across types of twins with known differences in genetic inheritance is sufficient. Alford and colleagues parceled out the proportion of variation in attitudes that is due to genetic heritability versus the twins' **shared environment** (primarily parental and family socialization but also shared school environments and exposure to the same media) versus their **unshared environment** (any unique experiences, socialization that occurred after adolescence, and so on). The statistical techniques they used are too complex to describe here, but a key premise of their analysis is important to understand. If a political attitude is genetically inherited, then monozygotic twins will be more likely (than dizygotic twins) to share the attitude with each other because monozygotic twins share more genetic material. For attitudes that originate with environmental factors rather than genes, the likelihood that a pair of twins will have the same attitude will not differ across monozygotic and dizygotic twins.

So, what do Alford, Funk, and Hibbing conclude? They find that a portion of political attitudes is genetically inherited, although the role of genetic inheritance differs across types of attitudes (see Figure 2.4). Of the three attitudes that they examined, the largest effect of genetic transmission occurs for political **ideology** (whether one is conservative or liberal). Just over 40 percent of the variation in whether these twins are liberal or conservative is due to genetic inheritance, compared with about one-third for their unshared environment and about one-quarter for the shared environment. In contrast, the unshared environment contributes a much larger share toward **political opinionation** (or whether individuals have opinions on political matters), with genetic factors accounting for just over

Figure 2.4   Genetic versus Environmental Factors Influencing Political Opinions

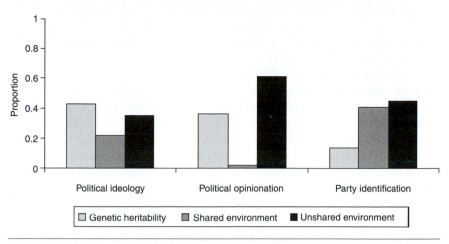

Source: Data from John R. Alford, Carolyn L. Funk, and John R. Hibbing, "Are Political Orientations Genetically Transmitted?" *American Political Science Review* 99 (2005), 160.

Note: Bars represent the proportion of estimated variability in political opinions due to each of the three types of factors.

one-third, and a negligible role for the shared environment. The attitude that is least likely to be genetically inherited is party identification. The twins' shared environment (which is assumed to be largely parental socialization) is a much stronger influence on party affiliation than are genetics (.41 versus .14, respectively). This finding reinforces one that you learned earlier in this chapter: parental socialization is an important source of individuals' partisanship.

The publication of Alford, Funk, and Hibbing's important study began a wave of other research exploring genetics and politics. In addition to political ideology, it appears that other attitudes also have a significant heritable component. These include the strength of a person's party identification, interpersonal trust, core values such as egalitarianism, and agreement that voting is a civic duty.[62] Voter turnout and other forms of political participation have also been linked to genetics.[63] Finally, Alford et al.'s finding that ideology is more closely related to genetics than party identification has been replicated with a sample that includes twins as well as nontwin siblings of twins.[64] Incorporating nontwins into this research is an important development, primarily because twin-only designs are open to generalizability critiques. In other words, we should be cautious in assuming that results gleaned from studies of twins apply to all people, twins and nontwins alike.

How are genes linked to political attitudes? Answering this question is not easy. The consensus now is that a complex chain is at work. Genes are known to influence many of our biological systems (such as dopamine reception). These systems can then condition our emotional reactions as well as the processing of incoming information, both of which are probably related to our personality traits and core values, which in turn are related to political ideology and issue attitudes. Throughout this sequence, environmental circumstances are also at work. Conceptually, this is how genes are thought to be related to political attitudes.[65] Research is now underway to explore some of the links in this chain. One intriguing study concludes that individual variation in a dopamine gene receptor is related to liberalism, but only for some people.[66] Here's how. Dopamine is a brain neurotransmitter. A specific gene influences the transmission of dopamine. Because this gene has multiple variants, individuals differ in their reception of dopamine, depending on their genetic makeup. Variation in dopamine reception is related to novelty seeking—individuals with greater reception are more likely to seek out new situations. As it turns out, openness to new experiences is also related to liberalism. Linking all of this together, researchers found variation in dopamine reception is related to having a liberal ideology, but only under certain circumstances. Specifically, the number of friendships a person had as an adolescent matters. For individuals with greater dopamine reception, those who had more friends were more liberal as young adults, whereas those with fewer adolescent friends were more conservative. In other words, when the social environment of these individuals allowed them to be exposed to more new experiences because of their greater number of friends, they were more liberal. Among people with less reception of dopamine, ideology was not related to the number of friends. In short, it is the *interaction* between genetics and environment that matters, not genetic makeup or environmental circumstances alone.

The link between genetics and politics is one of the most active areas of public opinion scholarship today. Despite this, not everyone has climbed aboard the genetics train.[67] In their 2005 article, Alford, Funk, and Hibbing correctly predicted that some people would greet their finding of a genetic source for political attitudes as "far-fetched, odd, even perverse."[68] Up until that time, much public opinion research, certainly including political socialization, focused on environmental sources of attitudes. That is, factors external to the individual were thought to play the largest role in developing political opinions. Peering internally, all the way down to our genes, has the potential to upend conventional wisdom regarding opinion formation.[69] On the other hand, some socialization scholars have been open to this new research. Kent Jennings, for instance, describes the genetics work as a "provocative addition to the political socialization literature" and has called for integrating it with traditional approaches for studying socialization.[70]

CONCLUSION

The acquisition of political attitudes begins fairly early in life and often with positive feelings toward the nation and idealized views of political leaders. Would democratic elitists thus be satisfied with the socialization of children in the United

States today? Although it is true that levels of system support tend to be high among children, as these theorists would hope, support is not uniformly high across all children. For some children, such as those who are older, black, Latino, Native American, or from impoverished backgrounds, childhood attitudes are less benevolent. More worrisome for elite democrats is that over recent decades children are more likely to hold cynical attitudes toward those holding political power. Elite democrats assume that citizens are neither interested in nor knowledgeable about politics and rely on the expertise of elected officials to make governing decisions. As Americans, including young Americans, have come to hold these officials in lower esteem, there is less deference to political authority than elite democrats prefer. Even when children hold more uniformly positive attitudes toward leaders, however, there is good evidence that these attitudes do not persist into adulthood, further undermining elite democrats' hope for socialization to produce system-supporting adults. For instance, although the children of the 1950s trusted government and possessed idealized images of leaders then, they "wound up rioting in the streets of Chicago or smoking dope in Vietnam or working as carpenters under assumed names in Toronto" to avoid the Vietnam War draft.[71]

Adolescence brings with it the development of partisan leanings and opinions toward a variety of issues. The family plays an important socializing role, particularly when it comes to party identification. Other agents of socialization—schools, peers, and current political events—also shape political attitudes. Yet, over years of socialization research, the family continues to emerge as an important shaper of children's attitudes, whether through genetic transmission or postnatal socialization. The imprint of our parents' political attitudes is often still visible into adulthood, after a period of attitude instability that many of us experience in our early twenties.

Pluralists would be pleased by the fact that the transmission of party identification continues to be more complete than the transmission of other political attitudes. Pluralists, after all, hope for socialization to develop strong political identities before adulthood, chief among these being party identification. Yet the development of preadult partisanship is not as complete as pluralists would prefer, partly because the party affiliation of young adults is not entirely stable. This suggests that adolescents' party identification is not very crystallized, certainly not as crystallized as pluralists would want for citizens about to reach voting age. Also of concern for pluralists is the movement away from strong party affiliations that Americans have experienced over the past few decades. As generations of adolescents have been socialized during a time of weaker national political parties, the effect has been to produce more Independent voters who, in the pluralists' eyes, are less able to have their interests represented through the party system.

How would participatory democrats assess the state of political socialization? They would have a more difficult task, given that much political science research on this topic has generally not focused on the features of socialization that these theorists feel are most important. Having said this, we can point to one conclusion from the research that certainly troubles participatory democrats: the fact that children who are black, Latino, Native American, or poor develop less trusting attitudes toward government at an early age. The more trust in government citizens have, the more likely they will participate in politics throughout their life. Participatory democrats worry that children who trust government less will grow up to be adults who do not participate in politics, thus undermining the goal of political equality across citizens that participatory democrats value so strongly.

More centrally for participatory democrats, teaching children to be active participants in democracy is crucial. Most socialization research has not gauged the participatory skills and activities of children or adolescents, certainly not to the degree that participatory democrats would like. Rather than emphasizing which agents of socialization influence preadult attitudes most strongly, for example, researchers could focus on "how agents might successfully inspire the development of democratic citizenship values in children and adolescents."[72] This situation is changing somewhat, however, as political scientists begin to examine the many civic engagement and service learning programs that are scattered throughout the nation.[73] Such programs attempt to introduce young people (and young adults) to politics through hands-on experience and also to develop civic skills that are relevant for political participation. More thorough assessments of the quality of these programs would provide valuable information for participatory democrats.

KEY CONCEPTS

adolescent socialization / 52	Millennials / 62
adult socialization / 52	national probability sample / 53
attitude stability / 56	panel or longitudinal study / 57
benevolent leader imagery / 47	party identification / 53
childhood socialization / 47	period effect / 61
efficacy / 50	political generation / 62
family politicization / 56	political opinionation / 66
generational effect / 60	political reality explanation / 52
genetic inheritance / 65	political socialization / 46
ideology / 66	shared environment / 66
impressionable years model / 57	socialization agents / 46
life cycle effects / 58	trust / 50
malevolent leader imagery / 50	unshared environment / 66

SUGGESTED SOURCES FOR FURTHER READING

Alwin, Duane F., Ronald L. Cohen, and Theodore M. Newcomb. *Political Attitudes over the Life Span: The Bennington Women after Fifty Years.* Madison: University of Wisconsin Press, 1991.

A fascinating study of the social and political attitudes of women who attended Bennington College (Vermont) in the 1930s and 1940s, this book assesses these women's attitudes in 1984, approximately fifty years after their college graduation, examining the stability of their attitudes over time as well as the influence of the social environment on these women's political opinions.

Funk, Carolyn L. "Genetic Foundations of Political Behavior." In *The Oxford Handbook of Political Psychology*, 2nd ed., ed. Leonie Huddy, David O. Sears, and Jack S. Levy. Oxford: Oxford University Press, 2013.
Hibbing, John R. "Ten Misconceptions Concerning Neurobiology and Politics." *Perspectives on Politics* 11 (2013): 475–489.

Funk's chapter is a thorough and engaging review of the past decade of research on genetics and political behavior. As the title of Hibbing's article suggests, he rebuts ten common criticisms of biological approaches to politics. Acknowledging that "many in the political science mainstream view the [biology and politics] movement with concern or even horror" (p. 475), he argues that political scientists need to move beyond false assumptions regarding biological bases for political behavior and toward valid critiques of this approach. Not everyone agrees with Hibbing. His essay is followed by eight that collectively present a variety of contrary views.

Jennings, M. Kent, and Richard G. Niemi. *Generations and Politics: A Panel Study of Young Adults and Their Parents*. Princeton, NJ: Princeton University Press, 1981.
Jennings, M. Kent, Laura Stoker, and Jake Bowers. "Politics across Generations: Family Transmission Reexamined." *Journal of Politics* 71 (2009): 782–799.

Generations and Politics presents a thorough summary of the conclusions drawn from the 1965 and 1973 waves of the authors' survey of high school students and their parents, whereas the article by Jennings, Stoker, and Bowers discusses results from all four waves of this project. In this chapter, we have focused on parental transmission of party identification; these two works examine socialization processes for many political attitudes in addition to party affiliation.

Urbatsch, R. *Families' Values: How Parents, Siblings, and Children Affect Political Attitudes*. Oxford: Oxford University Press, 2014.

Families' Values extends socialization research into new, or previously understudied, directions. Urbatsch explores family socialization agents other than parents, such as brothers, sisters, spouses, and children, finding that each can influence our political attitudes. He also studies a wide range of political attitudes and behaviors, beyond the oft-studied topic of party identification.

"The Next America," Pew Research Center, 2015, http://www.pewresearch.org/packages/the-next-america

This section of the Pew Research Center's website presents results from their analyses of generational differences in the United States. Topics include how Millennials differ from older generations in terms of demographics, political attitudes and practices, and use of technology. Pew's site contains loads of other information about Millennials, with results from new surveys added often. Select "Millennials" under their "Topics" link from Pew's home page for the most recent additions.

CIRCLE (The Center for Information and Research on Civic Learning and Engagement), http://www.civicyouth.org

CIRCLE conducts and disseminates research related to the civic engagement of youth. Its website contains a wealth of information, including research reports, tools for engaging in political and civic activity, and links to other civic engagement sites.

CHAPTER 3

Mass Media

DRAMATIC technological changes in recent decades have had a major impact on how, when, and whether citizens receive news. From the explosion of cable channels to the proliferation of smartphones, citizens are able to get news when and how they want it, or they can choose to avoid news altogether. Also, through social media citizens have unprecedented opportunities to shape and make the news themselves. Despite these extraordinary changes in the media environment, traditional media outlets, such as network TV news and newspapers, are still influential, and powerful political elites and institutions are still key drivers of news content.

We begin with a discussion of what we should expect from the news media in a democratic society. Participatory democratic theorists have high expectations regarding the media's role in providing citizens with the information and tools they need to engage in the political process. Next, we examine general characteristics of mass media ownership that shape news coverage. The media in the United States are best described as corporate, concentrated, and conglomerate. We discuss the political implications of those characteristics. Specific features of the traditional news media also influence how stories are covered. We discuss the impact of news norms on the reporting of political events as well as whether those norms have been undermined by technological changes that allow for niche news. We also grapple with the effects of media coverage on citizens. We review how our understanding of media effects on public opinion has changed over time and discuss the potential for citizens to use social media to influence the political process. Along the way, we remind you that all media are not alike and illustrate how studying a variety of news media provides added insight. We close by reviewing the evidence and considering whether the media play their appropriate role in our democratic society.

WHAT SHOULD CITIZENS EXPECT FROM THE MASS MEDIA IN A DEMOCRACY?

Before reading this section, stop and ask yourself: What do you expect from the mass media in a democracy? How do you think the media should behave? Notice we are not asking how the media act in reality. We will get to that in a moment. For now, we are interested in your ideal vision of how the media should operate in a democratic society.

Probably the first thing that came to mind is that the media should be free from government control.[1] Freedom of the press, of course, is a fundamental tenet in a democracy. The government should not control the media by censoring stories or by forcing the publication of stories. Secretary of State John Kerry, for example, should not be able to stop the *Washington Post* from publishing a particular story, nor should he be able to require the newspaper to cover certain events. In a democracy, a free press should also be free from economic forces, such as market pressures and advertising dollars. Powerful economic forces should not be able to prevent the media from covering important issues of the day and thus limit debate.

A press free from governmental and economic control will have great benefits for citizens because such a press should have several key characteristics. First, the media should act as an **intermediary** between citizens and elites, providing both with the information essential for a well-functioning democracy. Specifically, media organizations should provide citizens with the information and analysis necessary to make smart decisions. Further, the media should cover how citizens think about issues so that elites will be able to make educated decisions on behalf of their constituents. Second, a free press should provide a **forum for diverse views**. Elite and citizen opinion from across the spectrum should be presented so that debate can be wide ranging and critical or alternative voices will be heard. Finally, the media should play a "**watchdog**" role.[2] Because citizens cannot attend every city council meeting or participate in every public hearing held by a federal agency, they rely on the media to scrutinize the actions of public officials. The media should provide citizens with the information necessary to hold government accountable and act as a check on the judicial, legislative, and congressional branches of government.

This vision of the media is most consistent with the one held by participatory democratic theorists. Participatory theorists, as you recall, want citizens to be actively engaged in the political process. By providing accurate information, the media create knowledgeable citizens ready to participate in the give-and-take of politics. Moreover, by presenting diverse viewpoints, the media ensure that both privileged and marginalized voices will be heard. This facilitates participation on the part of *all* citizens (thus redressing inequality in society, a core concern of participatory theorists). Participatory democratic theorists believe that political participation makes people better citizens, and they see the potential for the media to assist in that process.

Elite democrats, on the other hand, would be happy with a press relatively free from governmental control. We say "relatively free" because these theorists might argue that there are circumstances under which government officials should have influence over what the media publish. Take stories on national security, for example. Elite democratic theorists might prefer censorship of such stories because they think it is unnecessary for citizens to know the details about these policies. Elites are the decision makers, so there is no need for the media to risk undermining national security by revealing information to the public. Furthermore, elite democrats would be much less concerned with the effect of economic forces on the media. From their perspective, media outlets should be responsive to market pressures and advertising dollars so that citizens receive the kind of programming they want. As long as the media provide enough basic information to citizens so they can vote, these theorists are not concerned with the quality or diversity of news presented in the media.

This discussion of citizens' expectations regarding the mass media largely presumes a separation between citizens and the press. In today's media environment, however, the line between citizens and reporters, between news makers and news consumers, is sometimes blurred. The Internet and social media provide "new, breathtakingly dynamic, and radically decentralized means for people and organizations to communicate and cooperate with one another for political and civic ends."[3] This gives some observers great hope that citizens will be able to use these electronic tools to enrich the quality of democracy, whereas other observers caution that citizens are more likely to use these tools to seek news from and communicate with like-minded individuals, leading to fragmentation and polarization. Or perhaps even worse still, citizens will simply use the choices provided by new forms of media to pursue entertainment and eschew news altogether.[4]

WHAT GENERAL CHARACTERISTICS OF THE MASS MEDIA SHAPE NEWS COVERAGE?

Let's turn now to a discussion of the mass media in reality. Here we focus on general characteristics of mass media ownership that influence news content. In the United States, the mass media can best be characterized by the three Cs: corporate, concentrated, and conglomerate.[5]

The First C: Corporate

The first C is **corporate** because most media are owned by large companies. The primary goal of these corporations is to make money for their owners and shareholders, not to serve the interests of citizens in a democratic society. Because they are profit-driven companies, pleasing advertisers, not citizens, is their main objective. And this concerns critics who argue that advertisers prefer stories that put people in the mood to purchase their products rather than participate in politics. Moreover, in the world of advertising, certain people are more valuable than others. Broadcast networks, for example, are most interested in attracting viewers to their news programs who are between the ages of eighteen and forty-nine, particularly women, who hold the purse strings in many households.[6]

Although most of you will not recall (but your grandparents will), citizens used to turn en masse to one of three broadcast networks for their evening news: ABC, CBS, or NBC. That was it—the big three *were* television news. That seems strange today with literally hundreds of available channels, several of which are dedicated to news coverage. During this time period, these evening news broadcasts were shielded from profit expectations. This changed in the mid-1980s as new owners took over ABC, CBS, and NBC with an eye toward turning these evening news broadcasts into money-making enterprises.[7] Around the same time, technological changes occurred that led to an explosion of cable channels, resulting in a much more competitive environment. Not only were broadcast networks forced to compete with cable news outlets (such as CNN, which debuted in 1980), but they also had to contend with entertainment television (such as MTV, which debuted in 1981). Thus, just as the three broadcast networks were asked to bring home the bacon, the competition became even stiffer. Today the media environment is even more complex with traditional media, such as network television news, newspapers, and radio, competing not only with cable news but also with social media, including Facebook, YouTube, Twitter, and many other social networking sites.

The Pew Research Center has conducted several surveys of citizens' news habits since the early 1990s that demonstrate the highly competitive and changing

Figure 3.1   Where Do Citizens Regularly Turn for News?

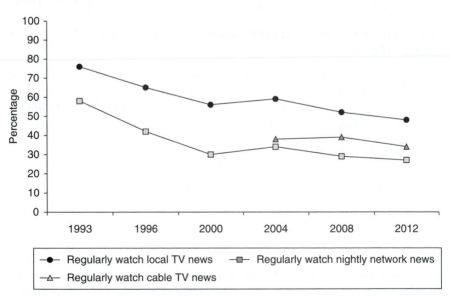

Source: Data from "In Changing News Landscape, Even Television Is Vulnerable," Pew Research Center, Washington, DC, September 27, 2012, http://www.people-press.org/files/legacy-pdf/2012%20News%20Consumption%20Report.pdf

nature of the news business (see Figure 3.1). Since 1993 traditional media platforms, such as local TV news and nightly network news, have suffered significant declines in the percentage of citizens who obtain news from these outlets "regularly." Since 2004 the percentage of citizens who obtain news from cable TV regularly has declined slightly.

To assess citizens' daily news habits, Pew asks citizens whether they received news from particular sources "yesterday." Here we see that daily viewership of TV news (with no distinction made for local, nightly, or cable) has not declined that much since 1996 (see Figure 3.2), whereas radio news and especially print newspapers have seen significant declines in their daily usage. Americans are increasingly obtaining news from the Internet and mobile devices. For instance, 39 percent of Americans in 2012 indicated they got news yesterday from Internet or mobile sources, including cell phones, tablets, or other mobile handheld devices. Pew's 2012 news survey revealed a particularly troubling phenomenon: 29 percent of young Americans aged eighteen to twenty-four reported they received no news yesterday. Among Americans of all ages, 17 percent received no news yesterday.[8] Participatory democratic theorists find these statistics deeply problematic.

A widely respected media scholar, Thomas Patterson, argues that traditional news organizations "softened" their coverage in response to the

Figure 3.2 Where Do Citizens Obtain News Daily?

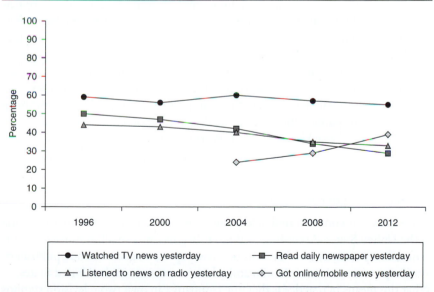

Source: Data from "In Changing News Landscape, Even Television Is Vulnerable," Pew Research Center, Washington, DC, September 27, 2012, http://www.people-press.org/files/legacy-pdf/2012%20News%20Consumption%20Report.pdf

increased competition.[9] In their rush to attract larger audiences, the media turned away from **hard news** coverage of important leaders and policies in favor of **soft news** without a connection to public policy. To examine this supposition, Patterson content analyzed a random sample of news stories from magazines, broadcast television networks, national newspapers, and local papers. He found that soft news increased from roughly 35 percent of all stories during the early 1980s to almost 50 percent of all stories by 1999.[10] Ironically, Patterson argued that this increase in soft news coverage, intended to draw in news audiences, actually drove people away from traditional platforms. For citizens who prefer hard news, the emphasis on soft news is a turnoff; for those who favor soft news—presumably due to its entertainment value—there are other, much more entertaining options available that will draw their attention in the long run. For example, 51 percent of Americans polled by the Pew Research Center in May 2011 said they had heard a lot about former California governor Arnold Schwarzenegger fathering a child with a member of his household staff, but only 25 percent had heard a lot about the debt ceiling debate.[11] Ultimately, if people prefer sensational stories about Arnold Schwarzenegger, there are much better places to turn for such news than the traditional news media.

Although many scholars view the increase in soft news coverage as alarming, others argue that citizens who turn to **soft news media** can actually learn about politics from those outlets.[12] In particular, politically inattentive citizens who have no desire to read the *New York Times*, for example, can still pick up information as an "incidental by-product" of exposure to entertainment-oriented media, such as daytime talk shows.[13] Deemed an "*Oprah* effect" (after Oprah Winfrey's popular and long-running talk show that sometimes touched on topics of a political nature), soft news media play a critical role in helping disinterested citizens gain some much-needed political knowledge.[14] Entertainment programs can also "provide deep and accessible insights into the impacts of policies, the prevarications and real goals of public officials, and the distribution of wealth and power."[15] In recent years *The Daily Show* and *The Colbert Report* come to mind as examples of such programming; these are shows that some of you, perhaps many of you, grew up watching regularly.[16]

The Second C: Concentrated

The second C is **concentrated**: a few large companies own the majority of media in the United States. According to Ben H. Bagdikian, a small number of multinational corporations own "most of the newspapers, magazines, book publishers, motion picture studios, and radio and television stations in the United States."[17] What this means in practice is that one company can own two television stations and six radio stations in the same community, as CBS does in Los Angeles.[18] Thus, what looks like a multiplicity of choices may actually be no choice at all.

In recent years, major media corporations have rushed to scoop up lucrative Internet companies. Many of you watch television shows or movies on Hulu, but do you know which major media corporations own stakes in the company? Hulu is jointly owned by 21st Century Fox, The Walt Disney Company, and NBCUniversal. All three of these corporations have extensive media holdings. For example, 21st Century Fox also owns the Fox Broadcasting Company, the Fox News Channel, the Fox Business Network, and numerous local television stations.[19] During summer 2011, News Corporation (which owned the Fox holdings at the time) closed one of its newspapers in the United Kingdom, *News of the World*, after it was revealed that employees of the paper had hacked the phones of crime victims and relatives of British soldiers killed in Iraq and Afghanistan.[20] The Fox News Channel was criticized heavily for downplaying this story while other major news organizations dedicated significant coverage to it.[21]

Some media critics might point to this example of Fox News ignoring the hacking scandal as evidence that media concentration affects news coverage and stifles discussion of important issues in a democracy. Diverse news content is impossible if just a few companies control the vast majority of the media, according to this perspective.[22] Since that time, News Corporation has split into two companies: 21st Century Fox, which has the television, film, and new media holdings, and News Corporation, which is the publishing arm.[23] Unfortunately, there is little systematic research on the effects of media ownership on news content. One study by Martin Gilens and Craig Hertzman, however, makes a substantial contribution to our understanding of this topic.[24]

Gilens and Hertzman conducted an innovative study of the influence of media concentration on news coverage of the 1996 Telecommunications Act. The Telecommunications Act had significantly different implications for those media corporations that owned television stations than for those that did not. Specifically, the Telecom Act loosened caps on television station ownership. Thus, media corporations that owned television stations benefited from the legislation, whereas other media corporations did not benefit and were perhaps even put at a disadvantage by the bill. As a result, Gilens and Hertzman hypothesized, newspapers owned by media companies with television interests would cover the Telecom Act more favorably than newspapers that did not have investments in television stations.

To test this hypothesis, Gilens and Hertzman identified newspapers owned by companies with no television stations and newspapers owned by companies with television stations. Then they collected 113 articles published in those newspapers between December 1, 1995, and February 28, 1996, that discussed the aspect of the Telecom Act dealing with loosening the caps on television ownership. Next, Gilens and Hertzman content analyzed the characteristics of the coverage dedicated to the ownership cap issue.

The researchers found that the different types of newspapers dedicated roughly the same amount of coverage to the ownership cap issue but that the tone of the coverage differed considerably. The newspapers with television holdings were more likely to focus on the positive impact of the Telecom bill and significantly less likely to mention the negative impact compared with the newspapers with no television ownership. For example, in newspapers without ties to television, 58 percent of the articles mentioned negative consequences of lifting the ownership caps, such as that the bill would decrease the diversity of viewpoints and dampen democratic debate in the media. In contrast, only 15 percent of the articles from those newspapers with substantial television interests mentioned any negative consequences. Also, newspapers with major television holdings were six times more likely than newspapers with no television interests to report a misleading claim about the impact of the Telecom Act.

This pattern of news coverage exposed by Gilens and Hertzman raises serious questions about the negative effects of media concentration on news content.[25] Gilens and Hertzman conclude their study on a pessimistic note: "Only the news media can provide the public with the information it needs to participate meaningfully in democratic government; a press that systematically slants the news to further its own business objectives threatens to undermine the very foundations of democracy."[26]

One final point here is that, ironically, whereas media ownership has become more concentrated, technological changes have enabled more media outlets. Citizens have more media choices than ever before (albeit many owned by the same relatively small set of corporations), providing many opportunities to choose news that caters to partisan or ideological views rather than news that is objective and balanced. In addition, citizens have unprecedented opportunities to choose entertainment rather than news, and as a result those citizens who are "entertainment fans are leaving news and politics behind altogether in the high-choice media environment."[27]

The Third C: Conglomerate

The third C is **conglomerate**. Not only do these large corporations own lots of different types of media, they own lots of *nonmedia* companies as well. For example, the same company—The Walt Disney Company—that airs ABC's *World News Tonight* also owns eight television stations in major cities across the country as well as ESPN, theme parks and resorts, movie studios, retail stores, and a variety of digital media, targeted to kids in particular. ABC News provides content to Yahoo! News, reaching up to "100 million people in the U.S. each month on PCs, mobile devices and tablets."[28] Many observers are concerned with this conglomeration. The "willingness to criticize and scrutinize those with political and economic power"[29] is expected from a free press, yet do media conglomerates hold their own accountable? Media critics from both ends of the ideological continuum worry about the effects of large, highly concentrated media conglomerates. Liberals might be concerned about whether ABC news outlets will report on environmental damage caused by Disney cruise ships, whereas conservatives might be concerned with the impact of violence in Disney films on our culture. People across the ideological spectrum might worry about whether ABC news outlets will report on The Walt Disney Company's lobbying efforts to limit government regulation of the amount of violence on television.[30]

Exceptions to the Three Cs

Although *corporate, concentrated,* and *conglomerate* characterize much of the news media in the United States, there are notable and important exceptions. National Public Radio (NPR) and the Public Broadcasting System (PBS) are *nonprofit media corporations* whose goal is to provide high-quality, noncommercial news and entertainment programming to American citizens. Both corporations are membership organizations and receive significant financial support from their member stations (public radio stations in the case of NPR and public television stations in the case of PBS). NPR and PBS are also underwritten by corporations and private foundations. These underwriters do not air advertisements in the traditional sense but do have their names mentioned during programming. A relatively small portion of NPR's and PBS's annual budgets comes from federal funds.[31] Conservative critics of NPR and PBS regularly work to pass legislation to defund NPR and PBS, much to the dismay of participatory democratic theorists because public radio and television stations play a crucial role in providing citizens with information necessary to make educated judgments about the most important issues of our day.[32] Several studies demonstrate that citizens who obtain their news from PBS or NPR are more informed about politics than citizens who get their news from commercial outlets (for more on this topic, see Chapter 8).[33] In a media environment dominated by conglomerates, noncommercial outlets are an essential source of reliable and accurate hard news.

Another noteworthy exception to the dominance of media conglomerates is the *minority press.* Let's take the black press as an example. Black newspapers tend to be independent or part of relatively small family-owned chains.[34] The black press is affected by economic forces, but it is also driven by a mission of advocacy. Its goal is to present the news from a "black" angle, and it tries to counter the often incomplete and erroneous coverage of minority communities that appears in the mainstream media.[35] As a result, the black press provides a diversity of voices that are not heard in the mainstream media.[36] Black citizens find this particularly important, especially during periods of racial strife.[37] The circulation of black papers also goes up during times of racial promise, as when Barack Obama won the presidency.[38] There are about two hundred African American newspapers in the United States. Just like mainstream newspapers, their circulation has decreased over time.[39] Nevertheless, by providing a forum for diverse points of view, black newspapers act as an important, albeit small, counterbalance to the nation's major media outlets.

Ethnic presses in other U.S. communities serve a similar function, and they are especially critical for citizens who prefer or need news in languages other than English.[40] As Latinos become an increasingly important electoral group, political scientists need to gain a better understanding of the content of Latino media as well as its effect on public opinion. In general, much more research is needed on media outlets that serve minority communities.

Finally, what about the *Internet* as an exception to the dominance of media conglomerates? Denis McQuail, a noted media scholar, argues that the Internet "can unlock secrets and make much arcane information readily available to ordinary people very rapidly, with an empowering effect."[41] The Internet provides unprecedented opportunities for citizens to discuss and make the news. Blogs, for example, turn readers into writers, and social media enable citizens to upload videos to YouTube, share political content on Facebook, and tweet their own political commentary as well as retweet news stories and the views of others.[42] Furthermore, because few resources are required to set up a website, independent media organizations can afford to establish a home on the Internet that would be impossible without the technology.

The Internet is not a panacea, however.[43] Citizens are much more likely to search the Internet for entertainment news than for political news.[44] Bloggers are not constrained by journalistic norms of accuracy and objectivity (which we discuss later), and many have no qualms about reporting gossip as fact or actively promoting falsehoods.[45] Furthermore, many citizens get news from online sources that share their point of view, undermining the potential of the Internet to provide a range of perspectives to the public.[46]

Media conglomerates have also planted their flags in cyberspace. The same companies that control much of the traditional news media also garner significant traffic on their Internet sites. These companies' "brands" are so powerful that citizens turn to them for information; it just happens to be on the Internet rather than on television or in print. **Legacy media outlets**—as the media organizations that existed before the Internet are sometimes called—dominate the top twenty online news entities. The top three are Yahoo!-ABC News Network, CNN Network, and NBC News Digital, and the *New York Times*, Washingtonpost.com, and NPR are all in the top twenty.[47] Nevertheless, the Internet provides countless opportunities for average citizens, if they so desire, to seek out information from social media; reputable bloggers; independent media organizations; and government, academic, and nonprofit websites.

Public Opinion in Comparative Perspective
Box 3.1 Social Media and the Arab Spring

"We use Facebook to schedule the protests, Twitter to coordinate, and YouTube to tell the world."[1]

This telling tweet from a female Egyptian activist captures two critical aspects of the "Arab Spring" protests that swept across North Africa and the Middle East beginning in spring 2011. First, social media played an important role in (a) identifying and communicating shared grievances among oppressed peoples, (b) organizing protests to articulate those grievances, and (c) publicizing those protests and governmental responses to them to people around the world. To put it quite simply, social media allowed lots of people to communicate very quickly with lots of other people. Individuals were able to share information, compare notes, find common ground, and inspire one another to challenge the authority of dictators in record speed. That brings us to the second point. All the tweets, Facebook posts, and videos uploaded to YouTube would have meant nothing if people had not been willing to hit the streets and risk their lives engaging in civil disobedience. Protesting in cyberspace would not have brought down Zine El Abidine Ben Ali in Tunisia or Hosni Mubarak in Egypt. It required people on the streets day after day, night after night willing to publicly protest these autocratic regimes. It required people willing to put their lives on the line to push their countries toward democracy. Facebook was critical in scheduling the protests, but it was the demonstrations themselves that led to the ousters of Ben Ali and Mubarak.

This Egyptian activist's tweet is insightful to be sure, but there is one critical aspect of the protests that it does not capture. Oppressive governments can also make use of social networking tools.[2] In Egypt, for example, Mubarak's government sent out text messages to try to mobilize pro-government rallies. Governments can use videos posted online to identify protesters, and they can track electronic activity to locate dissidents. Furthermore, governments can shut down access to the Internet and cut off phone lines. For instance, Mubarak's government blocked Internet and cell phone services for nearly a week during the protests calling for his removal. This likely backfired, however, because it brought more middle-class Egyptians into the streets as well as hampered government agencies supporting the regime.[3]

What role has social media played in fomenting change across North Africa and the Middle East? With Egypt currently led by a military strongman

(Continued)

BOX 3.1 (Continued)

after a coup d'état of its first elected president, it is too early to make a final judgment about this. We must be careful not to fall into the trap of assigning predominant influence to social media or assuming social media played no role at all in toppling autocratic rulers. Either of these assessments is too simple, especially if we also consider the widespread chaos in Libya, Syria, and Yemen in the wake of the Arab Spring. Time and further analyses will reveal the full complexity of social media's political role in the region.

Returning to the Tunisian example, it seems clear that a strong civil society has kept that country on a path to democracy. Four organizations—the Tunisian General Labor Union; the Tunisian Confederation of Industry, Trade, and Handicrafts; the Tunisian Human Rights League; and the Tunisian Order of Lawyers—making up the "National Dialogue Quartet" were key to resolving crises as Tunisia transitioned to a democratic form of government. The Quartet was awarded the Nobel Peace Prize in 2015.[4] Social media may be quite important, but it alone cannot transform an authoritarian state to a democracy.

1. Philip N. Howard, "The Arab Spring's Cascading Effects," *Pacific Standard*, February 23, 2011, http://www.psmag.com/business-economics/the-cascading-effects-of-the-arab-spring-28575
2. Simon Cottle, "Media and the Arab Uprisings of 2011: Research Notes," *Journalism* 12 (2011): 647–659.
3. Philip N. Howard and Muzamil M. Hussain, "The Upheavals in Egypt and Tunisia: The Role of Digital Media," *Journal of Democracy* 22 (2011): 35–48.
4. Sewell Chan, "Nobel Peace Prize Is Awarded to National Dialogue Quartet in Tunisia," *New York Times*, October 9, 2015, http://www.nytimes.com/2015/10/10/world/europe/national-dialogue-quartet-tunisia-nobel-peace-prize.html?_r=0

WHAT SPECIFIC CHARACTERISTICS OF THE TRADITIONAL NEWS MEDIA SHAPE THE REPORTING OF POLITICAL EVENTS?

In this section, we discuss **news norms** that influence the reporting of political events by traditional news organizations. Here we focus on norms that shape how journalists—not columnists or pundits—decide what's news, and we discuss which media organizations are constrained by these norms and which aren't. We also provide a critique of news norms.

News Norms

One of the most important norms that shapes news coverage is **objectivity**. In practice, journalists define objectivity as providing both sides of an issue. To uphold this norm, journalists strive for balance in their reporting. In the U.S.

political context, this often means that a Republican viewpoint is balanced with a Democratic one.[48]

A close cousin of objectivity is **neutrality**. According to this norm, journalists do not inject their personal opinions into news coverage. Instead, they report on political events by presenting others' viewpoints in their stories, especially the viewpoints of **official sources**. Official sources include primarily government officials but also other people who are powerful in society.[49] By relying heavily on official sources, journalists are able to do their jobs easily and efficiently. It also allows them to achieve the norm of **accuracy**. Journalists work hard to ensure the information they report is correct. They perceive official sources to be reliable, legitimate, and in the know; thus, journalists regularly turn to these sources in their news coverage.[50]

Assigning journalists to **newsbeats** is another journalistic norm.[51] Journalists are assigned to cover specific institutions or topic areas. These are called beats. For example, major news organizations assign journalists to the White House beat and the Pentagon beat. This allows journalists to gain expertise on certain topics; develop relationships with key players, which is obviously important because of the heavy reliance on official sources; and create familiar, reliable routines in a job where events are constantly changing.[52]

Journalists are also influenced by norms related to **newsworthiness**. Conflict garners significant attention because it is considered especially newsworthy. For example, media coverage of Congress focuses heavily on partisan conflict within the institution and strife between the Congress and the president.[53] The emphasis on conflict is also obvious in news coverage of political campaigns. The media tend to focus on the "**horse race**" aspect of campaigns: who's ahead in the polls and who's behind, who has momentum and who doesn't, and who's leading in fundraising and who's faltering.[54] Even once politicians gain office, the news media still assess their every move in terms of competition and gamesmanship rather than substance.[55]

These norms are a function of the traditional news media trying to reach as broad an audience as possible as efficiently as possible. Many media corporations want to advertise to large audiences, not just Republicans or Democrats. Thus, they provide objective news that will not tick off one side or the other (or at least tick off both sides equally). This was not always the case; newspapers early in U.S. history served the interests of powerful officials or political parties.[56] Technological changes during the mid-1800s, however, allowed publishers to print greater quantities of newspapers within a much shorter time frame. This technological advance allowed for high circulation, which encouraged businesses to own and advertise in newspapers. It became necessary for journalists to report the news in such a way that newspapers would appeal to a wide audience in an efficient manner; thus, journalists adopted the norms of objectivity, neutrality, accuracy, newsbeats, and newsworthiness.[57]

Do these news norms constrain the activities of all media organizations? No, they do not. Robert Entman distinguishes media sources based on the extent to which they adhere to news norms.[58] He argues that **traditional journalism** (such as the *New York Times* or the *CBS Evening News*) has a strong commitment to news norms, but **advocacy journalism** is committed to only some of these norms. Advocacy journalism includes magazines with an ideological bent, such as *The Nation* on the left and *The Weekly Standard* on the right. These magazines strive for accuracy but have no interest in balancing sources to follow the norm of objectivity. **Tabloid journalism** is much less committed, if at all, to news norms. Tabloid journalism includes cable programs such as the *O'Reilly Factor* on Fox News, which appeals to a conservative audience, and *The Rachel Maddow Show* on MSNBC, which speaks to a liberal audience. Over the last three decades, the explosion of cable channels has allowed for profitable niche programming. And because these programs do not need to appeal to a wide audience, the norms of objectivity, neutrality, and accuracy have gone by the wayside. In fact, the draw of these cable news programs tends to be the bombastic commentary of their hosts. The Internet, of course, has also provided a platform on which tabloid journalism can thrive, and social media allow anyone to create "news" without regard for journalistic norms of appropriate behavior.

If you are under the age of twenty-five, you may be quick to dismiss the importance of these news norms because you are more likely to get your news from digital platforms than traditional news outlets.[59] Keep in mind, however, that on a daily basis many more citizens get news on TV than online and that 29 percent of Americans still read a daily newspaper (see Figure 3.2). Moreover, as mentioned earlier, many of the online news sites that draw substantial traffic provide content from traditional news organizations that still practice these norms.

That said, even in traditional journalism, the commitment to these news norms seems to be weakening. Research suggests that the agenda of traditional news outlets is being influenced by tabloid journalists, which can undermine the norm of accuracy. For example, in 2008, a large community organizing group, ACORN (Association of Community Organizations for Reform Now), rocketed from near obscurity to widespread notoriety on the basis of misinformation and edited videos designed to smear the organization.[60] By blogging on corporate-sponsored websites, "opinion entrepreneurs" circulated inaccurate information about the organization's voter registration activities, including accusing ACORN of perpetuating voter fraud.[61] This voter fraud frame was picked up by traditional news outlets, including the *New York Times*, the *Wall Street Journal*, NPR, and the broadcast TV networks. Many journalists did little or no fact checking to determine whether the allegations against ACORN were true; instead, they simply repeated assertions made by politicians and bloggers despite a lack of evidence supporting their claims and sometimes even in the face of evidence contradicting their claims.[62] Under pressure to compete in a 24/7 media environment, traditional journalists working for national news organizations abandoned the norm of accuracy and covered ACORN in tabloid fashion or worse.

Critiques of News Norms

Our discussion of news norms may have raised some concerns in your mind. On the one hand, these news norms enable journalists to appeal to a wide audience, provide accurate information, and do their work in an efficient manner. The norms also ensure that powerful political elites will be able to get their messages out to the public, thus pleasing elite democratic theorists. On the other hand, *some* of these news norms make it difficult, if not impossible, for the news media to live up to the ideal standards proposed by participatory democratic theorists.

To begin, the norm of objectivity requires journalists to present two sides of an issue. But what if there are more than two sides? Take abortion, for example. The debate is often characterized in the media as pro-life versus pro-choice, with Republican elites supporting life and Democratic elites supporting choice. Among the public, however, 43 percent of Americans do not fall neatly into either camp. Instead, they believe that abortion should be available under certain circumstances, such as rape, incest, danger to the life of the mother, or when some other clear need has been established. Furthermore, another 44 percent say that a woman should always be able to obtain an abortion as a matter of choice. Because journalists rely so heavily on official, partisan sources, the abortion debate looks as if it is pro-life versus pro-choice, yet only 12 percent of Americans believe abortion should never be permitted.[63] If journalists paid more attention to the opinions of average Americans, the news coverage would focus on the circumstances under which abortion should be allowed rather than whether it should be allowed. For many citizens, the issue is more complex and nuanced than simply for or against, which actually suggests there might be room for compromise—something you would never know from media coverage of the issue.

We have discussed the limitations of objective reporting when there are more than two sides to an issue, but what about when elites are in agreement and thus there is only one side of an issue? In those circumstances, one of two things happens. Either important issues simply go unreported by the media because there is no conflict to draw the attention of journalists, or, if the issue does get covered, it appears as if there is no debate on the topic even though plenty of debate may be occurring among those who are not powerful enough to be included as official sources. In matters of foreign policy and national security especially, it is not uncommon for elites to stake out uniform positions.[64] Thus, on some of the most important issues of our day—war, terrorism, and international trade—elites often present a united front, which leads the press to act more as a tool of government than a watchdog. Indeed, in 2004, both the *New York Times* and the *Washington*

Post expressed regret for not publishing stories that challenged the George W. Bush administration's justifications for going to war in Iraq.[65]

The assignment of journalists to newsbeats results in journalists developing close relationships with government officials on those beats, leading to the concern that journalists may become too cozy with those officials. From this perspective, journalists act more like lapdogs than watchdogs. Newsbeats can also lead to **pack journalism** as journalists assigned to the same beat end up covering the same set of stories from the same perspective. Further, newsworthy events may be happening that do not get reported because there is no journalist assigned to that newsbeat.[66] For example, news organizations regularly assign journalists to cover the Pentagon. Those journalists become familiar with weapons systems, military buildups, and troop deployments; they attend press conferences; and they cultivate key sources. Not surprisingly, stories emanating from the Pentagon are regularly featured in news coverage. Reporters are not assigned to cover the Department of Veterans Affairs as a beat, however. As a result, significant stories may be overlooked. An important story about the shoddy treatment of wounded soldiers at Walter Reed Army Medical Center was missed for months, if not years.[67] And, of course, some stories may never be reported.

The norm of newsworthiness leads journalists to favor coverage of conflict and the strategic aspects of political campaigns and governance over substantive issues. This is highly problematic for those citizens who want journalists to cover the issues so they can evaluate whether political leaders are addressing their problems.[68] It is also troubling for participatory democratic theorists, who see a sharp disconnect between what information journalists deem newsworthy and what information citizens need to function effectively in a democratic society.

Finally, a recent study by Amber Boydstun demonstrates that news norms and economic incentives to be efficient lead media organizations to focus on only a few issues in an "explosion" of coverage while most issues receive little to no attention. Boydstun argues that media organizations draw attention to an issue by sounding an "alarm" that influences other journalists' behavior due to pack journalism. Momentum produces media fixation so that journalists "patrol" the issue, delving into details and developing stories on various aspects of the issue. This continues until the next hot topic comes along, which leads to an explosion of coverage of that issue. Importantly, what may look like an erratic pattern of news coverage can be explained by a few key factors. Specifically, momentum (i.e., prior attention to the issue), the attention of policymakers, citizens' concerns about a policy, and a diverse range of perspectives on the issue are more likely to result in significant media attention—for a while anyway.[69]

ARE CITIZENS AFFECTED BY THE MASS MEDIA?

In this chapter, we have discussed what citizens should expect from the media in a democracy, and we have addressed the empirical reality of the media in the

United States. By now, you should have a good feel for the general and specific characteristics of the media that shape news coverage. The question remains, however, whether citizens are affected by the mass media. That is the topic we turn to in this section.

The Hypodermic Model

Imagine you are going to the doctor to receive your annual flu shot. The doctor uses a hypodermic needle to inject you with the vaccine. You leave her office with the medicine coursing through your veins ready to fight off any flu bug that might come your way. Receiving a shot in a doctor's office is an (often unpleasant) experience to which we can all relate.

Now, let's translate this phenomenon to the political arena. Take yourself back in time to the Great Depression. Imagine you and your family sitting in your living room listening attentively to one of President Franklin D. Roosevelt's "fireside chats" on the radio. Or imagine you are in Munich, Germany, during roughly the same period. Picture yourself reading newspapers over which Adolf Hitler has exerted complete control. Are you being injected with messages from the mass media in the same way a doctor injects you with medicine? Are the media messages so powerful and you so weak that resistance is futile?

Bring yourself to the present and take a look around. Why are so many of your friends (and maybe even you) wearing Under Armour apparel or carrying iPhones with the name brands prominently displayed? Is it possible that the advertising campaigns of these companies have "injected" your friends with their messages, thus getting them to buy overpriced products and provide free advertising for the company all at the same time?

These examples illustrate what has been called the **hypodermic model** of media effects.[70] The early to mid-1900s saw a huge growth in advertising, numerous technological changes that allowed average citizens access to the media, two world wars, the rise of dictators across Europe, and a powerful president at home. All these factors led some observers to fear that the media could control citizens. Underlying this fear were two assumptions: (1) that the media are extremely powerful and (2) that citizens are not sophisticated enough to ward off media messages. The hypodermic model is certainly a compelling metaphor, but is there evidence to support its view of media effects on citizens? It turns out that systematic support for such wide-ranging, persuasive effects of the media never panned out. Instead, scholars came to the conclusion that the media have relatively minimal effects on citizens' political attitudes.

Minimal Effects Model

Whereas the hypodermic model viewed citizens as blank slates waiting to be written on by the mass media, the **minimal effects model** of media influence has a more nuanced understanding of citizens. From the minimal effects perspective, citizens' slates are already marked up with a whole host of prior attitudes and predispositions when they encounter media messages. Citizens rely on these existing attitudes to help them sift through, evaluate, and often filter out media content. Thus, citizens are not passively injected with messages from the media; instead, they are active receivers or rejecters of these messages depending on their predispositions. As a result, the media have minimal effects on citizens' political attitudes.

Evidence of the media's minimal effects was provided by Paul Lazarsfeld, Bernard Berelson, and Hazel Gaudet in their classic study of Erie County, Ohio, during the 1940 presidential campaign between Franklin Roosevelt and Wendell Wilkie.[71] Lazarsfeld et al. trained local interviewers to conduct several in-home interviews with a representative sample of Erie County residents between May and November 1940. To be precise, this panel survey included six hundred people, each of whom was interviewed six times over the course of the campaign. Thus, the design of the study allowed the researchers to track residents over time to determine why people voted the way they did in November. In particular, Lazarsfeld and colleagues were interested in the influence of campaign messages on citizens' vote choices. By studying one community in depth, the scholars were able to assess the campaign messages that were circulating in the local media environment and examine what effect, if any, those messages had on voters. In this way, Lazarsfeld et al.'s research provides evidence that allows us to assess the power of the media to influence citizens' political attitudes.

Lazarsfeld et al.'s research findings are striking. First, they discovered that a remarkable 50 percent of citizens already knew in May for whom they were going to vote in November. Obviously, the campaigns' media messages were not changing people's choices because they had already made up their minds before the campaign even got started. Nevertheless, Lazarsfeld et al. argued that political communication still played an important role because it reinforced people's existing decisions. Hence, this was labeled the **reinforcement effect**.

Lazarsfeld et al. also identified an **activation effect** among those people who were initially undecided about which candidate to support. The researchers demonstrated that campaign messages aroused interest in citizens, which led them to pay more attention to the election; however, the fascinating thing was that citizens did not pay attention to all aspects of the campaigns. Instead, citizens honed in on particular magazine articles and newspaper stories that corresponded with their political predispositions. In other words, citizens with Republican-leaning characteristics were more likely to seek out Republican-leaning campaign news, whereas Democratic-inclined citizens sought out pro-Democratic media content. This selective attention to the media activated citizens' prior attitudes, which served to remind citizens why they held those attitudes in the first place.[72] Thus, citizens' latent predispositions were stimulated and strengthened by the news stories. Rarely were those predispositions challenged, and when they were, citizens were anchored by their predispositions and therefore resistant to change. By November, citizens' preexisting attitudes became crystallized, encouraging them to vote for the presidential candidate who was consistent with their values and predispositions all along.

Finally, Lazarsfeld and colleagues found little evidence of a **conversion effect**. In other words, very few citizens actually changed from one candidate to another during the course of the campaign. We might expect that citizens who had few existing attitudes would be susceptible to campaign messages and thus to conversion; however, those same citizens who did not have strong predispositions also did not expose themselves to campaign news. In other words, those most likely to be persuaded were the least likely to come across the persuasive messages. Conversion, then, was a rare phenomenon.

Lazarsfeld et al. also argued that the media's influence was limited because many citizens relied on conversations with politically engaged friends and family, rather than the mass media, to obtain information about the presidential campaign. The researchers described the process as a "**two-step flow of communication**."[73] First, highly interested citizens would gather campaign information from newspapers and the radio. These people were called "opinion leaders."[74] Second, the opinion leaders would talk about the election with their friends and family, passing on information about candidates and issues to those who were much less caught up in the campaign. Therefore, Lazarsfeld et al. did not dismiss the influence of the media entirely because clearly the opinion leaders were gathering information from news organizations, but they did emphasize that personal contacts were more influential for most everyday, average citizens.

Subtle Effects Model

When scholars did not find evidence that the media had widespread persuasion effects, many lost interest in studying the influence (or lack thereof) of the media. Research in this area was dormant for quite a while. Maxwell McCombs and Donald L. Shaw reversed that trend, however, with their research on the agenda-setting role of the media in the 1968 presidential election.[75] McCombs and Shaw acknowledged that the media cannot change people's minds on the issues of the day, but they argued that *"the mass media set the agenda for each political campaign, influencing the salience of attitudes towards the political issues."*[76] Their study marks the beginning of the **subtle effects model** era of media research.

Agenda Setting. McCombs and Shaw's argument was based on a comparison between what a random sample of Chapel Hill, North Carolina, voters said were the key issues in the 1968 presidential election and the actual campaign coverage in the news media relied on by voters in that community. McCombs and Shaw found a strong relationship between the issues emphasized by the media and those issues deemed important by the voters. For example, the mass media devoted a significant amount of coverage to foreign policy and law-and-order issues, and

Chapel Hill voters indicated those topics were major campaign issues. Thus, the media set the agenda by establishing which campaign issues are considered important in the minds of voters. The media "may not be successful much of the time in telling people what to think, but it is stunningly successful in telling its readers what to think *about*."[77]

McCombs and Shaw's research breathed new life into the study of media effects and spurred a new generation of scholars to further investigate **agenda-setting effects**.[78] In 1982, Shanto Iyengar, Mark Peters, and Donald Kinder, for example, tackled a significant question left unanswered by McCombs and Shaw's research. Because McCombs and Shaw's conclusions were based on comparing aggregated cross-sectional survey data to media content, they were not able to demonstrate that media coverage *caused* voters to consider certain issues more important than others. To explain further, McCombs and Shaw had surveyed Chapel Hill voters at one time (therefore collecting what scientists call cross-sectional data) and then lumped them all together (meaning they aggregated the voters) to compare what voters as a group indicated were their campaign priorities with what issues were covered by the media. Thus, their research was not able to establish that the news coverage *caused* individual voters to consider particular issues important. Why not? Because perhaps it was the case that the media simply reflected the priorities of the voters. The media might have anticipated the interests of voters and therefore covered those issues they thought would draw the largest audience. Figure 3.3 illustrates this conundrum. Thus, the question remains: Do the media cause voters to think certain issues are important, or do voters think certain issues are important and the media cover those issues as a result?

To untangle this causal relationship, Iyengar, Peters, and Kinder conducted an agenda-setting experiment using citizens of New Haven, Connecticut, as subjects.[79]

Figure 3.3   Sorting Out Causal Relationships

Cross-sectional data do not allow us to sort out the causal relationship between two variables. Let's say we see an association between the amount of media coverage of global warming and the importance citizens assign to that issue. Does the association occur because the media coverage causes people to think global warming is important? Or does the association occur because people think global warming is important, which causes the media to devote more attention to the issue? This is known as the reverse causality problem. To solve this problem (and thus establish the direction of the causal arrow), scholars often use experimental research designs.

By paying subjects $20 to participate in their experiment, they were able to recruit a group of participants who mirrored the characteristics of New Haven citizens. Six days in a row during November 1980, subjects reported to an office at Yale University that had been transformed into a casual setting for television viewing. The researchers "encouraged participants to watch the news just as they did at home."[80] In this way, they tried to make the context as natural as possible to ensure their results could be generalized beyond the experimental setting. Therefore, by recruiting a mix of people to participate in their study and creating a comfortable setting for watching the news, Iyengar et al. took steps to ensure their experiment was high in external validity.

When the subjects arrived on the first day, they were asked to complete a questionnaire on political topics. Embedded in this survey were questions that asked subjects to rate the importance of several national problems. Over the next four days, subjects watched videotapes of the prior evening's network newscast, or so they thought. On the last day, subjects completed another questionnaire that repeated the problem-importance questions.

Now, there are three crucial details here. First, the newscasts were not truly from the night before. Instead, the experimenters created newscasts based partially on what had been shown the night before but with specific types of stories either added or deleted. Second, the experimenters created two different versions of the newscast. In one version, stories describing problems with U.S. defense capabilities were inserted in the middle of the broadcast, whereas no such stories were included in the other version. Thus, the researchers had complete control over the characteristics of the experimental treatment (the newscasts). And third, subjects were randomly assigned to view either the newscasts that emphasized weaknesses in U.S. military preparedness or the newscasts that did not mention the issue. In other words, it was chance alone that determined whether subjects saw the defense-related news stories or whether they saw newscasts without those stories. As a result of this random assignment, the subjects in the two conditions were essentially the same. Overall, then, this process of random assignment of subjects to conditions and experimenter control over the treatment ensured that the only difference between the two groups was that one viewed newscasts with the defense stories and the other did not. Thus, if the subjects in the two conditions expressed different opinions on the final questionnaire, we know that it is due to the experimental treatment because all other factors were held constant.

And, indeed, this was just the case. Subjects who viewed the newscasts emphasizing the problems with U.S. military preparedness changed their opinions and rated defense issues as much more important in the postexperiment questionnaire than in the initial questionnaire. Before viewing the newscasts, the subjects ranked defense as the sixth most important out of eight problems. After watching the newscasts, defense jumped to the second most important problem. Furthermore, their attitudes on the importance of other issues did not change, and subjects in the control condition did not change their ranking of the importance of defense as a national problem.

Priming. In addition to studying agenda setting, Iyengar and colleagues examined media **priming** in their experiments.[81] The researchers hypothesized a priming effect whereby the issues emphasized by the media would become the same issues citizens used to evaluate political leaders. For example, if the media covered defense topics, then a president's performance on that issue would become a salient factor shaping opinion toward the president in general. This is exactly what they found. After viewing stories on the inadequacies in the defense system, subjects' views of President Jimmy Carter on *that issue* were a stronger predictor of their overall evaluation of Carter than in the condition in which subjects did not see stories on defense. In other words, the defense stories *primed* citizens to evaluate the president along those lines.

In addition to priming issues, the media can also highlight particular traits, such as experience or competence, on which citizens will evaluate political leaders. For example, a study by Jody Baumgartner, Jonathan Morris, and Natasha Walth examined the effect of Tina Fey's *Saturday Night Live* (*SNL*) impersonation of Sarah Palin on public opinion.[82] Baumgartner et al. hypothesized that *SNL's* parody of Sarah Palin's debate performance primed citizens to view her as an "uninformed political novice,"[83] which would negatively affect their opinion of her and the likelihood they would vote for John McCain. To test this hypothesis, the researchers conducted an online panel survey of young adults during the 2008 campaign season. Their sample was not a representative one, but Baumgartner et al. argue that it is nonetheless informative because young people are the primary consumers of political humor. By comparing survey respondents who saw the *SNL* skit of Palin's debate performance to those who were exposed to other media coverage of the debate (and by taking into account respondents' prior attitudes toward Palin), the researchers found that those who viewed the *SNL* spoof were more likely to disapprove of Sarah Palin as McCain's vice-presidential candidate and less likely to say they would vote for McCain as a result of her nomination. Interestingly, viewing the *SNL* skit did not have much influence on the attitudes of Democrats, probably because they had already found reasons to dislike Sarah Palin. Among Republicans and independents, however, Palin's image suffered as a result of viewing Tina Fey's impersonation.

In a recent study, Michael Tesler demonstrates that political messages are especially likely to *prime* well-crystallized attitudes, such as partisanship, religiosity, values, and group-based attitudes.[84] These attitudes are formed early in life and tend to be stable. In contrast, less crystallized attitudes, such as issue opinions, are likely to *change* in response to political communication. For example, Tesler shows that President Obama's announcement on May 9, 2012, in favor of same-sex marriages primed citizens' underlying attitudes toward gays and lesbians. Specifically, citizens' evaluations of gays and lesbians had a larger effect on Obama's approval ratings immediately following his announcement than before or several days after. The priming effect diminished as media attention turned to other topics, suggesting that communication effects fade unless messages continue to be salient.

Tesler also examined the relationship between attitudes toward government health insurance and preferences for Barack Obama between 2008 and 2012.[85] Attitudes toward government health insurance were not crystallized before the issue received significant attention during President Obama's first term. Tesler uses panel survey data from 2008 and 2012 to show that attitudes toward government health insurance were no more closely linked to Obama evaluations in 2012, when health care was so tied to him that it was called Obamacare, than in 2008 when the issue was not yet his signature policy; thus, there was no evidence of a priming effect. Instead, citizens changed their positions on government health insurance over time to bring them in line with their vote choice in 2008. McCain voters in 2008, for example, changed their opinions on government health insurance between 2008 and 2012, becoming substantially less supportive of it as the policy became associated with Barack Obama.[86]

Framing. In addition to agenda setting and priming, scholars have also identified media **framing effects**. Framing is defined as "the process by which a communication source, such as a news organization, defines and constructs a political issue or public controversy."[87] Media frames identify which aspects of a problem are relevant and important, and they imply which characteristics of a problem are not significant. They also influence which aspects of a story are remembered.[88] A framing effect occurs when media frames influence public opinion on the issue being framed. To illustrate frames and framing effects, we turn to another classic study conducted by Shanto Iyengar.[89]

Iyengar examined television news framing of poverty between 1981 and 1986. He identified 191 poverty-related stories on CBS, NBC, and ABC news during this period. The stories were framed in either episodic or thematic terms. *Episodic frames* focused on individual poor people, whereas *thematic frames* emphasized poverty as a societal problem. For example, an episodic story on poverty might focus on a young single mother who is trying to make ends meet after losing her job. In contrast, a thematic story might discuss the nation's poverty rate. Obviously the topic of both stories is poverty, but one focuses your attention on the characteristics of the poor person, whereas the other leads you to think about poverty as a problem faced by the country as a whole. Iyengar found that the episodic frame dominated news coverage during the early to mid-1980s—two-thirds of the stories on poverty were framed in terms of particular victims of poverty.

Do these media frames influence public opinion? Iyengar answered this question by conducting an experiment to test whether the different frames influenced how people assign responsibility for poverty. Iyengar recruited subjects from the

Suffolk County, New York, area and paid them $10 to watch a twenty-one-minute videotape containing seven news stories. Subjects were randomly assigned to view either a thematic or episodic story on poverty, which was embedded as the fourth story in the broadcast. After viewing the video, subjects completed a questionnaire asking about responsibility for the problem of poverty. Specifically, to measure *causal responsibility*, individuals were asked, "In your opinion, what are the most important causes of poverty?"[90] And to measure *treatment responsibility*, individuals were asked, "If you were asked to prescribe ways to reduce poverty, what would you suggest?"[91] Iyengar then coded up to four responses for each question. The responses fell into one of two categories, citizens assigning responsibility either to individual poor people or to more general societal factors.

Did the frames influence how citizens attributed responsibility for poverty? Indeed they did. Subjects exposed to the episodic frame were significantly more likely to hold individuals responsible for causing and treating their own poverty and less likely to point to societal factors. The reverse occurred when subjects were exposed to the thematic frame; when the coverage emphasized the general phenomena of poverty, citizens were more likely to point to societal causes and solutions and less likely to hold individuals responsible for their poverty. Ironically, media coverage that highlights individual people and their plight leads citizens to point the finger of blame at the poor themselves. Overall, then, the dominance of the episodic frame in media coverage of poverty has clear implications for how citizens think about the issue.[92]

Another important aspect of Iyengar's study is the influence of race on public opinion. In the episodic framing condition, Iyengar also varied whether the poor person depicted in the news story was black or white. When the poor person was black, subjects were significantly more likely to indicate that poor people should solve their own problems and less likely to point to societal solutions for poverty. Thus, citizens' responses to poverty are at least partially driven by whether the poor person is black or white.

Thomas Nelson, Rosalee Clawson, and Zoe Oxley also examined media framing effects, but they took the research a step further by specifying the psychological mechanism that leads to such effects.[93] These scholars studied media coverage of a Ku Klux Klan (KKK) rally held in Chillicothe, Ohio. They identified two frames used by local television news stations to cover the event: *free speech* and *public order*. A newscast using the free speech frame emphasized the right of the KKK to speak and included images of KKK leaders speaking before a microphone. Several Klan supporters were interviewed and said they wanted to hear the KKK's message. One man said, "I came down here to hear what they have to say and I think I should be able to listen if I want to."[94] In contrast, a newscast with the public order frame focused on the possibility that violence would erupt at the rally between protestors and the KKK. The news story included images of police officers standing between the Klan members and the protesters. A bystander who was interviewed said, "Here you have a potential for some real sparks in the crowd."[95]

To examine what impact these frames had on tolerance for the KKK, Nelson et al. conducted an experiment using actual news coverage of the rally. They recruited college students enrolled in introductory political science courses to participate in the experiment. These subjects were randomly assigned to view either the free speech frame or the public order frame and then were asked to complete a survey that included a variety of questions, including two measuring tolerance for the KKK. The first question asked, "Do you support or oppose allowing members of the Ku Klux Klan to hold public rallies in our city?" The second asked, "Do you support or oppose allowing members of the Ku Klux Klan to make a speech in our city?"[96] Subjects responded on 7-point scales ranging from *strongly oppose* (1) to *strongly support* (7). Those exposed to the free speech frame were significantly more likely to support the KKK's right to rally and speak than those in the public order condition (see Figure 3.4). The free speech frame increased political tolerance for the KKK by more than one-half of a point on a 7-point scale. This is both a statistically and substantively significant increase in support for the KKK's right to participate in the public arena.

Nelson et al. also collected data in their experiment to understand the psychological mechanism leading to these framing effects. Previous scholars had hypothesized an **accessibility model** to explain why priming and framing effects occur. This perspective emphasizes that citizens are limited information processors operating in a complex political world. Because there is no way people can deal

Figure 3.4   Political Tolerance by Framing Condition

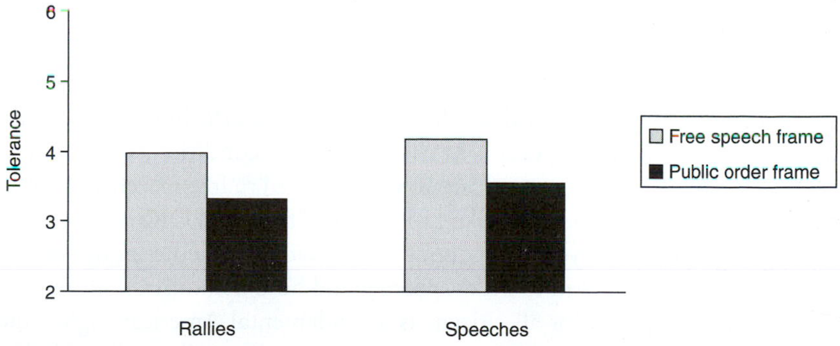

Source: Data from Thomas E. Nelson, Rosalee A. Clawson, and Zoe M. Oxley, "Media Framing of a Civil Liberties Conflict and Its Effect on Tolerance," *American Political Science Review* 91 (1997): 572.

Note: Higher numbers on 7-point scales indicate greater tolerance.

with all the information in their environment, they make judgments based on the most readily available considerations. The political context, such as news frames, makes certain concepts more accessible than others. In turn, these accessible concepts influence how citizens evaluate the issue that is being framed. For example, the free speech frame makes concepts such as freedom and liberty accessible. Thus, when citizens are asked whether the KKK should be allowed to rally after exposure to the free speech frame, freedom and liberty are uppermost in their minds. These accessible concepts encourage citizens to support the KKK's rights. At least that is the mechanism according to the proponents of the accessibility model.

Nelson, Clawson, and Oxley, however, suggest an **importance model** instead. They argue that not all equally accessible concepts have an equal effect on political evaluations. In other words, just because freedom and liberty are accessible does not mean they will automatically influence citizen judgment. Nelson et al. propose a more thoughtful model of information processing, which says that citizens will judge some accessible concepts more important than others. And those important or relevant concepts will be the ones that influence opinion.

To test these competing hypotheses, Nelson et al. randomly assigned subjects to either an accessibility or importance condition. In the accessibility condition, subjects were asked to respond to series of letter strings flashed on their computer screens. Subjects had to indicate whether each letter string was a word or a non-word. The task included words made accessible by the free speech frame (such as freedom, liberty, independence, and rights) and by the public order frame (such as violence, disorder, danger, and disturbance). How quickly subjects responded to the words indicates the accessibility of the words. This reaction time task is a standard method that psychologists use to measure accessibility.[97] Nelson et al. found that, regardless of the framing condition, the public order and free speech concepts were equally accessible. Thus, differences in accessibility could not explain why subjects were more tolerant in the free speech framing condition than in the public order framing condition.

Nelson and colleagues provide evidence, however, that the importance model explains how framing effects occur. In the importance condition, subjects were asked to evaluate the importance of certain values related to free speech and public order. For example, subjects were asked to indicate "how IMPORTANT each of these ideas is to you when you think about the question of whether or not the Ku Klux Klan should be allowed to make speeches and hold demonstrations in public": "Freedom of speech for all citizens is a fundamental American right" and "There is always a risk of violence and danger at Ku Klux Klan rallies."[98] The researchers found that public order values were deemed significantly more important after exposure to the public order frame and that free speech values were viewed as slightly more important in the free speech framing condition. As a result, these important values were weighted more heavily when determining support for the KKK's right to participate. In sum, frames influence which values citizens view as most important to the matter at hand, which leads to changes in public opinion regarding the issue.[99]

This research offers a more redeeming view of citizens. Rather than being buffeted around willy-nilly by whichever considerations are made most salient by a media frame, as suggested by the accessibility model, citizens engage in a more thoughtful process of weighing the importance of certain values as they form their opinions.[100]

Much of the work on framing effects has been done using experimental methods. Experiments, of course, are wonderful tools for testing causal hypotheses, but they are often more limited when it comes to generalizability because many experiments are conducted on college students. Paul Kellstedt's research on the impact of media framing on racial attitudes provides evidence that framing effects occur beyond the experimental laboratory, thus bolstering the case for the generalizability of these effects.[101]

Kellstedt argues that many citizens hold conflicting core values that influence their thinking on issues of race. On the one hand, citizens value *egalitarianism*; they believe everyone is of equal worth and should be treated the same before the law. On the other hand, citizens value *individualism*; they believe that people should get ahead through their own efforts and should pull themselves up by their own bootstraps. When it comes to racial policy preferences, egalitarians are more likely to support government activities designed to ensure blacks have the same opportunities as whites to succeed, whereas individualists are more likely to oppose such activities. But many citizens hold both values to be dear, so how do they figure out whether to support or oppose government programs intended to assist blacks? Kellstedt argues that citizens rely on egalitarian and individualist cues from the media to help determine their racial policy preferences.

To test this hypothesis, Kellstedt began by examining news coverage of race. Specifically, he content analyzed egalitarian and individualism frames in *Newsweek* stories on race between 1950 and 1994. He found that egalitarianism was a common frame during the 1960s but became less so after the mid-1970s. In contrast, individualism cues were fairly rare until the late 1970s, at which point they were used with greater regularity. The number of individualism cues peaked in the early 1990s.

Next, Kellstedt pulled together aggregate public opinion data on racial issues from this same period by relying on surveys from a variety of polling organizations. He showed that public opinion on issues of race fluctuated a great deal during this roughly forty-year period. Citizens were significantly more liberal on racial issues in the mid-1990s than they were in the early 1950s, but there was by no means a constant march in the liberal direction. Instead, we might think of the pattern as a dance step: for every two steps forward, you take one step—and sometimes more—back.

Last, Kellstedt compared the longitudinal data on media framing with these longitudinal public opinion data. He found that changes in media framing of values explain variations in racial policy preferences across time. When the egalitarian frame became more prominent in the media, citizens' racial attitudes became significantly more liberal. In contrast, the individualism frame led to slightly more conservative racial policy opinions. Thus, Kellstedt's "real-world" research confirms what many experimental researchers have found in the laboratory—media frames influence public opinion.

In sum, agenda setting, priming, and framing constitute what are known as subtle media effects. Researchers in this tradition have not found the widespread persuasion effects suggested by the hypodermic model, nor is their evidence consistent with the minimal effects model. Instead, researchers have shown how the media can influence public opinion by (1) affecting what the public thinks about, (2) affecting which issues and traits shape evaluations of leaders, and (3) affecting which considerations are viewed as most important when assessing a political issue.

Limits on Subtle Effects

Are there limits on subtle media effects? Can the media set the agenda to such an extent that we would consider them to be controlling the agenda? Can the media prime issues so much they overwhelmingly determine how candidates and politicians will be judged? Can the media frame political issues and therefore manipulate public opinion? These are important questions that emerge out of the research on subtle effects.

James Druckman moves us toward answering these questions by examining whether there are limits on framing effects.[102] Specifically, he asks, *who* can successfully frame an issue? He argues that citizens look to trusted, credible elites for guidance when determining their issue positions. He demonstrates that credible communication sources effectively frame public opinion, whereas less credible sources are not able to do so. As with Nelson, Clawson, and Oxley's research on framing effects, Druckman provides a more redeeming view of citizens. His study shows that citizens are not simply the victims of manipulation on the part of elites; instead, citizens react to cues that make sense—whether the elite is a credible source. Druckman and his colleagues also demonstrate that citizens respond to partisan cues.[103] They find that when citizens believe the issue at hand is one polarized along party lines, citizens will more likely follow a frame endorsed by their party even when that frame is a "weaker" one.

Additional work by Druckman and Chong reminds scholars that the real world of politics may put limits on framing not apparent in most research on framing effects.[104] In actual political debates, frames rarely go uncontested. Competing frames are part and parcel of political discourse. In many framing studies, however, participants are exposed to one-sided messages and then almost immediately asked their opinions on the issue at hand. Perhaps not surprisingly, researchers find that the messages shape public opinion. But what happens when citizens are faced with competing frames over the course of a policy debate or political campaign that might last weeks or months? Although the findings on this topic are quite complex, the simple answer is that when citizens are exposed to competing frames at one time, the messages tend to cancel each other out. When citizens receive messages at different times, however, they weigh the most recent message more heavily in their political judgments. Chong and Druckman conclude that, if you are an advocate of a particular frame, you would be well served to promote your message *early* to influence initial attitudes, *often* to combat other competing messages, and *late* to make sure your message is the last one heard by the public.[105]

MEDIA EFFECTS IN A CHANGING TECHNOLOGICAL ENVIRONMENT

As the media environment has evolved over the past few decades, technology has been a catalyst driving many changes. Partisan news outlets, for example, are more common than they used to be, in part because the explosion of cable channels has made it possible for companies to turn a profit even with small audiences. Whereas media organizations of the past had to attract large audiences to increase revenues, technological developments have made it cheaper to produce and disseminate news these days. Therefore, catering to a narrow partisan audience is a viable option. An even more significant new technology is, of course, social media. Social media platforms are ubiquitous in American society, but do they affect public opinion? We address social media effects on the public shortly. As for a discussion of the impact of partisan news on citizens' political attitudes, that appears in the Partisan News and Polarization section of Chapter 5. Finally, television is by no means a new technology, but television production techniques and values have certainly changed over time. We turn now to research that explores how these developments affect the public.

"In-Your-Face" Politics

Diana Mutz's path-breaking research examines the political impact of incivility on television.[106] Mutz starts with the premise that powerful social norms govern face-to-face interactions. These norms dictate the appropriate physical distance between people in a social interaction and guide us to distance ourselves from people with whom we disagree. Television violates these social norms in two ways. First, technological changes now enable cameras to shoot tight angles, bringing political figures into closer spatial proximity to television viewers than is normal for a face-to-face interaction. It is now commonplace for cameras to be "zoomed in so close that even portions of the speaker's head are routinely cut off and out of frame."[107] Second, norms of face-to-face social interaction require polite conversation. Much of the political discourse on television, however, is anything but polite. It is standard fare for politicians and pundits to disagree vehemently while shouting over one another. Discourteous interactions, not expressions of civility, are the norm. As a result of these two characteristics of political discourse on television, Mutz argues that citizens overwhelmingly experience politics as "in-your-face."

What is the impact of in-your-face politics? Mutz designed an experiment to investigate the effect of in-your-face politics on citizens. Specifically, she created her own television program modeled after standard political talk shows. She recruited two actors (equally attractive white males between the ages of 35 and 45) to play the part of congressional candidates competing for an open seat in Indiana. The two candidates and a moderator followed a script in which there was disagreement on several issues. In the "civil" condition, the candidates followed norms of politeness. For example, one candidate said, "I don't disagree with all of your points, Bob, but . . ." and then articulated his position. In the "uncivil" condition, the substantive content was the same, but it was no longer delivered in a polite way. Instead, the candidate said, "What Bob is *completely* overlooking is. . . ."[108] The experiment also included a manipulation of camera angles. In the "close-up" condition, the candidates' faces filled the screen, whereas tight close-ups were not included in the other condition, and the camera was at a "medium" distance. This experimental design resulted in four conditions. Subjects were randomly assigned to view either a civil, close-up program; a civil, medium program; an uncivil, close-up program; or an uncivil, medium program. Mutz found that subjects were more physically aroused by the close-ups and the uncivil discourse. These in-your-face conditions also caused subjects to list more of the candidates' arguments when asked to recall points made during the discussion. These findings suggest there are benefits to watching in-your-face programming. Arousal can lead to greater attention to politics, and recalling content from a political talk show can help citizens function effectively in a democracy.

Mutz was also concerned, however, about whether in-your-face politics would affect citizens' perceptions of the legitimacy of the opposition.[109] Here the effects are not so positive. In a second experiment using the same talk show stimulus, Mutz asked subjects to recall arguments made by the candidates, evaluate both candidates on a feeling thermometer, and indicate for which candidate they would vote if they had the opportunity to do so. Again in this experiment, Mutz found that subjects were able to recall more in the uncivil and close-up conditions, including better recall of arguments made by candidates they did not prefer. Importantly, when subjects were exposed to *both* the close-up shots and the uncivil exchange, their attitudes toward the candidate they didn't like were more negative and the arguments made by the disliked candidates were perceived as less legitimate. To summarize these findings, Mutz says subjects are "remembering more, but respecting it less."[110] In another experiment, Mutz shows that uncivil debates lower subjects' trust in politicians, political institutions, and the political system. Overall, Mutz's research suggests that televised in-your-face politics are problematic for constructive debate in a democratic society.

Social Media Effects

Social media have quickly become a mainstay of American politics. When both Republican and Democratic political leaders make active use of **social media** to connect with their supporters, you know it must play an important role in our contemporary political environment. Hillary Clinton announced her 2016 presidential bid in a video circulated on social media and regularly uses Twitter to weigh in on political issues of the day. Democratic candidate Bernie Sanders was dubbed "Facebook royalty" in a *New York Times* headline.[111] Republican presidential candidates use social media as well, with Donald Trump leading the pack in terms of the number of Twitter followers.[112]

It is clear that political elites are embracing social media as a technology to communicate with their supporters, but how many citizens use social media for political purposes? A 2014 study by the Pew Research Center shows that 16 percent of registered voters follow "candidates for office, political parties, or elected officials on social networking sites like Facebook or Twitter."[113] This is up dramatically from only 6 percent in 2010. Jason Gainous and Kevin Wagner argue that social media are particularly important to study despite the relatively low percentage of citizens who use it for political purposes because (a) these users are highly politically engaged, (b) even small numbers of citizens can influence elections in competitive districts, and (c) the number of users is increasingly rapidly.[114] Furthermore, Gainous and Wagner make several strong claims about the impact of social media on politics:

> Rather than simply being just the latest progression in communication technology, social media presents an entirely new paradigm on how people engage with each other. Instead of waiting for traditional media to explain limited elements of the news, the networker is interacting with not just the news itself but with entire networks of friends and acquaintances without limits from borders or geography. It is a network that lacks an editor or gatekeeper, and one that is governed by a new set of rules and codes of behavior that are only now being developed.[115]

As a two-way form of communication, social media allow users to choose what information to access and what to share with others. Importantly, citizens are able to embed themselves in a social network of like-minded individuals free from traditional journalistic gatekeeping. Gainous and Wagner demonstrate that many citizens prefer news that is consistent with their point of view, and those citizens are most likely to use Twitter and Facebook to gather political information. Social media provide citizens with the ideal tool to selectively expose themselves to information with which they agree. Political candidates, interest groups, and elected officials are all happy to accommodate this desire for agreeable content via social media because it also allows them to circumvent media gatekeepers. Why would Hillary Clinton or Donald Trump want to be asked questions at a news conference when they can simply tweet their message to their legions of followers?

Gainous and Wagner show that political users of social media are more likely to participate in politics by joining groups, which is a positive outcome. At the same time, citizens who use social media for political purposes also tend to have more extreme attitudes. This is probably not surprising because these individuals are largely opting for reassuring information from political elites who share their predispositions.

Conclusion

Do the mass media live up to democratic ideals? Overall, participatory democratic theorists would say no. In a perfect world, the media should be free from government and economic control, and they should inform and educate the public, provide a forum for diverse views, and hold government officials accountable. The reality is much different. The media in the United States are best characterized by the three Cs: corporate, concentrated, and conglomerate. Soft news is on the rise, tabloid journalism is increasingly influential, and in-your-face politics is problematic for democratic debate. Further, adherence to news norms often results in news that is biased toward the perspectives of powerful officeholders. Participatory democratic theorists would argue, however, that all is not lost because nonprofit media, the minority press, and the Internet offer alternatives to the dominance of conglomerates. Social media offer unprecedented opportunities for citizens to consume news and create and share their own political content, yet the reality is that many citizens use social media to simply seek out information that confirms their preexisting views, if they even encounter political information on social media at all.

Elite democratic theorists have a much different view about whether the media live up to democratic ideals. Compared with participatory democratic theorists, they have much lower expectations for citizens in a democracy, and as a result, they also have much lower expectations for the media. Because the media are relatively free from government control and provide citizens with enough information to go to the polls and cast a ballot, elite democrats are pleased. The influence of economic forces, the emphasis on official sources, and the increase in soft news, tabloid journalism, and in-your-face politics simply do not raise the same concerns for elite democrats.

Are citizens influenced by the mass media? The answer to that question has changed over time. Scholars originally proposed a hypodermic model of media effects, which said that the media were extremely powerful and would persuade unsophisticated citizens with their messages. This model went by the wayside, however, when little evidence was found to support it. Next, the minimal effects model emerged. This model argued that citizens would filter media messages through their preexisting attitudes. Instead of converting citizens to a new point of view, media messages were more likely to reinforce and activate current predispositions.

Most recently, scholars have found substantial evidence to support a subtle effects model of media influence. This tradition argues that the media influence citizens through agenda setting, priming, and framing; the media influence what citizens think about, which issues or traits citizens bring to bear when evaluating political leaders, and which considerations shape their thinking on political issues.

Overall, both participatory and elite democratic theorists can find things to like about the subtle effects model. On the one hand, elite democrats would find it natural for citizens to take cues from the media. Citizens are not expected to follow politics day in and day out; thus, it makes sense that the media would provide guidance for what issues are important and how politicians and issues should be evaluated. On the other hand, participatory democratic theorists would be pleased that citizens take in media messages in a thoughtful way and do not simply fall prey to elite manipulation.

KEY CONCEPTS

accessibility model / 97

accuracy / 85

activation effect / 90

advocacy journalism / 86

agenda-setting effects / 92

concentrated / 78

conglomerate / 80

conversion effect / 91

corporate / 75

forum for diverse views / 74

framing effects / 95

hard news / 78

horse race / 85

hypodermic model / 89

importance model / 98

intermediary / 74

legacy media outlets / 82

minimal effects model / 89

neutrality / 85

news norms / 84

newsbeats / 85

newsworthiness / 85

objectivity / 84

official sources / 85

pack journalism / 88

priming / 94

reinforcement effect / 90

social media / 103

soft news / 78

soft news media / 78

subtle effects model / 91

tabloid journalism / 86

traditional journalism / 86

two-step flow of communication / 91

watchdog / 74

SUGGESTED SOURCES FOR FURTHER READING

Iyengar, Shanto, and Donald R. Kinder. *News That Matters*. Chicago: University of Chicago Press, 1987.

In a series of classic experiments, these authors provide evidence of agenda setting, priming, and framing effects.

Parker, Emily. *Now I Know Who My Comrades Are: Voices from the Internet Underground*. New York: Sarah Crichton Books, 2014.

The author tells the stories of "citizens of the web" to argue that the Internet can be used to conquer the isolation, fear, and apathy sowed by authoritarian regimes.

Overholser, Geneva, and Kathleen Hall Jamieson, eds. *The Press*. Oxford: Oxford University Press, 2005.

Shapiro, Robert Y., and Lawrence R. Jacobs, eds. *The Oxford Handbook of American Public Opinion and the Media*. Oxford: Oxford University Press, 2011.

Essays in the Overholser and Jamieson edited volume examine the media as a critical institution in American democracy. The Shapiro and Jacobs edited volume pays particular attention to changes in technology and the mass media.

Matsaganis, Matthew D., Vikki S. Katz, and Sandra J. Ball-Rokeach. *Understanding Ethnic Media: Producers, Consumers, and Societies*. Thousand Oaks, CA: Sage, 2011.

This compelling text provides insight into the creation, nature, role, and consumption of ethnic media.

FAIR (Fairness & Accuracy in Reporting), www.fair.org
Media Matters for America, www.mediamatters.org

These two groups monitor the media from a progressive perspective.

Accuracy in Media, www.aim.org
Media Research Center, www.mrc.org

These two groups monitor the media from a conservative perspective.

Columbia Journalism Review, www.cjr.org/resources

If you are interested in "Who Owns What," check out this website. It provides detailed information on the holdings of major media corporations.

Pew Research Center, Journalism and Media, www.journalism.org

The Pew Research Center conducts empirical research on the news media and publishes annual "State of the News Media" reports. These reports provide all sorts of useful information about changes in American journalism, including ethnic media and digital news.

CHAPTER 4

Attitude Stability and Attitude Change

IN MID-APRIL 2011, public approval for President Barack Obama was at a fifty-two-week low, with only 41 percent of citizens saying they approved of his job performance. By the first week of May 2011, however, President Obama's ratings had jumped more than 10 percentage points, with 52 percent of citizens indicating they approved of the job he was doing as president. What caused this bump in support for President Obama? Quite simply, the increase resulted from a dramatic event that captured the attention of citizens across the country.

On the evening of May 1, 2011, President Obama announced, "Tonight, I can report to the American people and to the world that the United States has conducted an operation that killed Osama bin Laden, the leader of al Qaeda, and a terrorist who's responsible for the murder of thousands of innocent men, women, and children."[1] President Obama emphasized his role in finding bin Laden by saying, "Shortly after taking office, I directed Leon Panetta, the director of the CIA [Central Intelligence Agency], to make the killing or capture of bin Laden the top priority of our war against al Qaeda, even as we continued our broader efforts to disrupt, dismantle, and defeat his network."[2] The success of this daring and dangerous military mission made Obama look like a strong, decisive, and effective leader, which quickly translated into higher approval ratings. Did that bump in popularity last? Or was it fleeting? Do swings in public support for the president happen regularly, or are attitudes toward the president fairly stable?

More generally, do you think **attitude change** is common, or is **attitude stability** the norm? In Chapter 2, we learn how children and adolescents develop their political attitudes. After this early socialization, do political attitudes remain the same throughout an individual's adulthood? If attitude change occurs, what causes this change? And, from a normative standpoint, what does it say about the public if attitude instability is more common than stability? We address these questions in this chapter, first by examining some evidence for attitude change and some for attitude stability. Next, we discuss factors that explain fluctuations in presidential approval, one of the most important political attitudes held by citizens. In the remainder of the chapter, we draw heavily from the discipline of psychology as we overview theories of attitude formation and change that have greatly influenced how political scientists study public opinion.

ARE AMERICANS' ATTITUDES STABLE?

One way to assess whether people's attitudes remain the same over time is to survey people at one time about their political opinions and then ask them about the same opinions later. Recall from Chapter 2 that this approach, known as a panel study, was the one used by Kent Jennings and Richard Niemi to assess attitudes among high school seniors and their parents at various ages for both groups. Across the years, numerous panel studies have been conducted as part of the American National Election Study (ANES) series, allowing researchers to study attitude stability and change among the general public. ANES surveys have been carried out at least every two years, coinciding with presidential and congressional elections, since 1948.[3] Although in most years the ANES is a **cross-sectional study**—a survey using a new representative sample of adults—periodically since 1948 panel studies have been conducted whereby previous respondents are reinterviewed.

Individual Attitude Change

One of the very first empirical analyses of political attitude stability was conducted by Philip Converse using data from the ANES 1956, 1958, and 1960 panel study.[4] This study questioned respondents about salient political issues of the day in each of the three years. These issues included domestic and foreign policy issues such as school desegregation, federal aid to education, the creation of a fair employment practices commission to prevent racial discrimination in employment, and military aid to fight communism. Respondents were also asked their party identification. Comparisons of respondents' political attitudes in 1958 with their attitudes in 1960 are presented in Table 4.1. To measure the degree to which individuals' attitudes were stable, Converse calculated tau-b correlation coefficients, which are presented in the first column of Table 4.1. When tau-b equals 1.0, everyone's attitude was the same in 1960 as it had been in 1958. The smaller the value of tau-b, the more people's attitudes fluctuated over these two years. Another way to compare attitude stability over time is to determine how many people kept the same opinion at two times. We present our results from such an analysis in the second column of the table. The figures here are the percentage of respondents whose opinions stayed on the same side of an issue or whose party allegiance was to the same party (or who remained politically independent) from 1958 to 1960. Political attitudes are considered stable by this measure even if someone changed from strong to weak agreement or from strong to weak partisanship over time. The final column of the table presents the percentage of respondents who expressed no opinion toward the policy issues in either 1958 or 1960, or in both years.

As we see from the results in Table 4.1, party identification was the most stable political attitude over these two years. In fact, the value of tau-b for party identification is significantly higher than the tau-b for any of the other attitudes. For most people, their party affiliation remained the same from 1958 to 1960. Converse attributes this to the fact that attitudes and affect toward groups, such as political parties, help to organize the political opinions of many people. Because party identification was the only attitude surveyed "that touches on pure affect toward a visible population grouping," it came as no surprise to Converse that these attitudes remained quite stable over two years.[5]

In contrast, **attitude instability** was much more common for the policy issues, with only between 40 and 60 percent of the public holding the same opinion over time, versus nearly 86 percent for party allegiance. Among the policy issues queried, citizens' attitudes toward racial employment discrimination, isolationist foreign policy, and school desegregation were the least likely to change. Opinions about foreign aid and whether the federal government should be involved in providing housing and electric power were especially likely to fluctuate. To explain why there were these differences in attitude stability across issues, Converse points to the fact that some issues, even domestic ones, were less significant to citizens in the late 1950s.[6] Stable attitudes are more likely toward

Table 4.1   Stability of Individual Political Attitudes from 1958 to 1960

Political attitude	Correlation between attitudes in 1958 and 1960 (tau-b)	Percentage holding the same attitude in 1958 and 1960	Percentage having no opinion in at least one year
Party Identification	.73	85.7	N/A
School desegregation	.43	57.5	15.8
Employment discrimination	.41	60.0	17.9
Guaranteed employment	.41	56.5	15.2
Isolationism	.39	59.6	16.3
Federal aid to education	.38	57.2	13.8
Foreign economic aid	.34	48.0	21.4
Foreign military aid	.32	56.7	24.9
Federal housing	.29	40.7	33.9

Sources: Philip E. Converse, "The Nature of Belief Systems in Mass Publics," in *Ideology and Discontent*, ed. David E. Apter (New York: Free Press, 1964), 240; Analysis of American National Election Studies 1956–58–60 Panel Data File.

objects that tend to influence people's everyday lives (such as jobs or schools) or toward salient groups (such as blacks). When issues are more remote, attitude instability is more common.

People's political attitudes could change for a number of reasons. Citizens' opinions are susceptible to change, for instance, in the face of real-world events. Current events can provide new information to citizens as well as perhaps new understandings of issues, both of which can produce changes in attitudes. Converse considered this possibility but ruled it out as an explanation for the attitude instability he observed. In the late 1950s, high-profile news events did occur that could have influenced attitudes toward some issues that Converse studied, but not all. The public witnessed standoffs and violence in school desegregation cases in the southern United States, such as the integration of Central High School in Little Rock, Arkansas, in 1957 when army soldiers were required to escort black students into the formerly all-white high school. News also broke of waste in foreign aid spending during these years. Yet for one of the issues where the public's attitudes were the least stable, the role of the federal government in providing housing, there were no changes in federal policy or other relevant newsworthy items during these years that might have produced public attitude change. Converse also witnessed that the average correlations between people's attitudes were the same and were similarly low between 1956 and 1958, between 1958 and 1960, and between 1956 and 1960. We might expect that attitudes would fluctuate more the longer the interval between measuring the attitudes. This was not the case, leading Converse to turn to explanations for instability other than responses to changing events.

Ultimately, Converse concludes that many citizens' policy opinions are meaningless and might be better characterized as **nonattitudes** than attitudes.[7] Converse argues that "large portions of an electorate do not have meaningful beliefs, even on issues that have formed the basis for intense political controversy among elites for substantial periods of time."[8] If public attitudes were well developed, carefully considered, and based on detailed information, according to Converse, they probably would not change as much as he had observed. Converse's statements might seem extreme and unnecessarily harsh, especially when you consider that, according to Table 4.1, a majority of the public did continue to hold opinions on the same side of most issues between 1958 and 1960. Examining temporal attitude stability was only one portion of Converse's research, however, and his conclusions were based on a variety of other analyses. In particular, Converse demonstrated that most people's opinions are not well grounded in broader beliefs (such as liberalism or conservatism) and are not well organized.[9] We discuss these other conclusions more thoroughly in Chapter 5.

Yet, even thinking only about Converse's evidence of attitude change, it is fair to ask how many Americans should have stable attitudes for us to conclude that the public's policy opinions are meaningful. Is our standard 100 percent? If so, then any deviation from this might lead to conclusions similar to Converse's. In fact, it was empirical evidence such as this that fostered the development of the theories of democratic elitism and pluralism. Recall from Chapter 1 that these theorists compared empirical research about the public's capabilities with classical democratic theorists' expectations about the public and concluded that the public was not living up to the classical model. By using a different standard, however, perhaps one that recognizes some policy issues are complex and are not central to most people's daily lives, we may conclude that levels of attitude stability apparent in the late 1950s seem reasonable and not too low.

Collective Attitude Stability

We turn now to an examination of the stability of **collective public opinion**, that is, the aggregate political opinions of the public. In the most detailed analysis of collective opinion over time, Benjamin Page and Robert Shapiro analyzed results from public opinion surveys conducted over fifty years. Page and Shapiro's conclusions paint a very different picture than that emerging from studies of individuals. In their own words, "The American public, as a collectivity, holds a number of real, stable, and sensible opinions about public policy and . . . these opinions develop and change in a reasonable fashion, responding to changing circumstances and to new information."[10]

Page and Shapiro's evidence for this conclusion consists primarily of comparisons of responses to survey questions that were asked at least two different times between 1935 and 1990. For 58 percent of these questions, aggregate public opinion did not change significantly over time. For instance, in 1942, approximately 75 percent of the American public believed that the United States should have an active rather than isolationist foreign policy. Fourteen years later, the percentage of Americans holding this attitude was also about 75 percent. Opinions on this topic did fluctuate a bit in the intervening years, but within a narrow range of 72–80 percent supporting activism over isolationism.

Turning to domestic matters, Page and Shapiro observed that opinions about government spending on a variety of programs did not fluctuate very much during the 1970s and 1980s. Consistently high percentages of the public (68–77 percent) felt that the government was spending too little to fight crime, whereas consistently low percentages (12–25 percent) felt that government was spending too little on welfare (see Figure 4.1). Attitudes toward government spending on Social Security were especially stable during the late 1980s (the years for which opinion data are available). The item displayed in Figure 4.1 that shows the most variation was beliefs about education spending. Whereas about 49 percent of the public felt the government spent too little on education in the early 1970s, this percentage gradually increased during the time period, reaching 68 percent in 1989.

While Page and Shapiro found many examples of collective attitude stability, they also uncovered some instances of attitude change. Unlike what we might

Figure 4.1 Opinion toward Government Spending, 1971–1989

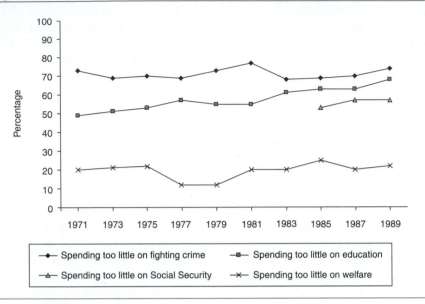

Source: Adapted from Figures 2.2, 4.1, and 4.3 of Benjamin I. Page and Robert Y. Shapiro, *The Rational Public: Fifty Years of Trends in Americans' Policy Preferences* (Chicago: University of Chicago Press, 1992), 49, 120, 126.

expect given Converse's results, however, Page and Shapiro observed that collective attitude change was often modest in size and that large attitude swings over short periods of time were not very common. Opinion change was more likely to be gradual (slow, steady shifts in Americans' beliefs, often in response to changes in the broader social or political climate) than to fluctuate (increases in support followed by decreases, or vice versa, over a short period of time). We just observed such a gradual increase with education spending. Americans' opinions have also changed slowly over time for other domestic policy issues, such as racial integration of schools and capital punishment. Only about 30 percent of white Americans supported the integration of schools in 1942, for example, compared with 90 percent in 1985. As for capital punishment, support for the death penalty steadily increased from 47 percent in 1966 to 78 percent in 1985. More recent research on death penalty attitudes shows that support for the policy continued to increase into the mid-1990s but then declined in the 2000s.[11] In 2014, the Gallup organization reported that 63 percent of Americans supported the death penalty for people convicted of murder.[12] Consistent with Page and Shapiro's argument that aggregate opinion responds to the political environment, the decline in support for the death penalty occurred as the media paid more attention to the "innocence frame,"[13] that is, the possibility that innocent people might be executed.[14]

Page and Shapiro also explored the prevalence of abrupt opinion changes among the public. Abruptness, or a change of at least 10 percentage points within a year, was especially likely for foreign policy issues. On closer examination of these cases, Page and Shapiro conclude that these sudden opinion changes often happened in the wake of real-world events: "wars, confrontations, or crises, in which major changes in the actions of the United States or other nations have understandably affected calculations about the costs and benefits of alternative policies."[15] Examples include a decline of 17 points in the percentage of Americans who sympathized with Israel regarding the long-running Arab-Israeli conflict. This decline was registered a few months after the Palestinian intifada (uprising) began in 1987 and the Israelis responded to the intifada with force, force that many felt was too severe.

Collective Public versus Individual Citizens

Throughout their book, Page and Shapiro contrast their image of aggregate public opinion as reasonable, meaningful, and largely stable with the image of the public presented in the empirical work of Converse and in the writings of America's founders, most especially James Madison and Alexander Hamilton, who asserted that the public was subject to fits of passion and that public opinion was expected to be volatile. How might we explain these discrepancies? Which view is correct?

To answer these questions, we should first consider the differences in examining individual opinions versus the aggregate opinion of the public. Aggregate opinion can appear quite stable even if many individuals change their opinions, provided that the individual changes cancel each other out. Imagine, for example, that we surveyed ten people in 2012, and six supported increasing government spending for fighting terrorism (see Table 4.2). Two years later, we surveyed the same ten people. Four respondents, Alonzo, Owen, Lei'ana, and Sadie, held the same attitudes, whereas the others had changed their minds. Madison, Cameron, and Kyree initially favored increasing spending but later supported spending decreases. Khalil, Jared, and Olivia wanted less spending in 2012 but favored spending more in 2014. Even with all these changes, our aggregate result is the same: six of ten respondents supported spending more money to fight terrorism in 2012 and 2014. The same phenomenon can occur when surveying representative samples of the American public. Many changes at the individual level over time can still result in temporal stability (or near stability) at the aggregate level. Thus, both Converse and Page and Shapiro are correct, in that their conclusions are appropriate for their level of analysis (individual or collective).

In describing the aggregation process, however, these researchers present different assumptions about what the aggregate results are really measuring. Page and Shapiro argue that individual changes, though perhaps frequent, are relatively minor deviations from true, enduring beliefs and values. Converse, in contrast, views the aggregation process as covering up the shallow, fleeting opinions of individual citizens. The sample quotations that follow present these contrasting views, with Page and Shapiro's appearing first:

> At any given moment, the random deviations of individuals from their long-term opinions may well cancel out over a large sample, so that a poll or survey can accurately measure collective preferences as defined in terms of the true or long-term preferences of many individual citizens.[16]

> It is quite possible, thanks to the hidden power of aggregation, to arrive at a highly rational system performance on the backs of voters, most of whom are remarkably ill-informed much of the time.[17]

Normatively, we might wonder whether it is better to think of the public as *individual citizens* or as a *collection of individuals*. Each approach is reasonable and well grounded in democratic theory. Many of these theories highlight the characteristics and capabilities of individual citizens, although theories reach different conclusions as to whether citizens are capable of ruling in a democracy or not. Yet, in positing a role for citizens to influence public policy, as most democratic theories do, these theories must also focus on aggregate public opinion. Discussions of whether and to what extent the wishes of the public should influence the decisions of elected officials naturally revolve around the wishes of the aggregate

Table 4.2 Aggregate Opinion Can Be Stable While Individual Attitudes Change

Ten survey respondents	Interviewed in 2012	Reinterviewed in 2014	Substantial individual change
Alonzo	Increase	Increase	Stable
Owen	Increase	Increase	Stable
Lei'ana	Increase	Increase	Stable
Madison	Increase	Decrease	Change
Cameron	Increase	Decrease	Change
Kyree	Increase	Decrease	Change
Khalil	Decrease	Increase	Change
Jared	Decrease	Increase	Change
Olivia	Decrease	Increase	Change
Sadie	Decrease	Decrease	Stable
Aggregate Stability	6 Increase, 4 Decrease	6 Increase, 4 Decrease	

public rather than the wishes of an individual citizen. Aggregating individuals' opinions is necessary for representation to occur, whether at the national, state, or congressional district level. In other words, if we want to know whether the national government is responsive to the wishes of the public when it comes to counterterrorism policies, for instance, we turn to aggregate measures of public opinion toward these policies. So whether we adopt Converse's conclusions that individual attitudes are unstable or Page and Shapiro's arguments that the aggregate public holds largely stable opinions depends in part on whether we are concerned about the democratic public as individual citizens or as a collective whose views might influence governmental decisions.

PRESIDENTIAL APPROVAL

One of the most important political attitudes studied by political scientists is presidential approval.[18] Politicians, journalists, and political junkies are also quite interested in this concept. **Presidential approval** refers to the public's level of approval or disapproval of the president's job performance. For decades, the Gallup organization has conducted daily telephone surveys with national, representative samples of U.S. citizens to track approval of the president. Gallup asks, "Do you approve or disapprove of the way [the incumbent] is handling his job as president?" Each day Gallup releases its latest approval numbers for the president based on a three-day rolling average of these **tracking polls**. The data are posted online at 1:00 p.m. EST on the Gallup website.[19] Some political observers are so obsessed with these numbers that they glue themselves to their computers or smartphones each afternoon waiting anxiously for the data to be released.

Why are these approval ratings so important? Because they speak volumes about a president's political power. Strong approval ratings are good news for a president's reelection chances, and they boost the electoral fortunes of members of Congress in his party who support his agenda.[20] Higher approval ratings also enable the president to be more successful in his interactions with Congress.[21] In general, high approval ratings can be thought of as a form of political capital that allows the president to pursue his goals.

Presidential approval ratings for George W. Bush and Barack Obama are presented in Figure 4.2. (Take a look at the Presidential Job Approval Center on the Gallup website for job approval ratings from Truman to Obama.[22]) The first thing that jumps out about these ratings is the way in which presidential approval declines over time. President George W. Bush started his presidency with approval ratings in the high 50s and low 60s but ended eight years later in the high 20s and low 30s. President Obama took office with approval ratings in the mid-60s, but those declined over time as well. This initial popularity is often referred to as the **honeymoon period**. Presidents take office with substantial goodwill from the public and, quite important, from other political elites. Some presidents who are reelected also see an uptick in their approval around the time of this reelection,

Figure 4.2   Presidential Approval for George W. Bush and Barack Obama

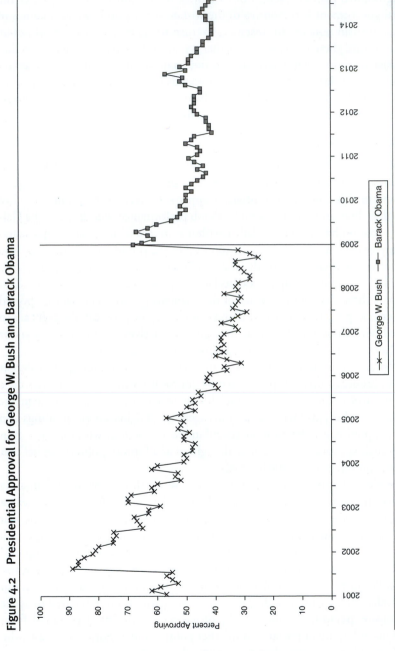

Source: "Presidential Job Approval Center," Gallup, Washington, DC, 2015, http://www.gallup.com/poll/124922/Presidential-Approval-Center.aspx

as President Obama did in the fall of 2012. As time goes by however, the president is faced with many difficult and controversial problems, and inevitably he makes decisions that tick off one group of people or another.[23] Although the average citizen may not track a president's every move, political elites are paying close attention, and some begin to complain about the president's decisions. The media transmit, and may even exaggerate, those criticisms, so that citizens are increasingly exposed to negative coverage of the president. As a result, public approval for the president falls over time.[24] Additionally, people tend to expect new presidents to be able to accomplish key policy goals and to have favorable personal characteristics, such as sound judgment and high ethical standards. Over time, as presidents fail to live up to these expectations, which can be unrealistically high, a public **expectations gap** emerges. The larger the gap between what the public expects of a president and what the president actually accomplishes, the lower the president's approval.[25]

Another noticeable feature of the presidential approval data is the way the public reacts to foreign policy events. Specifically, a **rally round the flag** effect occurs when presidential popularity surges in the wake of a foreign policy event involving the United States, especially an unexpected crisis.[26] After the 9/11 attacks, President George W. Bush's ratings soared to 90 percent approval as citizens' patriotism and feelings of unity were activated by the tragedy of that day.[27] As expected, over time President Bush's ratings declined from this extraordinarily high level, but he received another boost when he ordered the invasion of Iraq in March 2003. The capture of Saddam Hussein also provided a small lift to President Bush's ratings in December 2003, and as we already mentioned, President Obama's ratings rose in response to the killing of Osama bin Laden in May 2011.

Foreign policy events clearly benefited President George W. Bush's approval ratings on several occasions, but war also took a toll on his popularity. Battle deaths in Iraq, for example, had a significant negative effect on Bush's approval ratings.[28] More generally, a study of presidential approval ratings from 1948 through 2008 demonstrates that **war casualties** and the **financial costs of war** can dampen a president's popularity.[29]

Citizens' views of presidential job performance are influenced by another crucial factor—the economy. Whether scholars use **objective measures of economic well-being**, such as the unemployment rate, or citizens' **perceptions of the state of the economy** or both to explain presidential approval, it is clear that economic variables have a significant impact on citizens' evaluations.[30] As President Obama is well aware, a poor economy wreaks havoc on a president's popularity. The bump in approval President Obama experienced as a result of bin Laden's death quickly dissipated as economic conditions weighed heavily on many U.S. citizens during summer 2011. In fact, Obama's approval reached one of its low points in fall 2011 as citizens reacted to the acrimonious debate over raising the debt ceiling and the economy continued to sputter.

These factors can influence all members of the public in roughly the same fashion. During an international crisis, most citizens will rally around the president; when the economy nosedives, president approval declines for many.[31] Perhaps not surprisingly, though, there are also partisan differences in presidential popularity. Approval of Democratic presidents is higher among Democratic citizens. The same is true for Republicans. Near the end of President George W. Bush's time in office, for example, 86 percent of strong Republicans approved of his job performance compared to 4 percent of strong Democrats.[32] Contrast this with President Obama's ratings in early July 2015, when 81 percent of Democrats but only 10 percent of Republicans approved.[33] Partisan dynamics are also present when approval ratings change. In particular, citizens identifying with the party other than the president's display larger approval gains when the situation warrants (a rally effect or strong economy) than do members of the president's party. When conditions become less favorable for a president, declines in public approval are greatest for citizens of the opposite party.[34]

Overall, this aggregate-level research on presidential approval shows that it is not as stable as collective public opinion on issues tends to be. Yet at the same time, changes in presidential approval are not random but are reactions to political events and economic conditions, suggesting at least a somewhat sophisticated and capable citizenry. There is a caveat, however. Political elites and media organizations play a critical role in interpreting events and conditions for citizens as they evaluate the president.[35] For example, when a group of political elites start hammering a president on a particular issue and the media pick up that story line and run with it, an issue can quickly become prominent in the minds of citizens and influence their judgment of presidential performance. This is fine from a participatory democratic viewpoint if the media and political elites are focusing on important issues in an honest fashion, but what about when trivial issues are emphasized or reality is distorted? Citizens are ill served by such discourse and may find their evaluations of the president's job performance influenced by faulty evidence and reasoning.

PSYCHOLOGICAL APPROACHES TO ATTITUDES

Psychologists have studied attitudes more thoroughly than scholars in any other academic discipline and have provided important theories and approaches for political scientists who examine political attitudes. In trying to understand attitude formation and change, psychologists place primary emphasis on individuals. Some psychological theories, for instance, focus on the influence of individual characteristics, such as motivations and core values, on opinions. Other approaches examine how people learn and process new information, especially persuasive communication meant to change people's attitudes. Psychologists have also postulated many different routes to attitude change. Although we do not have space here to thoroughly review all the work on attitudes in psychology, we highlight approaches that are especially relevant to political attitude formation and change.[36]

Functions of Attitudes

One approach to understanding attitude formation is to consider the functions attitudes serve for individuals. **Functional theories** of attitudes highlight the motivations people have for holding the attitudes that they do.[37] For some people, attitudes serve a **utilitarian function**. People hold positive feelings toward objects that provide benefits, such as support for a tax policy that will increase their income. Negative attitudes are held toward objects that prevent people from satisfying their needs or that inflict punishment. A second type of function is **ego defense**. Attitudes fulfill this purpose by protecting an individual's ego or self-image from threats. These threats could be internal, such as denying certain negative characteristics about oneself. In particular, prejudice can result from ego-defense mechanisms: "When we cannot admit to ourselves that we have deep feelings of inferiority, we may project those feelings onto some convenient minority group and bolster our egos by attitudes of superiority toward this underprivileged group."[38]

Some individuals have a desire to understand the world around them, and attitudes can help to fulfill this goal. Attitudes can, in other words, serve a **knowledge function**. In particular, our existing attitudes can help us sort through newly encountered information. Imagine, for instance, that someone holds a positive attitude toward Democrats and learns that a Democratic politician is proposing a new policy toward immigration. He can use the knowledge that his attitude toward Democrats provides to arrive at support for the new immigration policy quickly without (or before) learning all the details of the new policy.

Attitudes that allow individuals to express their core beliefs and values perform a **value-expressive function**. A person who is deeply religious, for example, will feel that her identity is being actualized if she holds political views that reflect her religiosity, such as support for prayer in school. Somewhat related to a value-expressive motivation is **social adjustment**.[39] If social adjustment is an important goal for someone, he will express attitudes that conform to the views and values of peers in his social network.[40]

According to functional theories of attitudes, the reasons an attitude remains stable or the processes that result in attitude change depend on which function the attitude serves.[41] Attitudes that serve a value-expressive function, for instance, are not very likely to change because they are grounded in an individual's concept of self. Attitude change will only come about if a person's self-concept changes. Imagine a pacifist who, in the face of actual instances of unprovoked aggression toward a defenseless group, grows dissatisfied with holding pacifist values. As another example, attitudes that help a person make sense of the world will probably change when they cease to provide such knowledge, such as when the person's views toward a group are found to be based on incorrect information. If you believed that women are not as decisive as men, you would probably evaluate female politicians less positively than male politicians regardless of whether the specific politicians are decisive or not. Repeated encounters with decisive women might cause you to update your stereotype about women and then alter your attitudes toward female politicians.

Functional approaches to attitudes also suggest when persuasive appeals will succeed. Direct attempts to change someone's attitude will be more successful if the arguments are geared toward the function that the attitude is serving. One series of studies evaluated the success of different messages in persuading people for whom attitudes serve social adjustive versus value-expressive functions.[42] College students were exposed to arguments about the institutionalization of the mentally ill. Some participants were told that 70 percent of college students favored institutionalization. Information such as this resonated more strongly with participants for whom attitudes were presumed to fulfill a social adjustive function. In contrast, those holding attitudes for value-expressive reasons were more persuaded when told that support for institutionalization was based on values that these participants rated highly (particularly loving and responsibility). In other words, messages highlighting cherished values persuade people who hold value-expressive attitudes, whereas messages about the opinions of peer groups persuade people who express social adjustive attitudes.

Learning Theory

Learning theory provides another approach to attitudes. Some of our likes and dislikes are acquired through experience. When we are exposed to some stimuli, we receive positive reinforcement, such as feelings of happiness or rewards. With other stimuli, we receive negative reinforcement, such as a punishment or feelings of fear. A child, for instance, could learn to like the Republican Party because he hears his parents frequently saying positive things about the party. Likewise, a child who hears his parents using derogatory words to describe members of a minority group can develop prejudiced attitudes toward that group.

A basic premise of the **learning theory** of attitudes, then, is that, with repeated exposure to attitude objects paired with positive or negative adjectives, we can learn to like or to dislike those objects. More broadly, this theoretical approach assumes that attitudes are obtained much like habits are. In our daily lives, we learn about the attributes of attitude objects and the feelings associated with them; from these cognitions and affect, our attitudes develop. Attitudes are, in this view, a by-product of the learning process and individuals are rather passive actors in the acquisition of attitudes. Once attitudes are acquired in this way, they will tend to remain stable until new learning occurs.

According to learning theory, attitudes can also be influenced when the affect that is associated with one attitude object is transferred to a related object, a phenomenon called a **transfer of affect**. Individuals hold positive feelings toward objects that they like and negative feelings toward disliked objects. These feelings can be passed on to associated objects, resulting in either a new attitude or attitude change, depending on whether an attitude already exists for the associated object. In politics, this principle helps us understand why politicians try to connect their opponents to stimuli that induce negative emotions (such as fear and disgust) in most Americans. It also explains why politicians surround themselves with objects that evoke positive feelings for most people, such as the American flag. Politicians hope that the positive feelings citizens have for the flag will transfer to themselves, thus resulting in positive attitudes toward the politicians.

During the 2008 presidential primary season, a Republican candidate ran a Christmas-themed campaign advertisement to encourage the transfer of positive affect to himself. In an appeal to Christian conservatives, Governor Mike Huckabee aired an ad called "What Really Matters." In the ad, Huckabee wishes primary voters a Merry Christmas while a white cross appears to float behind his head. The ad immediately drew a great deal of attention. When asked about the advertisement, Huckabee said, "There was no hidden agenda. There was no floating cross. That is a bookshelf, but if people are seeing the cross in it, so be it."[43] Despite Huckabee's statement, many political observers concluded the ad was purposely designed to associate Huckabee with a symbol that holds great meaning for Christians.[44] (You can decide for yourself: see the ad on YouTube by searching for "Governor Huckabee" and "What Really Matters."[45])

A transfer of affect from one object to another can happen quite automatically, especially for attitude objects that are relatively unfamiliar. Even affect that is aroused subliminally can be transferred.[46] Researchers conducted an experiment in which participants viewed slides of an unknown woman engaged in a variety of daily activities (shopping, walking into her apartment, washing dishes, and so on). Immediately before each slide, a photo was flashed, but flashed so quickly that the participants were not consciously aware of it. For some participants, these subliminal photos were meant to arouse positive affect, whereas for others these photos were meant to arouse negative affect. Examples of the former include pictures of a child with a doll and a pair of kittens. Photos intended to arouse negative affect included a bucket of snakes, a dead body on a bed, and an opened chest during surgery.

After viewing the subliminal photos and the slides, participants were asked their attitudes about the woman whose image appeared in the slides. Participants for whom positive affect was aroused liked the woman more and rated her personality more positively than did those for whom negative affect was aroused. Keep in mind that the study participants did not learn anything about this woman other than what they had seen in the slides, so they had little information on which to base their attitudes. The temporal association between the subliminally presented images and the slides of the woman was sufficient, however, to allow the affect of the former to influence attitudes of the latter.

Communication-Induced Attitude Change

Much attention in psychology has been placed on understanding how and when communication can influence attitudes. Some of this communication is directly designed to change people's attitudes. In contrast to such explicitly persuasive communication, other messages can influence attitudes without necessarily attempting to do so. Examples of the latter include news media stories. By providing new information and understandings of issues, media coverage of current events can influence attitudes even if the journalists' intent is not to do so. Of the many models of communication and attitude change that exist, we highlight two that are especially relevant to understanding communication and political attitudes: Richard Petty and John Cacioppo's elaboration likelihood model of persuasion and John Zaller's receive-accept-sample model of attitude formation and change.

Petty and Cacioppo's Elaboration Likelihood Model. To understand persuasion, Petty and Cacioppo take a cognitive processing approach.[47] In particular, they consider the situations in which people will actively process persuasive communication versus the situations in which such processing will be unlikely. At times individuals are motivated to process thoroughly a persuasive message, such as when the issue is personally relevant to them, they will be held accountable for their decision, or they have a high need for cognition (they enjoy thinking things through). In one study, for example, college students were given a message supporting the university's adoption of comprehensive exams as a graduation requirement.[48] Students who were told that the policy was under consideration for the following year paid much closer attention to the arguments than did those students who were told the policy would not be implemented, if at all, until the following decade. For the former group, the policy proposal was more relevant because it might be enacted while the students were still at the university.

Regardless of motivation, individuals and situations also differ in whether the ability to process a message is present. People are better able to process a message when it is comprehendible and when they hold prior knowledge on the topic, are not distracted, and are under no time pressure. When someone is motivated and able to process persuasive communication, attitude change may come about through what Petty and Cacioppo term the **central route to persuasion**. If motivation or ability or both are lacking, then persuasion may occur via an alternative route, the **peripheral route**. Petty and Cacioppo's approach is called a dual processing model because it posits very different cognitive processes depending on which persuasion route is followed (see Figure 4.3 for an illustration of the model).

Figure 4.3   Petty and Cacioppo's Elaboration Likelihood Model

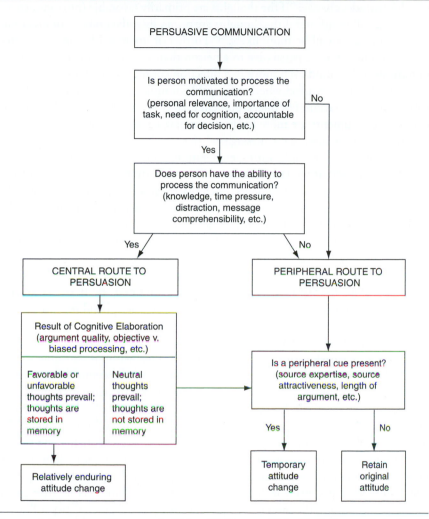

Sources: Adapted from Figure 9.3 in Richard E. Petty and John T. Cacioppo, *Attitudes and Persuasion: Classic and Contemporary Approaches* (Dubuque, IA: William C. Brown, 1981), 264; Figure 1-1 in Richard E. Petty and John T. Cacioppo, *Communication and Persuasion* (New York: Springer-Verlag, 1986), 4.

In the central route, people attend to the content of persuasive messages, think carefully about the pros and cons of the arguments, and generate thoughts (cognitive responses) to the initial communication. In other words, people engage in substantial elaboration on the communication in the central route (hence Petty and Cacioppo's choice of **elaboration likelihood** as the name of their model).

And it is their internally generated cognitive responses that influence whether people's attitudes change: "If the thoughts are primarily favorable (proarguments), persuasion will result: but if the thoughts are primarily unfavorable (counterarguments), resistance will be more likely."[49] Further, if unfavorable cognitions predominate and are more persuasive to a person than are the arguments presented to him, attitudes could even move in a direction counter to the message.

Some key factors affect whether favorable or unfavorable thoughts predominate during elaboration. For one, argument quality is very important. Strong and compelling arguments are more likely to generate cognitive responses that favor the viewpoint presented in the message, whereas weak arguments tend to generate counterarguments. Second, during elaboration, some people might be predisposed to generate either favorable or unfavorable thoughts, regardless of the content of the persuasive arguments. Such biased processing can occur for individuals who possess prior knowledge of the topic or for whom existing attitudes are closely associated with their core values.[50] In the end, and when taking into consideration these and other factors, if exposure to persuasive communication generates largely favorable thoughts or largely unfavorable thoughts that are stored in memory, attitudes will shift in favor of the tenor of these cognitive responses. If primarily neutral responses are generated, or if the cognitive responses are transitory and not stored into memory, peripheral processing will take over.

In contrast to the elaboration that occurs along the central route, the peripheral route to persuasion can result in attitude change "without engaging in any extensive cognitive work relevant to the issue under consideration."[51] Rather than attending to the content of the arguments contained in persuasive messages, individuals' attitudes can be influenced by incidental cues. Such cues include characteristics of the source of the message. Under peripheral processing, if the source is an expert or is attractive, attitudes are more likely to change in favor of the viewpoint of the communication compared with arguments delivered by nonexpert or nonattractive sources. Message length can also provide a peripheral cue: longer messages result in more favorable attitude change. Note that under peripheral processing the message length and the source characteristics influence attitudes regardless of whether the arguments contained in the message are strong or weak. When a cue is present during peripheral processing, attitudes are likely to change, but the resulting attitude will be quite shallow, temporary, and susceptible to change in the future. On the other hand, attitudes that have been influenced by persuasive communication in the central route are much more likely to endure and will be fairly resistant to change because more thought has been devoted to the content of the communication.

Zaller's Receive-Accept-Sample Model. Petty and Cacioppo's model of persuasion is broad enough to explain how a wide variety of attitudes can change, certainly including political attitudes. John Zaller's receive-accept-sample model, however, was designed more explicitly to account for the formation and change of attitudes in response to political communication.[52]

Zaller was interested in how the flow of political information can influence citizens' opinions. In particular, he examines political information that appears in the mass media. "This coverage," he writes, "may consist of ostensibly objective news reports, partisan argumentation, televised news conferences, or even paid advertisements, as in election campaigns."[53] Collectively, he refers to this communication as **elite discourse**, although he does not always specify whether the elites are politicians, candidates, news reporters, or experts quoted in news stories. In fact, he often means to convey that any and all of these types of elites can provide political information to the citizenry—information that may come to influence the public's opinions.

To understand the dynamics of public opinion formation and change, Zaller begins by focusing on the importance of **reception**. For people to be persuaded by a political message, they must first receive it. That is, they must be exposed to the message, and they must comprehend it. If this message reception does not occur, it would be impossible for the message to change citizens' minds.

In addition, Zaller argues that the effect of elite discourse on attitudes will not be the same for all people. In other words, key individual characteristics mediate the effects of communication on attitudes. Chief among these is **political awareness**, or the degree to which citizens follow political matters closely. Citizens who are politically aware are much *more likely* to receive political messages from elites than those who do not follow politics closely.

Once citizens have received a message, Zaller argues that persuasion can occur only if they also agree with the content of the message. Notably, at this **acceptance** stage of persuasion, political awareness works differently. Here awareness makes it *less likely* that an individual will accept the premise of an argument that he has received. Simply stated, people who pay more attention to politics are "better able to evaluate and critically scrutinize the new information they encounter."[54]

Given these two relationships between political awareness and reception, on the one hand, and acceptance, on the other, those who possess either low or high levels of awareness are not likely to have their attitudes influenced by elite discourse. Those with low levels of awareness are unlikely to receive political messages, whereas those highly aware are likely to rebut any political arguments they do receive. This means that those with the highest probability of having their attitudes changed by political discourse are people who possess moderate levels of awareness, a pattern displayed visually in Figure 4.4. Moderately aware citizens do receive some political messages but do not possess a large enough store of relevant knowledge with which to resist communication-induced attitude change.

As for other individual attributes that influence whether political messages will result in attitude change, Zaller focuses special attention on people's existing

Figure 4.4   Political Awareness in Zaller's Attitude Change Model

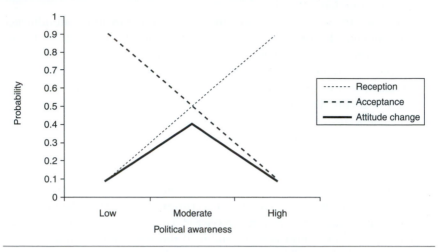

Source: Based on arguments contained in John R. Zaller, *The Nature and Origins of Mass Opinion* (Cambridge, UK: Cambridge University Press, 1992).

political orientations. These orientations, which he calls **political predispositions**, encompass core values, enduring beliefs, and experiences. Predispositions not only are the ingredients for specific policy opinions (those who value equality will have different political opinions from those who do not value equality, for example) but also mediate whether people accept the premises in elite discourse that they receive. Individuals are not likely to accept a message that is inconsistent with their predispositions. A conservative citizen who encounters a stream of liberal messages, such as arguments in favor of increasing government spending on social welfare policies, is unlikely to adopt the position of these messages because they conflict with her standing political views.

In Zaller's model, then, people are not necessarily passive vessels into which political opinions are poured. Instead, some citizens consider incoming arguments and decide whether to accept them. As Zaller correctly argues, however, the ability of a person to know which messages coincide with and which contradict his predispositions increases with political awareness. In other words, those who are more politically aware are better able to see the connections between elite discourse and their own predispositions, whereas "politically inattentive persons will often be unaware of the implications of the persuasive communications they encounter, and so often end up 'mistakenly' accepting them."[55] In addition, sometimes cues exist in the elite discourse to facilitate this connection. Such cues provide details regarding the implications of a political argument for a person's predispositions.

Often these cues are in the form of the partisan or ideological leanings of the source of the message. For example, when a Republican politician criticizes President Barack Obama's health care policy, a Republican citizen is more likely than a Democrat to accept this argument because she can assume, based on the source of the message, that the position advocated therein coincides with her existing political dispositions.

From this foundation, Zaller argues that citizens' opinions are not necessarily altered once they have received and accepted a political message. Instead, Zaller argues that individuals accept messages but only update their opinions when they are called on to do so, such as when discussing politics with friends or when asked by a polling organization to answer a survey question. At this point, people sample among the considerations that are stored in their memory related to the political issue at hand. **Considerations**, as Zaller defines them, are "any reason[s] that might induce an individual to decide a political issue one way or the other."[56] If, at the time the respondent must state her opinion, there are more considerations at the top of her head that favor the issue, she will indicate support for it. If she gathers more opposing considerations from her memory, however, an opposing opinion will result. This sampling is the final stage of Zaller's **receive-accept-sample model**.

What accounts for the balance of pro- versus anti- considerations that are accessible in people's minds at any one time? The content of elite discourse at the time influences which considerations come to mind. In particular, Zaller considers environments in which there is elite consensus on an issue so most messages articulated by elites favor the same side of the issue. At other times and for other issues, political elites will disagree over an issue and the flow of political information will contain messages both favoring and opposing the issue. When one message dominates elite discourse, there will be few details to cue citizens as to whether the arguments are consistent with their predispositions. This is because politicians from both dominant political parties and from varying ideological backgrounds will express support for an issue during times of elite consensus.

Therefore, in a one-message environment, more politically aware people will be more likely to receive and, due to the absence of key cueing details, accept the dominant message. Zaller calls this the **mainstream effect**. In contrast, elite disagreement over a policy issue, especially when the disagreement falls along party or ideological lines, results in the **polarization effect**. Attentive Democratic or liberal citizens will hold opinions that coincide with Democratic elites, whereas attentive Republican or conservative citizens will hold the opposing view. The opinions of those with lower levels of political awareness will not differ by political predispositions either because these people are unlikely to receive the countervailing messages or because they accept all received messages (because they are less able to discern the connection between the messages' arguments and their own predispositions).

The mainstream and polarization effects are illustrated in Figure 4.5. During the early years of American involvement in Vietnam, most political elites supported America's role. Consequently, in 1964, citizen support for the Vietnam War increased with political awareness, regardless of whether citizens were liberal or conservative. As the years passed, elite agreement disappeared, with more and more Democratic and liberal elites expressing opposition to the war. As a result, liberal citizens began to oppose the war whereas conservative citizens continued to express support for the war. This division existed, however, *only* among politically aware members of the public.

Resistance to Persuasion

Psychologists have also examined when people are especially likely to resist persuasive communication. The result of resistance is that attitude change will not occur in the face of persuasive messages. Scholars who explicitly focus on resistance, however, push beyond this outcome-focused definition. Instead, they discuss **resistance** in terms of the processes by which people ensure the persuasive communication will fail to change attitudes or individual motivations to withstand change.[57] Resistance is more likely (1) for people who consider themselves not easily susceptible to persuasion, (2) for attitudes that are linked to one's core values, and (3) when people have been forewarned that a persuasive message is coming.[58] In contrast, buttering people up before attempting to persuade them can reduce resistance. Why? Because one reason for resisting a persuasive message is a motivation to preserve a positive concept of oneself. If you have just been told that you possess a positive trait, this motivation is lessened and thus resistance to persuasion is less likely.[59]

How we *think of* our attitudes is also related to whether those attitudes are resistant to persuasion. Imagine for a minute that the 2016 Democratic presidential primary is occurring in your state and that the only two candidates on the ballot are Hillary Clinton and Bernie Sanders. If you prefer Clinton, this preference might exist because you *support* her or because you *oppose* Sanders. As it turns out, if you think about your opinion in terms of opposition, it will be more resistant to change. A series of experiments demonstrated this effect.[60] Participants were given information about fictitious candidates and were encouraged to think of their candidate preference in terms of support or opposition. Note that they were not encouraged to prefer a different candidate but, rather, to think about their attitude in terms of supporting their preferred candidate or opposing the preferred candidate's opponent. They were then exposed to a counterattitudinal message (such as learning that their preferred candidate had been involved in a scandal) and then asked their candidate preference again. Participants who thought of their initial attitude in terms of opposition showed less attitude change after receiving the counterattitudinal message. The researchers argue that this result occurs because negative information (such as opposition) is a more significant contributor

Figure 4.5   Zaller's Mainstream and Polarization Effects during Vietnam War Era

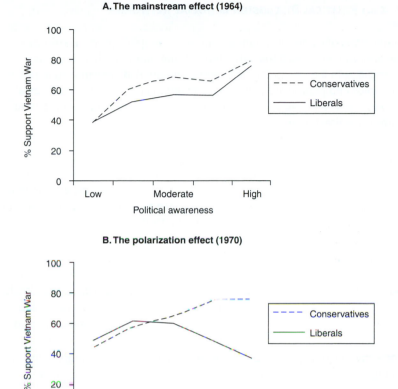

Source: Adapted from Figure 6.1 of John R. Zaller, *The Nature and Origins of Mass Opinion* (Cambridge, UK: Cambridge University Press, 1992), 103.

to attitudes than are positive details, thus making negatively framed attitudes more resistant to change.[61] In fact, the powerful effect of negative information on evaluations of politicians has been well documented in public opinion research, perhaps helping us to understand why negative campaign advertisements are effective.[62]

Attitudes Follow Behavior

Many people prefer to maintain consistency across their beliefs, attitudes, and attitude-relevant behaviors. Someone who attends a rally in support of the Republican Party, for example, probably has a positive attitude toward the group and

Public Opinion in Comparative Perspective
BOX 4.1 POLITICAL DISCUSSION IN SOCIAL NETWORKS

Many forms of communication can influence people's political attitudes. Persuasive messages transmitted through the mass media are just one example, albeit an important one. Some people also are exposed to political topics and arguments through conversations that occur in their social network. **Social networks** consist of "people with whom a person communicates on a direct, one-to-one basis."[1]

Conversations with family, friends, and others in one's network cover a wide range of topics, of course. How likely is it that politics is discussed? As it turns out, there is substantial variation across nations in how often people discuss politics with other citizens. Political conversations are common in Israel, Norway, the Netherlands, and Greece but much less likely to occur in Great Britain, Singapore, and Canada. The United States falls in between these nations. In comparison with eighty other nations, U.S. citizens engage in political discussions slightly more than average.[2]

Distinct from the frequency of political conversations is the composition of one's social network, particularly the degree to which citizens' social networks include people whose political views differ from their own. Examining survey data from twelve nations, Diana Mutz compared people's political beliefs with those of their conversation partners (excluding spouses).[3] The similarity of views is much higher across discussion partners in the United States compared with other nations. In other words, on a day-to-day basis, Americans are less likely to be exposed to political beliefs and arguments that differ from their own.

Why might there be this political similarity within social networks in the United States? Mutz speculates that Americans' residential choices are a contributing factor. Most people do not select their neighborhood based on the political views of their neighbors, of course. Yet this decision can be based on core values that are related to political beliefs. For example, some might prefer urban neighborhoods whereas others want a rural setting. Quality of schools, proximity to commercial services, and size of house lot are also factors influencing residential choice. As Mutz puts it, "People are likely to choose environments because they are populated by 'people like me' in the sense of shared lifestyles, values, or even market position."[4]

1. Diana C. Mutz, *Hearing the Other Side: Deliberative versus Participatory Democracy* (Cambridge, UK: Cambridge University Press, 2006), 10.
2. Ibid., Chap. 2.
3. Ibid.
4. Ibid., 47.

views the attributes of the party positively (such as believing that Republicans support policies that are good for the country). If inconsistencies exist among these elements, individuals will act to restore order. If someone else has negative attitudes toward the Republican Party but still attends a rally, perhaps at the request of a friend, she might change her attitude so that it is positive. These examples illustrate key postulates of **cognitive dissonance theory**, presented by Leon Festinger in the 1950s.[63] Festinger argued that when an individual holds cognitive elements (beliefs, attitudes, or knowledge of one's behaviors, for example) that are in opposition, cognitive dissonance exists. This dissonance produces negative arousal and the motivation to either eliminate the dissonance by changing the dissonant cognitive element or reduce the dissonance by adding more consonant elements. The person who attends the Republican Party rally but has a negative attitude toward the party might be unable to change this attitude but could instead reduce dissonance by thinking about the number of positive characteristics of the party. She might think that the Republican Party is better than the alternatives and that some Republican politicians are competent and pursue policies that are good for the country.

Festinger and colleagues conducted a number of studies in which they demonstrated that if people are forced to engage in behavior that contradicts their attitudes, their attitudes can change as a result. Once the behavior is performed, after all, it cannot be unperformed, so attitude change is one way to eliminate the discrepancy between the behavior and the attitude. In one of the more famous of these studies, carried out by Festinger and James Carlsmith, participants were asked to complete a number of tasks that were boring and toward which participants were expected to hold negative attitudes, such as putting objects into a tray, emptying them out, and putting them back in the tray again.[64] Participants were then paid either $1 or $20 to tell the next participant that the tasks were interesting and enjoyable. Finally, the participants were asked to assess the tasks. Those who earned $1 evaluated the tasks more positively than did those who earned $20. Festinger and Carlsmith argued that the cognitive dissonance resulting from stating that the tasks were interesting while actually believing the opposite led to attitude change for those earning $1. Those who earned $20, in contrast, did not experience dissonance. Instead, they attributed their behavior to the compensation they earned: they were paid $20 to say that the tasks were interesting.

In a challenge to cognitive dissonance theory, Daryl Bem proposed a different explanation to account for the findings from cognitive dissonance studies. Bem's approach, called **self-perception theory**, argued that attitude change such as that observed in Festinger and Carlsmith's research was not the result of correcting an unpleasant state of dissonance but, rather, occurred because people *infer their attitudes* from their behaviors. Bem describes his theory as follows:

> When we want to know how a person feels, we look to see how he acts. Accordingly, it seemed possible that when an individual himself wants to

know how he feels, he may look to see how he acts, a possibility suggested anecdotally by such statements as, "I guess I'm hungrier than I first thought." . . . Individuals come to "know" their own attitudes, emotions and other internal states partially by inferring them from observations of their own overt behavior and/or the circumstances in which this behavior occurs.[65]

Bem's self-perception theory does not presume that people use their behaviors as a guide to determine all their attitudes. Instead, the theory assumes that such self-perception is most likely when attitudes are weak or ambiguous. Because of this, some have argued that self-perception is better at accounting for attitude formation than attitude change.[66] If a person is uncertain about his attitude, using his recent behavior as a guide can help shape a new attitude. If, in contrast, the person's attitude is well developed and strong, it is unlikely to change in the face of a contradictory behavior. Perhaps more important, the stronger an individual's attitudes are and the more certain he is about his attitudes, the less likely he is to engage in behavior that contradicts them.

Whether through cognitive dissonance reduction or self-perception mechanisms, it seems as if attitudes can follow from behavior. Although these theories were not developed specifically for understanding political attitudes, political opinions clearly could be responsive to behavior, as the following examples demonstrate. First, imagine it is spring 2011 and a group of friends are discussing the uprisings occurring across the Arab world. During this conversation, a woman who had not previously thought very much about her opinion of the "Arab Spring" finds herself arguing that the U.S. government should do more to support democratic movements in Arab countries and should not be supporting dictators. After she speaks, she realizes that she must support the Arab democracy movements; otherwise, she would not have made the comments that she did. Second, through their membership in organizations such as churches, fraternities, or sororities, people sometimes agree to volunteer for a variety of activities (at soup kitchens or to clean up a city street). Such activity is not always motivated by positive attitudes toward volunteerism but, rather, because their group expects service from its members. After volunteering, however, positive attitudes toward service activities can develop simply because they have volunteered. As a final example, in some states and localities, people are required to recycle containers and newspapers. After engaging in such recycling, individuals can begin to think of themselves as recyclers and develop positive attitudes toward recycling and its environmental benefits, perhaps even forgetting that they began recycling not out of such attitudes but because of a legal mandate to do so.

CONCLUSION

In summarizing Bem's self-perception theory, psychologists Alice Eagly and Shelly Chaiken write:

> In general self-perception theory maintains that people function as relatively superficial information processors who merely generalize their attitudes from currently available external cues. By this account, people look to see what their recent behavior has been and assume that their attitudes are congruent with this behavior.[67]

This view of attitudes—as shallow and changeable—is also present in some of the other approaches that we have reviewed in this chapter. Zaller, for one, assumes that most people, especially those who are not highly politically aware, do not possess stable attitudes but, rather, hold a mix of attitude-relevant considerations in their heads. People's opinions at any point in time will reflect which of these considerations they bring to mind. For Petty and Cacioppo, attitudes that result from peripheral route processing will be rather ephemeral. Whether individuals engage in this type of processing depends, as you recall, on individual traits as well as issue characteristics, such as personal relevance. Both of these models thus provide support for elite democratic and pluralistic theorists' assumptions regarding the citizenry, especially their views that the public's political opinions are ill considered and subject to frequent changes. Yet both Zaller's and Petty and Cacioppo's models indicate that these conclusions are not appropriate for all people and for all situations. Reality, in other words, is more complex than some elite democrats and pluralists imply.

Eagly and Chaiken go on to describe another way of understanding attitudes: "A view of attitudes as relatively enduring tendencies suggests instead that people generalize their attitudes from internal data; they have stored their attitudes in memory and retrieve them from this internal source when called upon to make an attitudinal judgment."[68] From this description, we envision attitudes as enduring and stable, as judgments that are well linked to core values and beliefs. Attitudes with these characteristics occur when people process communication in the central route, argue Petty and Cacioppo. Enduring attitudes are also likely if these attitudes serve important functions for individuals. If people hold attitudes because they serve an ego-defensive or a value-expressive function, the attitudes will be fairly resistant to change. Learning theorists remind us that attitudes formed from repeated exposure to attitude objects have become habitual and are also unlikely to change. Even though these attitudes might be stable, the functional and learning approaches do not assume that all stable attitudes have been carefully considered. In contrast, learning theorists assume that people rather passively acquire attitudes without thinking through why they might like or dislike an attitude object. Ego-defensive attitudes, such as racial prejudice, provide similar examples of superficial thought. When feeling threatened, some individuals respond by expressing discriminatory attitudes toward members of other racial groups rather than considering the actual source of the threat, which could in fact be their own feelings of inferiority.

Some democratic theorists have assumed and some political scientists have demonstrated empirically that citizen attitudes are quite pliable. One of our goals in this chapter has been to present these arguments and this evidence. We also have presented alternative evidence to encourage you to consider whether attitude insta-bility should be viewed negatively, that is, as evidence that the citizenry is not living up to the model presented by classical democratic theorists. Page and Shapiro, for example, demonstrate that when collective opinion changes it is often in rational response to external cues, such as world events or a changed social climate. Likewise, presidential approval is often driven by events, including international crises and economic conditions. Further, we turned to psychology to demonstrate the variety of approaches available to understand the nature of attitudes and the mechanisms by which they can change. Models of communication-induced attitude change are especially relevant for political attitudes. Much political activity is designed to try to influence the opinions and judgments of political actors, whether they are citi-zens or politicians. Understanding when and how political communication influ-ences citizens' opinions has been the focus of much public opinion research.

At this point, you should have some thoughts about the following questions: Are citizen attitudes fleeting? If they are, do we care? In particular, does the pres-ence of unstable citizen attitudes undermine the public's ability to evaluate politi-cal issues and communicate its preferences to political leaders? Is democratic governance, in other words, threatened by attitude instability?

Key Concepts

SUGGESTED SOURCES FOR FURTHER READING

Ajzen, Icek. "The Theory of Planned Behavior." *Organizational Behavior and Human Decision Processes* 50 (1991): 179–211.

LaPiere, Richard T. "Attitudes vs. Actions." *Social Forces* 13 (1934): 230–237.

These two works examine the relationship between attitudes and behaviors, albeit drawing quite different conclusions. LaPiere traveled across the United States with a Chinese couple in the 1930s. In 251 situations when they asked for hotel accommodations or restaurant service, they were denied only once. Yet, when LaPiere sent questionnaires to these establishments after they visited, asking whether they would serve Chinese guests, over 90 percent said they would not. Ajzen's theory of planned behavior, in contrast, posits that behaviors can be predicted from relevant attitudes, provided that you factor in the degree to which an individual has control over behavior.

Banaji, Mahzarin R., and Larisa Heiphetz. "Attitudes." In *The Handbook of Social Psychology*, 5th ed., Vol. 1, ed. Susan T. Fiske, Daniel T. Gilbert, and Gardner Lindzey. Hoboken, NJ: John Wiley & Sons, 2010.

Maio, Gregory R., James M. Olson, and Irene Cheung. "Attitudes in Social Behavior." In *Handbook of Psychology*, 2nd ed., Vol. 5, Personality and Social Psychology, ed. Irving B. Weiner, Howard A. Tennen, and Jerry M. Suls. Hoboken, NJ: John Wiley & Sons, 2012.

These chapters provide detailed discussions of recent research on attitudes in the field of psychology.

Converse, Philip E. "The Nature of Belief Systems in Mass Publics." In *Ideology and Discontent*, ed. David E. Apter. New York: Free Press, 1964.

Converse, Philip E. "Attitudes and Non-Attitudes: Continuation of a Dialogue." In *The Quantitative Analysis of Social Problems*, ed. Edward R. Tufte. Reading, MA: Addison-Wesley, 1970.

These are classic studies of individuals' political attitudes, in which Converse concludes that the public's attitudes change frequently and are not well organized.

Gronke, Paul, and Brian Newman. "FDR to Clinton, Mueller to ?: A Field Essay on Presidential Approval." *Political Research Quarterly* 56 (2003): 501–512.

Waterman, Richard, Carol L. Silva, and Hank Jenkins-Smith. *The Presidential Expectations Gap: Public Attitudes Concerning the Presidency.* Ann Arbor: University of Michigan Press, 2014.

Gronke and Newman's article provides an excellent review of the research on presidential approval. Waterman, Silva, and Jenkins-Smith's book is a detailed exploration of one source of presidential approval: the expectations gap.

Page, Benjamin I., and Robert Y. Shapiro. *The Rational Public: Fifty Years of Trends in Americans' Policy Preferences.* Chicago: University of Chicago Press, 1992.

Stimson, James A. *Tides of Consent: How Public Opinion Shapes American Politics.* Cambridge, UK: Cambridge University Press, 2004.

After analyzing public opinion polls conducted between 1935 and 1990, Page and Shapiro conclude that public opinion at the aggregate level is quite stable over time. In addition, their book provides a detailed picture of the public's attitudes toward many important policy issues. Stimson also analyzes collective public opinion across the decades, although he focuses on opinion change rather than stability. He concludes that aggregate changes reflect reasonable responses to events or trends.

Petty, Richard E., and John T. Cacioppo. *Communication and Persuasion.* New York: Springer-Verlag, 1986.

Zaller, John R. *The Nature and Origins of Mass Opinion.* Cambridge, UK: Cambridge University Press, 1992.

Petty, Richard E., and Pablo Briñol. "The Elaboration Likelihood Model." In *The Handbook of Theories of Social Psychology*, Vol. 1, ed. Paul A.M. Van Lange, Arie W. Kruglanski, and E. Tory Higgins. London: Sage, 2012.

The Nature and Origins of Mass Opinion After 20 Years. Special issue of *Critical Review* 24 (2012).

Important insights into the effects of communication on attitudes are contained in these works. The first two books overview, respectively, Petty and Cacioppo's elaboration likelihood model and Zaller's receive-accept-sample model, which have greatly enhanced our understanding of persuasion and attitude change. The second two works are recent assessments of each model.

Gallup Presidential Job Approval Center, www.gallup.com/poll/124922/Presidential-Approval-Center.aspx

The American Presidency Project, www.presidency.ucsb.edu/data/popularity.php

These two websites provide extensive presidential approval data. The Gallup site allows you to analyze levels of presidential approval among Democrats, Republicans, and Independents.

PART III

Do Citizens Organize Their Political Thinking?

ARE PEOPLE'S POLITICAL opinions on different issues related to one another? That is, is there some consistency across views, or does knowing citizens' views on one issue not help predict their views on other issues? Assessing consistency can be tricky, but one common yardstick is political ideology. With this approach, a person with all conservative views would be considered to have more consistent attitudes than someone with a mixture of liberal and conservative views. But is ideology the best yardstick? And, if it is, what is the best way to measure the degree of ideological thinking and ideological organization of people's political opinions? The first chapter of this section opens with these topics. That chapter, as well as the other two chapters in this section, then move beyond ideology to consider a range of factors that might shape people's attitudes. Partisanship, personality, self-interest, core values, and social groups are among the topics explored.

Why should we care if the public organizes its political thinking? Answering this question brings us back to the normative topic of citizen competence. Can citizens function effectively in a democracy if their political views are not well organized? The chapters in this section speak to questions such as these; we hope you will ponder them as you proceed.

CHAPTER 5

Ideology, Partisanship, and Polarization

IN JUNE 2003, Bill O'Reilly and Al Franken appeared together at Book-Expo America, a convention for book publishers, sellers, and authors. O'Reilly, the host of *The O'Reilly Factor* on the Fox cable channel, and Franken, a former comedian on *Saturday Night Live* turned political commentator and, since 2009, a Democratic U.S. senator, were at Book-Expo to talk about their new books. Franken's book, *Lies and the Lying Liars Who Tell Them: A Fair and Balanced Look at the Right*, criticizes Republicans and right-leaning pundits and journalists, including those on Fox, for bending the truth to fit their aims. Not surprisingly, O'Reilly was annoyed by the arguments contained in Franken's book as well as its tone. Their appearance at the convention ended in a shouting match. *USA Today* began a news story about the event with this sentence: "Bill O'Reilly, the conservative talk show host, first decried political commentators who 'call people names.' Then he called Al Franken, the liberal humorist, an 'idiot.'"[1]

When reading that paragraph, what information was your mind drawn to? Maybe the ideological and partisan labels jumped off the page for you. If so, did they help you to understand the material better? In other words, was it useful to know that Franken is a Democrat or a liberal? Did characterizing O'Reilly as conservative, Republican, or right-leaning provide extra meaning? Alternatively, you might have focused on the disagreement between Franken and O'Reilly, particularly its uncivil nature. If so, did you take a side, either because the information cultivated a new evaluation or changed your mind? Perhaps, instead, your existing partisan or ideological leanings contributed to a positive evaluation of one man's behavior and negative evaluation of the other's. Or did you find yourself annoyed at both men and even perhaps the nastiness displayed between them that is not uncommon in American politics today?

This chapter takes up the topics hinted at in that series of questions. News coverage of politics and government often conveys the ideological or partisan leanings of political figures, such as members of Congress, Supreme Court justices, interest groups, and commentators. Are ideology and party also key identifications for citizens? That is, do members of the public think about politics in ideological terms or does ideology help to structure people's opinions toward specific issues? Not so much, as we discuss next. We then turn to the topic of partisanship, demonstrating that party affiliation is a core political identity for many Americans. We end with a discussion of political polarization. Our conclusions there might surprise you, especially if you hold the view that the nation is starkly divided into partisan (or ideological) camps. Throughout, as always, we will be tying specific topics to normative democratic theory.

CONVERSE'S CLAIM: IDEOLOGICAL INNOCENCE

Liberalism and conservatism are the two dominant ideologies in U.S. politics. A political **ideology** is "an interrelated set of attitudes and values about the proper goals of society and how they should be achieved."[2] Put another way, "If an attitude is a strand of feeling, then an ideology is a rope of intertwined attitudes and related fibers."[3] Two aspects of these definitions are worth emphasizing. First, an ideology consists of attitudes that are coherent and related to one another.[4] Second, an ideology does not refer to just any set of related attitudes but, rather, to beliefs about society and especially the proper role of government. In the American context, **conservatives** emphasize order, tradition, individual responsibility, and minimal government intervention, particularly in economic matters. **Liberals**, in contrast, believe that government intervention in the economy is sometimes necessary to combat features of the free market (such as discrimination and low wages). Liberals also value equality, openness to dissenting views, and civil rights.

According to many democratic theorists, citizens and politicians need to communicate effectively with one another so that, among other reasons, citizens can evaluate the performance of elected officials and these officials can know the political preferences of the citizens. Communication between citizens and leaders is enhanced if the two groups talk about politics using the same terms. This does not occur in the United States, however, at least according to Philip Converse's classic work on political ideology. Conducting his research in the late 1950s and early 1960s, Converse concluded that political elites are much more likely than citizens to organize the political world ideologically along a liberal-conservative continuum. Not only are citizens less likely to think about politics ideologically, the terms *liberal* and *conservative* carry little meaning for many people. Public understanding of political debates is threatened by such a lack of understanding. As Converse put it, "The more impoverished [a citizen's] understanding of the term [conservative or liberal], the less information [the term] conveys. In the limiting case—if he does not know at all what the term means—it conveys no information at all."[5] Further, low knowledge of ideology and uncommon ideological reasoning among the public is, at least to some, evidence that the public is not capable of democratic citizenship. Converse's work ignited a firestorm of research, with many scholars trying to resurrect a more respectable view of citizens' capabilities. After detailing Converse's original argument and the methodology on which his study relies, we discuss some of the research that challenges Converse's arguments.

The overarching goal of Converse's research was to examine the belief systems of citizens and elites. He defines a **belief system** as "a configuration of ideas and attitudes in which the elements are bound together by some form of constraint or functional interdependence."[6] Although Converse prefers the term *belief system* rather than ideology, he does admit that the two are closely related. Further, as we will soon see, to determine whether the public's beliefs are joined in coherent systems, he uses the liberal-conservative ideological dimension as one of his gauges. As for **attitude constraint**, Converse refers to the degree to which we could predict a specific attitude of someone knowing her attitude toward a different political object. When a belief system is present, "if a person is opposed to the expansion of social security," we can judge that "he is probably a conservative and is probably opposed as well to any nationalization of private industries, federal aid to education, sharply progressive income taxation, and so forth."[7] Constraint, for Converse, means that people's political attitudes are related to each other because they derive from an overarching worldview (such as a political ideology).

Do People Demonstrate Ideological Thinking?

Converse's overall conclusion, as we have already mentioned, was that elites were much more likely to possess belief systems compared with the general public. This conclusion is based primarily on his analyses of the 1956, 1958, and 1960 American National Election Studies (ANES) panel study. To understand and evaluate Converse's conclusions, you need to know what evidence he used to make his arguments. Thus, we summarize here Converse's study in depth. For his first analysis, Converse examined the degree to which respondents in 1956 used ideological language in response to questions about the political parties and the two major-party candidates for president. This series of questions began: "Is there anything in particular that you like about the Democratic Party? Is there anything in particular that you don't like about the Democratic Party?" Respondents were then asked for their likes and dislikes of the Republican Party and the candidates (Democrat Adlai Stevenson and Republican president Dwight Eisenhower).

Such **open-ended questions** allow respondents to discuss politics using their own terms and language, thus providing important insights into how people conceive of the political world. From his analysis of the responses, Converse categorized the public into five groups based on the degree to which people used an abstract benchmark, such as the liberal-conservative ideological continuum, to evaluate the parties and politicians.[8] Those individuals who did use this continuum, such as by differentiating the parties based on ideology and correctly linking specific policy positions of the parties to this ideology, were labeled Ideologues.[9]

The second group—Near Ideologues—included people who used ideological labels such as *liberal* or *conservative* but perhaps did not fully understand the meaning of these terms or did not use ideology as their primary tool for evaluating politics. One example here is a man who liked *both* the "liberalness" of the Democrats and the "conservative element in the Republican Party."[10] All told, only about 11.5 percent of the public was classified as either an Ideologue (2.5 percent) or a Near Ideologue (9 percent; see the lighter bars in Figure 5.1).

Far more common were people who conceptualized politics in terms other than ideology. The largest category was Group Interest citizens, who made up 42 percent of the respondents. These individuals tended to discuss the parties and candidates in terms of whether they favor the interests of specific groups, such as the man who disliked Republicans because "they are more for big business" or the woman who liked that the Democrats "have always helped the farmers."[11] *Nature of the Times* was the label Converse applied to his fourth group. People in this group (24 percent of the public) linked the parties or candidates with the current state of the nation. More specifically, parties in charge during times of peace or prosperity were evaluated more favorably than were those who ruled during war or economic downturns. An example from the 2000 ANES nicely illustrates this type of reasoning. One respondent explained his dislike of Republican candidate

Figure 5.1   Levels of Conceptualization among the American Public, 1956 and 2000

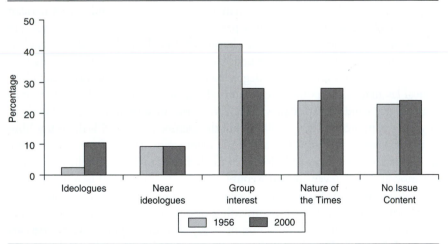

Sources: Adapted from Table I of Philip E. Converse, "The Nature of Belief Systems in Mass Publics," in *Ideology and Discontent*, ed. David E. Apter (New York: Free Press, 1964), 218, and Table 10.1 of Michael S. Lewis-Beck, Helmut Norpoth, William G. Jacoby, and Herbert F. Weisberg, *The American Voter Revisited* (Ann Arbor: University of Michigan Press, 2008), 279.

George W. Bush as follows: "He is a Republican. I have been in construction for the last 33 years and every time there has been a Republican in office, I've been in the unemployment line."[12]

The final group in Converse's classification evaluated the parties and candidates on grounds other than issues. No Issue Content citizens included those who used personal characteristics to evaluate candidates, were not sure what either political party stood for (even when they identified with one of the parties), or did not follow politics closely enough to discuss parties or candidates. One person in 2000, for instance, liked Bush because of "his sincerity. He surrounds himself with good people and he is well connected."[13] This final group made up 22.5 percent of the citizenry, nearly twice that of the Ideologues and Near Ideologues combined. To Converse, these results clearly demonstrated that most members of the public do not think about political parties and candidates ideologically.

Replication of this part of Converse's study in recent decades has been rare. Fortunately, however, Michael Lewis-Beck, William Jacoby, Helmut Norpoth, and Herbert Weisberg have done so, allowing us to see whether Converse's findings have stood the test of time.[14] Relying on the open-ended likes and dislikes questions in the 2000 ANES (regarding George W. Bush, Al Gore, and the Republican and Democratic parties), these researchers categorized respondents into the five groups first created by Converse. As demonstrated by the darker bars in Figure 5.1, the number of Ideologues among the public was higher in 2000 than in the 1950s, whereas the Group Interest category was smaller. Despite these changes, the two largest categories continued to be Group Interest and Nature of the Times, each containing 28 percent of the public. Following closely behind was No Issue Content with 24 percent. As was the case in the 1950s, in 2000 these three categories were all significantly larger than the Ideologues (10.5 percent) or Near Ideologues (9 percent).

Do People Recognize Ideological Terms?

Moving on and mostly moving away from open-ended questions, Converse next assessed the degree to which people could recognize the terms *liberal* and *conservative*. Even if ideological reasoning was uncommon among citizens, public understanding of these terms could be more common. To address this possibility, in 1960 Converse asked respondents, "Would you say that either one of the parties is more *conservative* or more *liberal* than the other?" Those answering yes were then asked which party is more conservative and then why they characterized that party as more conservative. Nearly 40 percent of the respondents either did not recognize these terms or were unable to attach any meaning to the terms.

Among those who did identify the ideological leanings of each party and did attempt to discuss the meaning of conservatism, there was variation in the correct use of the terms and in the breadth of ideological thinking apparent in the answers.

Converse concluded that about 17 percent did not correctly apply the terms or did not provide a correct meaning for conservatism, whereas 29 percent provided correct meaning but demonstrated only a narrow understanding of the ideologies. Typically, these respondents discussed ideology only in terms of which party spends more money and which saves more. Republicans are more conservative, one person explained, because "they vote against the wild spending spree the Democrats get on."[15] The remaining respondents, about 17 percent, recognized the ideological terms, identified the Democrats as liberal and the Republicans as conservative, and displayed a more thorough understanding of liberalism and conservatism. Although this number is larger than the 11.5 percent that displayed ideological thinking in response to the open-ended questions about parties and candidates, it is still a small percentage of the public.

Are Individuals' Attitudes Constrained and Stable?

So far, Converse's analyses suggest that most people do not use the liberal-conservative ideological spectrum to organize their political thinking. This, however, does not mean that the political views of most people are unorganized. Perhaps beliefs are organized along other criteria. Attitude constraint, in other words, may exist among the public even though the political worldview that is constraining the attitudes is not liberal or conservative ideology. Converse tested this assumption two ways. First, using the 1958 ANES data, he looked at the relationship between a number of issue opinions to see whether opinions toward an issue (such as federal education aid) correlated with opinions on another issue (such as public housing). Because liberals tend to support federal government spending on education and government provision of public housing, and conservatives tend to oppose both, if most of the public organize their issue opinions along this ideological continuum, we would expect these opinions to be highly correlated among the public. Yet what if people who support federal education aid also tend to oppose public housing? This would suggest a different organizing framework. If this is the case, we would still see high correlations between the attitudes, albeit in the opposite direction, with support for one issue correlated with opposition to the other.

Examining the relationships between four domestic issues and three foreign affairs issues, Converse in fact found very low correlations among the public, leading him to dismiss the possibility that the public's beliefs are constrained along any dimension. Further, he compared the correlations of the public with those of political elites (in this case, congressional candidates) and found that belief constraint is much higher among the elites. See Figure 5.2, which presents the average correlations (specifically, gamma coefficients) separately for domestic issues and foreign issues and then for a comparison between all domestic and all foreign issues. As you can see, correlations (and thus belief constraint) were higher among elites than the public for all three comparisons.

Figure 5.2   Relationships between Issue Opinions for the American Public and Political Elites, 1958

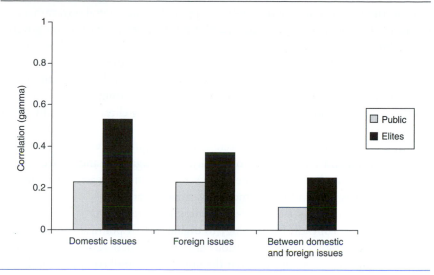

Source: Adapted from Table VIII of Philip E. Converse, "The Nature of Belief Systems in Mass Publics," in *Ideology and Discontent,* ed. David E. Apter (New York: Free Press, 1964), 229.

Second, Converse compared people's issue attitudes in 1956 with their opinions on the same issues in 1958 and again in 1960. This is the analysis we presented at the beginning of Chapter 4. As you recall, the levels of **attitude stability** were quite low. The correlation (expressed in this case with tau-b coefficients) between opinions on school desegregation in 1958 and 1960 was .43, whereas the correlation over time on the issue of federal housing assistance was .29. In contrast, respondents' party identification was much more stable across these two years (.73), demonstrating that party affiliation does not change as much as do issue opinions. Further, Converse found that people's issue opinions fluctuated as much between 1956 and 1958, and between 1958 and 1960, as they did between 1956 and 1960. Given the longer time frame of the last period, we might expect less stability than over a two-year period. But this pattern was not apparent in Converse's data, leading him to conclude that the public "contains significant proportions of people who, for lack of information about a particular dimension or controversy, offer meaningless opinions that vary randomly in direction during repeated trials over time."[16]

Groups as a Source of Belief Constraint

Although Converse argued that most Americans did not possess an ideologically constrained belief system, he did find one source of belief constraint among the public—attitudes toward social groups. Converse's respondents were asked two policy questions that referenced African Americans (or Negroes, the common label in the 1950s). One queried public support for the federal government to ensure public schools are desegregated, and the other assessed whether the government should ensure that African Americans are not discriminated against in employment and housing. The correlation between opinions on these two items was .57, much higher than the average relationship among public opinion toward the entire range of domestic policy issues that Converse examined (see Figure 5.2). Further, the correlation between these two items among elites was actually lower than for the public (.31).

In sum, Converse's conclusions were that (1) the public does not think about political parties and candidates ideologically, (2) recognition and correct use of the terms *liberal* and *conservative* are quite rare, (3) constraint across a variety of issue positions is low, and (4) attitude consistency over time is low. Citizens do appear, however, to organize their political opinions around views of prominent groups. Elites, in contrast, use ideology to organize their political thinking, as is evident by their higher levels of attitude constraint. If these results seem to confirm elite democrats' assumptions that the public is not well equipped for democratic governance, they should. In fact, empirical findings such as Converse's led to the development and refinement of the theory of democratic elitism. Elite democrats assume that the public is neither engaged in nor well informed about politics, which should contribute to their low levels of ideological understanding and use of ideology to organize their thinking. Other theorists, particularly those with a more optimistic view of the public's capabilities, found Converse's work limiting and looked to other explanations to account for his findings.

Critiques of Converse

Converse's research received much attention at the time of publication, has spurred countless commentaries and studies (some supporting and some opposing his conclusions), and is still influencing public opinion scholars today. His work was referred to as "celebrated" and "influential"; but it was also called "notorious" by one scholar,[17] and another described it as an "enduring milestone" and a "millstone," the latter because of the "misleading criteria Converse used to assess political competence and electoral responsibility."[18] As these quotations suggest, Conserve's work was not well received by all. Over the years, critiques have come from many quarters. We briefly summarize and evaluate key counterarguments.

Were Converse's results due to the nature of the times? Several people have argued that the 1950s was an especially nonideological time in the nation's politics, thus producing the low levels of ideological thinking measured by Converse. This was a decade of (relatively speaking) **consensual politics**. Disagreements between the political parties were minor, the political environment was not dominated by the discussion of conflictual issues, and the public was not very tuned in to politics. Politics during the 1960s and 1970s was much more **ideologically contentious**. Battles raged over civil rights, the United States was involved in what became a controversial war in Vietnam, the economy took a downturn, riots broke out in many cities, and President Richard Nixon was forced to resign as a result of the Watergate burglary. These salient issues increased public attention to political matters and divided the Democrats and Republicans quite publicly as the two parties openly debated their differences over these matters.

Did these more ideologically contentious times result in citizen views that were more ideologically grounded during this time period? Probably. Attitude constraint did tick up a bit in the 1960s and 1970s.[19] Some of the increase in 1972, for example, was due to the ideological nature of that year's presidential election.[20] The two candidates—Republican president Richard Nixon and Democrat George McGovern—proposed ideologically distinct platforms during their election campaigns. McGovern, in particular, was frequently described as representing the very liberal wing of the Democratic Party. The events of and debate over the Vietnam War also seemed to produce public attitudes that were more stable. In Converse's own words, "The crescendo of political turmoil associated with the later stages of the Vietnam war was producing somewhat firmer opinions on key subjects."[21] More generally, attitude constraint and stability are higher for certain types of issues. Issues that are grounded in religion, morality, or civil rights show less fluctuation over time and are more tied to ideological principles than are other types of issues (such as economic or foreign policy).[22] The former issues are more likely to be on the public agenda now than they were in the 1950s. As the issue context changes, then, public belief systems can become more constrained.

Even so, we have not witnessed very high levels of attitude constraint among the public in the decades since Converse's initial work. Figure 5.3 presents average correlation coefficients (Pearson's r) across pairs of issues for both 1980 and 2004. For each year, relationships between key issues of the day were examined.[23] In 1980, the average correlation between the issue pairs for the public was only .12, whereas it was .22 in 2004.[24] As for attitude stability over time, you can see in the figure that stability is higher than constraint (Converse also found this). However, levels of attitude stability are not terribly high. These results come from analyses of the 1972–1976 and the 2000–2004 ANES panel studies. For the first period, respondents were asked about three issues (abortion, school busing, and defense spending) using the same question wording in both 1972 and 1976. The average correlation (Pearson's r) between people's responses in these two years was .5.[25] More recently, respondents were asked about several policy issues using the same question wording in both 2000 and 2004. These included preferred levels of government spending on a variety of policies (such as environmental protections,

Figure 5.3   Attitude Constraint and Attitude Stability among American Public and Elites

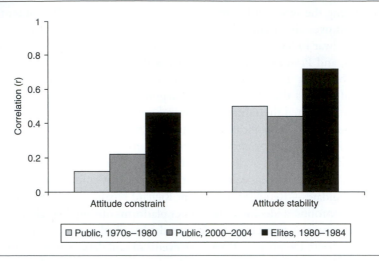

Sources: Attitude constraint for public (1980) and elites (1980) and attitude stability for public (1972–1976) and elites (1980–1984): Adapted from Figures 1 and 5 of M. Kent Jennings, "Ideological Thinking among Mass Publics and Political Elites," *Public Opinion Quarterly* 56 (1992), 426, 432. Attitude constraint for public (2004): Analysis of 2004 American National Election Study Data File. Attitude Stability for Public (2000–2004): Analysis of American National Election Studies 2000–02–04 Panel Data File.

welfare, child care, and aid to blacks) as well as abortion and legal protections against discrimination for homosexuals.[26] Stability over time across these four years was slightly lower than in the 1970s, with an average correlation of .44.

Recall that Converse compared attitude constraint for the public with that of the elites. Replications of this portion of his analysis have been rare, but one study did examine both elite and public attitude constraint and stability. The results from the public are the ones that we have been looking at in Figure 5.3; the elite results are also presented there. These elite data come from surveys of individuals attending the Democratic and Republican Party conventions in 1980 and 1984. Unfortunately, more recent analyses of elite opinion have not been conducted, so we must rely on this analysis. A quick glance back at this figure demonstrates that elites had higher levels of both constraint and stability than did the public during this time.[27] This result confirms one of Converse's key conclusions: elites possess more ideologically constrained belief systems than do citizens. This conclusion does not appear to be timebound, again suggesting that Converse's overall findings were not restricted to the 1950s.

Converse's method—survey research—has also come under attack. Some argue that asking citizens specific, focused questions does not allow them to reveal the complexity of their political thinking or the connections that they make across policy issues. Furthermore, questions that are designed to assess liberal or conservative ideologies are not likely to pick up the presence of other ideologies among the public. **Libertarians**, for example, prefer minimal government involvement in the economy but also believe that individual civil liberties need to be protected from government intrusion. These views are thus a mixture of liberalism and conservatism. If we used Converse's method for measuring attitude constraint (and his assumption that ideologies are arrayed along a liberal-conservatism continuum), libertarians would show low levels of constraint even though their attitudes are derived from an overarching ideology.[28]

To better measure other ideologies as well as to examine the process by which people reason about political matters, some researchers prefer **in-depth interviewing** over surveys.[29] During an interview session, a researcher asks someone very broad questions. The questions are designed to allow interviewees to discuss what is important to them rather than pointing them toward specific topics as surveys generally do. Furthermore, interviewing allows an examination of the reasoning process in addition to policy opinions, whereas survey research primarily assesses the latter. Put another way, political ideology might best be gauged through interviewing because this method provides for a contextual analysis of one's thoughts. Others have argued that listening to people discuss politics using their own terms and at their own pace is better than survey questions or even interviews for uncovering whether and how people organize politics ideologically. Thus, **ethnographic research** is preferred by some, whereby scholars place themselves in a setting or community, observe individuals, ask questions, and more generally interact with people.[30]

Finally, some argue that Converse overlooked ideological strains among minority communities. When he examined how people answered open-ended questions about political parties and candidates, the most common category of responses referred to groups (refer back to Figure 5.1). These Group Interest citizens did not display ideological thinking, at least according to Converse's standard. Others disagree, arguing that social groups play such a prominent role in American society and politics that group-linked political thinking should be considered ideological. In American society, this is particularly the case with race. As one scholar explains,

> If society is organized around race, and racial conflict is part of everyday life, and if our stories of the world are also organized around race, race is profoundly political and profoundly ideological. . . . To use Converse's language, there are a number of linking mechanisms between blacks' social

locations, their racial identities, and various (generally unsatisfactory) aspects of their social, economic, cultural and political worlds.[31]

Works examining **black political ideology** have identified a range of political ideologies among African Americans.[32] In contrast to how liberalism and conservatism were defined earlier in this chapter, black political ideologies encompass views toward the status of blacks in society and the proper strategies for improving this status, whites and other races, and blacks' interactions with the state (see Table 5.1). Group-based perspectives, in other words, play a prominent role in these ideologies. Delineating these ideologies is difficult using national surveys such as the

Table 5.1   Key Components of Black Political Ideologies

Ideology	Central beliefs
Radical egalitarianism (Dawson)/liberal integrationism (Harris-Lacewell)	Believes that racism is widespread in America and that it is spread primarily through racist institutions but that the nation's ideal of equality for all points toward a colorblind society. Black justice will only be achieved by demanding equality from the state and working across races.
Black nationalism	Views racial categorization and racial oppression as dominant features of society. Whites will oppose attempts by blacks to gain full equality. Proposes a black nation, generally not a separate political unit but instead a community within the broader society with separate cultural traditions and needs. Emphasizes strong unity among blacks.
Black feminism	Opposes the racism of whites and the sexism of white and black men. Race and gender intersect to oppress black women in multiple ways. Will form political alliances with nonblacks, unless racism is present.
Black conservatism	Believes in individual responsibility rather than government to improve the status of blacks. Faith that free markets do not discriminate. Black equality should be achieved through economic progress rather than through programs that provide blacks with special consideration, such as affirmative action.
Disillusioned liberalism (Dawson only)	Views racism among whites as ingrained and unlikely to disappear, so political alliances with whites are discouraged. Racial equality is to be pursued instead by increasing black political and economic power.

Sources: Michael C. Dawson, *Black Visions: The Roots of Contemporary African-American Political Ideologies* (Chicago: University of Chicago Press, 2001), Chaps. 1, 3–6; Melissa Harris-Lacewell, *Barbershops, Bibles, and BET: Everyday Talk and Black Political Thought* (Princeton, NJ: Princeton University Press, 2004), Chap. 1.

ANES because such surveys are often designed with the political views of majority whites in mind. Thus, researchers have designed and fielded surveys of blacks with questions that were created to tap into attitudes and concerns relevant to this community.

Summary

Some critics of Converse have chipped away at his conclusions. The levels of attitude constraint and stability that he documented were probably low because of the political environment of the 1950s. More ideologically polarizing times reveal more coherent belief systems among the public. The survey method also makes it difficult to uncover idiosyncratic ideologies or ideologies other than the dominant ones of liberalism or conservatism. On the whole, however, many of Converse's key findings have not been substantially undermined.[33] Constraint and stability have increased some over time, but not tremendously so, and public levels fall far short of elite levels for both. There is also little evidence that the public routinely thinks about politics ideologically. Remember that Converse's first attempt at examining ideological reasoning was to analyze responses to open-ended questions about presidential candidates and political parties. As we demonstrated earlier, Lewis-Beck and his colleagues' replication of this portion of Converse's research did identify more ideological thinking than the low levels found by Converse. Overall, however, the scholars conclude that "ideological awareness within the mass public is noticeably higher than during the 1950s, but still confined to a fairly small segment (i.e., about one-fifth) of the overall electorate."[34]

IDEOLOGICAL IDENTIFICATION

Another way to assess ideology among the American public is to examine levels of self-identification. Do Americans tend to identify more as liberals or conservatives or neither? The ANES has tracked ideological identification for the past few decades, showing respondents a scale and then asking where they fit on that scale. The exact wording of this question appears in Table 5.2. Note that there are three categories each for liberalism and conservatism, depending on the degree to which someone identifies with one of these ideologies. People whose ideological orientation is neither liberal nor conservative could select the midpoint on the scale (labeled "Moderate; middle of the road"). Finally, the end of the survey question explicitly encourages those who "haven't . . . thought much about" where they fall on the scale to say so.

Ideological identification from 1972 to 2012 appears in Figure 5.4.[35] The solid lines in this graph present trends over time in percentages of the public identifying as conservative, moderate, or liberal. In 1972 and 1976, the percentages of moderates and conservatives were nearly equal, at just over a quarter of the public each. Since then, conservatives have outnumbered both moderates and liberals. Nearly

Table 5.2   **Measuring Political Ideology**

"We hear a lot of talk these days about liberals and conservatives. Here is a seven-point scale on which the political views that people might hold are arranged from extremely liberal to extremely conservative."
"Where would you place yourself on this scale, or haven't you thought much about this?"

1. Extremely liberal
2. Liberal
3. Slightly liberal
4. Moderate; middle of the road
5. Slightly conservative
6. Conservative
7. Extremely conservative

Source: American National Election Studies Cumulative (1948–2012) data file codebook, http://www.electionstudies.org/studypages/anes_timeseries_cdf/anes_timeseries_cdf_codebook_var.pdf

Figure 5.4   **Ideological Identification over Time, 1972–2012**

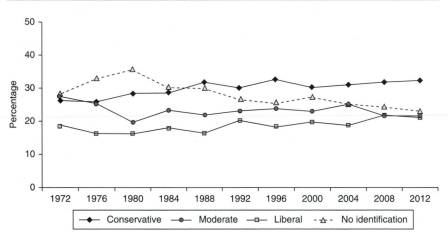

Source: Analysis of American National Election Studies Cumulative (1948–2012) data file.

one-third of the public identified as conservative in 2012. Liberals have been the smallest of the three ideological groups every year, although liberals and moderates were essentially the same portion of the public in 2008 and fairly close in 2012. The percentage of the public identifying as liberal has increased slightly over time, ranging from a low of 16 percent (in 1976 and 1980) to a high of 21 percent (in 2008 and 2012).

Focus your attention now on the dashed line, which demonstrates how many people did not know their political ideology or had not thought enough about it to classify themselves. Between 1972 and 1984 more people chose *not* to self-identify than did those who claimed any specific ideological identification. In other words, there were more "Haven't thought much about it" responses than either conservatives, liberals, or political moderates during these years. The number not classifying reached a high of 35.8 percent in 1980. Beginning in 1988, however, conservatives began to outnumber those without an ideology. The number of nonidentifiers has decreased gradually ever since. In 2004 and 2012, there were nearly identical percentages of moderates and nonidentifiers, with liberals not far behind in 2012. In fact, at 23 percent, 2012 saw the lowest proportion of the electorate indicating that they were not able to identify their ideology since the ANES began asking this question. Having said that, there is still nearly one-quarter of the public that has not thought enough about their ideology to self-identify. To us, this is further evidence in support of Converse's conclusions that a significant portion of the public does not think ideologically.

Symbolic versus Operational Ideology

With more self-identified conservatives than liberals or moderates among the public today, Americans must support conservative positions on specific policy issues. Not so, say Christopher Ellis and James Stimson.[36] In their work, Ellis and Stimson draw a clear distinction between symbolic and operational ideology. **Symbolic ideology** is what we have just been discussing, an individual's ideological identification (as conservative, moderate, or liberal). In contrast, **operational ideology** "is grounded more explicitly in concrete decisions, what citizens think the government should or should not be doing with respect to important matters of public policy."[37] In other words, operational conservatives favor conservative issue positions, such as increased spending on defense and crime, tax cuts, and the death penalty. In contrast, support for government social welfare policies, environmental protection, abortion, and gay rights are indicators of operational liberalism.

Ellis and Stimson's research highlights a paradox regarding ideology in the United States. Symbolically, Americans are most likely to be conservative (as we had demonstrated in Figure 5.4). Operationally, however, Americans tend toward liberalism.[38] To reach this latter conclusion, Ellis and Stimson examined responses to over 7,500 survey questions conducted between 1952 and 2010. These items queried public views toward a wide range of domestic issues. Across all of these questions, the public supported the liberal policy position 48 percent of the time compared to 34 percent for the conservative position. Furthermore, liberal positions were favored over conservative ones in every year except 1952. In addition to examining ideology for the entire nation, Ellis and Stimson also examined ideology at the individual level. Specifically, they grouped individuals based on their symbolic and operational ideologies.[39] They excluded moderates as well as those who did not self-identify an ideological orientation, thus leaving four possible combinations. People can have symbolic and operational ideologies that are both conservative or both liberal. These categories are labeled, respectively, consistent conservatives and consistent liberals. Two groups of ideological mismatches are also possible: symbolic conservatives who are operationally liberal or symbolic liberals who are operationally conservative. Figure 5.5 presents the classification of Americans into these four groups for 2008, the most recent year provided by Ellis and Stimson. Among those people whose symbolic and operational ideologies match, consistent liberals substantially outnumber consistent conservatives. Turning to those people whose symbolic and operational ideologies differ, the largest group is composed of symbolic conservatives who are operationally liberal. Indeed, this group is almost as numerous as consistent liberals. Finally, practically nonexistent are individuals with a liberal symbolic ideology paired with operational conservatism.

How might we explain these national and individual-level patterns of symbolic and operational ideology? Ellis and Stimson point to a number of factors. First, they emphasize that symbolic ideology is a personal identity, that it reflects how someone *thinks* of herself. As it turns out, more Americans are comfortable thinking of themselves as conservative than as liberal. This is due, in part, to the popularity of a conservative identity outside of politics, most notably in reference to religious worldviews and lifestyle choices. "Along with church on Sunday,"

Figure 5.5 Symbolic and Operational Ideology Classifications, 2008

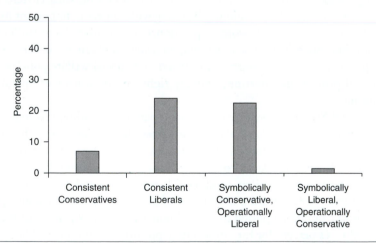

Source: Data from Figure 5.5 of Christopher Ellis and James A. Stimson, *Ideology in America* (Cambridge, UK: Cambridge University Press, 2012), 98.

write Ellis and Stimson, "imagine living by conventions—marriage, family, children, and work—and you have a lifestyle often called conservative. 'Conservative' in this context means conventional behavior and appearance, playing by the established rules, and fitting into established social patterns."[40] Some individuals who think of themselves as conservative in these nonpolitical domains transfer this identity to politics, thus self-identifying as politically conservative even if they do not hold conservative policy views.

Second, messages from the political environment also matter. Conservative politicians use the label "conservative" to describe themselves and their policy preferences, all the while decrying their opponents' "liberalism." Liberal politicians, in contrast, employ these ideological labels far less often. Thus the term *conservative* is used more commonly *and* more positively than is *liberal* in contemporary political debates. What type of language do liberal politicians use? They are more likely than conservatives to discuss the content of their policy proposals, such as by emphasizing the ends toward which these policies are geared. They state that they intend to "expand the economy," "improve education," "clean up the environment," or "build a social safety net," for example.[41] Because these goals are appealing to the public, conservative politicians generally opt not to debate the merits of the goals themselves. Put another way, liberal politicians prefer to describe their preferences in terms of operational ideology whereas conservatives lean toward symbolic ideological messages. As Ellis and Stimson conclude, "The result is a subset of the public that identifies and supports a 'conservative' approach to politics, while also supporting a wide range of 'liberal' public policies."[42]

PARTY IDENTIFICATION

As we have just seen, many citizens neither think ideologically nor organize their political attitudes along a single conservative-liberal dimension. In sharp contrast, party identification is one of the most meaningful political attitudes that individuals hold. As we discuss in Chapter 1, **party identification** refers to a person's psychological attachment to a political party or identification as independent of a party. Not surprisingly, party identification is the best predictor of which party a person will vote for in an election. Partisanship is also related to citizens' issue attitudes, as we demonstrate shortly. But party identification has effects that extend far beyond that; party identification also colors how citizens view political candidates and public policies.[43] For example, research shows that when citizens know a candidate's party identification, they rely on that knowledge to evaluate the candidate rather than relying on information about the candidate's issue positions, *even when* those positions are inconsistent with the party label.[44] In this section, we also discuss the theory of motivated reasoning, which helps us to understand how party identification can influence our perceptions and interpretations of new information, even factual information. Along the way, we will illustrate that party identification is a core identity for many Americans.

Party Identification and Issue Opinions

Party identification has a significant impact on a wide variety of policy opinions, as you can see from the 2012 ANES data presented in Figure 5.6. For these analyses, we have included leaners in with the partisan categories of Republican and Democrat. As you probably recall from Chapter 1, leaners are those individuals who first indicate they are politically independent but when then asked whether they lean toward one of the two parties, they identify one toward which they lean. To begin, let's consider the long-standing and fundamental difference between Democrats and Republicans on social welfare policies. Since the Great Depression, Democrats have championed more expansive social welfare programs than Republicans have. In 2012, for example, nearly a majority of Democrats supported more government services even if it meant an increase in spending, whereas only about 11 percent of Republicans favored that position. Note, however, that Republicans are not opposed to government spending across the board; a majority of Republicans supported greatly increasing government spending on defense, whereas just 26 percent of Democrats approved of increased spending in this area.

Since the 1960s, racial issues have been a key dividing point between the parties, with Democrats taking positions that are more pro–civil rights. In 2012, there was a large gap between partisans, 24 percentage points, in their support for efforts to improve the social and economic position of blacks. Notice, however, that neither Democrats nor Republicans seemed particularly interested in addressing the concerns of black Americans. In recent decades, cultural issues have divided Democrats and Republicans. Take abortion, for example. Fifty-nine percent of Democrats endorsed the most pro-choice stance when asked their views on abortion policy in 2012, whereas 29 percent of Republicans favored that position.

We would be remiss if we did not mention the policy attitudes of the 14 percent of Americans who identified as pure Independents in 2012. As the data in Figure 5.6 demonstrate, Independents are independent for a reason. They do not consistently side with one party or the other. On military spending, their views are more similar to Democrats, whereas they look somewhat more like Republicans on the issues of abortion and aid to blacks. When it comes to more government services, their opinions fall in between Democrats and Republicans.

Motivated Reasoning and Party Identification

When forming political opinions, most people are motivated in pursuit of one or more goals. Psychologists and political scientists have identified two types of goals that are particularly likely to motivate political reasoning: accuracy goals and directional goals. The former motivate people "to seek out and carefully consider relevant evidence so as to reach a correct or otherwise best conclusion" whereas directional goals direct a person to "apply their reasoning powers in defense of a

Figure 5.6   Party Differences in Issue Opinions, 2012

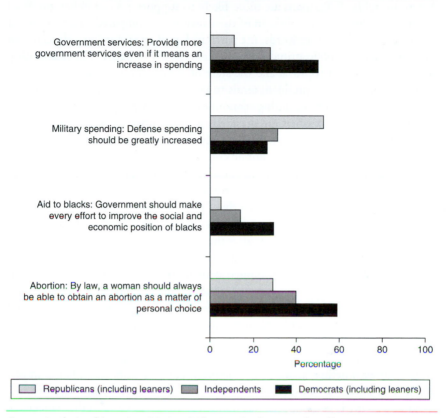

Source: Analysis of American National Election Studies 2012 data file.

Notes: Respondents placed themselves on 7-point scales for the government services, military spending, and aid to blacks questions. The bars represent the percentage of respondents who placed themselves on the more-government-services, more-spending, and more-government-effort side of the scales. For the abortion question, the bars represent the percentage of respondents who chose the most pro-choice stance from a list of four options.

prior, specific conclusion."[45] In the American context, where so much of politics is organized around political parties, this specific conclusion is often one that is consistent with one's partisanship. When **partisan motivated reasoning** occurs, citizens will search out information that coincides with their partisanship and quickly accept such supporting information without giving it much thought. At the same time, reasoners motivated by directional goals "strive to maintain their existing evaluations [by] discounting, counterarguing, and otherwise dismissing information running counter to their preferences."[46] In these ways, party identification can act as a screen through which incoming information is filtered.

We could provide many examples of partisan motivated reasoning among the American public.[47] Partisans are more likely to support a novel policy proposal when it is endorsed by a politician of their own party compared to a member of the other party.[48] In other words, the partisanship of an endorsing politician can strongly influence public attitudes toward a new policy initiative. The relationship between presidential approval and the state of the economy is another example. People's approval of the president tends to be more favorable when the economy improves and less favorable during economic declines. Among partisans, however, this pattern only exists when the president is of the opposite party. Approval of presidents who share one's own partisanship is not only generally high but also not responsive to changes in economic conditions.[49]

Partisan motivated reasoning can also influence the interpretation of factual information, as demonstrated by Brian Gaines, James Kuklinski, Paul Quirk, Buddy Peyton, and Jay Verkuilen's study of public opinion about the Iraq War.[50] Gaines et al. conducted panel surveys with University of Illinois students between October 2003 (roughly six months after the U.S. invasion of Iraq) and December 2004 (soon after the United States turned authority over to the Iraqi Provisional Government). These scholars examined whether partisanship influenced (1) citizens' factual beliefs about the situation in Iraq, (2) the interpretation of those facts, (3) opinions about President George W. Bush's handling of the war in Iraq, and (4) the relationship among facts, interpretations, and opinions about President Bush.

First, Gaines et al. asked participants to identify their party affiliation. Next, they examined whether factual beliefs varied by party identification. For example, they analyzed whether some partisan groups were more accurate than others when asked how many U.S. troops had been killed in Iraq. They found that citizens of all partisan stripes were fairly accurate in assessing the number of casualties. Moreover, as the number of troops killed in action increased over time, citizens updated their estimates accordingly, regardless of their party identification. Gaines et al. noted that this was an especially interesting finding for strong Republicans because they were the group that would be most motivated to distort reality because it was a Republican president who had led the country into war.

Despite the accuracy of their beliefs about the number of troop casualties, citizens' opinions of President Bush's handling of the war diverged a great deal based on partisanship. Strong Republicans were the most approving of President Bush, with weak Republicans the next most supportive group. At the other end of the continuum, strong Democrats were the most disapproving of the president, with weak Democrats not too far behind.

Now, all groups basically agreed on the number of casualties, so why did their opinions of President Bush differ so much? To answer that question, Gaines et al. examined how the partisan groups *interpreted* the factual information about casualties. Specifically, they asked, "When you think about [the number of]

U.S. troops being killed in the military action in Iraq since the May announcement that major combat operations had ended, do you think of that number as very large, large, moderate, small, or very small?"[51] An overwhelming proportion of strong Democrats indicated that the number of casualties was either very large or large. Weak Democrats generally agreed with strong Democrats, although they were a bit more likely to say the number was moderate. In sharp contrast, approximately 80 percent of strong Republicans saw the casualties as moderate, small, or very small. Even as casualties rose across time, strong Republicans did not change their interpretation of the number of casualties. Weak Republicans demonstrated a different pattern. They were more likely than strong Republicans to see the number of casualties as large or very large at the beginning of the study (although the percentage was not as high as for Democrats), and as more deaths occurred, an even greater percentage of weak Republicans interpreted the number killed in action as large or very large. Therefore, the views of weak Republicans were more responsive to the facts on the ground than the views of strong Republicans. Overall, the results clearly suggest that citizens' party affiliations shaped how they interpreted the number of casualties.

Thus far, the results we have discussed compare the beliefs, interpretations, and attitudes of different partisan *groups*. Gaines et al. also conducted an *individual-level* analysis to sort out whether it was the factual beliefs or the interpretation of those beliefs that influenced citizens' attitudes toward President Bush's handling of the war. They found that factual beliefs about the number of casualties had no effect on citizens' evaluations of the president, whereas people's interpretation of how large the casualties were had a substantial influence on their views of the president. "In other words, the meanings that people gave to their factual beliefs about troop losses, not the beliefs themselves, drove their opinions toward the war."[52] Notably, these meanings were heavily influenced by party identification and, thus, can explain why Republicans viewed Bush's handling of the war much more favorably than did Democrats. In sum, this study demonstrates that party identification functions as a critical filter for citizens. Partisans, especially strong ones, are motivated to interpret the world in a way that is consistent with their predispositions. As a result, Democrats and Republicans may agree on the facts in a situation yet still have very different understandings of what those facts mean.

POLARIZATION

"With just over two weeks to go until Election Day, the country looks and sounds more like the Divided States of America," opened an October 2014 analysis on the NBC News website.[53] The topic of that piece was, of course, **political polarization**. The headline of the article summed up the key points contained in it: polarization is "worse than ever" and "here to stay." Polarization refers to a gap in political opinions whereby Americans are divided in their preferences. Furthermore, as commonly understood, polarization implies not a narrow gap but instead a chasm with the public divided into camps on opposing sides. Such polarization could occur for opinions toward specific policy issues, for ideological orientations, or for partisanship. To illustrate, we drew a stylized graph of polarization (see panel C of Figure 5.7), in this case exploring the relationship between partisanship and ideology. The lighter bars present ideological categories among self-identified Democrats whereas the darker bars do the same for Republicans. Note that in this illustration all of the Democrats are liberal and all of the Republicans are conservative. This is what we usually mean by polarization: people are divided into extreme camps with no one in the middle.

Contrast this image of polarization with the other two panels of Figure 5.7. These are also hypothetical graphs, presenting possible distributions of ideology separately for Democrats and Republicans. The top panel shows ideology and partisanship to be rather intermingled. Democrats are arrayed along the entire ideological spectrum, as are Republicans. The most common ideological identification for both is moderate, yet there are liberal Democrats and liberal Republicans as well as conservative Democrats and conservative Republicans. Focus your attention now on the middle panel. Here we still see rather wide ideological distributions for both partisan groups. However, some shifting has occurred: Democrats have moved to the left as Republicans have shifted right. The distributions are no longer centered on moderate. Instead, the Democrats are centered on the slightly liberal category. The Republican distribution peaks at conservative. Finally, there are more liberals than conservatives among Democrats whereas conservatives outnumber liberals among Republicans.

Which of these possible options most accurately portrays the American public today? The middle one. Indeed, the stylized graph in panel B is fairly close to the actual relationship between ideology and partisanship that existed in 2012. Panel A, in contrast, is not that far off from the American public of 1972. Put another way, over the past few decades, partisans have sorted themselves more clearly into their proper ideological camps. A number of public opinion scholars have identified this trend, including Matthew Levendusky in his book *The Partisan Sort*.[54] Levendusky further demonstrates that partisan sorting is driven by people changing their ideological identification rather than their partisanship.[55] Over time, for instance, Republicans have been more likely to self-identify as conservative rather than moderate or liberal. The phenomenon of conservatives opting to change their partisanship from Democratic to Republican has been much rarer. This result should not be surprising, given our earlier discussion that partisanship is more likely than ideology to be a central political identity for most Americans.

Another way to explore political polarization among the public is to examine opinions toward specific issues. Is the public divided over key political issues of the day with two groups clustering on opposite sides of these issues? Not really. As it turns out, for many issues, more Americans take centrist than extreme views,

Figure 5.7   Stylized Portraits of the American Public

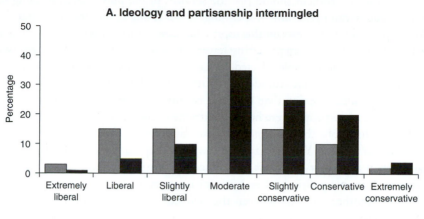

A. Ideology and partisanship intermingled

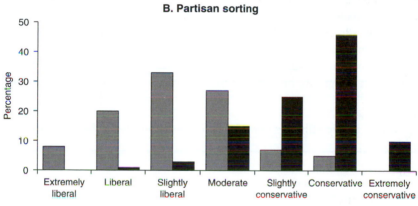

B. Partisan sorting

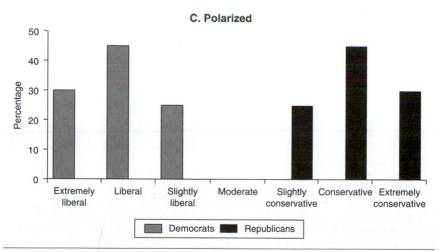

C. Polarized

Democrats   Republicans

Source: Figure created by authors.

a pattern that has not changed very much over time. Take attitudes toward whether the government should provide services to the public, even if doing so would require extra government spending. In 1984, one of the first years that the ANES probed public views on this topic, the most common response was smack dab in the middle between preferring fewer versus more government services (see Figure 5.8). Very few people selected either of the options at the extreme ends of this response scale. Public attitudes were little changed in 2012. Sure, fewer people selected the middle option than they had twenty-eight years earlier, but this was not because more people were holding extreme opinions. Instead, between 1984 and 2012, the public shifted somewhat toward preferring fewer rather than more government services. Yet in 2012 more people still opted for the middle position rather than any other one. This preference for centrism rather than extremism exists across many political issues. Even for issues over which Americans disagree with one another, the gap between the two sides tends not to be very large.[56] Opinions toward abortion are illustrative of this point. If the public were polarized on this issue, we would see a group of pro-choice Americans who support a woman's right to obtain an abortion in all circumstances and a pro-life group who do not support abortion in any circumstances. Instead, some people are pro-choice (44 percent in 2012), some are pro-life (12 percent), and others support abortion in some circumstances but not others (43 percent).[57] Even on a

Figure 5.8 Public Attitudes toward Government Provision of Services, 1984 and 2012

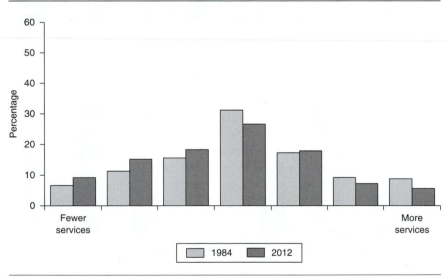

Source: Analysis of American National Election Studies Cumulative (1948–2004) and American National Election Studies 2012 data files.

hot-button issue such as this, disagreement does not often take the form of deep division. This is further evidence that Americans are not polarized.

If the public is not polarized, why do so many people assume that polarization exists in America? One reason is that U.S. politicians have become more polarized in recent decades. A few decades ago, the ideology of members of Congress were fairly well, but not perfectly, sorted by partisanship. Most Republicans were conservative, although a few liberal Republicans served in Congress. Similarly, whereas there were some conservative Democrats in the House and the Senate, most were best characterized as liberal. Members of Congress, in other words, looked like the middle panel of Figure 5.7. Today, panel C of that figure is a more accurate representation of political elites.[58] Democrats in Congress are liberal; Republicans are conservative. That is, partisans in Congress are divided into polarized ideological camps. This elite polarization has not gone unnoticed by the news media or the public. Polarization among national political elites is a much more common topic among news reporters than was the case a few decades ago.[59] Coupling this with the tendency of the news media to highlight conflict, and a portrait of a society deeply divided with strong rhetoric coming from both sides emerges in daily newscasts.[60] Perhaps it is not surprising then that the public is more likely now than in past decades to believe the parties are different from one another.[61] Fully 80 percent of citizens saw important differences in the stances of the parties in 2012 compared to only 58 percent in 1998. The perceived ideological distance between the parties has also grown over those same years. The public sees the Republicans as more conservative than they used to, all the while classifying Democrats as more liberal today than in the past. Finally, this elite polarization has contributed to the partisan sorting of the public. In the words of Levendusky, "As elites pull apart to the ideological poles, they clarify what it means to be a Democrat or a Republican. Ordinary voters use these clearer cues to align their own partisanship and ideology."[62]

In short, elites are polarized but the public is not, at least when it comes to holding extreme political opinions. As for *feelings* toward parties and politicians, however, we do see evidence of public polarization. **Affective polarization**, the combination of dislike of one's political opponents and favorable feelings toward political allies, is on the rise. One common method for measuring feelings toward political groups and politicians is via a feeling thermometer. This survey question asks respondents whether they feel warm, cold, or neither toward specific groups. The warmest rating on this thermometer is 100 degrees; the coldest is 0 degrees. Over time, partisans in the public have given colder ratings to the opposite party.[63] During the 1980s, for instance, the average Republican rating of Democrats was 45 degrees whereas the average Democratic rating of Republicans was 44 degrees. In 2008, these ratings were, respectively, 30 and 34 degrees. In 1980, the most common 10-degree interval selected by Democrats to rate Republicans was 41–50 degrees. By 2012, the most common interval was 0–10 degrees, the lowest possible interval. The exact same pattern existed for Republican assessments of Democrats. Across these decades, in contrast, partisan feelings toward their own party remained relatively stable. That tells us that Democrats and Republicans do not feel colder toward both parties, but only toward the opposing party.

Affective polarization is apparent in other ways as well. Stereotyping of party supporters is more common today than it used to be, in ways that favor one's own party.[64] In particular, American partisans are more likely in recent times to believe that typical supporters of their party possess positive personal traits. Supporters of the other party are, you guessed it, stereotyped more negatively. In an "us versus them" mentality, "they" are presumed to be closed-minded, hypocritical, and selfish whereas "we" are honest, intelligent, and open-minded. Furthermore, partisan sorting and affective polarization are related. People whose party and ideology align display more affective polarization than do those who are not partisan sorted. Partisan sorted individuals are more likely than the nonsorted to articulate a greater ratio of disliking than liking comments about their out party and to feel angry toward presidential candidates from the opposite party.[65]

Outside of the political realm, discomfort with interparty marriage is on the rise.[66] In 2010, one-third of Democratic parents indicated they would be somewhat or very unhappy if one of their children were to marry a Republican. Meanwhile, nearly one-half of Republicans would be unhappy to see their son or daughter marry a Democrat. In 1960, Americans were not much concerned about marriage across partisan lines, with only 5 percent of partisans expressing displeasure at the thought of a child marrying someone affiliated with the other party. Feelings toward partisans may even crop up when reviewing resumes. One experimental study asked participants to review the credentials of two (hypothetical) finalists for a college scholarship. Both of the finalists were high school seniors. One was the president of the Young Democrats, the other the president of the Young Republicans. Nearly 80 percent of the Democrats and Republicans in this study selected the finalist with the same partisanship as him or her, even when the finalist from their own party had a lower grade point average than the out-party finalist.[67] Thus, we see significant evidence of affective polarization, for both political and nonpolitical judgments. "Americans increasingly dislike people and groups on the other side of the political divide and face no social repercussions for the open expression of these attitudes."[68]

Partisan News and Polarization

Turn on cable television news stations Fox or MSNBC any weeknight and you will see talk show hosts and guests launching criticisms at their political opponents, akin to the O'Reilly-Franken debate profiled in the opening to this chapter. The same is true if you visit many online political blogs, where the tone of the posts is often nastier and more vitriolic than are the cable shows. Surely, then, the media have played a role in polarizing the attitudes of the public. In particular,

Public Opinion in Comparative Perspective
BOX 5.1 PARTY POLARIZATION ACROSS THE GLOBE

The United States is not the only democracy where party elites are polarized. In many other nations, political parties within a country take very different policy stances from one another. Yet, in some countries, party convergence exists, whereby party platforms are rather more similar to each other. Such natural variation in the degree of party polarization across nations allows scholars to examine whether elite polarization influences public opinion. In the most comprehensive such analysis to date, Noam Lupu examines one effect of polarization: the likelihood that citizens will identify with a political party.[1] In his study, Lupu analyzes 37 nations from across the globe. All are democracies, although there is a mix of newer and older, more established democracies. For data, he relies primarily on nationally representative surveys from each country, conducted between 1996 and 2011.

Across these nations and years, Lupu concludes that party polarization is indeed related to partisanship among the public. In nations where the parties are more polarized, more citizens affiliate with a political party than in nations with less polarization. Furthermore, individual citizens who perceive that their country's parties are polarized are more likely to be partisans than are people who believe the parties of their nation are similar to each other. Why might polarization affect partisanship holding? The "further apart the political parties, the easier it may be for citizens to distinguish among their electoral options. And if citizens can more clearly distinguish parties, they may find it easier to form a party attachment."[2] Put another way, if national parties hold similar positions, it can be hard for a voter to figure out which of those parties would best represent his issues and interests.

Ultimately, Lupu argues that polarization can be positive for democracy. When parties take clearly divergent views in a nation, the populace knows where the parties stand. This not only makes it easier for citizens to predict what a party will do if elected, but also makes it easier to then hold these elected officials accountable when the next election rolls around.

---

1. Noam Lupu, "Party Polarization and Mass Partisanship: A Comparative Perspective," *Political Behavior* 37 (2015): 331–356.
2. Ibid., 334.

scholars and others have presumed that **partisan news**, or media outlets that cover and present the news from a specific political point of view, fuel polarization. As it turns out, reality is more complex. Let's not forget that, as we just demonstrated, citizens are not actually polarized when it comes to issue opinions.

Perhaps, though, partisan news has the *potential* to polarize the public, and thus if our political news becomes even more partisan, issue polarization could emerge in the future. We discuss research that speaks to that topic. First things first, though: how many people actually consume partisan news?

Compared with prior decades, partisan or ideologically oriented news outlets are definitely more common today. Whether it be cable television stations, talk radio, or Internet blogs, citizens now have many choices for strictly liberal or strictly conservative news.[69] Not only do these liberal and conservative media sources exist, but people's choice of news sources is related, at least in part, to their own political predispositions. This process is known as **selective exposure**, whereby people choose to consume news that coincides with their existing political views.[70] Some people search out like-minded news, in other words. In 2014, for example, the audiences of the Fox News cable channel and Rush Limbaugh's radio show were filled with conservatives (46 and 83 percent, respectively). Liberals were much more prevalent among viewers of shows on the MSNBC cable channel or Comedy Central's *The Daily Show with Jon Stewart* (48 and 72 percent, respectively).[71] We do need to be careful not to dwell on these patterns of selective news exposure, however, particularly because the audiences for partisan outlets are still smaller than for mainstream news. The average daily combined viewership of the evening news on ABC, NBC, and CBS was 24 million in 2014, whereas just shy of 3 million people tuned into cable television news on a typical evening that year.[72] The audiences for most online political blogs are smaller still. For the *entire month* of January 2015, 3.3 million people visited the left-leaning Talking Points Memo website, one of the more popular political blogs. The average length of time for each visit to this site was 1.6 minutes.[73]

Determining whether consumption of partisan news leads to issue polarization is tricky. Many viewers of *The Daily Show* do not become liberal because they watch the show, after all, but rather watch the show because they are already liberal. Comparing the political views of liberal versus conservative news consumers is thus not a good approach for determining whether these news outlets polarize the public. Instead, as we discuss in Chapter 3, experiments are better methods for examining whether news content influences people's attitudes. By randomly assigning people to watch a conservative or a liberal news show, we can conclude whether the content of these shows changed attitudes and, specifically, whether these attitudes became more extreme. Using this approach, scholars have demonstrated that partisan news can lead to issue polarization. In particular, when liberals watch liberally oriented news, their views become even more liberal. Conservatives hold even more conservative views after consuming conservative news.[74]

These results are based on having study participants watch partisan news regardless of what their normal viewing habits are. That is, think of these results as demonstrating what can happen to attitudes when people are *forced* to watch partisan news. But what happens when you take into account the fact that some people prefer to watch partisan news whereas others much prefer entertainment over any type of news? One set of experiments demonstrates that partisan news viewing leads to opinion polarization only among those who prefer entertainment, most likely because they are not familiar with the political rhetoric and arguments present in the shows.[75] They are more open to persuasion and end up holding more extreme attitudes after watching partisan news. For those preferring news, in contrast, opinions do not become more extreme. "Ideologically congenial shows appear to have relatively small effects among those who choose to watch them . . . these shows end up preaching to the choir."[76] Taking these experimental results out of the lab, it appears as if partisan news could, in real life, polarize the opinions of those people who generally prefer to watch entertainment shows. Yet these are precisely the citizens who are unlikely to consume partisan news because they much prefer entertainment over news. If they do not watch Bill O'Reilly on Fox or Rachel Maddow on MSNBC, their opinions cannot be directly influenced by these shows. In short, then, partisan news shows do not seem to produce issue polarization in the real world. On the other hand, the nasty tone and fiery rhetoric hurled at political opponents on these shows has likely contributed to affective polarization, as we discuss in Chapter 3.

CONCLUSION

Few, if any, works have influenced public opinion scholarship as much as Converse's "The Nature of Belief Systems in Mass Publics." The piece has been called the "foundation stone of political-behavior research,"[77] and a veritable cottage industry of research on public ideology arose after its 1964 publication. Many of Converse's core conclusions have stood the test of time. Chief among these is that members of the public tend not to see the political world in ideological terms. One of Converse's primary concerns, of course, was the degree to which citizens and elites think about and discuss politics using the same terms. Converse found that elites are much more likely to possess ideologically constrained belief systems. Elite constraint has rarely been studied since Converse's work was published, but research examining this topic has confirmed Converse's finding. As one public opinion scholar writing a recent review of belief systems research put it, "Subsequent work has tended to confirm Converse's picture of a tiny stratum of well-informed ideological elites whose passionate political debates find little echo, or even awareness, in the mass public."[78] This empirical evidence, as we noted earlier in the chapter, is in line with one of the key tenets of elite democratic theory. In contrast, if citizens do not understand the nature of elite policy decisions, it might become more difficult for them to evaluate and constrain, if necessary, elite behavior. This undermines democratic governance, certainly the type of governance assumed by participatory democrats, who hope that citizens will fairly routinely monitor the actions of leaders.

Converse also concluded that group-oriented thinking is common among the public. Nowhere is this reality more obvious than in the case of partisan affiliation. Political parties are the main groups active in American politics, and much political activity is organized by or around the parties, from elections to legislative bodies in state capitals and Washington, DC. As one public opinion scholar put it, "Elite competition is partisan competition: Democrats and Republicans define the issues of the day and set the terms of the debate. . . . For ordinary citizens, party is how they understand the political world."[79] Just as pluralists expect, political parties help to orient the public toward political debates and structure public thinking about issues.

What do democratic theorists make of partisan sorting and increased affective polarization among the public? To the degree that partisan sorting has enabled citizens to line up their ideology and issue preferences with their partisanship, participatory democrats and pluralists would be pleased, especially if such sorting allows the public to better recognize their issue preferences within the dominant elite discussions and then act on these preferences in the voting booth. On the other hand, affective polarization worries participatory democrats. Animosity toward one's opponent is not typically a precursor to meaningful political involvement. In fact, high levels of negativity and distrust on all sides might just turn citizens away from politics.

Finally, if the public tends not to think ideologically and if many members of the public do not organize their beliefs along an ideological continuum, is it fair to conclude that public attitudes are fleeting and not well reasoned? As our discussion of party identification might have suggested, we are not yet prepared to draw that conclusion, and we hope you will wait as well. In the next two chapters, we describe other sources of people's political beliefs. Chapter 6 examines personality, values, self-interest, and historical events. We return to the topic of groups in Chapter 7, in this case membership in and attitudes toward demographic groups. Whether these alternative sources are as politically meaningful as or more meaningful than ideology and whether they revive a view of the public as more competent for democratic politics than Converse concluded are topics that we encourage you to consider as you read Chapters 6 and 7.

KEY CONCEPTS

affective polarization / 163	ideologically contentious / 147
attitude constraint / 141	ideology / 140
attitude stability / 145	in-depth interviewing / 149
belief system / 141	liberals / 140
black political ideology / 150	libertarians / 149
consensual politics / 146	open-ended questions / 141
conservatives / 140	operational ideology / 153
ethnographic research / 149	partisan motivated reasoning / 157

SUGGESTED SOURCES FOR FURTHER READING

Arceneaux, Kevin, and Martin Johnson. *Changing Minds or Changing Channels? Partisan News in an Age of Choice*. Chicago: University of Chicago Press, 2013.

Levendusky, Matthew. *How Partisan Media Polarize America*. Chicago: University of Chicago Press, 2013.

Stroud, Natalie Jomini. *Niche News: The Politics of News Choice*. Oxford: Oxford University Press, 2011.

If you want to learn more about partisan news and polarization, these books are good places to start. Stroud examines the phenomenon of partisan selective exposure. She demonstrates not only that some people do indeed choose news outlets based on the partisan perspective presented in the news but that these news choices have consequences for citizens' attitudes and behaviors. The other two books ask whether partisan news polarizes the public. Yes, concludes Levendusky. No, say Arceneaux and Johnson.

Converse, Philip E. "The Nature of Belief Systems in Mass Publics." In *Ideology and Discontent*, ed. David E. Apter. New York: Free Press, 1964.

Lewis-Beck, Michael S., William G. Jacoby, Helmut Norpoth, and Herbert F. Weisberg. *The American Voter Revisited*. Ann Arbor: University of Michigan Press, 2008.

Is Democratic Competence Possible? Special issue of *Critical Review* 18 (2006).

The first source is Converse's classic study, in which he outlines his argument for ideological innocence and presents survey data as evidence to support his conclusions. The second is a replication of a seminal work in voting behavior, *The American Voter*, published in 1960. Lewis-Beck et al. update this earlier book, using data from 2000 and 2004. Chapters 9 and 10 replicate portions of Converse's 1964 study. The special issue of the journal *Critical Review* contains a republication of Converse's 1964 "Nature of Belief Systems" paper (which is currently out of print) along with twelve essays that comment on research conducted on this topic since 1964. The issue ends with an interesting response essay by Converse in which he addresses some of the arguments of his critics.

Dawson, Michael C. *Black Visions: The Roots of Contemporary African-American Political Ideologies*. Chicago: University of Chicago Press, 2001.

Harris-Lacewell, Melissa. *Barbershops, Bibles, and BET: Everyday Talk and Black Political Thought*. Princeton, NJ: Princeton University Press, 2004.

Lane, Robert E. *Political Ideology: Why the American Common Man Believes What He Does*. New York: Free Press, 1962.

The authors of these books discuss and examine political ideology in ways quite different from Converse. Lane and Harris-Lacewell argue that ideology is best uncovered using methods other than surveys, such as interviews or ethnographic research. Dawson and Harris-Lacewell further demonstrate that group-based thinking should indeed be considered political ideology.

Hajnal, Zoltan L., and Taeku Lee. *Why Americans Don't Join the Party: Race, Immigration, and the Failure (of Political Parties) to Engage the Electorate.* Princeton, NJ: Princeton University Press, 2011.
Lavine, Howard G., Christopher D. Johnston, and Marco R. Steenbergen. *The Ambivalent Partisan: How Critical Loyalty Promotes Democracy.* Oxford: Oxford University Press, 2012.

Whereas our discussion of party identification focused primarily on partisans, these two books devote significantly more attention to those with weak, nonexistent, or shifting partisan ties. Hajnal and Lee identify the pathways to partisanship and nonpartisanship separately for African Americans, Latinos, Asian Americans, and whites. The authors of *The Ambivalent Partisan* analyze individuals who experience a mismatch between their party identification and their current evaluations of the Democratic and Republican parties.

Noel, Hans. *Political Ideologies and Political Parties in America.* Cambridge, UK: Cambridge University Press, 2013.

Noel traces the origins of American conservatism and liberalism, most notably the forging and development of these ideologies among activists, intellectuals, and political commentators. His work also demonstrates that the dominant parties have not always aligned along ideological lines to the degree they do today.

Thurber, James A., and Antoine Yoshinaka, eds. *American Gridlock: The Sources, Character, and Impact of Political Polarization.* Cambridge, UK: Cambridge University Press, 2015.

This excellent collection of essays presents up-to-date scholarly analyses of many facets of political polarization.

"Beyond Red vs. Blue: The Political Typology," Pew Research Center, 2014, http://www.people-press.org/2014/06/26/the-political-typology-beyond-red-vs-blue
"Where News Audiences Fit on the Political Spectrum," Pew Research Center, 2014, http://www.journalism.org/interactives/media-polarization

These Pew Research Center websites present interesting data on the ideology and news habits of the American public. The first summarizes Pew's efforts to classify Americans into one of eight political typologies. These typologies include some ideologically based ones (Steadfast Conservatives, Business Conservatives, and Solid Liberals, for example). For a fun exercise, click on the "Take the Typology Quiz" link, answer the questions that appear, and find out your political type. The second is an interactive site, containing graphs of the sizes and ideological orientations of the audiences for thirty-two distinct news sources. It's pretty cool—check it out!

CHAPTER 6

Pluralistic Roots of Public Opinion: Personality, Self-Interest, Values, and History

AFTER THE PUBLICATION of Philip Converse's path-breaking research in 1964, which we discussed at length in the previous chapter, much of the debate among public opinion scholars was driven by his findings regarding the public's lack of ideological sophistication. In fact, some observers argued that too much attention was paid to this debate over ideology, distracting scholars from how citizens really *do* think about politics.[1] In this chapter, we move beyond Converse and his critics to address this question: If ideology doesn't organize most citizens' opinions, what does? Donald Kinder has offered an answer to that question. He encourages scholars to consider the **pluralistic roots** of public opinion.[2] Specifically, he suggests five factors that might influence citizens' attitudes: personality, self-interest, values, historical events, and group attitudes.

The research on the public's lack of ideological sophistication leaves us with a view of citizens as not being competent to play an active role in governance, which bolsters the elite democratic theorists' argument that citizens should be removed from the policymaking process. In contrast, the research on the pluralistic roots of public opinion resurrects a more positive view of the average citizen. From this perspective, citizens are capable of holding reasoned, complex opinions derived from meaningful political factors, such as values and group identity. Pluralists are especially pleased by the reliance on group-based thinking. Participatory democratic theorists are also encouraged that citizens' opinions have some logic underlying them, yet we will see they are not always thrilled by the particular logic that drives public opinion.

In this chapter we discuss four of the five factors—personality, self-interest, values, and historical events—that shape public opinion. Each section focuses primarily on one of the factors, but you will quickly notice that these forces are not mutually exclusive. In many instances, more than one of the factors influences public opinion on a particular issue. In the next chapter, we focus on the fifth factor by discussing the central role of groups in shaping public opinion.

PERSONALITY

Let's begin with a discussion of how personality influences public opinion. In 1950, Theodor Adorno and his colleagues introduced the concept of an "authoritarian personality."[3] They defined authoritarianism as a *set* of personality traits, including submissiveness to authority, a desire for a strong leader, general hostility and cynicism toward people, strict adherence to convention, and a belief that people should be roundly punished if they defy those conventions.[4] These traits appear most often in people exposed to strict and rigid child-rearing practices. In other words, children whose parents dole out a "relatively harsh and threatening type of home discipline" are more likely to have authoritarian personalities as adults.[5]

This harsh upbringing leads to frustration among children, which ultimately gets redirected toward outgroups; anger and resentment toward parents becomes displaced onto people who are considered weak and inferior. As a result, authoritarians demonstrate high levels of intolerance for outgroups. This theory was developed shortly after World War II as a way to make sense of anti-Semitism. Over the years, Adorno et al.'s work on the authoritarian personality has been challenged on a number of theoretical and methodological fronts.[6] Nevertheless, the concept has continued to be a compelling one for social scientists.

More than fifty years after the publication of Adorno's research, Karen Stenner's work reinvigorated the study of authoritarianism.[7] According to Stenner, "Authoritarianism is an individual predisposition concerned with the appropriate balance between group authority and uniformity, on the one hand, and individual autonomy and diversity, on the other."[8] She labels people who value sameness and conformity to group norms as **authoritarians** and people who value diversity and individual freedom as **libertarians**.

Stenner takes pains to point out that the differences between authoritarians and libertarians are not simply a matter of political ideology.[9] In earlier research, some scholars had conflated conservatism and authoritarianism. But there is an important distinction. For example, people whom Stenner labels as "status quo conservatives" do not mind diverse viewpoints, as long as that diversity is stable over time. In contrast, authoritarians are bothered by the diversity in and of itself. Another way to think of the distinction is that status quo conservatives do not like change, whereas authoritarians are pleased with change as long as it moves people toward greater "oneness and sameness."[10] (Also note that we briefly discuss libertarians in Chapter 5. There we discuss libertarianism as a political ideology, whereas here Stenner is using the term to refer to a personality predisposition.)

Stenner argues that authoritarianism and libertarianism constitute very broad, normative worldviews about the way society should function and that these worldviews influence citizens' opinions across a wide range of political, racial, and moral issues. Because authoritarians value conformity and obedience to authority, they favor policies that stifle diversity and enforce sameness across citizens. On the other end of the continuum, libertarians value freedom and difference and thus oppose coercive government policies or policies that discourage individuality.

Stenner provides evidence of the impact of authoritarianism on public opinion by analyzing national survey data from the General Social Survey (GSS). But before we dive into Stenner's research findings, we must first discuss how she measures the concept of authoritarianism. Stenner argues that the best way to determine whether someone is an authoritarian is to examine his or her beliefs about child-rearing practices. Child-rearing values "can effectively and unobtrusively *reflect one's fundamental orientations* toward authority/uniformity versus autonomy/difference."[11] The GSS asks respondents to rank child-rearing values by indicating which qualities are "most desirable" for a child to have and which ones are "least important" (see Table 6.1). According to Stenner, authoritarians place a high value on obedient, neat, and well-mannered children, whereas libertarians are partial to inquisitive and responsible children with good judgment.[12]

Stenner examined data from surveys conducted by the GSS between 1990 and 2000; she focused her attention solely on white respondents.[13] Her analysis showed that authoritarians are significantly more likely than libertarians to be

Table 6.1 Measuring Authoritarianism

Authoritarian child-rearing values	*Libertarian child-rearing values*
"That a child obeys his or her parents well"	"That a child is interested in how and why things happen"
"That a child is neat and clean"	"That a child has good sense and sound judgment"
"That a child has good manners"	"That a child is responsible"

Sources: Karen Stenner, *The Authoritarian Dynamic* (New York: Cambridge University Press, 2005), 164–165; "General Social Surveys, 1972–2014: Cumulative Codebook," National Opinion Research Center, September 2015, http://publicdata.norc.org:41000/gss/documents/BOOK/GSS_Codebook.pdf, 356–360.

Note: The General Social Survey asks respondents to rank order thirteen child-rearing values using a series of questions: (a) "Which three qualities listed on this card would you say are the most desirable for a child to have?" (b) "Which one of these three is the most desirable of all?" (c) "All of the qualities listed on this card may be desirable, but could you tell me which three you consider least important?" (d) "And which one of these three is least important of all?" Stenner constructed her authoritarianism scale based on the ranking of the six values presented in this table.

racially, morally, and politically intolerant. In terms of race, authoritarian citizens tend to oppose interracial marriage, support housing segregation, and say they would not vote for a black presidential candidate. When it comes to moral issues, authoritarians oppose homosexuality, believe in compulsory school prayer, and think that pornography should be banned. Citizens who are authoritarian are also opposed to civil liberties for groups from both the left and right sides of the ideological spectrum. For example, authoritarians do not think that homosexuals or racists should be allowed to teach in a college or university. In addition, authoritarians are more punitive than libertarians. Authoritarians are more likely to support the death penalty, believe that courts are too soft on criminals, support wiretapping, and own a gun. Taken as a whole, Stenner provides strong evidence that white authoritarian citizens abhor difference and diversity and believe people should be harshly punished for disobedience.

Our discussion of Stenner's research has probably raised an important question in your mind: What about authoritarianism among nonwhite Americans? Presumably some African American, Hispanic, Asian American, and Native American citizens value oneness and sameness over diversity and difference just as some whites do. And if authoritarianism is a basic and universal personality predisposition, as Stenner suggests, then wouldn't we expect it to influence the policy opinions of nonwhite citizens as well?[14] Perhaps authoritarian blacks would not see voting for a black presidential candidate as a violation of oneness and sameness (or perhaps they would, given that the political system is dominated by whites and therefore a black presidential candidate might be seen as disruptive), but it seems likely, for example, that authoritarian blacks would be more opposed to homosexuals and racists in the classroom than libertarian blacks. Unfortunately, we do not know for certain because Stenner's research does not shed light on authoritarianism among minority citizens in the United States.

Stenner's research also examined the effect of **normative threats** on citizens with authoritarian predispositions. To authoritarians, a normative threat is a situation in which oneness and sameness are called into question. It is worth quoting Stenner at some length on her definition of normative threats:

> In diverse and complex modern societies, the things that make us *one and the same* are common authority and shared values. The conditions most threatening to oneness and sameness, then, are questioned or questionable authorities and values: that is, disrespect for leaders or leaders unworthy of respect and lack of conformity to or consensus in group values, norms, and beliefs.[15]

When citizens are faced with normative threats, authoritarianism becomes activated and thus has a stronger effect on intolerance of difference. In other words, those citizens with an authoritarian bent become even more intolerant when they are in a situation in which "diversity and freedom 'run amok.'"[16]

In a series of survey-based experiments, Stenner provides evidence to support this interaction between authoritarianism and normative threats. In one condition, interviewers read subjects a (fictitious) news story about how public opinion is increasingly divided in the United States on important political issues. This news story represents a normative threat to oneness and sameness because it focuses on division among the public. After exposure to the story, authoritarians became more intolerant and libertarians became more tolerant when asked their opinion about whether whites have a right to keep blacks out of their neighborhoods. In another condition, interviewers read subjects a (fictitious) news story about how strong and trustworthy U.S. presidents have been and how citizens can expect high-quality presidential candidates in the future. This story is a normatively reassuring one to authoritarians because it emphasizes authority. After exposure to this normative reassurance, authoritarianism and libertarianism were in effect deactivated, and the two groups became more similar in terms of their levels of racial tolerance as a result. As Stenner puts it, "They each let down their defenses in the wake of such reassurance, rendering authoritarians calmed and libertarians complacent, the latter fairly characterized as 'asleep at the wheel'" in this condition.[17]

Stenner also examined the interaction of authoritarianism with normative threats in other domains (political and moral) and found the same pattern of results: normative threats activated authoritarianism and thus led people with authoritarian leanings to be more intolerant and people with libertarian predispositions to be more tolerant. These research findings are problematic for participatory democratic theorists. Recall that participatory democratic theorists believe that citizens can come together to discuss political issues in a productive way. Citizens can learn from one another, which will help them look beyond their self-interest and gain an understanding of what is best for the nation as a whole. Stenner's research, however, pokes a big hole in this argument. Her findings suggest that if authoritarians are exposed to diverse viewpoints during conversations with their fellow citizens, they would view that as normatively threatening and thus become even more intolerant; however, participatory democratic theorists can take some solace from Stenner's results showing that libertarians exposed to diverse viewpoints become more tolerant.

Marc Hetherington and Jonathan Weiler also examine authoritarianism and its impact on policy attitudes by analyzing data from national surveys conducted in the 1990s and 2000s. These scholars argue that authoritarianism is best thought of as a worldview about what is right and what is wrong.[18] Like Stenner, they measure authoritarianism by assessing citizens' child-rearing values. Those who "score high in authoritarianism have (1) a greater need for order and, conversely, less tolerance for confusion or ambiguity, and (2) a propensity to rely on established authorities to provide that order."[19] Hetherington and Weiler demonstrate that authoritarians and nonauthoritarians (that is, those whom Stenner would call libertarians) have very different attitudes toward many of the most prominent issues of our day. Figure 6.1 shows a few examples. Only 19 percent of the citizens who score the highest on the authoritarian scale support same-sex marriage, whereas 71 percent of those who score lowest support marriage equality. Over one-half of the most authoritarian individuals support wiretaps without a warrant and believe the war in Iraq was not a mistake; just one-fifth of nonauthoritarians hold those views. Eighty-two percent of authoritarians believe illegal immigrants are lawbreakers, whereas only 38 percent of nonauthoritarians believe that is the case. Taken as a whole, these are striking differences in opinion based on citizens' level of authoritarianism. Furthermore, difference in issue opinions between authoritarians and nonauthoritarians have existed for decades.[20]

Figure 6.1   The Effect of Authoritarianism on Political Attitudes

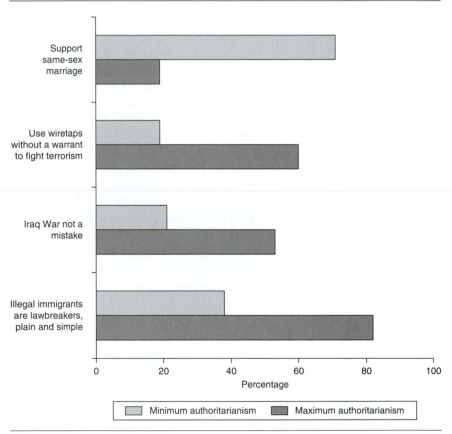

Source: Adapted from Tables 5.1A, 5.3, 5.4, and 8.1 of Marc J. Hetherington and Jonathan D. Weiler, *Authoritarianism and Polarization in American Politics* (New York: Cambridge University Press, 2009), 92, 99, 100, 169.

In addition to providing further evidence that authoritarianism affects attitudes toward a range of issues, Hetherington and Weiler make two new contributions to the study of authoritarianism. First, the scholars argue that studies showing nonauthoritarians become more tolerant in the face of threats are flawed because nonauthoritarians do not actually perceive the information they are exposed to as threatening. To illustrate this point, consider Stenner's experiment again. The normative threat she exposed her subjects to was disagreement among the public, which is a threat to the oneness and sameness valued by authoritarians. Divided public opinion, however, is *not* a threat to libertarians; in fact, they probably appreciate diversity in citizens' views. According to Hetherington and Weiler, when nonauthoritarians are confronted with truly threatening situations, they become more authoritarian, not more tolerant. Indeed, the scholars demonstrate that nonauthoritarians who are very worried about the war on terror (and therefore presumably feel threatened by it) are much more likely to support warrantless wiretapping than nonauthoritarians who are not worried at all about the war on terror. In fact, worried nonauthoritarians are as supportive of wiretapping as authoritarians, who are pro-wiretapping regardless of their level of concern about the war on terror. This finding helps explain why the percentage of citizens who were willing to forgo civil liberties increased after the terrorist attacks of 9/11. Authoritarians were already willing to sacrifice civil liberties for security prior to 9/11, but nonauthoritarians weren't willing to do so until they felt threatened by the tragic events of that day. They changed their minds and moved in a more authoritarian direction, which led to an aggregate increase in support for security over civil liberties (see Chapter 9 for further discussion of attitudes toward civil liberties post-9/11).

Hetherington and Weiler's second contribution connects authoritarianism and political parties. They argue that the most prominent issues of our day are ones on which authoritarianism matters a great deal, such as gay rights, race, immigration, and the war on terror. Political parties have taken distinct positions on these issues, with the Republican Party taking the authoritarian stance and the Democratic Party taking the nonauthoritarian perspective. Even though citizens tend to be fairly moderate on these issues, over the last two decades they have "sorted" themselves into one party or another so that their authoritarian leanings correspond with their party identification. In other words, authoritarians are increasingly aligning themselves with the Republican Party and nonauthoritarians are increasingly identifying with the Democratic Party.[21] As a result, because authoritarianism is a fundamental worldview, not simply different policy preferences, the gap between the two parties seems quite large. Among citizens, the average Republican and average Democrat may not be all that different, but their differences stem from deep-seated understandings of right and wrong, making American politics seem quite polarized.

Authoritarianism is not the only personality predisposition examined by political scientists. In recent years, scholars have also investigated the relationship

Public Opinion in Comparative Perspective
BOX 6.1 AUTHORITARIANISM ACROSS THE WORLD

In her book *The Authoritarian Dynamic*, Karen Stenner argues that the concept of authoritarianism helps us understand intolerance of difference not just in the United States but across the world "from Switzerland to China to Nigeria to Azerbaijan."[1] She analyzed the World Values Survey, which includes survey data collected from over 110,000 people in fifty-nine nations between 1990 and 1998. She measured authoritarianism based on people's evaluation of child-rearing practices. Across all these nations, Stenner demonstrated that authoritarians are more likely to be intolerant across a range of racial, political, and moral issues. For example, authoritarian people are more opposed to homosexuality, abortion, divorce, and racial integration than libertarians. Further, authoritarians are more likely to believe that jobs should be reserved for the native-born, that maintaining order is more important than free speech, and that fighting crime is more important than progressing toward a humane society.

What is so fascinating about Stenner's work is that she demonstrates the linkage between authoritarianism and intolerance in a wide variety of countries across the globe. This is noteworthy because conflict within countries is often attributed to factors specific to that country. So, for example, when observers try to explain the breakup of Yugoslavia during the 1990s, they often point to long-standing ethnic hatreds that were unleashed after the 1980 death of Tito, the country's powerful and charismatic communist leader. In France, conflict surrounding the assimilation of North African immigrants is most often explained by cultural and religious factors unique to that country and those particular immigrants. But Stenner argues that regardless of the particular groups involved or whether difference is based on culture, religion, race, ethnicity, or tribes, the primary factor that explains intolerance is authoritarianism. Why? Because authoritarianism is a universal personality predisposition. Stenner concludes, "Authoritarianism rather consistently produces a predictable cluster of sociopolitical stances varying in target and form, but never in function: the animating spirit throughout is to limit difference in people, beliefs, and behaviors."[2]

1. Karen Stenner, *The Authoritarian Dynamic* (New York: Cambridge University Press, 2005), 129.
2. Ibid., 116.

between specific **personality traits** and political attitudes. There are five traits, the **Big Five**, that personality researchers have identified as fundamental to understanding individuals' attitudes and behaviors: openness to experience, conscientiousness, agreeableness, extraversion, and emotional stability (see Table 6.2). These traits stem from genetic differences, and they form early in childhood, remaining largely stable throughout a person's lifetime. Scholars measure these personality characteristics by asking survey respondents to indicate whether particular traits apply to themselves (see Table 6.3).[22] For example, a respondent is conscientious if she thinks of herself as dependable and self-disciplined *and* does not consider herself disorganized and careless. Someone open to new experiences would also think of himself as complex but neither conventional nor uncreative.

Look around your dorm room or apartment (or, if you are not in your living space now, imagine its contents). Do you see calendars, an iron, and a laundry basket? What about books and music—are there many types of books and CDs, or are your book and music collections rather homogeneous? Do you have any art supplies in your room or evidence of travel (such as an airline ticket, travel books, or souvenirs)? Are your living quarters neat or messy? Well lit or quite dark? According to research in psychology, your answers to these questions are likely to be related to whether you are conservative or liberal.[23] A study of college students and new college graduates demonstrates that conservatives tend to have neater, better lit, and better organized (hence the presence of calendars and laundry supplies) residences. Liberals, on the other hand, live in messier and darker rooms that contain a wider variety of books, music, and artistic supplies as well as travel literature and souvenirs.

This intriguing work demonstrates that personality traits can be linked to both ideological leanings and behavior. Being open to new experiences is related not

Table 6.2　Big Five Personality Traits

Personality trait	Description
Openness to experience	Individuals with this trait respond positively to a wide range of experiences; they appreciate complexity and novelty.
Conscientiousness	Individuals with this trait engage in socially prescribed impulse control; they appreciate rules and norms.
Agreeableness	Individuals with this trait are kind and communal; they are not antagonistic toward others.
Extraversion	Individuals with this trait are active and energetic; they are sociable and outgoing.
Emotional stability	Individuals with this trait are steady and resilient; they are not nervous and anxious.

Source: Based on Alan S. Gerber, Gregory A. Huber, David Doherty, Conor M. Dowling, and Shang E. Ha, "Personality and Political Attitudes: Relationships across Issue Domains and Political Contexts," *American Political Science Review* 104 (2010): 111–133.

Table 6.3   Ten-Item Personality Inventory

"Here are a number of personality traits that may or may not apply to you. Please write a number next to each statement to indicate the extent to which you agree or disagree with that statement. You should rate the extent to which the pair of traits applies to you, even if one characteristic applies more strongly than the other."

Disagree strongly	Disagree moderately	Disagree a little	Neither agree nor disagree	Agree a little	Agree moderately	Agree strongly
1	*2*	*3*	*4*	*5*	*6*	*7*

I see myself as:
1. _____ Extraverted, enthusiastic.
2. _____ Critical, quarrelsome.
3. _____ Dependable, self-disciplined.
4. _____ Anxious, easily upset.
5. _____ Open to new experiences, complex.
6. _____ Reserved, quiet.
7. _____ Sympathetic, warm.
8. _____ Disorganized, careless.
9. _____ Calm, emotionally stable.
10. _____ Conventional, uncreative.

Source: Samuel D. Gosling, "Ten Item Personality Measure (TIPI)," http://gosling.psy.utexas.edu/scales-weve-developed/ten-item-personality-measure-tipi

Note: Each of the Big Five personality dimensions is measured by answers to two of the trait pairs: Openness to experiences: agreeing with 5, disagreeing with 10; Conscientiousness: agreeing with 3, disagreeing with 8; Agreeableness: agreeing with 7, disagreeing with 2; Extraversion: agreeing with 1, disagreeing with 6; and Emotional stability: agreeing with 9, disagreeing with 4.

only to having a messier room and owning more books but also to holding a liberal ideology. Conscientious individuals are neater, more organized, and more likely to be conservative. The openness-liberalism and conscientiousness-conservatism connections are quite robust, having been found in a number of studies.[24] To explain these relationships, one scholar pointed to features of these two ideologies: "Liberalism is conceived of embracing change and proactive policies, whereas conservatism is likened to personal responsibility, caution, and maintaining order."[25]

Personality traits are also associated with party identification. Given that the Democratic Party is the more liberal party in the United States, it should come as no surprise to learn that the trait of openness is related to Democratic Party identification. Republican identifiers are quite high in conscientiousness, again not surprisingly.[26] Beyond which party a person identifies with, Big Five traits are also related to the strength of one's party identification and whether someone even identifies with a party.[27] People high in extraversion or high in agreeableness are more likely to have a partisan identity and have stronger party identifications than do those who are low in either trait. Extraverts are sociable whereas agreeable individuals are communal, thus likely leading them to be "drawn to the affective, social benefits of party identification . . . [or] to the communal and cooperative components of joining a political 'team.'"[28] In contrast, those high in openness to new experiences are less likely to affiliate with a political party. Partisan ties help to structure the political world, providing cues and context with which to interpret political debates and events. Those who are high in openness do not desire structure to the degree that those low in openness do, perhaps making partisanship less appealing to the former.

According to research conducted by Alan Gerber and his colleagues, the Big Five also have a substantial impact on citizens' issue opinions, particularly toward economic and social policies.[29] The scholars measured economic policy attitudes by assessing citizens' views on the proper role of government in the provision of health care and attitudes toward taxes on the wealthy. Social policy attitudes were measured by asking citizens about their abortion attitudes and whether they supported civil unions for gay and lesbian couples. They find that citizens who are open to experiences are more liberal on economic and social issues, probably because they respond more positively to new programs and initiatives. Conscientious individuals, however, are more conservative on economic and social issues; they are rule followers and value self-discipline, which makes them more amenable to conservative policies. People who are agreeable have more liberal economic attitudes, most likely because they view those policies as helpful to others, yet they are more conservative on social issues, perhaps because they see social policies such as same-sex marriage as disruptive to the community. In contrast, emotionally stable citizens are more conservative on economic policy. Because they are less anxious, they are less likely to see the need for government to step in and regulate the economy. In terms of social policy, emotionally stable individuals are a bit more conservative, but it is unclear why that is the case. Finally, extraversion is related to conservative views on social and economic policies; however, the relationships are weak ones, and the researchers are not certain why being sociable and energetic is associated with conservatism.

Gerber et al. also consider whether the relationship between personality traits and political attitudes differs for whites and blacks. Why might the relationship differ for the two groups? Because whites and blacks operate in substantially different political environments and the effects of personality on policy attitudes is context-specific. That is, political context influences how individuals interpret government policies, which then affects whether a particular personality trait leads to more or less support for those policies. For example, given historical and current discrimination against black Americans, blacks perceive liberal economic policies as helping those who have been systematically denied opportunities to succeed in the marketplace. Thus, compared with whites, conscientious blacks see liberal economic policies as "dutiful, (e.g., helping those who are in bad circumstances through no fault of their own) rather than as undermining social norms (e.g., work hard and you will get ahead)."[30] As a result, conscientiousness does *not* lead to strong support for conservative economic policies among blacks as it does for whites. Blacks tend to support liberal economic policies regardless of their level of conscientiousness.

Much of this work linking Big Five traits with political predispositions is fascinating. This has been a very productive area of public opinion scholarship of late with, undoubtedly, more projects currently underway. To date, scholars have focused primarily on identifying which traits are related to which opinions.[31] In contrast, more work is needed to fully understand why certain personality traits lead to particular positions, whether traits interact with each other in politically consequential ways, and how the political and nonpolitical contexts influence the relationship between traits and political attitudes.[32]

SELF-INTEREST

It seems incredibly intuitive that **self-interest** would have an important effect on our policy attitudes. When considering human nature, it certainly seems as if people are looking out for number one. Indeed, James Madison argued that a representative form of government is the best form of government because citizens are too focused on their narrow self-interest, whereas representatives have the wisdom to "best discern the true interest of their country."[33] Elite democratic theorists have used this argument to justify why elites (rather than citizens) should have central decision-making roles in politics.

Despite the intuitive—even compelling—nature of the claim that citizens follow their self-interest, there is actually quite limited evidence to support the proposition. On policy opinions ranging from government spending to government health insurance to race and gender issues to foreign policy, scholars have found only weak or nonexistent effects of self-interest.[34] For example, several studies showed that white nonparents were as likely to oppose school busing as a means to achieve racial integration as white parents with school-age children.[35] Instead of self-interest, racial prejudice was a key factor influencing attitudes on school busing: prejudiced citizens were more opposed to busing, whereas non-prejudiced citizens were more supportive of the policy (regardless of whether the citizens had kids or not). Other research indicates that citizens' evaluations of the nation's economy are more important than their own personal economic circumstances when assessing the political party in power.[36] In other words, general concerns about society—what political scientists call **sociotropic concerns**—trump **pocketbook issues** when citizens evaluate their government.

There are a few instances, however, when self-interest does influence citizens' policy attitudes. Homeowners are more likely to favor property tax cuts than nonhomeowners.[37] Smokers are more opposed to cigarette taxes and bans on smoking than nonsmokers.[38] And gun owners are less supportive of gun restrictions than people who do not own guns.[39] These examples illustrate the conditions under which self-interest can be influential: when the effects of a policy are *visible, tangible, large,* and *certain.*[40] The innovative studies we profile next provide further evidence of such conditions triggering self-interest.

Robert Erikson and Laura Stoker demonstrate that self-interest can have powerful and long-lasting effects when citizens are faced with circumstances in which their lives might be severely disrupted and even put in jeopardy.[41] Specifically, Erikson and Stoker examine what happens to the political attitudes of young men when they are faced with the prospect of being drafted for military service. In 1969 in the midst of the Vietnam War, Republican president Richard Nixon instituted a new policy that assigned numbers (1 through 366) to draft-eligible men based on their birth dates. The men assigned low numbers were called up first for duty, whereas the men assigned high numbers were virtually assured they would *not* be drafted. The policy in effect randomly assigned some men to be vulnerable to being sent to war in Vietnam and others not to be. This was a perfect case in which self-interest should have shaped public opinion because those with low draft numbers faced "a (relatively) high likelihood of being forced to abandon all personal plans and undertakings and to take part in a potentially life-threatening war. As one's lottery number increased, one's vulnerability decreased."[42]

As luck would have it, a representative sample of young men affected by this draft policy were interviewed in 1965 and reinterviewed several times later as part of an ongoing panel study to examine political attitudes and socialization. (This is the Jennings and Niemi panel study we discuss at some length in Chapter 2.) The data collected included the respondents' birth dates, which allowed Erikson and Stoker to determine the draft number assigned to each male respondent. As a result, the researchers were able to use these data to investigate whether vulnerability to the draft changed young men's political attitudes. Indeed, they found striking evidence that being assigned a lower draft number influenced attitudes in several ways. When reinterviewed in 1973, men with lower numbers were more likely to think the war in Vietnam was a mistake than those with higher numbers. In addition, compared with the men who held high draft numbers, the men vulnerable to the draft were less likely to have voted for Nixon for reelection and were more likely to express a liberal ideology and liberal issue positions. Remarkably, when interviewed twenty-four years later in 1997, the men who had been assigned low numbers continued to be more likely to report that the war was a mistake than those assigned high numbers. Erikson and Stoker also present evidence that the vulnerable men reconsidered their partisanship, which led them to become more Democratic and largely stay that way into later adulthood. Finally, it was not only these men who were politically affected by their draft numbers. Their parents were as well.[43] Parents of sons who had low draft numbers were more likely to vote in the 1972 presidential election than were parents of sons with high numbers, especially if the families with low-draft-number sons lived in a town where at least one soldier had been killed in the Vietnam War.

High-profile events can sometimes bring into sharp relief the ties between a policy domain and one's economic interests. Such was the case with the *Deepwater Horizon* oil spill, according to Bradford Bishop.[44] In April 2010, there was an explosion on the *Deepwater Horizon*, an oil rig drilling one mile from the shore in the Gulf of Mexico. The rig sank, leaving an uncapped well. Crude oil flowed out of that well into the ocean, nearly 5 million barrels worth before the well was sealed a few months later. Oil washed up along hundreds of miles of shoreline in the Gulf Coast states of Louisiana, Mississippi, Alabama, and Florida, damaging coastal ecosystems and wildlife. This incident was, in the words of President Obama, "the worst environmental disaster America has ever faced."[45]

Bishop's research uncovers interesting effects of this environmental disaster on public opinion. Overall, the American public became more concerned about the environment and less supportive of offshore oil drilling. Self-interested concerns came into play, however, among those people living in offshore drilling communities. These are coastal regions where the oil industry is a large component of the local economy. There are drilling communities in various areas of the nation, including those along the Gulf Coast that were directly affected by the *Deepwater Horizon* spill. Offshore drilling exists or is planned in other regions as well, such as in parts of Texas, California, and Alaska. Compared to the rest of the nation, people residing in any of these offshore drilling communities were more supportive of offshore drilling in the wake of the *Deepwater Horizon* disaster. Importantly, before this event, people living in drilling regions were not more pro-drilling than those living elsewhere, despite the fact that their economic livelihoods might have depended on offshore drilling. Bishop attributes this change to the fact that the *Deepwater Horizon* spill served as a focusing event, drawing the public's attention to topics such as offshore drilling, pollution, and environmental regulation. This event activated "latent forms of self-interest among citizens who do not ordinarily connect abstract debates over public policy to considerations relevant to their communities."[46] When offshore drilling was in danger of becoming more tightly regulated, personal and community economic considerations came to the fore among people residing in drilling communities. During more conventional times, however, there is little evidence that self-interest plays a role in forming citizens' environmental policy preferences,[47] just as self-interest plays a minimal role in most other policy domains.

VALUES

Values are "general and enduring standards."[48] They are abstract beliefs about how the world *should* work. As such, values constitute citizens' core principles, guiding their understanding of right and wrong. Thus, it makes sense that citizens' values would influence their specific policy positions.[49]

Scholars have identified two fundamental values that influence public opinion: egalitarianism and individualism.[50] **Egalitarianism** is the belief that citizens should be equal regardless of their personal characteristics.[51] In the U.S. context, egalitarianism emphasizes equality of opportunity, not necessarily equality of results. In other words, egalitarianism is the belief that all citizens should have the *chance* to achieve rather than the belief that all citizens should be guaranteed equal outcomes. **Individualism** is the belief that citizens should get ahead by virtue of their own hard work; people should "pull themselves up by their own bootstraps" and rely on their own ingenuity.

Egalitarianism and individualism are abstract concepts and therefore difficult to measure. Nevertheless, political scientists have devised a set of survey questions to assess these concepts. In particular, Stanley Feldman analyzed citizens' levels of agreement with several statements that were included on a pilot study for the 1984 ANES to come up with the best way to measure egalitarianism and individualism.[52] He identified three statements that provide a valid measure of egalitarianism (see Table 6.4 for the wording of these items). The first two items seem to focus on support for equal opportunity, whereas the third is more ambiguous. Some people might infer that treating people "more equally" means ensuring

Table 6.4 Measuring Egalitarianism and Individualism

"I am going to read several statements. After each one, I would like you to tell me whether you agree or disagree. I would also like to know whether you agree or disagree strongly or not strongly."

Egalitarianism	Individualism
"Our society should do whatever is necessary to make sure that everyone has an equal opportunity to succeed."	"Any person who is willing to work hard has a good chance of succeeding."
"One of the big problems in this country is that we don't give everyone an equal chance."	"If people work hard, they almost always get what they want."
"If people were treated more equally in this country, we would have many fewer problems."	"Most people who don't get ahead should not blame the system; they really have only themselves to blame."
	"Hard work offers little guarantee of success."
	"Even if people try hard, they often cannot reach their goals."

Source: Stanley Feldman, "Structure and Consistency in Public Opinion: The Role of Core Beliefs and Values," *American Journal of Political Science* 32 (1988): 421.

equal results, whereas others might think the statement simply refers to providing people with equal opportunities. Feldman also identified five statements that provide a valid measure of individualism (again, see Table 6.4 for the wording of these items). These statements emphasize the personal effort that is needed for someone to get ahead in life. (Note that agreeing with the first three statements is the individualistic response, whereas disagreeing with the last two statements is the individualistic response.) What do you think—do these statements do a good job measuring individualism and egalitarianism?

Feldman analyzed the impact of egalitarianism and individualism on citizens' policy attitudes.[53] He demonstrates that egalitarianism is closely related to citizens' opinions on a wide range of policies. For example, egalitarian citizens are more likely to support welfare programs; increased government spending on health and education; and government efforts to improve the societal position of African Americans, women, and the poor. Thus, across many different policy areas, egalitarianism leads to more progressive political views. In contrast, individualism has an effect in only a few policy areas; nevertheless, its influence is still noteworthy. Individualistic citizens are more likely to oppose welfare spending and prefer a more limited role for the federal government (compared with state governments) in handling social and economic problems.

Political values also influence public opinion in the domain of gay rights.[54] Egalitarianism has a strong effect on support for gay rights. Specifically, citizens who are more egalitarian tend to favor laws that protect homosexuals against job discrimination and believe that homosexuals should be allowed to serve in the military. Individualism, especially as this value highlights personal freedom, is related to support for same-sex marriage and favoring laws allowing same-sex couples to adopt children. Another influential value—moral traditionalism—is highlighted by Paul Brewer's research.[55] **Moral traditionalism** refers to citizens' "underlying predispositions on traditional family and social organization."[56] Moral traditionalists prefer stable, two-parent—one male and one female, that is—families and are opposed to changing norms regarding family structure and acceptable lifestyles. See Table 6.5 for the statements used to measure moral traditionalism.[57] (Note that agreeing with the first and third statements is the morally traditional response, whereas disagreeing with the second and fourth statements is the morally traditional response.)

Analyzing ANES data from 1992, 1996, and 2000, Brewer found that citizens who are moral traditionalists are more likely to oppose laws to protect homosexuals from job discrimination and to think that homosexuals should not be allowed to serve in the armed forces. This held for all three years under study, but moral traditionalism was a more influential factor explaining attitudes toward gay rights in 1992 and 1996 than in 2000.

Although the primary focus of this section is on values, we would be remiss if we failed to discuss Brewer's other important findings regarding support for gay rights.

Table 6.5   Measuring Moral Traditionalism

"Now I am going to read several statements. After each one, I would like you to tell me whether you agree strongly, agree somewhat, neither agree nor disagree, disagree somewhat, or disagree strongly with this statement. The first statement is . . ."
"The newer lifestyles are contributing to the breakdown of our society."
"The world is always changing and we should adjust our view of moral behavior to those changes."
"This country would have many fewer problems if there were more emphasis on traditional family ties."
"We should be more tolerant of people who choose to live according to their own moral standards, even if they are very different from our own."

Source: Paul R. Brewer, "The Shifting Foundations of Public Opinion about Gay Rights," *Journal of Politics* 65 (2003): 1218.

First, Brewer suggests that moral traditionalism had less of an impact on citizens' views in 2000 because of people's reactions to *historical events.* He points to the brutal murder of Matthew Shepherd as an event that probably shaped how citizens thought about gay rights. Matthew Shepherd was a college student at the University of Wyoming. In 1998, he was kidnapped, viciously beaten, tied to a fence, and left to die. His death received extensive media coverage. Why would this tragedy influence public opinion on gay rights? Because Matthew Shepherd was gay. Brewer speculates that this repugnant act might have led some people to question whether their traditional moral views should be linked to opposing gay rights.

Second, Brewer shows that *attitudes toward gays and lesbians* are an important predictor of opinion on gay rights. Citizens who have negative feelings toward gays and lesbians are more likely than those who have positive feelings to oppose employment rights for the group. This was true each year under study, although attitudes toward homosexuals became a less important predictor of gay rights opinion across the time period. Again, Brewer links this decrease in the importance of attitudes toward gays and lesbians to the public responding to historical events. As gays and lesbians became more visible on television (at the time *Ellen* and *Will and Grace*, both with lesbian and gay lead characters, were popular sitcoms), Brewer argues that people became more familiar with homosexuals, therefore breaking down stereotypes and reducing hostility. Citizens began to see gays and lesbians as individual people rather than an undifferentiated mass. As a result, citizens were less likely to derive their opinions on gay rights from their feelings toward gays and lesbians as a group.

Moral traditionalism also has an impact on attitudes toward same-sex marriage, a particularly contentious issue in American politics in recent years. An analysis of data from the 2004 ANES showed that citizens who endorsed moral traditionalism were significantly more likely to oppose same-sex marriage than citizens who did not agree with that value.[58] Even though the public has become much more supportive of same-sex marriage over time (see Chapter 10), it is likely the issue will continue to be visible and vexing for those who feel a core value is at stake.

In sum, several scholars have demonstrated the important role of values in shaping citizens' issue attitudes. Individualism, egalitarianism, and moral traditionalism are all abstract, enduring standards that influence public opinion. Brewer's research on attitudes toward gay rights also points toward two additional factors that are key to understanding public opinion: historical events and group attitudes. We discuss the effects of historical events in the next section and the influence of groups in the next chapter.

HISTORICAL EVENTS

Citizens' attitudes are also shaped by **historical events**, a phenomenon we touched on earlier. For example, recall that international crises have an impact on public approval of the president.[59] Presidents typically get a boost in popularity in the wake of a foreign policy–related crisis, known as a rally-round-the-flag effect (for further detail, see Chapter 4). As noted earlier in this chapter, high-profile events (e.g., the *Deepwater Horizon* disaster) can heighten self-interest considerations, whereas others (e.g., the brutal murder of Matthew Shepherd) can lessen the connection between core values and issue opinions.

The battle over civil rights also influenced political attitudes beyond party identification. In a groundbreaking study, Taeku Lee demonstrated the impact of **social movements**, particularly the civil rights movement, on public opinion.[60] Specifically, Lee argues that events initiated by social movements can have a more powerful effect on public opinion than events initiated by political elites. He argues that too often public opinion research focuses on how attitudes are shaped by elite actions and does not dedicate enough attention to the influence of nonelites, such as movement activists. Furthermore, Lee makes the case that political scientists rely too heavily on public opinion polls to assess citizens' attitudes. He maintains that public opinion polls are not well suited for the task of distinguishing between elite and nonelite influences on the public.

To illustrate the effect of nonelite events on public opinion, Lee conducted an in-depth analysis of the civil rights movement between 1948 and 1965. Lee shows that political events initiated by movement activists galvanized the black public, which then led to a backlash from white Southerners who opposed the goals of the civil rights movement. This, in turn, led to national elites reacting to the events on the ground in the South, as well as racially liberal white citizens from across the country responding sympathetically to the plight of black citizens.

Lee tracked this chain of events not by monitoring public opinion data from polls but by examining letters written to the president of the United States during this period. Lee argues that constituency mail measures **activated mass opinion**, which is "beliefs and sentiments that are at once *salient* in the mind and *impel* one to political action."[61] He shows that letter writing to the president increased in response to events initiated by civil rights activists. For example, the Montgomery bus boycott, Freedom Summer, and especially Bloody Sunday in Selma stimulated an outpouring of letters from citizens.[62] In contrast, the passage of the Civil Rights Act of 1964, the presidential election of 1964, and the Voting Rights Act of 1965—all elite-driven events typically considered watershed moments in the push for civil rights—did not inspire citizens to write the president.[63]

Lee also examined the race of the correspondent, which was identifiable in about 47 percent of the letters, and the timing of the letter writing.[64] He found that blacks, who were universally sympathetic to the civil rights activists, were the first to be activated by movement events. This was followed by sympathetic Northern whites who wrote to the president outraged by the extremely violent backlash of white Southerners against blacks participating in the civil rights movement. Next, white Southerners were motivated to write the president in strong opposition to elite actions at the national level to end racial segregation. Finally, racially liberal whites from across the nation (except the South) wrote to the president in support of integration. Based on this pattern of letter writing, Lee does not dismiss the importance of elite events entirely but concludes that a "movement-initiated, movement-elite interaction" model best describes the events that influenced public opinion on racial issues during this period.[65] In other words, citizens' opinions were affected by movement events, *and* their opinions were shaped by elite activities *in response* to movement events.

Lee's research speaks to one of the most important debates within the study of public opinion: the capability of citizens to function effectively in a democratic society. Elite democratic theorists, of course, argue that citizens do not have the ability or the desire to participate in the rough-and-tumble of politics. But Lee's important work suggests that is not always the case. Lee concludes that "ordinary citizens, under appropriately compelling circumstances, *will* take an active part in crafting politics rather than merely consuming the political outputs of elite actors."[66] These are heartening words to the ears of participatory democratic theorists.

Long-term developments also influence political attitudes. As we note in Chapter 2, party identification among many white Southerners changed from Democratic to Independent or even Republican after the national Democratic Party became the party of civil rights during the 1960s. Immigration and the increased racial diversity of American society have also contributed to changes in partisanship among whites. Zoltan Hajnal and Michael Rivera reach this conclusion after analyzing ANES and other national survey data collected between 1970 and 2012.[67] As Hajnal and Rivera note, the racial composition of America has changed over the past few decades, most especially due to the growth in the Latino population. This demographic change has been accompanied by a number of political party developments. The Democratic and Republican parties now have different immigration policy positions, with the Democrats being more favorable toward immigration and immigrants. Latinos are much more likely to identify with the Democratic than the Republican Party. Overall, immigration has become an issue that divides the parties more and more, a reality that has influenced the opinions of whites. "In short," write Hajnal and Rivera, "many white Americans will see that America is changing, will believe that immigration is driving many of the negative changes they see, and will know that one party is backed by immigrants and stands largely on the side of immigrants, whereas the other party is opposed by almost all immigrants and stands largely in opposition to immigration. For many white Americans, this may be a powerful motivation to defect to the Republican Party."[68]

Hajnal and Rivera uncover a number of ways that public opinion has been affected by these changing demographic patterns. People holding negative views of illegal immigrants and Latinos are more likely to be Republican and are also more likely to vote for Republican candidates. This relationship between attitudes toward Latinos and partisanship appears to be slightly stronger than it was a few decades ago. Finally, immigration-related attitudes are one factor driving a long-term trend in the partisanship of white Americans: the move away from Democratic and toward Republican party identification. Put more broadly, "the ongoing transformation of the United States by immigrants and Latinos helps to explain the partisan transformation of white America."[69]

CONCLUSION

Do citizens organize their political attitudes in any kind of coherent way? Yes, the research we have discussed in this chapter suggests that public opinion is derived from several factors. Therefore, instead of a single ideological dimension underlying public opinion (à la Converse), it is more appropriate to think in terms of the pluralistic roots of public opinion. The research on authoritarianism provides compelling evidence that personality predispositions influence a wide range of attitudes on moral, political, racial, and foreign policy issues. Further, core personality traits, including openness to experiences and conscientiousness, shape attitudes toward ideology, partisanship, and issue opinions. Self-interest, in contrast, has a much more limited effect on public opinion. In certain circumstances, however, self-interest does matter. When the effects of a policy are clear, large, and salient, self-interest can kick in and influence public opinion. In addition, citizens' values play an important role in shaping political attitudes. Egalitarianism, for instance, influences public opinion on a number of political issues, and moral traditionalism drives opinion toward gay rights policies. Public opinion is also molded by historical events. The civil rights movement affected citizens' political attitudes, as has America's increased racial diversity.

Elite democratic theorists would be surprised by the limited role that self-interest plays in shaping public opinion. Their justification for the centrality of elites in the political system is based at least in part on the argument that citizens are too self-interested to be intimately involved in decision making. The research suggests, however, that their argument is more of a rationalization than a justification. Taeku Lee's research also delivers a body blow to the elite democratic theorists. His research shows quite convincingly that elite actions are not always central to the lives of citizens. Instead, events initiated by social movement activists have an important effect on public opinion.

Participatory democratic theorists are delighted that the studies discussed in this chapter demonstrate that citizens are capable of holding reasoned opinions derived from important political factors. The research on the pluralistic roots of public opinion revives an image of citizens as more sophisticated than the one suggested by Converse's research. This research, however, does not put participatory democratic theorists completely at ease. The opposition of moral traditionalists to gay rights is troubling. Further, the intolerant reaction of authoritarians to diverse viewpoints undermines the faith that participatory democratic theorists have in citizens coming together to work on political problems in a constructive way.

KEY CONCEPTS

activated mass opinion / 189	normative threats / 174
authoritarians / 172	personality traits / 178
Big Five / 178	pluralistic roots / 171
egalitarianism / 185	pocketbook issues / 182
historical events / 188	self-interest / 182
individualism / 185	social movements / 188
libertarians / 172	sociotropic concerns / 182
moral traditionalism / 186	values / 184

SUGGESTED SOURCES FOR FURTHER READING

Adorno, T. W., Else Frenkel-Brunswik, Daniel J. Levinson, and R. Nevitt Sanford. *The Authoritarian Personality.* New York: Harper & Brothers, 1950.

Altemeyer, Bob. *Enemies of Freedom: Understanding Right-Wing Authoritarianism.* San Francisco: Jossey-Bass, 1988.

Stenner, Karen. *The Authoritarian Dynamic.* New York: Cambridge University Press, 2005.

Hetherington, Marc J., and Jonathan D. Weiler. *Authoritarianism and Polarization in American Politics.* New York: Cambridge University Press, 2009.

In these four books, the authors grapple with the concept of authoritarianism. Adorno and his colleagues argue that authoritarianism is a deeply rooted set of personality traits stemming from exposure to harsh child-rearing practices, whereas Altemeyer asserts that authoritarianism develops through social learning.

Stenner emphasizes that authoritarianism has a stronger effect on attitudes when citizens are faced with normative threats. Hetherington and Weiler argue that differences in levels of authoritarianism are a key reason why citizens disagree about the most vexing issues of our day.

Brewer, Paul R. *Value War: Public Opinion and the Politics of Gay Rights*. Lanham, MD: Rowman & Littlefield, 2008.

Feldman, Stanley. "Political Ideology." In *Oxford Handbook of Political Psychology*, 2nd ed., ed. Leonie Huddy, David O. Sears, and Jack S. Levy. Oxford: Oxford University Press, 2013.

Brewer uses a variety of methods (surveys, experiments, and content analysis) to examine how the public debate over gay rights has shaped citizens' attitudes. In particular, he highlights the importance of values in molding citizens' beliefs about gay rights. Feldman's chapter devotes significant attention to values as sources of ideology.

Mondak, Jeffery J. *Personality and the Foundations of Political Behavior*. Cambridge, UK: Cambridge University Press, 2010.

Caprara, Gian Vittorio, and Michele Vecchione. "Personality Approaches to Political Behavior." In *Oxford Handbook of Political Psychology*, 2nd ed., ed. Leonie Huddy, David O. Sears, and Jack S. Levy. Oxford: Oxford University Press, 2013.

Mondak thoroughly reviews the Big Five trait framework and explores the relationship between these traits and a variety of political attitudes and behaviors. In their chapter, Caprara and Vecchione discuss traits and authoritarianism as well as other personality characteristics that are related to political attitudes and behaviors.

Sears, David O., and Jack Citrin. *Tax Revolt: Something for Nothing in California*. Enlarged ed. Cambridge, MA: Harvard University Press, 1985.

Lau, Richard R., and Caroline Heldman. "Self-Interest, Symbolic Attitudes, and Support for Public Policy: A Multilevel Analysis." *Political Psychology* 30 (2009): 513–537.

Sears and Citrin's classic book examines citizens' opinions on taxes and government spending in California during the "tax revolt" of the late 1970s. The authors demonstrate that both self-interest and symbolic racism influenced support for the tax revolt. Lau and Heldman document the limited effects of self-interest on policy attitudes between 1972 and 2004.

SDA: Survey Documentation and Analysis, http://sda.berkeley.edu

This website allows you to easily analyze survey data from the American National Election Studies and the General Social Survey. Let's say you are interested in whether authoritarians were less likely than nonauthoritarians to vote for Barack Obama in 2012. You could conduct that analysis using the American National Election Study 2012, which is available in the SDA Archive. This example is just the tip of the iceberg. The SDA website allows you to do all kinds of fun and informative data analysis. Check it out.

CHAPTER 7

Pluralistic Roots of Public Opinion: The Central Role of Groups

THE ROOTS OF public opinion are best described as pluralistic.[1] Personality, self-interest, values, and historical events shape policy attitudes, as we discuss in Chapter 6. Groups also play a central role in opinion formation, which thrills pluralists because these theorists view groups as fundamental to political life in a democratic society.

Political scientists have paid particular attention to two ways in which groups influence public opinion. First, scholars have examined whether political attitudes vary by **group membership**. "Group membership refers to the assignment of an individual into a particular group based on characteristics that are specific to that group, in accordance with widely held intersubjective definitions."[2] In other words, group membership is based on ascription, that is, how others describe a person based on social norms and legal definitions, rather than on a person's identification with a group. Public opinion scholars have investigated the views of members of many different groups. For instance, researchers have examined and compared the attitudes of members of different racial groups.

The second way in which scholars have tackled the influence of groups on public opinion is by examining the impact of **attitudes toward groups** on citizens' issue opinions. Attitudes toward groups is a broad concept that includes citizens' *prejudice toward* and *stereotypes about* groups, as well as their *identification with* groups. These attitudes play an incredibly important role in shaping political views because many public policies can be thought of in terms of the groups that are affected by the policy.[3] Here are some examples: equal pay policy has clear implications for women; welfare policy has a direct effect on poor people; and Social Security policy has an impact on elderly people. In each of these instances, attitudes toward the groups involved drive opinion on these issues.[4] Scholars have dedicated significant effort to understanding how group attitudes influence policy opinions.

It is interesting, of course, to analyze how attitudes differ by *group membership*, and we do that in this chapter by examining the attitudes of different racial and ethnic groups and assessing gender differences in opinion. It is more enlightening, however, to understand *why* groups differ. To get a handle on that, it is important to consider *attitudes toward groups*. Black-white differences in public opinion, for example, can largely be explained by racial prejudice among some whites and high levels of group identity among blacks. Another example is gender differences in opinion, which can partially be explained by a feminist consciousness among some women. We discuss these examples in much greater detail next.

RACE AND PUBLIC OPINION

Race is an enduring cleavage among American citizens. As a result, racial groups often differ in their policy opinions and party preferences. Public opinion scholars have examined black-white differences in opinion, successfully identifying key factors, including racial prejudice and identity, that lead the two groups to diverge. Less is known about public opinion among Latinos and Asian Americans, although recent scholarship has begun to fill this gap in our knowledge.

Black-White Differences in Party Identification and Issue Opinions

In the United States, blacks and whites hold very different opinions, especially when it comes to party identification and racial issues. In the 1960s, the partisanship of blacks was heavily influenced by the national Democratic Party's support of the civil rights movement and the party's push for legislation to end discrimination against blacks. As a result, African Americans who came of age during the civil rights movement have the strongest identification with the Democrats. Younger cohorts of African Americans who were socialized after the civil rights movement have demonstrated a small yet significant move toward identification with the Republican Party.[5] Nevertheless, in 2012, an overwhelming majority of blacks continued to identify with the Democratic Party (see Figure 7.1). As we discuss in Chapter 6, the civil rights movement also influenced the party identification of some white citizens as they opposed the pro-equality position of the national Democratic Party and changed their allegiance to the Republican Party. In 2012, just 38 percent of whites identified with the Democratic Party.

In addition to party identification, blacks and whites also differ in their issue opinions, as you can see in Figure 7.1. Blacks are more supportive of social welfare programs than whites. In 2012, a majority of blacks favored more government services even if it meant an increase in spending, whereas only 25 percent of whites endorsed that position. There was a smaller, yet still meaningful, difference between blacks and whites on support for military spending; 32 percent of blacks favored increased defense spending, whereas 39 percent of whites held that view. Blacks and whites tend to differ a great deal when the issue domain is racial policies. For instance, 42 percent of blacks supported government efforts to improve the social and economic position of their group in 2012; only 11 percent of whites agreed that the government should make such efforts.

Figure 7.1   Black-White Differences in Party Identification and Issue Opinions, 2012

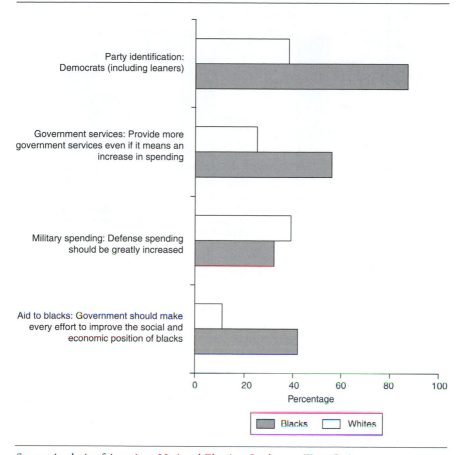

Source: Analysis of American National Election Study 2012 Time Series.

Notes: Respondents placed themselves on 7-point scales to answer these questions. The bars represent the percentage of respondents who placed themselves on the Democratic, more government services, more military spending, and more effort side of the scales.

What explains these black-white differences in issue opinions? A critical reason why blacks and whites disagree on racial and social welfare policies is because they hold different political values dear.[6] In particular, blacks are substantially more likely to endorse **egalitarianism** than whites (see Figure 7.2). For example, 85 percent of African Americans believe that society should take whatever steps are necessary to ensure equal opportunity, whereas 71 percent of whites support that view. There is an even larger racial gap—more than 20

Figure 7.2   Egalitarianism among Blacks and Whites, 2012

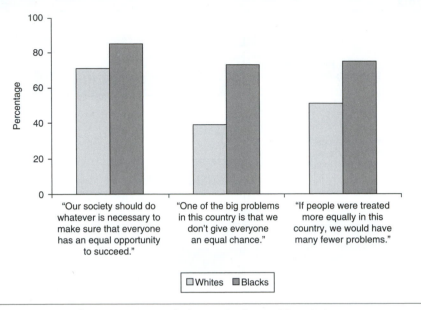

Source: Analysis of American National Election Study 2012 Time Series.

Note: Bars represent the percentage of respondents who indicated they "agree somewhat" or "agree strongly" with each statement.

percentage points—in agreement on the two statements that measure beliefs about how serious of a problem inequality is in the United States.

These racial differences in support for egalitarianism are extremely important because they translate into differences in policy opinions between blacks and whites. Greater egalitarianism among blacks leads them to be more supportive than whites of a wide variety of racial and social programs, including government programs that assist blacks as well as federal spending on education, aid for college students, the poor, the homeless, and the unemployed. Egalitarianism is a key factor that creates this racial gap in opinion, but other factors, such as racial prejudice among whites and racial identification among blacks, also help explain the divergent views between the two groups.[7] These are topics we discuss next.

White Racial Prejudice and Race-Targeted Policy Opinion

One of the most controversial areas of public opinion research is the study of racial prejudice and its impact on policy attitudes. Racial prejudice is a complex concept, and thus debates over its definition and measurement have raged for several decades. One school of thought among public opinion scholars is that racism is significantly different today from what it once was. Researchers from this camp argue that there is a distinction between old-fashioned racism and new racism. **Old-fashioned racism** is a set of beliefs about the innate inferiority of black Americans. These beliefs served as a justification for segregating blacks and whites. Old-fashioned racism led to separate blood supplies for blacks and whites, white fears of miscegenation, the segregation of public accommodations (such as restrooms, hotels, and restaurants), and legal discrimination against black Americans. Over time, these beliefs about black inferiority were discredited by scientific research (which is ironic because for many years "scientific" arguments were used to justify old-fashioned racism). Consequently, white citizens are much less likely to endorse old-fashioned racism these days than they did fifty years ago. For example, today 84 percent of white Americans say they approve of marriage between blacks and whites, whereas only 17 percent approved of interracial marriage in 1969.[8]

Although old-fashioned racism has decreased considerably, many scholars contend that a different, more subtle form of racial prejudice has emerged.[9] Donald Kinder and Lynn Sanders argue that a "new form of prejudice has come to prominence, one that is preoccupied with matters of moral character, informed by the virtues associated with the traditions of individualism. At its center are the contentions that blacks do not try hard enough to overcome the difficulties they face and that they take what they have not earned."[10] Kinder and Sanders label this new form of prejudice **racial resentment**.[11] Instead of blaming biological or genetic factors for black inferiority, as old-fashioned racism does, racial resentment blames a lack of work ethic for the continued inequality between blacks and whites in our society.

Kinder and Sanders make the case that racial resentment developed among whites in response to the success of the civil rights movement. As discriminatory laws were knocked down by the Supreme Court and Congress passed civil rights legislation, white Americans began to think that racial problems were solved. Yet five days after the 1965 Voting Rights Act was signed by President Lyndon B. Johnson, riots broke out in Watts, a South Central neighborhood in Los Angeles. The uprising went on for days, and other riots followed in major cities across the country over the next few years. This social disorder appalled Americans across the racial divide, but many blacks understood the uprisings as legitimate protests based on long-standing grievances, whereas many whites saw the riots as inexcusable criminal behavior. Many whites felt that blacks should be grateful for government efforts on their behalf and should take advantage of the opportunities now open to them rather than continuing to complain about discrimination.

Kinder and Sanders argue that racial resentment is fairly widespread among white citizens and that it has a strong influence on policy opinions dealing with race. Before we discuss the impact of racial resentment on policy attitudes, we need to review the way Kinder and Sanders measured racial resentment. They used four survey statements (included on the ANES) to tap into this concept (see Figure 7.3 for the wording of these survey items). Because racial resentment is a subtle form of prejudice, Kinder and Sanders asserted that a "roundabout" approach is the most appropriate way to measure the concept.[12] Thus, their survey statements did not require whites to agree that blacks are outright lazy or that blacks are simply hucksters trying to con white America into giving them something they don't deserve. No, nothing of the sort. Instead, the statements used subtle language to get whites to reveal their bias. And, indeed, many whites demonstrated racial resentment, according to Kinder and Sanders's research.

In 1986, for example, roughly 60 percent of whites endorsed racially resentful responses when asked whether (1) blacks should work their way up without special favors, (2) blacks should try harder to be as well off as whites, and (3) blacks have

Figure 7.3   Racial Resentment among Whites, 1986 and 2012

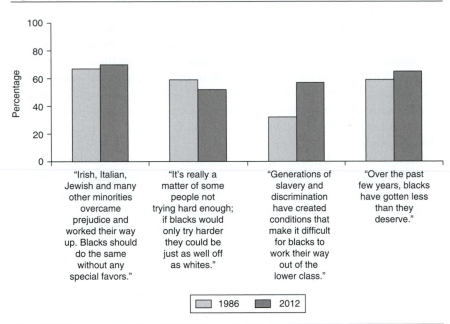

Sources: Donald R. Kinder and Lynn M. Sanders, *Divided by Color* (Chicago: University of Chicago Press, 1996), 107; analysis of American National Election Studies 2012 Time Series.

Note: Bars represent the percentage of white respondents who gave racially resentful responses. For the first two statements, the racially resentful response is agreeing "strongly" or "somewhat" with each statement. For the last two statements, the racially resentful response is disagreeing "strongly" or "somewhat" with each statement.

gotten less than they deserve (see Figure 7.3). The only question on which a majority of whites did not give the resentful response was with regard to the lingering effects of slavery and discrimination. Just over 30 percent were resentful on that question.[13]

Kinder and Sanders's data are from thirty years ago, so perhaps levels of racial resentment have decreased since the mid-1980s? That does not seem to be the case. Compared with 1986, survey data from the 2012 ANES show that white citizens were less resentful when asked whether blacks should try harder, yet were a bit more racially resentful when asked whether blacks have gotten less than they deserve and whether they should work their way up without special favors. The most striking difference is the increase in the percentage who *disagreed* that slavery and discrimination have created conditions making it difficult for blacks to succeed. On all four questions, a majority of white Americans provide racially resentful responses. Overall, it appears that racial resentment is as prevalent, if not more so, in recent years as it was in 1986. Indeed, some scholars argue that racial prejudice increased after President Obama took office in 2008.[14]

Let's turn to the impact of racial resentment on white citizens' attitudes toward race-targeted policies. **Race-targeted policies** are those designed to specifically aid black Americans, such as affirmative action and government steps to ensure fair treatment in employment. Kinder and Sanders analyzed the influence of racial resentment on race-targeted policy attitudes using ANES data from 1986, 1988, and 1992. They found that white citizens who were more racially resentful were more opposed to a variety of race-targeted policies. For example, racially resentful whites were significantly more likely to oppose affirmative action in college admissions and employment than whites who did not hold such attitudes.[15] The relationship held between racial resentment and policy opinions even though other important variables were taken into account, such as self-interest, individualism, egalitarianism, and demographic characteristics. More recent research confirms that racial resentment continues to shape citizens' attitudes toward race-targeted policies in contemporary times.[16]

Ultimately, it is not that surprising that attitudes toward blacks influence white citizens' opinions on race-targeted policies. Pluralists, in particular, would view this as entirely appropriate given the emphasis these theorists put on groups as the primary organizers of political life in the United States. Participatory democratic theorists, in contrast, would not be thrilled with the way in which *prejudicial* group attitudes drive the policy positions of whites. Because the participatory democratic theorists care a great deal about equality, they would be very concerned about the level of racial resentment among whites and the extent to which racial resentment influences white policy opinions. What is even more troubling to participatory democratic theorists is the power of racial prejudice to shape attitudes on policies beyond those directly tied to African Americans. We turn to research on that topic next.

Race-Neutral Policy Opinion or Race-Coded?

A distinction is often made between social policies that are race-targeted and social policies that are race-neutral. As we just discussed, race-targeted policies are ones that directly affect African Americans. In contrast, **race-neutral policies** are ones that affect citizens regardless of race. For example, government assistance to help blacks is a race-targeted policy, whereas government assistance to help poor people is a race-neutral policy. Research by Martin Gilens, however, leads us to consider another possibility—race-coded policies.[17] **Race-coded policies** are race-neutral, yet have become linked with black Americans in the minds of white citizens. Gilens argues that welfare is an example of such a policy.[18] Gilens maintains, "Although political elites typically use race-neutral language in discussing poverty and welfare, it is now widely believed that welfare is a 'race-coded' topic that evokes racial imagery and attitudes even when racial minorities are not explicitly mentioned."[19] Thus, because welfare is linked to race, Gilens hypothesizes that opposition to welfare policy among whites largely stems from their racial attitudes.

To test this hypothesis, Gilens analyzed data from the 1991 National Race and Politics Study, a national representative survey. To measure attitudes toward welfare spending, Gilens used this question: "Suppose you had a say in making up the federal budget, would you prefer to see more spent, less spent, or the same amount of money spent on welfare as it has been?"[20] To measure racial attitudes, Gilens focused on the stereotype that blacks are lazy. Specifically, Gilens asked respondents to assess the work ethic of blacks by indicating whether terms such as *lazy* and *hardworking* characterize the group. Gilens found that white citizens who endorsed the view of blacks as lazy and not hardworking were significantly more opposed to welfare spending than white citizens who rejected that stereotype. The relationship between racial stereotypes and welfare attitudes held even when Gilens took into account other variables that might influence welfare attitudes, such as perceptions of welfare recipients as undeserving, individualism, party identification, ideology, and demographic characteristics.[21]

How did a seemingly race-neutral issue like welfare become a race-coded issue? Gilens argues that news media coverage of poverty and welfare disproportionately focuses on black Americans, which leads to this linkage between race and poverty in the minds of white citizens.[22] To provide evidence to support this contention, Gilens analyzed newsmagazine stories on poverty between 1950 and 1992. He identified every poverty-related story in *Time*, *Newsweek*, and *U.S. News & World Report* during this period. Then, he examined every picture within the poverty stories. He coded whether the race of each poor person pictured was black, nonblack, or undeterminable; he also coded whether the topic of the poverty story was sympathetic (such as old-age assistance) or unsympathetic (such as the underclass, which refers to people who belong to the lowest socioeconomic class and who are often stereotyped as deviant).

Gilens found that whites were the dominant image of poverty in the 1950s and early 1960s. In 1965, however, the racial makeup of the poor in these magazine stories on poverty changed quite dramatically. The representation of blacks jumped from 27 percent of the poor in 1964 to 72 percent in 1967. From 1967 on, blacks tended to dominate the coverage of poverty, averaging 57 percent of the poor portrayed by these newsmagazines between 1967 and 1992. To illustrate the skewed nature of this media coverage, Gilens compared the true percentage of blacks among the poor (based on data from the U.S. Census Bureau) with the racial makeup of the poor depicted in the newsmagazines. In reality, blacks only made up about 29 percent of the poor during this period. Thus, the magazines' depiction essentially doubled the proportion of blacks among the poor. Gilens also found that the overrepresentation of blacks became even more extreme when unsympathetic topics were covered. For example, blacks made up 100 percent of the poor people pictured in stories on the underclass and 84 percent of the poor in stories on urban problems. In contrast, there were no blacks pictured in stories on old-age assistance and only about one-quarter of the poor were black in stories on hunger and medical care.[23]

Rosalee Clawson and her colleagues have updated and extended Gilens's study by examining the representation of poverty in five newsmagazines between 1993 and 2010.[24] They analyzed the same three magazines as Gilens, as well as two additional newsmagazines, the *New York Times Magazine* and *Business Week*. They found that blacks continued to be grossly overrepresented in pictures of the poor, making up over 50 percent of the magazine poor during this period. Bas van Doorn also demonstrates that Hispanics are underrepresented in newsmagazine pictures of poverty, a finding he attributes to the common stereotype that Hispanics have a stronger work ethic than other racial groups, whites included.[25] This enduring **racialization of poverty** in the news media helps us understand why stereotypes about the work ethic of blacks continued to shape citizens' welfare attitudes in the 1990s and 2000s.[26]

Even more problematic is a recent experimental study of how people evaluate applicants for welfare assistance. This research demonstrates that white applicants who are described as "excellent" workers are rewarded with much greater financial assistance than equivalent black applicants who are described that way.[27] At the same time, whites who are characterized as "poor" workers are penalized only a small amount, whereas blacks described that way are punished a great deal. The experimental subjects who held racially resentful attitudes were those most likely to allocate money to white applicants and withhold funds from black applicants. "In an age when some argue that we have moved beyond the importance of race, this article shows just how much race still colors Americans' beliefs about work ethic and the deserving poor. While some may be opposed to welfare spending on purely fiscal and race-neutral grounds, the average American still believes blacks deserve less than whites, all else equal."[28]

An issue that has recently become race-coded is health care policy, according to Michael Tesler.[29] Tesler argues that health care is now a racialized issue because it is linked with President Obama in the minds of American citizens, a phenomenon he refers to as the *spillover of racialization*.[30] Because President Obama is black, racialized considerations are activated in discussions of health care reform. As a result, racial prejudice shapes white citizens' views on health care policy proposals. Using survey data between 1988 and 2009, Tesler demonstrates that racial resentment became a powerful predictor of white opposition to health care reform *after* the policy became associated with President Obama. In fact, racial resentment came to trump other considerations, including party identification and ideology, in white citizens' thinking about Obamacare. Furthermore, Tesler argues that black attitudes toward health care policy were also shaped by President Obama's advocacy of the issue. He demonstrates that blacks supported President Obama's health care plan at double the rate of whites; around 80 percent of blacks approved compared with approximately 40 percent of whites. Of course it's not surprising that blacks favored health care reform more than whites given their greater Democratic leanings, but the size of the gap is staggering. In the early 1990s when President Bill Clinton, also a Democrat, was pushing health care reform, the difference between blacks and whites was substantial (around 26 percentage points), but not nearly as extreme as the Obamacare gap.[31]

Racial Attitudes of Young White Adults

Are young white Americans less prejudiced than older white Americans? Yes, young whites are less likely than older cohorts to endorse old-fashioned racism, as you can see in Table 7.1. Specifically, survey data from 2014 show that young whites are less likely to endorse the notion that blacks are unintelligent and less likely to think that blacks differ from whites due to inborn abilities. These views have nearly faded away for the youngest generation.

Young whites are also less likely than older citizens to endorse beliefs consistent with symbolic racism, a concept very similar to racial resentment. **Symbolic racism** refers to the beliefs that blacks do not work hard enough and that black disadvantage cannot be explained by racial discrimination. Unlike old-fashioned racism, however, symbolic racism has not faded away among the youngest cohort. Over 20 percent of young whites endorse the stereotype that blacks are lazy, and 41 percent believe that racial differences are due to a lack of motivation on the part of blacks. Over one-half deny the effect of discrimination on black-white differences. These views are more prevalent among middle-age and older citizens, but symbolic racism still finds plenty of adherents among young whites today.

Scott Blinder argues that this pattern of prejudice among young white people is the result of a two-tracked process of socialization.[32] On one track, children are explicitly taught about principles of equality by their parents, through the media, and in the school system. As a result, children learn to accept antiracist norms.

Table 7.1   White Support for Old-Fashioned Racism and Symbolic Racism by Age, 2014

Type of racism	18–29	30–49	50+
Old-fashioned racism			
Blacks are unintelligent	7%	12%	16%
Differences between blacks and whites due to inborn ability	4	6	9
Symbolic racism			
Blacks are lazy	22	28	33
Differences between blacks and whites are due to lack of black motivation	41	42	49
Differences between blacks and whites are *not* due to discrimination	56	73	73

Source: Analysis of General Social Survey 1972–2014 Cumulative Datafile.

On another track, children pick up implicit messages—also from their parents, the media, and the schools—about differences among racial groups. "For example, it is easy to imagine—or even recall from personal experience or observation—White American parents telling their children to treat everyone equally regardless of race but balking at the thought of passing through a so-called 'bad' neighborhood where Black people live."[33] Consequently, young whites no longer accept beliefs consistent with old-fashioned racism, yet some continue to endorse racial stereotypes consistent with symbolic racism.

Group Consciousness among Blacks

Attitudes toward groups also shape the opinions of minority citizens. Here the research has primarily focused on the effects of group consciousness on black public opinion.[34] **Group consciousness** refers to a politicized awareness of how membership in a particular group shapes the "lives and fortunes" of individuals.[35] Many scholars agree that group consciousness is made up of several components, including group identity and perceived discrimination.[36]

In separate research, two prominent scholars, Michael Dawson and Katherine Tate, provide insight into the critical role of racial group identity in shaping black public opinion. They demonstrated that **racial identity** is an important determinant of policy opinions. Blacks who have higher levels of racial identity, as measured by the extent to which they perceive their fate is directly tied to the fate of their race, are more likely to support social welfare policies and government programs to assist blacks. They are also more likely to favor the drawing of congressional districts in such a way that increases the likelihood a minority will be elected.[37]

Dawson refers to this belief that people's life chances are tied to the fate of their group as **linked fate**. He argues that blacks use information about how their racial group as a whole is faring to make sense of their own position in society. Therefore, blacks use racial group interests as a cue to determine their own issue opinions and party preferences. Dawson calls this phenomenon the **black utility heuristic** and argues that "as long as race remains dominant in determining the lives of individual blacks, it is 'rational' for African Americans to follow group cues in interpreting and acting in the political world."[38] Not all blacks agree, of course, that their fate is tied to their group, but most do think that is the case. In three national surveys of African Americans conducted in the 1980s and 1990s, roughly 80 percent agreed that "what happens generally to Black people in this country will have something to do with what happens" in their own lives. Further, in each survey, over 60 percent indicated that it will affect them "a lot" or "some."[39] National survey data from the early 2000s demonstrate the continuing importance of racial identity to African Americans. Fifty-four percent of African Americans said they feel "very close" to black people in the United States, and another 37 percent said they feel "fairly close."[40]

One question that arises with the study of group consciousness is whether minorities with high levels of consciousness are hostile toward whites. Some observers argue that race consciousness leads to separatism and a pursuit of divisive politics by minority citizens, whereas others argue that race consciousness is empowering to minorities and has very little to do with their attitudes toward whites. Mary Herring, Thomas Jankowski, and Ronald Brown put these contradictory propositions to the test by investigating the relationship between African Americans' racial identification and their attitudes toward whites.[41] Herring et al. analyzed the 1984 National Black Election Study (NBES), a national representative survey of black Americans. The NBES included a set of questions about racial identity and evaluations of whites. They examined several measures of racial identity and found little evidence to support the claim that high levels of racial identification are closely associated with hostility toward whites. For example, Herring et al. demonstrated that there was no relationship between blacks feeling close to their racial group and the belief that whites keep blacks down.

Melanye Price argues that to understand differences of opinion *within* the black community, political scientists need to move beyond studies of linked fate.[42] She views linked fate as essentially a constant and therefore argues the concept does little to explain why blacks differ on a range of policies. Using focus groups conducted in Columbus, Ohio, and national survey data, she explores **black nationalism**. Black nationalism is best defined as an identity based on adherence to four principles: support for black self-determination; support for black economic and social independence in the form of self-help programs; distance from whites and white supremacy; and support for a global black community (also see

Dawson's definition of black nationalism in Chapter 5).[43] Only a minority of blacks fully endorse black nationalism. Those who do, however, hold more negative feelings toward white Americans than those who reject the identity. Price argues that many black Americans endorse certain tenets of black nationalism, such as self-help, yet they don't only blame whites and systemic discrimination for their group's economic and social situation. In focus group conversations, statements of black blame are often intermingled with a discussion of obstacles faced by black Americans. Price argues that as long as blacks continue to face discrimination and inequality, black nationalism has the potential to be a potent political force. Similarly, other scholars show that black citizens who have felt discrimination against themselves because of their race are more likely to identify as blacks first rather than Americans first.[44]

In sum, black-white differences in public opinion are quite large. Blacks overwhelmingly identify with the Democratic Party, whereas whites tend to lean Republican; blacks also hold more liberal issue positions than whites. Racial differences in egalitarianism help explain these divergent views, as does racial prejudice among whites and racial identity among blacks. Racial resentment and racial stereotypes are robust and enduring predictors of white public opinion on race-targeted and race-coded issues. A sense of linked fate with their racial group drives the policy positions of black Americans, although the concept cannot fully explain intragroup differences.

Latino Public Opinion

Scholarship on race and public opinion has primarily focused on blacks and whites, constructing a dichotomous political world that largely ignores other minority groups. This is highly problematic because Latinos are increasingly influential in national politics and they constitute the largest minority group in the United States.[45] Latinos now make up 17 percent of the U.S. population.[46] In recent years, national surveys of Latinos have provided insight into their political attitudes.

The first question to answer with regard to Latinos is whether it even makes sense to talk about them as a coherent political group. Latinos in the United States may have arrived yesterday, or their families may have been here since long before the United States was the United States. Latinos come from more than twenty different national origin groups, with individuals of Mexican, Puerto Rican, Cuban, Dominican, and Salvadoran descent making up the largest proportion of Latinos in the United States. Many speak Spanish, others are bilingual, and some are primarily English speakers.[47] Despite this variety, national public opinion surveys suggest that Latinos do have a shared, although certainly not uniform, view of the political world. In the 2006 Latino National Survey, respondents were asked in separate questions about the degree to which they identified with (1) their country of origin and (2) Latinos. Eighty-five percent of respondents said they "very strongly" or "somewhat strongly" identified with their nation of origin, and

88 percent said the same about Latinos. Thus, Latinos certainly feel tied to their own national origin group, but the vast majority also have a sense of identification with a broad ethnic group, a **pan-ethnic identity**. In addition, many respondents indicated their fate was linked to other Latinos. Seventy-eight percent of respondents said that what happens generally to Latinos will have at least a little effect on their lives, with 63 percent saying it will affect them "some" or "a lot."[48] Note that these levels of *linked fate* among Latinos are quite similar to the levels among black Americans.

One of the most interesting patterns of public opinion among Latinos is their strong support for government social programs, even though they lean toward a moderate or even conservative ideological identification.[49] For example, large majorities of Latinos favor government spending on education, health care, and government services generally, and these are the issues that a majority of Latinos deem as extremely important to them personally.[50] Latinos tend to support affirmative action policies more than whites, although not to the same extent as black Americans.

Immigration is another important issue to Latinos. In 2014, 66 percent of Latino voters said that passing new immigration legislation soon was extremely or very important to them.[51] Latinos are more favorable toward immigrants than non-Latinos, and they "prefer immigration reforms that take into account the integration and stabilization of the lives of undocumented immigrants."[52] For example, 86 percent of Latinos indicate that a path to citizenship should be most important or as important as border security when dealing with illegal immigration; only 10 percent of Latinos thought that border security should be the top priority. In contrast, 64 percent of the general population prioritized a path to citizenship as the most important or as important as border security with 33 percent saying that border security comes first. Deportations from the United States are at a record high in recent years, and about one-quarter of Latinos say they know someone who has been deported or detained in the last twelve months. As a result, Latinos have significant concerns about deportation policy. Fifty-six percent say that it is more important for undocumented immigrants in the United States to be able to live and work in the country without the threat of deportation than to have a pathway to citizenship.[53] Latino voters who know someone who is an undocumented immigrant or someone who has been deported or detained are more likely to say that immigration is an important issue that should be addressed by Congress and the president.[54] Given the growing importance of Latino voters, immigration issues are likely to be front and center during the 2016 presidential election.

On immigration, the economy, and foreign policy, Latinos say that Democrats will do a better job than Republicans dealing with the issue.[55] Furthermore, Latinos identify with the Democratic Party more than the Republican Party (see Table 7.2). A notable exception is Cubans, who have historically leaned Republican, although that is less true today.[56] At the same time, more than 40 percent of

Table 7.2   Latino and Asian American Party Identification

Party identification	Latinos (2014)	Asian Americans (2012)
Republicans (including leaners)	25%	18%
Democrats (including leaners)	58	35
Independents	15	25
Nonidentifiers	2	22

Sources: Latino data from Mark Hugo Lopez, Ana Gonzalez-Barrera, and Jens Manuel Krogstad, "Latino Support for Democrats Falls, but Democratic Advantage Remains: Immigration Not a Deal-Breaker Issue for Half of Latino Voters," Pew Hispanic Center, Washington, DC, October 29, 2014, http://www.pewhispanic.org/files/2014/10/2014-10-29_NSL-latino-politics.pdf. Asian American data from the 2012 Asian American and Pacific Islander Post-Election Survey, http://www.naasurvey.com/resources/Presentations/2012-aapipes-national.pdf

Latinos identify themselves as conservative, which is a higher rate of conservatism than among whites. It's also strikingly more conservative than African Americans, with whom Latinos share many similarities in issue opinions. Public opinion scholars explain this disconnect partially by pointing to Latinos' greater conservatism on social issues such as abortion and gay rights, but researchers also think that political socialization plays a role. Latinos adopt this mix of liberal issue opinions and conservative ideological leanings because others in their community hold a similar combination of views.

Asian American Public Opinion

Asian Americans are another fast-growing group in the United States. They make up a relatively small proportion of the U.S. population (roughly 6 percent), but their concentration in particular geographical areas makes them a powerful political group in certain counties and states.[57] Moreover, Asian Americans are becoming increasingly dispersed, which means their potential for influence across the nation is growing.[58] Like Latinos, Asian Americans are a diverse group. Some are recent immigrants; others are in families who have been in the United States for generations. Asian Americans come from many different national origin groups, ranging from China and Japan to India and Pakistan. Unlike Latinos, who primarily speak Spanish or English, Asian Americans speak a wide range of languages.

Do Asian Americans form a cohesive political group and have political attitudes in common? The evidence is somewhat mixed based on recent surveys. In 2008, slightly less than a majority of Asian Americans agreed that what happens generally to other Asians in the United States affects what happens in their own lives.[59] That is a lower level of *linked fate* than African Americans and Latinos have with their groups. Furthermore, Asian Americans were divided when it came to abortion. Yet Asian Americans overwhelmingly agreed that the U.S. government should end the war in Iraq and provide universal health care. In 2012, two-thirds supported tax increases on the wealthy to reduce the federal deficit and considered themselves environmentalists.[60]

In 2012, 58 percent of Asian Americans favored a path to citizenship for undocumented immigrants.[61] In 2008, only about one-third of Asian Americans held that position. This shift toward a more liberal position on immigration may continue as some leaders in the Republican Party speak about Asian immigrants in derogatory terms. In 2015, for instance, during the Republican presidential nomination process, candidate Jeb Bush said that Asian people were coming to the United States to have "anchor babies" to gain U.S. citizenship for their children. In response, Michael Kwan, a leader of an Asian American advocacy organization, said, "Jeb Bush and other political candidates who embrace such demeaning labels should understand that the majority of Asian Americans will not support you with either our votes or our dollars when you espouse rhetoric which dehumanizes and degrades us."[62] Perhaps not surprisingly, Asian Americans prefer the Democratic Party over the Republican Party (see Table 7.2).[63]

Particularly noteworthy about Asian Americans' partisanship is the large proportion of people who did not identify with either party in the 2012 Asian American and Pacific Islander Post-Election Survey. Twenty-five percent of Asian Americans identified as Independents, and another 22 percent did not identify with either major party or as Independents. Instead, many respondents, especially Asian-language respondents, indicated they did not think in terms of political parties at all. This suggests there is room for either party to speak to the concerns of Asian Americans and pull them into their partisan fold. The party leaders who realize this and conduct language-targeted and culturally sophisticated outreach efforts will reap the benefits of support from this fast-growing group.[64] Overall, the current picture of Asian Americans is of a political group that shares many important political attitudes while exhibiting intragroup differences as well.

GENDER AND PUBLIC OPINION

Do women and men differ in their political attitudes? The quick answer is, it depends. On some issues, women and men consistently differ, but on other issues, gender has little effect on opinions. When women and men do differ, those differences are often fairly small, especially compared to differences in opinion based on membership in other groups such as racial groups. In this section, we examine the effects of gender on public opinion and discuss explanations for why women and men differ in some instances but not in others.

Gender Differences in Party Identification and Issue Opinions

Since the early 1980s, there has been a modest but consistent **gender gap in party identification**, with women leaning more Democratic than men.[65] As you can see in Figure 7.4, the difference between women and men was 5 percentage points in 2012.

Figure 7.4   Gender Differences in Party Identification and Issue Opinions, 2012

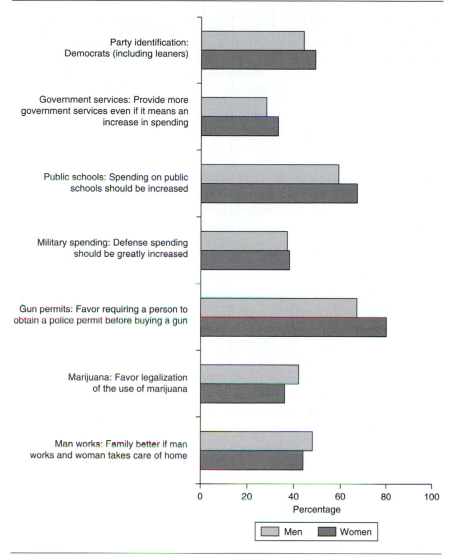

Sources: Data for Party identification, Government services, Public schools, Military spending, Marijuana, and Man works are from analysis of American National Election Study 2012 Time Series. Data for Gun permits are from *GSS Cumulative Datafile* 1972–2014—*Quick Tables,* SDA: Survey Documentation and Analysis, http://sda.berkeley.edu/archive.htm

Notes: Respondents placed themselves on 7-point scales for the Party identification, Government services, Military spending, and Man works questions. The bars represent

(Continued)

Figure 7.4 (Continued)

the percentage of respondents who placed themselves on the Democratic, more-spending, and family-better-if-man-works side of the scales. For Public schools, respondents were asked whether federal spending on schools should be increased, decreased, or kept the same. The bars represent the percentage of respondents who favored more spending. For Marijuana, respondents were asked whether they favor or oppose the use of marijuana being legal. The bars represent the percentage of respondents who favored legalization. For Gun permits, respondents were asked whether they favor or oppose a law requiring people to obtain gun permits before buying a gun. The bars represent the percentage of respondents who favored gun permits.

That is not a huge difference, and it is dwarfed when compared to the partisan difference between blacks and whites (refer to Figure 7.1). Nevertheless, the difference between men and women is meaningful, particularly when we consider the impact that party identification has on vote choice. In fact, since the 1980s, women have regularly voted for Democratic presidential and congressional candidates at higher rates than men.[66]

In terms of policy opinions, women and men tend to differ on what political scientists call compassion issues.[67] **Compassion issues** are social welfare policies that help others, including programs to aid children, the elderly, the homeless, and the poor. Generally women are several percentage points more likely to support these policies than men.[68] In Figure 7.4, for example, we see that 33 percent of women favored more government services in 2012, even if it meant an increase in spending, whereas only 28 percent of men agreed with that position. When it comes to increasing government spending for schools, 67 percent of women wanted more money spent on public education compared to 59 percent of men, an 8 percentage point gap. There tend to be even larger differences between women and men on **use-of-force issues**.[69] Women are more opposed to war than men, and they are less supportive of the death penalty. Women are also more likely to support gun control measures. In 2012, for instance, 80 percent of women favored requiring a person to obtain a police permit before buying a gun, whereas 67 percent of men supported that position. Historically women have been less supportive of military spending than men, although in 2012 the level of support was nearly even (see Figure 7.4). Men's support of defense spending is the lowest this century, bringing them in line with the views of women.

A new use-of-force issue on which remarkably large gender differences have emerged is drone strikes. In a 2013 Pew Research Center survey, 53 percent of women approved of U.S. drone strikes, whereas 70 percent of men did so. This large gap between women and men in the United States is mirrored in countries around the world. What is different globally, however, is that a majority of citizens in most countries surveyed by the Pew Research Center oppose U.S. drone strikes. The United States is one of only three countries where a majority of citizens approve U.S. drone strikes. The other two countries are Israel and Kenya. In most countries, drone strikes are "widely unpopular," and even more so among women.[70]

On compassion issues and use of force, women tend to take more liberal positions than men, but on at least some **moral issues**, women are more conservative than men.[71] Women are more supportive of government restrictions on pornography, more supportive of prayer in school, and more opposed to marijuana legalization than men. In 2012, for example, 36 percent of women favored legalizing the use of marijuana, whereas 42 percent of men supported legalization (see Figure 7.4).

Although these gender gaps in public opinion are certainly worth noting, we should not overstate the differences between women and men. Women and men overlap in their views much more than they diverge.[72] Also, gender differences are not constant over time, and subgroups of women (based on race, class, age, religion, marital status, or sexual orientation) often vary in their attitudes as much as, if not more than, women and men. For instance, the party identification of white women looks *much more similar* to white men than it does to black women. Further, when it comes to **women's issues** on which we might think gender differences would be quite large, men's and women's opinions tend to be fairly similar. An examination of abortion attitudes over time, for example, shows that roughly 10 percent to 15 percent of both women and men believe abortion should never be permitted.[73] In Figure 7.4, we see a 4 percentage point difference between men and women on whether they think it is better for the family as a whole if the man works outside the home and the woman takes care of the home and family.

Why is it that men and women differ on compassion, use-of-force issues, and moral issues? Scholars have provided a variety of explanations for these gender differences.[74] First, girls and boys are *socialized* differently. Anyone who has ever walked into a store and looked at children's toys knows that gender norms are heavily enforced still today. Girls are encouraged to play with dolls and dress up like princesses, whereas boys are encouraged to play with balls and fight with lightsabers. Gendered socialization practices in childhood may result in differences between men and women in adulthood. Girls are taught to be caring and nurturing, which may translate into greater support for compassion issues among women; boys are taught to be competitive and aggressive, which may evolve into greater support for the use of force among men.

A second explanation for gender differences in public opinion emphasizes that women and men often play different *roles in society* and have different *economic interests*. Women are expected to be caregivers for children and other family members, and they are more likely to work in low-paying service-sector jobs than men. As a result, women are in poverty and make use of social welfare programs at higher rates than men. All this may lead women to be more supportive of social welfare policies than men. Further, women's caregiver roles may make them more concerned about protecting their families from moral decay, which may lead to their greater conservatism on moral issues.

A third explanation for gender differences focuses on how a *feminist consciousness* may shape citizens' political attitudes, especially party identification. The Democratic Party has been the party of women's rights for over three decades now, which leads feminists to identify as Democrats more than Republicans.[75] A feminist consciousness can also shape women's (but not men's) attitudes toward war.[76] For example, feminist women are less opposed to war when the stakes are humanitarian than when military action is taken for economic reasons.

Overall, these three factors—socialization, roles and interests, and a feminist consciousness—help explain the gender gaps in public opinion. Much more research is needed, however, to fully understand the differences *and* similarities between women and men. Finally, it is important to note that, although gender differences in public opinion tend to be fairly modest, they can still have a big impact because women make up more than half of the U.S. population and they turn out to vote at higher rates than men.

Public Opinion in Comparative Perspective
BOX 7.1 THE CROSS-NATIONAL GENDER GAP ON USE-OF-FORCE ISSUES

Is the gender gap on use-of-force issues unique to the United States, or is it a broader political phenomenon? To answer that question, we turn to recent research by Richard Eichenberg and Blair Read.[1] Analyzing surveys conducted in twenty-nine countries in 2013, Eichenberg and Read find that men are consistently more supportive of war than women. For example, in every country men are more likely than women to agree that "under some conditions war is necessary to obtain justice." The size of the difference between men and women, however, varies across countries. In Belgium and Sweden, men and women are more than 20 percentage points apart, whereas they only differ by 4 percentage points in China, Romania, and Turkey.

In addition, Eichenberg and Read examined gender differences in support for military action in Libya in fourteen democratic nations, including twelve European countries as well as the United States and Turkey. They found that men were at least 5 percentage points more supportive of military attacks on the Gaddafi regime in 2011 than women. Turkey was the lone exception where men and women were comparable in their low level of support for military action in Libya.

Gender Gap in Approval for Military Action in Libya, 2011

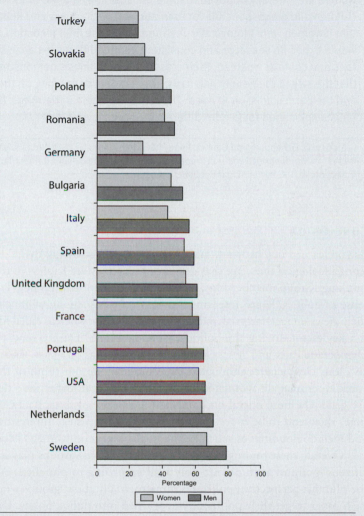

Source: Adapted from Table 1 of Richard C. Eichenberg and Blair M. Read, "Gender Difference in Attitudes towards Global Issues" in *Handbook of Gender in World Politics*, eds. Jill Steans and Daniela Tape (Cheltenham, UK: Edward Elgar Publishers, 2015).
Note: Bars represent the percentage of respondents who support military action.

(Continued)

BOX 7.1 (Continued)

Some observers have argued that women are less supportive of war and violence than men due to biology. This *essentialist* view states that women are naturally opposed to force because they are the ones who bear children and are responsible for their survival. Eichenberg and Read argue that if women were biologically destined to oppose military action, then we would expect to see large and consistent gender differences across countries and contexts. Instead, their cross-national analysis demonstrates that the size of the gender gap varies a great deal depending on the country and the particular issue at hand. Thus, their research undermines the essentialist explanation for gender differences in public opinion.

1. Richard C. Eichenberg and Blair M. Read, "Gender Difference in Attitudes towards Global Issues" in *Handbook of Gender in World Politics*, eds. Jill Steans and Daniela Tape (Cheltenham, UK: Edward Elgar Publishers, 2015).

CONCLUSION

As you learned in Chapter 5, many citizens do not structure their issue attitudes along ideological lines. Yet that does not mean they are hapless in their political thinking. Group memberships, attachments, and antipathies help citizens make sense of politics. Racial resentment and stereotypes among white citizens shape their views on race-targeted and race-coded policies, whereas racial identification is a key factor driving the political views of blacks. Latinos tend to prefer the Democratic Party and generally take liberal positions on issues. Asian Americans also lean Democratic, although a large minority do not think of themselves in partisan terms at all. Women identify as Democrats at higher rates than men and are generally more liberal on compassion and use-of-force issues. At the same time, they tend to be more conservative on moral issues. Interestingly, women and men do not differ as much as one might expect on women's issues.

Overall, these findings about the central role that groups play in organizing citizens' political attitudes are not at all surprising to pluralists. According to the pluralist perspective, politics is fundamentally about groups wrangling with each other to get their points of view turned into public policy. Debate, competition, and compromise among groups are what make a democracy function. Factors other than groups, such as personality, values, historical events, and self-interest, also shape citizens' attitudes, but group attitudes constitute the most profound root of public opinion. In addition to the groups discussed in this chapter, we reinforced this conclusion with our discussion of party identification in Chapter 5.

Whereas pluralists are delighted with the critical role of groups in U.S. politics, participatory democrats are more ambivalent. On the one hand, public opinion differences based on group membership and group attitudes confirm participatory democratic theorists' views that citizens are able to organize their opinions in a meaningful way. Reliance on group cues, such as the black utility heuristic, provides a reasonable means by which citizens can navigate the political world. On the other hand, group-based thinking results in powerful stereotypes and prejudice shaping some white citizens' views on key political issues, a situation that is not compatible with participatory democratic theorists' desire for greater equality among citizens.

KEY CONCEPTS

attitudes toward groups / 193

black nationalism / 204

black utility heuristic / 204

compassion issues / 210

egalitarianism / 195

gender gap in party identification / 208

group consciousness / 203

group membership / 193

linked fate / 204

moral issues / 211

old-fashioned racism / 197

pan-ethnic identity / 206

race-coded policies / 200

race-neutral policies / 200

race-targeted policies / 199

racial identity / 203

racial resentment / 197

racialization of poverty / 201

symbolic racism / 202

use-of-force issues / 210

women's issues / 211

SUGGESTED SOURCES FOR FURTHER READING

Barreto, Matt, and Gary M. Segura. *Latino America: How America's Most Dynamic Population Is Poised to Transform the Politics of the Nation.* New York: Public Affairs, 2014.

Masuoka, Natalie, and Jane Junn. *The Politics of Belonging: Race, Public Opinion, and Immigration.* Chicago: University of Chicago Press, 2013.

Wong, Janelle, S. Karthick Ramakrishnan, Taeku Lee, and Jane Junn. *Asian American Political Participation: Emerging Constituents and Their Political Identities.* New York: Russell Sage Foundation, 2011.

These books provide a thorough examination of Asian American and Latino political behavior.

Dawson, Michael. *Behind the Mule: Race and Class in African-American Politics.* Princeton, NJ: Princeton University Press, 1994.

In this classic book, Dawson argues that many black Americans see their own interests as closely tied to the interests of their racial group because of historical and current experiences with discrimination. Thus, blacks feel a sense of linked fate with other black citizens, which influences their policy positions (even when taking into account class differences).

Huddy, Leonie, Eric Cassese, and Mary-Kate Lizotte, "Gender, Public Opinion, and Political Reasoning." In *Political Women and American Democracy*, ed. Christina Wolbrecht, Karen Beckwith, and Lisa Baldez. Cambridge, UK: Cambridge University Press, 2008.

The authors provide an excellent discussion of gender differences in public opinion, emphasizing that the differences are modest yet politically important.

Nelson, Thomas E., and Donald R. Kinder. "Issue Frames and Group-Centrism in American Public Opinion." *Journal of Politics* 58 (1996): 1055–1078.

In this classic article, Nelson and Kinder use a series of experiments to show that group attitudes have a stronger effect on policy opinion when issues are framed in such a way that highlights the beneficiaries of the policy.

Shapiro, Robert Y., and Lawrence R. Jacobs. *The Oxford Handbook of American Public Opinion and the Media*. Oxford: Oxford University Press, 2011.

This handbook includes relevant chapters on groups and public opinion that are worth reading.

Walsh, Katherine Cramer. *Talking about Race*. Chicago: University of Chicago Press, 2007.

In this innovative study, Walsh uses participant observation to analyze how citizens talk about racial issues while participating in community programs designed to foster dialogue among citizens from different racial groups.

Politics, Groups, and Identities

Politics, Groups, and Identities is the official journal of the Western Political Science Association. It presents the best scholarship on social groups, exploring the politics of gender, race, ethnicity, religion, sexuality, class, and other dimensions of identity and structural disadvantage.

Project Implicit, www.implicit.harvard.edu

This is a fascinating website on which you can complete tasks to assess whether you have hidden biases. The Implicit Association Test was developed by social scientists as a way to measure implicit attitudes, that is, those attitudes that people are either unable or unwilling to report in a survey.

AAPI DATA, www.aapidata.com

This website provides extensive data on Asian American and Pacific Islander politics and public opinion.

Latino Decisions, www.latinodecisions.com

This website provides "everything Latino politics." It is the go-to website for data on Latino public opinion.

PART IV

Do Citizens Endorse and Demonstrate Democratic Basics?

CERTAIN FEATURES OF a democratic society place expectations on the citizenry. Popular sovereignty, for example, puts some decision making in the hands of the citizens. To exercise this duty, must democratic citizens be knowledgeable about and attentive to politics? A democratic society also guarantees a number of freedoms for citizens, such as freedom of speech and religion, and ensures that citizens are equal before the law. These are known as civil liberties and civil rights, respectively. In a democracy, however, how important is it for citizens to support civil liberties and civil rights?

Not surprisingly, the answers to these two questions differ depending on which type of democratic theorist is responding. The normative debates over these key democratic basics (knowledge, interest, attentiveness, support for civil liberties, and support for civil rights) are profiled in this section. In the chapters that follow, we also pay particular attention to whether citizens endorse these democratic basics in the abstract and demonstrate them in practice.

CHAPTER 8

Knowledge, Interest, and Attention to Politics

DO YOU KNOW how many of the nine U.S. Supreme Court justices are women? Do you know which political party controls the U.S. Senate? Do you know with which country the United States recently re-established diplomatic relations? If you are like two-thirds of Americans, you do not know that three women serve on the Supreme Court as of 2015. It is likely that many of you do not know that the Republican Party holds more seats in the U.S. Senate than the Democratic Party; only about half of Americans know that. You probably identified Cuba as the country with which the United States recently re-established diplomatic relations given that about three-quarters of citizens are aware of that fact. Notably, 84 percent of men answer the "Cuba" question correctly, whereas only 68 percent of women do so. Such a gender gap in knowledge is not unusual, although note that men and women are just as likely to know how many women serve on the Court.[1] See Table 8.1 to learn more about what citizens do and do not know about politics, according to a Pew Research Center poll conducted in March 2015.

Political scientists often define **political knowledge** as "the range of factual information about politics that is stored in long-term memory."[2] Does it matter that many citizens are not highly knowledgeable about key political figures and facts? Participatory democratic theorists say yes. "Political information is to democratic politics what money is to economics: it is the currency of citizenship."[3] Thus, without knowledge, citizens cannot function effectively. From this perspective, democracy *requires* informed citizens, as well as interested and attentive ones.

Other scholars argue that citizens can make reasonable decisions without being knowledgeable about or particularly interested in and attentive to politics. Citizens can use informational shortcuts, such as cues from individuals or groups they trust, to form their political opinions.[4] Because many of the cues citizens rely on come from elites, this perspective is in line with the thinking of elite democratic theorists. A more extreme position taken by some elite democratic theorists is that citizen ignorance actually allows democracies to flourish.[5] Clearly, elite

Table 8.1   Political Knowledge in Pictures, Words, Maps, and Graphs, March 2015

"Here are some questions about people and things that have been in the news. Please answer the questions as best as you can. If you don't know the answer to a question, just move on to the next one. We will reveal the correct answers at the end of the survey."

What the public does and does not know	Answered correctly	Answered incorrectly	Don't know/ refused to answer
Name this person (photo)? (Martin Luther King, Jr.)	91%	6%	3%
Need to indicate health insurance coverage on? (Taxes)	84	10	6
Leader of what country (Kim Jong-un photo)? (North Korea)	82	14	4
Where is Guantanamo located? (Cuba, from map)	78	13	9
U.S. re-established relations with? (Cuba)	76	18	6
Route of Keystone XL pipeline? (map of route)	73	17	10
Unemployment rate '06–'15? (chart of trend)	72	17	12
Who is Malala Yousafzai (photo)? (2014 Nobel Prize winner)	63	23	14
Senate party balance? (from set of four charts)	52	37	11
Pope Francis is from? (Argentina, from map)	52	36	11
Elizabeth Warren? (from set of four photos)	51	31	18
Number of women U.S. Supreme Court Justices? (three)	33	57	10

Source: "What the Public Knows—In Pictures, Words, Maps and Graphs, Pew Research Center News IQ Quiz," Pew Research Center, Washington, DC, April 28, 2015, http://www.people-press.org/2015/04/28/what-the-public-knows-in-pictures-words-maps-and-graphs

Note: Correct answers are in parentheses.

democratic theorists and participatory democratic theorists have very different views on how engaged the public should be.

In this chapter, we discuss the competing visions of elite democratic theorists and participatory democratic theorists regarding levels of citizen knowledge, interest, and attention to politics. Next, we examine how knowledgeable citizens actually are about politics. As with so many concepts, there is controversy over how to measure political knowledge; we discuss that debate. Then we turn to an analysis of why some citizens are more knowledgeable than others. We consider the effect of individual characteristics and political context on knowledge. We also examine the consequences of political knowledge and ignorance. Finally, we discuss how interested citizens are in politics and whether some individuals might best be considered bystanders to democracy. We conclude the chapter by considering whether citizens are knowledgeable enough, interested enough, and attentive enough to function effectively in a democracy.

HOW KNOWLEDGEABLE, INTERESTED, AND ATTENTIVE SHOULD CITIZENS BE IN A DEMOCRACY?

Democratic theorists debate about how much knowledge, interest, and attention to politics is necessary for citizens to function effectively in a democracy.[6] Participatory democratic theorists argue that citizens should have high levels of knowledge and be actively engaged in the political world so they can hold elites accountable. Citizens should be well informed so they can (1) figure out their interests, (2) recognize which policies serve those interests, and (3) identify which political parties, interest groups, and politicians are pursuing those policies. These theorists argue that citizens need to be on the ball because elites may try to misrepresent the facts or may not even know the facts to begin with.

Participatory democratic theorists assume that all citizens have the ability to understand what is going on in the political arena. Thus, if citizens are *not* knowledgeable, interested, and attentive, there must be barriers that keep citizens from engaging. For example, participatory democratic theorists might point to the shortcomings of the media as an obstacle to citizens acquiring the knowledge they need to successfully evaluate elite behavior.

Elite democrats, on the other hand, are not particularly concerned about levels of citizen knowledge, interest, and attention to politics. In fact, some scholars argue that it is *irrational* for citizens to spend time on politics.[7] Why is that the case? First, there are substantial costs to acquiring information about politics. It takes significant time for citizens to arm themselves with the knowledge necessary to form opinions, evaluate policy proposals, and understand the political process. Staying informed also requires financial resources. Buying newspapers or traveling to public meetings, for example, entails a monetary commitment on behalf of citizens. Second, citizens can expect very little in return for becoming knowledgeable. The voice of a citizen would be just one of many; thus, it is extremely unlikely that a single person could influence the adoption of a particular policy or the outcome of an election. If citizens were assured a payoff from becoming informed, it would be rational for them to invest in gathering information. But because that is not the case, it does not make sense for them to spend time and money becoming knowledgeable. In the words of acclaimed rational choice theorist Anthony Downs, "In general, it is irrational to be politically well-informed because the low returns from data simply do not justify their cost in time and other scarce resources."[8]

Even though it is irrational to become knowledgeable about politics, citizens can still function in a democracy because they can rely on cues in their environment to make reasonable political judgments.[9] Citizens can use **heuristics** (shortcuts), such as party identification and ideology, to figure out where they stand on issues. They can take cues from trusted groups and individuals to determine which politicians best represent their interests. Scholars refer to this as **low-information rationality**. From this perspective, citizens can get by with fairly minimal levels of knowledge. As long as they know enough to take cues from political parties, interest groups, and other elites, citizens can function effectively. Note that taking cues from interest groups is consistent with the pluralist vision of a democratic society.

Other scholars emphasize that citizens use heuristics not because it is irrational to become informed but because it is *impossible* for citizens to become fully informed. The political world is extremely complex, and citizens are **limited information processors**. They simply do not have the cognitive abilities to systematically process the vast amounts of political information out there. Instead, they rely on whatever shortcuts are available to simplify complex material and thus function efficiently, if not always accurately.[10] Indeed, a recent study found that inaccurate heuristics are particularly problematic for those who are most informed. The most informed are typically able to make the best use of heuristics due to their preexisting knowledge. For example, well-informed citizens know the party identification of various politicians and can therefore use that information to predict their votes on issues. But relying on that heuristic can lead the most informed astray *when a representative votes against his party.*[11]

Hard-core elite democrats make a different argument about citizen knowledge, interest, and attention to politics. They believe that democratic nations are actually better off when citizens are apathetic and ignorant. From this perspective, elites do the heavy lifting, and citizen engagement would just complicate matters. These theorists remind us that many features of the U.S. government, such as the Electoral College and the Supreme Court, were specifically intended to keep citizens at bay. Moreover, because the institutions of government were designed to check and balance each other, it is not necessary for citizens to hold elites accountable. Some citizens might be political junkies, but most people are not interested in, and many are even turned off by, the conflict and compromise that are part and parcel of democratic decision making.[12] And that's a good thing according to some elite democratic theorists.

Are Citizens Knowledgeable about Politics?

"Nothing strikes the student of public opinion and democracy more forcefully than the paucity of information most people possess about politics."[13] In this section, we discuss the empirical evidence that speaks to this claim. Is it the case that citizens are uninformed about politics? Also, are citizens misinformed about politics? Have citizens become more or less knowledgeable over time?

Are Citizens Informed or Uninformed?

As we have briefly discussed in the introduction to this chapter, citizens are not deeply informed about politics. Only about one-half of citizens can identify Senator Elizabeth Warren from a set of four photos, and even fewer know the number of women Supreme Court justices (refer back to Table 8.1). Yet over 90 percent of Americans recognize a photo of Martin Luther King Jr., and 84 percent know that citizens need to indicate on their taxes whether they have health insurance. Seventy-three percent can identify the route of the Keystone XL pipeline on a map, which suggests that political knowledge is not simply a function of *ability* and *motivation* but also of *opportunity*. The Keystone XL pipeline is a controversial issue that has received significant news coverage in recent years. Overall, the Pew Research Center poll results presented in Table 8.1 show that citizens are well informed about certain political facts but that there are also gaping holes in citizens' knowledge.

To delve further into this topic, we turn to the classic research of Michael X. Delli Carpini and Scott Keeter, whose work established the definition of political knowledge as "the range of factual information about politics that is stored in long-term memory."[14] To be knowledgeable about politics, Delli Carpini and Keeter argue citizens should be well informed in three areas: (1) the rules of the game, (2) the substance of politics, and (3) the people and players (including parties and groups).[15] To assess citizen knowledge in these areas, Delli Carpini and Keeter pulled together fifty-four years of national survey data. They examined numerous polls conducted between 1940 and 1994, which included over 2,000 questions regarding factual knowledge of politics.

Overall, Delli Carpini and Keeter found a mixed bag when it comes to levels of citizen knowledge.[16] On the one hand, citizens clearly did not live up to the standards set by participatory democratic theorists. "Only 13 percent of the more than 2,000 questions examined could be answered correctly by 75 percent or more of those asked, and only 41 percent could be answered correctly by more than half the public."[17] Furthermore, many citizens did not even know enough to use heuristics. For example, bare majorities of the public could identify party positions on key issues. Thus, for those who didn't know party positions, it would be impossible to use party as a cue. On the other hand, citizens were not as ignorant of politics as suggested by some observers. Most citizens were aware of some basic facts, such as the length of a presidential term (96 percent), the name of their governor (86 percent), that there is no religious test for political candidates (81 percent), that Cuba is a communist country (82 percent), and that Social Security does not provide job training (89 percent).

Citizens did best at answering questions about the **rules of the game**. This is probably due to the fact that the institutions and processes of politics rarely change over time. Further, this is the type of knowledge citizens are exposed to in high school civics classes. Turn to Table 8.2 for some examples of what citizens knew and didn't know. In 1985 virtually everyone knew that the United States was a member of the United Nations, but in 1989 hardly anyone could name two Fifth Amendment rights. Before you make fun of the public, can you name two Fifth Amendment rights?

Table 8.2   Examples of Political Knowledge and Ignorance, 1940–1994

Knowledge of	Answered correctly
Rules of the game	
U.S. is a member of the UN (1985)	96%
Accused are presumed innocent (1983)	50
Name all three branches of government (1952)	19
Name two Fifth Amendment Rights (1989)	2
Substance of domestic politics	
What is the steel dispute about (1952)	96
What is greenhouse effect (1988)	50
What is Watergate about (1972)	22
Percentage of population that is black (1990)	8
Substance of foreign affairs	
Ozone damage affects whole world (1988)	94
Black South Africans can't vote (1985)	51
Number of U.S. soldiers killed in Vietnam (1965)	17
Describe Glasnost (1987)	11
People and players	
U.S. president (1986)	99
Andrew Young (1977)	48
Republican party stance: pro-life amendment (1980)	21
President of Mexico (1991)	3

Source: Michael X. Delli Carpini and Scott Keeter, *What Americans Know about Politics and Why It Matters* (New Haven: Yale University Press, 1996). Copyright © 1996 by Yale University.

Citizens were a bit less knowledgeable when it came to the **substance of politics** and the **people and players**. Again, Table 8.2 contains several examples. Citizens were well informed about the steel dispute back in 1952 but shockingly uninformed about Watergate in 1972. In terms of foreign affairs, only about one-half of the public knew that black South Africans could not vote in 1985, and a mere 11 percent could describe Glasnost—a Soviet policy of openness—in 1987. Basically everyone could identify Ronald Reagan as president in 1986, but only 3 percent could name the president of Mexico in 1991.

Are Citizens Misinformed?

James Kuklinski, Paul Quirk, Jennifer Jerit, David Schwieder, and Robert Rich make an important distinction among people who are **informed**, **uninformed**, and **misinformed**.[18] They explain the differences this way:

> To be *in*formed requires, first, that people have factual beliefs, and second, that the beliefs be accurate. If people do not hold factual beliefs at all, they are merely *un*informed. They are, with respect to the particular matter, in the dark. But if they firmly hold beliefs that happen to be wrong, they are *mis*informed—not just in the dark, but wrongheaded.[19]

Using survey data from a representative sample of Illinois residents, Kuklinski et al. demonstrated that citizens were largely misinformed about welfare policy.[20] For example, citizens were asked what percentage of the federal budget is spent on welfare. The survey used a multiple-choice format and provided the following options: 1 percent, 5 percent, 8 percent, 11 percent, or 15 percent. The correct answer is 1 percent, but a whopping 90 percent of the respondents selected one of the other options. Although citizens were the most misinformed about this fact, more than a majority of citizens demonstrated they were "not just in the dark, but wrongheaded" on five other questions regarding welfare. Furthermore, when asked how confident they were of their answers, a majority of citizens said they were very or fairly confident about their responses. Thus, many citizens were not just wrong, they were quite confident in their wrongheadedness.

In general, citizens tended to be misinformed in an antiwelfare direction. For example, believing that a much higher percentage of the budget is spent on welfare than actually is would probably make people less supportive of welfare. Indeed, Kuklinski et al. found that misinformation led people to be more opposed to welfare spending than they otherwise would be. Because Kuklinski et al.'s survey respondents were from Illinois, the authors were careful not to generalize their findings to American citizens in general. Nevertheless, their research raises significant concerns about the public's ability to understand and evaluate important public policies.

In an important study of misperceptions regarding the war in Iraq, Steven Kull, Clay Ramsay, and Evan Lewis found that many citizens were confused about facts pertaining to the war.[21] These scholars collected survey data from a random sample of 1,362 respondents between June and September 2003. They were interested in whether citizens had misperceptions about the war and whether citizens receiving news from particular sources were more likely to hold those misperceptions. Kull, Ramsay, and Lewis crafted three questions to measure misperceptions:

> Is it your impression that the US has or has not found clear evidence in Iraq that Saddam Hussein was working closely with the al Qaeda terrorist organization?

> Since the war with Iraq ended, is it your impression that the US has or has not found Iraqi weapons of mass destruction? (Note that the end of the war wording here refers to the end of major combat operations, as declared by President George W. Bush in May 2003.)

> Thinking about how all the people in the world feel about the US having gone to war with Iraq, do you think: The majority of people favor the US having gone to war; The majority of people oppose the US having gone to war; or Views are evenly balanced.[22]

Because the United States did not find a clear link between Saddam Hussein and al-Qaeda or weapons of mass destruction in Iraq (despite occasional Bush administration statements implying otherwise), answering "has" to the first two questions were coded as misperceptions. Saying world opinion favored the war in response to the third question was also coded as a misperception because public opinion polls showed that most people around the world opposed the war. Kull et al. found that 60 percent of Americans held one or more of these misperceptions about the war.

Next, Kull et al. examined whether citizens' levels of misperceptions varied with their news source. Indeed, they found stark differences in beliefs about the war based on where citizens tended to get their news (see Figure 8.1). Viewers of Fox News were particularly likely to believe one or more of the misperceptions. More than a majority of CBS, ABC, CNN, and NBC viewers held one or more of these misperceptions; slightly less than a majority of print media users were confused about the facts. Three-fourths of the NPR and PBS audience did not hold any misperceptions. The relative accuracy of the NPR and PBS audience demonstrates the importance of noncommercial outlets in a media environment dominated by conglomerates.

What makes the high level of misperceptions among the public particularly troublesome is that the more misperceptions citizens held, the more they

Figure 8.1   Misperceptions by News Source

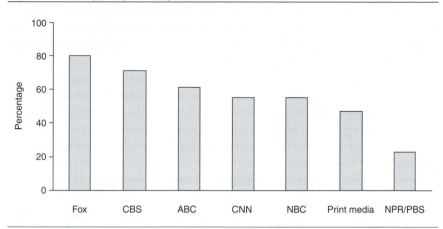

Source: Data from Steven Kull, Clay Ramsay, and Evan Lewis, "Misperceptions, the Media, and the Iraq War," *Political Science Quarterly* 118 (2003–2004): 582.

Note: Bars represent the percentage of people holding at least one misperception about the Iraq War by primary news source.

supported the war in Iraq. For example, only 23 percent of citizens who had no misperceptions supported the war, whereas 86 percent of those with three misperceptions supported it. Importantly, this relationship held even when taking into account citizens' party identification and intention to vote for President Bush. Kull et al. did not demonstrate that the news sources *caused* the misperceptions or that the misperceptions *caused* support for the war. Nevertheless, the associations between news sources and misperceptions and between misperceptions and support for the war raise serious questions about the sources, extent, and effect of misinformation in a democratic society.

Clay Ramsay and his colleagues conducted a similar survey of citizens' misperceptions shortly after the 2010 midterm elections.[23] The survey included eleven questions asking about citizens' knowledge of issues debated during the campaign, such as the recently enacted health care reform law, climate change, campaign contributions by the U.S. Chamber of Commerce, and President Barack Obama's place of birth. Many citizens were misinformed on these issues. Take Obama's place of birth, for example. Fifty-six percent of citizens knew that Obama was born in the United States, but 27 percent said it was not clear whether he was born in the United States and another 15 percent said he was not born in the United States. This is a striking level of ignorance about the president of the United States. Citizens were also quite ill-informed when it came to perceptions of expert opinion. When asked about economists' views of the health care reform law on the federal budget deficit, only 13 percent of citizens knew that more economists estimated the act would not increase the deficit over the next ten years. Citizens were more knowledgeable about expert opinion on climate change, but still 45 percent incorrectly believed that scientists were evenly divided or that most did not think that climate change is occurring.

The average level of misperception-holding was higher in 2010 than in the 2003 study of misperceptions about Iraq for all news sources.[24] "Consumers of all sources of media evidenced substantial misinformation, suggesting that false or misleading information is widespread in the general information environment."[25] In most cases, citizens with more exposure to news sources were better informed; however, those who watched Fox News almost daily were significantly more likely to be misinformed on several topics than those who never watched it. To illustrate, 63 percent of daily Fox News viewers did not know that President Obama was born in the United States, compared with 32 percent of citizens who never watched Fox News.[26] In general, citizens were most likely to be well-informed if they got their news from NPR and PBS or MSNBC, although a majority of their audiences incorrectly believed that the U.S. Chamber of Commerce was spending foreign money to back Republican candidates.

In a recent study, Josh Pasek, Gaurav Sood, and Jon Krosnick expressed concerns about misperceptions of the Affordable Care Act (ACA), i.e., Obamacare.[27] Using an online survey, they asked a nationally representative sample of Americans to identify whether a list of eighteen provisions were or were not included in the ACA. Twelve of the provisions truly were in the ACA, and six were not. They also asked respondents to indicate how sure they were in their judgment. Similar to Kuklinski et al., they argue that it is important to make the distinction between (1) simply being incorrect and unsure and (2) being *incorrect and certain* about that belief. They found that many Americans were unsure about aspects of the ACA. For example, slightly less than one-half of respondents correctly identified that the ACA required companies that sell health insurance to pay new fees to the federal government each year, and most of the people who answered incorrectly indicated they felt unsure about their response. What made Pasek, Sood, and Krosnick concerned was that some people were incorrect and certain on a set of items about which opponents of the law had spread false information. For example, 53 percent of Americans incorrectly believed that the ACA required doctors and hospitals to treat illegal immigrants free of charge if they cannot afford to pay. Of those 53 percent, 18 percent held that incorrect view with certainty. In addition, the scholars examined knowledge of the ACA in 2010 and 2012 and found that such misperceptions were prevalent at both times. The good news is that "where correct information was widely disseminated, respondents increasingly held correct beliefs with confidence."[28]

Have Levels of Political Knowledge Changed over Time?

To examine whether citizens have become more knowledgeable over time, Delli Carpini and Keeter collected national survey data from randomly selected respondents in 1989. Their survey included political knowledge questions matching those asked on surveys from the 1940s and 1950s. Thus, Delli Carpini and Keeter were able to compare levels of political knowledge across time. Before we turn to their results, let's discuss why we might expect citizens to be more informed in 1989 than fifty years earlier as well as why we might expect citizens to be less informed.

There are certainly reasons to believe that citizens would be significantly more informed in 1989.[29] First, citizens' ability to understand politics should have increased because levels of formal education have risen dramatically over the years. Second, citizens' motivation to understand politics should have increased because the government has become significantly "bigger" over the last few decades. Both domestically and on the world stage, the U.S. government plays a much larger role today than it did in the 1940s. Thus, citizens should be more concerned with all the ways the government affects their daily lives and how U.S. power is wielded around the world. Third, citizens should have more of an opportunity to learn about politics given the huge leaps in communication that have occurred since the 1940s.

But let's not get too far ahead of ourselves. There are also reasons to suspect that citizens would be less knowledgeable in 1989 than in the 1940s.[30] Although levels of formal education have increased, that does not necessarily mean a corresponding increase in civics education. Moreover, some observers have lamented the low quality of education in today's schools. More students may be graduating, but with fewer skills and knowledge than once was the case. As for motivation, it may be that a larger and more visible government turns citizens off rather than encouraging engagement. And certainly changes in communication technology provide citizens greater access to news, but they also provide greater access to entertainment that draws attention away from the politics of the day.

So there are arguments in both directions regarding whether citizens should be more knowledgeable in 1989 than several decades ago, but ultimately this is an empirical question. By comparing levels of knowledge in 1989 to roughly fifty years earlier, Delli Carpini and Keeter found that "the level of public knowledge has remained remarkably stable."[31] For example, over 90 percent of the public knew that a presidential term lasts four years, and roughly two-thirds of citizens knew which party controlled the House in both 1947 and 1989. There were some questions on which people demonstrated significant increases or decreases in knowledge, but many of these changes seem understandable given varying patterns of media coverage and elite emphasis over time.

More than twenty years have passed since Delli Carpini and Keeter conducted their 1989 study, and during that time the Internet revolution has occurred, providing citizens with unprecedented access to information. With a few keystrokes on the computer or a smartphone in hand, citizens can hunt down political information at the drop of a hat. Have citizens become more knowledgeable as a result? Perhaps Delli Carpini and Keeter's conclusions about the stability of political knowledge are **timebound**.

We turn to survey data collected by the Pew Research Center to address this issue. Pew conducted knowledge surveys in 1989 and 2007 that included nine identical or comparable questions.[32] The Pew data do not show that citizens have become markedly more knowledgeable in recent years; instead, citizens were more knowledgeable about some topics in 2007 but less informed about others (see Table 8.3). Citizens were less likely to correctly name the vice president, their state's governor, the president of Russia, and an administration official involved in a scandal (Scooter Libby in 2007, who was in the midst of a trial for perjury

Table 8.3   Political Knowledge, 1989–2007

Political knowledge	1989	2007	Difference
Percentage who could correctly name:			
The vice president	74%	69%	−5
Their state's governor	74	66	−8
The president of Russia[a]	47	36	−11
Percentage who knew:			
U.S. has a trade deficit	81	68	−13
The party controlling the House	68	76	+8
The chief justice is conservative	30	37	+7
Percentage who could correctly identify:			
Tom Foley/Nancy Pelosi	14	49	+35
Richard Cheney/Robert Gates	13	21	+8
John Poindexter[b]/Scooter Libby	60	29	−31

Source: "Public Knowledge of Current Affairs Little Changed by News and Information Revolutions," Pew Research Center, Washington, DC (April, 2007), http://www.people-press.org/2007/04/15/public-knowledge-of-current-affairs-little-changed-by-news-and-information-revolutions/

[a] Data in first column from 1994.
[b] Data in first column from 1990.

and obstruction of justice in a case involving the outing of a CIA agent, and John Poindexter in 1990, who was in the midst of a trial for involvement in the Iran-Contra scandal). They were also less likely to know the United States has a trade deficit. On the upside, the public was more aware of which party controlled the House and the ideology of the chief justice. They were also more likely to identify the Speaker of the House and the secretary of defense. Overall, the Pew surveys suggest citizens have not become more knowledgeable as a result of technological changes making information easier to access. Therefore, it seems that Delli Carpini and Keeter's research findings are not timebound; levels of citizen knowledge have stayed roughly the same from the 1940s until the present.

MEASURING POLITICAL KNOWLEDGE

When it comes to measuring political knowledge, a key question is whether citizens are generalists or specialists. A **generalist** would be knowledgeable across all political topics. In contrast, a **specialist** would have knowledge on some topics but not others. For example, a specialist might be well informed about foreign affairs but pay little attention to domestic politics.

If it is the case that people specialize, then measuring political knowledge would be quite difficult. It would require lots of survey questions covering a wide range of political topics. Survey researchers would need to include multiple questions on the substance of domestic and foreign policy, rules of the game (both domestic and foreign), and people and players (again both domestic and foreign). If, on the other hand, citizens are generalists, then a relatively small set of survey questions would provide a valid and reliable measure of political knowledge.

Delli Carpini and Keeter analyzed a variety of survey data to determine whether citizens are generalists or specialists.[33] They found that citizens can best be characterized as generalists.[34] In other words, the same person who can name the president of Russia also tends to know which party controls the House, who declares war, what a recession is, and whether the United States has a trade deficit. Likewise, a person who does *not* know the Russian president doesn't know other political facts either. As a result, Delli Carpini and Keeter argued it is possible to successfully measure political knowledge using a small set of items. Based on their extensive analyses, they recommended using five questions to measure political knowledge.[35] Those items, as well as the introduction they suggested, are presented in Table 8.4.

There are two noteworthy exceptions to the argument that citizens are generalists. First, Delli Carpini and Keeter's research shows that some people specialize in state or local politics.[36] These citizens are knowledgeable about political events and issues in their states or in their local communities but are not as aware of national politics. Consequently, Delli Carpini and Keeter's measure of political knowledge may classify some people who are highly informed about state and local politics as ill informed. Thus, their measure is not a good indicator of state

Table 8.4   Measuring Political Knowledge

"Last, here are a few questions about the government in Washington. Many people don't know the answers to these questions, so if there are some you don't know just tell me and we'll go on."

"Do you happen to know what job or political office is now held by [insert name of current vice president]?"

"Whose responsibility is it to determine if a law is constitutional or not . . . is it the president, the Congress, or the Supreme Court?"

"How much of a majority is required for the U.S. Senate and House to override a presidential veto?"

"Do you happen to know which party had the most members in the House of Representatives in Washington before the election this/last month?"

"Would you say that one of the parties is more conservative than the other at the national level? Which party is more conservative?"

Source: Michael X. Delli Carpini and Scott Keeter, *What Americans Know about Politics and Why It Matters* (New Haven, CT: Yale University Press, 1996), 305–306.

and local political knowledge; instead, it assesses *"national political competence* rather than *citizen competence."*[37]

Second, some people may specialize in knowing about issues and people particularly pertinent to them or groups to which they belong. Delli Carpini and Keeter's research, for example, shows that blacks have lower levels of political knowledge than nonblacks, in general, but are just as knowledgeable on race-related issues.[38] Similarly, in a 2007 poll, the Pew Research Center found that blacks identified then-senator Barack Obama and then–secretary of state Condoleezza Rice at the same level as whites but that blacks were less informed than whites in other areas.[39] A study conducted a few months after the al-Qaeda attacks on the World Trade Center and the Pentagon showed that citizens living in the Northeast were more knowledgeable about the events of 9/11 than people living in other parts of the country but not better informed about politics in general.[40] Overall, then, the research demonstrates that some citizens have domain-specific knowledge in areas that are particularly important to them.

Delli Carpini and Keeter's method of measuring political knowledge has greatly influenced how political scientists study the concept. Not all scholars agree, however, that their conceptualization and measurement are the best. Indeed, research conducted by Kathleen Dolan raises concerns about Delli Carpini and Keeter's narrow definition of politics and the gender differences in knowledge that result from that limited understanding of politics.[41] In addition, several scholars have demonstrated that levels of citizen knowledge are underestimated by the open-ended type of questions recommended by Delli Carpini and Keeter.[42] Yet another scholar, Doris Graber, argues that Delli Carpini and Keeter's emphasis on factual knowledge measured through surveys is misplaced.[43] We discuss these critiques next.

Gender-Relevant Domains of Knowledge

Noting that many studies have documented that men are more knowledgeable about politics than women, Kathleen Dolan argues that scholars should broaden their conceptualization of political knowledge to include "gender relevant domains of knowledge."[44] Delli Carpini and Keeter's understanding of politics emphasizes electoral politics and the institutions of government, but those are not the aspects of politics most important to women. Women are more likely to be interested in government programs, women's issues, and female leaders. Therefore, questions that measure knowledge about these topics should be included on surveys, which would reduce, if not reverse, the **gender gap in political knowledge**.[45]

To test this proposition, Dolan conducted an online survey of a random sample of 1,039 adults. The survey included several items designed to measure gender-relevant knowledge, including asking respondents the name of the Speaker of the House (who was a woman at the time), the name of any woman serving in the U.S. Congress, the number of women Supreme Court justices, and the percentage of women serving in Congress. For comparison purposes, the survey also included one traditional political knowledge item that asked respondents which party held a majority in the U.S. House of Representatives. In Table 8.5, we see that women were significantly less informed about who controlled the House but comparable to men in terms of naming Nancy Pelosi as House Speaker, naming

Table 8.5 Traditional and Gender-Relevant Political Knowledge

	Answered correctly	
	Women	*Men*
Traditional political knowledge		
Majority in House	**58%**	**68%**
Gender-relevant political knowledge		
Speaker of House	39	39
Woman member of Congress	51	54
Women on Supreme Court	43	47
Percentage women in Congress	**34**	**28**

Source: Adapted from Table 1 of Kathleen Dolan, "Do Women and Men Know Different Things? Measuring Gender Differences in Political Knowledge," *Journal of Politics* 73 (2011), 102.

Note: The boldface percentages indicate statistically significant gender differences.

a woman House member, and knowing how many women were on the Supreme Court. Further, the gender gap was reversed when it came to knowing the percentage of women serving in Congress. Women members made up 16 percent of Congress at the time, so Dolan coded any answer between 15 and 20 percent as correct. Women were significantly more likely than men to answer correctly, whereas men were more likely than women to underestimate the presence of women in Congress. Dolan's point that survey researchers should conceptualize and measure political knowledge in a way that represents the experiences of men and women is well taken; nevertheless, even with gender-relevant items included, the conclusion is still that political knowledge among the American public is modest at best and woefully low at worst.

Public Opinion in Comparative Perspective
Box 8.1 Gender and Political Knowledge in Canada

Canadian political scientists have also raised concerns about traditional measures of political knowledge. Similar to Kathleen Dolan, Dietlind Stolle and Elisabeth Gidengil argue that the conventional conceptualization and measurement of knowledge are too narrow because of the focus on electoral politics and government institutions.[1] They prefer a broader measure that assesses citizens' knowledge of government programs and services. Such knowledge is practical and useful; it helps citizens "know how to access welfare and other government services that are essential to their own well-being and that of their families."[2] This knowledge is especially critical for women, who use government services at a higher rate, are more likely to have jobs in the public sector, and support welfare state policies more than men.

Because this information is so relevant to women, Stolle and Gidengil argue that women are as knowledgeable as men, if not more informed, about important government services and benefits. Thus, the typical gender gap in knowledge will disappear when a wider range of questions is used to measure political knowledge. To investigate this issue, Stolle and Gidengil conducted a survey of Canadian citizens living in Montreal and Toronto. The survey included traditional questions about key political leaders and political parties, but it also included questions measuring knowledge of several government programs, such as legal aid, the availability of free health-screening tests, and where to turn if someone knew of a child being abused.

Stolle and Gidengil found that men and women were comparable in their knowledge of high-profile political leaders, such as the prime minister, but

	Answered correctly	
	Women	*Men*
Traditional political knowledge		
Prime minister	91%	92%
Party forming official opposition	**56**	**73**
Female cabinet minister	**38**	**44**
Knowledge of government programs		
Legal aid	83	81
Health-screening tests	**76**	**50**
Child abuse	**68**	**62**

Source: Dietlind Stolle and Elisabeth Gidengil, "What Do Women Really Know? A Gendered Analysis of Varieties of Political Knowledge," *Perspectives on Politics* 8 (2010): 99.

Note: The boldface percentages indicate statistically significant gender differences.

that women tended to be less knowledgeable than men on the other measures of conventional political knowledge. In sharp contrast, women generally outperformed men when it came to knowledge of government services and benefits. For example, women were much more likely to know about free health-screening tests available through their health care plans than men.

Stolle and Gidengil acknowledge that knowledge of conventional politics is important but argue quite persuasively that practical knowledge is also essential in democratic societies. Thus, they recommend including questions that measure both types of information on surveys assessing political knowledge.

1. Dietlind Stolle and Elisabeth Gidengil, "What Do Women Really Know? A Gendered Analysis of Varieties of Political Knowledge," *Perspectives on Politics* 8 (2010): 93–109.
2. Ibid., 94.

Recall versus Recognition

Another concern with the measurement of political knowledge is the use of **short-answer questions**.[46] People are more likely to say "don't know" to these questions than to **multiple-choice questions**. People who are semiconfident may not be willing to toss out an answer with a short-answer question but will articulate a response once they hear the option mentioned in a multiple-choice format. Further, multiple-choice questions may jog people's memories, allowing them to recognize the correct answer.

Table 8.6 presents survey data from the Pew Research Center that illustrate the differences between short-answer and multiple-choice questions.[47] Note the data presented here are not from a split-half survey in which respondents were randomly assigned to receive one type of question or another. Instead, they are drawn from two national representative surveys, one conducted in February and the other in March 2007. Thus, it could be the case that factors other than the question format affected levels of political knowledge. We should be cautious in interpreting these results; nevertheless, the data suggest that format matters. On both items, citizens appear more knowledgeable with a multiple-choice question. And notice the dramatic difference on the question about the president of Russia—citizens go from being fairly ignorant to fairly well informed with the switch in format.

Table 8.6   The Perils of Measuring Political Knowledge: Short-Answer versus Multiple-Choice Questions

	Short-answer format February 1–13, 2007	Multiple-choice format March 9–12, 2007
	"Can you tell me who Robert Gates is?"	"Is Robert Gates the U.S. Secretary of Defense? A senator from Michigan? The chairman of General Motors? Or is he something else?"
U.S. secretary of defense	21%	37%
Anything else/don't know/refused	79	63
	"Can you tell me the name of the president of Russia?"	"Can you tell me who is the president of Russia? Is it Boris Yeltsin? Vladimir Putin? Mikhail Gorbachev? Or is it someone else?"
Vladimir Putin	36%	60%
Anything else/don't know/refused	64	40

Source: "Public Knowledge of Current Affairs Little Changed by News and Information Revolutions," Pew Research Center, Washington, DC, April 15, 2007, 23–33, http://people-press.org/2007/04/15/public-knowledge-of-current-affairs-little-changed-by-news-and-information-revolutions

Too Much Emphasis on Factual Knowledge?

Doris Graber raises an even more fundamental concern with Delli Carpini and Keeter's measure of political knowledge.[48] She argues that political scientists should focus on what citizens *need to know* to function in a democracy rather than emphasizing "precisely remembered factual knowledge about historically important past and current events."[49] Why? Because citizens are *limited information processors*. Graber reviews research by communication scholars, psychologists, biologists, and neuroscientists and concludes that it is simply not possible for citizens to remember every little detail about politics because our brains are not designed to do so. Moreover, our brains are not set up to quickly recall political knowledge in the context of a survey.[50]

This does not mean, however, that citizens are clueless about politics. Instead, they pay attention to issues that are relevant to them. People are interested in understanding the impact of political events on their lives and on the well-being of the country, not on memorizing the names of politicians or constitutional rights. Citizens want *useful* information, not factoids. Graber argues, for example, "There may be areas of knowledge where the poor, trained in the school of hard knocks, may excel. But scores of streetwise knowledge are not usually gathered and reported."[51] To substantiate her claims, Graber analyzed transcripts of nine **focus groups** conducted in the Chicago area.[52] The ninety-eight focus group participants ranged from suburban voters to city voters to young people to homeless people. The focus groups began with the moderator asking, "What are the issues that are most important to you in your community, however you define that? What would you tell an elected official?"[53] Graber coded for whether participants' responses were "simple," such as statements of fact or description, or "complex," such as statements that showed understanding of a variety of perspectives and drew connections among different ideas.

Here is an example of a black voter discussing economic problems using complex statements: "I would like to hear a political person say that one of the viable alternatives to crime in our neighborhoods is really lobbying for minimum wage standards . . . not just talking about minimum wage but how do we get people who have smaller stores to expand and employ more people. . . . How do we talk to Sears about having part-time staff with no benefits?"[54] Overall, Graber found that people often made complex statements or a mix of complex and simple statements when talking about political topics. Simple statements dominated the discussion in only 18 percent of the issue areas discussed by the focus groups.

Graber admits these people would not score well on Delli Carpini and Keeter's measure of political knowledge, but she does not expect them to given the inherent limitations of the brain. Instead, Graber argues that the focus group participants "possess reasonably sophisticated, politically useful knowledge about current problems that confront them and that the issue areas covered by this knowledge are generally quite well suited to carrying out the actual tasks of citizenship that most Americans perform."[55] Participatory democratic theorists would prefer, of course, that American citizens perform a wider variety of citizenship tasks than they currently perform and thus would argue that citizens need substantially greater political information than what Graber thinks is necessary.

WHY ARE SOME CITIZENS MORE KNOWLEDGEABLE THAN OTHERS?

In this section, we turn our attention to understanding why some citizens are more informed than other citizens. Citizens vary in political knowledge based on their abilities, motivations, and the opportunities available. We begin with a discussion of the relationship between demographic characteristics and political knowledge. Next we examine the role of motivation. Then we turn to a discussion of contextual factors that affect political knowledge.

Demographic Groups and Political Knowledge

Several studies have demonstrated substantial differences in political knowledge across demographic groups.[56] We have already discussed the gender gap in political knowledge at some length and mentioned the **racial gap in political knowledge** on issues that are not race related. It is also important to mention that these gender and racial gaps extend to young people. A study of students at six middle schools in Maricopa County, Arizona, showed that white adolescents were significantly more knowledgeable about politics than African American, Latino, and Native American adolescents.[57] Further, a national representative survey of high school seniors demonstrated that boys have slightly more civics knowledge than girls and that whites have substantially more civics knowledge than Hispanics and African Americans.[58]

Levels of political knowledge also differ across age groups. In general, older folks are better informed than younger ones. This appears to be due to both life cycle and generational effects. As people progress through the life cycle, they are simply exposed to more political information. Older citizens have experiences, such as buying a house and paying property taxes, that younger people are less likely to have. These experiences result in an increase in political knowledge. Also, older people were raised in a more politically engaged era than today's young people. Accordingly, this early socialization put the older generation on a track to pay attention to, and thus be knowledgeable about, politics throughout their lives.

Income and education also matter. Wealthy citizens are better informed than their poorer counterparts. Similarly, citizens with higher educations are substantially more knowledgeable than those with a minimal education, especially when it comes to rules of the game and people and players.[59] Education is critical, of course, because it improves citizens' cognitive abilities to learn about politics. But it also boosts interest in politics, which motivates citizens to become more knowledgeable. In addition, education affects the opportunities citizens have to become informed; formal education allows people to obtain jobs in which politics matter on a regular basis (such as lawyers, business executives, and political science professors) and places people in social networks that value political knowledge. Indeed, "formal education is the single most important factor differentiating those who know more about politics from those who know less. Citizens who spend more years in school simply know a lot more about politics."[60]

In Table 8.7, we illustrate demographic differences in political knowledge by examining citizens' familiarity with the party makeup of the U.S. Senate. The March 2015 poll conducted by the Pew Research Center asked respondents to identify the chart (from four choices) that showed the correct partisan breakdown of the Senate. We see that 52 percent of citizens correctly identified the chart that showed 54 Republicans, 44 Democrats, and 2 Independents. There is striking variation, however, across sex, age, and education. Men, older citizens, and those who were better educated were more likely to answer correctly. Notice in particular the large impact of education on political knowledge.

Table 8.7   Demographic Differences in Political Knowledge

"Which of the following [charts] shows the number of seats each party holds in the U.S. Senate?"

Characteristics	Answered correctly
Total	52%
Sex	
Male	59
Female	46
Age (in years)	
18–29	44
30–49	53
50+	57
Education	
High school or less	38
Some college	55
College graduate	70

Source: "The News IQ Quiz Results," Pew Research Center, Washington, DC, http://www.pewresearch.org/quiz/the-news-iq-quiz/results

Motivation and Political Knowledge

People also differ in how motivated they are to learn about politics. Citizens who are interested in and attentive to politics are significantly more knowledgeable than those who just don't care.[61] This finding extends to young people. Among high school seniors, students who expressed an interest in studying government were substantially more likely to have a grasp of civics knowledge than other students. Political discussion is also a factor. A study of citizens in the United States and Great Britain found a significant link between discussing politics with family and friends and being well informed about politics.[62]

A recent experiment demonstrated that citizens who had the opportunity to interact in an e-townhall with their member of Congress and other constituents about a controversial issue—immigration—became more knowledgeable about the issue.[63] Having the chance to interact with their representative motivated citizens to seek out information and to discuss the issue with additional people. Thus, motivation should not be considered a static characteristic of individuals; instead, citizens have the capacity to learn about politics and can be motivated to do so through electronic deliberation with elected officials and fellow citizens.

Context and Political Knowledge

Political knowledge is not simply a function of individual characteristics and motivation. To become knowledgeable about politics, citizens must also have the opportunity to do so.[64] Some political contexts offer greater opportunities for citizens to become informed than others. Richard Niemi and Jane Junn emphasize the influence of **civic education** on political knowledge.[65] They analyzed survey data from a national representative sample of high school seniors and found that students who had more civics classes and more recent civics instruction were more knowledgeable than others. Furthermore, the particular type of curriculum mattered— students who were exposed to a wide variety of topics and discussed current events in their classes were more likely to be knowledgeable about politics.

The **political structure** also influences citizens' levels of political knowledge. Because political structures differ across nations, scholars can compare the effects of different institutional arrangements and electoral systems on political knowledge cross-nationally.[66] For example, in a nation with competitive elections, parties are motivated to provide information to citizens, and citizens find the information useful. In such a political context, citizens are more knowledgeable about politics. Similarly, in the United States, competitive House races lead to more local news coverage, which then results in citizens being better informed about the congressional election.[67] Unfortunately there are many uncompetitive congressional districts in the United States, so this is a significant hindrance to citizen knowledge.

Jennifer Jerit, Jason Barabas, and Toby Bolsen examined how the **information environment** affects citizens' political knowledge.[68] They argue that citizens will be better informed about politics when the information environment is rich. In other words, when the media pay a great deal of attention to political issues, the public becomes more knowledgeable as a result. An information-rich environment, however, helps the better educated more than their less-educated counterparts. Thus, information does not level the playing field; instead, well-educated citizens are better equipped to integrate new knowledge into their existing stores of information, which allows them to move even further ahead of those who are less educated. Thus, the knowledge gap between the less educated and better educated is exacerbated by an information-rich environment.

Does it matter whether the information-rich environment is created by news stories in print or on television? Yes, it does. Jerit et al. examined the relationship between different types of media coverage and political knowledge of forty-one issues, ranging from understanding how the West Nile virus is spread to knowledge of the Supreme Court's ruling on partial-birth abortion to knowing about President George W. Bush's drug plan. The researchers found that on issues with low levels of media attention (such as Bush's drug plan), highly educated people were only slightly more likely to answer questions correctly than those with less education, whereas there was a large knowledge gap on issues receiving a great deal of media attention (such as how the West Nile virus is spread). Furthermore, this knowledge gap was exacerbated when the issue received extensive coverage in the print media. In contrast, for issues receiving extensive television coverage, both less-educated and highly educated people gained. A knowledge gap remained, of course, but the important point is that the gap was not increased by the television coverage.[69] Media critics have complained about the simplicity and inanity of television news compared with print, but these findings suggest that television presents information in a way that benefits those who are least knowledgeable.

The political context in the United States is dominated by men, which has an effect on levels of political knowledge among women. A study by Nancy Burns, Kay Schlozman, and Sidney Verba asked the question, "What if politics weren't a man's game?"[70] Burns et al. found that women living in states with a female senator or a female Senate candidate were substantially more knowledgeable about politics than women living in states without those characteristics. Specifically, only 51 percent of women from male-dominated states could name one of their U.S. senators, whereas 79 percent of women could do so when the political context included powerful female politicians.[71] This is a huge difference and suggests that the knowledge gap between men and women could close if more women served in elective office. There is also evidence that women's political participation would be higher if there were more women senators because more knowledgeable citizens also tend to be more involved citizens.[72]

Overall, these studies suggest the political context matters a great deal. Citizens are more knowledgeable when the political context is a favorable one. This is consistent with the views of participatory democratic theorists. If you are interested in boosting levels of political knowledge, as participatory democratic theorists are, then it makes sense to structure the political environment in a way that encourages and enables citizens to easily and efficiently acquire information.

WHAT ARE THE CONSEQUENCES OF POLITICAL KNOWLEDGE?

Does it matter whether citizens are politically knowledgeable or ignorant? This is a normative question to be sure. As we have already discussed, different democratic theorists have different views on the consequences of political ignorance. But it is also an empirical question. By examining the differences between those who are knowledgeable and those who are not, we can get a handle on the consequences of political ignorance.

Delli Carpini and Keeter identify a number of ways in which knowledgeable citizens differ from others.[73] First, well-informed citizens are more likely to demonstrate political tolerance, a fundamental norm in a democratic society. Second, knowledgeable citizens participate at higher rates than their counterparts. Third, knowledgeable citizens are more likely to have stable issue opinions and structure their opinions along a liberal-conservative continuum. Fourth, informed citizens are more likely to recognize their interests, bring their issue positions into line with their party identification, and vote accordingly. Fifth, knowledge begets knowledge. In other words, knowledgeable citizens are able to handle new information with ease; existing knowledge allows citizens to efficiently incorporate new tidbits into their belief systems. All these things are critical in a democracy, according to Delli Carpini and Keeter. "Because so many of these differences bear on the issue of political power, a key implication of these findings is that the maldistribution of political knowledge has consequences: it threatens the basic democratic principle of political equality among citizens."[74] Delli Carpini and Keeter find this maldistribution particularly alarming because those who are already less powerful in society (such as women, minorities, the poor, the less educated, and young people) are the ones who are less knowledgeable.

Political ignorance also has an effect on policy attitudes and vote choice. Recall the studies on misinformation we discussed earlier in the chapter.[75] The Kuklinski et al. study showed that incorrect beliefs led citizens to be more opposed to welfare spending than they otherwise would be, and the Kull et al. research demonstrated that citizens who held more misperceptions about the war in Iraq were more likely to support the war. Another study used an experimental design to show that when citizens were provided with accurate information about the decrease in crime in recent years, they were more likely to say the government was spending too much money on building prisons.[76] Other scholars have demonstrated that uninformed citizens would vote for different candidates if they were fully informed.[77] Thus, this research highlights the important policy and electoral impact of citizens' lack of knowledge.

ARE CITIZENS INTERESTED IN AND ATTENTIVE TO POLITICS?

Are citizens interested in politics and political campaigns? Do they pay attention to politics, or are they disengaged? These are important questions because citizens who are interested in and attentive to politics tend to have higher levels of political knowledge than citizens who are not engaged.[78] And, as we just discussed, knowledge has important political consequences.

Interest in Politics and Political Campaigns

Let's first examine public **interest in politics**, or the degree to which people find politics appealing. In a 2012 ANES survey, 17 percent of citizens said they always pay attention to what's going on in government and politics; 31 percent said most of the time; 22 percent said about half of the time; 28 percent said some of the time; and only 3 percent said never.[79] How does this compare to prior years? As you can see from the note to Figure 8.2, the interest-in-politics question wording and response options changed in 2012. One of the most important changes was that respondents in 2012 were offered five response options, whereas they were offered only four in prior years. Unfortunately that makes the comparison between 2012 and earlier years problematic. To make that clear in the figure, the interest in politics data for 2012 are not connected to the time series lines. In the 2008 ANES, 26 percent of citizens said they "follow what's going on in government and politics most of the time." Another 37 percent indicated they were interested "some of the time" (see the solid lines in Figure 8.2). Despite the different question wordings, it seems that *modestly interested* is the best way to characterize citizens' interest in politics in recent years. Historically the proportion of citizens highly interested in politics was larger. In the 1960s and 1970s, roughly one-third of respondents said they were following politics most of the time. From the 1980s until 2008, it was only about one-quarter.[80]

What about interest in political campaigns? In 2012, citizens were quite interested.[81] Forty-one percent said they were "very much interested" and another 42 percent said they were "somewhat interested" (see the dotted lines in Figure 8.2). Note that 2008 was the highest level of interest in political campaigns recorded since the survey's inception in 1952. It at least partially reflects the Obama campaign's ability to mobilize young people and minority groups during his first run for the presidency. As Figure 8.2 shows, there is quite a bit of variation in campaign interest over time. As in 2004, 2008, and 2012, citizens indicated significant interest in 1992, but they were less engaged in 1996 and 2000. Nevertheless, in every presidential election year since 1964, at least 70 percent of respondents have said they were somewhat or very much interested in political campaigns. Overall, then, citizens seem to perk up during the

Figure 8.2   Interest in Politics and Current Campaign, 1964–2012

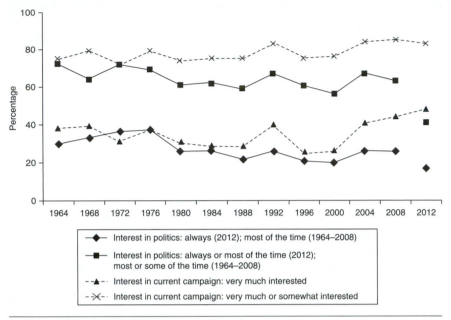

Source: The American National Election Studies (www.electionstudies.org), *The ANES Guide to Public Opinion and Electoral Behavior* (Ann Arbor: University of Michigan, Center for Political Studies, producer and distributor); Analysis of American National Election Study 2012 Time Series.

Notes: Interest in Politics question wording: In 2012: "How often do you pay attention to what's going on in government and politics? Always, most of the time, about half the time, some of the time, or never"; 1964–2008: "Some people seem to follow (1964: think about) what's going on in government and public affairs most of the time, whether there's an election going on or not. Others aren't that interested. Would you say you follow what's going on in government and public affairs most of the time, some of the time, only now and then, or hardly at all?"

Interest in Current Campaign question wording: "Some people don't pay much attention to the political campaigns. How about you, would you say that you have been/ were very much interested, somewhat interested, or not much interested in (1964–2008: following) the political campaigns (so far) this year?"

presidential campaign season but are somewhat less engaged when it comes to day-to-day politics.[82]

As with political knowledge, levels of interest vary across demographic groups.[83] Men and whites are generally more interested in politics. Likewise, those with more education and higher incomes are more concerned with political happenings. Age, in particular, has a strong relationship with political interest; older individuals follow politics more than young people. Partisans and ideologues are also much more likely to follow politics than independents or moderates.

The political context also matters. During the 2008 presidential campaign, for example, 51 percent of blacks said they were very much interested in the campaign compared with only 44 percent of whites. Further, in 2004, only 32 percent of blacks said they were very much interested in the campaign. Clearly having Barack Obama on the ballot stimulated a great deal of interest among black Americans in 2008, a pattern that continued in 2012.[84] Similarly, in states where females hold statewide offices (such as senator or governor), women are significantly more interested in politics than in states without such female representation.[85] Likewise, women in states with competitive female candidates are more likely to discuss politics and try to convince others to support a political candidate than women in states without viable female contenders.[86] The political context is also important for adolescents. Girls, for example, are more likely to anticipate future political involvement when they see women run high-profile, viable political campaigns.[87]

What do democratic theorists have to say about variation in levels of political interest? Participatory democratic theorists would be concerned with the demographic differences in political interest, and they would argue that changes in the political context are necessary to ensure all citizens are interested in politics. Some elite democrats, on the other hand, would wonder why so many citizens are interested in politics. From their point of view, it is irrational for citizens to spend time on politics. The likelihood that a citizen, even an interested and informed one, could make a difference is so small that it simply doesn't make sense for him or her to devote resources to such an endeavor.

Bystanders

Do citizens pay **attention to politics**? According to a 2014 survey conducted by the Pew Research Center, 77 percent of the public say they "follow what's going on in government and public affairs" most or some of the time.[88] Some citizens, however, are largely inattentive to politics. Indeed, the Pew data demonstrate that 10 percent of the public are best characterized as **bystanders**.[89] Pew comes to this conclusion by creating a political typology that sorts individuals into groups according to responses to a series of questions about political attitudes, values, and engagement. By definition, bystanders are not registered to vote. They are politically disengaged, with almost three-quarters of bystanders saying they have *no* interest in politics and virtually none ever contributing money to a political candidate. In the words of the Pew Research Center, bystanders "don't give a hoot about politics."[90] Instead, they are interested in health, celebrities, and entertainment. They are more likely to be young, Hispanic, and foreign born than other groups identified in the political typology. They are also more likely to answer "don't know" or to skip questions altogether when responding to the survey.

What do we make of the fact that 10 percent of the American public are totally disengaged from politics? Should we look at this as *only* 10 percent are inattentive so it's no big deal, or should we be concerned that a meaningful minority of citizens are much more interested in Dr. Oz than Obamacare? Participatory democrats would certainly have higher expectations for the public and would be especially concerned that bystanders are disproportionately young, Hispanic, and foreign born. Elite democrats would be less concerned yet would be bothered that members of this group are not even registered to vote, a minimal threshold these bystanders do not cross.

CONCLUSION

Are citizens highly knowledgeable about politics? No, many people are not particularly well informed, and some citizens are outright misinformed about important political issues. Nevertheless, people are not as ignorant about politics as some observers have suggested. Further, citizens have not become more ignorant over time; levels of political knowledge have been remarkably stable over the last seventy years. There is a controversy about how to measure political knowledge, with several scholars arguing that Delli Carpini and Keeter's method is too narrow or that it underestimates citizen competence. Indeed, Graber argues that citizens do know useful political information but do not have the brain capacity to deal with every little detail.

Why are some citizens more knowledgeable than others? Citizens differ in ability, motivation, and opportunity. Formal education, for example, provides citizens with the cognitive ability to become informed about politics. Other demographic characteristics matter as well; men, whites, higher-income, and older people are more likely to be knowledgeable. Motivational factors, such as interest, attention, and discussion, lead citizens to be informed. The political context also acts as either a facilitator or inhibitor of political knowledge.

Are there consequences of political knowledge? Yes, indeed there are. Citizens who are knowledgeable are more likely to endorse democratic values and participate in political activities. They have opinions on issues that are more stable and more closely linked to their ideology and party identification. In addition, knowledgeable citizens are capable of dealing with new information in an efficient manner, making it easier for them to learn even more about politics. And perhaps most important, informed citizens hold different issue opinions than they otherwise would. Thus, political knowledge has significant ramifications for policy preferences among the public.

Are citizens interested in and attentive to politics? Citizens demonstrate modest interest in politics and fairly high interest in political campaigns. A small subset of the population indicate they basically do not pay attention to politics at all. They are bystanders to democracy.

Overall, do people live up to the democratic ideal of knowledgeable, engaged citizens? Participatory democratic theorists would say no. They would argue that citizens should be more knowledgeable so they can play an active role in the democratic process. Informed and engaged citizens are at the heart of a democracy. They are necessary to influence elite behavior and hold elites accountable. Participatory democratic theorists find the demographic differences in political knowledge especially troubling because they are concerned with inequalities in society. These theorists do not blame individuals for their lack of political savvy and interest, however. Instead, they point to the barriers that limit citizen engagement and knowledge.

In sharp contrast, some elite democratic theorists are curious about why citizens are interested and knowledgeable at all, given the low odds that their voices will be influential. In their minds, the puzzle is not why so many people lack knowledge but why so many people are informed. Elite democrats who think government works best when the public interferes least would probably be satisfied with the low levels of knowledge and modest levels of political interest. Scholars who emphasize that citizens can make sensible political decisions by using heuristics would be troubled by the lack of knowledge about such things as party stances on the issues. Some citizens can use cues to effectively muddle their way through, but many people do not even have those basic insights.

You are an expert now on political knowledge, interest, and attention. You understand the different normative approaches to citizen competence, and you have a good grasp of the empirical research findings. So what do you think? Are citizens knowledgeable enough, interested enough, and attentive enough to function effectively in a democracy?

KEY CONCEPTS

attention to politics / 245
bystanders / 245
civic education / 240
focus groups / 237
gender gap in political
knowledge / 233
generalist / 231
heuristics / 222
information environment / 240
informed / 225
interest in politics / 243
limited information processors / 222
low-information rationality / 222

misinformed / 225
multiple-choice questions / 235
people and players / 225
political knowledge / 219
political structure / 240
racial gap in political
knowledge / 238
rules of the game / 224
short-answer questions / 235
specialist / 231
substance of politics / 225
timebound / 230
uninformed / 225

SUGGESTED SOURCES FOR FURTHER READING

Boudreau, Cheryl, and Arthur Lupia. "Political Knowledge." In *Handbook of Experimental Political Science*, eds. James Druckman, Donald P. Green, James H. Kuklinski, and Arthur Lupia. New York: Cambridge University Press, 2013.

Luskin, Robert C., and John G. Bullock. "'Don't Know' Means 'Don't Know':
DK Responses and the Public's Level of Political Knowledge." *Journal of
Politics* 73 (2011): 547–557.

Boudreau and Lupia review experimental research that provides insight into the
measurement and conceptualization of political knowledge. Luskin and Bullock
use experimental data to examine an ongoing debate among scholars of political
knowledge: Should respondents be encouraged or discouraged from providing
"don't know" responses to knowledge questions?

Davis, Darren W., and Brian D. Silver. "Stereotype Threat and Race of
Interviewer Effects in a Survey on Political Knowledge." *American Journal
of Political Science* 47 (2003): 33–45.
McGlone, Matthew S., Joshua Aronson, and Diane Kobrynowicz. "Stereotype
Threat and the Gender Gap in Political Knowledge." *Psychology of Women
Quarterly* 30 (2006): 392–398.

These scholars argue that stereotype threat explains at least part of the racial and
gender gap in political knowledge. Stereotype threat occurs when blacks and
women feel pressure to perform well on political knowledge questions because
they are aware of negative stereotypes about their intellectual abilities. As a result
of stereotype threat, blacks and women do worse on political knowledge tests—
not because they are less knowledgeable but because the stress of the situation
interferes with their ability to answer correctly.

Niemi, Richard G., and Jane Junn. *Civic Education: What Makes Students Learn.*
New Haven, CT: Yale University Press, 1998.

Niemi and Junn's book shows that civic education in high schools can bolster
political knowledge. If you are an education major, you will find this book particularly interesting.

Pew News IQ Quiz, http://pewresearch.org/newsiq

Check out this website for an online news quiz. Take the quiz and then compare
your performance with that of other American citizens.

The American National Election Study Guide to Public Opinion and Electoral
Behavior, www. electionstudies.org/nesguide/nesguide.htm

This website provides public opinion data from national, random samples of U.S.
citizens. See the "Political Involvement and Participation in Politics" section for
a set of questions that measure citizens' levels of engagement in politics. Question
wording and response choices are included. Both tables and graphs present the
data. There are also tables that show how different demographic groups respond
to the questions.

CHAPTER 9

Support for Civil Liberties

AS LEADER OF the National Socialist Party of America (Nazis), Frank Collin requested permission for his group to demonstrate in Skokie, Illinois, in 1977. The Nazis had been planning to protest against racial integration in Chicago, but a policy there required them to have a $250,000 insurance bond before they would be given a permit to demonstrate. Because they were not able to post this bond, they turned to a number of Chicago suburbs, including Skokie. Collin indicated that the Nazis would carry signs expressing their white supremacist beliefs (such as "Free Speech for the White Man") and that they would be wearing uniforms that would include swastikas.

Response to Collin's request was swift and negative. Skokie was home to thousands of Jewish residents, including survivors of the World War II Nazi concentration camps. Many of these survivors spoke out publicly against the Nazis' march and tried to influence public officials to prevent the march. The mayor of Skokie was persuaded to fight against the Nazis' request after a Holocaust survivor told him that a concentration camp guard had killed his two-year-old daughter in front of him. By recounting this episode, the man hoped to convince the mayor of the "emotional reaction . . . [he] might have to the sight of a group of men marching in [this] community wearing the swastika symbol."[1] The survivor was successful; the mayor agreed to fight strongly against the Nazi march.

Shortly thereafter, village leaders in Skokie unanimously adopted a number of ordinances designed to prevent the Nazis from marching. These new policies required demonstrators to have $350,000 worth of insurance and allowed village officials to deny a permit to any group that promoted hostility toward individuals based on their race, ethnicity, or religious affiliation. A further ordinance, even more clearly directed toward the Nazi party, banned anyone from participating in a demonstration "as a member or on behalf of any political party while wearing a military-style uniform."[2] The American Civil Liberties Union (ACLU), representing the Nazi party, filed suit, declaring that the Skokie ordinances were unconstitutional in that they were designed to restrict free speech. By working to protect the Nazis' freedom of expression, the ACLU received much negative publicity and suffered significant membership declines. Some ACLU members felt they could no longer support an organization that would stand up for the rights of a group with views as distasteful as those of the Nazis. In the end, however, the federal courts agreed with the ACLU's legal arguments and nullified the village ordinances. Meanwhile, the Chicago requirement of insurance for demonstrators was also declared unconstitutional, paving the way for the Nazis to hold their demonstration there, which they did in 1978, thus ending one of the most notable free speech controversies of the past few decades.

Alongside the principle of majority rule, democracies guarantee the political rights of those individuals or groups holding unpopular viewpoints. In fact, this protection of minority views is one key characteristic of democratic nations and is the principle that the courts upheld during the Skokie controversy. Because of the courts' decisions, the Nazis did hold their march in Chicago despite the fact that opposition to the march came from many quarters, including elected officials, community leaders, and citizens.

In the United States, the rights of freedom of speech, freedom to assemble, freedom of religion, and freedom to petition the government are protected by the First Amendment of the Constitution. These rights, and others in the Constitution, are known as **civil liberties**, which are defined as rights granted to citizens that are protected from government suppression. Public support for civil liberties is known as **political tolerance**. Yet we do not commonly refer to someone as tolerant if she supports the exercise of civil liberties only for those who share her political beliefs. More typically, tolerance refers to extending freedoms to individuals or groups with whom one disagrees: "a willingness to 'put up with' those things that one rejects. Politically, it implies a willingness to permit the expression of those ideas or interests that one opposes."[3] Or, in the more direct phrasing of Samuel Stouffer, the author of a groundbreaking book on political tolerance, "If I am tolerant, there are rights which I will grant, within the law, even to those whom I most condemn."[4]

For classical and participatory democratic theorists, a key characteristic of democracy is the active engagement of the public. Citizens should debate issues and share their preferences with politicians, and the policy that results should reflect the wishes of the people. Political equality is also important to these theorists; all citizens should be able to share their views in the public forum regardless of the content of these views. Equality is important because, among other matters, only when there is such a free **marketplace of ideas** will leaders be able to discern what is in the public's interest. For such equality to exist in practice, support for freedom of expression must be high among the public. Although these theorists do not necessarily assume that everyone will be tolerant, high levels of public intolerance would be counter to the democratic principles they espouse. Participatory democratic theorists have focused particularly on the importance of civil liberties for democracy. They further believe that with more formal education, greater involvement in politics, and more exposure to democratic principles, citizens can learn to tolerate the political expressions of all, even those with whom they vehemently disagree. Thus, participatory democrats value educational and political opportunities for the public to learn key democratic norms.

In contrast, elite democrats are not nearly as optimistic about the citizenry. In fact, given these theorists' beliefs that the public is uninformed about and uninterested in politics and their assumption that when citizens do participate they do so only to further their own interests, democratic elitists expect the public to be intolerant of political viewpoints that differ from their own. How, then, can a democracy that values minority rights continue to function given high levels of public intolerance? To answer this question, democratic elitists, and also pluralists, turn to elites. Elites, they argue, strongly support minority rights and ensure that these rights are upheld. The elites, these theorists contend, are aware of the importance of civil liberties and further understand the consequences to democracy if civil liberties were to be eroded. Democratic regimes will be stable, even in the face of widespread public intolerance, as long as the political elites support civil liberties and ensure that the principle of minority rights is applied to all.

Not all variants of democratic elitism and pluralism have such faith in the good judgment of elites, however. In particular, James Madison, at the time of the writing and ratification of the U.S. Constitution, made a forceful case that all people, elites included, could not be trusted to welcome the political expression of all viewpoints.[5] Madison's remedy to this problem was the creation of a political system that, first, divided power among three branches of government and, second, ruled over such a large population that diverse interests would be represented in the national government. These characteristics of the **constitutional framework** would ensure that leaders would need to compromise with others—others who were representing a multitude of different interests—in the policymaking process. Interacting with their opponents repeatedly would instill in these leaders an appreciation for the value of tolerating diverse viewpoints. Occasionally, elites might even need to join in coalition with individuals who hold very different views than they do. Madison's was thus a pragmatic approach to ensuring that in America civil liberties would be ensured, rooted as they were in the political system rather than in the natural virtue of either the public or the elites.

In this chapter, we discuss attitudes toward civil liberties and tie this evidence back to the normative debates about support for civil liberties in a democracy. More specifically, we discuss levels of tolerance in the United States, sources of tolerance, and differences between elites and citizens in their support for civil liberties. Much of our attention will be on views toward the freedoms of expression contained in the First Amendment because this has been the topic of most public opinion research on civil liberties. The first ten amendments of the Constitution (the **Bill of Rights**) list a number of other civil liberties such as the right to bear arms and some rights of people accused of crimes, including the rights against self-incrimination and unreasonable searches and seizures. Historically, less scholarly attention has focused on public support for these liberties. That changed, however, in the wake of the September 11, 2001, al-Qaeda attacks and increased national attention on how to effectively capture terrorists. The national debate has largely swirled around the proper balance between protecting civil liberties and promoting national security. The implications of this changed climate on public support for civil liberties since the 9/11 attacks are discussed later in the chapter.

ARE AMERICANS TOLERANT?

Public support for many civil liberties principles in the abstract is very high. In the late 1930s and early 1940s, for example, over 95 percent of survey respondents answered yes to the following question: "Do you believe in freedom of speech?"[6] Across the decades, similarly high percentages of citizens have agreed that "people in the minority should be free to try to win majority support for their opinions," agreed that "[no] matter what a person's political beliefs are, he is entitled to the same legal rights and protections as anyone else," and believed in "free speech for all, no matter what their views might be."[7] Yet support for the application of these principles in specific circumstances tends to be lower, sometimes substantially so.[8] As one scholar put it, "Americans believe in free speech in theory, but not always in practice. Many would like to see controversy limited and the Bill of Rights tailored to the times and to the occasion. Very few have ever accorded complete freedom of expression to political extremists."[9] In other words, tolerance for the practice of civil liberties, especially among those with unpopular viewpoints, tends not to be very high. Furthermore, the public is not equally tolerant of all types of political acts. Support for certain acts, such as blocking entrances to government buildings or violent demonstrations, is quite low.[10]

Have levels of public tolerance changed over time? This question is not so easy to answer. As we will see, specific conclusions about whether levels of tolerance among the citizenry have changed across the decades depend, in part, on how tolerance is assessed.

Stouffer's Classic Study

In one of the very first empirical analyses of public support for civil liberties, Samuel Stouffer assessed tolerance toward individuals holding unconventional political views.[11] It was the 1950s, and Stouffer was interested in probing a variety of public attitudes toward communism. A primary goal of his analysis was determining levels of tolerance toward communists and two other groups, socialists and atheists. During this era, known as the Red Scare, political leaders at both the national and state levels, prominently led by U.S. senator Joseph McCarthy, had taken actions to restrict the rights of communists. Suspected communists were jailed, blacklisted, and, in some cases, deported. Stouffer wanted to explore whether the public was intolerant of communists and, if so, what measures might be taken to increase public tolerance.

Stouffer's conclusions are based on results from two public opinion polls conducted in 1954. Survey respondents were selected from a national probability sample. Their responses, therefore, can be generalized to the entire nation. For each of the three nonconformist groups under study, Stouffer queried respondents' willingness to tolerate specific activities performed by group members. The survey questions used by Stouffer to assess tolerance toward these groups have been repeated over the years by many others researching civil liberties. The questions have also come under criticism, as we will soon see. Thus, it is important that we consider how these questions were worded. Table 9.1 presents the questions regarding **atheists**. As you can see, the term *atheist* does not appear in the question. Instead, an atheist's *beliefs* were presented (specifically, "somebody who is against all churches and religion"). Furthermore, these questions assessed tolerance for three specific activities: making a speech, keeping a published book in the public library, and teaching at a university. The first two are clearly examples of freedom of expression, a civil liberty protected by the Bill of Rights. Following these were questions gauging tolerance of the same three activities for the other two groups. As with atheists, Stouffer described the *views* of **socialists** (those favoring "government ownership of all the railroads and all big industries") rather than using the group name. In contrast, he referred to **communists** directly by name, instead of presenting their views. Presumably citizens were more familiar with communists than with the other two groups, given the national attention devoted to communism during the 1950s. Asking the public about socialists or atheists without describing the views of these two groups might therefore have been unproductive. On the other hand, we cannot be certain whether respondents

Table 9.1   Assessing Public Tolerance of Atheists: Stouffer's Survey Questions

"There are always some people whose ideas are considered bad or dangerous by other people. For instance, somebody who is against all churches and religion."

   "If such a person wanted to make a speech in your city (town, community) against churches and religion, should he be allowed to speak, or not?"

   "Should such a person be allowed to teach in a college or university, or not?"

   "If some people in your community suggested that a book he wrote against churches and religion should be taken out of your public library, would you favor removing this book, or not?"

Source: Samuel A. Stouffer, *Communism, Conformity, and Civil Liberties: A Cross-Section of the Nation Speaks Its Mind* (Garden City, NY: Doubleday, 1955), 252.

in that era knew what communists believe and were expressing tolerance toward those beliefs or were only responding to the group name.

Levels of public tolerance toward these groups in 1954 are presented in Figure 9.1. The bars represent the percentage of the public who would tolerate the specific act for each group. At first glance, it is clear that levels of tolerance toward these groups were not very high. In fact, the public might best be described as intolerant, especially toward communists and atheists. At most, only about one-quarter of the public supported any of the three rights for communists, with only 6 percent of the citizens feeling that communists should not be fired from college teaching. Public support for civil liberties toward atheists was somewhat higher, with just over one-third feeling that atheists should be able to make speeches or have their books kept in the local library. Only 12 percent of the public, however, would support the right of atheists to teach college courses. Tolerance was highest for socialists, with a slight majority of the public expressing support for two of the rights. As with communists and atheists, however, the public was much less supportive of socialists teaching compared with the other two acts.

Overall, then, although public tolerance was quite low in 1954, citizens did make distinctions across the political groups. Support for the civil liberties of socialists was highest, possibly because atheists and communists were perceived to be further from the mainstream and also because communism was viewed by

Figure 9.1   Tolerance of Political Minorities, 1954

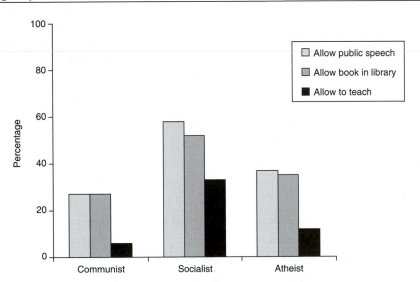

Source: Data from Samuel A. Stouffer, *Communism, Conformity, and Civil Liberties: A Cross-Section of the Nation Speaks Its Mind* (Garden City, NY: Doubleday, 1955), Chap. 2.

many to be a threat to the American way of life. Levels of tolerance also varied across the specific acts, with tolerance consistently higher for the two freedoms of expression than for holding a teaching job. University teaching, with its potential to indoctrinate young adults, was thought to be more risky for society than speechmaking or book publishing; hence it was less tolerated.

Trends in Political Tolerance

Have Americans become more or less tolerant since the 1950s? Fortunately, we can directly compare levels of tolerance in that decade with more recent years because Stouffer's tolerance questions have appeared on the General Social Survey (GSS) many times since this survey began in 1972. Every year at first, then biennially since 1994, a national sample of adults has been asked their attitudes toward a variety of social and political objects.[12] The GSS is a cross-sectional study, which means that different people are surveyed each year. Many of the same questions have been asked over the years, so we can compare the responses of one year with responses in other years to determine whether the attitudes of Americans have changed. Keep in mind that the GSS is not a panel study; in other words, the same people are not surveyed every time. Instead, each time the GSS is conducted, a new national probability sample of adults is contacted. Based on this sampling design, we can assume that the results for a given GSS represent the opinions of all American adults for the year of the specific study.

By using Stouffer's questions, tolerance of the speechmaking rights of a variety of political minority groups has been assessed. Figure 9.2 presents results from these surveys for selected years. First, let's consider the three groups that Stouffer examined. Public levels of tolerance toward these groups were much higher in 1972 compared with 1954. For communists and atheists, tolerance increased further through 1990 and has remained relatively stable since then.[13] It is very possible that tolerance of socialists has also increased, but because the GSS stopped asking questions about this group in 1974, we cannot be certain about this.

Beginning in the 1970s, the GSS also queried the public about its tolerance of three other groups: **racists** (described in the GSS question as "a person who believes that blacks are genetically inferior"), **militarists** ("a person who advocates doing away with elections and letting the military run the country"), and male **homosexuals**. Levels of tolerance for these three groups appear in Figure 9.2 as dashed lines. Tolerance gains have been largest for homosexuals. In 2014, 90 percent of citizens supported speechmaking by homosexual men, making tolerance of this group higher than the other groups included on the GSS. The public is also more supportive of civil liberties for militarists now than was the case a few decades ago. In contrast, tolerance of racists has not increased. Slightly more people tolerated racists in 1990 compared to the 1970s, but since 1990 public support for racists' speechmaking has actually declined.[14] Finally, in 2008 the GSS began assessing tolerance toward **Muslim extremists** (specifically, "a Muslim

Figure 9.2   Tolerance of Speechmaking, 1954–2014

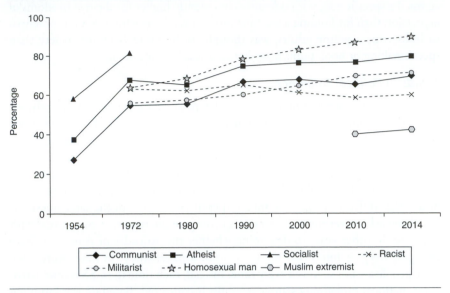

Sources: Data for 1954 from Samuel A. Stouffer, *Communism, Conformity, and Civil Liberties: A Cross-Section of the Nation Speaks Its Mind* (Garden City, NY: Doubleday, 1955), Chap. 2. Data for all other years from an analysis of the General Social Survey Cumulative Data File, 1972–2014.

Note: 1972 data for racist and militarist are actually from 1976; 1972 data for homosexual man are actually from 1973.

clergyman preaching hatred toward the United States"). As demonstrated in Figure 9.2, tolerance toward this group was significantly lower than for the others.[15] Only 42 percent would allow such a Muslim clergyman to make a speech in their communities in 2014, one percentage point higher than in 2010.

It is now the case that majorities of citizens, sometimes more than 70 percent, support the practice of civil liberties for some individuals professing unconventional views, those that are outside of the political mainstream. Yet variation in tolerance does vary across groups, and for no group or act is support unanimous. Thus, is it accurate to conclude that U.S. citizens are generally a tolerant lot? Certain democratic theorists, especially participatory democrats, would be reluctant to offer such a rosy conclusion. They would be pleased to see the increasing levels of tolerance toward some groups but would probably prefer even more citizens to possess tolerant attitudes. Furthermore, the empirical evidence demonstrating increases in tolerance since Stouffer's original analysis has come under criticism, most notably by John Sullivan, James Pieresen, and George Marcus.

Sullivan, Piereson, and Marcus: Tolerance of Least Liked Groups

To be tolerant, an individual must allow the behavior of those whom he opposes. To Sullivan, Piereson, and Marcus, this is a crucial component of tolerance, yet it is one that is not captured by Stouffer's survey questions.[16] Although many Americans probably disagree with communists or atheists, Stouffer's questions do not directly probe for whether the public dislikes these groups. To compensate, Sullivan et al. used an alternative method for assessing public tolerance, one that they argue more faithfully represents a definition of tolerance as support for the rights of those holding repugnant political views.

Sullivan et al.'s measures of tolerance have come to be called the "**least liked group**" approach, based on the wording of their survey questions. Rather than listing specific groups that they assumed the public would not support, they asked survey respondents to identify which political group they liked the least from a list of potentially unpopular groups. Individuals were also allowed to suggest a group that was not on the list, in the hope that respondents would select the group that they most strongly disliked. As the respondents perused a printed list of the groups, survey interviewers asked this question:

> I am giving you a list of groups in politics. As I read the list please follow along: socialists, fascists, communists, Ku Klux Klan, John Birch Society, Black Panthers, Symbionese Liberation Army, atheists, pro-abortionists, and anti-abortionists. Which of these groups do you like the least? If there is some group that you like even less than the groups listed here, please tell me the name of that group.[17]

In addition to the three groups analyzed by Stouffer, included in this list are groups from the political left (Black Panthers and Symbionese Liberation Army) and right (fascists, Ku Klux Klan, and John Birch Society), as well as two groups on opposite sides of the abortion debate. This question was first used by Sullivan and colleagues in the 1970s, so the groups selected are ones that were salient at that time. For example, the Symbionese Liberation Army, perhaps best known for kidnapping newspaper heiress Patty Hearst in 1974, combined urban guerilla tactics with calls for a black revolution. On the other end of the political spectrum, the John Birch Society is a very conservative organization that promotes individual freedom and a limited government, and that was formed to protect the Constitution from communism. More contemporary research conducted by James Gibson contains a somewhat different list of groups.[18] As demonstrated in Table 9.2, Gibson examined some of the same groups that Sullivan and his colleagues did but also included new ones (such as gay rights activists and radical Muslims).

Which groups does the American public like the least? Sullivan et al. included their original list of groups on a national survey of the American public in 1978. Gibson did so in 2005. In 1978, the most commonly disliked group was communists, followed closely by the Ku Klux Klan (KKK). By 2005, the KKK was far and away the most disliked group in the nation. Whereas 44 percent of Gibson's respondents selected the KKK as their most disliked group, the next two groups (radical Muslims and Nazis) were selected by only 13 and 12 percent. Another notable change across these years is that the public was much more likely

Table 9.2   Least Liked Political Groups, 1978 and 2005

	Percentage selecting group as their least liked	
Political group	1978	2005
Stouffer's groups		
Communists	29	4
Atheists	8	6
Socialists	1	
Other groups on political left		
Symbionese Liberation Army	8	
Black Panthers	6	
Gay rights activists		4
Groups on political right		
Ku Klux Klan	24	44
Fascists (1978)/Nazis (2005)	5	12
John Birch Society	1	
Radical Muslims		13
Militarists		6
Christian fundamentalists		1
Abortion groups		
Pro-abortionists	4	3
Anti-abortionists	2	2
Other group	2	N/A
Don't know	10	N/A

Sources: Data from John L. Sullivan, James Piereson, and George E. Marcus, "An Alternative Conceptualization of Political Tolerance: Illusory Increases 1950s–1970s," *American Political Science Review* 73 (1979): 790; James L. Gibson, "Intolerance and Political Repression in the United States: A Half Century after McCarthyism," *American Journal of Political Science* 52 (2008): 102.

to select groups on the political right than the left as their least liked in 2005. The opposite was true in 1978. Focusing on Stouffer's primary groups, two results are noteworthy. First, although communists were the most disliked group in 1978, only 29 percent disliked this group the most. In other words, over 70 percent of people *did not* choose communists as the group they liked the least. Second, by 2005, only 10 percent selected one of Stouffer's three groups. If tolerance is best understood as supporting freedom of expression for those individuals whose speech citizens strongly dislike, then focusing only on tolerance for communists, atheists, and socialists will suggest the public is more politically tolerant than they really are.

Although this examination of which groups Americans dislike most is interesting, the heart of Sullivan et al.'s and Gibson's research focused on whether the public was *tolerant* of those groups that they disliked. Thus, after being asked which group they disliked most, both sets of survey respondents were asked whether they would support certain activities performed by members of the selected group, such as holding rallies and making speeches. All participants were also asked whether they would tolerate the following activities for communists and atheists: speechmaking (in 1978) and holding rallies (in 2005). This clever research design allows us to compare public levels of tolerance toward least liked groups with two of the groups that were the focus of Stouffer's research. The results to facilitate such a comparison are presented in Figure 9.3.

For both activities and in both 1978 and 2005, we see that public tolerance is higher for communists and atheists than it is for people's self-selected least liked group.[19] Regardless of which group was selected, in 1978, only 50 percent of the public would support speechmaking for their least liked group, whereas 63 percent and 65 percent would support such rights for communists and atheists, respectively. By 2005, tolerance of speechmaking for least liked groups had declined to 36 percent. A similar pattern exists for tolerance of rallies: less tolerance toward least liked groups in 2005 versus 1978 and more tolerance toward communists and atheists versus least liked groups.

Sullivan et al.'s new measures of tolerance significantly altered research on political tolerance and changed many people's conclusions about how tolerant Americans are. Their results, and Gibson's more recent work, seem to indicate that the public has not become significantly more tolerant over time, in contrast to the conclusions of those who updated Stouffer's analysis beginning in the 1970s. Such apparent increases in tolerance were misleading, argue Sullivan and colleagues, and were the result of less negative attitudes toward the groups under study rather than the result of more support for civil liberties among the public. During the Cold War of the 1950s, the **political times** produced especially high levels of intolerance toward communists and groups with similar ideologies. Yet, as time passed and the threat of communism receded in many people's minds, the public was more likely to support freedom of expression for these groups.

Figure 9.3 Tolerance of Least Liked Groups, Communists, and Atheists, 1978 and 2005

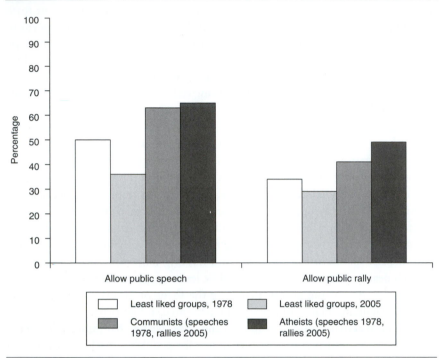

Least liked groups, 1978   Least liked groups, 2005

Communists (speeches 1978, rallies 2005)   Atheists (speeches 1978, rallies 2005)

Sources: Data from John L. Sullivan, James Piereson, and George E. Marcus, "An Alternative Conceptualization of Political Tolerance: Illusory Increases 1950s–1970s," *American Political Science Review* 73 (1979): 787; James L. Gibson, "Intolerance and Political Repression in the United States: A Half Century after McCarthyism," *American Journal of Political Science* 52 (2008): 104.

Concurrently, other political groups became the focus of public intolerance. By assessing public attitudes toward a variety of groups, and especially by allowing individuals to select which groups they strongly disliked, Sullivan et al. were able to pick up public intolerance that other researchers missed.

These high levels of intolerance would certainly disappoint classical democratic and participatory democratic theorists because the results indicate majorities of the public would restrict the rights of those individuals whose opinions they oppose. Further, when Sullivan and his colleagues asked whether least liked groups should be outlawed, over two-thirds of the public felt their most disliked group should not even be allowed to exist. Democracy, these theorists argue, requires the free exchange of ideas and the opportunity for political minorities to have their views represented in public forums.

Sullivan et al. did not view their findings quite as pessimistically for the prospect of democracy. Rather than leveling intolerance toward only one group, they concluded that **pluralistic intolerance** best describes Americans' attitudes toward civil liberties. Collectively, the public selects a number of groups to not tolerate. With intolerance spread around, it is not the case that only one group's rights are undermined by the tyranny of the majority. In other words, "the diversity of the targets selected works against and mitigates to some extent the rather high levels of intolerance."[20] On the other hand, Gibson draws quite a different conclusion about the effects of pluralistic intolerance. With more groups being disliked, it is more likely that any one person will think her civil liberties are under attack. As Gibson puts it, "Because some Communists are not tolerated and do not feel free, and because some Religious Fundamentalists are not tolerated and do not feel free, and because some of those sympathetic to other groups are not tolerated and do not feel free, the cumulative effect is more widespread feelings of lack of freedom today than in the McCarthy era."[21]

SOURCES OF TOLERANT ATTITUDES

There are many reasons why some people are more tolerant than others. Chief among these is a person's years of **formal education**. Just as theorists of participatory democracy hope and predict, the more education a person has, the more likely he will be tolerant toward people with unpopular political views. This relationship between education and tolerance has been uncovered by many researchers, beginning with Stouffer's study and continuing since.[22] Furthermore, some researchers have even concluded that education is the strongest predictor of how tolerant a person is.[23] Although there has been the rare challenge to this consensus, the overwhelming evidence is that more education leads to greater tolerance.[24] Why would this be? It is generally assumed that cognitive development accompanies formal education. More years of education can result in "greater acquaintance with the logical implications of the broad democratic principles."[25] Similarly, some suggest that education promotes "knowledge, a flexible cognitive style, and a broadened cultural sophistication."[26] In one of the few analyses to directly examine this assumption, people with more years of education were found to be more cognitively sophisticated (more intellectually engaged and more able to reason about complex concepts) and thus more tolerant of diverse viewpoints.[27]

Greater exposure to different ideas and people is another presumed outcome of more education. With **exposure to diversity** often comes greater acceptance of difference, as manifested in greater levels of tolerance.[28] For example, one study demonstrates that urban dwellers and white-collar workers were more tolerant than, respectively, rural residents and blue-collar employees.[29] This finding confirms Stouffer's assumption that group differences in tolerance levels are due to the fact that some demographic groups are less likely than others to come into contact with people unlike them. More recently, Diana Mutz explored the influence of exposure to diverse political perspectives on tolerance. She finds that people who have political discussion partners who hold views different than their own are more tolerant than are those who discuss politics only with like-minded individuals.[30] Repeated exposure to political difference, Mutz argues, translates into more support for the free expression rights of political groups, even those groups that an individual dislikes.

Other characteristics that predict whether a person will be tolerant include psychological features, most especially **personality traits**. People with low levels of self-esteem tend to be less tolerant, presumably because such negative attitudes toward self interfere with the learning of social norms, including tolerance. Further, dogmatic individuals are less likely to be tolerant, especially when compared with those who are more open-minded. In the words of Sullivan and his colleagues, "Persons with flexible, secure and trusting personalities are much more likely to be tolerant."[31]

Certain political attitudes, such as **support for democratic norms**, are also related to tolerance. People who tend to support civil liberties in the abstract, such as the principle of freedom of speech, and to support democratic procedural norms, such as majority vote, are more tolerant toward specific groups or acts.[32] **Political expertise** is also relevant. The more knowledgeable about and interested in politics a person is, the more tolerant she will be.[33]

Last but by no means least, **threat perceptions** are a particularly strong predictor of tolerance. Many researchers, beginning with Stouffer, have found that the more a person believes that a particular group is threatening, the less tolerant she is toward the group.[34] She might feel that the group threatens the American way of life and would threaten the stability of the government if the group becomes too powerful, engages in violent tactics and thus could threaten people and property, or is personally threatening to her because of the nature of the group's political views. Regardless of the exact nature of the threat, however, perceiving that a particular group is threatening can significantly reduce a person's tolerance of group members.

These predictors of tolerance can help us to understand one demographic group difference: women tend to be less tolerant than men. To explain why, Ewa Golebiowska compared the sources of women's tolerance judgments with the sources of men's.[35] Compared to men, women display lower support for democratic norms, in part because women are less likely to be politically knowledgeable and engaged. Furthermore, women are more likely than men to feel threatened by disliked groups. Heightened threat perceptions and lessened support for democratic norms both explain why women's support for free expression rights is lower than men's.

CONTEXTUAL INFLUENCES ON TOLERANCE JUDGMENTS

You have just learned that there are many individual-level attributes and attitudes that influence people's tolerance for political diversity. Certain features of the

context external to individuals also affect whether someone is tolerant. Contemporary events, both national and global, are relevant, as nicely illustrated by an examination of tolerance for communists.[36] Shortly before World War II, at a time of alliance between the Nazis in Germany and the communist-led government of the Soviet Union, tolerance for communists was fairly low in the United States. This was probably due to Americans feeling their democracy was especially threatened by both the Nazis and the Soviets. During the war, the Nazi-Soviet pact collapsed and the Soviet Union became an ally of the United States; then tolerance for communists increased. Once the war ended, tensions between the Soviet Union and the United States escalated. The public began to display lower support for civil liberties for communists because some citizens perceived an external threat from the Soviet Union and an internal threat from communists in the United States. As national attention, from both politicians and the news media, to domestic communism faded in the 1960s and 1970s, tolerance for the expression of communist beliefs increased.

One of the most systematic analyses of the influence of context on public tolerance was conducted by George Marcus, John Sullivan, Elizabeth Theiss-Morse, and Sandra Wood, results of which were published in their book *With Malice toward Some*.[37] Marcus and his colleagues carried out a series of experiments in which they manipulated two characteristics of groups involved in hypothetical civil liberties controversies. The first was whether the group violated norms regarding appropriate political activity. Was the group respectful and law-abiding or reckless and violent? Second, the likelihood of the group gaining political power was also manipulated. Marcus and colleagues found that participants who learned the group was likely to violate key norms expressed lower levels of tolerance than those who were reassured that the group would conduct its rallies peacefully and lawfully. The probability of power manipulation did not influence tolerance judgments.

Therefore, Marcus and his coauthors demonstrate that some features of the context surrounding a civil liberties controversy can influence tolerance. They do not conclude, however, that tolerance is related only to this contextual information. In fact, their model of tolerance judgments considers the roles that both individual predispositions (such as support for abstract democratic principles) and contextual information play. They conclude that "some people *tend* to be tolerant while others *tend* to be intolerant, but contemporary information . . . can elicit judgments that differ from people's standing decisions."[38] In other words, people who are predisposed to be tolerant can become less tolerant when presented with certain types of information.

Support for freedom of expression is an important value in democratic societies, but it is not the only one. This value can come in direct conflict with others, such as a desire for public order. Individuals can differ in which of these two they regard more highly, with consequences for their tolerance. A survey of members of the Houston Gay Political Caucus, for example, shows that caucus members who opposed the right of the Ku Klux Klan to march in opposition to homosexuality in a Houston gay neighborhood did so largely because they feared violence would break out at the march. Supporters of the Ku Klux Klan's right to march, however, were not so worried about potential violence and, instead, strongly supported freedom of expression for all.[39]

Significantly, the broader context can, at times, influence which of these competing values is most dominant. One source of this influence is the news media. Recall the Nelson, Clawson, and Oxley study about media framing of a Ku Klux Klan rally that we discuss in Chapter 3. That study demonstrated the effects of different media frames on levels of tolerance for the KKK. To briefly summarize, Nelson et al. conducted an experiment and showed that subjects exposed to a media frame emphasizing the disorder that might result from a KKK rally were significantly more intolerant of the KKK than subjects exposed to a media frame emphasizing freedom of speech for the KKK. This research demonstrates that journalists' choices regarding how to present the news can influence support for civil liberties. A steady stream of stories stressing groups' free speech rights would probably increase tolerance levels. Given the media's proclivity for airing stories that highlight violence and public disruption, however, a more likely outcome is lower levels of public tolerance toward all types of groups in the political minority.

Methods to Increase Tolerance

What other contextual features can increase tolerance? Among adolescents, exposure to a **tolerance curriculum** can produce greater tolerance of disliked groups. This is particularly likely if the lessons are designed to link democratic principles and the American legal system with specific examples of speech by unpopular groups, such as a case study of the Nazi-Skokie controversy.[40] In contrast, curricula that highlight only abstract democratic norms or that focus on the Bill of Rights (such as its history or related court cases) tend not to change support for civil liberties.[41]

Being reminded of the ideals of free expression can also increase tolerance. Marcus and his colleagues, in addition to the experiments already described, also conducted a study in which they controlled whether the participants were exposed to information extolling the virtues of free expression. In this new study, everyone read about a hypothetical group espousing unpopular political views. Some participants' scenarios included details that were meant to remind them of the **value of free expression**. The societal importance of open public debate was highlighted via statements such as "No matter how much I dislike these jerks [the hypothetical group], I feel strongly that they should have the freedom to say what they want to" or "People should have access to a variety of ideas, so that they can make up their minds based on full information."[42] Being exposed to such statements resulted in higher levels of tolerance. Although this conclusion was drawn from a laboratory experiment, Marcus and his coauthors conclude that in real-life civil liberties controversies, such as that which occurred when the Nazis wanted to march in Skokie, political elites could discuss these democratic principles more often: "Framing the issues in terms of a marketplace of ideas, stressing the positive role of dissent, and noting historic freedoms in the United States can increase support for tolerance, even when the group involved is extremely unpopular."[43]

ARE ELITES MORE TOLERANT?

Do elites express greater support for civil liberties than citizens do, as assumed by the theory of democratic elitism? Yes, according to a number of empirical analyses of this topic, beginning with Stouffer's important work. In addition to his public opinion poll of adults across the nation, Stouffer surveyed 1,500 local leaders from cities with populations between 10,000 and 150,000. For this portion of his research, he selected political elites (such as mayors and the chairs of county Democratic and Republican Party committees), community activists (such as the president of the women's club and president of the Parent-Teachers' Association), and people holding other top positions in these communities (including the Chamber of Commerce president and the publisher of the local newspaper).[44] The local leaders responded to the same tolerance questions contained on the public opinion poll. Results of the comparison between these elites and the mass public are clear—the leaders are much more tolerant of political minorities.[45] For example, whereas 84 percent of the leaders supported the right of a socialist to make a speech in the community, only 58 percent of the public did. Similarly, 51 percent of elites supported communists' speechmaking rights, whereas only 27 percent of the public expressed such support. This greater support for civil liberties among elites is a very robust finding. It has been demonstrated a number of other times, and it holds for many different types of elites, including national party activists and members of Congress.[46]

Explanations for Higher Elite Tolerance

Why would elites be more tolerant of minority viewpoints than citizens? One possible explanation focuses on differences in demographic characteristics of leaders versus the mass public. In general, political elites tend to possess characteristics, such as higher levels of education, that are related to higher levels of tolerance. A nice illustration of this pattern comes from research conducted by Robert Jackman.[47] Using Stouffer's data, Jackman compared the characteristics of the community leaders with the citizens who responded to Stouffer's poll. He found that the community leaders were more educated, more male, and less likely to live in the South. Forty-five percent of the leaders possessed a college degree, for example, whereas only 7.5 percent of the public did. Further, a majority of the leaders were men (77 percent), whereas only 47 percent of the public survey respondents were male. Because men, those with more education, and those living outside of the South are more tolerant than their counterparts, differences in these characteristics of the two samples accounted for their differing levels of support for civil liberties. When comparing leaders with members of the public with similar characteristics, Jackman noticed no sizable differences in levels of tolerance. In other words, community leaders who were male, nonsouthern, and college graduates expressed similar levels of tolerance as members of the public with the same characteristics. Similarly, female southern leaders with a high school diploma displayed roughly equivalent support for civil liberties as did female southern citizens with a high school diploma.

A second explanation for elite-public disparities posits that elites have higher levels of tolerance because of their direct involvement in politics.[48] Leaders experience specific adult socialization effects through their political activity, learning to become more tolerant. This increased tolerance occurs for a number of reasons:

> Greater and more intimate contact with ideological diversity decreases authoritarianism and increases tolerance; the necessity to compromise with individuals who disagree strongly with oneself can lead to a more realistic and less dramatic view of the threat presented by nonconformist groups and their ideas; the great responsibility of having actually to govern, of seeing the consequences of one's view enacted into policy and of shaping others' lives can lead to a "sober second thought" about the consequence of one's own intolerance.[49]

Support for this political socialization explanation was found in an examination of attitudes of politicians in four nations: Britain, Israel, New Zealand, and the United States. The elites in the study, all members of their national legislature, displayed more tolerance than would be expected given their levels of education, support for democratic norms, and personality traits such as dogmatism. In other words, the reason why elites are more tolerant is not only because they differ from the general public in certain characteristics that we know to be related to tolerance (such as having more education or being less dogmatic) but also because their engagement with politics socializes them differently than other adults. Note, however, that this finding contradicts Jackman's, but that is probably because of the different types of elites that were studied. Whereas Jackman's elites were local community leaders who were engaged in political activity to some degree, politics was not the primary career for many of these leaders, and they were certainly devoting less time and attention to politics than were national legislators. This suggests that the differential adult socialization of elites versus citizens will only emerge for elites at extremely high levels of political activity.

Public Opinion in Comparative Perspective
BOX 9.1 POLITICAL TOLERANCE IN DENMARK AND POLAND

Political tolerance in Europe was the focus of two books published in 2014. One examines a nation (Denmark) in the midst of a freedom of expression controversy. The other is a broad assessment of tolerance in Poland, a nation known for public intolerance.

Satirical cartoons depicting the prophet Mohammed were published in a Danish newspaper in 2005. The ensuing controversy pitted the value of free expression against respect for Mohammed and Islam. Leaders of Muslim countries demanded an apology from the Danish government, which was refused. Protests occurred throughout the Muslim world and Danish embassies in Syria and Pakistan were attacked. How did the Danish public respond to this series of events? First and foremost, by supporting the rights of Muslims in their country. While the cartoon crisis was still unfolding, public tolerance of the free expression rights of Muslims was high and equal to that of other minority groups such as Christian fundamentalists, according to Paul Sniderman, Michael Bang Petersen, Rune Slothuus, and Rune Stubager.[1] This result would not have been expected by many, given weariness in many European nations regarding Muslim immigration and rising levels of anti-immigrant sentiment more broadly in Denmark.

Why were the Danes so supportive of Muslims' rights? Sniderman and his colleagues argue that the Danish public view Muslims as a group that is legitimate even though they possess nonmainstream views. Contrast this with transgressive groups, those "that are not merely critical or out of step with the society but also actively pit themselves against it."[2] An example of such a group is Islamic fundamentalists. Throughout the cartoon crisis, the Danish public made clear distinctions between Muslims and Islamic fundamentalists, displaying far lower levels of tolerance toward the latter. The Danes thus were not tolerant of free expression rights for all. Yet they did not transfer their attitudes toward Islamic fundamentalists to all Muslims.

"Poland—an almost uniformly Catholic and ethnically Polish country, which experienced a lengthy period of authoritarian rule in the post-WWII period has a reputation for being intolerant, anti-Semitic, and homophobic."[3] So Ewa Golebiowska begins her book *The Many Faces of Tolerance*. The rest of the book tests this assumption by analyzing levels of tolerance in Poland toward a wide range of groups. Along the way,

(Continued)

Box 9.1   (Continued)

Golebiowska uncovers many pockets of intolerance. Support for the civil liberties of gays and lesbians and some political minority groups (militarists, Nazis, and racists especially) is low in Poland. Additionally, many Poles would prefer that women focus on home and family rather than engage in politics.

   On the other hand, Poles' tolerance of ethnic minority groups as well as women's political involvement has increased somewhat of late. Golebiowska credits these small changes in part to Poland's recent transition to democracy and accompanying institutional protection of political minority groups. As for the sources of public tolerance in Poland, Golebiowska finds that tolerance is higher among Poles that have more formal education, are younger, are less religious, are less authoritarian, and are more supportive of democratic norms in the abstract. Many of these characteristics, as you now know, also predict tolerance in the United States. In the end, the portrait presented by Golebiowska demonstrates that "there is more than a kernel of truth to the stereotype of Poland as a sanctuary for intolerance" but that the overall "picture is far more complex."[4]

---

1. Paul M. Sniderman, Michael Bang Petersen, Rune Slothuus, and Rune Stubager, *Paradoxes of Liberal Democracy: Islam, Western Europe, and the Danish Cartoon Crisis* (Princeton, NJ: Princeton University Press, 2014).
2. Ibid., 24.
3. Ewa A. Golebiowska, *The Many Faces of Tolerance: Attitudes Toward Diversity in Poland* (New York: Routledge, 2014), 1.
4. Ibid., 10.

Civil Liberties Post-9/11

Not surprisingly, in response to the September 11, 2001, al-Qaeda attacks on New York City and Washington, DC, national leaders made some significant changes to **counterterrorism policies** (policies designed to identify and capture suspected terrorists). Along with these changes came concerns that the new policies were infringing on individual liberty. The ensuing, and continuing, debate regarding the proper balance between protecting the homeland and upholding civil liberties is summarized well by public opinion scholar Darren Davis:

> Unequivocal support for democratic rights, in the context of terrorism, has been seen as tantamount to *constitutional suicide*—that is, the ultimate demise of society because strict adherence to civil liberties and rights makes it impossible to detect potential threats. And yet allowing the government and law enforcement to usurp individual liberties may potentially jeopardize

liberty for everyone. Innocent and law-abiding citizens would be threatened not only by terrorists, but also by their government.[50]

What has the public thought about balancing civil liberty and national security in the post-9/11 era? Thanks to pollsters at the Pew Research Center, we can find out. Over nearly fifteen years, Pew asked respondents the following question: "In order to curb terrorism in this country, do you think it will be necessary for the average person to give up some civil liberties, or not?" The percentages of the public thinking it necessary to give up liberties appear in Figure 9.4 (the solid line). In the late 1990s, only around 30 percent of the public thought Americans would need to sacrifice some civil liberties to fight terrorism. This figure shot up to 55 percent immediately after the 2001 al-Qaeda attacks. It has declined fairly steadily since, with only 27 percent of the public holding this view in 2009.

Figure 9.4   Public Opinion: Civil Liberties versus National Security

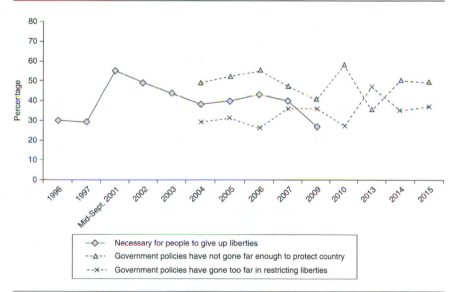

Sources: Data from "Independents Take Center Stage in Obama Era: Trends in Political Values and Core Attitudes: 1987–2009," Pew Research Center, Washington, DC, May 21, 2009, http://people-press.org/2009/05/21/independents-take-center-stage-in-obama-era; "Terrorism Worries Little Changed; Most Give Government Good Marks for Reducing Threat," Pew Research Center, Washington, DC, January 12, 2015, http://www.people-press.org/2015/01/12/terrorism-worries-little-changed-most-give-government-good-marks-for-reducing-threat/#views-of-governments-handling-of-terrorist-threat

Note: 2007 data for dashed lines are actually from 2008.

Since 2004, Pew has also asked respondents to assess the government's policies to combat terrorism using the civil liberties versus national security yardstick. Specifically, the surveys asked, "What concerns you more about the government's anti-terrorism policies: That they have gone too far in restricting the average person's civil liberties [or] That they have not gone far enough to adequately protect the country?" Results for both of these options are presented in Figure 9.4 (dashed lines). Between 2004 and 2009, Americans were more likely to think that antiterrorism policies were not protecting the nation than that the policies were restricting civil liberties, with the gap between these two narrowing somewhat.

Public attitudes have fluctuated since then, in response to national and international events. In January 2010, the gap blew wide open, with over twice as many people more concerned that policies did not protect the nation than that they restricted liberties (58 versus 27 percent). Why this change? On Christmas 2009, an alleged al-Qaeda member, Umar Farouk Abdulmutallab, hid explosives in his underwear and attempted to blow up a Northwest Airlines plane flying from Amsterdam to Detroit. Abdulmutallab failed. Yet his near success and the fact that he was able to board a plane with explosives on his body raised concerns about the effectiveness of the nation's counterterrorism policies. Three years later, and for the only time since 2004, the public was more concerned with protecting civil liberties than national security. Credit should go to Edward Snowden for this reversal. Snowden, a former contractor with the National Security Agency, leaked documents in 2013 revealing that the NSA had been collecting telephone and Internet data from millions of Americans. Whereas the public had been willing to support many government actions in the fight against terrorism, many felt this NSA activity was a step too far. Throughout 2014 and 2015, Americans' focus shifted to potential terrorist activity, producing a return to favoring security over civil liberties. In particular, many citizens were worried about the growing power in the Middle East of ISIS (the Islamic State of Iraq and Syria, also known as the Islamic State of Iraq and the Levant or ISIL). A militant extremist group, ISIS aims to create an Islamic state. Its tactics have included kidnappings, beheadings, and mass executions.

Taken together, the results in Figure 9.4 present a portrait of citizens who generally, although not always, think current terrorism policies do not unduly restrict liberties. Furthermore, the changes over time in all three lines make sense, given what we know about the role of threat in civil liberties judgments. Americans tend to be more willing to sacrifice civil liberties when they feel threatened than when they feel secure.[51] This was the case, for example, after Timothy McVeigh bombed the Oklahoma City federal building in 1995, purportedly in retaliation for federal authorities raiding the compound of a religious group, the Branch Davidians, near Waco, Texas. The Oklahoma City bombing resulted in the deaths of 168 people, making it the deadliest domestic terrorist act in the United States. Shortly after the Oklahoma City bombing, nearly one-half of the public felt that giving up some civil liberties would be necessary to fight terrorism.

Two years later, however, during which time no other acts of terrorism occurred on U.S. soil, only 29 percent of the public was willing to sacrifice these liberties.[52] We see a similar trend in the years since the 9/11 attacks. When terrorism is in the news, as was the case with the Christmas 2009 failed airliner bombing or the more recent actions of ISIS, the balance between prioritizing security or liberty tips more toward security.

Which Americans are most willing to trade civil liberties for protecting the nation from terrorism? Not surprisingly, people who feel most threatened by terrorism. As Darren Davis and Brian Silver explain, "The 9/11 attacks . . . caused widespread anxiety and concern among Americans. One emotional response to threat is to try to reduce the discomfort by increasing personal security, increasing physical and psychological distance, or eliminating the threatening stimuli."[53]

In probing post-9/11 attitudes toward civil liberties, however, Davis and Silver reveal that threat perception is only one piece of the puzzle. Trust in government, especially law enforcement, is also relevant. Considering only those people who place a lot of trust in the government, support for civil liberties is lowest for citizens who are very concerned that another terrorist attack might occur. However, people who display little trust in government demonstrate stronger support for civil liberties whether they fear another terrorist attack or not. In other words, for people who are distrustful of government, this distrust overrides their concern about future terrorist activity, and they are less willing to trade civil liberties for security. Finally, Davis and Silver conclude that personal characteristics, especially political ideology and race, also influenced how citizens responded to the 9/11 attacks. Liberals were consistently less willing to support restrictions on civil liberties than were conservatives, and African Americans expressed stronger pro–civil liberties positions than either whites or Latinos. Davis and Silver attribute this latter finding to African Americans' "struggle for civil rights and . . . distrust of government. As a result, African Americans may be reluctant to concede rights that they have worked hard to achieve or to empower a government in which they have little confidence, even for the sake of personal security."[54]

Public Opinion's "Dark Side"

A variety of specific counterterrorism policies were implemented by the national government in the weeks and years after the 9/11 attacks. One was the **USA Patriot Act** (Uniting and Strengthening America by Providing Appropriate Tools Required to Intercept and Obstruct Terrorism). This legislation, passed in October 2001, made it easier for federal authorities to issue telephone wiretap orders, conduct searches, and obtain the records (financial, library, Internet usage, and so on) of individuals. Since 2001, the federal government has been classifying some suspected terrorists as **enemy combatants**. Enemy combatants, according to federal policy, can be held without being charged with a specific crime and can be tried by a military commission without some of the civil liberties afforded to citizens who are accused of committing crimes. Many of these enemy combatants are still being held at a U.S. military prison in Guantanamo Bay, Cuba. Furthermore, people with the same racial or religious characteristics as the 9/11 hijackers have been targeted by airport security screeners and law enforcement officials. Such **racial profiling**, which involves selecting someone for questioning or extra scrutiny on the basis of race or ethnicity, had historically been used most commonly in the United States to target African Americans. In the wake of the 9/11 attacks, however, profiling is used in an attempt to identify suspected terrorists.

Does the public support these and other counterterrorism policies? Answering this question is the primary goal of Clem Brooks and Jeff Manza's book *Whose Rights?*[55] Indeed, their research is one of the most comprehensive analyses of public opinion, civil liberties, and counterterrorism policy in the post-9/11 era.[56] Overall, Brooks and Manza conclude that the "attitudes and beliefs of Americans have a dark side, a willingness to suppress otherwise strong support for civil rights and liberties in the name of national crisis and perceived threats."[57] Their evidence comes from nationally representative surveys that they conducted in 2007, 2009, and 2010. In these surveys, they assessed public support for a wide range of counterterrorism policies (see Figure 9.5). The bars in this figure represent the average level of support for each policy, measured on a scale from zero to one. A score of zero represents strong opposition to the policy whereas one equals strong support. Results greater than .5 thus demonstrate that the public is, on average, more approving than disapproving of the policy.

A few aspects of these results are noteworthy. First, Americans are not equally supportive of all policies. The public is most supportive of the NSA surveillance policy (as of 2009). The lowest support was registered for two policies: the use of waterboarding on suspected terrorists and torture for the purpose of gathering information to prevent a future attack. Second, the average level of support was greater than .5 for seven of the nine counterterrorism policies. Indeed, the average was lower for only the waterboarding and torture policies. Third, these public attitudes were assessed not in the immediate aftermath of the 9/11 attacks but rather nearly ten years later. The high level of support for most of these policies coupled with the time delay since the 2001 attacks were two factors contributing to Brooks and Manza's categorization of these attitudes as representing a dark side of the public. Furthermore, they speculate that "support for coercive policies may become relatively enduring, persisting beyond the initial context in which political leaders offered their original justifications."[58]

Pushing beyond overall support for counterterrorism policies, Brooks and Manza explore whether public attitudes vary depending on the identity of the groups targeted by the policies. To do so, they embedded experiments within their surveys. **Survey-based experiments** enable researchers to manipulate the wording of questions on a survey administered to a national representative sample of Americans. Respondents are randomly assigned to receive one out of multiple

Figure 9.5   Public Support for Counterterrorism Policies, 2009 and 2010

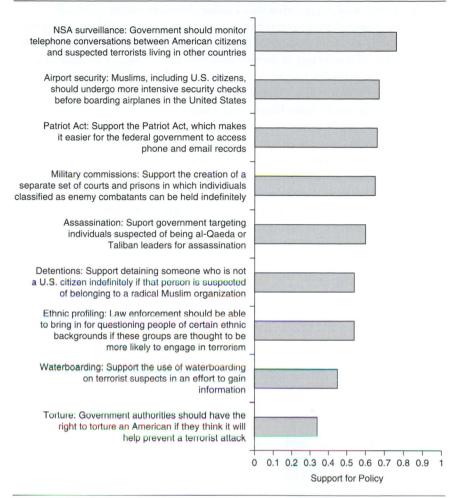

Source: Clem Brooks and Jeff Manza, *Whose Rights? Counterterrorism and the Dark Side of Public Opinion* (New York: Russell Sage Foundation, 2013), Chap. 3.

Note: Data for NSA surveillance and Military commissions from 2009; all others from 2010.

versions of a question. In Brooks and Manza's case, they altered who was targeted by a specific policy. One version of a question assessing attitudes toward the use of military commissions asked "should the government move *American citizens* who are terrorism suspects to special military prisons and rely on military courts?"[59] Some respondents received that military commissions question, whereas others received a question asking about *foreign nationals* rather than U.S. citizens. The third version of this question asked about *American citizens of Middle Eastern background.* Other than the group target, these three versions of the question were worded exactly the same. Because of this and because respondents were randomly assigned to receive only one of the versions, Brooks and Manza are able to assess whether public attitudes toward this policy depend on which groups of people are being targeted for military commissions.

Some of the results from Brooks and Manza's survey experiments appear in Figure 9.6. The public is more supportive of using military prisons and trials for suspected terrorists who are foreign nationals versus those who are American citizens. For this policy, support was not significantly different for American citizens of Middle Eastern background compared to all American citizens. This latter distinction did matter when it came to NSA surveillance. Average public support was twice as high when the American citizens being monitored by the government have a Middle Eastern background. In contrast, the identity of Americans who would be subject to torture in pursuit of preventing future attacks did not influence public support for this policy. When it comes to torturing American citizens, the public's opinions are not very malleable. In other words, people seem to either

Figure 9.6   Counterterrorism Policy Opinions Vary by Identity of Target

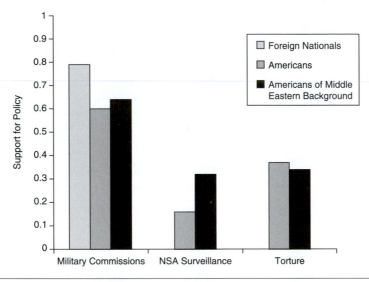

Source: Clem Brooks and Jeff Manza, *Whose Rights? Counterterrorism and the Dark Side of Public Opinion* (New York: Russell Sage Foundation, 2013), 103, 121, 137.

Note: Bars represent the average support for each item.

support torture or oppose torture no matter the identity of the suspect. Unfortunately, we do not know whether the public would be more supportive of torture (or, for that matter, NSA surveillance) if the policy were directed at citizens from other nations. These two survey experiments did not contain a condition for foreign nationals.

Brooks and Manza's broad conclusion from across their set of experiments is that the public tends to be more supportive of policies that are more obviously directed toward foreigners or toward those with the same ethnic characteristics as the 9/11 hijackers.[60] Given the history of citizens displaying lower levels of tolerance for the civil liberties of unpopular groups, these results are not unexpected. Finally, you might have noticed that support for NSA surveillance is much lower in this figure than in Figure 9.5. This is likely explained by differences in question wording. The results presented in Figure 9.5 demonstrate support for monitoring telephone conversations between U.S. citizens and suspected terrorists *who live abroad*. The survey experiment instead queried support for monitoring "telephone conversations, banking transactions, and email between American citizens [or American citizens of Middle Eastern background] in the United States."[61] Not only is the sweep of government monitoring broader in the second version, but only U.S. citizens would be targeted. The different results from these two questions likely capture the public's greater willingness to support counterterrorism policies that target foreign nationals, especially those who are suspected of terrorism.

CONCLUSION

Are Americans tolerant of nonconformity? Is the public more or less tolerant than elites? What are the sources of tolerance and intolerance? Does public support for civil liberties change as political times do? These questions motivated Samuel Stouffer to write *Communism, Conformity, and Civil Liberties* almost sixty years ago. Although the answers have changed somewhat and certainly have become more complex since, these questions continue to be the focus of most political tolerance research today. Stouffer was also worried about the implications of public intolerance for the nation and therefore proposed solutions for increasing levels of tolerance. Discussing whether the level of tolerance is high or low enough in a polity is, of course, at the heart of democratic theorists' writings on civil liberties. It is to democratic theory that we now turn, particularly evaluating the assumptions of both elite and participatory theories of democracy in light of conclusions drawn from political science studies of tolerance.

Elite Democracy

Elite democrats expect the public to be intolerant toward those whose views they reject, especially because of the public's self-interested proclivities and disengagement from political forums where opposing views are aired. Thus, these theorists would not be terribly surprised by Stouffer's findings of widespread public intolerance, similar conclusions drawn by Sullivan and colleagues and by Gibson, and post-9/11 public support for restricting the civil liberties of those who are thought to be sympathetic to or engaged in terrorist activities. Moreover, democratic elitists argue that the leaders of a nation will display more support for civil liberties than the public, a point that is also supported by the empirical political science research. Recall that these theorists went one step further, arguing that the leaders' support for civil liberties would ensure that these liberties are protected, even in the face of much public intolerance. Yet, even though elites do profess more attitudinal support for civil liberties than the citizens do, the *actions* of elected officials do not always coincide with their expressed support for civil liberties in the abstract. When the Nazi party requested permission to march in Skokie, for example, it was the city's politicians who enacted local laws designed to prevent the march. After the 9/11 attacks, it was members of Congress who passed and President Bush who signed the USA Patriot Act of 2001, which allowed the federal government more latitude in collecting information on citizens. Many of Bush's counter-terrorism policies have continued under President Obama, such as the NSA phone and Internet surveillance program and the detention of suspected terrorists in Guantanamo Bay. These examples remind us that elite democratic theory has perhaps overstated its case that elites will ensure the maintenance of civil liberties in a democracy.

More recently, elected elites have taken action on the issue of immigration in a way that restricts civil liberties. Anti-immigration laws that curtail individual freedoms have been passed in a handful of states. In April 2010, for instance, Arizona passed a law that would, in the words of one reporter, "hand the police in the state broad power under state law to check the legal status of people they reasonably suspect are illegal immigrants."[62] Specifically, the law requires police officers to request immigration documents from people they have stopped if they are suspected of being in the nation illegally, a provision that was upheld by the U.S. Supreme Court in 2012.[63] Opponents argue that the law will lead to racial and ethnic profiling, with Hispanics in Arizona, including U.S. citizens, facing discriminatory treatment. Supporters counter that laws such as this are necessary for identifying and, eventually, deporting illegal immigrants.

Participatory Democracy

Beyond their faith in elites, there is another reason why elite democrats do not worry very much about high levels of public intolerance. Because, according to these theorists, citizens are generally too apathetic to engage in political activity, the likelihood that the public will engage in any behavior to actually limit the civil liberties of others is low. "Apathy . . . furnishes its own partial corrective by keeping the [intolerant] from acting upon their differences. In the United States, at least, their disagreements are *passive* rather than active, more the result of political ignorance and indifference than of intellectual conviction."[64] Such a viewpoint maddens theorists of participatory democracy. A nation's continued commitment to support for minority rights and other civil liberties should not be predicated on the apathy of a segment of the citizenry, argue participatory democrats. Among the key democratic goals for these theorists is the full involvement of the citizenry, so they find any argument that applauds the political uninvolvement of the public worrisome.

In contrast, participatory democrats want the public to be more involved in politics, believing that people can learn to become more tolerant through political activity. Thus, participatory democrats are quite pleased with the empirical evidence that formal education leads to more tolerant attitudes and the conclusion that political leaders are more tolerant than the public because of the leaders' exposure to political activity, especially bargaining and compromising with their opponents. These two findings are promising for increasing citizen tolerance in that they suggest routes to pursue this goal. Further, the fact that specific types of high school curricula can increase tolerance is especially relevant to participatory democrats' arguments and demonstrates the role that the educational system could play: "If civic education were to include a systematic examination of the role of dissent in a democratic society, young people might develop a commitment to protect civil liberties that would ultimately engender a more fully democratic citizenry."[65]

As should be clear, most participatory democrats assume that high levels of public tolerance are ideal for a democracy. It is worth considering, however, whether supporting the free expression rights of some groups might actually undermine tolerance. Take a group that advocates white supremacy and hatred of blacks, such as the KKK. If the KKK speaks out in favor of curtailing the political rights of blacks, and if this speech then reduces the participation of blacks or removes the viewpoints of blacks from the marketplace of ideas, is it tolerant to support the views of the KKK? Or take an issue that has been on the agenda of a few state legislatures recently: religious freedom. On their face, religious freedom laws may seem to protect the free exercise of religion by preventing the government from interfering with this right. Yet recent versions of these laws, such as the one passed in Indiana in March 2015, have come under fire because they appear to legalize discrimination against groups toward which a person or business might have religious objections.[66] If such a law exists, opponents argue, what's to stop owners of a reception hall or catering business from refusing to provide wedding services to same-sex couples in the name of religious freedom?

These debates suggest that tolerance might not require supporting the political expression of all viewpoints in a democracy, that some viewpoints are "uniquely undeserving of First Amendment protection."[67] In other words, are "the citizens of a democracy obliged to tolerate those who, if they prevailed, would destroy the practice of tolerance? If tolerance is among the highest values in democratic regimes, does it make sense to tolerate those who threaten this very principle?"[68] To some people, however, particularly those for whom the freedom of expression of all groups is an absolute necessity, raising such questions is downright intolerant. This debate, which, by the way, was prevalent during the Skokie-Nazi controversy, will exist as long as differing understandings of tolerance and intolerance exist in society.

Key Concepts

atheists / 253	personality traits / 262
Bill of Rights / 251	pluralistic intolerance / 261
civil liberties / 250	political expertise / 262
communists / 253	political times / 259
constitutional framework / 251	political tolerance / 250
context / 263	racial profiling / 272
counterterrorism policies / 268	racists / 255
enemy combatants / 271	socialists / 253
exposure to diversity / 261	support for democratic norms / 262
formal education / 261	survey-based experiments / 272
homosexuals / 255	threat perceptions / 262
least liked group / 257	tolerance curriculum / 264
marketplace of ideas / 250	USA Patriot Act / 271
militarists / 255	value of free expression / 264
Muslim extremists / 255	

Suggested Sources for Further Reading

Barnum, David G. "Decision Making in a Constitutional Democracy: Policy Formation in the Skokie Free Speech Controversy." *Journal of Politics* 44 (1982): 480–508.

Gibson, James L., and Richard D. Bingham. "Skokie, Nazis, and the Elitist Theory of Democracy." *Western Political Quarterly* 37 (1984): 32–47.

These two articles discuss the Skokie free speech controversy and its implications for the theory of democratic elitism.

Brooks, Clem, and Jeff Manza. *Whose Rights? Counterterrorism and the Dark Side of Public Opinion.* New York: Russell Sage Foundation, 2013.

Davis, Darren W. *Negative Liberty: Public Opinion and the Terrorist Attacks on America.* New York: Russell Sage Foundation, 2007.

Merolla, Jennifer L., and Elizabeth J. Zechmeister. *Democracy at Risk: How Terrorist Threats Affect the Public*. Chicago: University of Chicago Press, 2009.

These books are all detailed examinations of public support for civil liberties and counterterrorism policies in the post-9/11 era.

Marcus, George E., John L. Sullivan, Elizabeth Theiss-Morse, and Sandra L. Wood. *With Malice toward Some: How People Make Civil Liberties Judgments*. Cambridge, UK: Cambridge University Press, 1995.

In a series of experiments, the authors demonstrate that new information about unpopular political groups (such as whether they intend to hold a rally that will be violent) can interact with people's existing beliefs (such as whether they support freedom of expression in the abstract) to influence tolerance judgments.

Stouffer, Samuel A. *Communism, Conformity, and Civil Liberties: A Cross-Section of the Nation Speaks Its Mind*. Garden City, NY: Doubleday, 1955.

In this classic study, Stouffer thoroughly examines Americans' tolerance toward nonconformists. More broadly, the book provides a portrait of the public's views toward communism, communists, and the communist threat in the 1950s.

Sullivan, John L., James Pierson, and George E. Marcus. *Political Tolerance and American Democracy*. Chicago: University of Chicago Press, 1982.
Gibson, James L. "Measuring Political Tolerance and General Support for Pro-Civil Liberties Policies: Notes, Evidence, and Cautions." *Public Opinion Quarterly* 77 (2013 Special Issue): 45–68.

In *Political Tolerance and American Democracy*, the authors present their least liked group measure of tolerance, explain why it is a better measure than others, and discuss many sources of political tolerance. Gibson's article compares measures of tolerance, including the least liked group approach, and attitudes toward civil liberties policies.

American Civil Liberties Union, www.aclu.org

One of the nation's leading organizations supporting civil liberties, the ACLU aims, in a variety of ways, to ensure the individual protections provided for in the U.S. Constitution are upheld. Its website details the organization's activities and presents a wealth of information about many civil liberties issues, such as free speech, religious liberty, mass incarceration, the death penalty, and immigrants' rights.

Teaching Tolerance, www.tolerance.org

A program of the Southern Poverty Law Center, this website provides many free resources, including teaching tools, for people who wish to fight bias and promote respect for diversity in their communities.

"What Americans Think About Privacy," Pew Research Center, http://www .pewinternet.org/2014/11/12/what-americans-think-about-privacy

This interactive website allows you to compare views toward privacy and government surveillance of digital communication for different Americans (e.g., young vs. old, women vs. men, social media users vs. nonusers). Results on the site are based on surveys and focus groups conducted by the Pew Research Center.

CHAPTER 10

Support for Civil Rights

DURING SUMMER 2015, Hillary Clinton was the frontrunner for the Democratic Party's 2016 presidential nomination. Clinton, who had nearly universal name recognition as a former first lady who went on to serve as a U.S. senator from New York and as secretary of state in the Obama administration, was raising substantial sums of money and leading in the polls in Iowa, the first caucus state. If Clinton were to win the Democratic nomination, let alone win the presidency, history would be made. A woman has never won a major-party nomination or been elected president. History was already made in 2008 when Barack Obama became the first African American president of the United States and again in 2012 when Republican Mitt Romney became the first Mormon to win a major-party nomination. Will 2016 be another first? What does the public think of this turn of events? How supportive are citizens of candidates who break the mold?

One marker of a democratic society is the openness of its political system to citizens from many different walks of life. If elected officials only come from a narrow stratum of society, it raises questions about how representative the institutions of government truly are. In the United States, the institutions of government do not accurately reflect the diversity of the citizenry. Take gender, for example. As of 2015, the U.S. Congress is 19 percent female.[1] Obviously that is low given the proportion of women in society. It is also low compared with many other countries around the world. The United States ranks 75th out of 190 countries in terms of female representation in its legislature.[2] And of course the presidency is the ultimate bastion of male dominance. Running for vice president on a major-party ticket is the closest women have made it to the presidency, and only two women have achieved that, Representative Geraldine Ferraro (D-N.Y.) in 1984 and Alaska governor Sarah Palin in 2008. Certainly there are no laws on the books that stop women or minorities from seeking political office, so why is there this inequality in officeholding? Are citizens' attitudes toward women and minorities partially to blame for the lack of diversity in our institutions?

In this chapter, we discuss how supportive citizens are of political rights for women and minorities, specifically in terms of holding the office of president. If even a small segment of society is biased against women and minorities, it can have huge electoral implications. Over the last two decades, presidential elections have been decided by differences in the popular vote of fewer than 10 percentage points. In 2000, the difference between Al Gore and George W. Bush was 0.5 percentage point; in 2004, the difference between John Kerry and George W. Bush was 2.5 percentage points; in 2008, the difference between John McCain and Barack Obama was 7.3 percentage points; and in 2012, the difference between Barack Obama and Mitt Romney was 3.9 percentage points.[3] Given such an evenly split electorate, hesitation on the part of citizens to vote for someone due to a particular characteristic could spell disaster for that candidate.

Political rights are a specific type of civil right we discuss in this chapter, but we also examine support for other **civil rights**. "Civil rights are government guarantees of equality for people in the United States with regard to judicial proceedings, the exercise of political rights, treatment by public officials, and access to and enjoyment of the benefits of government programs."[4] In particular, we examine public opinion concerning civil rights policies geared toward two groups: African Americans and gays and lesbians.

We focus on African Americans because they are an important group in the United States, both historically and in contemporary society. African Americans have had to fight for their civil rights since the founding of this nation, and the struggle has been a long and hard one. Today African Americans still battle to preserve their civil rights and work to expand them further. In addition, we highlight opinion toward policies dealing with African Americans for practical reasons. Social scientists have collected extensive public opinion data on issues dealing with African Americans; unfortunately, other racial minority groups have not received nearly as much attention.

In comparison with African Americans, the movement for gay and lesbian rights is a more recent phenomenon. Over the last few decades, gay and lesbian issues have become quite prominent. In the 1980s, fear of AIDS led to concerns about job discrimination against gays and lesbians. The "Don't Ask, Don't Tell" policy that allowed gays and lesbians to serve in the military as long as they did not reveal their sexual orientation was an extremely divisive issue in the 1990s. In the 2000s, same-sex marriage became a heated issue in the United States, but then in the early 2010s, the repeal of "Don't Ask, Don't Tell" allowed gays and lesbians to serve openly in the military. By 2015 the U.S. Supreme Court had upheld same-sex marriage as the law of the land. We examine how public opinion shifted on these issues across time.

Controversies over civil rights concern participatory democratic theorists a great deal. Participatory democratic theorists worry about equality in the political sphere and, thus, are concerned when the path to leadership is not open to all citizens. To these theorists, opposition to civil rights reflects the fact that many citizens are not actively involved in politics. If all citizens participated in political decision making, then women and minorities would have more power within the political system and thus would be able to successfully push for civil rights. Furthermore, participatory democratic theorists believe that participation in and of itself produces better citizens. That is, political interactions with many different types of people allow citizens to see beyond their narrow worlds and to gain a better understanding of what's good for other citizens and for the nation as a whole. As a result, citizens would probably demonstrate greater support for civil rights.

In contrast, elite democratic theorists are not particularly concerned with equality in society. Indeed, some elite democratic theorists *expect* that certain inequities will exist in the political system. Thus, they would not be surprised that our institutions of government do not reflect the diversity of society. Other elite democratic theorists are not concerned about opposition to civil rights among the public because these theorists emphasize that elites are the key political players. Because the elites appreciate and support the rights of minorities, the public's views on the subject don't really matter.

PUBLIC OPINION AND PRESIDENTIAL CANDIDATES

There are very few formal qualifications to run for president of the United States. A person must be a natural-born citizen, at least thirty-five years of age, and a resident of the United States for fourteen years to be eligible for the presidency. That's it. In practice, however, the story is much different. The youngest president ever elected was John F. Kennedy at forty-three years old, and the oldest was Ronald Reagan at sixty-nine. The majority of presidents have been between the ages of fifty and fifty-nine when elected. Only one president has been Catholic, and two have been Quakers. Just one has been African American, and no woman has ever been elected to the highest office in the land. What explains why presidents have come from such a limited pool of citizens? We turn to some fascinating public opinion data to help answer this question.

Religion and Presidential Candidates

For several decades, the Gallup organization has asked citizens whether they would vote for particular types of candidates if nominated by their party.[5] Let's first examine support for candidates of different religious faiths (see Figure 10.1). Support for Baptist presidential candidates has been high since the question was first asked in 1958.[6] In contrast, support for a Catholic was modest in 1937 but has climbed steadily since then. Support for a Jewish candidate was under 50 percent in 1937 but has also increased over time. In 2015, over 90 percent of citizens said they would vote for a well-qualified Catholic or Jew if nominated by their party.

Support for a Mormon president has stayed remarkably steady over time. The question was first asked in 1967 when George Romney (Mitt Romney's father) ran for the Republican presidential nomination. At that time, 75 percent of

Figure 10.1   Support for Presidential Candidates, 1937–2015: Religion

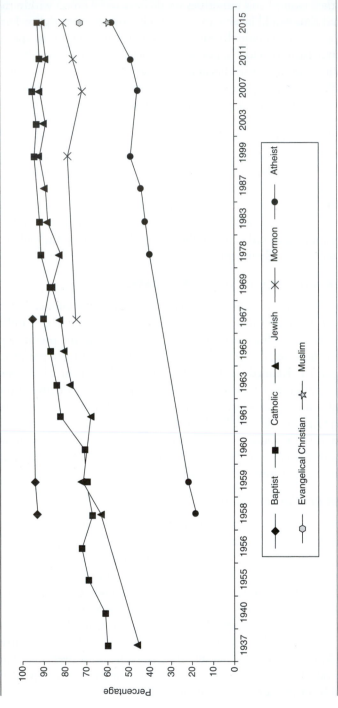

Sources: Lydia Saad, "Support for Nontraditional Candidates Varies by Religion," Gallup, June 24, 2015, http://www.gallup.com/poll/183791/support-nontraditional-candidates-varies-religion.aspx; Mariana Servín-González and Oscar Torres-Reyna, "Trends: Religion and Politics," *Public Opinion Quarterly* 63 (1999): 610–611.

Note: Gallup's question wording has varied over time. The question wording from the 2015 Gallup poll: "Between now and the 2016 political conventions, there will be discussion about the qualifications of presidential candidates—their education, age, religion, race, and so on. If your party nominated a generally well-qualified person for president who happened to be a _____, would you vote for that person?" These questions were asked on more than one Gallup poll in 1958 and 1959. The data presented here come from the September 10–15, 1958, poll and the December 10–15, 1959, poll.

Americans said they would vote for a Mormon nominated by their party. Nearly fifty years later, support for a Mormon has increased by just a few percentage points. Thus, there remains significant opposition to a Mormon becoming president of the United States.

A Mormon's chances look good, however, compared with an atheist's chances. In the late 1950s, support for an atheist presidential candidate was very weak at 18 percent, and although it has tripled since then, it is still fairly low. In June 2015, only 58 percent of Americans said they would vote for a well-qualified atheist if nominated by their political party. Gallup only recently started measuring attitudes toward Muslim and evangelical Christian candidates, so unfortunately we don't know how those attitudes have changed over time. Only 60 percent of Americans said they would support a well-qualified Muslim nominated by their party in 2015, and 73 percent indicated they would vote for an evangelical Christian. Perhaps not surprisingly, there are large partisan differences in attitudes toward atheist, Muslim, and evangelical Christian candidates with Republicans much more supportive of evangelical Christian candidates than Democrats, and Democrats much more supportive of atheists and Muslims than Republicans.[7]

Another way to examine support for candidates with various religious affiliations is to ask citizens whether they would be *more or less likely* to support a candidate with particular characteristics. The Pew Research Center conducts polls doing just that (see Table 10.1). In recent years, Pew has asked about support for

Table 10.1 Religion and Likelihood to Vote for a Presidential Candidate

"We'd like to know how you generally feel about some different traits. Would you be more likely or less likely to support a candidate for president who is _____, or wouldn't this matter to you?"

Response	Evangelical Christian (2014)	Mormon (2011)	Muslim (2007)	Does not believe in God (2014)
More likely to support	21%	5%	1%	5%
Less likely to support	17	25	46	53
Wouldn't matter	58	68	49	41
Don't know/refused	4	3	4	2

Sources: "Voters Remain in Neutral as Presidential Campaign Moves into High Gear," Pew Research Center, February 23, 2007, http://people-press. org/2007/02/23/voters-remain-in-neutral-as-presidential-campaign-moves-into-high-gear; "Candidate Traits: D.C. Experience Viewed Less Positive," Pew Research Center, June 2, 2011, http://people-press.org/files/legacy-pdf/06-02-11%202012%20Campaign%20Release.pdf; "For 2016 Hopefuls, Washington Experience Could Do More Harm than Good," May 19, 2014, Pew Research Center, http://www.people-press.org/files/legacy-pdf/5-19-14%20Presidential%20Traits%20Release.pdf

evangelical Christian, Mormon, Muslim, and atheist presidential candidates. For 58 percent of people, whether a candidate is an evangelical Christian wouldn't matter; when it does matter, being a Christian is slightly more likely to help the person than hurt him or her. Sixty-eight percent of people said it wouldn't matter if a candidate were Mormon, but when it does matter, it works strongly against the candidate. Twenty-five percent said they would be less likely to support a Mormon, whereas only 5 percent said they would be more likely to support a Mormon. Just less than one-half of Americans indicated that a candidate being Muslim wouldn't matter to them, whereas 46 percent said they would be less likely to support such a candidate. Still, being a Muslim puts a candidate at an advantage over an atheist. Fifty-three percent of Americans said they would be less likely to support a candidate who does not believe in God. Given these current levels of public opposition, it seems unlikely that the United States will have either a Muslim or an atheist president any time soon.

Race, Ethnicity, and Presidential Candidates

What about citizens' attitudes toward presidential candidates who are racial or ethnic minorities? In 1958, Gallup first asked citizens whether they would support a well-qualified black candidate nominated by their party for the presidency. Less than 50 percent of Americans said they would do so (see Figure 10.2). This percentage increased gradually but steadily over time with 79 percent of Americans saying they would support a black candidate in 1987. The question was not asked again until 1997, at which time support had jumped to 93 percent. Since then, support has remained in the low- to mid-90 percent range.

Not long before Obama won the 2008 presidential election, citizens were asked whether they would be more or less likely to support a black candidate. Almost 90 percent said it would make no difference, and only 4 percent said less likely.[8] In 2011, a similar picture emerged, with nearly 90 percent of citizens saying that it wouldn't matter (see Table 10.2).

In recent years, the Gallup poll has also asked citizens whether they would vote for a well-qualified Hispanic for president if nominated by their party. In 2007, 87 percent said they would do so (see Figure 10.2). By 2015, this percentage had inched up to 91 percent. When respondents were asked whether they would be more or less willing to support a Hispanic presidential candidate, 80 percent said it wouldn't matter, but 9 percent said they would be less likely to support such a candidate (see Table 10.2). On the whole, these public opinion data raise questions about whether a Hispanic candidate can win the presidency. Despite Bobby Jindal, the Indian American governor of Louisiana, running for the 2016 Republican presidential nomination, Asian Americans are so far off the radar screen that polling organizations generally do not ask respondents about their support for such candidates. The same is true for Native Americans.

Figure 10.2 Support for Presidential Candidates, 1937–2015: Gender, Race, Ethnicity, and Sexual Orientation

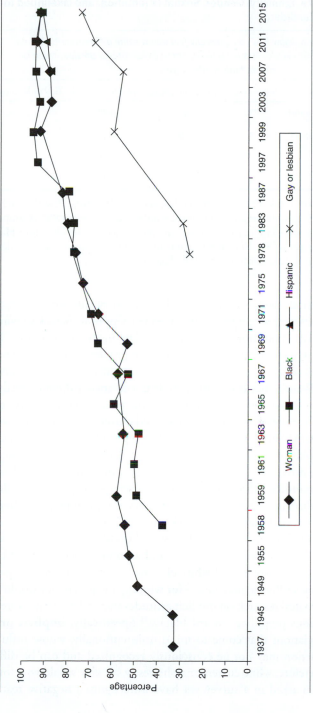

Source: Lydia Saad, "Support for Nontraditional Candidates Varies by Religion," Gallup, June 24, 2015, http://www.gallup.com/poll/183791/support-nontraditional-candidates-varies-religion.aspx

Note: See note for Figure 10.1.

Table 10.2   Race, Ethnicity, Gender, Sexual Orientation, and Likelihood to Vote for a Presidential Candidate

	"We'd like to know how you generally feel about some different traits. Would you be more likely or less likely to support a candidate for president who is _____, or wouldn't this matter to you?"			
Response	*Black (2011)*	*Hispanic (2014)*	*Woman (2014)*	*Gay or lesbian (2014)*
More likely to support	7%	9%	19%	5%
Less likely to support	3	9	9	27
Wouldn't matter	89	80	71	66
Don't know/refused	1	1	1	2

Source: "Candidate Traits: D.C. Experience Viewed Less Positive," Pew Research Center, June 2, 2011, http://people-press.org/files/legacy-pdf/06-02-11%202012%20Campaign%20 Release.pdf; "For 2016 Hopefuls, Washington Experience Could Do More Harm than Good," May 19, 2014, Pew Research Center, http://www.people-press.org/files/legacy-pdf/5-19-14%20Presidential%20Traits%20Release.pdf

Some political observers, including the authors of this book, were skeptical that an African American could win the presidency prior to Barack Obama's 2008 victory even with opposition to a black candidate in the single digits. Why the skepticism? First, these survey questions asking respondents to directly report their attitudes toward a black candidate may underestimate opposition because **social desirability** pressures may lead some people not to answer them honestly. Many citizens recognize that it is socially unacceptable to say they wouldn't vote for a candidate just because of race. Thus, prejudiced citizens, unwilling to reveal their true preferences to a survey interviewer, might simply refuse to answer the question or say they would vote for a black candidate even when they have no intention of doing so in the privacy of the voting booth. Survey questions such as these measure **explicit prejudice**, which is "consciously endorsed negative attitudes based on group membership."[9] Second, other measures of explicit prejudice find significantly higher levels of bias against blacks. In 2008, survey questions measuring racial stereotypes showed that more than one-third of white citizens rated blacks as less intelligent than they rated whites, and around 50 percent rated blacks as lazier than they rated whites.[10] If white citizens were to apply these negative stereotypes to Barack Obama, his chances for winning the presidency would be hurt. Third, psychological research on implicit attitudes shows that many white citizens hold unconscious prejudice toward blacks.[11] Specifically, **implicit prejudice** "refers to associations that come to mind unintentionally, whose influence on thought and action may not be consciously recognized and can be difficult to control."[12] Therefore, white citizens may honestly say they would vote for a black candidate when asked in a survey yet have unrecognized negative reactions to blacks that would lead them to oppose such a candidate in reality. In other words, automatic or unintentional biases can shape citizens' political judgments without them even knowing it's happening.

Important research conducted since President Obama's victory speaks to these concerns about public opinion and support for a black candidate. As Barack Obama led in the polls in the months and weeks before the 2008 election, many political junkies debated whether or not social desirability was inflating levels of support for Obama. In particular, Obama supporters worried that there would be a gap between where Obama stood in the polls leading up to the election and the actual vote on Election Day. This phenomenon is known as the "**Bradley effect**," because Tom Bradley, a black candidate for California governor in 1982, led comfortably in preelection polls but ended up losing the election to a white opponent.[13] An analysis of polling and election outcomes showed that black candidates experienced the Bradley effect until the mid-1990s; however, in more recent elections, including the 2008 contest, polling provided accurate estimates of voters' support for black candidates.[14] Therefore, concerns about the effects of social desirability on Obama's poll results were unfounded.

There is evidence, however, that explicit prejudice dampened support for Barack Obama in both polls and on Election Day. For example, one study showed that white citizens who rated blacks as less intelligent and lazier than whites were less likely to vote for Obama than white citizens who did not endorse those stereotypes.[15] This effect was particularly strong among Independents and Democrats, whereas Republican opposition to Obama was already so pervasive that prejudiced Republicans were only slightly more likely to oppose Obama than nonprejudiced Republicans.[16] Another study demonstrated that white citizens who expressed racial resentment were more likely to oppose Obama than white citizens who did not express those views. The pattern was different among Latinos, however. Latinos held roughly the same level of racial resentment as non-Hispanic whites, but those sentiments did *not* shape their attitudes toward Obama.[17] In yet another study drawing on three national surveys, Keith Payne and his colleagues analyzed several questions measuring explicit prejudice and demonstrated that such attitudes made citizens less likely to vote for Barack Obama and more likely to vote for John McCain.[18]

Several scholars have examined whether implicit prejudice influenced citizens' attitudes and vote choices in 2008 and 2012.[19] These scholars assessed citizens' implicit prejudice using an innovative measurement technique called the **affect misattribution procedure** (AMP).[20] The AMP asks respondents to look at a computer screen and evaluate "drawings" of letters from the Chinese alphabet shown on it. Specifically, in the 2008 American National Election Study, the instructions were, "Just tell us whether you think each drawing is more pleasant than average or less pleasant than average."[21] Psychologists consider this an ambiguous evaluative task, meaning there is no obvious basis on which respondents can judge these abstract Chinese symbols. As a result, respondents' evaluations of how pleasant or unpleasant a particular Chinese letter is will be influenced by affective reactions primed in their brains, which is where prejudice comes into play.[22] Before each Chinese letter is shown on the computer, respondents are quickly, but not subliminally, exposed to a photograph of the face of a black man or a white man. Although respondents can only briefly see the photographs, they elicit affective reactions that subsequently influence respondents' evaluations of the Chinese letters. This procedure is called affect misattribution because people mistakenly rely on their affective reactions to the faces when they evaluate the abstract symbols, even when they are specifically instructed not to let the images influence their judgment of the drawings. Now, to the extent that negative evaluations of the symbol are associated with exposure to black faces, researchers can infer negative affective reactions to blacks. Alternatively, if positive evaluations of the symbol are associated with black faces, then scholars can infer positive affect toward blacks. And the same holds true for exposure to white faces. (This task may seem a bit confusing, so we recommend looking at the instructions provided to survey respondents and examples of the pictures and Chinese letters on the ANES questionnaire.[23]) Initial studies using the AMP to measure implicit attitudes among American citizens found that citizens who were high in implicit prejudice toward blacks were less likely to vote for Obama.[24] After further analyses of survey data from 2008 *and* 2012, scholars concluded that implicit prejudice had little if any systematic influence on citizens' voting behavior. Implicit prejudice exists among some citizens, but it appears not to creep into political judgments, such as vote choice, that require cognitive effort. Scholars continued to find strong evidence, however, of the influence of explicit prejudice on evaluations of Obama and vote choice.[25]

Obviously, despite the impact of explicit prejudice on citizens' vote choices, Barack Obama did win the 2008 presidential election and was reelected in 2012. His historic candidacy in 2008 benefitted from a unique set of political and economic conditions, according to a group of scholars who specialize in forecasting elections. These researchers concluded that Barack Obama should have won an overwhelming victory in 2008 given the record-low popularity of the sitting president, George W. Bush, and the biggest economic crisis since the Great Depression. They estimate that racial prejudice depressed Obama's vote by 5 percentage points, which was not enough to cost him the election but enough to deny him a landslide.[26] An analysis of 2012 data suggests that racial prejudice cost President Obama votes in his reelection bid as well.[27]

Gender and Presidential Candidates

Since 1937, the Gallup organization has asked citizens whether they would vote for a well-qualified woman nominated by their party for the presidency. Only one-third of Americans said they would do so in 1937 (see Figure 10.2). During the 1950s and 1960s, support for a woman candidate hovered in the 50 percent range. Coinciding with the women's movement, support for women candidates increased significantly in the 1970s. By 1975, 73 percent of citizens said they would support a well-qualified woman for the presidency. This percentage increased to 92 percent by 1999, only to fall back a few percentage points in the 2000s.

Why did support for a woman candidate drop after 1999? It is difficult to answer that question by examining the Gallup data because the organization did not ask the question between 1999 and 2003. Another polling organization, however, did ask the question of a representative sample of citizens in August and September 2002. In that poll, only 65 percent of respondents said they would vote for a qualified woman candidate nominated by their party for the presidency. Seven percent said they would not do so, and 28 percent said they were unsure.[28] What led to all this uncertainty about a woman candidate? What happened between 1999 and 2002 that might have led citizens to be hesitant about electing a woman as president?

On September 11, 2001, terrorists struck the World Trade Center and the Pentagon, a tragic event that is etched in the minds of most Americans. From that fateful day until the economic crisis of 2008, foreign policy issues, especially the war on terrorism, dominated American politics. Why would this influence whether citizens would be willing to support a woman candidate? Because many citizens believe male politicians are more competent than female politicians when it comes to issues relating to terrorism and national security. For example, in the 2002 poll just mentioned, 35 percent of citizens said that men would be more competent to punish the people responsible for the September 11 attacks, and 40 percent indicated that men were more capable of protecting the homeland from future attacks. Nearly a decade later, a 2010 survey found that 42 percent of the public think male elected officials are better able than elected females to handle the issue of national security.[29] In both years, virtually everyone else said that women and men would be equally competent to deal with these issues, with only a tiny percentage indicating women would be more competent. It turns out that the same citizens who doubted the competency of women were the ones more likely to indicate they would not vote for a woman candidate or were unsure whether they would do so.[30]

Thus, these data suggest that in an atmosphere focused on war and terrorism, women candidates might be at a severe disadvantage because of the endorsement of **gender stereotypes** by a significant minority of the American people. On the other hand, recent research suggests that when voters are faced with a choice between real-life candidates on Election Day, gender stereotyping is not very likely.[31] The Gallup question and the policy competence items we just mentioned ask about *hypothetical* candidates. For actual candidates, voter determinations about whether a candidate is competent to handle certain issues are not strongly driven by the sex of the candidate. In other words, in a contest between Jane

Williams and Richard Jones, Richard is not likely to be seen as better to handle national security simply because he is a man. Furthermore, when deciding whether to vote for Jane or Richard, voters are more influenced by factors such as the party and incumbency of the candidate or the competitiveness of the race than gendered expectations about the candidates. This conclusion is based on contests for the U.S. Senate, U.S. House, and state governor offices. What about the highest seat in the land? Because as of 2012 there had never been a female major-party nominee for president in the United States, we cannot say whether gender stereotyping of women matters in an actual contest for the presidency. If Hillary Rodham Clinton secures the Democratic nomination in 2016, you can be sure scholars will be addressing this topic. The good news for Clinton and other women candidates is that the Gallup polls indicate support for a woman has recovered and stands at 92 percent in 2015. The bad news is that some scholars believe that number is inflated due to social desirability effects. One study, for example, demonstrated that as many as 26 percent of citizens were "angry or upset" by the notion of a woman president, sentiments that are not revealed on surveys because citizens do not want to appear sexist.[32]

Sexual Orientation and Presidential Candidates

In 1978, the Gallup organization asked citizens for the first time about voting for a "homosexual" presidential candidate. Only 26 percent of Americans said they would vote for such a candidate (refer back to Figure 10.2). Over time, that percentage changed substantially as did the language used to characterize such a candidate. In 2015, 74 percent indicated they would vote for a "gay or lesbian" candidate nominated by their party for the presidency. When asked if it would matter whether a candidate was homosexual, 66 percent of citizens said it wouldn't matter, yet 27 percent said it would make them less likely to support the candidate (see Table 10.2). Although a great deal of prejudice remains, this is a significant improvement from 2007, when 46 percent said they would be less likely to support a homosexual candidate. Overall, these polling data suggest that Americans are becoming more open to a gay or lesbian candidate; nevertheless, it seems unlikely that such a candidate could win the White House any time soon.

SUPPORT FOR CIVIL RIGHTS POLICIES

"Equal Justice Under Law" are the words majestically incised above the entrance of the U.S. Supreme Court building. This simple phrase captures the essence of civil rights, as suggested by the more detailed definition of civil rights that we presented at the beginning of the chapter. In this section, we discuss public support for African American rights and how support for those rights has changed over time. We also examine public attitudes toward gay and lesbian rights and how those attitudes have changed since the 1970s.

Support for Civil Rights for African Americans

Are citizens supportive of civil rights for black Americans? In principle, the answer is yes. Both white and black Americans overwhelmingly endorse **principles of equality**. In practice, however, the answer is much more complex. Support drops significantly among whites when it comes to the **implementation** of civil rights policies, especially if the implementation means that blacks will receive preferential treatment or redress for past harms.[33] Blacks also demonstrate less support for civil rights in practice than in principle, but a majority still supports the enforcement of civil rights policies.

Support for School Integration. Let's first discuss **attitudes toward school integration** to illustrate support for the principles of equality. When white citizens were first asked in 1942 whether they thought Negro and white students should go to the same or separate schools, only one-third supported integration (see Figure 10.3). White opinion on this issue has shifted dramatically over time, with virtually all whites supporting integration in 1995. Some scholars have characterized this change in attitudes as a "revolution."[34] Indeed, the GSS has stopped asking the question because support for equality is so high. Regrettably, this question was not asked of blacks until 1972. Black support for integration was nearly universal at that time and has remained so ever since.

In sharp contrast to their support for equality in principle, whites show much less support for putting this principle into practice. Given high levels of racial

Figure 10.3   Support for Same Schools, by Race

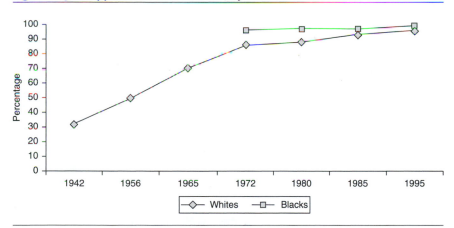

Source: Howard Schuman, Charlotte Steeh, Lawrence Bobo, and Maria Krysan, *Racial Attitudes in America* (Cambridge, MA: Harvard University Press, 1997), 104–105, 240–241.

Note: Here is the General Social Survey question wording: "Do you think white students and (Negro/black) students should go to the same schools or to separate schools?"

segregation in residential patterns, it was rare that white and black students attended the same neighborhood schools. Thus, to achieve school integration, several communities enacted busing plans during the 1970s. In other words, some cities bused white children to schools in black neighborhoods and black children to schools in white neighborhoods as a way to end segregation. Schools became more integrated as a result, but these policies were highly unpopular with white citizens. When asked whether they favored or opposed "the busing of Negro and white school children from one school district to another," only 14 percent of white Americans supported the policy in the 1970s (see Figure 10.4). Over time, white support for busing doubled, but it was still quite low at 30 percent the last time the question was asked in 1996. Compare these low levels of support for busing with the high levels of support white Americans voiced for whites and blacks going to the same schools (refer back to Figure 10.3). There is a huge gap between how whites think about equality in theory versus what policies they are willing to support in practice.

Blacks also demonstrate lower levels of support for the implementation of school integration policies than they do for integration in principle. During the 1970s, 53 percent of blacks supported school busing (see Figure 10.4). By the 1990s, black support for busing had increased to 61 percent. Although this percentage is lower than the almost universal support among blacks for the abstract

Figure 10.4   Support for School Busing, by Decade and Race

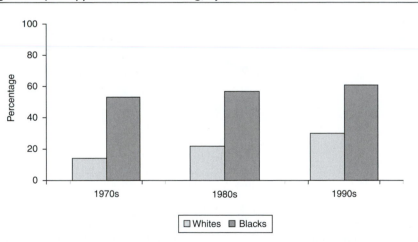

Source: Analysis of General Social Survey Cumulative Data File, 1972–2004.

Note: Here is the General Social Survey question wording: "In general, do you favor or oppose the busing of (Negro/black/African-American) and white school children from one school district to another?"

notion of the two groups attending school together (refer to Figure 10.3), black support for busing is still double the level of white support.

This lack of support for busing, especially among whites, at least partially explains why schools continue to be highly segregated. In many cities, whites protested against busing, brought lawsuits to end the policy, and moved to the suburbs in a practice called "white flight." Further, in 2007, the Supreme Court struck down voluntary school desegregation plans that took into account race in assigning students to schools.[35] As a result, not only has progress in integrating schools stalled, but resegregation is occurring in school systems across the country.[36] "Nearly 40 years after the assassination of Dr. Martin Luther King Jr., we have now lost almost all the progress made in the decades after his death in desegregating our schools."[37]

Support for Affirmative Action. *Affirmative action* is an umbrella term for a variety of policies that ensure equal treatment of minorities and whites in education and employment. Affirmative action policies range from a job advertisement that includes a declaration that the company is an equal opportunity employer to a business taking race into account when making hiring decisions to a college considering race as a factor in admissions. Some affirmative action policies ensure equal opportunity, whereas other policies take special steps to turn the principle of equal opportunity into practice by encouraging equal outcomes.[38]

Affirmative action policies have been justified primarily on two grounds. First, they are intended to make up for past and continuing discrimination against racial minorities in our society. And second, they are designed to ensure that the diversity of the United States is reflected in our colleges and universities, government institutions, and workplaces. Policies to ensure equal treatment between men and women are also referred to as affirmative action policies.

As with other civil rights policies, **attitudes toward affirmative action** are more positive in principle than in practice. In 1995 and in 2007, the Pew Research Center asked citizens whether they supported "affirmative action programs designed to help blacks, women and other minorities get better jobs and education." This question focuses on the principle of enhancing opportunities rather than providing special treatment. As a result, a majority of whites and almost all blacks supported the policy. Specifically, 53 percent of white citizens favored such programs in 1995.[39] By 2007, the level of support had increased to 65 percent. The fact that the question refers to both blacks *and* women also boosts white support for the policy.[40] Among blacks, support for this type of affirmative action policy was nearly universal in both 1995 and 2007 (94 and 93 percent).

Similarly, 60 percent of citizens support the idea of affirmative action programs on college campuses. According to a 2014 Pew Research Center survey, 55 percent of whites said that "affirmative action programs designed to increase the number of black and minority students on college campuses are a good thing."

Eighty-four percent of blacks agreed with that sentiment as did 80 percent of Hispanics. A large majority of Democrats (78 percent) and Independents (62 percent) agreed; it was only among Republicans that less than a majority (43 percent) thought such programs were a good thing.[41]

Citizens' support for affirmative action, however, falls dramatically when the policies refer to specific steps to ensure the equal treatment of blacks. In surveys conducted between 1986 and 2008, the American National Election Study asked respondents whether "blacks should be given preference in hiring and promotion." In 1986, only 14 percent of white Americans supported such policies. White levels of support have varied little over time, and a mere 11 percent favored preferential treatment in 2008 (see Figure 10.5). Among blacks, we also see less support for affirmative action policies designed to put equality into practice. Nevertheless,

Figure 10.5   Support for Preferences in Hiring and Promotion for Blacks

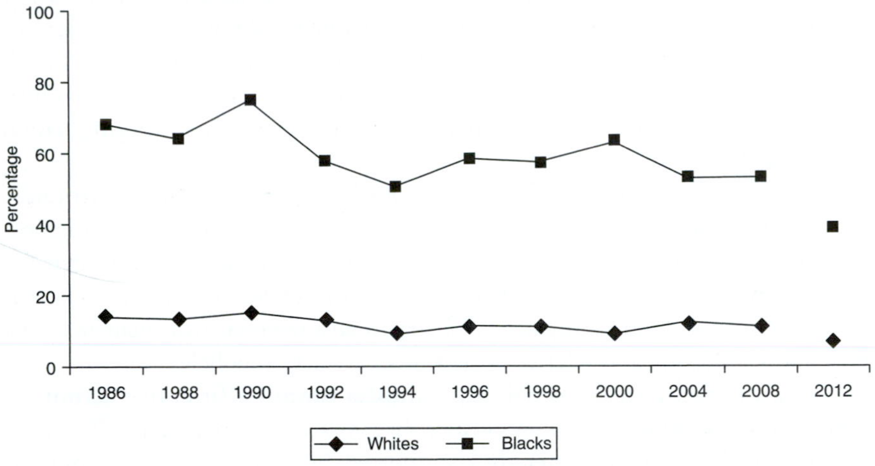

Sources: Howard Schuman, Charlotte Steeh, Lawrence Bobo, and Maria Krysan, *Racial Attitudes in America* (Cambridge, MA: Harvard University Press, 1997), 174–175, 268–269; analysis of American National Election Studies Cumulative Data File, 1948–2004; analysis of American National Election Studies 2008 Data File; analysis of American National Election Study 2012 Time Series.

Note: Here is the American National Election Study question wording for 1986–2008: "Some people say that because of past discrimination, blacks should be given preference in hiring and promotion. Others say that such preference in hiring and promotion of blacks is wrong because it gives blacks advantages they haven't earned. What about your opinion—are you for or against preferential hiring and promotion of blacks?" For 2012: "Do you favor, oppose, or neither favor nor oppose allowing companies to increase the number of black workers by considering race along with other factors when choosing employees?"

two-thirds of blacks supported these policies in 1986, and a majority continued to favor these types of policies in 2008.

In 2012 the ANES used a different question to measure citizens' support for affirmative action in practice. The new question says: "Do you favor, oppose, or neither favor nor oppose allowing companies to increase the number of black workers by considering race along with other factors when choosing employees?" This wording results in significantly less support for affirmative action among black respondents, 39 percent, compared to the over 50 percent who favored such policies in 2008. Is this a question wording effect, or does this illustrate true attitude change among blacks? It is most likely an artifact of the question wording. The old question links preferences to "past discrimination" (see old question wording below Figure 10.5). That wording primes blacks to think about discrimination they have faced, which likely increases their support for measures to correct past injustices. Regardless of the exact question wording, only a small percentage of white citizens favor concrete, affirmative steps to diversify the workforce. Likewise, when asked a similar question about considering race in college admissions, whites are not nearly as supportive as they are when evaluating college affirmative action programs in principle. In 2012, only 9 percent of whites said they favored "allowing universities to increase the number of black students studying at their schools by considering race along with other factors when choosing students." Among blacks, 37 percent favored such programs, considerably greater support than among white citizens.[42] But still, the bottom line is that white and black support for affirmative action in practice is below what it is for affirmative action in principle.

Support for Reparations. Since 1989, Congressman John Conyers (D-Mich.) has proposed the Commission to Study Reparation Proposals for African Americans Act in every Congress, and he says he will continue to do so until the bill, HR 40, is passed into law. HR 40 would establish a commission to examine the effects of slavery on African Americans living today and make recommendations regarding appropriate remedies to address slavery's harmful effects. Such remedial policies are referred to as reparations.

In a 2014 article in *The Atlantic*, Ta-Nehisi Coates drew significant attention to the issue by presenting a powerful case for reparations.[43] Coates argued that America began "in black plunder and white democracy, two features that are not contradictory but complementary," and detailed the ways in which black lives and livelihoods continued to be plundered through the present. He also lamented that most Americans are not interested in debating the issue. "Perhaps after a serious discussion and debate—the kind that HR 40 proposes—we may find that the country can never fully repay African Americans. But we stand to discover much about ourselves in such a discussion—and that is perhaps what scares us. The idea of reparations is frightening not simply because we might lack the ability to pay. The idea of reparations threatens something much deeper—America's heritage, history, and standing in the world."

In the wake of Ta-Nehisi Coates's article in *The Atlantic*, a survey was conducted to assess **attitudes toward reparations**. Respondents were asked whether they thought slavery and discrimination were major factors in lower average wealth levels of blacks. As you can see in Table 10.3, blacks and whites had very different views on these questions with blacks much more likely to say that slavery and discrimination were major factors. Blacks and whites also differed on whether the government should take steps to compensate black Americans for slavery. Around 60 percent of black Americans supported an apology for slavery, cash payments to descendants of slaves, and education and job training programs. In contrast, whites were particularly resistant to the notion of cash payments, and large majorities opposed an apology and education and job training programs. Overall, whites and blacks have strikingly different views on the subject of reparations for slave descendants.

Philip J. Mazzocco and his colleagues conducted a fascinating study to examine *why* whites oppose reparations for black Americans who are the descendants of slaves.[44] One possible reason for people to oppose reparations is that the crime

Table 10.3   White and Black Support for Reparations, 2014

	Percentage major factor	
Question	Whites	Blacks
"Do you think the impact of slavery is a major factor, a minor factor, or not a factor in lower average wealth levels for blacks in the United States today?"	14	48
"Do you think discrimination against blacks in the past is a major factor, a minor factor, or not a factor in lower average wealth levels for blacks in the United States today?"	29	62

	Percentage should	
	Whites	Blacks
"Do you think the federal government should or should not apologize to black Americans for the slavery that once existed in this country?"	21	60
"Do you think the government should or should not make cash payments to black Americans who are descendants of slaves?"	6	59
"Do you think the government should or should not set up education and job training programs for black Americans who are the descendants of slaves?	19	63

Source: Peter Moore, "Overwhelming Opposition to Reparations for Slavery and Jim Crow," Yougov, June 2, 2014, https://today.yougov.com/news/2014/06/02/reparations

of slavery happened long ago and neither the perpetrators of the crime nor the victims of the crime are alive today. Thus, reparations are not fair because they would benefit people who were not directly harmed and penalize people who had nothing to do with slavery. If this reasoning explains white opposition to reparations, then it makes sense that whites would oppose reparations for *any type* of crime that happened long ago, not just reparations for slavery. Is this the case?

To answer this question, Mazzocco et al. asked sixty-six white college students to read a scenario in which someone had done significant harm to their great-great-grandfather, including gaining financial advantage at the expense of their relatives. After reading the scenario, participants were asked whether they would join in a class action suit to try to recover some of their great-great-grandfather's assets. Here is the scenario:

> Imagine that about 150 years ago, in the mid 1800s, your great, great grandfather was kidnapped by Fineus Jones. Jones demanded a million dollars from your great, great grandfather's shipping business. The family borrowed the money and paid the ransom and your great, great grandfather was released. Jones escaped to Europe and was apprehended, but none of the million dollars was found. Your great, great grandfather lost his business to pay back the ransom loan and died in poverty. Recently it was proven that the lost money had been transferred to one of Fineus Jones's sons who started a successful banking company with a successor firm now worth 100 million dollars. Your cousins have found a respected attorney who will press a claim on the successor firm and will do the work on a contingency basis, that is, the attorney will receive a portion of the amount awarded by the court. If all costs are included in the claim, the amount awarded to each claimant will be about $5,000.00. Your cousins have asked if you would wish your name to be included on the list of claimants.[45]

What would you do? Would you allow your name to be included in the class action suit? Of the participants in the study, 61 percent said they would want their name to be listed in the lawsuit. Thus, it seems that many whites are not opposed to the notion of reparations in principle; rather, they are opposed to reparations for black Americans who are the descendants of slaves.

Mazzocco et al. argue that this opposition to reparations for blacks stems from white Americans underestimating racial disparities in the United States. Across many areas of society—health care, criminal justice, education, and the economy—blacks are at a disadvantage relative to whites. But because many whites do not seem to understand or appreciate the cost of being black in our society, they do not support reparations.

The research by Mazzocco et al. was not conducted on a random sample of white citizens. Thus, we should be cautious about generalizing these results to whites in general. Nevertheless, it is striking how similar the level of white support for reparations based on the scenario is to the percentage of blacks who supported cash payments to the descendants of slaves in the 2014 poll (refer back to Table 10.3). Ideally, future research will examine the reaction of a representative sample of whites to these types of scenarios.

Support for Civil Rights for Gays and Lesbians

Do citizens support civil rights for gays and lesbians? It depends on which type of right. Citizens largely oppose discrimination in employment but are less supportive of gay rights when it comes to the legality of intimate relationships between homosexuals. Furthermore, **attitudes toward gay and lesbian rights** have changed a great deal over time, with support for such rights increasing dramatically since citizens were first polled on these issues in the 1970s.

Support for Equality in Employment. Let's begin with a discussion of attitudes toward equality for gays and lesbians in the workplace. In 1977, the Gallup organization began asking citizens whether they think "homosexuals should or should not have equal rights in terms of job opportunities." A majority of Americans, 56 percent, supported such rights in 1977 (see Figure 10.6). By the mid-1990s, support for equal job rights had jumped to over 80 percent. As of 2008, almost nine out of every ten Americans supported equal job opportunities for gays and lesbians. This is a large shift in public opinion over time.[46] As a result of the substantial agreement on the issue, Gallup has not included the question on recent surveys.

It is both ironic and troubling that despite widespread public support for gay rights in employment, there is no federal or constitutional ban against employment discrimination based on sexual orientation. In other words, federal law and the U.S. Constitution allow employers to fire employees simply because they are gay or lesbian. To ensure this does not happen, some states, localities, universities, and corporations have instituted bans on discrimination based on sexual orientation. As a result, whether gay rights are protected depends on where you live and where you work in the United States. We will use ourselves to illustrate this point. Zoe Oxley lives in New York, a state that has a law that bans employment discrimination based on sexual orientation. In contrast, Rosalee Clawson lives in Indiana, a state that does not ban such employment discrimination, yet the city she lives in, Lafayette, Indiana, *does* have a gay rights ordinance barring job discrimination. Both Clawson and Oxley work at universities where discrimination based on sexual orientation is prohibited.

A particular type of employment received a great deal of attention in the 1990s and 2000s—gays and lesbians serving in the U.S. military. Since 1977, the Gallup poll has asked citizens whether they thought homosexuals should or should not be hired for the armed forces. Just over one-half of citizens believed gays and lesbians should be allowed to serve in the military at that time (see Figure 10.6). Over the next three decades, support for gays and lesbians in the armed forces increased substantially. By 2003, support reached 80 percent. In 2005, the last time the question was asked by Gallup, support had declined a bit, with 76 percent of Americans saying they would support the right of gays and lesbians to serve in the military. Overall, these data suggest many Americans have come to the conclusion that "you don't have to be straight to shoot straight."[47]

Despite this level of public support for hiring gays and lesbians in the armed forces, the U.S. government maintained a policy against gays and lesbians serving openly until President Obama signed legislation repealing "Don't Ask, Don't Tell" in December 2010. The legislation did not go into effect immediately because the Department of Defense and the president were required to take a number of steps to ensure the military was prepared for the policy change. During summer 2011, President Obama certified that the military was ready, and as a result, gays and lesbians have served openly since September 20, 2011.

Support for Equality in Intimate Relationships. Although most people are opposed to discrimination in employment, public opinion has historically been much more divided when it comes to support for intimate relationships between gays and lesbians. Since 1977, the Gallup poll has asked citizens whether they think "homosexual relations between consenting adults should or should not be legal." Only 43 percent of citizens supported the rights of gays and lesbians to have sexual relations at that time (see Figure 10.6). The level of support dropped even lower in the mid-1980s when merely 33 percent of the public supported such rights. This drop in support might have been a reaction to the Supreme Court ruling on gay sex in 1986. In *Bowers v. Hardwick*, the Supreme Court ruled that the U.S. Constitution does not protect homosexual relations between consenting adults even in the privacy of their own homes.[48] Thus, the Court ruling might have given "permission" to citizens who were hesitant about gay rights to decide it was acceptable to oppose the legality of gay and lesbian sexual relationships. This was also a period during which people's fears about AIDS may have influenced their attitudes toward gay and lesbian rights.

By the late 1980s, support for homosexual relationships had gone back up and was at 47 percent. In May 2003, support for the legality of gay and lesbian relationships reached 60 percent, but again public opinion seemed to react to a Supreme Court decision on gay and lesbian rights, although this time the Court was in support of such rights. On June 26, 2003, the Supreme Court reversed its earlier decision on gay sex and ruled in *Lawrence v. Texas* that the U.S. Constitution protects consensual sexual relationships between two people of the same sex.[49] This ruling caused an immediate outcry from conservative activists, especially because many argued this ruling was the logical precursor to the legalization of same-sex marriage. Thus, some citizens thought the Court had overstepped its

Figure 10.6   Support for Gay Rights, 1977–2015

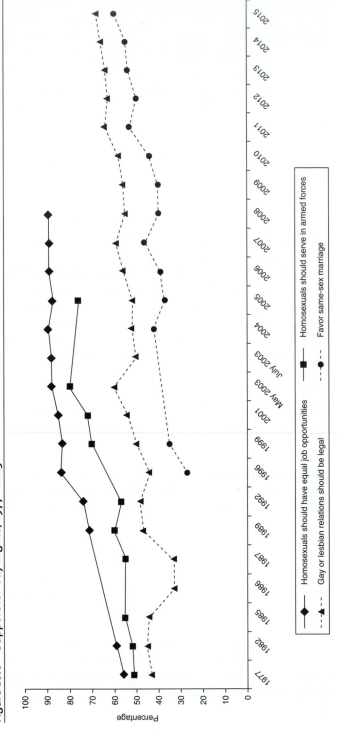

Source: Justin McCarthy, "Record High 60% of Americans Support Same-Sex Marriage," Gallup, Washington, DC, May 19, 2015, http://www
.gallup.com/poll/183272/record-high-americans-support-sex-marriage.aspx; "Gay and Lesbian Rights," Gallup, Washington, DC, http://www
.gallup.com/poll/1651/gay-lesbian-rights.aspx

Note: The solid lines indicate employment policies, and the dashed lines indicate policies concerning intimate relationships. There have been some
minor variations in question wording over time. The following are the most recent question wordings:

Job opportunities: "As you may know, there has been considerable discussion in the news regarding the rights of homosexual men and women. In
general, do you think homosexuals should or should not have equal rights in terms of job opportunities?"

Serve in armed forces: "Now, I'd like to ask you about the hiring of homosexuals in specific occupations. Do you think homosexuals should or should
not be hired for the following occupations: The Armed Forces?"

Relations between consenting adults: "Do you think gay or lesbian relations between consenting adults should or should not be legal?"

Marriage: "Do you think marriages between same-sex couples should or should not be recognized by the law as valid, with the same rights as traditional
marriages?"

bounds, and they rejected the Court's position. As a result, public support for homosexual relations between consenting adults dropped to 50 percent in a July 2003 Gallup poll. Over the last fifteen years, however, citizens' support for gay relationships has climbed up to 68 percent.[50]

In the prior (2013) edition of this book, we said: "That brings us to the most controversial gay rights issue of our times—gay marriage." In an incredibly short time period, same-sex marriage has gone from a highly controversial issue to one that is accepted by a sizable majority of citizens. Gallup surveys show that **attitudes toward same-sex marriage** have changed dramatically in the last

---

Public Opinion in Comparative Perspective
BOX 10.1 SUPPORT FOR GAY RIGHTS ACROSS THE WORLD

In 2012, the European Union commissioned a study of attitudes toward gay, lesbian, and bisexual political leaders. Respondents were asked to place themselves on a 1 to 10 scale with 1 meaning totally uncomfortable and 10 totally comfortable with having someone who is gay, lesbian, or bisexual in the highest elected political position in their country. The average rating for all citizens in the European Union was 6.6 on the 10-point scale. Support varied a great deal across countries within the European Union, ranging from a high of 8.9 in Denmark to a low of 3.2 in Latvia. The average rating of citizens in each country is presented in the table.[1]

Another way to examine the public's attitudes toward gay rights is to consider whether people believe homosexuality should be accepted by society. In 2013, the Pew Research Center conducted a Global Attitudes survey in thirty-nine nations. The survey asked respondents whether "homosexuality should be accepted by society." People in Middle Eastern, African, and some Asian countries were particularly opposed to homosexuality. Russians were also quite opposed. In contrast, a majority of citizens in Canada, the United States, and most European Union and Latin American countries deemed homosexuality acceptable.[2]

Average Rating of How Comfortable Europeans Feel with a Gay, Lesbian, or Bisexual Political Leader

Country	Rating
Denmark	8.9
Sweden	8.8

Country	Rating
Luxembourg	8.5
Netherlands	8.4
Ireland	8.2
Spain	7.9
United Kingdom	7.9
Belgium	7.7
France	7.3
Malta	6.8
European Union	6.6
Germany	6.4
Slovenia	6.2
Italy	5.8
Poland	5.8
Austria	5.7
Portugal	5.7
Finland	5.2
Czech Republic	4.9
Estonia	4.7
Greece	4.5
Hungary	4.2
Cyprus	4.1
Lithuania	4.1
Bulgaria	3.7
Romania	3.6
Slovakia	3.4
Latvia	3.2

Source: "Special Eurobarometer 393: Discrimination in the EU in 2012," European Commission, November 2012, http://ec.europa.eu/public_opinion/archives/eb_special_399_380_en.htm

(Continued)

Box 10.1   (Continued)

Should Homosexuality Be Accepted by Society?

	No	Yes
Spain	11	88
Germany	11	87
Canada	14	80
Czech Rep.	16	80
Australia	18	79
France	22	77
Britain	18	76
Argentina	21	74
Italy	18	74
Philippines	26	73
Chile	24	68
Mexico	30	61
Brazil	36	60
U.S.	33	60
Japan	36	54
Greece	40	53
Venezuela	42	51
Bolivia	49	43
Poland	46	42
Israel	47	40
S. Korea	59	39
El Salvador	62	34
S. Africa	61	32
China	57	21
Lebanon	80	18
Russia	74	16
Malaysia	86	9
Turkey	78	9
Kenya	90	8
Palest. ter.	93	4
Uganda	96	4
Egypt	95	3
Ghana	96	3
Indonesia	93	3
Jordan	97	3
Senegal	96	3
Pakistan	87	2
Tunisia	94	2
Nigeria	98	1

Source: "The Global Divide on Homosexuality," Pew Research Center, Washington, DC, June 4, 2013, http://www.pewglobal.org/2013/06/04/the-global-divide-on-homosexuality

Note: Some responses do not sum to 100 percent because of refusals or "don't knows." In some countries, this constitutes a significant minority of the responses.

twenty years. In 1996, Gallup asked citizens for the first time, "Do you think marriages between same-sex couples should or should not be recognized by the law as valid, with the same rights as traditional marriages?" At that time only 27 percent said they supported same-sex marriage (see Figure 10.6). When the question was asked again in 1999, 35 percent of Americans said they would support same-sex marriage. Between 2004 and 2010, support for same-sex marriage bounced around the 40 percent level, and then for the first time in 2011 a majority of Americans came around to the marriage equality point of view. By 2015 support had reached an all-time high of 60 percent favoring same-sex marriage. Interestingly, an analysis of the remarkable change in attitudes toward same-sex marriage over time concluded that the transformation was overwhelmingly due to people changing their minds on the issue (rather than simply generational replacement of older cohorts by younger and more progressive citizens), thereby reflecting a "cultural shift."[51]

It was not particularly surprising when the U.S. Supreme Court upheld same-sex marriage on June 26, 2015, in the landmark case *Obergefell v. Hodges*, because Court rulings are consistent with public opinion roughly two-thirds of the time.[52] To be sure, Democrats and Republicans continue to differ on the issue, but with nearly 80 percent of young adults under 30 in support of same-sex marriage, not to mention same-sex couples across the country exercising their newly won right, marriage equality is here to stay.[53]

CONCLUSION

Are citizens hesitant about supporting women and minority candidates? Well, it depends. If you are a Muslim or an atheist, your chances for winning the presidency seem quite slim. The public is not predisposed to favor such a candidate. If you are a Mormon, an evangelical Christian, or gay, you also have an uphill battle. Your prospects are better if you are a woman, a Jew, or a racial or ethnic minority, but still there are some citizens who say they will not support someone like you. The good news is that over time citizens have become increasingly more likely to say they would vote for a woman or minority candidate, with one notable exception. Public support for a Mormon candidate has budged only slightly over the last fifty years. But these survey questions ask about hypothetical candidates; an actual flesh-and-blood person who happens to be a nontraditional candidate might be able to win despite stereotypes and prejudices—just ask President Barack Obama.

What about citizens' support for civil rights for black Americans? When it comes to equality for blacks, citizens' attitudes depend heavily on two factors. First, support varies based on whether the policy at hand refers to equal rights in principle or equal rights in practice. People tend to support the goals of equal rights, yet support drops when the focus is on implementation. Second, levels of support for civil rights differ a great deal between black and white citizens. Both groups support the principle of equal rights more than specific policies designed to achieve those rights, yet support for civil rights in principle is basically universal among blacks, and many support policies to implement civil rights. In contrast, a majority of whites supports civil rights in principle (in some cases, a very large majority), yet support drops precipitously when it comes to putting the principle into action.

What about public support for gay rights? Citizens demonstrate strong support for equal job opportunities for gays and lesbians. Further, three-fourths of Americans think that gays and lesbians should be able to serve in the military. Citizens' support for gay and lesbian sexual relationships has increased substantially over time, with over two-thirds now saying those relationships should be legal. Until recently citizens have been reluctant to extend marriage rights to gays and lesbians, yet in 2015 public support hit 60 percent. The bottom line is that a sea change in attitudes toward rights for gays and lesbians has occurred over the last forty years.

Overall, these findings certainly provide some encouragement to participatory democratic theorists. That citizens have become more supportive of women and minorities holding office and that citizen support for several civil rights policies has increased over the years are heartening to theorists who worry about inequality in society. Nevertheless, the news is not all good for participatory democratic theorists. A meaningful minority (especially given the closeness of presidential races) still opposes women and minorities running for the highest office in the land. Moreover, the influence of explicit prejudice on vote choice during the 2008 and 2012 presidential elections is also extremely troubling. Further, the hesitancy to support the implementation of civil rights policies on the part of whites raises serious doubts about whether our society provides "equal justice under law," as proclaimed by the words on the Supreme Court building.

Because elite democratic theorists expect some inequality in society, they are not shocked by opposition to women and minority candidates or by the lack of support among white Americans for implementing civil rights policies or by the remaining opposition to same-sex marriage. As we discussed earlier, elite democratic theorists emphasize that it is fine if the public doesn't support civil rights because elites hold the power. Because elites are more sophisticated, they appreciate the importance of civil rights in a democratic society and are therefore better equipped to protect the rights of marginalized or unpopular groups. Political theories, however, do not always accurately capture the practice of politics. Take the issue of gay rights. For a long time elites in both the Republican and Democratic parties opposed marriage rights for gays and lesbians. Most Democratic leaders have finally changed their position, but many Republican officials continued to speak out against same-sex marriage even after the Supreme Court ruled it constitutional in 2015. Clearly these elites are no more protective of this particular civil right than those citizens who persist in opposing same-sex marriage.

Key Concepts

affect misattribution procedure / 289
attitudes toward affirmative
action / 295
attitudes toward gay and lesbian
rights / 300
attitudes toward reparations / 298
attitudes toward same-sex
marriage / 304
attitudes toward school
integration / 293

Bradley effect / 289
civil rights / 282
explicit prejudice / 288
gender stereotypes / 291
implementation / 293
implicit prejudice / 288
principles of equality / 293
social desirability / 288

Suggested Sources for Further Reading

Doan, Alesha E., and Donald Haider-Markel. "The Role of Intersectional Stereotypes of Evaluations of Gay and Lesbian Political Candidates." *Politics & Gender* 6 (2010): 63–91.

Dolan, Kathleen. *When Does Gender Matter? Women Candidates and Gender Stereotypes in American Elections.* Oxford: Oxford University Press, 2014.

These studies provide insight into the influence of stereotypes on the evaluation of political candidates.

Schneider, Monica C. and Angela L. Bos. "Measuring Stereotypes of Female Politicians." *Political Psychology* 35 (2014): 245–266.

This innovative research investigates stereotypes of female politicians compared to other relevant groups, including politicians, male politicians, and female professionals.

Streb, Matthew J., Barbara Burrell, Brian Frederick, and Michael A. Genovese. "Social Desirability Effects and Support for a Female American President." *Public Opinion Quarterly* 72 (2008): 76–89.

This article uses a "list experiment," which is an unobtrusive method to measure attitudes, to assess prejudice toward a female presidential candidate. The researchers find substantial evidence of prejudice.

Redlawsk, David P., Caroline J. Tolbert, and Natasha Altema McNeely. "Symbolic Racism and Emotional Responses to the 2012 Presidential Candidates." *Political Research Quarterly* 67 (2014): 680–694.

The authors demonstrate how racial prejudice and emotions (both positive and negative) interact to influence evaluations of President Obama.

Schuman, Howard, Charlotte Steeh, Lawrence Bobo, and Maria Krysan. *Racial Attitudes in America*. Rev. ed. Cambridge, MA: Harvard University Press, 1997.

This classic book examines trends in racial attitudes since the early 1940s. The authors analyze the racial attitudes of both blacks and whites.

Human Rights Campaign, www.hrc.org

The Human Rights Campaign is the largest civil rights organization working for lesbian, gay, bisexual, and transgender (LGBT) equality. This website contains information about LGBT issues, such as marriage, adoption, and workplace discrimination. You can look up LGBT policies in your state and community on this site.

National Association for the Advancement of Colored People (NAACP), www .naacp.org

Founded in 1909, the NAACP is the nation's oldest civil rights organization. Its website contains both historical and contemporary information about civil rights issues. The site includes a "Youth & College" section that students will find of particular interest.

National Council of La Raza, www.nclr.org

The National Council of La Raza is the largest national Latino civil rights organization in the United States. This website contains information about civil rights, including racial profiling, criminal justice issues, and voting rights.

Campaign Zero, www.joincampaignzero.org

This grassroots organization focuses on ending police violence, a civil rights issue that has recently gained significant national attention. This website provides information on political leaders' positions on a range of policies, including body cameras for police, community oversight, and demilitarization of police departments.

Gender and Multicultural Leadership: The Future of Governance, www.gmcl.org

This website provides state-by-state data on more than 10,000 elected officials of color.

PART V

What Is the Relationship between Citizens and Their Government?

DO U.S. CITIZENS trust the government? Do they support the institutions of government and the people who occupy key political offices? Does the government respond to the policy preferences of the public? If so, do all citizens' opinions weigh equally, or do the views of some matter more? Alternatively, is policy not related to public opinion but, rather, influenced by the wishes of others, such as interest groups or elected officials' own goals?

All of these questions point, in one way or another, to the relationship between citizens and their government, the focus of this section. In addition to these empirically oriented questions, we also consider many normative ones. How important to democratic governance is citizens' trust in their government? Can a democracy survive without it? What if citizens display little support for the institutions of government? Are there worrisome implications that arise under this situation? Finally, why does it matter whether public opinion influences public policy? Are there some circumstances where the public should have a large influence? A small one? No influence?

CHAPTER 11

Trust in Government, Support for Institutions, and Social Capital

LET'S RECAP MAJOR national events of the last decade or so. Hurricane Katrina hit America's Gulf Coast in 2005. This massive storm caused widespread damage, yet relief efforts, from the national, state, and local governments, were slow in coming. The financial and subprime mortgage crises of 2008 kick-started the worst economic downturn since the Great Depression. For weeks during the summer of 2011 President Barack Obama and congressional leaders engaged in a long and, let's face it, not very pretty debate over raising the federal government's debt ceiling. An agreement was finally reached, but only hours before the government would have been prevented from borrowing money to pay its bills. Two years later, the debt ceiling was on the agenda again. Both sides hunkered down yet again. Leaders failed to reach an agreement on this or the nation's annual budget, leading to the federal government shutting down. For sixteen days. Around the same time, the government website meant to allow Americans to sign up for health insurance under Obamacare was launched. The site was plagued with problems. By some accounts, only six people successfully completed enrollment on the site during its first day of operation.[1] In the summer of 2014, police officers in Ferguson, Missouri, shot and killed Michael Brown, an unarmed black man. The deaths of other African American men in police custody, including Eric Garner in New York City and Freddie Gray in Baltimore, received widespread national attention in 2014 and 2015.

This is admittedly only a partial list of recent events, and, by design, they are all negative. Even so, is it any wonder the American public does not view the government and public officials very favorably these days? One important feature of democratic public opinion is citizen assessment of government. Furthermore, democratic citizens are expected to not only evaluate their government and their political leaders but also have the means to enact change if they are dissatisfied. Citizens can hold elected officials accountable by voting for their opponents on Election Day. Severe dissatisfaction with the government could lead to calls for changing governmental procedures or even for replacing the structure of government with a new one. This type of citizen control is one key characteristic of democracies, as so clearly stated by Thomas Jefferson in the Declaration of Independence. "Whenever any Form of Government becomes destructive of these ends [securing individual rights]," wrote Jefferson, "it is the Right of the People to alter or abolish it, and to institute new Government."[2] Furthermore, a belief that the government is legitimate is related to citizen obedience to authorities and to laws, whereas alienation from government may suppress involvement in political activities.[3] Given its importance to democratic functioning, therefore, public opinion scholars have long been interested in whether citizens demonstrate support for their government.

There are, of course, many aspects of government toward which the public holds attitudes, including constitutional principles, day-to-day functioning, governmental institutions, governmental decisions, and the performance of elected and appointed officials. One useful way to categorize these diverse attitude objects was presented by political scientist David Easton in the 1960s.[4] Easton suggests there are two types of public support for political systems: diffuse support and specific support. **Diffuse support** refers to public opinions about the political system, such as contentment with the form of government and attachment to the norms and structure of the regime. In contrast to this broad attitude, the public also holds attitudes toward the performance of incumbent political leaders and governmental outputs, such as public policies. Easton calls this **specific support**. As for the relationship between the two, Easton has this to say: "One major characteristic [of diffuse support] is that since it is an attachment to a political object for its own sake, it constitutes a store of political good will. As such, it taps deep political sentiments and is not easily depleted through disappointment with outputs."[5] In other words, if citizens are unhappy with governmental policy decisions, specific support for the government will be low, but diffuse support can remain high.

In this chapter, we discuss attitudes tapping both diffuse and specific support for government. We first examine public trust in government, which encompasses characteristics of diffuse and specific support. We demonstrate that public trust in government has declined over time, present explanations to account for changing levels of trust, and discuss the implications of lower trust levels. Second, we examine confidence in particular governmental institutions: the executive branch, Congress, and the Supreme Court. Public faith in those institutions is also a function of both diffuse and specific support. We also demonstrate that attitudes toward the *members* of the institutions are distinct from attitudes toward the *institutions* themselves. In the final section, we move away from an assessment of public evaluations of government to explore citizen interaction with other citizens. Social capital, or the degree to which people connect with and trust other citizens and engage in civic activities, is related to both trust in government and support for government institutions. As we will see, however, social capital has other important consequences for the public and for democratic governments. Also, as with trust in government, the stock of social capital in America has declined of late, a trend we examine. Finally, to help us think through the importance and implications of public trust in government, support for national institutions, and social capital, we turn to relevant democratic theories throughout the chapter.

TRUST IN GOVERNMENT

Although a number of different definitions of **trust in government** have been proposed, scholars generally agree that trust refers to "the public's basic evaluative orientation toward the government in Washington."[6] As such, trust seems to be a measure of diffuse support for government. Consider, however, the more focused definition provided in the 1970s by Arthur Miller, a leading researcher of public trust: "The belief that the government is operating according to one's normative expectations of how government should function."[7] More recently, trust has been described "as a pragmatic running tally of how people think the government is doing at a given point in time."[8] These definitions suggest that public trust involves assessing the performance of government. The attitude of trust therefore can also be classified as a measure of specific support because it involves some evaluation of governmental outputs. The lack of trust is commonly referred to as cynicism or distrust.[9] Following from Miller's definition of trust, **cynicism** "reflects the belief that the government is not functioning in accordance with individual expectations of efficiency, honesty, competence and equity."[10]

Many democratic theorists agree that public trust in government is important for democratic societies. Citizens place governing duties in their elected representatives and appointed officials. Given their distance from government and their lack of knowledge regarding the many complex policy matters that leaders must address, citizen trust in leaders and governing institutions is a salient feature of democratic decision making.[11] If citizens trust their government, they will accept and comply with its decisions, leading to a stable democracy. If, on the other hand, citizens do not trust their government, it might be difficult for government to enforce the law, leading to political and social disruption.[12]

Proponents of participatory democracy and related variants, such as deliberative democracy, further emphasize that citizen trust in government reacts to the political environment. Trust can increase the more that government procedures are transparent and the more that citizens become involved in debating issues. "Deliberative arenas . . . provide opportunities to explain oneself, one's group, one's problems," leading to greater understanding of the views of others and perhaps engendering trust in others' motives.[13] An obvious extension of this view is that declines in public trust, whether of the diffuse or specific support variety, could be indicative of too little involvement of the public in decision making.

Elite democratic theorists have a more nuanced view of trust in government. One key feature of liberal democracy, a theoretical precursor to contemporary elite democracy, is a presumption that citizens should distrust the people in government.[14] After all, the Federalists designed the complex checks and balances of the U.S. political system with the presumption that political leaders would not pursue the public good but would, rather, look out solely for their own interests. Yet the founders wanted citizens to trust the representative institutions of government so that people would not feel it necessary to pursue direct democracy, which was anathema to the founders.[15] Thus, elite democrats would expect the public to place less trust in government leaders than in the institutions and procedures of government that were established to hold leaders in check. In other words, low specific support would be acceptable, but diffuse support should remain high.

Measuring Public Trust

To measure public trust in government, survey researchers working on the American National Election Studies (ANES) developed four specific questions in the early 1960s.[16] These questions are the ones most commonly used to examine trust, so it is worth considering the content of the survey items in detail. The complete wording of these questions appears in Table 11.1. The first question asks respondents directly how often they trust the national government. The next two items query people about the behavior of politicians, specifically whether they waste taxpayer money and whether they work for "the benefit of all the people" or only a "few big interests." The final question originally required respondents to assess

---

Table 11.1 Assessing Public Trust: Survey Questions from the American National Election Studies

"How much of the time do you think you can trust the government in Washington to do what is right—just about always, most of the time, or only some of the time?"

"Do you think that people in government waste a lot of the money we pay in taxes, waste some of it, or don't waste very much of it?"

"Would you say the government is pretty much run by a few big interests looking out for themselves or that it is run for the benefit of all the people?"

"Do you think that quite a few of the people running the government are crooked, not very many are, or do you think hardly any of them are crooked?" (before 2012); "How many of the people running the government are corrupt? All, most, about half, a few, or none?" (in 2012)

Source: American National Election Studies Cumulative Data File, 1948–2012, http://www.electionstudies.org/studypages/anes_timeseries_cdf/anes_timeseries_cdf.htm

whether politicians were crooked. In 2012, this question was changed slightly. *Corrupt* replaced *crooked*, perhaps because the latter is an outdated term.

What specific criteria were these four items intended to assess? Donald Stokes, one of the creators of the questions, points to "the honesty and other ethical qualities of public officials" as well as "the ability and efficiency of government officials and the correctness of their policy decisions."[17] To be sure, these are varied criteria. Despite this, Stokes's analysis indicated that public responses to the individual questions correlated strongly with each other to form a general evaluation of government, usually referred to as the **trust in government scale**.

Although the ANES questions are often used by scholars, many acknowledge they are not perfect measures of trust. The first item, with its explicit focus on trusting "the government in Washington," most closely resembles the notion of trust as a characteristic of the political regime. The other items, however, appear to tap specific attitudes toward politicians' actions and motives. Because of this, argued Jack Citrin, an early critic of the ANES measures, the survey questions register "mere disapproval of incumbent political leaders" rather than "alienation from the political regime."[18] This seems especially likely because the attitude objects that are the focus of these questions alternate between the general government and politicians ("the government in Washington" versus "the people running the government," for example). In place of these survey items, Citrin preferred questions asking respondents whether they favored changing the form of government or whether they were proud about the form of government. For Citrin, such questions better tap individuals' views of the political regime than do the ANES items. In contrast, because the ANES questions specifically mention politicians, Citrin viewed these as measures solely of specific support. Most public opinion researchers, however, accept that the ANES items tap a combination of diffuse and specific support.[19] Finally, this debate is about more than simply how to measure trust in government on a public opinion survey. As we see later in this chapter, disagreement also exists over how to *interpret* public attitudes toward government when these survey questions are used.

Decline in Public Trust

One benefit of the ANES trust questions is that they have been asked of the American public since 1964, allowing us to examine levels of public trust over many decades. The graph in Figure 11.1 displays public responses to the four ANES items in presidential election years since 1964. The most obvious conclusion to be drawn from this figure is that public trust has declined considerably. Nearly 80 percent of the public felt that government could be trusted to do the right thing most of the time or just about always in 1964 (refer to the solid line). This percentage steadily declined to 25.7 percent in 1980. Public trust increased quite a bit by 1984, with 44.9 percent of the public trusting the government, but then declined in 1988 and 1992. Between 1992 and 2004 slightly and steadily increasing percentages of the public demonstrated trust in the government. Trust has decreased since then. Indeed, in 2012 only 22.1 percent of Americans trusted the government, far lower than in 1964. Turning to the other three trust questions (the dashed lines in Figure 11.1), the overall trends are very similar to each other. Significant increases in negative evaluations occurred between 1964 and 1980, followed by somewhat more positive assessments in the mid-1980s and between 1992 and 2004. Evaluations have been more negative since. Overall, for three of the four items, the lowest levels over the entire time period occurred in 2012.

What explains this variation in public trust over time? The large and steady decline in trust that ended in 1980 began, in part, with the tumultuous events that occurred during the 1960s and 1970s. U.S. involvement in and ultimate withdrawal from Vietnam demonstrated the inability of the American military to succeed in this conflict. The urban uprisings of the late 1960s were visible manifestations that the government was incapable of preventing social unrest. The Watergate scandal further quickened the pace of decreasing public trust. The burglary of the Democratic National Committee headquarters in the Watergate complex occurred in 1972. This was followed two years later by President Richard Nixon resigning his office among allegations of abuse of power and trying to cover up his involvement in the burglary. Thus, it is perhaps not surprising that the largest four-year decline in the trust-in-government item occurred between 1972

Figure 11.1   Public Trust in Government, 1964–2012

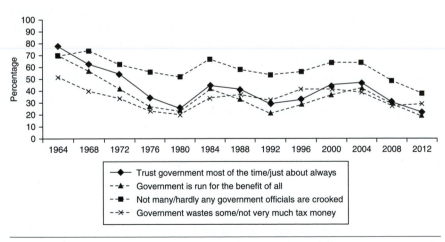

Source: Analysis of American National Election Studies Cumulative (1948–2004), American National Election Studies 2008, and American National Election Studies 2012 data files.

Note: For 2012, the result for "Not many/hardly any government officials are crooked" corresponds to "A few/no people running the government are corrupt."

and 1976, when the percentage of the public who believed government could be trusted always or most of the time fell from 54.2 to 34.5 percent.

Presidential scandals are also cited to explain later trust declines, such as those witnessed between 1984 and 1988 and again at the beginning of Bill Clinton's first term in office.[20] In 1986, the public became aware that members of President Ronald Reagan's administration had sold arms to Iran to help fund a group (the Contras) fighting the communist government in Nicaragua. Details relating to these events, known as the Iran-Contra scandal, dogged Reagan for the rest of his time in office. Clinton was embroiled in a number of scandals shortly after assuming office, including allegations that he and his wife Hillary were involved in a shady real estate deal (the Whitewater development), the firing of the entire White House travel office, and continued rumors of his marital infidelities. These scandals contributed to a decline in trust between 1992 and 1994. By 1996, however, the news was dominated by other topics, and trust in government had increased.

Quite notably, public trust in government did not drop during President Clinton's biggest scandal—the Monica Lewinsky affair, an affair with a White House intern, which eventually led to unsuccessful impeachment proceedings. Why might that be the case? According to one political scientist, President Clinton's approval ratings withstood the scandal because the economy was strong, the country was at peace, and Clinton pursued moderate policies.[21] Perhaps these factors also kept trust in government from declining. We have already mentioned how military involvement lowers trust, and shortly we discuss how good economic times and moderate policies might increase trust among the public.

Other explanations for the long-term decline in trust include **changes in public expectations of government**. In particular, Jane Mansbridge focuses on broader societal and cultural changes to explain why government increasingly does not meet public expectations.[22] Societal changes force new problems onto the government's agenda, problems that the public expects the government to address but that the government might not necessarily be equipped to solve. When these problems persist over time, as Mansbridge argues has been the case with crime and childhood poverty, government is perceived as being unable to solve problems. Public distrust results.

The increase in public trust during the 1980s has been attributed to two factors: President Reagan and an improved national economy. After Reagan took over the White House from Jimmy Carter, public trust in government increased, in large part due to the differing personas of these two presidents. Reagan was viewed by many as an inspiring, strong leader. Further, his "apparent self-assurance, good humor, decisiveness and . . . communicat[ion of] a sense of pride in the nation and its past" contrasted strongly with Carter, who was perceived as weak and lacking in the self-confidence that Reagan possessed.[23] Improved assessments of the president and his abilities led directly to increasing faith in the government.

Improved economic conditions also increased trust in the 1980s. The high inflation and high unemployment rates of the 1970s turned around in the 1980s. Public perceptions of government's handling of the economy became more favorable, leading to increased trust in government.[24] Economic performance and the public's evaluations of the government's economic policies have been correlated with public trust at other times as well. Declines in trust often accompany a poorly performing economy, as was the case in the 1970s and during President George H. W. Bush's term in office (1989–1993), whereas trust rebounds when the economy improves (such as between 1992 and 2000).[25] The impact of the economy on trust is not symmetrical, however. Trust does indeed increase when the economy improves, yet trust declines more significantly when the economy is poor. Why? "When the economy is performing badly, more people care about it, which increases its (negative) effect on trust. Since fewer people care about the economy when times are good, trust increases less in periods of prosperity than it decreases in periods of weakness."[26]

Furthermore, the state of the national economy and public trust in government do not always move in tandem. Economic conditions as well as public perceptions of the economy worsened in 2000, for instance, yet the increase in trust that had begun in the mid-1990s continued. This was largely because of the September 11, 2001, attacks and the attention placed on terrorism, foreign policy, and domestic security that resulted. Upsurges in trust follow events that place public attention squarely on terrorism and foreign affairs, such as the 9/11 attacks themselves or the 2002 congressional resolution giving President George W. Bush the authority to begin the war in Iraq.[27] It is not only during the post-9/11 era when we see that trust is influenced by foreign affairs. Over the past few decades, whenever the public has been especially concerned about global issues and national security, trust in government has increased.[28] This is largely due to the propensity of the public to rally around the president during times of crisis or threat and to the public's positive evaluation of the U.S. military.

How can we account for the recent drop in trust? Analyzing this downward trend in 2010, the Pew Research Center identified "a perfect storm of conditions associated with distrust of government—a dismal economy, an unhappy public, bitter partisan-based backlash, and epic discontent with Congress and elected officials."[29] At the time of that Pew survey, an immediate source of discontent with politicians was the high-profile and often divisive debate over the passage of the Affordable Care Act ("Obamacare"). Yet the seeds of public distrust had been sown in earlier years. Perceptions of poor government performance related to the war in Iraq and the response to Hurricane Katrina as well as the financial meltdown of 2008 all contributed to decreased trust.[30] And, as we indicated in the opening of this chapter, there has been much to dislike about the activities of national politicians of late. In fact, the lowest levels of trust in government that Pew has ever recorded came about during the debt ceiling debate of 2011 and the

2013 government shutdown. During both episodes, only 19 percent of Americans felt they could trust the national government to do the right thing.[31]

Contemporary distrust is especially high among supporters of the **Tea Party movement**. In 2013, whereas 80 percent of the overall public trusted the federal government only some of the time or never, fully 96 percent of Tea Party supporters expressed this view.[32] The Tea Party movement emerged in 2009, shortly after President Obama's inauguration. For the purposes of public opinion, this movement is best described as a set of not always well-connected local groups, the members of which possess conservative views toward government. That is, at the grassroots level, the hundreds of Tea Party organizations that exist operate largely independent of each other. Having said that, national Tea Party organizations do exist. They are funded by wealthy business interests, and their activities have consisted largely of organizing national bus tours as well as supporting candidates for office.[33] Demographically, citizen Tea Partiers are overwhelmingly white, majority male, and typically over the age of fifty.[34] Politically, they are conservative.[35] Although some have categorized Tea Partiers as straight-up antigovernment, their views are more complex than this. Tea Party supporters tend to oppose government programs directed toward groups that they consider not deserving of assistance (for example, social welfare programs for younger, able-bodied citizens or affirmative action for racial minorities). At the same time, they support federal entitlement programs such as Social Security and Medicare as well as oppose cuts to defense spending.[36] As for why their trust in government is lower than that of the broader public, one analysis pointed to two key factors: "deep pessimism about the direction of the country and the conviction that the policies of the Obama administration are disproportionately directed at helping the poor rather than the middle class or the rich."[37]

Sources of Trust

Citizens' trust in government arises from a variety of sources. We encountered some of these in the preceding discussion of variation in public trust over time, such as real-world events and government activities, evaluations of the personal characteristics of the president, the state of the economy, and assessments of governmental economic policy performance. Public trust is also related to evaluations of governmental policymaking across many other domains. In other words, people's *assessments of the products of government* (especially public policies) influence whether they trust the government. Generally speaking, distrust rises for citizens whose policy preferences are furthest from the policy decisions enacted by leaders or the platforms of the parties. Between 1964 and 1970, this meant that people with strongly liberal or strongly conservative views were the most distrusting because government policy was increasingly centrist, or moderate, rather than either liberal or conservative.[38] During this time, liberal cynics expected the government to address forcefully and quickly a number of social problems (such as poverty, inflation, and unemployment), but policymakers enacted more moderate policies instead. Conservative cynics also felt let down by government because they believed the policies favored by both the Republican and Democratic parties were too liberal (such as not using substantial police force to stop urban riots). By the 1990s, however, both parties had become more ideologically extreme. The Democratic Party platform was more liberal than it had been, and the Republican platform was more conservative. During this time, however, the ideological and policy preferences of the citizens did not change substantially. So, as the parties drifted more to the extremes, centrist citizens became the ones who felt removed from the parties' goals and who trusted government less.[39] In this continuing era of party polarization, trust among centrist citizens seems unlikely to have increased.

Public attitudes toward government are also shaped by *messages from the political environment*. When news media coverage becomes more cynical toward leaders and more questioning of politicians' motives, as has been the case over the past few decades,[40] public trust declines. Not all news outlets present the same level of cynicism toward politics, of course, but people who read more critical newspapers are less trusting of government.[41] Other changes to the media landscape also have consequences for political trust. For instance, political television is more likely today than in the past to contain uncivil political discussions. Diana Mutz and Byron Reeves wondered whether "watching politicians and pundits hurl insults at one another on television . . . [has] consequences for how people think about politics and government."[42] Their research shows that it does. Watching an uncivil versus a polite political discussion results in lower trust in government and in politicians among viewers.[43] Finally, watching faux news shows, such as *The Daily Show with Jon Stewart*, can increase cynicism. To demonstrate this, Jody Baumgartner and Jonathan Morris conducted an experiment in which participants (all young adults) viewed clips of the 2004 presidential election from either *The Daily Show* or *CBS Evening News*.[44] Compared to watching election coverage on the traditional news show, viewers of *The Daily Show* clip had less faith in the electoral system. Baumgartner and Morris explain this by pointing to Jon Stewart's tendency to portray candidates' shortcomings in sarcastic and often exaggerated ways. For example, whereas *CBS Evening News* raised questions about George W. Bush's competency to govern by drawing on examples from his first term as president, *The Daily Show* presented Bush as a "dimwitted fraternity boy."[45]

The media are not the only source of information about government. Political leaders themselves communicate their views about the government to the public. It is not uncommon for candidates, especially newcomers to national politics, to run for office by criticizing the government and portraying themselves as outsiders. This was the successful strategy pursued by Jimmy Carter, former governor of Georgia, when he ran for president in 1976, and the strategy of some of the candidates vying to be the 2016 Republican presidential nominee. For instance, Scott Walker, the governor of Wisconsin, displayed the following quotation prominently on his presidential campaign website in the summer of 2015: "In America we celebrate our independence from the government, not our dependence on it."[46] Sitting presidents have also been known to speak harshly about government, as did Ronald Reagan when during his first inaugural address he stated, "Government is not the solution to our problems; government is the problem."[47]

With such attacks on government delivered by politicians, it is perhaps not surprising that public trust is low. Could a more positive tone toward government increase trust? An experiment conducted by Shmuel Lock, Robert Shapiro, and Lawrence Jacobs suggests that it could. During the course of a telephone survey, Lock, Shapiro, and Jacobs asked all of their respondents, "How much confidence do you have in the federal government's ability to run its national programs?"[48] For half of the respondents, questions about the government's ability to run specific programs (the military, Social Security, and Medicare) were asked before the general confidence item. These respondents displayed greater confidence in government than did those for whom the specific policy questions appeared *after* the general item. Lock et al. attribute this difference to the fact that those receiving the questions about government policy in specific domains were reminded about government programs that are generally regarded as successful. With thoughts of successful government activities at the forefront of their minds, people displayed greater confidence in government. This research suggests that if elite and media communication more often contained details of well-regarded government policies, levels of trust among the public could rise.

Citizen experiences with government and government officials also influence trust, in both positive and negative ways. Every year, the Social Security Administration sends information to Americans between the ages of twenty-five and sixty-five. This mailing contains general details about Social Security (such as benefits and eligibility) as well as personal details regarding the recipients' contributions and anticipated monthly payment on retirement. In 1999, the Gallup organization was surveying the public about their knowledge of and attitudes toward the Social Security program at the same time that the annual statements were being mailed. Some survey respondents had received their statement before they were polled, whereas others had not. This reality allowed researchers to examine whether receiving the mailing influenced trust toward Social Security. It did. Compared to those who had not received their statement, individuals who had received it were more knowledgeable about Social Security, which in turn led to greater faith that the Social Security Administration would provide future benefits.[49]

On the other hand, when citizens interact with the criminal justice system, their trust in government can decline. The more serious the contact with the justice system, the lower the trust in government. For example, a national survey of adults in their twenties demonstrates that, for those who had not had any encounters with the criminal justice system, only 18 percent distrusted the federal government.[50] But nearly 30 percent of the young adults who had been questioned by police or arrested were distrustful. Being convicted of a crime or serving jail time further increased distrust (conviction, 31 percent distrustful; incarceration, 43 percent; and more than one year in jail or prison, 55 percent). The authors of this study argue that "punitive encounters with the state foster mistrust of political institutions," and their results demonstrate that the mistrusting attitudes extend to political institutions and actors (that is, the federal government) beyond the police officers, local courts, and correctional facilities of the criminal justice system.[51]

One factor that is not strongly related to people's trust attitudes is their demographic characteristics. Beginning with the initial analyses of the ANES trust items and continuing on to more recent times, many scholars have found that levels of trust do not differ substantially across subgroups of people.[52] As you can see from Figure 11.2, in 2012 levels of trust in government were not significantly different for women and men. Trust also was quite similar for people of different income levels and of different education levels. Differences across age were not that large, although we do see that younger adults were the most trusting.[53]

Racial differences in trust did emerge in 2012. Whites were the least trusting of government, followed by Hispanics and then blacks. One explanation for Hispanics' higher level of trust hinges on the more recent arrival in the United States of some Hispanics. Newly arrived immigrants generally have more positive views toward the government than do individuals who have been in the country longer. Because a larger proportion of Hispanics are foreign-born than are whites and blacks, trust levels among Hispanics have been, on average, higher than among the other two groups.[54] We see this same trend in 2012, but only when Hispanics are compared to whites. Unlike in the past, Hispanics did not display higher levels of trust than did African Americans, largely because trust in government has been increasing among blacks. Historically, blacks tended to be less trusting of government than either whites or Hispanics.[55] Most explained this difference using the **political reality model**.[56] With less political power than whites in the United States and a government less responsive to their needs, blacks were more distrustful. As the face of government literally changes, however, so can levels of trust. Black citizens have been found to display higher levels of trust in areas where there is a larger proportion of black elected officials.[57] As for assessments of the federal government, blacks have higher trust in black politicians than politicians of other races.[58] Finally, and not surprisingly given that blacks are much more likely to be Democratic than Republican, blacks have displayed higher trust in the government when the president is Democratic. Ever since the inauguration of the nation's first African American president, who also happens to be

Figure 11.2   Trust in Government for Specific Demographic Groups, 2012

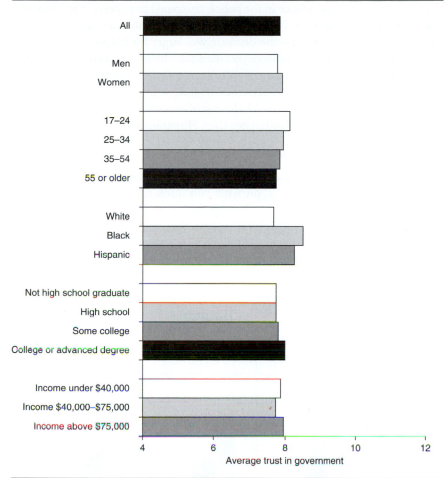

Source: Analysis of American National Election Studies 2012 data file.

Note: For these comparisons, we constructed an index of trust by adding up people's responses to the four ANES trust items. The possible range of the index was from 4 to 14, with higher numbers indicating more trust. The average for all respondents was 7.84.

Democratic, blacks have been more likely to trust the federal government to do what is right.

At the same time, trust and confidence in law enforcement are lower among blacks than among other racial groups. These racial differences are not new,[59] although they have received renewed attention in the wake of the 2014 shooting death of Michael Brown in Ferguson, Missouri. Gallup surveys fielded in 2014 and 2015 found that, on average, only 30 percent of African Americans had a great deal or quite a lot of confidence in the police, compared to 52 percent of Hispanics and 57 percent of whites (see Figure 11.3). Confidence among all three groups has declined since 2012, although the decrease was larger for blacks and Hispanics (6 and 8 percentage points, respectively) than for whites (3 percentage points).[60] Late 2014 polling conducted by the *Washington Post* and ABC News assessed confidence in two specific police activities: treating whites and blacks equally and receiving sufficient training to avoid the use of excessive force. For both, blacks display much lower levels of confidence than Hispanics and, especially, whites.

Implications of Declining Public Trust

What are we to make of the decline in public trust since the 1960s? Answers to this question depend, in part, on what you think the trust survey questions

Figure 11.3   Racial Differences in Confidence in the Police

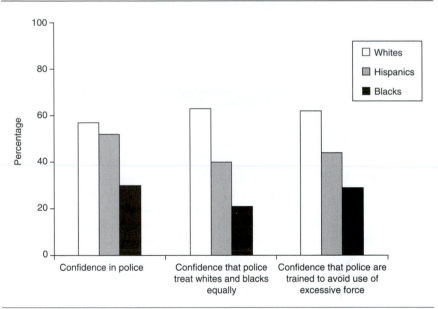

Sources: Jeffrey M. Jones, "In U.S., Confidence in Police Lowest in 22 Years," Gallup, Washington, DC, June 19, 2015, http://www.gallup.com/poll/183704/confidence-police-lowest-years.aspx?utm_source=position3&utm_medium=related&utm_campaign=tiles; "*Washington Post*–ABC News Poll, December 11–14, 2014," *The Washington Post*, January 4, 2015, http://www.washingtonpost.com/politics/polling/washington-postabc-news-poll-december-1114/2014/12/16/b6f831be-8518-11e4-abcf-5a3d7b3b20b8_page.html

Note: Bars represent the percentage having "a great deal" or "quite a lot" of confidence for the first item and being "very" or "somewhat" confident for the other two items.

are measuring. Thus, we return to the debate between Arthur Miller and Jack Citrin. Recall that Miller believes the ANES questions tap into system-level attitudes toward government. For him, then, a sustained decline in public trust suggests an unhealthy democracy. Miller also worries that a long-term decline in trust might lead citizens to demand radical change to the democratic political system.[61] In contrast, according to Citrin such consequences are unlikely to result from declines in trust as measured by the ANES because these measures primarily register assessments of incumbent politicians rather than evaluations of the broader political system. To Citrin, expressions of cynicism are "ritualistic rather than genuine . . . to agree verbally that many people 'running the government' are corrupt, incompetent, or untrustworthy is like shouting 'Kill the umpire!' at a baseball game. Bloodthirsty rhetoric threatens neither the life expectancy of umpires nor the future of the national pastime."[62]

Even with sustained low levels of public trust in government, there is little evidence that the serious consequences predicted by Miller and others have resulted. Public levels of patriotism remain high, support for antidemocratic measures and activities has not noticeably increased, and pleas for radical changes to the governmental system are uncommon. Despite registering very low levels of public trust, a 2013 Pew survey also recorded that Americans are not so much angry with the federal government as frustrated.[63] This, however, does not mean that cynical attitudes are largely ritualistic and without any effects. Research conducted by Marc Hetherington demonstrates a variety of repercussions. Lower levels of trust can lead to poorer evaluations of presidential performance and less support for the institutions of government, thus making it more challenging for political leaders to govern.[64]

Hetherington's most provocative argument is that declining public trust has contributed to the increase in conservative public policies adopted by the national government.[65] Liberal solutions to public problems generally involve government, such as federal intervention to prevent racial discrimination or the provision of public money and subsidies to fight poverty. Conservatives, in contrast, tend to prefer minimal government involvement in the economic sector, so they generally favor policies that pursue this goal. Such conservative policies have been more common in the United States since the 1960s, especially in contrast to President Lyndon Johnson's Great Society legislation, which established a variety of government programs to fight racism and poverty. Public policy could have taken a conservative turn because citizens' attitudes became more conservative toward all issues over this time. Hetherington, however, demonstrates this is not the case. The public has not become less supportive of government funding for Social Security, Medicare, transportation, and education, for example.

Public opinion has fluctuated, however, toward certain social welfare policies, especially those that require most people to sacrifice so that others (such as the poor and racial minorities) will benefit. And these fluctuations have been largely driven by levels of public trust. When trust is higher, the public supports liberal antipoverty and racial policies. As trust declines, public support for these policies is much lower. Most citizens believe that poverty and racism should be eliminated—they simply do not believe the government is capable of solving these problems. Hetherington shows that decades of increasing public distrust in government have "undermined public support for federal programs like welfare, food stamps, and foreign aid, not to mention the entire range of race-targeted programs designed to make equality between the races a reality."[66]

Finally, some have argued that public distrust is a good thing, so we should not worry about any negative implications. As liberal democratic theorists posit, suspicion of those in power can be healthy for democracy, and thus declining trust might be a reasonable reaction to government actions.[67] Further, public distrust in the past has contributed to the inclusion of new groups into democratic decision making. Political movements such as the women's movement, the civil rights movement, and the environmental movement rose up to challenge existing power arrangements, in part because members of these groups lost trust in the government's willingness to address the groups' concerns.[68] Increasing public distrust has also been mentioned as an indicator of the level of development of a nation. When a society's basic needs must be met by the government, trust in the government is expected to be high. Yet, "as material well-being increases, trust in political institutions and elites is likely to decline as publics begin to evaluate their leaders and institutions by more demanding standards."[69]

Public Opinion in Comparative Perspective
Box 11.1 Levels of Public Trust in Other Nations

Declining levels of public trust are not a uniquely American phenomenon. In fact, across many advanced industrial democracies, trust in government has declined over the past decades. In 2012, for example, only 13 percent of Greeks and 35 percent of the Irish had confidence in their national government. Similarly low levels of confidence were recorded in other European nations as well as around the globe, including in Japan (17 percent), South Korea (23), Chile (32), Mexico (33), and Israel (34).[1] Furthermore, for many nations public trust was lower than it had been in 2007, substantially so for some. The nations experiencing the largest percentage point drops were Ireland (28 points), India (27), and Greece (25).

Writing about a decade ago, Russell Dalton pointed to three key explanations for the over-time decline.[2] First, contemporary democratic publics have higher expectations for government and the democratic process than their governments are meeting. Second, governments' policy agendas have expanded. As a government tries to address more societal problems, some groups of the public will inevitably be unhappy with the resulting solutions. Third, more and more, the mass media and the public are holding political officials accountable for their unethical behavior. Finally, we need to add one more explanation to account for the recent decline in trust: the global economic recession and public perceptions that governments have not dealt adequately with the crisis.[3]

The fact that many democracies have witnessed declines in public trust could be good news for those in the United States who worry about public distrust and wonder what is wrong in America that has caused trust to drop. Yet Dalton reminds us of an alternative, less sanguine interpretation: "The commonality of these trends suggests that no one has found a way to restore public confidence in politicians, parties and political institutions . . . which implies that low levels of support may be a continuing feature of advanced industrial democracies."[4]

---

1. "Confidence in Government Falls in Much of the Developed World," Pew Research Center, Washington, DC, November 21, 2013, http://www.pewresearch.org/fact-tank/2013/11/21/confidence-in-government-falls-in-much-of-the-developed-world
2. Russell J. Dalton, *Democratic Challenges, Democratic Choices: The Erosion of Political Support in Advanced Industrial Democracies* (Oxford: Oxford University Press, 2004).
3. Antonis A. Ellinas and Iasonas Lamprianou, "Political Trust *in Extremis*," *Comparative Politics* 46 (2014): 231–250; Mariano Torcal, "The Decline of Political Trust in Spain and Portugal: Economic Performance or Political Responsiveness?," *American Behavioral Scientist* 58 (2014): 1542–1567.
4. Dalton, *Democratic Challenges*, 208.

SUPPORT FOR INSTITUTIONS

In addition to understanding citizens' trust in government in general, it is important to examine attitudes toward individual aspects of the political system, especially the institutions of government. We begin with a discussion of citizens' levels of confidence in the Supreme Court, the executive branch, and Congress. As with trust in government, confidence in institutions is an important underpinning of a democratic nation. If citizens do not support governmental institutions, they are less likely to accept and comply with the outputs of those institutions. For example, citizens who lack confidence in institutions might be more willing to protest Supreme Court decisions or ignore legislation passed by Congress and signed into law by the president.[70] The questions used to measure confidence, however, tap into both attitudes toward the institutions and attitudes toward members of those institutions. Thus, it is difficult to know what to make of these low levels of confidence. Do they suggest a crisis for American democracy? Or do the low levels simply reflect citizens' dislike of the individuals within those institutions? We now address these questions.

Confidence in Institutions

How much confidence do citizens have in the Supreme Court, the executive branch, and Congress? Not much, according to national survey data collected by the General Social Survey (GSS). Since the early 1970s, citizens have been asked the following:

> I am going to name some institutions in this country. As far as the people running these institutions are concerned, would you say you have a great deal of confidence, only some confidence, or hardly any confidence at all in them? . . . Executive branch of the federal government . . . U.S. Supreme Court . . . Congress.[71]

Of the three branches, citizens have the most **confidence in the Supreme Court** (see Figure 11.4). Between 1973 and 2014, 33 percent of citizens, on average, said they had a great deal of confidence in the Court. Support for the Supreme Court was at its all-time high in 1991 when 39 percent of citizens said they had a great deal of confidence in the institution. Its lowest point came in 2014, when only 24 percent felt that way.

Figure 11.4   Confidence in the Supreme Court, Executive Branch, and Congress, 1974–2014

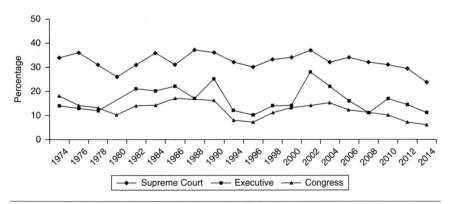

Source: Analysis of General Social Survey Cumulative Data File, 1972–2014.

Note: Data points are the percentage of respondents who had "a great deal" of confidence in each institution.

Confidence in the executive branch has been quite a bit lower and not as stable as in the Supreme Court. On average, 17 percent of Americans said they had a great deal of confidence in the executive branch between 1973 and 2014. The executive branch was held in highest esteem in 1973, when 29 percent of citizens said they had a great deal of confidence in the institution. The Watergate scandal was playing out at that point, yet confidence in the institution was high, relatively speaking. Unfortunately, the GSS did not ask the question prior to 1973, so we do not know whether the Watergate scandal had already taken a toll on confidence in the executive branch. By 1974, however, it is clear the scandal had tainted the presidency—confidence dropped to 14 percent. The low point for the executive branch came in 1996, when only 10 percent said they had a great deal of confidence. Twice in recent years—2008 and 2014—this figure was only slightly higher, at 11 percent.

Confidence in Congress is lower than in both the Supreme Court and the executive branch. Similar to the executive branch, confidence in Congress is more volatile than support for the Supreme Court. On average, only 13 percent of citizens said they had a great deal of confidence in Congress between 1973 and 2014. Congress's high point was in 1973 at 24 percent. One low point was in 1993 when a mere 7 percent said they had a great deal of confidence in the legislative body. The voters expressed their displeasure at the ballot box in 1994. That year, the "Republican Revolution" occurred, with the Republicans taking over the House of Representatives from the Democrats for the first time in forty years. Throughout much of the 1990s, public support for Congress was dismal. It bounced back in the early 2000s, only to decline since 2004. In short, disdain for Congress is high, especially these days. Only 6 percent of the public, the lowest level ever recorded by the GSS, had a great deal of confidence in this institution in 2014.

As you have probably already noticed, the question wording used to measure confidence in these institutions conflates diffuse and specific support.[72] The survey question refers to "institutions" (thus implying diffuse support) *and* to "the people running these institutions" (thus implying specific support). Consequently, these data make it impossible to sort out whether American citizens have very limited faith in the fundamental institutions of our government, whether they simply hold political leaders in low esteem, or both. This is problematic because, if we are interested in combating low levels of confidence, we need to know what is driving the discontent. We would come up with very different solutions if the target of citizens' wrath was the institution versus the politicians themselves. We now turn to an important research project that tackles this issue.

Approval of Political Institutions and Their Members

John Hibbing and Elizabeth Theiss-Morse argue that political scientists must make a distinction between citizens' **attitudes toward the institutions of government** and their **attitudes toward institutional members**.[73] To sort this out,

Hibbing and Theiss-Morse designed and implemented their own national survey of 1,433 randomly selected respondents in 1992. In this survey, citizens were asked about their approval of each institution and their approval of members of each institution. See Table 11.2 for the wording of the questions used in this survey.

When attitudes toward the institutions are separated from attitudes toward the people running the institutions, you can immediately see that citizens are actually quite supportive of the institutions: 88 percent or more of the respondents approved of each of the three institutions (see Figure 11.5).[74] Attitudes toward the people running these institutions, however, are a different story. With a 73 percent approval rating, support for the Supreme Court justices was the highest, followed closely by approval of the respondents' own member of Congress. In contrast, less than one-quarter of citizens approved of members of Congress, and less than one-half approved of the way the president was handling his job. Based on these data, Hibbing and Theiss-Morse conclude that the "confidence" questions overstate people's displeasure with the *institutions* of government.[75] Indeed, they argue citizens see the constitutional system of three branches of government as "goodness and light."[76]

Table 11.2 Survey Questions Assessing Approval of Institutions and Members of Institutions

Approval of institutions:

"I have a few more questions about the institutions of the government in Washington—that is, the presidency, the Supreme Court, and Congress. In general, do you strongly approve, approve, disapprove, or strongly disapprove of the institution of the presidency, no matter who is in office?"

"What about the Supreme Court, no matter who the justices are?"

"What about the U.S. Congress, no matter who is in office?"

Approval of members of institutions:

"Again, thinking about people in government, please tell me if you strongly approve, approve, disapprove, or strongly disapprove of the way the people are handling their jobs. How do you feel about the way the nine justices on the Supreme Court have been handling their job?"

"What about President George Bush?"

"What about the 535 members of Congress?"

"What about your own representative in the U.S. House of Representatives?"

Source: John R. Hibbing and Elizabeth Theiss-Morse, *Congress as Public Enemy: Public Attitudes toward American Political Institutions* (Cambridge: Cambridge University Press, 1995), 166. © Cambridge University Press 1995. Reprinted with the permission of Cambridge University Press.

Figure 11.5 Approval of Institutions and Members of Institutions, 1992

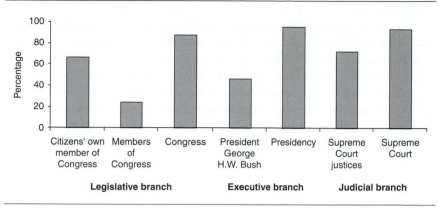

Source: John R. Hibbing and Elizabeth Theiss-Morse, *Congress as Public Enemy: Public Attitudes toward American Political Institutions* (Cambridge: Cambridge University Press, 1995), 45. © Cambridge University Press 1995. Reprinted with the permission of Cambridge University Press.

Note: Bars represent the percentage of respondents who either "strongly approve" or "approve" of each attitude object.

Hibbing and Theiss-Morse's survey was conducted in 1992, so you might be wondering whether their findings still apply today. Unfortunately, researchers have rarely probed the public's views of government institutions separately from the people serving in those institutions. Pew surveys conducted between 2010 and 2014 have done this, at least for Congress. Pew asked respondents whether "Most members of Congress have good intentions, it's the political system that is broken" or "The political system can work fine, it's the members of Congress that are the problem."[77] In 2010, a slight majority of respondents (52 percent) felt congressional representatives were the problem, with just 38 percent evaluating the political system more negatively than members of Congress. Three years later, the public was even more likely to view congressional members as causing problems (58 percent) versus believing that the system is broken (32 percent). A 2014 Pew survey contained two questions that allow us to compare the public's views of all members of Congress to their own representative. When asked whether "most members of Congress" should be reelected, 23 percent said yes. In contrast, 48 percent wanted their own representative to win reelection.[78] Note that 48 percent is somewhat low by historical standards, yet it is still significantly higher than the percentage of the public that wanted most of the representatives to be reelected. Overall, these Pew survey results essentially confirm Hibbing and Theiss-Morse's regarding Congress. Without similar questions assessing views toward the presidency and Supreme Court, however, we cannot say whether

Hibbing and Theiss-Morse's earlier conclusions still apply to these two branches of government.

So why doesn't the public like members of Congress? To address this question, let's return to Hibbing and Theiss-Morse's research. They wanted to explore citizens' attitudes toward institutions more deeply than surveys will allow. Thus, Hibbing and Theiss-Morse conducted eight focus groups in four areas of the country: southeast Nebraska, Minneapolis–St. Paul, Houston, and upstate New York. Each focus group was made up of six to twelve participants. Responding to a facilitator's broad questions about support for political institutions, the groups had open, free-flowing discussions that lasted about two hours each.[79] The participants in the focus groups echoed many of the survey research findings but also added richness to our understanding of why citizens find members of Congress particularly distasteful. In particular, Hibbing and Theiss-Morse conclude that "Congress is an enemy of the public *because* it is public."[80] Congress is an open institution; debates and decision making are on full display for the public to see. The gridlock, the partisan bickering, the compromises, and conflict—they're all there for citizens to evaluate.[81] Furthermore, citizens are turned off by what they perceive as the inappropriate influence of lobbyists and interest groups on members of Congress. People are angered by members acting on behalf of interest groups in exchange for perks and ignoring the interests of common citizens. Table 11.3 contains quotations from focus group participants that illustrate these points.

But if citizens are so turned off by members of Congress, why do they like their *own* representative? Because members of Congress are an undifferentiated mass of people who do things the public does not like, whereas citizens have individuating information about their own representative that makes them like

Table 11.3 Focus Group Discussions of Members of Congress

Participant from New York: "In Congress, they got cobwebs on their arms from sitting in chairs for three years. They got no new ideas. They just keep going back to the old stuff that keeps putting money in their pockets."

Participant from Texas: "These guys are up there, pardon my language, like fat cats as they've been called, doing this, that, and the other, and they're hobnobbing with who? The people who have the influence, and who has the influence? The people with the money."

Participant from Nebraska: "I think Congress . . . has gotten too big for their britches. They got used to all the freebies, the perks, the nice things that come to them, the power, and it's just become taken for granted. It's become abused."

Source: John R. Hibbing and Elizabeth Theiss-Morse, *Congress as Public Enemy: Public Attitudes toward American Political Institutions* (Cambridge: Cambridge University Press, 1995), 97–99. © Cambridge University Press 1995. Reprinted with the permission of Cambridge University Press.

him or her. A citizen might know, for example, that her representative tracked down Grandpa Dale's lost farm subsidy check, or another citizen might know that his representative secured funding to build a new bridge in the community. Of course, when citizens see *other* members of Congress bringing home money to their districts, they often refer to it derisively as "pork," but projects brought to their *own* districts are considered sensible uses of taxpayer money.

Whereas Congress is the most open institution, the Supreme Court is at the other end of the continuum. The president falls between these two extremes.[82] The Court is the least public institution, heavily shielded from the media and citizens. Debate occurs and votes are taken behind closed doors; the justices' own clerks are not even present during conferences. As for the executive branch, internal debates and disagreement within this branch are not as visible as those in Congress. Furthermore, many people view the president as a symbolic leader or a figurehead. Interest groups do try to influence judicial decision making as well as executive agencies, yet this activity occurs largely out of the public eye. Interest groups do not, for example, take Supreme Court justices on golfing junkets or give money to reelection campaigns because justices never run for election to this position. Lobbying of the White House happens behind closed doors rather than in public hearings, as it does on Capitol Hill.

For these reasons, the Supreme Court and its membership are perceived as different than the other branches of government, as above the hurly-burly of politics.[83] The Court is perceived as a defender of the Constitution neutrally applying legal guidelines rather than as a political actor.[84] At least that used to be the case. Recent research demonstrates that a not insubstantial segment of the public views the Court as a political institution.[85] Even though changes might be afoot, citizens still feel substantially more favorable toward the Supreme Court and justices than toward Congress and its membership. Finally, the less public, more ceremonial nature of the presidency makes it more palatable than the open divisiveness of Congress. Of course, attitudes toward the president are another matter. For more on this, see the discussion of presidential approval in Chapter 4.

Overall, Hibbing and Theiss-Morse conclude that citizens do not like democratic processes, which leads them to view members of Congress with particular disdain. These scholars do not excuse the bad behavior on the part of some members of Congress, but they do argue that citizens should be better educated about how democracy actually works. Democratic processes are "inevitably unruly."[86] If citizens had a better understanding of that, they might not be so turned off by the bickering and deal making occurring in the legislative branch. Ironically, citizens blame the members of Congress rather than the institution of Congress for the messy way in which democracy works. They do not seem to understand that Congress, not to mention the entire U.S. system of government, was designed to ensure conflict and compromise. If they did realize that, would citizens be as supportive of the constitutional system as they currently are? Would education lead people to appreciate members of Congress, or would it lead citizens to lose respect for the institutions of democracy? These are hypothetical questions we cannot answer, but they are certainly important to consider.

Hibbing and Theiss-Morse's results are particularly troubling to pluralists and participatory democratic theorists. Pluralists, of course, think that citizens can be well represented by interest groups, but citizens don't agree. During Hibbing and Theiss-Morse's focus groups, one of the strongest complaints was that interest groups do not represent the views of ordinary Americans. As a result of interest group influence, members of Congress pass legislation to please powerful groups but not to serve the interests of the people, according to many citizens. Participatory democratic theorists are challenged by the extreme dislike of politics that citizens revealed in the focus group discussions.[87] Participatory democratic theorists believe that citizens would be more engaged and participate at higher levels if they just had the opportunity to do so. Hibbing and Theiss-Morse's participants, however, were not interested in debate, conflict, uncertainty, and compromise—democracy, in other words. Citizens dislike democracy in practice and want no part of it. Instead, the public wants "government to do its job quietly and efficiently, sans conflict and sans fuss."[88] Thus, these findings undermine the arguments of participatory democratic theorists.

Elite democratic theorists would be most pleased with the findings discussed in this section. They believe citizens should have a healthy skepticism toward political leaders yet maintain support for the institutions of government. That seems to best characterize citizens' attitudes toward institutions and the members of those institutions.

SOCIAL CAPITAL

For most people, interactions with other individuals (at dinner, over the water cooler at work, or while volunteering to clean up a park) are more frequent and more significant than are their interactions with government. Social connectedness not only is important for people but also can be beneficial to a community, as observed nearly one hundred years ago by the rural schools supervisor in West Virginia:

> The individual is helpless socially, if left to himself. . . . If he comes into contact with his neighbor, and they with other neighbors, there will be an accumulation of social capital, which may immediately satisfy his social needs and which may bear a social potentiality sufficient to the substantial improvement of living conditions in the whole community.[89]

Contemporary definitions of **social capital** share much in common with this first use of the term. For political scientist Robert Putnam, the most visible writer on this topic, "social capital refers to connections among individuals—social networks and the norms of reciprocity and trustworthiness that arise from them."[90] Social capital has two broad components: **civic engagement** (activities intended to solve public or community problems) and **interpersonal trust** (the degree to which people think others can be trusted, are fair, and are helpful). Communities with high social capital consist of many citizens engaged in group activities and a public that has high levels of trust in other people.

Researchers have identified a number of specific consequences of social capital. Recent declines in social capital, which we outline in the next section, have contributed to the lower levels of trust in government witnessed over the past few decades. Why? "When citizens disengage from civic life and its lessons of social reciprocity, they are unable to trust the institutions that govern political life."[91] Confidence in national institutions, particularly the legislature, is higher in nations with greater social capital.[92] Social capital is also related to political behavior. Recent research by Emily Farris and Mirya Holman illustrates this relationship for one specific group of Americans: black women.[93] Black women belong to and engage with community groups at a rate higher than white women or men (whether black or white). Such social capital is also more strongly linked to participation in more explicitly political activities (e.g., voting, attending a political meeting) for black women. Put another way, social capital spurs political activity for black women to a higher degree than for black men or whites.

Many other benefits are presumed to accrue to communities with high levels of social capital, largely because such capital allows members to work together to address community problems. Compared with U.S. states with low social capital, for example, those with high levels contain less violent crime, better environments for children (e.g., lower infant mortality rates, fewer children living in poverty), healthier citizens, and improved status for women (e.g., increased economic autonomy, better health and well-being).[94] Furthermore, communities with more social capital can recover more quickly from natural disasters, as was the case along the Gulf Coast after Hurricane Katrina hit.[95] Community ties, trust in one's neighbors, and connections to civic associations can help both in the immediate aftermath of a disaster as well as in the slow process of recovery.

Is social capital important for democratic governance? Democratic theorists disagree on this, largely because they differ on the proper level of citizen political engagement. Elite and pluralist democrats both propose that the public be minimally involved in governmental decision making, with the public's views represented via elected officials or interest groups, respectively. Pluralists emphasize the importance of group activity in politics, as do social capital theorists, but they disagree over the role of groups in democracy. Pluralists argue that competition among groups over governmental policy produces stable democracies by preventing one set of interests from becoming too powerful. The study of social capital, in contrast, emphasizes the benefits to individuals who participate in civic groups as well as the benefits to the community of having people engaged in politics.[96]

These last views, of course, more closely resemble the theory of participatory democracy than pluralism. Participatory democrats stress the importance of a politically active public and thus would view social capital as valuable for democratic health. In particular, participatory democrats extol the virtues of citizen engagement with one another. Working with others can teach people tolerance of opposing views, trust in other people, and cooperation—qualities that are important for democratic governance. Communicating with others can also contribute to learning about politics and fine-tuning an individual's political attitudes. In addition to these individual benefits, participatory democrats believe that a citizenry more engaged in political activities and debate is good for democracy in that this is more likely to result in citizen views influencing government decisions. These normative theories of democracy, then, differ in whether they consider citizen connectedness important for democracy. What of the reality of social capital in the United States today? We answer that question next by summarizing an influential study that tracked levels of social capital over the past few decades.

Putnam's Bowling Alone

Did you know that bowling was one of the most popular competitive sports in the United States near the end of the twentieth century? Between 1980 and the mid-1990s, the number of people who bowled increased by 10 percent. At the same time, however, participation in bowling leagues decreased by 40 percent. So more Americans were bowling, but they were increasingly bowling on their own rather than as members of established leagues.[97] This fact led to the title of Robert Putnam's book examining social capital, *Bowling Alone.* At this point, you might be wondering what the connection between bowling and social capital is. For Putnam, the decline in league bowling was one of many indications that informal social connections among Americans were waning. Compared with nonleague bowlers, people who bowl in leagues not only bowl at the alley but also are much more likely to hang out together over food and drink. Connections are made and conversations—about bowling and many other topics—ensue. So the imagery of bowling is particularly useful for illuminating one of the main themes of Putnam's book: rather than joining with others in a variety of political, social, and leisure activities, the American public is increasingly acting alone.

To demonstrate that social capital is on the decline, Putnam and his research assistants marshaled an impressive amount of data covering many manifestations of social capital. The centerpiece of this analysis examines membership in **chapter-based civic associations**, such as parent-teacher associations, the American Legion, and the Jaycees, where members meet regularly in their local communities. For many of these groups, membership increased fairly steadily from 1900 to 1945 and then grew tremendously until the mid-1960s. After a period of stability lasting through the 1970s or later, most groups saw their membership numbers decrease substantially. Membership declines for a variety of civic associations are illustrated in Figure 11.6. These percentages represent the decline in membership rates for each association from the year of their highest membership until 1997. The number of people belonging to each group declined, quite significantly for some, during this time period. For example, the American Association of University Women's membership rate is 84 percent lower than it was, and membership in the National Association for the Advancement of Colored People (NAACP) and the Elks each dropped 46 percent. The smallest decline presented here, at 25 percent, occurred for the Rotary Club.

In contrast, during these same decades some **national mass membership organizations** witnessed tremendous growth. Major environmental organizations, including the Sierra Club and National Wildlife Federation, saw their membership increase from 2 million in 1980 to 6.5 million in 1990, before leveling off.[98] One of the largest organizations in the nation, the American Association of Retired Persons (AARP), counted 33 million members in the mid-1990s, up from 400,000 in 1960. This expansion was remarkable and has contributed to the

Figure 11.6 Membership Declines for Civic Associations between Peak Year of Membership and 1997

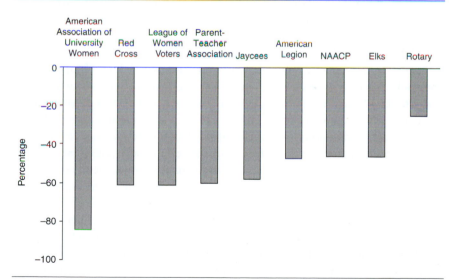

Source: Adapted from Appendix 3 of Robert D. Putnam, *Bowling Alone: The Collapse and Revival of American Community* (New York: Simon and Schuster, 2000), 438–439.

Note: Bars represent the percentage decline in membership rate (based on size of population eligible for membership) from the year of highest membership rate for each organization to 1997.

lobbying clout exercised by the AARP in Washington.[99] Yet, from a social capital perspective, membership in these types of organizations does not resemble belonging to an association with local chapters. For many who belong to mass membership organizations, participation entails sending in annual dues and perhaps reading newsletters, e-mail messages, and other communication sent by the national headquarters. The connection between members of the AARP or the National Audubon Society is "like the bond between any two Red Sox fans . . . they root for the same team and they share some of the same interests, but they are unaware of each other's existence. Their ties, in short, are to common symbols, common leaders, and perhaps common ideals, but not to one another."[100] Belonging to such groups, in other words, does not develop social capital.

Putnam's analysis did not stop with civic and political associations; he also considered other indicators of social capital's decline. Participation in religious activities (such as attending religious services) and groups (such as the B'nai B'rith and the Knights of Columbus) is lower than in prior decades. Labor union membership is down, as is membership in many professional organizations, including the American Nurses Association and the American Bar Association. In addition to membership in formal organizations, **informal social interaction** has also declined. Compared with past years, Americans are less likely to socialize with their neighbors, entertain friends at their house, or be entertained at a friend's house. As Putnam concluded, "We spend less time in conversation over meals, we exchange visits less often, we engage less often in leisure activities that encourage casual social interaction. . . . We know our neighbors less well, and we see old friends less often."[101]

Bowling Alone made a huge splash when it was published. Unlike most scholarly books, it received considerable national attention in the press and was read by many nonacademics, including politicians, activists, and leaders of associations. Putnam's work has thus been very influential in our thinking about social capital, and many people do support his conclusions. Yet his research was not well received by everyone. In particular, some feel he overstated his case that social capital is declining, such as by being too quick to dismiss national mass membership organizations as contributors to social capital. A closer look at the governing structures of and individual activities within these organizations demonstrates that some do indeed provide opportunities for members to interact with one another in pursuit of common goals.[102] In short, check writing is not the only activity of members.

Putnam also missed some examples of citizen engagement. Even though Americans are less likely to join the traditional civic associations that Putnam profiles, participation in small, less formal groups has increased. These include support groups (such as Alcoholics Anonymous), book clubs, coffee house gatherings, and tenants' associations.[103] Putnam acknowledges these groups are common but argues they do not contribute to social capital in the same way that civic associations do because members of these types of small groups do not translate their participation into forms of civic engagement. Instead, the groups primarily provide an important support and caring network for members.[104] Putnam is correct, yet these small groups do provide meaningful person-to-person interaction and would seem to build interpersonal trust, one key feature of social capital.

By focusing so much attention on formal civic organizations, Putnam also overlooked social capital among citizens who have been marginalized in society. Marginalized citizens often create social networks and social capital from their own locations, rather than only, or even primarily, through the type of civic associations favored by those in the majority. Participation in such groups, notably African American civic organizations, has been shown to facilitate engagement in majority civic life.[105] Furthermore, historical exclusion from many political and civic activities led to blacks forming bonds with each other in locales that Putnam neglected to examine, including homes, neighborhoods, black churches, the streets (especially during social protests), and possibly even prison. Although prison might not seem an obvious venue for building social capital, one scholar argues that "the prison is increasingly a venue of black civic action."[106] Some black organizations are active inside and outside prison, fostering links between prisoners and those on the outside. This has increased attention throughout the black community to issues related to prison life (including racial bias in the criminal justice system that leads to higher incarceration rates of blacks versus whites). Political activism around criminal justice has been one result.

Putnam's book was published over fifteen years ago and his conclusions are based on data that are older still. Has the decline in social capital he documented persisted since then? Generally yes, say Putnam and a colleague.[107] Yet society has changed since then in one major way related to social connectedness: the use of the Internet, especially **social media** sites such as Facebook and Twitter, has exploded. Can interacting with others virtually, through a computer or smartphone, produce the same social capital benefits that face-to-face communication is presumed to? Although attempts to answer this question have, to date, been few, there is preliminary evidence that some types of social media usage can indeed develop social capital. Two scholars did a side-by-side comparison of in-person versus virtual group participation. Examples of the latter include becoming more involved online with organizations to which one belongs offline or interacting online with others who share one's views or interests. Both online and in-person group activity were found to be related to a sense that citizens should be politically engaged and to heightened political participation.[108] A different set of scholars examined the use of Twitter for political activism, including during the 2011 Occupy movement in the United States. They concluded that Twitter can develop social capital, most notably building interpersonal trust among the movement's online participants.[109] These are two examples out of a few initial forays exploring social media and social capital. It seems likely that time spent on social media will displace activities that would contribute to social capital. You might say that social media is the new entertainment television in this regard. On the other hand, social media might present new opportunities to engage citizens and foster social capital, opportunities that have yet to be fully realized. More experience with these new media, as well as more scholarly research, is needed before we draw any firm conclusions.

Why Has Social Capital Declined?

To explain the widespread and significant decline in social capital, Putnam considered many possible factors, ultimately concluding that four played contributing roles. The two that account for the smallest portion of the downward trend in social capital are changes in work patterns and the movement of people to the suburbs. With more women in the paid labor force and more two-career families than in the past, adults, especially women, have less time to devote to civic engagement, entertaining at home, and communal leisure activities. Suburbanization has played a role in decreasing social capital, in part because those who live in the suburbs spend more time commuting to work, which eats into their time available for other activities. Suburbs contain not only residential areas but increasingly jobs and shops. The result can be a separation of people's home, work, and consumer lives. We might live in one town, work in a second, and do most of our shopping in a third. Further, our neighbors (or spouses!) might work in a fourth town and prefer to shop in a fifth. This leaves people without a strong attachment to any particular community, weakening social bonds and discouraging participation in local civic activities.

Although these two are important contributors to the decline in social capital, Putnam identifies a third, generational replacement, as more significant. Those who were born in the 1920s were especially civic minded and active, much more so than any generation born since. Putnam suggests that entering adulthood, a particularly formative period in a person's life, during World War II separates this generation from others. Many members of this generation served in the military during the war, and the war was also felt on the home front. Factories were turned over to wartime production, people were asked to donate scrap metal and rubber when national supplies ran low, food and other goods were rationed, and volunteers participated in activities from civil defense to mailing books to service members overseas. Levels of patriotism and feelings of shared adversity were very high. Putnam argues that these experiences translated into a lifetime of civic participation and social connectedness.

There is another crucial difference between this generation and ones that were born later: the former did not grow up watching television. Television viewing, Putnam's fourth factor, increased over the same decades that social capital was declining. More important, people who watch television a lot or rely on TV as their main form of entertainment are less likely to engage in a variety of social and civic activities, including attending meetings, going to church, and volunteering. In contrast, newspaper readership is related to belonging to civic organizations.[110] The relationship between TV watching and social capital is complex, however, in that not all types of TV shows depress social capital. In particular, the effect is greatest among those who view entertainment shows. As watching daytime television (soap operas, talk shows, and so on) increases, civic engagement decreases. On the other hand, watching news and current affairs programs on TV leads to increased civic participation.[111]

To his credit, Putnam did examine many reasons for social capital's decline, but he overlooked some. The increase in public disillusionment with government in the wake of political scandals and government corruption has probably contributed to the decrease in explicitly political forms of civic engagement.[112] Messages from the political environment also probably played a role, such as conservative attacks on the protest movements of the 1970s and criticisms of the welfare state in the 1980s. Both types of rhetoric could have contributed to lowering civic engagement (particularly among conservative citizens) and increasing mistrust across social groups.[113] Finally, Putnam underemphasized an important trend—globalization. As the world becomes more connected economically and transnational entities (including corporations, media conglomerates, and trade bodies) become more prominent internationally, "traditional communal values of cooperation, solidarity, and civic participation are trumped by competitive market norms."[114]

What connects these additional explanations for the erosion of social capital is that they highlight structural or environmental causes, whereas Putnam focused his attention on individual people, implying that it was Americans' fault for social capital's decline. As one critic pointed out, it seems that Putnam's take-home point is this: "We watch television instead of joining groups, and we have the wrong attitude to make democracy flourish."[115]

CONCLUSION

Do citizens trust their government? Not all that much, it turns out. If citizens do not have high levels of trust for the government in general, perhaps they have confidence in specific governmental institutions? Again, the answer is no. Scholars have demonstrated, however, that citizens actually have a great deal of support for the basic institutions of government but are not as fond of the people running those institutions, particularly members of Congress. Turning away from evaluations of government and institutions, what about citizen engagement with other citizens? The story here is also one of decline; the stock of social capital is smaller in the United States than it once was.

Trust, support for institutions and their members, and social capital are all interrelated. Declines in social capital lead to less trust and less confidence in institutions, and low levels of trust lead to less support for institutions and their members. But do low trust and social capital matter? Should we be concerned about citizens' disapproval of the people running government institutions (especially members of Congress)? Or should we be consoled by the high levels of approval for the institutions of government? Elite democratic theorists would not be concerned with a lack of social capital because they do not envision an active role for citizens. They would be pleased that citizens have a healthy skepticism toward members of institutions yet maintain a high regard for the three branches of government. This support for the basic institutions of government will lead people to obey the law, thus creating a stable democracy, even if people do not like the particular people running the government.

In contrast, participatory democratic theorists would be troubled by low levels of trust and social capital and little faith in politicians because these indicate citizens are not actively engaged in politics. If citizens were involved, they could ensure that government officials were not crooked or wasting money or working on behalf of a few big interests. Thus, they could trust government to do what is right. Further, if citizens trusted government and the people running it, then more citizens would be willing to run for political office, something that would please participatory democratic theorists.

Democratic theorists of all stripes would be concerned if trust in government and confidence in the people running institutions became so low that the government could not function. Government officials might avoid trying to solve intractable problems (especially if solving them meant short-term pain) if they thought citizens would not support their efforts over the long haul. In fact, some saw a precursor to this situation during the 2011 debate over the federal government's debt ceiling. Even though President Obama and Congress reached a deal to raise the ceiling, one credit rating agency was not pleased with the result. Days after the agreement was reached, Standard and Poor's downgraded the U.S. government's credit rating, arguing that the deal "falls short of what, in our view, would be necessary to stabilize the government's medium-term debt dynamics." They went on: "The political brinksmanship of recent months highlights what we see as America's governance and policymaking becoming less stable, less effective, and less predictable than what we previously believed."[116] The polarization and political shenanigans that led to the 2013 government shutdown did nothing to increase confidence in America's political leaders, among credit rating agencies or the public. Should the actions of national politicians move away from such brinkmanship, however, history suggests that public evaluations of government are likely to improve.

Key Concepts

attitudes toward institutional members / 331

attitudes toward the institutions of government / 331

Suggested Sources for Further Reading

Atkeson, Lonna Rae, and Cherie D. Maestas. *Catastrophic Politics: How Extraordinary Events Redefine Perceptions of Government.* Cambridge, UK: Cambridge University Press, 2012.

Mutz, Diana C. *In-Your-Face Politics: The Consequences of Uncivil Media.* Princeton, NJ: Princeton University Press, 2015.

These books contain sections exploring public trust in government. Atkeson and Maestas do so through the lens of catastrophic events, more specifically Hurricane Katrina. The topic of Mutz's book is conflict on television political shows. She concludes that the lack of civility displayed on many of these shows can decrease trust.

Caldeira, Gregory A., and James L. Gibson. "The Etiology of Public Support for the Supreme Court." *American Journal of Political Science* 36 (1992): 635–664.

Bartels, Brandon L., and Christopher D. Johnston. "On the Ideological Foundations of Supreme Court Legitimacy in the American Public." *American Journal of Political Science* 57 (2013): 184–199.

Clawson, Rosalee A., and Eric N. Waltenburg. *Legacy and Legitimacy: Black Americans and the Supreme Court.* Philadelphia: Temple University Press, 2009.

These three works explore public opinion toward the Supreme Court. Caldeira and Gibson's classic article develops a measure of diffuse support for the Supreme Court. Bartels and Johnston explore the relationship between legitimacy of the Court and public perceptions of the ideological direction of the Court's decisions. Legitimacy is lower when people perceive ideological distance between the Court's rulings and their own personal preferences. Clawson and Waltenburg's book presents a comprehensive overview of black Americans' opinions of the Court.

Durr, Robert H., John B. Gilmour, and Christina Wolbrecht. "Explaining Congressional Approval." *American Journal of Political Science* 41 (1997): 175–207.

Ramirez, Mark D. "The Dynamics of Partisan Conflict on Congressional Approval." *American Journal of Political Science* 53 (2009): 681–694.

Ramirez, Mark D. "The Policy Origins of Congressional Approval." *Journal of Politics* 75 (2013): 198–209.

Public approval of Congress is the topic of these three works. Durr and his co-authors find that support for the institution declines when it carries out its duties as a legislative and representative body. Ramirez's first article concludes that Congressional approval declines when the degree of partisan conflict in the legislative body increases. His second piece demonstrates that approval is influenced by public evaluations of the policies passed by Congress.

Hetherington, Marc J. *Why Trust Matters: Declining Political Trust and the Demise of American Liberalism.* Princeton, NJ: Princeton University Press, 2005.

Hetherington, Marc J., and Jason A. Husser. "How Trust Matters: The Changing Political Relevance of Political Trust." *American Journal of Political Science* 56 (2012): 312–325.

Hetherington focuses on the implications of declining public trust in government. In his book, he presents a convincing case that lower levels of trust are responsible for the conservative shift in domestic public policy that has occurred since the 1960s. Hetherington and Husser extend this conclusion to foreign policy.

Nunnally, Shayla C. *Trust in Black America: Race, Discrimination, and Politics.* New York: New York University Press, 2012.

As the title suggests, Nunnally's book explores trust among blacks in America. Her thorough examination covers both social and political trust, trust toward members of many different racial groups, and differences within the black community.

Putnam, Robert D. *Bowling Alone: The Collapse and Revival of American Community.* New York: Simon and Schuster, 2000.

Castiglione, Dario, Jan W. van Deth, and Guiglielmo Wolleb. *Handbook of Social Capital.* Oxford: Oxford University Press, 2008.

In *Bowling Alone*, Putnam provides a wealth of information documenting recent declines in social capital and civic engagement. He also presents explanations for and describes many implications of these declines. The *Handbook of Social Capital* contains essays covering a wide range of topics and research related to social capital.

"Public Trust in Government, 1958–2014." Pew Research Center, http://www.people-press.org/2014/11/13/public-trust-in-government.

This interactive website contains survey data regarding the public's trust in government. You can graph changes in trust over time alongside other measures, such as consumer confidence, or explore trust among Democrats versus Republicans. Check it out.

CHAPTER 12

Impact of Public Opinion on Policy

ON THE EVE of the U.S. invasion of Iraq in March 2003, nearly 60 percent of the American public supported U.S. military intervention to force Saddam Hussein from power.[1] In fact, according to polls conducted by the Pew Research Center, a majority of the public had favored sending troops into Iraq since November 2001 (see Figure 12.1). Polls conducted by other organizations showed "exceptionally consistent" results, with *all* demonstrating majority support for using U.S. troops to unseat Hussein.[2] With public support on his side (as well as congressional approval), President George W. Bush ordered the military into Iraq on March 19, 2003. In a nationally televised speech that evening, Bush announced this action as follows: "My fellow citizens, at this hour, American and coalition forces are in the early stages of military operations to disarm Iraq, to free its people and to defend the world from grave danger."[3]

During the first eighteen months of the war, most Americans continued to express support for Bush's decision. Beginning in October 2004, however, less than 50 percent of the public felt that using military force in Iraq was the "right decision."[4] As the months ticked by, more and more Americans concluded that military action in Iraq should not have happened. By January 2007, only 40 percent labeled the military intervention as the right decision, whereas a slight majority (51 percent) believed it was the wrong decision. Furthermore, over these years, gradually increasing percentages of the public supported bringing U.S. troops home from Iraq. Whereas only 32 percent of people expressed this view in September of 2003, nearly 50 percent did by the beginning of 2007.[5]

It was in this climate of decreased public support for the Iraq War that Bush proposed sending more than 20,000 additional troops to Iraq to serve alongside the approximately 140,000 servicemen and -women already there. At the outset of 2007, he argued that these extra troops were necessary to combat sectarian violence between Shiite and Sunni Muslims in Iraq and therefore improve safety and security in the nation, particularly in Baghdad.[6] Given the public's dissatisfaction with the war and increasing preference to return troops to the United States, it is not surprising that support for the proposed surge was not high. In fact, only

Figure 12.1 Public Opinion and the Iraq War

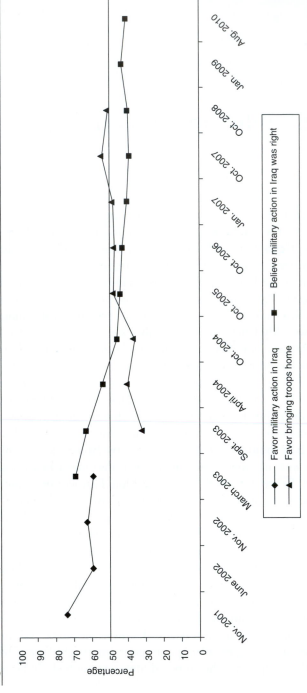

Sources: Data for "Favor military action in Iraq" from "Different Faiths, Different Messages," Pew Research Center, Washington, DC, March 19, 2003, http://people-press.org/2003/03/19/different-faiths-different-messages. Data for "Believe military action in Iraq was right" from "Independents Oppose Party in Power . . . Again," Pew Research Center, Washington, DC, September 23, 2010, http://people-press.org/2010/09/23/independents-oppose-party-in-power-again. Data for "Favor bringing troops home" from "Growing Doubts about McCain's Judgment, Age and Campaign Conduct," Pew Research Center, Washington, DC, October 21, 2008, http://people-press.org/2008/10/21/growing-doubts-about-mccains-judgment-age-and-campaign-conduct

31 percent of the public favored this proposal in January 2007. And of those who opposed it, fully 69 percent believed that Congress should actively try to prevent Bush from implementing his plan, even by withholding funding for the troops if necessary.[7] Despite this lack of public support, Bush did order more troops into Iraq.

Throughout 2007 and 2008, even more citizens began to support bringing U.S. military troops home from Iraq. In fact, a majority of the public held this view during most of those two years (refer to Figure 12.1). Also, only a minority of the public believed that military action in Iraq had been the right decision, a trend that continued through 2010. Clearly, public support for U.S. military involvement in Iraq was not high. In one of his first major foreign policy speeches as president, Barack Obama announced in February 2009 that U.S. combat forces would be gradually removed from Iraq. His goal, ultimately met, was to remove all such forces by August 31, 2010, while retaining up to 50,000 members of the military in Iraq after that date to support the Iraq government and its military.[8] Drawing down troop levels in Iraq was favored by the public. In both April 2009 and August 2010, clear majorities (74 and 68 percent, respectively) of the public approved of "Obama's decision to end the combat role of U.S. troops and remove most but not all U.S. troops from Iraq by August 31, 2010."[9]

In subsequent years, Obama's attention turned to other nations in the Middle East, notably Iran. In July 2015, the president announced that the United States and five other nations had negotiated an agreement with Iran over that country's nuclear program. Years-long economic sanctions against Iran would be lifted in exchange for Iran agreeing to restrict its capability of acquiring or producing nuclear fuel, fuel that could be used for a nuclear bomb. International weapons inspectors would also be given greater access inside Iran. Initial public views toward this deal tended toward opposition. Polling indicated that, among those Americans who had heard about the agreement with Iran, 48 percent disapproved of the plan compared to 38 percent who approved.[10] Furthermore, 73 percent had no or not very much confidence that "Iran's leaders will uphold their side of the agreement."[11] When asked whether Congress should approve or reject the Iran nuclear deal, 52 percent supported rejection.[12]

These four examples of policy decisions made by Bush and Obama present contrasting views of the relationship between public opinion and public policy. Bush's choice to engage in military action in Iraq and Obama's decision to remove combat troops from Iraq both coincided with the public's preferences. In contrast, Bush's troop surge decision went against the wishes of a majority of Americans and Obama did not have the public firmly on his side for his negotiated nuclear deal with Iran. Which is more common? Do policymakers generally enact policies that a majority of citizens support? Or is the discounting of public opinion more common? Under what circumstances will policy reflect the public's policy opinions? Does the type of policy matter? Are officials more or less likely to be responsive to public opinion when formulating foreign versus domestic policy? We address these questions in this chapter.

For a minute, however, let's think about the first and last examples a bit more carefully. Before the Iraq War began, Bush attempted to persuade the public and other policymakers (notably members of Congress) that the United States should invade Iraq and topple Saddam Hussein. He presented two primary reasons why he felt this action was necessary.[13] First, he warned that Hussein was developing weapons of mass destruction and America's safety depended on stopping this effort. Second, he argued that Hussein must be removed from power because he was connected with al-Qaeda, the group responsible for the 9/11 attacks. A few weeks after announcing the Iran nuclear deal, Obama delivered a high-profile speech designed to influence the opinions of the public and members of Congress. Calling discussion of this agreement "the most consequential foreign policy debate that our country has had since the invasion of Iraq," he outlined the reasons why he believed the deal to be the best option for halting Iran's development of a nuclear weapon.[14] Did Bush and Obama's arguments convince the public to support their plans? If so, are these examples of presidents responding to public opinion or shaping opinion to support their own goals? These questions suggest that to truly understand the role of public opinion in policymaking, we must consider how officials monitor and use public opinion to further their own policy preferences, topics that we also take up in this chapter. First, however, we summarize democratic theorists' views on the role of the public in policymaking.

Should Public Opinion Influence Policy?

Regardless of whether public policy does respond to the wishes of the public, *should* it? As you have no doubt guessed by now, democratic theories provide quite different answers to this question. Before discussing these differences, recall that all democratic theorists support **popular sovereignty**. This is the belief that power in a democratic society ultimately rests with the citizenry. Differences across the theories emerge over how the people should exercise their power and how capable the public is for democratic governance.

Participatory democrats expect the influence of the public on policy to be quite substantial. Policymakers should, in their view, enact policy that coincides with the wishes of the majority. These theorists further believe that officials should debate policy openly, providing the public with meaningful and relevant information about policy options. Leaders should not attempt to manipulate or mislead the public. After listening to an information-rich policy debate, the public can form opinions about public policy, opinions that they communicate to the leaders. Because political equality is also important to participatory democrats, they expect that policymakers will respond to the wishes of the entire public, not only those citizens who are especially involved in politics or who have the financial means to express their opinions most loudly (such as by contributing to candidates for elective office).

Pluralists expect that public policy will reflect public opinion, but they prefer that citizens be somewhat removed from the policymaking process. For them, opinions are best expressed via *organized groups*.[15] Whereas citizens are not knowledgeable enough about policy issues to express clear preferences to officials, pluralists assume interest group representatives are. These groups lobby policymakers directly, trying to convince them to support policy that is in the interest of the group's members. Pluralists also argue that citizens are not attentive enough to politics to follow the goings-on of their elected officials but that interest group representatives do this and communicate details back to their members. Through the interest group link, however, only those people who are represented by groups are likely to have their preferences communicated to officials. This model thus privileges the opinions of those who are organized over those who do not have a group actively involved in lobbying government officials.

Of the democratic theories we have been profiling in this book, elite democrats posit the smallest role for the public in policymaking. These theorists believe that the public should be involved in electing officials but should then leave the policy details up to the leaders. Elite democrats view citizens as disinterested in following politics closely enough to make decisions about complex policy matters and as incapable of seeing beyond their own interest to make choices that are in the best interest of the nation. Thus, elite democrats prefer to leave policymaking to those with expertise—the leaders. Policymakers can attempt to educate the public about the best policy option, but at the end of the day, the officials should do as they see fit. This view was clearly expressed in an opinion column written by the late David Broder, a former *Washington Post* journalist. After describing examples in which the "dangerously compliant congressional leadership" followed the wishes of the public by not enacting policies that Broder thought would be good for the country, he concluded, "Politicians are wise to heed what people want. But they also have an obligation to weigh for themselves what the country needs. In today's Washington, the 'wants' of people count far more heavily than the nation's needs."[16]

Despite this view, elite democrats expect that policy might minimally correspond with public preferences. They see this outcome occurring via *elections*. Citizens elect leaders who they hope will follow their general policy preferences and then have the chance to remove these officials from office if they do not. Thus, elections can produce a connection between the opinions of voters and policy. The voters have control over who is elected, and officials have an incentive to keep the preferences of voters in mind or risk losing their jobs come Election Day. Finally, elite democrats do not hope for or expect that the preferences of all members of the public will be expressed through elections but, rather, only the wishes of those who are most attentive to and involved in politics. For elite democrats, it is perfectly fine, even preferred, if the opinions of other members of the public do not influence policy decisions.

Judgments about politicians' responses to public opinion are not restricted to democratic theorists. Everyday conversations include negative descriptions of leaders who do not adopt the speaker's preferred behavior. Politicians who are perceived to follow the public's wishes too quickly and uncritically are said to *pander*, whereas those who make decisions contrary to public opinion are decried as *shirkers* or worse. Indeed, you might have strong preferences about whether officials should or should not enact policy that corresponds with the wishes of the public. Whether you do or not, we encourage you to ponder the normative democratic theories as we present findings from empirical research on public opinion and public policy.

Is Public Opinion Related to Policy?

As one scholar puts it, "No one believes that public opinion always determines public policy; few believe it never does."[17] True enough, but sorting out how often public opinion is related to policy is not an easy task. Numerous decisions need to be made, including whether to examine public opinion for one or more issues and whether to focus on national or state policymaking. Thus, researchers have taken very different approaches to studying the relationship between opinion and policy. One method that has been used is a **case study**, which entails an in-depth analysis of one policy area (such as health care policy) or one policy decision (the passage of a specific bill). Although many case studies of the opinion-policy relationship have been conducted,[18] we instead focus our attention in this section on research that examines many different policy areas and decades at once. After all, if a case study of tax policy in the 2000s finds that opinion influenced policymaking, we cannot be certain that this relationship exists for other issues or for other time periods. In contrast, **aggregate studies**, which examine many issue domains and years, provide more conclusive evidence about the overall relationship between public opinion and public policy.

Before moving on to review research on this topic, we have a spoiler alert. Early on, scholars concluded that public views are indeed related to the government's policy decisions. We briefly review this research to give you a sense of the range of work that coalesced around the finding of substantial opinion-policy consistency. Over the past decade or so, however, that conclusion has unraveled in the face of new and contrary evidence. Believe it or not, one of these newer studies was so noteworthy that its authors (two political science professors no less!) discussed their work on *The Daily Show with Jon Stewart*.

The Old View: Opinion Is Related to Policy

When public support toward an issue changes, does policy then change? This question was addressed by Benjamin Page and Robert Shapiro.[19] They examined public opinion survey data between 1935 and 1979 and identified 357 cases in which policy preferences changed significantly over time. Page and Shapiro then studied national and state policies for each case at the time of the first public opinion measure and then again one year after the second measure to see if there had been any change in the policy. Their goal was to assess **opinion-policy congruence**. For example, imagine that the percentage of the public that wanted the government to spend more money to protect the environment increased from 48 percent in 1978 to 58 percent in 1983. To assess the relevant government policy, Page and Shapiro compared the level of actual spending on the environment in 1978 with that in 1984. Such an approach allowed them to determine whether public policy changed in the same direction as the opinion change (this is congruence), changed in the opposite direction, or did not change. Across all their cases, Page and Shapiro found that when both opinion and policy changed, 66 percent of these changes were congruent. They further demonstrated that congruence was more likely the larger the opinion change.

A related approach to assessing the opinion-policy relationship is to examine public *preference for change* rather than actual opinion change. This was the approach favored by Alan Monroe. Perusing the results from public opinion polls, Monroe identified many examples of questions asking about policy change. He did this for two time periods: 1960–1976 and 1980–1993.[20] To assess consistency (Monroe's term for congruence), Monroe compared public preferences for change with actual policymaking for each policy issue in his analysis. When a majority of the public favored policy change and change did occur in the direction of the public's wishes, opinion-policy consistency was present. Similarly, consistency also occurred when the majority opinion favored the status quo (no change) and policy did not change. Overall, Monroe concluded that public preferences and policy were consistent 64 percent of the time for the first time period and 55 percent for the second. As you can see in Figure 12.2, however, the preferences of the public were more in line with public policy when the public favored the status quo.[21] Between 1980 and 1993, for instance, when the public preferred that a specific policy not change, this policy stayed the same in 70 percent of the cases Monroe analyzed. When the public wanted change, they got it only 45 percent of the time. This **status quo bias** is perhaps not surprising. The U.S. political system with its three branches of government that share power and check each other's power was set up to make policy alterations occur slowly, if at all.

Other studies of the opinion-policy relationship used broader measures of public opinion. This approach assumes that when formulating policies, policymakers focus on general **opinion trends** (such as liberal or conservative swings) in public opinion rather than opinion toward specific policy issues.[22] One broad measure of public opinion used in opinion-policy studies is labeled **policy mood** or **policy sentiment**.[23] The measure is obtained by aggregating across opinion toward dozens of specific issues. It captures whether the public feels that the government, in general, is doing too much or not doing enough. In other words,

Figure 12.2 Consistency between Public Opinion and Public Policy

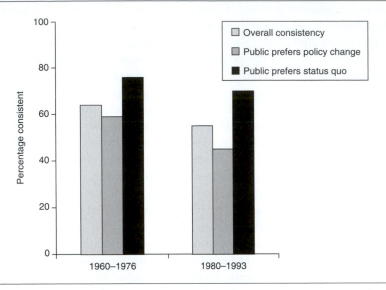

Sources: Data for 1960–1976 from Table 1 of Alan D. Monroe, "Consistency between Public Preferences and National Policy Decisions," *American Politics Quarterly* 7 (1979): 9. Data for 1980–1993 from Table 1 of Alan D. Monroe, "Public Opinion and Public Policy, 1980–1993," *Public Opinion Quarterly* 62 (1998): 13.

it measures "global preferences for a larger, more active federal government as opposed to a smaller, more passive one across the sphere of all domestic policy controversies."[24] Are changes in the public's policy sentiment accompanied by changes in public policy? Yes, according to research conducted by Robert Erikson, Michael MacKuen, and James Stimson.[25] These authors assessed the direction of policymaking by determining the ideological direction of key laws passed by Congress (and not vetoed by the president) between 1954 and 1996. When comparing policy direction with public views, Erikson et al. found that when the public mood changed (refer to the solid line in Figure 12.3) public policy generally followed in the same direction (see the dotted line). In other words, a liberal shift in the public mood was followed by a liberal shift in policy; likewise, conservative opinion shifts were accompanied by policy moving in a conservative direction.

More recently, Stuart Soroka and Christopher Wlezien used a similar dynamic approach to assess policy responsiveness to public opinion.[26] They explored public opinion toward government spending in specific policy domains (such as defense, social welfare, health, education, and foreign aid) between 1973 and 2004. They compared trends over time in public preferences for spending to trends over time

Figure 12.3   Correspondence between Public Mood and Policy

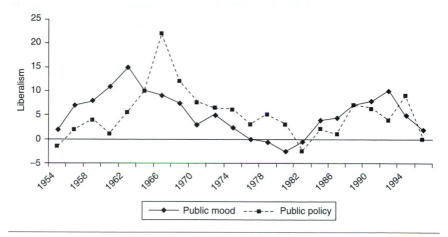

Source: Figure 2.2 of "Public Opinion and Policy: Causal Flow in a Macro System Model" by Robert S. Erikson, Michael B. MacKuen, and James A. Stimson, in *Navigating Public Opinion: Polls, Policy, and the Future of American Democracy*, ed. Jeff Manza, Fay Lomax Cook, and Benjamin I. Page (Oxford: Oxford University Press, 2002), 43. By permission of Oxford University Press, USA.

in actual spending by the national government. Their conclusion? Policy responds to public views. When the public prefers more spending in a domain, actual spending often does increase. When the public holds the opposite preference, spending is likely to decrease.

Despite the dissimilarities in research designs and goals, all these scholars concluded that national public opinion and public policy tend to be related.[27] Others have explored the U.S. states, finding a correspondence between opinion and policymaking at that level of government also.[28] Finally, researchers have identified characteristics that influence the degree of opinion-policy congruence. First, **issue salience** matters. The more that the public is especially concerned about an issue or the more that an issue receives national attention, such as in the news media, the more likely it is that public opinion about the policy will closely match actual policy.[29] **Public attentiveness** is also relevant. Congruence is higher for citizens who follow politics closely than for citizens who pay less attention.[30] Members of the public who care deeply about a policy area as well as the attentive public are likely to know how their elected officials stand on issues and to take this into consideration when they vote.[31] Elected officials also know this, and if they wish to remain in office, they pay attention to the wishes of their aware and engaged constituents. Officials are also vigilant about especially salient issues.

Such issues can provoke those citizens who are normally only marginally attentive to politics to tune in and become informed about the topics.[32] And if these citizens do not like their representatives' positions on salient issues, they can vote them out of office.

A New View: Opinion-Policy Congruence Is Probably Overstated

Turning now to the research findings that call into question whether the public's views are indeed closely related to public policy, we begin where we ended the last section, on the topic of issue salience. As we noted, past work did explore opinion-policy consistency for issues that the public cares greatly about versus those that the public cares about less. In his 2014 book, Paul Burstein goes a step further to also consider issues that are so low in salience that most members of the public would not even know they are on the policymaking agenda.[33] Scholars who study the opinion-policy relationship generally begin by collecting information about public opinion. Burstein's work began at the other end of the relationship, by collecting information about policies. His goal was to assess public views toward those issues that policymakers thought it important to address. To do so, he selected a random sample of sixty policy proposals that were introduced in the 101st Congress (1989–1990). He then followed these proposals over time (for most, a few years) focusing on whether they passed and, crucially, whether a majority of the public supported passage.

Among those proposals for which Burstein could determine the opinions of the public, the levels of consistency between opinion and policy mirrored those of the studies we profiled in the prior pages. For about 40 percent of the proposals, however, public opinion data were not available.[34] In other words, the opinions of the public were not readily discernable for these policy proposals, by Burstein or, presumably, by members of Congress. Burstein admits that we do not know whether policy reflects the public's wishes for this 40 percent, yet he suspects that it would not. These issues tend to be ones that are important to a very small segment of the public (less than 1 percent) and for which many citizens likely do not have firm opinions. On the one hand, policymakers cannot be responsive to the citizenry if they do not have opinions to respond to. On the other hand, because the issues are of such low salience, officials might think they have loads of wiggle room to decide as they see fit, without worrying about public preferences.

More broadly, Burstein cautions us to be careful in interpreting results from other studies of opinion-policy congruence, such as Page and Shapiro's or Monroe's.[35] These scholars only examined issues for which there was opinion polling data. As it turns out, and for quite obvious reasons, polling firms tend to survey the public only for issues that are relatively high profile (e.g., of great public concern, in the news, the focus of policymakers' attention). Questions about policy issues of very low salience tend not to appear on polls. Thus, as a by-product of the research design, most examinations of the link between opinion and policy contain only a subset of all possible policy issues. In other words, **sampling bias** might be at work. Rather than representing the entire universe of issues, these designs overrepresent salient issues. With strong reasons to believe that congruence will be lower for nonsalient issues, the earlier research by Page and Shapiro and by Monroe probably overstates actual congruence across the entire set of issues that policymakers consider.

Another New View: Opinions of the Wealthy Matter Most

An emerging body of work suggests that the more income a person has, the more likely that public policy corresponds to his or her preferences, for both national[36] and state public policies.[37] The most systematic of these analyses has been conducted by Martin Gilens, on his own and in collaboration with Benjamin Page. In research for his book *Affluence and Influence*, Gilens compiled public preferences for policy change and actual policy outcomes for nearly 1,800 cases between 1981 and 2002.[38] His study was very similar to Monroe's with one notable exception. Rather than opinion for the entire public, Gilens segmented opinion by income levels so that he could examine the opinion-policy connection separately for low-, middle-, and high-income citizens. He concluded, as we already mentioned, that the wealthy are more likely to see their views enshrined in policy.[39] This finding is particularly striking when we consider instances in which the preferences of high-income Americans differ from the opinions of either low- or middle-income Americans. In such situations, public policy is significantly likely to be related to the opinions of the high-income group but is *unrelated* to the preferences of people with lower incomes. Or, as Gilens put it, "For Americans below the top of the income distribution, any association between preferences and policy outcomes is likely to reflect the extent to which their preferences coincide with those of the affluent."[40]

Using Gilens's dataset of policy outcomes and public opinion by income level, he and Page added information regarding the policy preferences of two types of interest groups: those representing business interests and mass-based groups (such as AARP, the National Rifle Association, or labor unions).[41] They then analyzed whether enacted policy reflects the views of the following: affluent Americans, average citizens (those at the middle of the income distribution), business interest groups, or mass-membership interest groups. Their approach is noteworthy because they consider the *comparative* influence of each, whereas most studies of the opinion-policy relationship have examined only whether public opinion influences policy. In reality, policymakers have many people and groups attempting to sway their policy decisions, so Gilens and Page's research design more closely matches actual policymaking conditions. They concluded, as demonstrated in Figure 12.4, that wealthy citizens have the strongest impact on public policy. Both types of interest groups have significant influence as well, although the effect is larger for business groups. The preferences of the average member of the public regarding policy change bear essentially no relationship to whether the policy is changed or not. This study is thus further evidence that governmental policy more closely resembles the wishes of the wealthy than of other Americans. By the way, did you guess that this is the study that was profiled on *The Daily Show*? We present the link to that segment at the end of this chapter, should you want to watch Jon Stewart talk to Gilens and Page about their research.

These findings concern proponents of participatory democracy greatly. Not only do the research conclusions suggest that not all Americans' preferences are equally likely to be related to the policy decisions of leaders, but they also suggest that **economic inequalities** are one source of such differing levels of responsiveness. This provides further evidence to these theorists that inequalities among the public need to be minimized. Elite democrats, in contrast, would likely applaud the findings. These theorists prefer that, if the government's policies do match the preferences of the public, the opinions of the most involved and more aware citizens are followed. These citizens, after all, are most likely to have well-considered opinions on policy matters, according to elite democrats. Finally, pluralists would not be surprised to learn that the preferences of interest groups are reflected in public policy, although many strains of pluralism would not predict that the views of one type of group (business) would so dominate those of another type (mass-based).

Figure 12.4   Citizen and Interest Group Influence on Public Policy

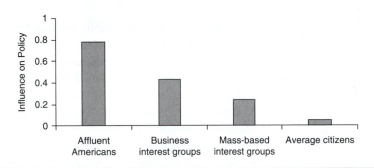

Source: Data from Table 4 of Martin Gilens and Benjamin I. Page, "Testing Theories of American Politics: Elites, Interest Groups, and Average Citizens," *Perspectives on Politics* 12 (2014): 575.

Note: Bars represent regression coefficients predicting the impact on policy change of the policy preferences of each group.

Public Opinion in Comparative Perspective
BOX 12.1 COMPARING OPINION-POLICY CONGRUENCE ACROSS DEMOCRACIES

The likelihood that governmental policy is responsive to citizen preferences is not the same across nations. Comparative politics scholars have uncovered a few reasons why. First, whether the country has a parliamentary or presidential system seems to matter. For example, the United States has higher levels of policy responsiveness than nations with parliamentary governments (specifically, Denmark, Great Britain, and Canada).[1] In presidential systems, power is separated between the executive and the legislature. Not only are both branches of government involved in policymaking, but the executive and members of the legislature are all directly elected. This seems to create incentives for these officials to be more responsive to public wishes when formulating policy.

Among parliamentary democracies, electoral rules and the degree of party polarization come into play. In the past, the congruence between the preferences of the public and elected officials was greater for proportional representation than single-member-district electoral systems. Over time, congruence for nations using single-member districts has increased, in part because parties in such nations have tended to become less polarized.[2] As parties converge toward the middle of a nation's ideological spectrum, the likelihood increases that the ruling party's platform will coincide with the preferences of the citizenry. In contrast, parties in the United States have become more polarized in recent decades, perhaps contributing to a decline in opinion-policy congruence.[3]

Finally, some features of public opinion matter also. In both parliamentary and presidential systems, policy is more likely to reflect public preferences when the popularity of the executive is low.[4] This is probably because the president or prime minister is worried about remaining in power and wants to keep the public happy. In the domain of social welfare policy, government spending is more likely to reflect the public's wishes in nations where the citizens prefer high levels of social welfare spending.[5] Put another way, when citizens send a signal to leaders that they want a high level of social welfare spending, they are more likely to get the policy they prefer than when the signal is for low spending levels.

1. Sara Binzer Hobolt and Robert Klemmensen, "Government Responsiveness and Political Competition in Comparative Perspective," *Comparative Political Studies* 41 (2008): 309–337; Stuart N. Soroka and Christopher Wlezien, *Degrees of Democracy: Politics, Public Opinion, and Policy* (Cambridge, UK: Cambridge University Press, 2010), Chap. 7.
2. G. Bingham Powell Jr., "Representation in Context: Election Laws and Ideological Congruence between Citizens and Government," *Perspectives on Politics* 11 (2013): 9–21.
3. Robert Y. Shapiro and Lawrence Jacobs, "Simulating Representation: Elite Mobilization and Political Power in Health Care Reform," *The Forum* 8, no. 1 (2010): Article 4.
4. Hobolt and Klemmensen, "Government Responsiveness."
5. Clem Brooks and Jeff Manza, "Social Policy Responsiveness in Developed Democracies," *American Sociological Review* 71 (2006): 474–494.

Do Politicians Follow or Lead the Public?

Before public policy is changed, politicians unveil proposals and publicly debate their preferred policies. The news media often cover these developments. While politicians are debating the merits of various policy proposals, the public thus has the opportunity to learn about the pros and cons of each. And, because it can take many weeks, months, or even years before policy is changed, the opinions of the public can be influenced by the policymaking process. For example, as we suggest at the beginning of this chapter, Bush's appeals to the public to support his plan to invade Iraq probably influenced public opinion on this matter.

Why do we care about this? It is important to sort out the precise nature of the opinion-policy connection for many reasons, not least of which are democratic theory implications. **Democratic responsiveness** refers to leaders enacting policy that the public wants. Such responsiveness assumes that governmental policy reflects the *genuine opinions* of the public. This is what participatory democrats hope for. However, what if the public opinion that the officials seem to be responding to was actually largely created by these officials? If policymakers persuade the public to support the officials' preferred policy and then policymakers enact this policy, can we conclude that democratic responsiveness has occurred? It depends. If public support for the proposal is genuine, then politicians' influence on public opinion would not worry participatory democrats so much. What if, however, the public has been *manipulated*? Manipulation occurs when leaders use "false or misleading arguments or information to turn the public against its true interests (the preferences it would hold if information were accurate and complete)."[42] Such a circumstance would undermine participatory democrats' goal of responsiveness. Thus, it is important to know whether leaders are truly responding to the public or are trying to shape, or even manipulate, citizens' opinions.

Unlike participatory theorists, elite democrats actually prefer that public preferences be shaped by leaders. The leaders, after all, are the ones who are most aware of what is in the best interests of the nation and who have the expertise to put forth specific policy proposals. Policymakers should share their proposals and reasons for supporting them to the public, thus providing **opinion leadership**. According to this view, educating the public is an important goal for leaders. If policy reflects the wishes of the public at all, according to elite democrats, it is best if the public's preferences have been influenced by the wisdom and expertise of the leaders.

To navigate among these competing theories, it is important to consider the context in which public policy opinions are formed, especially the goals and actions of politicians. This entails asking different questions and using different research methods than the aggregate studies of opinion and policy we already profiled. In particular, interviews of policymakers and **archival research** (interpreting documents from historical collections, such as a past president's papers) are well suited for these tasks, as you will see in the following sections. We first focus on research that examines how leaders learn about public opinion. Then, we discuss what politicians do with this public opinion information. Do they use it to inform their policy decisions? Or do they use it to try to direct public opinion? Many of the examples on the following pages are from past decades. Please do bear in mind, however, that that is the reality of archival research. Analyzing historical documents can only occur once they are made available, oftentimes years after policymakers served in office.

How Do Politicians Learn about Public Opinion?

One way that politicians try to determine the opinions of the public is through opinion polls. This is especially the case with presidents. Before modern opinion polling techniques were developed in the 1930s, presidents used other means to learn of public preferences. These included reading letters that were sent to the White House, talking to citizens, reading newspapers, interpreting past election outcomes, and counting the number of people attending rallies.[43] Franklin Roosevelt was the first president to hire a pollster to conduct private polls for him.[44] Presidents Harry S. Truman and Dwight Eisenhower chose not to follow Roosevelt's lead, but presidential opinion polling returned with the election of John F. Kennedy. With Kennedy's inauguration in 1961, "the White House became a veritable warehouse stocked with the latest public opinion data."[45]

Presidential Polling. All presidents since Kennedy have relied on **private polls** to gauge public opinion. These private polls are conducted specifically for the president and contain the questions designed by his personal pollster(s) and advisors. One reason why presidents use private polls is that they consider their own polls more trustworthy and of higher quality than other sources of public opinion.[46] Opinion information collected by others (for example, members of Congress, the news media, and interest groups) probably reflects the goals of the collector. Thus, relying on private polls gives the president an independent means to determine the public's wishes.[47]

Although private polling is now a permanent and institutionalized feature of presidential administrations, some presidents have commissioned more polls than others. Presidents tend to keep details of their private polling secret, but one way to track this activity is to consider how much money was spent on the president's polls. Two studies have done just this, beginning with Jimmy Carter and concluding with the first two years of the George W. Bush administration. Three results from these studies are noteworthy. First, the amount spent on polls increases gradually every month that a president is in office.[48] Second, presidents spend more on polling during their reelection year than during other years, presumably to track voter support for them and their opponents.[49] Third, not all presidents devote the same amount of attention to polling in nonelection years. Specifically, Jimmy Carter's and George H. W. Bush's annual spending was lower than Ronald Reagan's, Bill Clinton's, and George W. Bush's.[50]

A variety of opinions are collected by presidents, including, not surprisingly, public support for specific policy issues. One analysis of the content of polls used by Presidents Richard Nixon through George H. W. Bush demonstrates that policy questions appeared more than other types of questions for Jimmy Carter, Ronald Reagan, and George H. W. Bush.[51] These items encompassed a wide range of domestic and foreign policies, although opinions on specific policies were most likely to be gathered for especially salient issues.[52] Richard Nixon and Gerald Ford were more interested in popularity data. Their polls contained more items assessing public approval of their own and Congress's job performance than items about policy matters. This discrepancy was especially clear for Nixon.[53] Finally, presidential polls also collect demographic information about respondents, allowing presidents to assess the opinions of subgroups of the citizenry (e.g., partisans, political independents, and the wealthy).[54]

Other Sources of Public Opinion. Although commonly used by presidents, opinion polls are not the most frequent source of public opinion for all politicians. One reason is cost. Polling is very expensive, and not all officials have access to funds to pay for polls.[55] Some politicians, however, simply believe that there are better sources of information on public preferences. Reliance on polls appears to be less common in Congress than in the White House for this reason. Communicating in person as well as examining mail and phone calls received from constituents provides important information to representatives about the issue opinions, concerns, and intensity of feeling among members of the public. Polls are perceived by members of Congress to be especially poor at registering how strongly the public cares about an issue.[56]

In an analysis of the sources of public opinion information among staff members in the Illinois legislature, Susan Herbst finds that two stand out: the news media and interest groups.[57] These staffers assume that media presentations of policy issues (whether in news stories or editorials) reflect public sentiment on the issues. So if newspapers positively portray a reform measure to make criminal sentences harsher, the legislative assistants infer that the public also perceives this policy favorably, regardless of what citizen views actually are. More interesting, however, are Herbst's findings about interest groups as proxies for the public's attitudes. Consider the following two quotations from people she interviewed:

> Interest groups. That's how we gauge public opinion. . . . I would have to say that from a public opinion standpoint, we don't really care what the average Joe thinks. I don't say that as if we're not representing them, but we're representing the people who represent them. It's one step removed from the general public.

Obviously I think that the lobbyists and organized groups are much more effective [than average citizens] because they have an organized message. They have money and they're here. Whereas a lot of people, I think there's a lot of people in the state that just really don't care what goes on in Springfield.[58]

The sentiments expressed here are pluralism in action. The legislative staff members saw interest group positions as a better measure of public opinion than the *actual opinions* of the citizenry. The groups are organized, their messages are coherent, and their members are more knowledgeable and attentive to politics than is the general public. So when a representative from an interest group, such as an agricultural or labor organization, communicates the group's position on an issue, legislative aides assume this is the same position held by farmers or union workers.

How Do Politicians Use Public Opinion Data?

After investing millions of dollars in private polls, what do politicians and their advisors do with the detailed public opinion information they receive? Two influential books, both coauthored by Lawrence Jacobs, argue that politicians use these details to try to influence public opinion. In other words, responsiveness to wishes of the majority is not the main goal.

Priming Popular Issues and Personal Characteristics. Peering inside the Oval Offices of three former presidents, James Druckman and Lawrence Jacobs illuminate many aspects of presidential decision making.[59] They collected private polling data from the archives of Presidents Lyndon Johnson, Richard Nixon, and Ronald Reagan. In an attempt to understand why certain questions were asked as well as how the results were interpreted and toward what ends they were used, Druckman and Jacobs reviewed internal White House memos, analyzed public statements made by the presidents, and interviewed former staff members of these presidents. One of their most intriguing findings is that presidents try to divert the public's attention away from unpopular topics and toward those that portray the president in a more favorable light. This is known as **priming**, whereby leaders attempt to alter the criteria by which members of the public evaluate those same leaders.

As Druckman and Jacobs demonstrate, presidents use two different methods in their attempts to prime the public: issue priming and image priming.[60] No matter how popular a president is in the eyes of the public, citizens do not judge the president's handling of all issues the same. On some issues, a majority of the public agrees with the president's positions, whereas the president is out of step with the public on others. Presidents and their advisors not only know this, but, thanks to their private polls, they also know toward which issues the president is evaluated more or less favorably. In their public statements, presidents can increase the number of times they discuss the more popular issues, in the hope that the public will focus their overall evaluation of the president on the president's handling of these issues. President Johnson, for example, "deliberately made more public comments about pushing legislation through Congress to help the poor and create Medicare than about Vietnam in order to shift attention away from the politically damaging situation in Southeast Asia."[61] This is issue priming.

In contrast, image priming involves attempting to shape the public's assessment of the president's personal characteristics, such as competence, strength, or warmth. One way to do this is to emphasize issues that portray the desired image of the president. In the words of, respectively, President Nixon and one of his advisors, public statements were to feature "issues that will give us a sharp image" or that "convey the true image of a President."[62] For Nixon, this meant emphasizing his foreign policy activity. When his polling indicated that public assessments of his competence were on the decline, Nixon would devote more attention in his speeches to his foreign affairs and diplomatic accomplishments, such as those in China. The intent was to remind voters of his competence in these policy domains. President Reagan also image primed. He talked about his economic policies, emphasizing how they improved the nation's economic health, when public assessments of his strength flagged. Mentions of his diplomatic goals in the foreign policy realm increased when the public thought Reagan was lacking in personal warmth. In the end, Druckman and Jacobs argue, such presidential actions undermine democratic responsiveness. Rather than enacting the public's preferences into law, "elites widen their latitude on policy . . . by priming what issues are salient, and by triggering the public to evaluate them on their *perceived personality* rather than on policy issues."[63]

Crafted Talk and Health Care Reform. In their book *Politicians Don't Pander*, Lawrence Jacobs and Robert Shapiro argue that polling results are used to create **crafted talk**, rhetoric and messages that officials communicate to the public.[64] Opinion polls demonstrate to officials which features of a proposal citizens support, which they oppose, and which they are uncertain about and thus open to persuasion on. Polling also helps politicians "identify the words, arguments and symbols about specific policies that the centrist public finds most appealing and that they believe to be most effective in changing public opinion to support their policy goals."[65] If politicians are successful at cultivating public support their proposals might become law. Rather than democratic responsiveness, however, Jacobs and Shapiro call this outcome **simulated responsiveness**.

To provide evidence in support of their crafted talk theory, Jacobs and Shapiro conducted a detailed case study of the formulation of and debate over President Clinton's proposal to reform health care in 1993–1994.[66] To determine how Clinton used public opinion, they interviewed key Clinton advisors; reviewed White House documents; examined public statements made by Clinton and others about health care reform; and considered poll results, including Clinton's private polls. They found that, although Clinton polled extensively on health care, he did not do so to help him determine the details of his reform proposal. Instead, the policy details were driven by Clinton's own policy goals, his ideology, and the preferences of key interest groups. Once the specifics of the proposal had been decided on, Clinton's private pollster (Stanley Greenberg) was asked to gather public opinion data. Rather than finding out the public's opinions about health care policy, he instead "polled the *presentation* of the policy."[67] In other words, polling data were used to make decisions about how to sell Clinton's proposal to the public. And getting the public behind his proposal was very important on the assumption that it would put pressure on Congress to pass Clinton's plan.

How exactly did public opinion shape Clinton's presentation of his proposal? It helped Clinton and his advisors identify which aspects of the complex plan were especially popular.[68] One of Clinton's policy goals was to provide universal health care coverage for all Americans, a goal that the public also supported. Thus, the overarching theme used to describe his proposal was "Security for All." Clinton also felt that health care reform was necessary to slow down the increase in health care costs. Because the public was less concerned about this problem, he deemphasized this aspect of his plan when discussing the proposal with the public.

Meanwhile, opponents of Clinton's reforms (primarily congressional Republicans and interest groups representing business and health insurers) were not silent. In fact, they were also relying on polling data to determine how to communicate their message to the public.[69] Their polls demonstrated that the public was concerned about too much government control over their own health care decisions. Clinton's plan was thus described as mandating a substantial increase in the government's health care bureaucracy. Furthermore, knowing that citizens were generally happy about their own health coverage but also uneasy about how their coverage might change, Clinton's opponents emphasized the possible negative effects they would witness under Clinton's policy.

Responsiveness, Opinion Leadership, and Manipulation. In the end, public support for Clinton's plan declined from nearly 60 percent in favor in September 1993 to 40 percent the following July. The reform plan died in Congress before it reached the floor for a formal vote. This could be interpreted as evidence of opinion leadership and democratic responsiveness. Perhaps the public listened to the politicians' policy debate, were more persuaded by Clinton's opponents than by Clinton and his supporters, and changed their opinions accordingly. This interpretation further implies that policymakers responded to the well-informed and meaningful wishes of the public in deciding not to enact Clinton's reforms.

Jacobs and Shapiro draw quite a different conclusion from their case study. They argue that the public's preferences were manipulated by the policy debate. Citizens grew to oppose Clinton's plan, not because of the plan's actual content but because of the rhetoric that opponents used to undermine the plan. The results from one opinion poll demonstrate this point quite clearly. In March 1994, when respondents were asked whether they supported "the Clinton health plan," less than a majority did. Yet when asked what they thought about a plan that provided coverage for all people, promoted competition in the health care industry, required employers to provide insurance for their employees, and gave government some power to control health care costs, 76 percent felt that plan had "a great deal" or "some" appeal.[70] The details of this hypothetical plan were actually the exact provisions contained *in Clinton's plan*. In other words, the public wanted the features of Clinton's proposal, but not if it were described as "Clinton's plan." This could be seen as evidence that the public did not learn enough from the elites' health care policy debate to develop meaningful opinions about Clinton's plan.

If this interpretation is correct, participatory democrats should be concerned. Perhaps more disturbing for them is the reality that politicians often feel it is more important to try to shape public opinion, whether through priming or crafted talk, than to respond to the public. Druckman and Jacobs label this the "chronic *intent* to manipulate."[71] This perspective would please elite democrats, however, because it coincides with these theorists' beliefs that the public's capabilities are minimal and that officials should thus discount public opinion when making policy.

Jacobs and Shapiro's case study of the 1993–1994 health care reform debate was extensive and intensive. They have also explored a more recent case of health care policymaking: the debate over and successful passage of health care reform legislation early in President Obama's administration.[72] Unlike their prior work, they did not conduct interviews of key policymakers for the 2009–2010 debate. Instead, they relied on publicly available opinion polls and journalistic accounts of the use of polls by Obama and congressional leaders. Their conclusions are thus a bit more speculative. Nonetheless, they argue that the evidence they collected paints a picture consistent with the conclusions of health care policymaking during Clinton's presidency. Obama as well as Democrats and Republicans in Congress closely followed public opinion polls regarding health care reform and then used the polling results to design messages to influence the citizenry. Obama and his Democratic allies in Congress emphasized that leaving problems with the health care system unfixed was too risky and that reform needed to rein in the selfish tactics of private health insurance companies. Republican opponents, in contrast, argued that Obama's approach would amount to the government taking over health care, perhaps even to the point of convening "death panels" to determine which patients would receive health care. Elite policymaking of this nature, argue Shapiro and Jacobs, "becomes a tug-of-war between teams of intense partisans intent on their divergent policy goals and on treating the public as a pawn in their intense power struggles."[73]

So is it safe to conclude that democratic responsiveness is rare and that manipulation of public opinion is the norm? There is not a clear consensus on this topic. For instance, some scholars have concluded that presidents are responsive to public opinion, especially for salient policies, for domestic policy issues, among electorally important segments of the public, or when large majorities (more than 70 percent) of the public support an issue.[74] Other research demonstrates that, even though presidents do collect opinion data in order to market their preferred policies, the mere collection of the data allows them to monitor the public's attitudes. This monitoring can result in presidents responding to the public's wishes, and it also helps presidents determine when the public is unlikely to be swayed by crafted talk.[75] Even Jacobs and Shapiro uncover some evidence of policymakers (particularly congressional Republicans) responding to public preferences during the health care debate.[76] Finally, and probably not surprisingly, the likelihood that elected officials will respond to, rather than attempt to lead, public opinion varies throughout their terms. Responsiveness to public wishes increases as Election Day nears.[77] We need to continue to explore these topics if we want to link the empirical study of public opinion to normative democratic theory. From a normative standpoint, it is not enough to know that opinion and policy are sometimes related. We also need to know how the opinions of the public are influenced by policymakers, what the quality of public opinion is, and what the officials do once they know public preferences.

PUBLIC OPINION AND FOREIGN POLICY

There are many reasons to suspect that governmental policy might be more likely to follow public opinion for domestic policy than for foreign policy.[78] For one, foreign policies are often less salient for the public than are domestic policies. Some people, including policymakers, believe that, because the public is not knowledgeable or sophisticated enough to hold coherent, well-reasoned foreign policy opinions, foreign policy officials should discount public preferences. Compared with other issue domains, policymakers might be more likely to rely on arguments and evidence from experts (intelligence analysts, military officials, and so on) when it comes to foreign policy. Furthermore, public opinion manipulation by policymakers might be especially likely in foreign affairs: "Foreign policy issues are often obscure, distant from everyday life, and the executive often enjoys a high degree of information control as well as substantial bipartisan deference from other elites."[79]

Finally, elected officials might feel as if they have the flexibility to ignore the public when it comes to foreign policy and not suffer electoral consequences. Given that foreign policies are removed from the day-to-day lives of most Americans, some leaders think they can be successful at educating the public on these issues. Consider, for example, the following comments of former representative Brian Baird (D-WA). When asked in summer 2007 how he would justify to his constituents his view that U.S. troops needed to stay in Iraq longer when he had initially been an opponent of military intervention in Iraq, Baird responded:

I would just say to people who are upset, if you could take the time that I have taken over the last number of months to meet with, not only the Iraqi leaders on all sides but our military troops on the ground, their leaders, our ambassadors, leaders from throughout the region, I think you'd have a different impression—I certainly do. And my hope would be people would say someone who's been there on the ground several times now, met with people throughout the region, may have a different insight than just someone who's reading about it second or third hand in the media.[80]

Despite these assumptions that opinion-policy congruence might be lower for foreign compared with domestic policy, early aggregate analyses did not provide supporting evidence.[81] Monroe even concluded that foreign policy was *more* likely than domestic issues to reflect public preferences.[82] Further, case studies of specific policy topics tended to confirm that opinion does influence foreign policy. Public preferences for defense spending are related to the size of the defense budget, for example, and public opinion has constrained policymakers' decisions regarding U.S. military interventions, such as during the 1991 Persian Gulf War.[83]

Reconsiderations of Public Influence

As is the case with the broader opinion-policy research we profiled earlier in the chapter, a number of more recent studies paint a somewhat different picture of the relationship between the public and foreign policy. Archival research of Clinton's decisions to launch military interventions in Somalia and Bosnia demonstrates a lack of responsiveness to public opinion. In both cases, Clinton made these decisions despite his own polling evidence showing that the public did not support either intervention.[84] Finally, a very interesting analysis of the mail received by President Lyndon Johnson uncovers a key relationship between the views expressed by certain letter writers and Johnson's decisions regarding the Vietnam War.[85] Even though a majority of the American public did not support Johnson escalating the war, his public statements and military policy became more "hawkish" when he received more letters encouraging him to step up military activity in Vietnam. In this way, Johnson did follow public opinion, but only the opinions of the especially attentive and informed public rather than the wishes of the broader populace.

Benjamin Page, one of the coauthors of an aggregate analysis of opinion-policy congruence, has even reconsidered his earlier conclusion that congruence is similar for domestic and foreign policies.[86] In two separate projects, he has provided compelling empirical evidence that public preferences shape foreign policy minimally, if at all. In the first, Lawrence Jacobs and Page examine the influence of the public, business interests, labor unions, and foreign policy experts (academics, think-tank researchers, and leaders of foreign policy organizations) on foreign policy officials' views.[87] For data, they relied on surveys conducted by the Chicago Council on Foreign Relations (CCFR). The CCFR is a nonpartisan organization that analyzes and disseminates information about foreign policy issues. Between 1974 and 2002, the CCFR measured the opinions of government officials engaged in foreign policymaking (from presidential administrations, the Senate, and the House of Representatives). Note that the data do not indicate which *policy decisions* government officials made but, rather, what their views are. Although this limits somewhat Jacobs and Page's conclusions about what influences foreign policy, they are probably correct when they argue that "the survey-expressed policy preferences of government officials can be used as reasonable indicators of the policies that they enact or pursue."[88]

The CCFR also gathered the foreign policy opinions of the public, business and labor representatives, and foreign policy experts. Jacobs and Page compared the opinions for each of those groups with the opinions of the government officials. So which has the strongest influence on the views of foreign policy officials? Business. As Jacobs and Page put it, "Internationally oriented business leaders exercise strong, consistent, and perhaps lopsided influence on the makers of U.S. foreign policy."[89] The effect of business leaders on officials in presidential administrations was especially strong. Foreign policy experts were also influential, but less so than business leaders. Further down the influence ladder came labor unions, and weakest of all was the public. Public preferences were more consequential in influencing the opinions of members of the House, for highly salient issues, and for economic matters. Yet, overall, these effects were dwarfed by the substantial impact of business leaders on foreign policy officials.

Results from Page's second project appear in his book with Marshall Bouton.[90] This book provides a careful and thorough analysis of the content of the public's foreign policy attitudes. For their data, they relied on CCFR surveys conducted between 1974 and 2004, with a particularly strong emphasis on the 2002 survey results. They draw two key conclusions regarding the foreign policy opinions of the public. First, of the many possible goals Americans could want U.S. foreign policy to pursue, three broad goals are most important: security from attack, domestic well-being, and international justice and humanitarianism.[91] The first column of Table 12.1 presents the five specific goals most supported by the public in 2002 for each of these three categories. Some of these, as you can see, fulfill more than one broad goal, so they are listed in two of the three categories. Very large majorities (90 percent or more) of the public viewed the security goals of fighting terrorism and stopping the spread of nuclear weapons as very important. Close behind, however, was support for such domestic well-being goals as protecting jobs and preventing illegal drugs from entering the nation (85 and 81 percent, respectively). Although the public believed that the foreign policy goal of international justice and humanitarianism is less important than security or domestic well-being, this goal is not unimportant. Indeed, 61 percent of Americans believed U.S. foreign policy should aim to fight world hunger, and

Table 12.1   Americans' Foreign Policy Goals, 2002 and 2014

Foreign policy goal	2002	2014
Security from attack		
Combat international terrorism	91	61
Prevent spread of nuclear weapons	90	73
Maintain superior military power worldwide	68	52
Strengthen UN (also justice goal)	57	37
Defend U.S. allies' security (also justice goal)	57	38
Domestic well-being		
Protect jobs of U.S. workers	85	76
Stop flow of illegal drugs into U.S.	81	N/A
Secure adequate energy supplies	75	66
Control and reduce illegal immigration	70	47
Improve global environment (also justice goal)	66	N/A
International justice and humanitarianism		
Combat world hunger	61	42
Promote and defend human rights in other nations	47	32
Strengthen international law and institutions (also security goal)	43	N/A
Protect weaker nations against aggression	41	25
Promote market economies abroad (also domestic goal)	36	N/A

Source: Data for 2002 from Table 2.1 of Benjamin I. Page with Marshall M. Bouton, *The Foreign Policy Disconnect: What Americans Want from Our Leaders but Don't Get* (Chicago: University of Chicago Press, 2006), 41; 2014 data from "United in Goals, Divided on Means: Opinion Leaders Chicago Council Survey Results 2014," Chicago Council on Global Affairs, June 2, 2015, http://www.thechicagocouncil.org/publication/united-goals-divided-means

Note: Entries are the percentage of the public agreeing goal should be "very important foreign policy goal of the United States."

47 percent viewed the promotion of human rights in other nations as very important. The CCFR, now known as the Chicago Council on Global Affairs, queried the foreign policy opinions of the public again in 2014.[92] As the last column in Table 12.1 demonstrates, the percentage of the public identifying each goal as very important declined. Yet the relative ranking of specific goals within each of the three categories is largely the same in 2014 as twelve years earlier. Furthermore,

the public continues to prioritize security and domestic well-being goals over justice goals.

In terms of which specific foreign policies the United States should pursue to meet these goals, the public has a preference for **multilateralism**.[93] This is Page and Bouton's second primary conclusion about foreign policy opinions. Multilateral foreign policies emphasize working with other nations and international bodies such as the United Nations rather than "going it alone." Support for a multilateral approach was evident in the buildup to the Iraq War. Although majorities of the public did support sending the U.S. military to Iraq (as we documented at the beginning of the chapter), when asked whether the U.S. military should be the sole force in Iraq or whether the United States "should only invade Iraq with UN approval and the support of its Allies," 65 percent preferred the latter while only 20 percent supported the former.[94] More broadly, the public has consistently supported (1) U.S. alliances, (2) participating in UN peacekeeping missions, (3) engaging in diplomacy (with allies and adversaries) rather than using force, (4) using international legal bodies for people who violate human rights, and (5) entering into international treaties to solve global problems, such as the Kyoto Protocol to reduce global warming.

Do the public's preferences coincide with U.S. foreign policy? Not so much, say Page and Bouton. They provide numerous examples of actual foreign policy decisions that have differed from the public's wishes. These include privileging the policy goal of security from attack over domestic well-being, stopping the payment of dues to the UN in the 1990s, the decades-long refusal to engage in diplomatic relations with Cuba, and President George W. Bush's decisions not to sign the Kyoto Protocol or the International Criminal Court treaty.

In a more systematic analysis, Page and Bouton compare citizens' and policymakers' responses to the CCFR surveys.[95] These are the same surveys that Jacobs and Page used. And, in line with these earlier findings, Page and Bouton conclude that the policy opinions of policymakers often diverge from those of the public. For instance, the public is significantly more likely than foreign policy officials in Congress, the Defense Department, or the White House to believe protecting domestic jobs and strengthening the UN are very important U.S. foreign policy goals. Citizens also display more support for the Kyoto Protocol, the International Criminal Court, and decreasing legal immigration. Foreign policy officials are more likely than the public to believe the United States should pursue **unilateral foreign policies** ("go it alone"), to think that the North American Free Trade Agreement is good, and to support the elimination of tariffs on imported goods. Some of these differences in opinions between the public and policymakers are substantial. Compared to policymakers, the public was 42 percentage points more likely to want foreign policy to prioritize the protection of U.S. jobs, for instance, and 51 percentage points less likely to favor ending tariffs. It is because of findings such as these that

Figure 12.5   Foreign Policy Preferences of Public versus Council on Foreign Relations Members, 2013

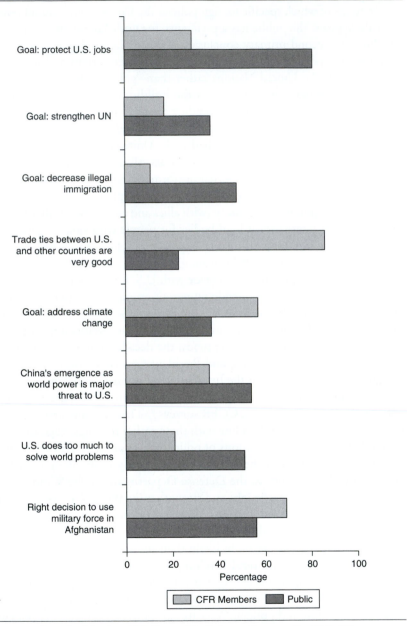

Source: Data from "Public Sees U.S. Power Declining as Support for Global Engagement Slips," Pew Research Center, December 3, 2013, http://www.people-press.org/2013/12/03/public-sees-u-s-power-declining-as-support-for-global-engagement-slips

Page and Bouton subtitled their book "What Americans Want from Our Leaders but Don't Get."

More recent research demonstrates findings similar to those of Page and Bouton. In 2013, the Pew Research Center surveyed the opinions of the public and members of the Council on Foreign Relations (CFR; an organization much like the CCFR).[96] CFR members include current and former public officials, academics, journalists, and business leaders, among others. Thus, not all members are foreign policymakers. Some are, to be sure, but others are better classified as foreign policy specialists.

How do the opinions of CFR members compare to those of the public? Among the topics that were also explored by Page and Bouton, the public continues to be more likely than foreign policy experts to want jobs in the United States protected, to strengthen the United Nations, and to decrease immigration (in this case, illegal immigration; see Figure 12.5). On the other hand, CFR members are much more supportive of international trade than citizens are. As for other topics, compared to CFR members, the public was less likely to say addressing global climate change should be a top foreign policy goal, more worried about China's growing power, more likely to think the United States does too much to solve world problems, and less likely to think U.S. military involvement in Afghanistan had been the right thing to do.

Finally, one area where the 2013 Pew survey differs from Page and Bouton's results is public attitudes toward unilateralism. A slight majority of the public supported unilateral foreign policies, the highest ever recorded in nearly 50 years of tracking this opinion. In contrast, only 33 percent of the public felt the United States should "go it alone" internationally in 2002, according to Page and Bouton.[97] This new isolationist mood among the public was probably driven by fatigue from prolonged military involvement in Iraq and Afghanistan and the recent economic recession in the United States, leading citizens to be more focused on solving domestic rather than foreign problems. Time will tell whether this public move toward unilateralism was a momentary blip or a permanently changed public outlook. The Pew survey did not ask CFR members a comparable question, so we cannot be sure whether public and CFR views toward unilateralism differ. Yet public support for unilateral policies was much higher in 2013 than in 2002, perhaps even reaching the level of foreign policymakers.

CONCLUSION

Does public opinion influence public policy? As you learned at the beginning of this chapter, aggregate empirical studies had demonstrated that policy is related to opinion more often than not. This congruence between opinion and policy is highest for salient issues. Congruence also varies across individuals; attentive and higher-income people are most likely to have their preferences realized in public policy. Indeed, there is a strong indication that affluent Americans are driving the policymaking process, with the views of lower-income citizens coinciding with enacted policies only if they share the same views as their wealthier counterparts.

Considering whether policymakers try to influence public opinion during policymaking encouraged us to examine how leaders use information about public opinion. Ample evidence suggests that officials, particularly the president, collect public opinion for the dual purposes of *responding to* and especially *shaping* public opinion. When policies reflect the preferences of the public after the public's opinions have been influenced, perhaps even manipulated, by leaders, we hesitate to conclude that democratic responsiveness has occurred. Finally, recent scholarship on foreign policy demonstrates that public opinion influences policies in this domain less than was once thought. Business interests and policy experts exert a stronger influence over foreign policy, which perhaps explains why policy decisions are often out of step with public preferences. Overall, then, we agree with others that, when it comes to control over public policy, citizens are "semi-sovereign."[98] In other words, public policy only sometimes coincides with the public's policy opinions.

What do democratic theorists make of these empirical findings? Elite democrats would likely be most satisfied. When public policy does coincide with the preferences of the public, it is best that the views of the most attentive citizens are heeded. The fact that politicians are increasingly using polls to try to shape public opinion to support policy options that the politicians have already designed (without following the wishes of the public to do so) would please elite democrats. They would also be heartened to learn that leaders appear to be exercising discretion in the realm of foreign policy and are more likely to rely on the views of business leaders and policy experts than the uninformed public.

The empirical research also provides some, albeit limited, support for the views of pluralists. Those officials who do not conduct private polls appear to rely on interest groups to assess the public's wishes. The nation's public policies also are more likely to match the preferences of interest groups than the public. Yet it does not appear to be the case that a variety of groups actively advocate on behalf of the public's views, as pluralism would suggest. Indeed it tends to be business-oriented groups that have the largest influence over public policy.

Finally, there is much in this chapter to worry participatory democrats. The greater influence of wealthy citizens on policy undermines these theorists' goal of political equality. Also problematic is the evidence that politicians believe there are times they should not follow the wishes of the public. Whether ignoring the public, as seems to be the case in foreign policymaking, or trying to alter citizens' views with crafted rhetoric and perhaps misleading information, the end result is a lack of democratic responsiveness.

KEY CONCEPTS

aggregate studies / 352
archival research / 360
case study / 352
crafted talk / 364
democratic responsiveness / 360
economic inequalities / 358
issue salience / 355
multilateralism / 371
opinion leadership / 360
opinion-policy congruence / 353
opinion trends / 353

policy mood / 353
policy sentiment / 353
popular sovereignty / 350
priming / 363
private polls / 361
public attentiveness / 355
sampling bias / 357
simulated responsiveness / 364
status quo bias / 353
unilateral foreign policies / 371

SUGGESTED SOURCES FOR FURTHER READING

Berinsky, Adam J. *In Time of War: Understanding American Public Opinion from World War II to Iraq.* Chicago: University of Chicago Press, 2009.
Gries, Peter Hays. *The Politics of American Foreign Policy: How Ideology Divides Liberals and Conservatives over Foreign Affairs.* Stanford, CA: Stanford University Press, 2014.
Holsti, Ole R. *American Public Opinion on the Iraq War.* Ann Arbor: University of Michigan Press, 2011.

These books explore citizens' foreign policy opinions. Berinsky and Holsti focus on the content and sources of opinions toward war. Gries examines a wide range of foreign policy views, concluding that ideology is a key driver of these attitudes.

Druckman, James N., and Lawrence R. Jacobs. *Who Governs? Presidents, Public Opinion, and Manipulation.* Chicago: University of Chicago Press, 2015.
Jacobs, Lawrence R., and Robert Y. Shapiro. *Politicians Don't Pander: Political Manipulation and the Loss of Democratic Responsiveness.* Chicago: University of Chicago Press, 2000.

These scholars argue that policy does not necessarily respond to the wishes of the American public. Both books demonstrate that politicians can be motivated to manipulate public opinion rather than enact policies the public truly wants.

Enns, Peter K., and Christopher Wlezien, eds. *Who Gets Represented?* New York: Russell Sage Foundation, 2011.
Gilens, Martin. *Affluence and Influence: Economic Inequality and Political Power in America.* Princeton, NJ: Princeton University Press, 2012.

The essays in *Who Gets Represented?* explore a variety of topics related to equality in the opinion-policy relationship. Notably, the authors explore group differences in policy opinions and whether some segments of the public are more likely to have their views reflected in policy. Gilens also focuses on equality and concludes that policy is more similar to the preferences of the rich than the poor.

Erikson, Robert S., Michael B. MacKuen, and James A. Stimson. *The Macro Polity.* Cambridge, UK: Cambridge University Press, 2002.

Page, Benjamin I., and Robert Y. Shapiro. "Effects of Public Opinion on Policy." *American Political Science Review* 77 (1983): 175–190.

Soroka, Stuart N., and Christopher Wlezien. *Degrees of Democracy: Politics, Public Opinion, and Policy.* Cambridge, UK: Cambridge University Press, 2010.

These influential studies demonstrate that national policies do correspond with the wishes of the public. Soroka and Wlezien's book also demonstrates that changes in policy (specifically, government spending) influence public opinion.

The Daily Show with Jon Stewart, http://thedailyshow.cc.com/videos/kj9zai/ martin-gilens—benjamin-page

This link will take you to the 2014 appearance of Martin Gilens and Benjamin Page on *The Daily Show with Jon Stewart.* These political scientists discussed their study that we profiled in this chapter. Check it out!

Chicago Council on Global Affairs, www.thechicagocouncil.org
Council on Foreign Relations (CFR), www.cfr.org

These websites each contain a wealth of information about contemporary foreign policy issues. The Chicago Council on Global Affairs, formerly the Chicago Council on Foreign Relations, was formed in 1922, whereas the CFR is one year older. Both have been analyzing global affairs and U.S. foreign policy since they were created.

PART VI

What Do We Make of Public Opinion in a Democracy?

CHAPTER 13

Conclusion

CITIZENS MATTER in a democratic society. The word *democracy* comes from the Greek words *demos* and *kratein*. *Demos* means "the people," and *kratein* means "to rule." Thus, by definition, democracy is rule by the people. Now, to what extent citizens should rule in a democratic nation depends largely on your normative perspective, as we have discussed in this book at some length.

In this concluding chapter, we grapple with what to make of public opinion in a democracy. Specifically, we address the five questions that have organized our discussion throughout this book: What should the role of citizens be in a democratic society? Are citizens pliable? Do citizens organize their political thinking? Do citizens endorse and demonstrate democratic basics? And what is the relationship between citizens and their government? We base our answers to these overarching questions on the empirical research and in light of normative democratic theories. But, ultimately, we ask you to judge the evidence, weigh the theories, and draw your own conclusions regarding the capacity of citizens to function effectively in a democracy.

WHAT SHOULD THE ROLE OF CITIZENS BE IN A DEMOCRATIC SOCIETY?

This question cuts to the heart of the matter. Should citizens be at the center of decision making, or should they be at the periphery of power? The answer, of course, depends on your normative perspective. Classical democratic theorists envisioned a fundamental role for citizens. Citizens should be informed, interested, and intimately involved in political decision making. By engaging in political activities, people would become good citizens with concerns beyond their own narrow self-interest. Yet empirical evidence suggests that many—if not most—people are not the ideal citizens specified by the classical democratic theorists. Most citizens are not intensely interested in politics, nor are they particularly well informed about the issues of the day. Further, many citizens dislike politics and do not want to be involved with decision making on a regular basis; rather, they prefer representatives to act on their behalf.

In response to the empirical evidence on the limitations of citizens, elite democratic theories sprung up. Elite democratic theorists stressed that democracy is still possible even though citizens do not meet the high expectations of classical democratic theory. Instead of citizens directly influencing governmental decision making, elite democratic theorists argued that citizens should exert indirect control by voting in competitive elections. Citizens are only expected to participate in elections, not to fully engage in the ins and outs of policymaking. From this perspective, the goal of democracy is system stability rather than the development of good citizens. Pluralists also envisioned a more limited role for citizens, but they emphasized interest groups as fundamental intermediaries linking the public to elites. According to pluralists, citizens can still have their views articulated to elites through the actions of interest groups without becoming knowledgeable about issues themselves.

Participatory democratic theories were developed to challenge the narrow role of citizens asserted by elite democratic theorists. Although acknowledging that direct democracy is not feasible in a nation as geographically large and highly populous as the United States, participatory democratic theorists emphasized a much more central place for citizens. Indeed, these theorists argued that citizens *could* live up to the ideals of classical democratic theorists *if* systemic barriers keeping people from reaching their potential were removed. Participatory democratic theorists emphasized the benefits that would accrue to individuals as they participated in politics; citizens would learn more about politics and become more knowledgeable about the interests of others and therefore become more open and tolerant. These theorists also stressed that all citizens, not just the advantaged in society, should have a voice. If participation were widespread, inequities in society would be redressed.

By now you are an expert on these varying theoretical approaches. You probably even have a favorite theoretical lens through which to assess the empirical evidence. In the next sections, we rely on these theories as we review the research that addresses the question posed at the beginning of each section.

Are Citizens Pliable?

Yes, to some extent citizens are pliable. That is not to say they are completely malleable. Citizens do not enter the political arena as blank slates simply waiting to be written on by interested political elites. Nevertheless, they are influenced by the environment around them, including sometimes being swayed by elite behavior.

Children are shaped by agents of socialization, including schools, peers, and political events. Parents in particular have an effect on their children's political development. In their early twenties, young adults go through a period of attitude instability, yet remnants of their childhood socialization tend to stick with people throughout their lives. We can think of the predispositions developed early on—especially party identification—as anchors that keep citizens from being buffeted too much by elite storms of influence. The Millennial generation is much less likely to identify with a party than earlier generations, which suggests the potential for greater pliability in their political attitudes.

The Internet and social media provide unparalleled opportunities for citizens to be exposed to information that might change their attitudes. For the most part, however, citizens prefer news that is consistent with their preexisting views. More broadly, the mass media are not able to simply inject citizens with their messages, yet citizens are not fully constrained by their existing attitudes either. The subtle effects model best characterizes the influence of the media on citizens. That is, citizens are affected by the media through agenda setting, priming, and framing, but this influence often works in ways that make sense, for example, through credible sources or a thoughtful process of weighing which values are most important.

Now, it is important to recognize that the extent to which citizens are pliable differs across individuals. Research on attitude stability and change, for example, shows that politically unaware citizens tend to hold unstable attitudes. Citizens' predispositions also matter. Citizens who are aware rely more on their predispositions (such as party identification) to decide whether to accept messages from elites compared with those who are less aware. Attitude stability is also influenced by the different ways in which citizens process persuasive messages. That is, citizens who process political messages quickly and without much detailed thought (that is, using a peripheral route) tend to end up with unstable attitudes. In contrast, citizens who process messages using a central route, which involves more careful consideration of persuasive messages, are more apt to have durable attitudes.

Elite democratic theorists would assess the empirical evidence and focus on the movement of citizens' attitudes. They would conclude that citizens do not have well-considered, meaningful opinions and thus should rightly take cues from more rational political elites. Participatory democratic theorists, on the other hand, would emphasize the structural factors that lead citizens to have unstable attitudes. For example, they might point to the media's preference for soft news as a barrier to citizens having informed, stable opinions. Moreover, participatory democratic theorists would argue that not all attitude change is bad. Citizens should learn from political events and experiences, perhaps changing their attitudes as a result. Fluctuations in presidential approval in response to political events and economic conditions, for example, demonstrate the public's ability to assess and evaluate the political environment. Citizens who never modify their opinions in response to new information are close-minded and short-sighted, not thoughtful and reasonable. Thus, participatory democratic theorists would argue that both "excessive instability and excessive stability of public opinion can be liabilities in a democracy."[1] What do you think? Does the pliability of the

American public constitute excessive instability? Or do the levels of pliability indicate citizens are open to information from the environment yet anchored by meaningful predispositions?

DO CITIZENS ORGANIZE THEIR POLITICAL THINKING?

According to Philip Converse, the answer is a resounding no. His research demonstrates quite persuasively that citizens do not organize their political thinking along a liberal-conservative dimension. Other scholars, however, counter that view by relying on a broader understanding of ideology. Further, if we move beyond ideology and look to other factors that might structure citizens' issue positions, we see there are a variety of forces that influence citizens, including attitudes toward social and political groups, values, personality, historical events, and occasionally self-interest. Thus, it seems that citizens organize their thinking a lot more than Converse's original research would lead us to believe.

Nevertheless, Converse's work raises serious questions about how well citizens and elites can communicate in that they are not speaking the same ideological language. Moreover, how can citizens hold elites accountable if they are not on the same ideological page? Both participatory and elite democratic theorists worry about accountability, so neither is comforted by Converse's findings. Pluralists, however, point out it is not surprising that groups play such an important role in organizing citizens' political thinking. From the pluralist perspective, of course, groups are central to politics. Thus, Converse's early findings that citizens conceptualize politics in terms of groups and more recent scholars' findings that group attitudes, especially party identification, racial prejudice, and racial identity, have a strong influence on citizen thinking allow pluralists to resurrect a more optimistic view of citizen capabilities. But is the heavy reliance of citizens on group-based thinking good enough for participatory democratic theorists? Probably not, especially given that stereotypes and prejudice against blacks play such a large role in shaping the attitudes of many white Americans. Increased affective polarization is also a concern because animosity toward one's opponent does not lead to the kind of constructive democratic engagement desired by participatory democrats.

DO CITIZENS ENDORSE AND DEMONSTRATE DEMOCRATIC BASICS?

To answer this question, we really need to separate it into two propositions. First, do citizens *endorse* democratic basics? Yes, citizens endorse many fundamental democratic principles. In the abstract, citizens show high levels of support for civil liberties. People believe, for example, in freedom of speech and legal rights for citizens regardless of their political views. Similarly, many people approve of civil rights in principle. For instance, citizens are highly supportive of blacks and whites attending the same school.

But do citizens *demonstrate* democratic basics? The answer to this question is often no. Citizens do not show much support for civil liberties in practice, especially during times of war and for groups they despise. Likewise, citizens are significantly less supportive of civil rights in practice than in principle. For example, when it comes to school busing to ensure school integration, the majority of white citizens are not on board. And although a majority of blacks support busing, it is a much smaller proportion than the number of blacks who favor school integration in theory. Overall, then, most citizens endorse civil liberties and civil rights in the abstract, but many do not demonstrate support for the implementation of these principles.

Since we wrote the first edition of this book, there has been a striking way in which citizens have endorsed equal rights in principle *and* demonstrated them in practice. We are referring, of course, to the election of Barack Obama as the first black president of the United States. An overwhelming majority of citizens had been telling pollsters since the late 1990s of their willingness to support a black candidate if nominated by their party. Given continuing racial prejudice among some whites, however, many political observers did not think electing a black president was possible. It is likely that a unique set of events (a lousy economy, two wars, and an unpopular two-term president from the other party) made it possible for Obama to win the presidency in 2008, and racial prejudice probably kept him from achieving a landslide; nevertheless, in electing and reelecting Barack Obama to the presidency, citizens demonstrated their ability to put principle into practice.

A remarkable feature of public opinion in recent years is the change in attitudes toward same-sex marriage. Over a relatively short period of time Americans demonstrated a cultural shift in their views such that a majority are now in favor of same-sex marriage. Public policy has changed as well with the Supreme Court upholding same-sex marriage as the law of the land in 2015. This opinion shift, and related policy change, pleases participatory democrats as it is a big step in the direction of fully protecting the rights of gays and lesbians.

When it comes to political interest and knowledge, however, the disconnect between principle and practice is still quite evident. Citizens express at least modest interest in politics and are quite attentive to political campaigns. Thus, citizens seem to realize the importance of politics in theory. Yet in practice, many citizens lack the political knowledge needed to participate effectively in a democratic society, and too many can be characterized as complete bystanders to the political process.

Elite democratic theorists look at the limited levels of political knowledge and low levels of support for civil rights and liberties in practice and conclude that citizens are not capable of a central role in democratic governance. In the minds of these theorists, the lack of support for democratic basics justifies elites dominating decision-making processes. In contrast, participatory democratic theorists lament the democratic deficiencies of the American people yet see hope in the high levels of support for democratic principles. Participatory democratic theorists argue that if barriers were removed and citizens got the chance to participate more actively, then they would learn how to put their support of democratic principles into practice.

What Is the Relationship between Citizens and Their Government?

If we were to think about the relationship between citizens and their government in the same way we think about a marital relationship, we would characterize it as on the rocks and possibly heading for divorce court. Many citizens do not trust the government, with levels of distrust on the rise. Furthermore, the public does not have much respect for the people running the government, especially members of Congress as a whole. The one saving grace is that citizens support the basic institutions of government. This may be what keeps the relationship from completely falling apart.

Participatory democratic theorists argue that low levels of trust in government and citizens' disapproval of the people running government institutions stem from people not participating in the political process. If more people were involved, government would be more responsive and citizens would feel more trusting. This would lead to a virtuous circle of influence because more trust would lead to more participation, which would lead to more trust, and so forth. Unfortunately, the empirical evidence suggests more of a vicious circle, with less trust leading to lower approval of political leaders, which leads to less participation, which feeds back into less trust, and the pattern repeats. Elite democratic theorists are not overly concerned by this vicious circle. They expect citizens to be skeptical of their government. But if trust were to become so low as to undermine the stability of the political system, elite democratic theorists would be concerned. For example, low levels of trust and confidence in law enforcement among African Americans—and the disparate treatment that leads them to hold those views—raise serious questions about the health of our democracy. To return to our marriage analogy, if citizens actually decided to divorce the government, it would most definitely get the attention of elite democratic theorists.

Are elected officials responsive to the public? The evidence on this point is most consistent with the views of elite democratic theorists. The research shows that citizens have a fairly minimal effect. When the public does have an impact, it is most often the voices of the attentive and especially the wealthiest individuals who are most influential. There is an exception to this general pattern of elite unresponsiveness to citizens: when issues—either foreign or domestic—are highly salient, policy is more likely to follow the wishes of the public.

Overall, elite democratic theorists are pleased by the limited role citizens play in shaping policy outcomes, and pluralists appreciate the prominence of interest groups in formulating foreign policy. Participatory democratic theorists, on the other hand, are troubled that the general public has so little influence on the policymaking process. They are especially concerned by the power of affluent individuals to drive the policymaking process. In addition, the evidence that elites try to manipulate public opinion is disconcerting to participatory democratic theorists.

WHAT DO WE MAKE OF PUBLIC OPINION IN A DEMOCRACY?

At the end of the day, what do we make of public opinion? There is empirical evidence that provides support for elite democratic theorists, pluralists, and participatory democratic theorists. In our view, the evidence is most consistent with elite and pluralist views of politics. Additional public opinion research is needed to determine why citizens don't meet the ideals of participatory democratic theorists. A better understanding of the obstacles to citizen competence and engagement would be helpful. Participatory democratic theorists look to greater political participation as a route through which people can become better citizens—more knowledgeable, tolerant, and respectful of civil rights, for example. But does greater participation actually have that effect on citizens? More research in this area would certainly help us evaluate whether participation is the panacea suggested by these theorists.

In closing, you are now an expert on normative democratic theories and the empirical research on public opinion. Which normative democratic theory is most appealing to you? How do you assess the empirical evidence? In short, what do *you* make of public opinion in a democracy?

Notes

CHAPTER 1

1. "Remarks by the President on the Supreme Court Decision on Marriage Equality," June 26, 2015, https://www.whitehouse.gov/the-press-office/2015/06/26/remarks-president-supreme-court-decision-marriage-equality (accessed July 7, 2015).
2. "Remarks by the President at LGBT Pride Month Reception," June 24, 2015, https://www.whitehouse.gov/the-press-office/2015/06/25/remarks-president-lgbt-pride-month-reception (accessed July 7, 2015).
3. "Remarks by the President in a Discussion on the Affordable Care Act – Nashville, TN," July 1, 2015, https://www.whitehouse.gov/the-press-office/2015/07/02/remarks-president-discussion-affordable-care-act-nashville-tn (accessed July 7, 2015).
4. "Statement by the President on the Re-Establishment of Diplomatic Relations with Cuba," July 1, 2015, https://www.whitehouse.gov/the-press-office/2015/07/01/statement-president-re-establishment-diplomatic-relations-cuba (accessed July 7, 2015).
5. "Remarks by the President to U.S. Conference of Mayors," June 19, 2015, https://www.whitehouse.gov/the-press-office/2015/06/19/remarks-president-us-conference-mayors (accessed July 7, 2015).
6. William E. Hudson, *American Democracy in Peril: Seven Challenges to America's Future,* 2nd ed. (Chatham, NJ: Chatham House, 1998), 2.
7. David Held, *Models of Democracy,* 2nd ed. (Stanford, CA: Stanford University Press, 1996).
8. These and other features of classical democracy are outlined by Aristotle in *The Politics,* especially the beginning of Book VI, pp. 359–367. Aristotle was not a proponent of this form of democracy, however, in part because he preferred that those with wealth have more control over decision making. Aristotle, *The Politics,* trans. T. A. Sinclair (Middlesex, UK: Penguin Books, 1986).
9. In Thucydides, *History of the Peloponnesian War, Books I and II,* trans. Charles Forster Smith (Cambridge, MA: Harvard University Press, 1991), 2.37.2, 2.40.3–5.
10. Jean-Jacques Rousseau, *The Social Contract,* trans. Maurice Cranston (London: Penguin Books, 1988), 69, 136.
11. Ibid., 72.
12. Held, *Models of Democracy,* 44.
13. Philip Green, "'Democracy' as a Contested Idea," in *Democracy: Key Concepts in Critical Theory,* ed. Philip Green (Atlantic Highlands, NJ: Humanities Press, 1993); Held, *Models of Democracy.*
14. Held, *Models of Democracy*; C. B. Macpherson, *The Life and Times of Liberal Democracy* (Oxford: Oxford University Press, 1977).
15. Held, *Models of Democracy.*
16. Hudson, *American Democracy in Peril,* 5. See also Held, *Models of Democracy.*
17. Joseph A. Schumpeter, *Capitalism, Socialism and Democracy,* 5th ed. (London: Allen and Unwin, 1976), 269.
18. Robert A. Dahl, *Who Governs? Democracy and Power in an American City* (New Haven, CT: Yale University Press, 1961); David B. Truman, *The Governmental Process* (New York: Knopf, 1951).

19. Bernard R. Berelson, Paul F. Lazarsfeld, and William N. McPhee, *Voting: A Study of Opinion Formation in a Presidential Campaign* (Chicago: University of Chicago Press, 1954), 307.

20. Berelson, Lazarsfeld, and McPhee, *Voting*; Macpherson, *Life and Times*; Jack L. Walker, "A Critique of the Elitist Theory of Democracy," *American Political Science Review* 60 (1966): 285–295.

21. Henry S. Kariel, "The Democratic Revisionists," in *Frontiers of Democratic Theory*, ed. Henry S. Kariel (New York: Random House, 1970); Macpherson, *Life and Times*.

22. Robert A. Dahl, *A Preface to Democratic Theory* (Chicago: University of Chicago Press, 1956), 63.

23. Held, *Models of Democracy*.

24. Alexander Hamilton, James Madison, and John Jay, *The Federalist Papers*, ed. Clinton Rossiter (New York: Penguin, 1961), 78.

25. Ibid., 79.

26. Ibid., 82.

27. Schumpeter, *Capitalism, Socialism and Democracy*, 283.

28. Dahl, *Who Governs?*

29. Peter Slevin and Robin Wright, "Pentagon Was Warned of Abuse Months Ago; U.S. Officials, Rights Groups Sought Changes," *Washington Post*, May 8, 2004, A12.

30. Robinson Meyer, "People of the Internet: 1, Cable Industry: 0," *The Atlantic*, February 4, 2015, http://www.theatlantic.com/technology/archive/2015/02/how-activists-rescued-net-neutrality-and-the-modern-internet/385185/ (accessed July 8, 2015).

31. E. E. Schattschneider, *The Semi-Sovereign People: A Realist's View of Democracy in America* (New York: Holt, Rinehart and Winston, 1960), 35.

32. Dahl, *Who Governs?* 228. See also Dahl, *Preface to Democratic Theory*.

33. Held, *Models of Democracy*.

34. Hudson, *American Democracy in Peril*.

35. Walker, "Critique of the Elitist Theory," 289. For a similar argument, see Peter Bachrach, *The Theory of Democratic Elitism: A Critique* (Washington, DC: University Press of America, 1980).

36. Walker, "Critique of the Elitist Theory," 288–289.

37. Macpherson, *Life and Times*; Carole Pateman, *Participation and Democratic Theory* (Cambridge, UK: Cambridge University Press, 1970).

38. Macpherson, *Life and Times*, 94.

39. Held, *Models of Democracy*.

40. Benjamin Barber, *Strong Democracy: Participatory Politics for a New Age* (Berkeley: University of California Press, 1984), 272.

41. Walker, "Critique of the Elitist Theory."

42. Held, *Models of Democracy*; Macpherson, *Life and Times*.

43. Barber, *Strong Democracy*; Pateman, *Participation and Democratic Theory*.

44. Bachrach, *Theory of Democratic Elitism*, 101.

45. Bachrach, *Theory of Democratic Elitism*.

46. Macpherson, *Life and Times*; Pateman, *Participation and Democratic Theory*.

47. Hudson, *American Democracy in Peril*, 21.

48. Raymond E. Wolfinger and Jonathan Hoffman, "Registering and Voting with Motor Voter," *PS: Political Science and Politics* 34 (2001): 85–92; Cynthia Rugeley and Robert A. Jackson, "Getting on the Rolls: Analyzing the Effects of Lowered Barriers on Voter Registration," *State Politics and Policy Quarterly* 9 (2009): 56–78.

49. John R. Hibbing and Elizabeth Theiss-Morse, *Stealth Democracy: Americans' Beliefs about How Government Should Work* (Cambridge, UK: Cambridge University Press, 2002); Diana C. Mutz, *Hearing the Other Side: Deliberative versus Participatory Democracy* (Cambridge, UK: Cambridge University Press, 2006).

50. V. O. Key Jr., *Public Opinion and American Democracy* (New York: Alfred A. Knopf, 1961), 14.

51. Alan D. Monroe, *Public Opinion in America* (New York: Dodd, Mead, 1975), 6.

52. Herbert Blumer, "Public Opinion and Public Opinion Polling," *American Sociological Review* 13 (1948), 544.

53. Ibid., 547.

54. Ibid., 546.

55. Philip E. Converse, "Changing Conceptions of Public Opinion in the Political Process," *Public Opinion Quarterly* 51 (1987): S12–S24. For a critique of the dominance of polls in the study of public opinion, see Taeku Lee, "The Sovereign Status of Survey Data," in *Navigating Public Opinion: Polls, Policy, and the Future of American Democracy*, ed. Jeff Manza, Fay Lomax Cook, and Benjamin I. Page (Oxford: Oxford University Press, 2002).

56. Susan Herbst, "(Un)Numbered Voices? Reconsidering the Meaning of Public Opinion in a Digital Age," in *Political Polling in the Digital Age: The Challenge of Measuring and Understanding Public Opinion*, ed. Kirby Goidel (Baton Rouge: Louisiana State University Press, 2011).

57. Ibid., 92.

58. Kirby Goidel, "Transitioning into a New Era of Public Opinion Research," in *Political Polling in the Digital Age: The Challenge of Measuring and Understanding Public Opinion*, ed. Kirby Goidel (Baton Rouge: Louisiana State University Press, 2011), 126.

59. Robert Weissberg, *Polling, Policy, and Public Opinion: The Case against Heeding the "Voice of the People"* (New York: Palgrave Macmillan, 2002).

60. Ibid., 139.

61. Daniel Yankelovich, *Coming to Public Judgment: Making Democracy Work in a Complex World* (Syracuse, NY: Syracuse University Press, 1991), 6. See also Daniel Yankelovich and Will Friedman, eds., *Toward Wiser Public Judgment* (Nashville, TN: Vanderbilt University Press, 2010).

62. Gordon W. Allport, "Attitudes," in *A Handbook of Social Psychology*, ed. Carl Murchison (Worcester, MA: Clark University Press, 1935), 804.

63. Alice H. Eagly and Shelly Chaiken, *The Psychology of Attitudes* (Fort Worth, TX: Harcourt Brace Jovanovich College, 1993), 1.

64. Richard E. Petty and John T. Cacioppo, *Attitudes and Persuasion: Classic and Contemporary Approaches* (Dubuque, IA: William C. Brown, 1981), 7.

65. Jon A. Krosnick, "Government Policy and Citizen Passion: A Study of Issue Publics in Contemporary America," *Political Behavior* 12 (1990): 59–92.

66. James H. Liu and Bibb Latané, "The Catastrophic Link between the Importance and Extremity of Political Attitudes," *Political Behavior* 20 (1998): 105–126.

67. Martin Gilens, *Why Americans Hate Welfare* (Chicago: University of Chicago Press, 1999).

68. Milton Rokeach, *The Nature of Human Values* (New York: Free Press, 1973), 5.

69. Donald R. Kinder and David O. Sears, "Public Opinion and Political Action," in *Handbook of Social Psychology*, Vol. 2, 3rd ed., ed. Gardner Lindzey and Elliot Aronson (New York: Random House, 1985), 674.

70. Kinder and Sears, "Public Opinion and Political Action."

71. Rokeach, *The Nature of Human Values*; Stanley Feldman, "Structure and Consistency in Public Opinion: The Role of Core Beliefs and Values," *American Journal of Political Science* 32 (1988): 416–440.

72. Donald R. Kinder, "Pale Democracy: Opinion and Action in Postwar America," in *The Evolution of Political Knowledge: Theory and Inquiry in American Politics*, ed. Edward D. Mansfield and Richard Sisson (Columbus: Ohio State University Press, 2004).

73. Mahzarin R. Banaji and Larisa Heiphetz, "Attitudes," in *Handbook of Social Psychology*, Vol. 1, 5th ed., ed. Susan T. Fiske, Daniel T. Gilbert, and Gardner Lindzey (Hoboken, NJ: John Wiley & Sons, 2010), 358.

74. Angus Campbell, Philip Converse, Warren Miller, and Donald Stokes, *The American Voter* (New York: John Wiley, 1960), 121.

75. This question appears on the American National Election Studies (ANES), conducted between 1948 and 2004 at the Center for Political Studies, University of Michigan. These surveys are now jointly conducted by the University of Michigan and Stanford University. For more information about the ANES, visit http://www.electionstudies.org

76. This wording is used on General Election Exit Polls, conducted in past years by the Voter News Service and in recent years by the National Election Pool, http://www.edisonresearch.com/election_polling.php

77. Philip E. Converse, "The Nature of Belief Systems in Mass Publics," in *Ideology and Discontent*, ed. David E. Apter (New York: Free Press, 1964); Philip E. Converse and Gregory B. Markus "Plus ça change . . .: The New CPS Election Study Panel," *American Political Science Review* 73

(1979): 32–49; Donald P. Green, Bradley Palmquist, and Eric Schickler, *Partisan Hearts and Minds: Political Parties and the Social Identities of Voters* (New Haven, CT: Yale University Press, 2002).

78. Macpherson, *Life and Times*, 4.

APPENDIX

1. Jeffrey M. Jones, "Americans' Support for Death Penalty Stable," Gallup, Washington, DC, http://www.gallup.com/poll/178790/americans-support-death-penalty-stable.aspx?utm_source=position4&utm_medium=related&utm_campaign=tiles (accessed May 22, 2015).

2. Ibid.

3. Mark Peffley and Jon Hurwitz, *Justice in America: The Separate Realities of Blacks and Whites* (Cambridge, UK: Cambridge University Press, 2010).

4. Jones, "Americans' Support for Death Penalty Stable."

5. Lydia Saad, "U.S. Death Penalty Support Stable at 63%," Gallup, Washington, DC, http://www.gallup.com/poll/159770/death-penalty-support-stable.aspx?utm_source=position8&utm_medium=related&utm_campaign=tiles (accessed May 22, 2015).

6. Robert M. Bohm and Brenda L. Vogel, "More Than Ten Years After: The Long-Term Stability of Informed Death Penalty Opinions," *Journal of Criminal Justice* 32 (2004): 307–327.

7. Don A. Dillman, Jolene D. Smyth, and Leah Melani Christian, *Internet, Mail, and Mixed-Mode Surveys: The Tailored Design Method*, 4th ed. (Hoboken, NJ: Wiley, 2014).

8. Frank E. Dardis, Frank R. Baumgartner, Amber E. Boydstun, Suzanna De Boef, and Fuyuan Shen, "Media Framing of Capital Punishment and Its Impact on Individuals' Cognitive Responses," *Mass Communication and Society* 11 (2008): 115–140.

9. The Dardis et al. study actually had two additional conditions, but we discuss only the morality and innocence frames here to keep the example simple.

10. Donald R. Kinder and Thomas R. Palfrey, "On Behalf of an Experimental Political Science," in *Experimental Foundations of Political Science*, ed. Donald R. Kinder and Thomas R. Palfrey (Ann Arbor: University of Michigan Press, 1993).

11. Martin Gilens, "An Anatomy of Survey-Based Experiments," in *Navigating Public Opinion: Polls, Policy, and the Future of American Democracy*, ed. Jeff Manza, Fay Lomax Cook, and Benjamin I. Page (Oxford: Oxford University Press, 2002), 232.

12. Peffley and Hurwitz, *Justice in America*.

13. In fact, Peffley and Hurwitz's national survey oversampled black Americans. As a result, they have representative samples of blacks and whites in their study, which allows them to generalize to both groups.

14. Sandra J. Jones, *Coalition Building in the Anti-Death Penalty Movement* (Lanham, MD: Lexington Books, 2010).

15. Ibid., 197.

16. James M. Carlson and Mark S. Hyde, *Doing Empirical Political Research* (Boston: Houghton Mifflin, 2003), 297.

17. Diana L. Falco and Tina L. Freiburger, "Public Opinion and the Death Penalty: A Qualitative Approach," *Qualitative Report* 16 (2011): 830–847, http://www.nova.edu/ssss/QR/QR16-3/falco.pdf

18. Bernard R. Berelson, *Content Analysis in Communications Research* (New York: Free Press, 1952), 18. See also Klaus Krippendorff, *Content Analysis: An Introduction to Its Methodology* (Newbury Park, CA: Sage, 1980).

19. For a list of the arguments coded in the Dardis et al. study and in an extension of that study, see Frank R. Baumgartner, Suzanna L. De Boef, and Amber E. Boydstun, *The Decline of the Death Penalty and the Discovery of Innocence* (Cambridge, UK: Cambridge University Press, 2008), 246–251.

CHAPTER 2

1. The original interview aired on National Public Radio's *All Things Considered* on February 11, 1987. The interview was re-aired by *This American Life* in 2007 and is available at http://www.thisamericanlife.org/radio-archives/episode/339/break-up (accessed August 9, 2011).

2. Richard M. Merelman, "Revitalizing Political Socialization," in *Political Psychology*, ed. Margaret G. Hermann (San Francisco: Jossey-Bass, 1986), 279.

3. See, for example, Herbert H. Hyman, *Political Socialization* (Glencoe, IL: Free Press, 1959).

4. Virginia Sapiro, "Not Your Parents' Political Socialization: Introduction for a New Generation," *Annual Review of Political Science* 7 (2004), 2.

5. David Easton and Jack Dennis, *Children in the Political System: Origins of Political Legitimacy* (New York: McGraw-Hill, 1969).

6. Merelman, "Revitalizing Political Socialization."

7. Fred I. Greenstein, *Children and Politics*, rev. ed. (New Haven, CT: Yale University Press, 1969), 1.

8. Robert D. Hess and Judith V. Torney, *The Development of Political Attitudes in Children* (New York: Anchor Books, 1968).

9. Fred I. Greenstein, "The Benevolent Leader: Children's Images of Political Authority," *American Political Science Review* 54 (1960): 934–943.

10. Robert D. Hess and David Easton, "The Child's Changing Image of the President," *Public Opinion Quarterly* 24 (1960): 632–644.

11. See also Roberta S. Sigel, "Image of a President: Some Insights into the Political Views of School Children," *American Political Science Review* 62 (1968): 216–226.

12. Greenstein, "Benevolent Leader."

13. Amy Carter and Ryan L. Teten, "Assessing Changing Views of the President: Revisiting Greenstein's *Children and Politics,*" *Presidential Studies Quarterly* 32 (2002): 453–462.

14. Hess and Easton, "Child's Changing Image"; Hess and Torney, *Development of Political Attitudes.*

15. Greenstein, "Benevolent Leader," 941.

16. Hess and Torney, *Development of Political Attitudes.*

17. Dean Jaros and Bradley C. Canon, "Transmitting Basic Political Values: The Role of the Educational System," *School Review* 77 (1969): 94–107.

18. Richard G. Niemi and Jane Junn, *Civic Education: What Makes Students Learn* (New Haven, CT: Yale University Press, 1998).

19. Roberta Sigel and Marilyn Brookes, "Becoming Critical about Politics," in *The Politics of Future Citizens,* ed. Richard G. Niemi (San Francisco: Jossey-Bass, 1974).

20. Fred I. Greenstein, "The Benevolent Leader Revisited: Children's Images of Political Leaders in Three Democracies," *American Political Science Review* 69 (1975): 1371–1398.

21. Carter and Teten, "Assessing Changing Views of the President."

22. Greenstein, "Benevolent Leader"; Hess and Easton, "Child's Changing Image"; Sigel and Brookes, "Becoming Critical about Politics"; Dean Jaros and Kenneth L. Kolson, "The Multifarious Leader: Political Socialization of Amish, 'Yanks,' Blacks," in *The Politics of Future Citizens,* ed. Richard G. Niemi (San Francisco: Jossey-Bass, 1974); Sarah F. Liebschutz and Richard G. Niemi, "Political Attitudes among Black Children," in *The Politics of Future Citizens,* ed. Richard G. Niemi (San Francisco: Jossey-Bass, 1974).

23. Hess and Easton, "Child's Changing Image," 640.

24. Dean Jaros, Herbert Hirsch, and Frederic J. Fleron Jr., "The Malevolent Leader: Political Socialization in an American Sub-Culture," *American Political Science Review* 62 (1968): 564–575.

25. Hess and Easton, "Child's Changing Image."

26. Greenstein, "Benevolent Leader Revisited."

27. Jaros and Kolson, "Multifarious Leader"; Liebschutz and Niemi, "Political Attitudes among Black Children."

28. Paul R. Abramson, "Political Efficacy and Political Trust among Black Schoolchildren: Two Explanations," *Journal of Politics* 34 (1972): 1243–1275.

29. Kim L. Fridkin, Patrick J. Kenney, and Jack Crittenden, "On the Margins of Democratic Life: The Impact of Race and Ethnicity on the Political Engagement of Young People," *American Politics Research* 34 (2006): 605–626.

30. Christia Spears Brown, Rashmita S. Mistry, and Rebecca S. Bigler, "Hurricane Katrina: African American Children's Perceptions of Race, Class, and Government Involvement Amid a National Crisis," *Analyses of Social Issues and Public Policy* 7 (2007): 191-208.

31. Abramson, "Political Efficacy and Political Trust"; Fridkin, Kenney, and Crittenden, "On the Margins of Democratic Life."
32. Jaros, Hirsch, and Fleron, "Malevolent Leader," 565.
33. Fridkin, Kenney, and Crittenden, "On the Margins of Democratic Life."
34. M. Kent Jennings and Richard G. Niemi, "The Transmission of Political Values from Parent to Child," *American Political Science Review* 62 (1968), 169.
35. Jennings and Niemi, "Transmission of Political Values."
36. Ibid., 173.
37. M. Kent Jennings, Laura Stoker, and Jake Bowers, "Politics across Generations: Family Transmission Reexamined," *Journal of Politics* 71 (2009): 782–799.
38. Ibid., 787.
39. Laura Stoker and M. Kent Jennings, "Of Time and the Development of Partisan Polarization," *American Journal of Political Science* 52 (2008): 619–635. See also M. Kent Jennings and Gregory B. Markus, "Partisan Orientations over the Long Haul: Results from the Three-Wave Political Socialization Panel Study," *American Political Science Review* 78 (1984): 1000–1018; Richard G. Niemi and M. Kent Jennings, "Issues and Inheritance in the Formation of Party Identification," *American Journal of Political Science* 35 (1991): 970–988.
40. Stoker and Jennings, "Of Time"; Jennings, Stoker, and Bowers, "Politics across Generations."
41. Jennings and Markus, "Partisan Orientations"; Paul Allen Beck and M. Kent Jennings, "Family Traditions, Political Periods, and the Development of Partisan Orientations," *Journal of Politics* 53 (1991): 742–763.
42. Donald R. Kinder, "Politics and the Life Cycle," *Science* 312 (2006): 1905–1908; M. Kent Jennings, "Political Socialization," in *The Oxford Handbook of Political Behavior*, ed. Russell J. Dalton and Hans-Dieter Klingemann (Oxford: Oxford University Press, 2009); Elias Dinas, "Opening 'Openness to Change': Political Events and the Increased Sensitivity of Young Adults," *Political Research Quarterly* 66 (2013): 868–882.
43. Jennings, Stoker, and Bowers, "Politics across Generations."
44. Ibid., 793.
45. Niemi and Jennings, "Issues and Inheritance."
46. Elias Dinas, "Why Does the Apple Fall Far from the Tree? How Early Political Socialization Prompts Parent-Child Dissimilarity," *British Journal of Political Science* 44 (2013): 827–852; Elias Dinas, "The Long Shadow of Parental Political Socialization on the Development of Political Orientations," *The Forum* 12 (2014): 397–416.
47. Dinas, "Why Does the Apple Fall Far from the Tree?," 848.
48. Paul R. Abramson, "Generational Change and the Decline of Party Identification in America: 1952–1974," *American Political Science Review* 70 (1976): 469–478.
49. Danny Osborne, David O. Sears, and Nicholas A. Valentino, "The End of the Solidly Democratic South: The Impressionable-Years Hypothesis," *Political Psychology* 32 (2011): 81–107.
50. Abramson, "Generational Change."
51. Osborne, Sears, and Valentino, "End of the Solidly Democratic South."
52. Ibid., 104.
53. Laura Stoker, "Reflections on the Study of Generations in Politics," *The Forum* 12 (2014): 378.
54. "Millennials in Adulthood: Detached from Institutions, Networked with Friends," Pew Research Center, Washington, DC, March 7, 2014, http://www.pewsocialtrends.org/2014/03/07/millennials-in-adulthood/#fnref-18663-1 (accessed July 1, 2015).
55. Ibid.; David Madland and Ruy Teixeira, *New Progressive America: The Millennial Generation*, Center for American Progress, Washington, DC, May 2009, https://cdn.americanprogress.org/wp-content/uploads/issues/2009/05/pdf/millennial_generation.pdf (accessed July 1, 2015).
56. See also "Millennials in Adulthood" and Clyde Wilcox and Patrick Carr, "The Puzzling Case of Abortion Attitudes in the Millennial Generation," in *Understanding Public Opinion*, 3rd ed., Barbara Norrander and Clyde Wilcox (Washington, DC: CQ Press, 2010).

57. For an excellent review of the challenges inherent in studying generations, see Stoker, "Reflections on the Study of Generations in Politics."

58. Tatishe M. Nteta and Jill S. Greenlee, "A Change Is Gonna Come: Generational Membership and White Racial Attitudes in the 21st Century," *Political Psychology* 34 (2013): 877–895.

59. "Millennials in Adulthood"; Madland and Teixeira, *New Progressive America.*

60. John R. Alford, Carolyn L. Funk, and John R. Hibbing, "Are Political Orientations Genetically Transmitted?" *American Political Science Review* 99 (2005): 153–167. See also John R. Alford and John R. Hibbing, "The Ultimate Source of Political Opinions: Genes and the Environment," in *Understanding Public Opinion*, 3rd ed., ed. Barbara Norrander and Clyde Wilcox (Washington, DC: CQ Press, 2010).

61. This equal environment assumption is not accepted by all scholars. The key points of disagreement between proponents and detractors are presented in four articles appearing in the Exchange section of the June 2008 issue of *Perspectives on Politics* (pp. 299–343) as well as in two articles in the Comments section of the December 2008 issue of *Perspectives on Politics* (pp. 785–797).

62. For party identification, see Peter K. Hatemi et al., "Is There a 'Party' in Your Genes?" *Political Research Quarterly* 62 (2009): 584–600; Jaime E. Settle, Christopher T. Dawes, and James H. Fowler, "The Heritability of Partisan Attachment," *Political Research Quarterly* 62 (2009): 601–613. For interpersonal trust, see Patrick Sturgis et al., "A Genetic Basis for Social Trust?" *Political Behavior* 32 (2010): 205–230. For egalitarianism, see Carolyn L. Funk et al., "Genetic and Environmental Transmission of Political Orientations," *Political Psychology* 34 (2013): 805–819. For voting as a duty, see Peter John Loewen and Christopher T. Dawes, "The Heritability of Duty and Voter Turnout," *Political Psychology* 33 (2012): 363–373.

63. James H. Fowler, Laura A. Baker, and Christopher T. Dawes, "Genetic Variation in Political Participation," *American Political Science Review* 102 (2008): 233–248; James H. Fowler and Christopher T. Dawes, "Two Genes Predict Voter Turnout," *Journal of Politics* 70 (2008): 579–594; Christopher T. Dawes and James H. Fowler, "Partisanship, Voting, and the Dopamine D2 Receptor Gene," *Journal of Politics* 71 (2009): 1157–1171.

64. Peter K. Hatemi et al., "Not by Twins Alone: Using the Extended Family Design to Investigate Genetic Influence on Political Beliefs," *American Journal of Political Science* 54 (2010): 798–814.

65. Alford and Hibbing, "Ultimate Source of Political Opinions"; Kevin B. Smith et al., "Linking Genetics and Political Attitudes: Reconceptualizing Political Ideology," *Political Psychology* 32 (2011): 369–397; Peter K. Hatemi et al., "A Genome-Wide Analysis of Liberal and Conservative Political Attitudes," *Journal of Politics* 73 (2011): 271–285.

66. Jaime E. Settle, Christopher T. Dawes, Nicholas A. Christakis, and James H. Fowler, "Friendships Moderate an Association between a Dopamine Gene Variant and Political Ideology," *Journal of Politics* 72 (2010): 1189–1198.

67. See, for example, Evan Charney and William English, "Candidate Genes and Political Behavior," *American Political Science Review* 106 (2012): 1–34; the "Debate Over Genopolitics" Forum in the May 2013 issue of the *American Political Science Review* (pp. 362–395); and the Reflections Symposium in the June 2013 issue of *Perspectives on Politics* (pp. 475–524).

68. Alford, Funk, and Hibbing, "Are Political Orientations Genetically Transmitted?," 153.

69. Evan Charney, "Genes and Ideologies," *Perspectives on Politics* 6 (2008): 299–319.

70. Jennings, "Political Socialization," 40; see also Laura Stoker and Jackie Bass, "Political Socialization: Ongoing Questions and New Directions," in *The Oxford Handbook of American Public Opinion and the Media,* ed. Robert Y. Shapiro and Lawrence R. Jacobs (Oxford: Oxford University Press, 2011).

71. David O. Sears, "Whither Political Socialization Research? The Question of Persistence," in *Political Socialization, Citizenship Education, and Democracy*, ed. Orit Ichilov (New York: Teachers College Press, 1990), 75.

72. Diana Owen, "Service Learning and Political Socialization," *PS: Political Science and Politics* 33 (2000), 639.

73. Sapiro, "Not Your Parents' Political Socialization"; Jennings, "Political Socialization."

CHAPTER 3

1. This section draws heavily from Denis McQuail, *Media Accountability and Freedom of Publication* (Oxford: Oxford University Press, 2003); David Croteau and William Hoynes, *By Invitation Only: How the Media Limit Political Debate* (Monroe, ME: Common Courage, 1994). See also James Curran, "What Democracy Requires of the Media," in *The Press*, ed. Geneva Overholser and Kathleen Hall Jamieson (Oxford: Oxford University Press, 2005).

2. W. Lance Bennett and William Serrin, "The Watchdog Role," in *The Press*, ed. Geneva Overholser and Kathleen Hall Jamieson (Oxford: Oxford University Press, 2005).

3. Larry Diamond, "Introduction," in *Liberation Technology: Social Media and the Struggle for Democracy*, ed. Larry Diamond and Marc F. Plattner (Baltimore: Johns Hopkins University Press, 2012), ix.

4. For a discussion of how media choice allows entertainment fans to pursue their interests rather than politics, see Markus Prior, *Post-Broadcast Democracy* (New York: Cambridge University Press, 2007).

5. Robert G. Picard, "Money, Media, and the Public Interest," in *The Press*, ed. Geneva Overholser and Kathleen Hall Jamieson (Oxford: Oxford University Press, 2005); Michael Schudson and Susan E. Tifft, "American Journalism in Historical Perspective," in *The Press*, ed. Geneva Overholser and Kathleen Hall Jamieson (Oxford: Oxford University Press, 2005).

6. James T. Hamilton, *All the News That's Fit to Sell: How the Market Transforms Information into News* (Princeton, NJ: Princeton University Press, 2004), Chap. 4.

7. For a fascinating history of these events, see Ken Auletta, *Three Blind Mice: How the TV Networks Lost Their Way* (New York: Random House, 1991).

8. "In Changing News Landscape, Even Television Is Vulnerable," Pew Research Center, Washington, DC, September 27, 2012, http://www.people-press.org/files/legacy-pdf/2012%20News%20Consumption%20Report.pdf (accessed October 4, 2015).

9. Thomas E. Patterson, "Doing Well and Doing Good: How Soft News and Critical Journalism Are Shrinking the News Audience and Weakening Democracy—And What News Outlets Can Do about It" (Cambridge, MA: Harvard University, Joan Shorenstein Center on the Press, Politics and Public Policy, John F. Kennedy School of Government, 2000), http://shorensteincenter.org/wp-content/uploads/2012/03/soft_news_and_critical_journalism_2000.pdf (accessed October 4, 2015).

10. Ibid., 3. See also Martin Gilens, Lynn Vavreck, and Martin Cohen, "The Mass Media and the Public's Assessments of Presidential Candidates, 1952–2000," *Journal of Politics* 69 (2007): 1160–1175.

11. "Public Stays with bin Laden Story; Media Focus Shifts," Pew Research Center, Washington, DC, May 25, 2011, http://people-press.org/2011/05/25/public-stays-with-bin-laden-story-media-focus-shifts/ (accessed October 4, 2015).

12. Matthew A. Baum, "Sex, Lies, and War: How Soft News Brings Foreign Policy to the Inattentive Public," *American Political Science Review* 96 (2002): 91–109.

13. Ibid., 96; Matthew A. Baum and Angela S. Jamison, "The *Oprah* Effect: How Soft News Helps Inattentive Citizens Vote Consistently," *Journal of Politics* 68 (2006): 946–959.

14. Baum and Jamison, "*Oprah* Effect," 946.

15. Robert M. Entman, "The Nature and Sources of News," in *The Press*, ed. Geneva Overholser and Kathleen Hall Jamieson (Oxford: Oxford University Press, 2005), 62.

16. "In Changing News Landscape, Even Television Is Vulnerable."

17. Ben H. Bagdikian, *The New Media Monopoly* (Boston: Beacon Press, 2004), 3.

18. "Who Owns What," *Columbia Journalism Review*, February 27, 2013, http://www.cjr.org/resources/?c=cbs (accessed October 4, 2015).

19. "Who Owns What," *Columbia Journalism Review*, May 2, 2014, http://www.cjr.org/resources/?c=21st_century_fox (accessed October 4, 2015).

20. Mark Hughes, Duncan Gardham, John Bingham, and Andy Bloxham, "Phone Hacking: Families of War Dead 'Targeted' by News of the World," *Daily Telegraph*, July 7, 2011, http://www.telegraph.co.uk/news/uknews/phone-hacking/8621797/Phone-hacking-families-of-war-dead-targeted-by-News-of-the-World.html (accessed October 4, 2015).

21. "Reliable Sources," CNN, July 17, 2011, http://transcripts.cnn.com/TRANSCRIPTS/1107/17/rs.01.html (accessed October 11, 2015); "Updated Report: How CNN, MSNBC, and Fox Are Continuing to Cover the News Corp. Hacking Scandal," Media Matters for America, July 20, 2011, http://mediamatters.org/research/201107200021 (accessed October 11, 2015).

22. Croteau and Hoynes, *By Invitation Only*, 23.

23. "Who Owns What," *Columbia Journalism Review*, May 2, 2014, http://www.cjr.org/resources/?c=21st_century_fox (accessed October 4, 2015).

24. Martin Gilens and Craig Hertzman, "Corporate Ownership and News Bias: Newspaper Coverage of the 1996 Telecommunications Act," *Journal of Politics* 62 (2000): 369–386.

25. See also Hamilton, *All the News*, Chap. 5. Hamilton finds that television stations held by companies owning multiple stations provide significantly less hard news coverage on their local broadcasts than those stations that are not part of concentrated media companies.

26. Gilens and Hertzman, "Corporate Ownership and News Bias," 383.

27. Prior, *Post-Broadcast Democracy*, 281.

28. The Walt Disney Company, Our Businesses, Media Networks, https://thewaltdisneycompany.com/disney-companies/media-networks (accessed October 12, 2015).

29. McQuail, *Media Accountability and Freedom of Publication*, 80.

30. OpenSecrets.org, Center for Responsive Politics, http://www.opensecrets.org/orgs/summary.php?id=d000000128 (accessed October 12, 2015).

31. See the PBS and NPR websites for more detailed information, http://www.npr.org/about-npr/178660742/public-radio-finances and http://www.pbs.org/producing/funding/ (both accessed October 12, 2015).

32. To be sure, public radio and television have critics beyond conservative lawmakers. For example, see Croteau and Hoynes, *By Invitation Only*, Chap. 5; Ralph Engelman, *Public Radio and Television in America: A Political History* (Thousand Oaks, CA: Sage, 1996), Chap. 10.

33. Steven Kull, Clay Ramsay, and Evan Lewis, "Misperceptions, the Media, and the Iraq War," *Political Science Quarterly* 118 (2003–2004): 569–598; Clay Ramsay, Steven Kull, Evan Lewis, and Stefan Subias, "Misinformation and the 2010 Election: A Study of the U.S. Electorate," World Public Opinion.org, Program on International Policy Attitudes, Washington, DC, December 10, 2010, http://www.worldpublicopinion.org/pipa/pdf/dec10/Misinformation_Dec10_rpt.pdf (accessed October 12, 2015).

34. Roland Edgar Wolseley, *The Black Press, U.S.A.*, 2nd ed. (Ames: Iowa State University Press, 1990), Chap. 5.

35. Ronald N. Jacobs, *Race, Media, and the Crisis of Civil Society: From Watts to Rodney King* (Cambridge, UK: Cambridge University Press, 2000); Pamela Newkirk, "The Minority Press: Pleading Our Own Cause," in *The Press*, ed. Geneva Overholser and Kathleen Hall Jamieson (Oxford: Oxford University Press, 2005).

36. Rosalee A. Clawson, Harry C. "Neil" Strine IV, and Eric N. Waltenburg, "Framing Supreme Court Decisions: The Mainstream versus the Black Press," *Journal of Black Studies* 33 (2003): 784–800; Michael Huspek, "Black Press, White Press, and Their Opposition: The Case of the Police Killing of Tyisha Miller," *Social Justice* 31 (2004): 217–241.

37. Jacobs, *Race, Media*, 52.

38. Emily Guskin, Paul Moore, and Amy Mitchell, "African American Media: Evolving in the New Era," The State of the News Media 2011, Pew Research Center's Project for Excellence in Journalism, Washington, DC, 2011, http://stateofthemedia.org/2011/african-american/ (accessed October 12, 2015).

39. Nancy Vogt, "African-American Media: Fact Sheet," The State of the News Media 2015, Pew Research Center, Washington, DC, http://www.journalism.org/2015/04/29/african-american-media-fact-sheet/ (accessed October 12, 2015).

40. Katerina Eva Matsa, "Hispanic Media: Fact Sheet," The State of the News Media 2015, Pew Research Center, Washington, DC, http://www.journalism.org/2015/04/29/hispanic-media-fact-sheet/ (October 12, 2015).

41. McQuail, *Media Accountability and Freedom of Publication*, 58.

42. John Carey and Nancy Hicks Maynard, "The Future of News: The Future of Journalism," in *The Press*, ed. Geneva Overholser and Kathleen Hall Jamieson (Oxford: Oxford University Press, 2005); Curran, "What Democracy Requires of the Media."

43. Matthew Hindman, *The Myth of Digital Democracy* (Princeton, NJ: Princeton University Press, 2009).
44. Hamilton, *All the News*, Chap. 7.
45. Schudson and Tifft, "American Journalism in Historical Perspective," 40–41.
46. Jason Gainous and Kevin M. Wagner, *Tweeting to Power: The Social Media Revolution in American Politics* (New York: Oxford University Press, 2014), 35.
47. Kenneth Olmstead and Elsa Shearer, "Digital News—Audience: Fact Sheet," State of the News Media 2015, Pew Research Center, Washington, DC, April 29, 2015, http://www.journalism .org/2015/04/29/digital-news-audience-fact-sheet/ (accessed October 12, 2015).
48. Entman, "Nature and Sources of News"; Herbert J. Gans, *Deciding What's News*, 25th anniversary ed. (Evanston, IL: Northwestern University Press, 2004), 175–176.
49. Gans, *Deciding What's News*; Leon Sigal, *Reporters and Officials* (New York: D. C. Heath, 1973); Entman, "Nature and Sources of News"; W. Lance Bennett, "Toward a Theory of Press-State Relations in the United States," *Political Communication* 40 (1990): 103–125.
50. Timothy E. Cook, *Governing with the News*, 2nd ed. (Chicago: University of Chicago Press, 2005).
51. Timothy E. Cook, "Domesticating a Crisis: Washington Newsbeats and Network News after the Iraqi Invasion of Kuwait," in *Taken by Storm*, ed. W. Lance Bennett and David L. Paletz (Chicago: University of Chicago Press, 1994).
52. Gaye Tuchman, *Making News* (New York: Free Press, 1978).
53. Jonathan S. Morris and Rosalee A. Clawson, "Media Coverage of Congress in the 1990s: Scandals, Personalities, and the Prevalence of Policy and Process," *Political Communication* 22 (2005): 297–313.
54. Michael Robinson and Margaret Sheehan, *Over the Wire and on TV: CBS and UPI in Campaign '80* (New York: Russell Sage Foundation, 1980). Similarly, Patterson argues that journalists use a "game schema" to organize their reporting of political campaigns; Thomas E. Patterson, *Out of Order* (New York: Alfred A. Knopf, 1993).
55. Joseph N. Cappella and Kathleen Hall Jamieson, *Spiral of Cynicism* (New York: Oxford University Press, 1997).
56. Cook, *Governing with the News*.
57. See Hamilton, *All the News*, Chap. 2.
58. Entman, "Nature and Sources of News."
59. "In Changing News Landscape," 10.
60. Peter Dreier and Christopher R. Martin, "How ACORN Was Framed: Political Controversy and Media Agenda Setting," *Perspectives on Politics* 8 (2010): 761–792.
61. Ibid., 762.
62. Local newspapers were the exception to this general pattern because they checked the allegations with local election officials to verify whether voter fraud had indeed occurred.
63. Based on analysis of the American National Election Studies 2012 Time Series data.
64. Daniel Hallin, *The Uncensored War* (Cambridge, UK: Cambridge University Press, 1986); John R. Zaller, *The Nature and Origins of Mass Opinion* (Cambridge, UK: Cambridge University Press, 1992).
65. Howard Kurtz, "The Post on WMDs: An Inside Story," *Washington Post*, August 12, 2004, A1; "The Times and Iraq," *New York Times*, May 26, 2004, A10.
66. Bennett and Serrin, "Watchdog Role."
67. Dana Priest and Anne Hull, "Soldiers Face Neglect, Frustration at Army's Top Medical Facility," *Washington Post*, February 18, 2007, A1.
68. Patterson, *Out of Order*.
69. Amber Boydstun, *Making the News* (Chicago: University of Chicago Press, 2013).
70. Denis McQuail, *Mass Communication Theory: An Introduction* (Beverly Hills, CA: Sage, 1984), Chap. 7.
71. Paul F. Lazarsfeld, Bernard R. Berelson, and Hazel Gaudet, *The People's Choice: How the Voter Makes Up His Mind in a Presidential Campaign,* 2nd ed. (New York: Columbia University Press, 1948). See also Bernard R. Berelson, Paul F. Lazarsfeld, and William N. McPhee, *Voting: A Study of Opinion Formation in a Presidential Campaign* (Chicago: University of Chicago Press, 1954).

72. For a discussion of selective exposure, selective perception, and selective retention, see Joseph T. Klapper, *The Effects of Mass Communication* (New York: Free Press, 1960), Chap. 2.
73. Lazarsfeld, Berelson, and Gaudet, *People's Choice*, 151.
74. Ibid.
75. Maxwell E. McCombs and Donald L. Shaw, "The Agenda-Setting Function of Mass Media," *Public Opinion Quarterly* 36 (1972): 176–187.
76. Ibid., 177; emphasis in original.
77. Bernard C. Cohen, *The Press and Foreign Policy* (Princeton, NJ: Princeton University Press, 1963), 13; emphasis in original.
78. For a discussion of agenda-setting research conducted in other countries, see David Weaver, Maxwell McCombs, and Donald L. Shaw, "Agenda-Setting Research: Issues, Attributes, and Influences," in *Handbook of Political Communication Research*, ed. Lynda Lee Kaid (Mahwah, NJ: Erlbaum, 2004), 257–282.
79. Shanto Iyengar, Mark D. Peters, and Donald R. Kinder, "Experimental Demonstrations of the 'Not-So-Minimal' Consequences of Television News Programs," *American Political Science Review* 76 (1982): 848–858.
80. Ibid., 851.
81. Iyengar, Peters, and Kinder, "Experimental Demonstrations."
82. Jody C Baumgartner, Jonathan S. Morris, and Natasha L. Walth, "The Fey Effect: Young Adults, Political Humor, and Perceptions of Sarah Palin in the 2008 Presidential Election Campaign," *Public Opinion Quarterly* 76 (2012): 95–104.
83. Ibid., 96.
84. Michael Tesler, "Priming Predispositions and Changing Policy Positions: An Account of When Mass Opinion Is Primed or Changed," *American Journal of Political Science* 59 (2014): 806–824.
85. Ibid.
86. Also see Gabriel S. Lenz, "Learning and Opinion Change, Not Priming: Reconsidering the Priming Hypothesis," *American Journal of Political Science* 53 (2009): 821–837.
87. Thomas E. Nelson, Rosalee A. Clawson, and Zoe M. Oxley, "Media Framing of a Civil Liberties Conflict and Its Effect on Tolerance," *American Political Science Review* 91 (1997): 567.
88. Adam J. Berinsky and Donald R. Kinder, "Making Sense of Issues through Media Frames: Understanding the Kosovo Crisis," *Journal of Politics* 68 (2006): 640–656.
89. Shanto Iyengar, "Framing Responsibility for Political Issues: The Case of Poverty," *Political Behavior* 12 (1990): 19–40.
90. Ibid., 25.
91. Ibid.
92. For a more recent analysis of the influence of episodic frames on public opinion, see Lester K. Spence, "Episodic Frames, HIV/AIDS, and African American Public Opinion," *Political Research Quarterly* 63 (2010): 257–268.
93. Nelson, Clawson, and Oxley, "Media Framing."
94. Ibid., 571.
95. Ibid.
96. Ibid.
97. Russell H. Fazio, "A Practical Guide to the Use of Response Latency in Social Psychological Research," in *Review of Personality and Social Psychology*, Vol. 11: *Research Methods in Personality and Social Psychology*, ed. Clyde Hendrick and Margaret S. Clark (Newbury Park, CA: Sage, 1990).
98. Nelson, Clawson, and Oxley, "Media Framing," 579.
99. For additional evidence on this point, see Thomas E. Nelson and Zoe M. Oxley, "Issue Framing Effects on Belief Importance and Opinion," *Journal of Politics* 61 (1999): 1040–1067; James N. Druckman, "On the Limits of Framing Effects: Who Can Frame?" *Journal of Politics* 63 (2001): 1041–1066.
100. Other scholars have also provided a more redeeming view of the citizen by showing that accessibility does not lead to priming. Instead, citizens who are politically knowledgeable and who trust the media infer that issues covered by the media are important and thus rely on those issues when evaluating politicians. See Joanne M. Miller and Jon A. Krosnick, "News Media

Impact on the Ingredients of Presidential Evaluations: Politically Knowledgeable Citizens Are Guided by a Trusted Source," *American Journal of Political Science* 44 (2000): 301–315.

101. Paul M. Kellstedt, *The Mass Media and the Dynamics of American Racial Attitudes* (Cambridge, UK: Cambridge University Press, 2003).

102. Druckman, "On the Limits of Framing Effects."

103. On the importance and influence of partisan cues, see James N. Druckman, Erik Peterson, and Rune Slothuus, "How Elite Partisan Polarization Affects Public Opinion Formation," *American Political Science Review* 107 (2013): 57–79.

104. Dennis Chong and James N. Druckman, "Dynamic Public Opinion: Communication Effects over Time," *American Political Science Review* 104 (2010): 663–680.

105. Ibid., 679.

106. Diana C. Mutz, *In-Your-Face Politics: The Consequences of Uncivil Media* (Princeton, NJ: Princeton University Press, 2015).

107. Ibid., 25.

108. Ibid., 33.

109. Ibid., Ch. 3.

110. Ibid., 68.

111. Nick Corasaniti, "Seeking the Presidency, Bernie Sanders Becomes Facebook Royalty Through Quirky Sharing," *New York Times*, May 18, 2015, http://www.nytimes.com/2015/05/19/us/politics/bernie-sanders-wants-to-be-president-but-hes-already-facebook-royalty.html (accessed October 14, 2015).

112. Nicholas Wells, "Can Any Candidate Top @realDonaldTrump?," CNBC, October 8, 2015, http://www.cnbc.com/2015/10/07/the-4-types-of-republicans-on-twitter.html (accessed October 14, 2015).

113. Monica Anderson, "More Americans Are Using Social Media to Connect with Politicians," Pew Research Center, May 19, 2015, http://www.pewresearch.org/fact-tank/2015/05/19/more-americans-are-using-social-media-to-connect-with-politicians/ (accessed October 3, 2015).

114. Jason Gainous and Kevin M. Wagner, *Tweeting to Power: The Social Media Revolution in American Politics* (New York: Oxford University Press, 2014), 26.

115. Ibid., 3.

Chapter 4

1. Office of the Press Secretary, "Remarks by the President on Osama bin Laden," May 2, 2011, http://www.whitehouse.gov/the-press-office/2011/05/02/remarks-president-osama-bin-laden (accessed June 6, 2011).

2. Ibid.

3. For more details regarding the ANES series, visit www.electionstudies.org.

4. Philip E. Converse, "The Nature of Belief Systems in Mass Publics," in *Ideology and Discontent*, ed. David E. Apter (New York: Free Press, 1964).

5. Ibid., 240.

6. Ibid., 241.

7. Philip E. Converse, "Attitudes and Non-Attitudes: Continuation of a Dialogue," in *The Quantitative Analysis of Social Problems*, ed. Edward R. Tufte (Reading, MA: Addison-Wesley, 1970).

8. Ibid., 245.

9. Converse, "Nature of Belief Systems."

10. Benjamin I. Page and Robert Y. Shapiro, *The Rational Public: Fifty Years of Trends in Americans' Policy Preferences* (Chicago: University of Chicago Press, 1992), 1. For a similar conclusion, see James A. Stimson, *Tides of Consent: How Public Opinion Shapes American Politics* (Cambridge, UK: Cambridge University Press, 2004).

11. Frank R. Baumgartner, Suzanna L. De Boef, and Amber E. Boydstun, *The Decline of the Death Penalty and the Discovery of Innocence* (Cambridge, UK: Cambridge University Press, 2008).

12. Jeffrey M. Jones, "Americans' Support for Death Penalty Stable," Gallup, Washington, DC, October 23, 2014, http://www.gallup.com/poll/178790/americans-support-death-penalty-stable.aspx (accessed July 13, 2015).

13. Baumgartner, De Boef, and Boydstun, *Decline of the Death Penalty*, 4.

14. Ibid.

15. Page and Shapiro, *Rational Public*, 56.

16. Ibid., 16.

17. Philip E. Converse, "Popular Representation and the Distribution of Information," in *Information and Democratic Processes*, ed. John A. Ferejohn and James H. Kuklinski (Urbana: University of Illinois Press, 1990), 382.

18. For an excellent review of the research on presidential approval, see Paul Gronke and Brian Newman, "FDR to Clinton, Mueller to ?: A Field Essay on Presidential Approval," *Political Research Quarterly* 56 (2003): 501–512.

19. "How Does Gallup Daily Tracking Work?," Gallup, Washington, DC, 2015, http://www.gallup.com/174155/gallup-daily-tracking-methodology.aspx (accessed July 13, 2015).

20. Paul Gronke, Jeffrey Koch, and J. Matthew Wilson, "Follow the Leader? Presidential Approval, Perceived Presidential Support, and Representatives' Electoral Fortunes," *Journal of Politics* 65 (2003): 785–808.

21. Brandice Canes-Wrone and Scott de Marchi, "Presidential Approval and Legislative Success," *Journal of Politics* 64 (2002): 491–509; Bryan W. Marshall and Brandon C. Prins, "Strategic Position Taking and Presidential Influence in Congress," *Legislative Studies Quarterly* 32 (2007): 257–284.

22. See http://www.gallup.com/poll/124922/Presidential-Approval-Center.aspx.

23. John Mueller, *War, Presidents, and Public Opinion* (Lanham, MD: University Press of America, 1973).

24. Richard A. Brody, *Assessing the President: The Media, Elite Opinion, and Public Support* (Stanford, CA: Stanford University Press, 1991).

25. Richard Waterman, Carol. L. Silva, and Hank Jenkins-Smith, *The Presidential Expectations Gap: Public Attitudes Concerning the Presidency* (Ann Arbor: University of Michigan Press, 2014).

26. Mueller, *War, Presidents, and Public Opinion*.

27. Cindy D. Kam and Jennifer M. Ramos, "Joining and Leaving the Rally: Understanding the Surge and Decline in Presidential Approval Following 9/11," *Public Opinion Quarterly* 72 (2008): 619–650.

28. Richard C. Eichenberg, Richard J. Stoll, and Matthew Lebo, "War President: The Approval Ratings of George W. Bush," *Journal of Conflict Resolution* 50 (2006): 783–808.

29. Benny Geys, "Wars, Presidents, and Popularity: The Political Cost(s) of War Re-Examined," *Public Opinion Quarterly* 74 (2010): 357–374.

30. Eichenberg, Stoll, and Lebo, "War President"; Waterman, Silva, and Jenkins-Smith, *The Presidential Expectations Gap*.

31. Waterman, Silva, and Jenkins-Smith, *The Presidential Expectations Gap*.

32. Tiffany Harper and Barbara Norrander, "The Rise and Fall of George W. Bush: Popular Support for the President," in *Understanding Public Opinion*, 3rd ed., ed. Barbara Norrander and Clyde Wilcox (Washington, DC: CQ Press, 2010).

33. See http://www.gallup.com/poll/124922/Presidential-Approval-Center.aspx.

34. Matthew J. Lebo and Daniel Cassino, "The Aggregated Consequences of Motivated Reasoning and the Dynamics of Partisan Presidential Approval," *Political Psychology* 28 (2007): 719–746; Gerald T. Fox, "Partisan Divide on War and the Economy: Presidential Approval of G. W. Bush," *Journal of Conflict Resolution* 53 (2009): 905–933.

35. Brody, *Assessing the President*; Kam and Ramos, "Joining and Leaving the Rally."

36. A wonderful resource for understanding the vast psychology literature on attitudes is Alice H. Eagly and Shelly Chaiken, *The Psychology of Attitudes* (Fort Worth, TX: Harcourt Brace Jovanovich, 1993).

37. Daniel Katz, "The Functional Approach to the Study of Attitudes," *Public Opinion Quarterly* 24 (1960): 163–204.

38. Ibid., 172.

39. M. Brewster Smith, Jerome S. Bruner, and Robert W. White, *Opinions and Personality* (New York: John Wiley, 1956).

40. Mark Snyder and Kenneth G. DeBono, "A Functional Approach to Attitudes and Persuasion," in *Social Influence: The Ontario Symposium*, Vol. 5, ed. Mark P. Zanna, James M. Olson, and C. Peter Herman (Hillsdale, NJ: Erlbaum, 1987), 109.

41. Katz, "Functional Approach."

42. Snyder and DeBono, "Functional Approach to Attitudes." For a similar argument, see Gregory M. Herek, "The Instrumentality of Attitudes: Toward a Neofunctional Theory," *Journal of Social Issues* 42 (1986): 99–114.

43. Perry Bacon Jr., "The Unholy Truth? No Cross in Ad, Huckabee Says," *Washington Post*, December 21, 2007, A5.

44. Rebecca Sinderbrand, "New Huckabee Ad Appeals to Christian Conservatives," CNN.com, January 1, 2008, http://www.cnn.com/2008/POLITICS/01/01/huckabee.christians/index .html?iref=allsearch (accessed June 17, 2011).

45. "What Really Matters," Mike Huckabee campaign advertisement, http://www.youtube.com/ watch?v=8xn7uSHtkuA&NR=1 (accessed June 17, 2011).

46. Jon A. Krosnick, Andrew L. Betz, Lee J. Jussim, and Ann R. Lynn, "Subliminal Conditioning of Attitudes," *Personality and Social Psychology Bulletin* 18 (1992): 152–162.

47. Richard E. Petty and John T. Cacioppo, *Attitudes and Persuasion: Classic and Contemporary Approaches* (Dubuque, IA: William C. Brown, 1981); Richard E. Petty and John T. Cacioppo, *Communication and Persuasion* (New York: Springer-Verlag, 1986).

48. Richard E. Petty, John T. Cacioppo, and Rachel Goldman, "Personal Involvement as a Determinant of Argument-Based Persuasion," *Journal of Personality and Social Psychology* 41 (1981): 847–855.

49. Petty and Cacioppo, *Attitudes and Persuasion*, 225.

50. Eagly and Chaiken, *Psychology of Attitudes*.

51. Petty and Cacioppo, *Attitudes and Persuasion*, 256.

52. John R. Zaller, *The Nature and Origins of Mass Opinion* (Cambridge, UK: Cambridge University Press, 1992). It is important to note that Zaller's work draws heavily on the work of psychologist William McGuire. See, for example, William J. McGuire, "The Nature of Attitudes and Attitude Change," in *The Handbook of Social Psychology*, 2nd ed., Vol. 3, ed. Gardner Lindzey and Elliot Aronson (Reading, MA: Addison-Wesley, 1969).

53. Zaller, *Nature and Origins*, 1.

54. Ibid., 19.

55. Ibid., 44–45.

56. Ibid., 40.

57. Pablo Briñol, Derek D. Rucker, Zakary Tormala, and Richard E. Petty, "Individual Differences in Resistance to Persuasion: The Role of Beliefs and Meta-Beliefs," in *Resistance and Persuasion*, ed. Eric S. Knowles and Jay A. Linn (Mahwah, NJ: Erlbaum, 2004); Julia Zuwerink Jacks and Maureen E. O'Brien, "Decreasing Resistance by Affirming the Self," in *Resistance and Persuasion*, ed. Eric S. Knowles and Jay A. Linn (Mahwah, NJ: Erlbaum, 2004).

58. Briñol, Rucker, Tormala, and Petty, "Individual Differences in Resistance to Persuasion"; Kathleen Fuegen and Jack W. Brehm, "The Intensity of Affect and Resistance to Social Influence," in *Resistance and Persuasion*, ed. Eric S. Knowles and Jay A. Linn (Mahwah, NJ: Erlbaum, 2004); Jeffrey M. Quinn and Wendy Wood, "Forewarnings of Influence Appeals: Inducing Resistance and Acceptance," in *Resistance and Persuasion*, ed. Eric S. Knowles and Jay A. Linn (Mahwah, NJ: Erlbaum, 2004).

59. Jacks and O'Brien, "Decreasing Resistance by Affirming the Self."

60. George Y. Bizer and Richard E. Petty, "How We Conceptualize Our Attitudes Matters: The Effects of Valence Framing on the Resistance of Political Attitudes," *Political Psychology* 26 (2005): 553–568.

61. Ibid.

62. Richard R. Lau, "Two Explanations for Negativity Effects in Political Behavior," *American Journal of Political Science* 29 (1985): 119–138.

63. Leon Festinger, *A Theory of Cognitive Dissonance* (Stanford, CA: Stanford University Press, 1957).

64. Leon Festinger and James Merrill Carlsmith, "Cognitive Consequences of Forced Compliance," *Journal of Abnormal and Social Psychology* 58 (1959): 203–210.
65. Daryl J. Bem, "Self-Perception Theory," in *Advances in Experimental Social Psychology*, Vol. 6, ed. Leonard Berkowitz (New York: Academic Press, 1972), 5. See also Daryl J. Bem, "Self-Perception: An Alternative Interpretation of Cognitive Dissonance Phenomena," *Psychological Review* 74 (1967): 183–200.
66. Eagly and Chaiken, *Psychology of Attitudes*.
67. Ibid., 546.
68. Ibid.

Chapter 5

1. Bob Minzesheimer, "Insults Thrown, Left and Right," *USA Today*, June 1, 2003, http://www .usatoday.com/life/books/news/2003-06-01-book-expo_x.htm (accessed July 23, 2007).
2. Kent Tedin, "Political Ideology and the Vote," *Research in Micropolitics* 2 (1987): 65.
3. Mahzarin R. Banaji and Larisa Heiphetz, "Attitudes," in *Handbook of Social Psychology*, 5th ed., Vol. 1, ed. Susan T. Fiske, Daniel T. Gilbert, and Gardner Lindzey (Hoboken, NJ: John Wiley & Sons, 2010), 380.
4. Kathleen Knight, "Transformations of the Concept of Ideology in the Twentieth Century," *American Political Science Review* 100 (2006): 619–635.
5. Philip E. Converse, "The Nature of Belief Systems in Mass Publics," in *Ideology and Discontent*, ed. David E. Apter (New York: Free Press, 1964), 214.
6. Ibid., 207.
7. Ibid.
8. See also Angus Campbell, Philip E. Converse, Warren E. Miller, and Donald E. Stokes, *The American Voter* (New York: John Wiley, 1960), Chap. 10.
9. Converse used *Ideologue* to refer to those people who demonstrated the most abstract ideological thinking, even though this term is often reserved for people who display a dogmatic attachment to their beliefs. In other words, whereas Converse's ideologues displayed high levels of political reasoning, we more commonly think of ideologues as those who are not open-minded to new information or who do not think carefully about political matters. This distinction was not lost on Converse. Despite the potential confusion over his use of *ideologue*, he selected this term because he could not locate another term or short phrase that conveyed the meaning he intended. Philip E. Converse, "Democratic Theory and Electoral Reality," *Critical Review* 18 (2006): 297–329.
10. Campbell et al., *American Voter*, 231.
11. Ibid., 236.
12. Michael S. Lewis-Beck, Helmut Norpoth, William G. Jacoby, and Herbert F. Weisberg, *The American Voter Revisited* (Ann Arbor: University of Michigan Press, 2008), 275.
13. Ibid., 276.
14. Ibid., Chap. 10.
15. Converse, "Nature of Belief Systems," 223.
16. Ibid., 243.
17. Donald R. Kinder, "Belief Systems after Converse," in *Electoral Democracy*, ed. Michael B. MacKuen and George Rabinowitz (Ann Arbor: University of Michigan Press, 2003), 13.
18. Samuel L. Popkin, "The Factual Basis of 'Belief Systems': A Reassessment," *Critical Review* 18 (2006): 233–234.
19. Norman H. Nie, Sidney Verba, and John R. Petrocik, *The Changing American Voter*, enlarged ed. (Cambridge, MA: Harvard University Press, 1979), Chap. 8. For a contrary view, see John L. Sullivan, James E. Pierson, and George E. Marcus, "Ideological Constraint in the Mass Public: A Methodological Critique and Some New Findings," *American Journal of Political Science* 22 (1978): 233–249.
20. James A. Stimson, "Belief Systems: Constraint, Complexity and the 1972 Election," *American Journal of Political Science* 19 (1975): 393–417; Tedin, "Political Ideology and the Vote."

21. Converse, "Democratic Theory and Electoral Reality," 305. See also Stephen Earl Bennett, "Democratic Competence, before Converse and After," *Critical Review* 18 (2006): 105–141.

22. Philip E. Converse and Gregory B. Markus, "Plus ça change . . .: The New CPS Election Study Panel," *American Political Science Review* 73 (1979): 32–49; M. Kent Jennings, "Ideological Thinking among Mass Publics and Political Elites," *Public Opinion Quarterly* 56 (1992): 419–441; Converse, "Democratic Theory and Electoral Reality."

23. The seven issues for 1980 were defense spending, school busing, environmental regulations, relations with the Soviet Union, abortion, the Equal Rights Amendment, and inflation. Eight issues were analyzed for 2004: government provision of services, defense spending, government versus private medical insurance, government job guarantee, aid to blacks, environmental protection, death penalty, and women's roles.

24. The 1980 results are from Jennings, "Ideological Thinking."

25. Ibid.

26. We excluded three issues from our analysis because we worried that public responses to these items would have been affected by the events of September 11, 2001. The excluded items were spending on crime, foreign aid, and border security. When these items are included, the correlation decreases slightly from .44 to .40.

27. Jennings, "Ideological Thinking."

28. For a similar argument, see Edward G. Carmines, Michael J. Ensley, and Michael W. Wagner, "Political Ideology in American Politics: One, Two, or None?" *The Forum* 10, no. 3 (2012): Article 4 [online].

29. Robert E. Lane, *Political Ideology: Why the American Common Man Believes What He Does* (New York: Free Press, 1962).

30. Melissa Harris-Lacewell, *Barbershops, Bibles, and BET: Everyday Talk and Black Political Thought* (Princeton, NJ: Princeton University Press, 2004).

31. Michael C. Dawson, *Black Visions: The Roots of Contemporary African-American Political Ideologies* (Chicago: University of Chicago Press, 2001), 65.

32. Dawson, *Black Visions*; Melissa Harris-Lacewell, *Barbershops, Bibles, and BET*.

33. For similar conclusions, see Donald R. Kinder, "Belief Systems Today," *Critical Review* 18 (2006): 197–216; Bennett, "Democratic Competence, before Converse and After."

34. Lewis-Beck et al., *American Voter Revisited*, 293. See also Tedin, "Political Ideology and the Vote"; Kathleen Knight, "Ideology in the 1980 Election: Ideological Sophistication Does Matter," *Journal of Politics* 47 (1985): 828–853.

35. The 2012 ANES study used two interviewing modes: in person and on the web. Because the Internet version of the survey did not provide respondents with the option to indicate they have not thought much about their ideology, we have included results only from the face-to-face interviews in Figure 5.4.

36. Christopher Ellis and James A. Stimson, *Ideology in America* (Cambridge, UK: Cambridge University Press, 2012).

37. Ibid., 11.

38. Ibid., Chaps. 2–3.

39. Ibid., Chap. 5. For a similar analysis, see Christopher Claassen, Patrick Tucker, and Steven S. Smith, "Ideological Labels in America," *Political Behavior* 37 (2015): 253–278.

40. Ellis and Stimson, *Ideology in America*, 131.

41. Ibid., 158.

42. Ibid., 161.

43. For an early account of the influence of party identification on political attitudes, see Angus Campbell, Philip E. Converse, Warren E. Miller, and Donald E. Stokes, *The American Voter* (New York: John Wiley, 1960). It is important to note that issue attitudes can also influence party identification; see Logan Dancey and Paul Goren, "Party Identification, Issue Attitudes, and the Dynamics of Political Debate," *American Journal of Political Science* 54 (2010): 686–699.

44. Wendy M. Rahn, "The Role of Partisan Stereotypes in Information-Processing about Political Candidates," *American Journal of Political Science* 37 (1993): 472–496.

45. Charles S. Taber and Milton Lodge, "Motivated Skepticism in the Evaluation of Political Beliefs," *American Journal of Political Science* 50 (2006): 756. See also Milton Lodge and Charles S. Taber, *The Rationalizing Voter* (Cambridge, UK: Cambridge University Press, 2013).

46. David P. Redlawsk and Richard R. Lau, "Behavioral Decision-Making," in *The Oxford Handbook of Political Psychology*, 2nd ed., ed. Leonie Huddy, David O. Sears, and Jack S. Levy (Oxford: Oxford University Press, 2013), 151.

47. For a thorough review, see Thomas J. Leeper and Rune Slothuus, "Political Parties, Motivated Reasoning, and Public Opinion Formation," *Advances in Political Psychology* 35, Supplement 1 (2014): 129–156.

48. Toby Bolsen, James N. Druckman, and Fay Lomax Cook, "The Influence of Partisan Motivated Reasoning on Public Opinion," *Political Behavior* 36 (2014): 235–262.

49. Matthew J. Lebo and Daniel Cassino, "The Aggregated Consequences of Motivated Reasoning and the Dynamics of Partisan Presidential Approval," *Political Psychology* 28 (2007): 719–746.

50. Brian J. Gaines et al., "Same Facts, Different Interpretations: Partisan Motivation and Opinion on Iraq," *Journal of Politics* 69 (2007): 957–974.

51. Ibid., 972.

52. Ibid., 967.

53. Mark Murray, "A Long Division: Political Polarization Is Worse Than Ever, and Here to Stay," NBC News, October 17, 2014, http://www.nbcnews.com/politics/first-read/long-division-political-polarization-worse-ever-here-stay-n228441 (accessed September 19, 2015).

54. Matthew Levendusky, *The Partisan Sort: How Liberals Became Democrats and Conservatives Became Republicans* (Chicago: University of Chicago Press, 2009). See also Alan I. Abramowitz and Kyle L. Saunders, "Ideological Realignment in the U.S. Electorate," *Journal of Politics* 60 (1998): 634–652 and Morris P. Fiorina, with Samuel J. Abrams and Jeremy C. Pope, *Culture War? The Myth of a Polarized America*, 3rd ed. (Boston: Longman, 2011), Chap. 4.

55. Levendusky, *The Partisan Sort*, Chap. 6.

56. Fiorina, Abrams, and Pope, *Culture War?*; Levendusky, *The Partisan Sort*, Chap. 3. For a contrary view, see Alan I. Abramowitz, *The Disappearing Center: Engaged Citizens, Polarization, and American Democracy* (New Haven, CT: Yale University Press, 2010).

57. Analysis of American National Election Studies 2012 data file. See also Fiorina, Abrams, and Pope, *Culture War?*, Chap. 5.

58. Nolan McCarty, Keith Poole, and Howard Rosenthal, *Polarized Politics: The Dance of Ideology and Unequal Riches* (Cambridge: Massachusetts Institute of Technology Press, 2006); Sean Theriault, *Party Polarization in Congress* (Cambridge, UK: Cambridge University Press, 2008); Gary C. Jacobson, *A Divider, Not a Uniter: George W. Bush and the American People* (New York: Pearson Longman, 2007), Chap. 2.

59. Levendusky, *The Partisan Sort*, Chap. 2.

60. Fiorina, Abrams, and Pope, *Culture War?*, Chap. 2.

61. Howard J. Gold, "The Polls—Trends: Americans' Attitudes toward the Political Parties and the Party System," *Public Opinion Quarterly* 79 (2015): 803–819.

62. Levendusky, *The Partisan Sort*, 3.

63. The following results are from Marc J. Hetherington and Thomas J. Rudolph, *Why Washington Won't Work: Polarization, Political Trust, and the Governing Crisis* (Chicago: University of Chicago Press, 2015), Chap. 2. For a similar conclusion, see Shanto G. Iyengar, Guarav Sood, and Yphtach Lelkes, "Affect, Not Ideology: A Social Identity Perspective on Polarization," *Public Opinion Quarterly* 76 (2012): 405–431.

64. Iyengar, Sood, and Lelkes, "Affect, Not Ideology."

65. Lilliana Mason, "'I Disrespectfully Agree': The Differential Effects of Partisan Sorting on Social and Issue Polarization," *American Journal of Political Science* 59 (2014): 128–145.

66. Iyengar, Sood, and Lelkes, "Affect, Not Ideology."

67. Shanto Iyengar and Sean J. Westwood, "Fear and Loathing across Party Lines: New Evidence on Group Polarization," *American Journal of Political Science* 59 (2015): 690–707.

68. Ibid., 692.

69. Michael Schudson and Susan E. Tifft, "American Journalism in Historical Perspective," in *The Press*, ed. Geneva Overholser and Kathleen Hall Jamieson (Oxford: Oxford University Press, 2005).

70. Natalie Jomini Stroud, *Niche News: The Politics of News Choice* (Oxford: Oxford University Press, 2011); Shanto Iyengar and Kyu S. Hahn, "Red Media, Blue Media: Evidence of Ideological Selectivity in Media Use," *Journal of Communication* 59 (2009): 19–39.

71. Amy Mitchell, Jeffrey Gottfried, Jocelyn Kiley, and Katerina Eva Matsa, "Political Polarization & Media Habits," Pew Research Center, Washington, DC, October 21, 2014, http://www.journalism.org/2014/10/21/political-polarization-media-habits (accessed September 15, 2015).

72. Amy Mitchell, "State of the News Media 2015," Pew Research Center, Washington, DC, April 29, 2015, http://www.journalism.org/2015/04/29/state-of-the-news-media-2015 (accessed September 15, 2015).

73. "Digital: Top 50 Digital Native News Sites (2015)," Pew Research Center, Washington, DC, April 29, 2015, http://www.journalism.org/media-indicators/digital-top-50-digital-native-news-sites-2015 (accessed September 15, 2015).

74. Kevin Arceneaux and Martin Johnson, *Changing Minds or Changing Channels? Partisan News in an Age of Choice* (Chicago: University of Chicago Press, 2013); Matthew Levendusky, *How Partisan Media Polarize America* (Chicago: University of Chicago Press, 2013).

75. Arceneaux and Johnson, *Changing Minds or Changing Channels?*, Chap. 4.

76. Ibid., 88.

77. Bennett, "Democratic Competence, before Converse and After," 119.

78. Ibid., 105.

79. Levendusky, *The Partisan Sort*, 119.

CHAPTER 6

1. Donald R. Kinder, "Diversity and Complexity in American Public Opinion," in *Political Science: The State of the Discipline*, ed. Ada Finifter (Washington, DC: American Political Science Association, 1983).

2. Ibid., 401.

3. T. W. Adorno, Else Frenkel-Brunswik, Daniel J. Levinson, and R. Nevitt Sanford, *The Authoritarian Personality* (New York: Harper & Brothers, 1950).

4. Ibid., 228.

5. Ibid., 385.

6. See, for example, Richard Christie and Marie Jahoda, eds., *Studies in the Scope and Method of "The Authoritarian Personality": Continuities in Social Research* (Glencoe, IL: Free Press, 1954); Bob Altemeyer, *Right-Wing Authoritarianism* (Winnipeg, Canada: University of Manitoba Press, 1981).

7. Karen Stenner, *The Authoritarian Dynamic* (New York: Cambridge University Press, 2005).

8. Ibid., 14.

9. Ibid., Chap. 6.

10. Ibid., 177.

11. Ibid., 24; emphasis in original.

12. Unfortunately, these questions about child-rearing values were not available for all years of the General Social Survey. When these questions were not available, Stenner used a sophisticated statistical technique to impute authoritarianism scores for respondents. See ibid., 164–165.

13. Ibid., 190.

14. Ibid., 86.

15. Ibid., 17.

16. Ibid., 26.

17. Ibid., 292.

18. Marc J. Hetherington and Jonathan D. Weiler, *Authoritarianism and Polarization in American Politics* (New York: Cambridge University Press, 2009).

19. Ibid., 34.

20. Anne M. Cizmar, Geoffrey C. Layman, John McTague, Shanna Pearson-Merkowitz, and Michael Spivey, "Authoritarianism and American Political Behavior from 1952 to 2008," *Political Research Quarterly* 67 (2014): 71–83.

21. Hetherington and Weiler, *Authoritarianism and Polarization,* Chap. 7.

22. Samuel D. Gosling, Peter J. Rentfrow, and William B. Swann Jr., "A Very Brief Measure of the Big-Five Personality Domains," *Journal of Research in Personality* 37 (2003): 504–528.

23. Dana R. Carney, John T. Jost, Samuel D. Gosling, and Jeff Potter, "The Secret Lives of Liberals and Conservatives: Personality Profiles, Interaction Styles, and the Things They Leave Behind," *Political Psychology* 29 (2008): 807–840.

24. Ibid.; John T. Jost, "The End of the End of Ideology," *American Psychologist* 61 (2006): 651–670; Jeffery J. Mondak, *Personality and the Foundations of Political Behavior* (Cambridge, UK: Cambridge University Press, 2010), Chap. 5; Alan S. Gerber, Gregory A. Huber, David Doherty, and Conor M. Dowling, "Personality and the Strength and Direction of Partisan Identification," *Political Behavior* 34 (2012): 653–688; Jan-Emmanuel De Neve, "Personality, Childhood Experience, and Political Ideology," *Political Psychology* 36 (2015): 55–73.

25. De Neve, "Personality, Childhood Experience, and Political Ideology," 59.

26. Mondak, *Personality and the Foundations of Political Behavior*, Chap. 5.

27. Gerber, Huber, Doherty, and Dowling, "Personality and the Strength and Direction of Partisan Identification."

28. Ibid., 661.

29. Alan S. Gerber et al., "Personality and Political Attitudes: Relationships across Issue Domains and Political Contexts," *American Political Science Review* 104 (2010): 111–133. For additional analyses of traits and issue attitudes, see Mondak, *Personality and the Foundations of Political Behavior*, Chap. 5.

30. Gerber et al., "Personality and Political Attitudes," 117.

31. Other work has explored relationships between the Big Five and a range of political behaviors. On the topic of engaging in political discussions, see Matthew V. Hibbing, Melinda Ritchie, and Mary R. Anderson, "Personality and Political Discussion," *Political Behavior* 33 (2011): 601–624 and Alan S. Gerber, Gregory A. Huber, David Doherty, and Conor M. Dowling, "Disagreement and the Avoidance of Political Discussion: Aggregate Relationships and Differences across Personality Traits," *American Journal of Political Science* 56 (2012): 849–874. For effects of traits on news media use, political attentiveness, and political participation, see Mondak, *Personality and the Foundations of Political Behavior*, Chaps. 4 and 6.

32. For initial forays into these topics, see Mondak, *Personality and the Foundations of Political Behavior*; De Neve, "Personality, Childhood Experience, and Political Ideology"; and Alan S. Gerber, Gregory A. Huber, David Doherty, Conor M. Dowling, and Costas Panagopoulos, "Big Five Personality Traits and Responses to Persuasive Appeals: Results from Voter Turnout Experiments," *Political Behavior* 35 (2013): 687–728.

33. Alexander Hamilton, James Madison, and John Jay, *The Federalist Papers*, ed. Clinton Rossiter (New York: Penguin, 1961), 82.

34. For a review of this literature, see Jack Citrin and Donald P. Green, "The Self-Interest Motive in American Public Opinion," *Research in Micropolitics* 3 (1990): 1–28; David O. Sears and Carolyn L. Funk, "The Role of Self-Interest in Social and Political Attitudes," *Advances in Experimental Social Psychology* 24 (1991): 1–91. For an examination of the limited effects of self-interest across time, see Richard R. Lau and Caroline Heldman, "Self-Interest, Symbolic Attitudes, and Support for Public Policy: A Multilevel Analysis," *Political Psychology* 30 (2009): 513–537.

35. See, for example, David O. Sears, Carl P. Hensler, and Leslie K. Speer, "Whites' Opposition to 'Busing': Self-Interest or Symbolic Politics?" *American Political Science Review* 73 (1979): 369–384. Kinder and Sanders show the limited effect of self-interest on white and black opinion toward several racial issues; Donald R. Kinder and Lynn M. Sanders, *Divided by Color* (Chicago: University of Chicago Press, 1996).

36. Donald R. Kinder and D. Roderick Kiewiet, "Sociotropic Politics: The American Case," *British Journal of Political Science* 11 (1981): 129–161.

37. David O. Sears and Jack Citrin, *Tax Revolt: Something for Nothing in California*, enlarged ed. (Cambridge, MA: Harvard University Press, 1985).

38. Donald Philip Green and Ann Elizabeth Gerken, "Self-Interest and Public Opinion toward Smoking Restrictions and Cigarette Taxes," *Public Opinion Quarterly* 53 (1989): 1–16; Richard D. Dixon, Roger C. Lowery, Diane E. Levy, and Kenneth F. Ferraro, "Self-Interest and Public

Opinion toward Smoking Policies: A Replication and Extension," *Public Opinion Quarterly* 55 (1991): 241–254.

39. Robin M. Wolpert and James G. Gimpel, "Self-Interest, Symbolic Politics, and Public Attitudes toward Gun Control," *Political Behavior* 20 (1998): 241–262.

40. Citrin and Green, "Self-Interest Motive," 18.

41. Robert S. Erikson and Laura Stoker, "Caught in the Draft: The Effects of Vietnam Draft Lottery Status on Political Attitudes," *American Political Science Review* 105 (2011): 221–237.

42. Ibid., 223.

43. Tiffany C. Davenport, "Policy-Induced Risk and Responsive Participation: The Effect of a Son's Conscription Risk on the Voting Behavior of His Parents," *American Journal of Political Science* 59 (2015): 225–241.

44. Bradford H. Bishop, "Focusing Events and Public Opinion: Evidence from the *Deepwater Horizon* Disaster," *Political Behavior* 36 (2014): 1–22.

45. "Remarks by the President to the Nation on the BP Oil Spill," June 15, 2010, https://www .whitehouse.gov/the-press-office/remarks-president-nation-bp-oil-spill (accessed September 28, 2015).

46. Bishop, "Focusing Events," 2. Policy debates can also make self-interest considerations more salient. For examples, see Dennis Chong, Jack Citrin, and Patricia Conley, "When Self-Interest Matters," *Political Psychology* 22 (2001): 541–570 and William Franko, Caroline J. Tolbert, and Christopher Witko, "Inequality, Self-Interest, and Public Support for 'Robin Hood' Tax Policies," *Political Research Quarterly* 66 (2013): 923–937.

47. Eric R. A. N. Smith, *Energy, The Environment, and Public Opinion* (Lanham, MD: Rowman & Littlefield, 2002).

48. Kinder, "Diversity and Complexity," 406.

49. For reviews of the values literature, see Stanley Feldman, "Values, Ideology, and the Structure of Political Attitudes," in *Oxford Handbook of Political Psychology*, ed. David O. Sears, Leonie Huddy, and Robert Jervis (New York: Oxford University Press, 2003) and pp. 602–609 of Stanley Feldman, "Political Ideology," in *Oxford Handbook of Political Psychology*, 2nd ed., ed. Leonie Huddy, David O. Sears, and Jack S. Levy (Oxford: Oxford University Press, 2013).

50. Stanley Feldman, "Structure and Consistency in Public Opinion: The Role of Core Beliefs and Values," *American Journal of Political Science* 32 (1988): 416–440; Kinder and Sanders, *Divided by Color*. For an argument that other values compete with these two as core values for many Americans, see William G. Jacoby, "Is There a Culture War? Conflicting Value Structures in American Public Opinion," *American Political Science Review* 108 (2014): 754–771.

51. Feldman and Steenbergen make an interesting distinction between egalitarianism and humanitarianism; Stanley Feldman and Marco R. Steenbergen, "The Humanitarian Foundation of Public Support for Social Welfare," *American Journal of Political Science* 45 (2001): 658–677.

52. Feldman, "Structure and Consistency in Public Opinion."

53. Ibid.

54. Paul R. Brewer, "The Shifting Foundations of Public Opinion about Gay Rights," *Journal of Politics* 65 (2003): 1208–1220; Clyde Wilcox and Robin Wolpert, "Gay Rights in the Public Sphere: Public Opinion on Gay and Lesbian Equality," in *The Politics of Gay Rights,* ed. Craig A. Rimmerman, Kenneth D. Wald, and Clyde Wilcox (Chicago: University of Chicago Press, 2000); Stephen C. Craig, Michael D. Martinez, James G. Kane, and Jason Gainous, "Core Values, Value Conflict, and Citizens' Ambivalence about Gay Rights," *Political Research Quarterly* 58 (2005): 5–17.

55. Brewer, "Shifting Foundations"; Paul R. Brewer, *Value War: Public Opinion and the Politics of Gay Rights* (Lanham, MD: Rowman & Littlefield, 2008).

56. Herbert F. Weisberg, "The Structure and Effects of Moral Predispositions in Contemporary American Politics," *Journal of Politics* 67 (2005): 648.

57. Weisberg makes a distinction between moral traditionalism and moral judgment. He argues that moral judgment (that is, an evaluation of people's lifestyles) is a better predictor of attitudes on some cultural issues than moral traditionalism; Weisberg, "Structure and Effects."

58. Susan N. Gaines and James C. Garand, "Morality, Equality, or Locality: Analyzing the Determinants of Support for Same-Sex Marriage," *Political Research Quarterly* 63 (2010): 553–567.

59. John E. Mueller, *War, Presidents, and Public Opinion* (New York: John Wiley, 1973); Paul Brace and Barbara Hinckley, *Follow the Leader: Opinion Polls and the Modern Presidents* (New York: Basic Books, 1992).

60. Taeku Lee, *Mobilizing Public Opinion: Black Insurgency and Racial Attitudes in the Civil Rights Era* (Chicago: University of Chicago Press, 2002).

61. Ibid., 31; emphasis in original.

62. The Montgomery bus boycott was instigated by Rosa Parks's refusal to give up her bus seat to a white man on December 1, 1955. Some observers have characterized Parks's actions as the beginning of the modern civil rights movement; see Paula Giddings, *When and Where I Enter: The Impact of Black Women on Race and Sex in America* (New York: William Morrow, 1984). Freedom Summer refers to the events of summer 1964. During that summer, civil rights organizations registered and organized African Americans in Mississippi in the face of extreme brutality carried out by the white power structure. Bloody Sunday in Selma refers to the events of March 7, 1965. Civil rights activists were beaten mercilessly by white law enforcement officers as they attempted to march from Selma to Montgomery, Alabama.

63. Lee, *Mobilizing Public Opinion*, 127.

64. Ibid., 132.

65. Ibid., 123.

66. Ibid., 208; emphasis in original.

67. Zoltan Hajnal and Michael U. Rivera, "Immigration, Latinos, and White Partisan Politics: The New Democratic Defection," *American Journal of Political Science* 58 (2014): 773–789.

68. Ibid., 776.

69. Ibid., 786.

CHAPTER 7

1. Donald R. Kinder, "Diversity and Complexity in American Public Opinion," in *Political Science: The State of the Discipline*, ed. Ada Finifter (Washington, DC: American Political Science Association, 1983).

2. Paula D. McClain, Jessica D. Johnson Carew, Eugene Walton Jr., and Candis S. Watts, "Group Membership, Group Identity, and Group Consciousness: Measures of Racial Identity in American Politics?" *Annual Review of Political Science* 12 (2009): 473.

3. Thomas E. Nelson and Donald R. Kinder, "Issue Frames and Group-Centrism in American Public Opinion," *Journal of Politics* 58 (1996): 1055–1078.

4. See, for example, Pamela Johnston Conover, "The Role of Social Groups in Political Thinking," *British Journal of Politics* 18 (1988): 51–76; Fay Lomax Cook and Edith Barrett, *Support for the American Welfare State* (New York: Columbia University Press, 1992); James R. Kluegel and Eliot R. Smith, *Beliefs about Inequality* (New York: Aldine de Gruyter, 1986).

5. Samantha Luks and Laurel Elms, "African-American Partisanship and the Legacy of the Civil Rights Movement: Generational, Regional, and Economic Influences on Democratic Identification, 1973–1994," *Political Psychology* 26 (2005): 735–754.

6. Donald R. Kinder and Lynn M. Sanders, *Divided by Color* (Chicago: University of Chicago Press, 1996); Donald R. Kinder and Nicholas Winter, "Exploring the Racial Divide: Blacks, Whites, and Opinion on National Policy," *American Journal of Political Science* 45 (2001): 439–453.

7. Kinder and Winter demonstrate that black-white differences in egalitarianism and support for limited government explain nearly one-half of the racial gap in opinions on social welfare policies; Kinder and Winter, "Exploring the Racial Divide." They also provide further details on the principle of limited government. See also Jason Gainous, "The New 'New Racism' Thesis: Limited Government Values and Race-Conscious Policy Attitudes," *Journal of Black Studies* 43 (2012): 251–273.

8. Frank Newport, "In U.S., 87% Approve of Black-White Marriage, vs. 4% in 1958: Ninety-six Percent of Blacks, 84% of Whites Approve," Gallup, Princeton, NJ, June 25, 2013, http://www .gallup.com/poll/163697/approve-marriage-blacks-whites.aspx (accessed August 30, 2015); also

see Howard Schuman, Charlotte Steeh, Lawrence Bobo, and Maria Krysan, *Racial Attitudes in America*, rev. ed. (Cambridge, MA: Harvard University Press, 1997).

9. For a brief overview of the literature on new forms of racism, see Kinder and Sanders, *Divided by Color*, App. A, 291–294.

10. Ibid., 105–106.

11. Kinder and Sanders, *Divided by Color*.

12. Ibid., 106.

13. Ibid., 107.

14. Josh Pasek, Tobias H. Stark, Jon A. Krosnick, Trevor Tompson, and B. Keith Payne, "Attitudes Toward Blacks in the Obama Era: Changing Distributions and Impacts on Job Approval and Electoral Choice, 2008–2012," *Public Opinion Quarterly* 78 (2014): 276–302.

15. Kinder and Sanders, *Divided by Color*, 117.

16. Joshua L. Rabinowitz, David O. Sears, Jim Sidanius, and Jon A. Krosnick, "Why Do White Americans Oppose Race-Targeted Policies? Clarifying the Impact of Symbolic Racism," *Political Psychology* 30 (2009): 805–828.

17. Martin Gilens, *Why Americans Hate Welfare* (Chicago: University of Chicago Press, 1999).

18. The death penalty is another race-coded issue. See the Chapter 1 Appendix for a discussion of race and public opinion toward the death penalty.

19. Gilens, *Why Americans Hate Welfare*, 67.

20. Ibid., 81.

21. Ibid., 90.

22. For an experimental demonstration of the effect of racialized welfare images on public opinion, see James M. Avery and Mark Peffley, "Race Matters: The Impact of News Coverage of Welfare Reform on Public Opinion," in *Race and the Politics of Welfare Reform*, ed. Sanford F. Schram, Joe Soss, and Richard C. Fording (Ann Arbor: University of Michigan Press, 2003).

23. Gilens, *Why Americans Hate Welfare*, 128.

24. Rosalee A. Clawson and Rakuya Trice, "Poverty as We Know It: Media Portrayals of the Poor," *Public Opinion Quarterly* 64 (2000): 53–64; Rosalee A. Clawson, Mark Franciose, and Adam Scheidt, "The Racialized Portrayal of Poverty," paper presented at the annual meeting of the Midwest Political Science Association, Chicago, April 2007; Benjamin Floreancig and Michelle Masotto, "Race and Poverty in America Revisited: A Second Look at Media Representations of the Poor," poster presented at the annual meeting of the Midwest Political Science Association, Chicago, April 2011. See also Joshua J. Dyck and Laura S. Hussey, "The End of Welfare as We Know It? Durable Attitudes in a Changing Information Environment," *Public Opinion Quarterly* 72 (2008): 589–618, who examine the same three magazines as Gilens and find an overrepresentation of blacks between 1999 and 2004 but to a lesser extent.

25. Bas W. van Doorn, "Pre- and Post-Welfare Reform Media Portrayals of Poverty in the United States: The Continuing Importance of Race and Ethnicity," *Politics & Policy* 43 (2015): 142–162.

26. Ibid.; Dyck and Hussey, "End of Welfare."

27. Christopher D. DeSante, "Working Twice as Hard to Get Half as Far: Race, Work Ethic, and America's Deserving Poor," *American Journal of Political Science* 57 (2013): 342–356.

28. Ibid., 354.

29. Michael Tesler, "The Spillover of Racialization into Health Care: How President Obama Polarized Public Opinion by Racial Attitudes and Race," *American Journal of Political Science* 56 (2012): 690–704. Voter identification is yet another issue that has recently become race-coded. See David C. Wilson and Paul R. Brewer, "The Foundations of Public Opinion on Voter ID Laws: Political Predispositions, Racial Resentment, and Information Effects," *Public Opinion Quarterly* 77 (2013): 962–984; Antoine J. Banks and Heather M. Hicks, "Fear and Implicit Racism: Whites' Support for Voter ID Laws," *Political Psychology* (2015) doi/10.1111/pops.12292 (accessed September 8, 2015).

30. Tesler, "The Spillover of Racialization."

31. Ibid., 701; see also Antoine J. Banks, "The Public's Anger: White Racial Attitudes and Opinions Toward Health Care Reform," *Political Behavior* 36 (2014): 493–514.

32. Scott B. Blinder, "Dissonance Persists: Reproduction of Racial Attitudes among Post-Civil Rights Cohorts of White Americans," *American Politics Research* 35 (2007): 299–335.

33. Ibid., 304–305.

34. For a classic example, see Patricia Gurin, Shirley Hatchett, and James S. Jackson, *Hope and Independence* (New York: Russell Sage Foundation, 1989); for a recent review, see McClain et al., "Group Membership."

35. Patricia Gurin, "Women's Gender Consciousness," *Public Opinion Quarterly* 49 (1985): 144.

36. Note that whereas scholars tend to agree that there are several components of group consciousness, they often disagree about how many and what to label those components.

37. Michael C. Dawson, *Behind the Mule* (Princeton, NJ: Princeton University Press, 1994); Katherine Tate, *From Protest to Politics*, enlarged ed. (Cambridge, MA: Harvard University Press, 1994); Katherine Tate, "Black Opinion on the Legitimacy of Racial Redistricting and Minority-Majority Districts," *American Political Science Review* 97 (2003): 45–56. For a discussion of black feminist consciousness, see Evelyn M. Simien, *Black Feminist Voices in Politics* (Albany, NY: SUNY Press, 2006).

38. Dawson, *Behind the Mule*, 57–58.

39. Ibid., 78; Michael C. Dawson, *Black Visions: The Roots of Contemporary African-American Political Ideologies* (Chicago: University of Chicago Press, 2001), 327.

40. Michael C. Thornton, Robert Joseph Taylor, and Linda M. Chatters, "African American and Black Caribbean Mutual Feelings of Closeness: Findings from a National Probability Survey," *Journal of Black Studies* 44 (2013): 798–828.

41. Mary Herring, Thomas B. Jankowski, and Ronald E. Brown, "Pro-Black Doesn't Mean Anti-White: The Structure of African-American Group Identity," *Journal of Politics* 61 (1999): 363–386.

42. Melanye T. Price, *Dreaming Blackness: Black Nationalism and African American Public Opinion* (New York: New York University Press, 2009).

43. Ibid., 3–4.

44. Fredrick C. Harris and Brian D. McKenzie, "Unreconciled Strivings and Warring Ideals: The Complexities of Competing African-American Political Identities," *Politics, Groups, and Identities* 3 (2015): 239–254.

45. Jeffrey S. Passel, D'Vera Cohn, and Mark Hugo Lopez, "Hispanics Account for More than Half of Nation's Growth in Past Decade," Pew Hispanic Center, March 24, 2011, http://pewhispanic.org/reports/report.php?ReportID=140 (accessed August 26, 2011).

46. Renee Stepler and Anna Brown, "Statistical Portrait of Hispanics in the United States, 1980–2013," Pew Research Center, May 12, 2015, http://www.pewhispanic.org/2015/05/12/statistical-portrait-of-hispanics-in-the-united-states-1980-2013 (accessed September 5, 2015).

47. Ibid.

48. John A. Garcia, "Latino Public Opinion: Identity Politics and Policy Preferences," in *Understanding Public Opinion*, 3rd ed., ed. Barbara Norrander and Clyde Wilcox (Washington, DC: CQ Press, 2010).

49. Rodolfo O. De La Garza and Seung-Jin Jang, "Latino Public Opinion," in *The Oxford Handbook of American Public Opinion and the Media*, ed. Robert Y. Shapiro and Lawrence R. Jacobs (Oxford: Oxford University Press, 2011).

50. Ibid; Jens Manuel Krogstad, "Top Issue for Hispanics? Hint: It's Not Immigration," Pew Research Center, Washington, DC, June 2, 2014, http://www.pewresearch.org/fact-tank/2014/06/02/top-issue-for-hispanics-hint-its-not-immigration (accessed September 5, 2015).

51. Mark Hugo Lopez, Ana Gonzalez-Barrera, and Jans Manuel Krogstad, "Latino Support for Democrats Falls, but Democratic Advantage Remains: Immigration Not a Deal-Breaker Issue for Half of Latino Voters," Pew Research Center, Washington, DC, October 29, 2014, http://www.pewhispanic.org/files/2014/10/2014-10-29_NSL-latino-politics.pdf (accessed September 5, 2015).

52. Garcia, "Latino Public Opinion," 41.

53. Lopez, Gonzalez-Barrera, and Krogstad, "Latino Support for Democrats Falls."

54. Gabriel R. Sanchez, Edward D. Vargas, Hannah L. Walker, and Vickie D. Ybarra, "Stuck Between a Rock and a Hard Place: The Relationship between Latino/a's Personal Connections

to Immigrants and Issue Salience and Presidential Approval," *Politics, Groups, and Identities* 3 (2015): 454–468.

55. Lopez, Gonzalez-Barrera, and Krogstad, "Latino Support for Democrats Falls."

56. De La Garza and Jang, "Latino Public Opinion," 511–514.

57. "The Rise of Asian Americans," Pew Research Center, Washington, DC, June 19, 2012, http://www.pewsocialtrends.org/2012/06/19/the-rise-of-asian-americans (accessed August 30, 2015).

58. Jane Junn, Taeku Lee, S. Karthick Ramakrishnan, and Janelle Wong, "Asian-American Public Opinion," in *The Oxford Handbook of American Public Opinion and the Media*, ed. Robert Y. Shapiro and Lawrence R. Jacobs (Oxford: Oxford University Press, 2011).

59. Karthick Ramakrishnan, Jane Junn, Taeku Lee, and Janelle Wong, "National Asian American Survey, 2008 Codebook," http://www.icpsr.umich.edu/icpsrweb/ICPSR/studies/31481/documentation (accessed August 30, 2011).

60. Karthick Ramakrishnan and Farah Z. Ahmad, "Public Opinion," State of Asian American and Pacific Islanders Series, https://cdn.americanprogress.org/wp-content/uploads/2014/04/AAPI-PublicOpinion.pdf (accessed August 30, 2015).

61. Ramakrishnan and Ahmad, "Public Opinion."

62. Michael C. Bender, "Jeb Bush Brings Asian Immigrants Into 'Anchor Baby' Debate," Bloomberg Politics, April 24, 2015, http://www.bloomberg.com/politics/articles/2015-08-25/jeb-bush-brings-asian-immigrants-into-anchor-baby-debate (accessed September 5, 2015).

63. "Behind the Numbers: Post-Election Survey of Asian American and Pacific Islander Voters in 2012," Asian American Justice Center, Asian and Pacific Islander American Vote, and National Asian American Survey, April 2013, http://www.naasurvey.com/resources/Presentations/2012-aapipes-national.pdf (accessed August 30, 2015).

64. Ibid.

65. Janet M. Box-Steffensmeier, Suzanna De Boef, and Tse-min Lin, "The Dynamics of the Partisan Gender Gap," *American Political Science Review* 98 (2004): 515–528.

66. Leonie Huddy and Erin Cassese, "On the Complex and Varied Political Effects of Gender," in *The Oxford Handbook of American Public Opinion and the Media*, ed. Robert Y. Shapiro and Lawrence R. Jacobs (Oxford: Oxford University Press, 2011); see also "The Gender Gap: Three Decades Old, as Wide as Ever," Pew Research Center, March 29, 2012, http://www.people-press.org/2012/03/29/the-gender-gap-three-decades-old-as-wide-as-ever (accessed September 5, 2015).

67. Huddy and Cassese, "On the Complex and Varied Political Effects."

68. Richard L. Fox and Zoe M. Oxley, "Women's Support for an Active Government," in *Minority Voting in the United States*, Vol. I, ed. Kyle L. Kreider and Thomas J. Baldino (Santa Barbara, CA: Praeger, 2016).

69. Huddy and Cassese, "On the Complex and Varied Political Effects"; Virginia Sapiro and Shauna L. Shames, "The Gender Basis of Public Opinion," in *Understanding Public Opinion*, 3rd ed., ed. Barbara Norrander and Clyde Wilcox (Washington, D.C.: CQ Press, 2010).

70. "America's Global Image Remains More Positive than China's: Chapter 1. Attitudes toward the United States," Pew Research Center, July 18, 2013, http://www.pewglobal.org/2013/07/18/chapter-1-attitudes-toward-the-united-states/#drone-strikes (accessed September 5, 2015).

71. Huddy and Cassese, "On the Complex and Varied Political Effects."

72. Sapiro and Shames, "Gender Basis of Public Opinion."

73. The American National Election Studies (www.electionstudies.org), *The ANES Guide to Public Opinion and Electoral Behavior* (Ann Arbor: University of Michigan, Center for Political Studies, producer and distributor); The American National Election Studies (ANES; www.electionstudies.org), The ANES 2012 Time Series Study. Stanford University and the University of Michigan.

74. Sapiro and Shames, "Gender Basis of Public Opinion"; Huddy and Cassese, "On the Complex and Varied Political Effects."

75. Huddy and Cassese, "On the Complex and Varied Political Effects."

76. Deborah Jordan Brooks and Benjamin A. Valentino, "A War of One's Own: Understanding the Gender Gap in Support for War," *Public Opinion Quarterly* 75 (2011): 270–286.

Chapter 8

1. "What the Public Knows—In Pictures, Words, Maps and Graphs, Pew Research Center News IQ Quiz," Pew Research Center, Washington, DC, April 28, 2015, http://www.people-press .org/2015/04/28/what-the-public-knows-in-pictures-words-maps-and-graphs (accessed August 3, 2015).

2. Michael X. Delli Carpini and Scott Keeter, *What Americans Know about Politics and Why It Matters* (New Haven, CT: Yale University Press, 1996), 10.

3. Ibid., 8.

4. Samuel L. Popkin, *The Reasoning Voter* (Chicago: University of Chicago Press, 1994); Paul M. Sniderman, Richard A. Brody, and Philip E. Tetlock, *Reasoning and Choice: Explorations in Political Psychology* (New York: Cambridge University Press, 1991).

5. John A. Ferejohn, "Information and the Electoral Process," in *Information and Democratic Processes*, ed. John A. Ferejohn and James H. Kuklinski (Urbana: University of Illinois Press, 1990), Chap. 1.

6. This section draws heavily from Delli Carpini and Keeter, *What Americans Know.* Delli Carpini and Keeter provide an excellent review of the various strands of thought regarding levels of citizen knowledge.

7. Anthony Downs, *An Economic Theory of Democracy* (New York: Harper & Row, 1957).

8. Ibid., 259.

9. John A. Ferejohn and James Kuklinski, *Information and Democratic Processes* (Urbana: University of Illinois Press, 1990); Arthur Lupia and Mathew D. McCubbins, *The Democratic Dilemma* (Cambridge, UK: Cambridge University Press, 1998); Popkin, *Reasoning Voter.*

10. Susan T. Fiske and Shelley E. Taylor, *Social Cognition*, 2nd ed. (New York: McGraw-Hill, 1991); Doris A. Graber, *Processing Politics* (Chicago: University of Chicago Press, 2001).

11. Logan Dancey and Geoffrey Sheagley, "Heuristics Behaving Badly: Party Cues and Voter Knowledge," *American Journal of Political Science* 57 (2013): 312–325.

12. See John R. Hibbing and Elizabeth Theiss-Morse, *Stealth Democracy* (Cambridge, UK: Cambridge University Press, 2002).

13. Ferejohn, "Information and the Electoral Process," 3.

14. Delli Carpini and Keeter, *What Americans Know*, 10.

15. Ibid.

16. Ibid., Chap. 2.

17. Ibid., 101.

18. James H. Kuklinski et al., "Misinformation and the Currency of Democratic Citizenship," *Journal of Politics* 62 (2000): 790–816.

19. Ibid., 792–793; emphasis in original.

20. Also see Jennifer Jerit and Jason Barabas, "Bankrupt Rhetoric: How Misleading Information Affects Knowledge about Social Security," *Public Opinion Quarterly* 70 (2006): 278–303.

21. Steven Kull, Clay Ramsay, and Evan Lewis, "Misperceptions, the Media, and the Iraq War," *Political Science Quarterly* 118 (2003–2004): 569–598.

22. Kull, Ramsay, and Lewis do not provide the full text of this question in ibid., but it is available at http://www.pipa.org/OnlineReports/Iraq/IraqMedia_Oct03/IraqMedia_Oct03_rpt.pdf (accessed August 8, 2011).

23. Clay Ramsay, Steven Kull, Evan Lewis, and Stefan Subias, "Misinformation and the 2010 Election: A Study of the U.S. Electorate," WorldPublicOpinion.org, http://www.worldpublic opinion.org/pipa/pdf/dec10/Misinformation_Dec10_rpt.pdf (August 8, 2011).

24. Zoe M. Oxley, "More Sources, Better Informed Public? New Media and Political Knowledge," in *iPolitics: Citizens, Elections, and Governing in the New Media Era*, ed. Richard L. Fox and Jennifer M. Ramos (Cambridge, UK: Cambridge University Press, 2012).

25. Ibid., 19.

26. Ibid., 20–22.

27. Josh Pasek, Gaurav Sood, and Jon A. Krosnick, "Misinformed About the Affordable Care Act? Leveraging Certainty to Assess the Prevalence of Misperceptions," *Journal of Communication* 65 (2015): 660–673.

28. Ibid., 671.
29. Delli Carpini and Keeter, *What Americans Know*, 106–116.
30. Ibid.
31. Ibid., 116. But also see Bennett, who argues that citizens were slightly less informed in 1987 than they were in 1967; Stephen Earl Bennett, "Trends in Americans' Political Information, 1967–1987," *American Politics Quarterly* 17 (1989): 422–435.
32. "Public Knowledge of Current Affairs Little Changed by News and Information Revolutions," Pew Research Center Washington, DC, April 15, 2007, http://people-press.org/2007/04/15/public-knowledge-of-current-affairs-little-changed-by-news-and-information-revolutions (accessed August 8, 2011).
33. Delli Carpini and Keeter, *What Americans Know*, Chap. 4.
34. See also "Public Knowledge," 7–8.
35. Delli Carpini and Keeter, *What Americans Know*, App. 2.
36. Ibid., 147–151.
37. Lee Shaker, "Local Political Knowledge and Assessments of Political Competence," *Public Opinion Quarterly* 76 (2012): 534
38. Delli Carpini and Keeter, *What Americans Know*, 146. See also Vincent L. Hutchings, *Public Opinion and Democratic Accountability: How Citizens Learn about Politics* (Princeton, NJ: Princeton University Press, 2003).
39. "Public Knowledge," 7.
40. Markus Prior, "Political Knowledge after September 11," *PS: Political Science & Politics* 35 (2002): 523–529.
41. Kathleen Dolan, "Do Women and Men Know Different Things? Measuring Gender Differences in Political Knowledge," *Journal of Politics* 73 (2011): 97–107.
42. Jeffery J. Mondak, "Developing Valid Knowledge Scales," *American Journal of Political Science* 45 (2001): 224–238; James L. Gibson and Gregory A. Caldeira, "Knowing the Supreme Court? A Reconsideration of Public Ignorance of the High Court," *Journal of Politics* 71 (2009): 429–441.
43. Graber, *Processing Politics*.
44. Dolan, "Do Women and Men Know Different Things?" 99.
45. Also see Jason Barabas, Jennifer Jerit, William Pollock, and Carlisle Rainey, "The Question(s) of Political Knowledge," *American Political Science Review* 108 (2014): 840–855.
46. Jeffery J. Mondak and Belinda Creel Davis, "Asked and Answered: Knowledge Levels When We Will Not Take 'Don't Know' for an Answer," *Political Behavior* 23 (2001): 199–224; Mondak, "Developing Valid Knowledge Scales"; Jeffery J. Mondak and Mary R. Anderson, "The Knowledge Gap: A Reexamination of Gender-Based Differences in Political Knowledge," *Journal of Politics* 66 (2004): 492–512.
47. "Public Knowledge."
48. Graber, *Processing Politics*; Doris A. Graber, "Why Voters Fail Information Tests: Can the Hurdles Be Overcome?" *Political Communication* 11 (1994): 331–346.
49. Graber, *Processing Politics*, 7.
50. Ibid., Chap. 2.
51. Ibid., 30.
52. Ibid., Chap. 3. See also William A. Gamson, *Talking Politics* (Cambridge, UK: Cambridge University Press, 1992).
53. Graber, *Processing Politics*, 57.
54. Ibid., 56.
55. Ibid., 64.
56. Delli Carpini and Keeter, *What Americans Know*; Staci L. Rhine, Stephen Earl Bennett, and Richard S. Flickinger, "Gaps in Americans' Knowledge about the Bosnian Civil War," *American Politics Research* 29 (2001): 592–607; Bennett, "Trends in Americans' Political Information"; Jennifer Jerit, Jason Barabas, and Toby Bolsen, "Citizens, Knowledge, and the Information Environment," *American Journal of Political Science* 50 (2006): 266–282.
57. Kim L. Fridkin, Patrick J. Kenney, and Jack Crittendon, "On the Margins of Democratic Life: The Impact of Race and Ethnicity on the Political Engagement of Young People," *American Politics Research* 34 (2006): 605–626.

58. Richard G. Niemi and Jane Junn, *Civic Education: What Makes Students Learn* (New Haven, CT: Yale University Press, 1998).

59. Barabas et al., "The Question(s) of Political Knowledge."

60. Niemi and Junn, *Civic Education*, 13.

61. Delli Carpini and Keeter, *What Americans Know*, 182–184; Jerit, Barabas, and Bolsen, "Citizens, Knowledge, and the Information Environment."

62. Stephen E. Bennett, Richard S. Flickinger, and Staci L. Rhine, "Political Talk over Here, over There, over Time," *British Journal of Political Science* 30 (2000): 99–119.

63. Kevin M. Esterling, Michael A. Neblo, and David M.J. Lazer, "Means, Motive, and Opportunity in Becoming Informed about Politics: A Deliberative Field Experiment with Members of Congress and Their Constituents," *Public Opinion Quarterly* 75 (2011): 483–503.

64. Delli Carpini and Keeter, *What Americans Know*.

65. Niemi and Junn, *Civic Education*.

66. Stacy B. Gordon and Gary M. Segura, "Cross-National Variation in the Political Sophistication of Individuals: Capability or Choice?" *Journal of Politics* 59 (1997): 126–147.

67. Danny Hayes and Jennifer L. Lawless, "As Local News Goes, So Goes Citizen Engagement: Media, Knowledge, and Participation in US House Elections," *Journal of Politics* 77 (2015): 447–462.

68. Jerit, Barabas, and Bolsen, "Citizens, Knowledge, and the Information Environment."

69. Also see Rhine, Bennett, and Flickinger, "Gaps in Americans' Knowledge." These authors argue that the knowledge gap about the Bosnian civil war declined over time because television news provided significant coverage of the conflict.

70. Nancy Burns, Key Lehman Schlozman, and Sidney Verba, *The Private Roots of Public Action* (Cambridge, MA: Harvard University Press, 2001).

71. Ibid., 343.

72. Kim L. Fridkin and Patrick J. Kenney, "How the Gender of U.S. Senators Influences People's Understanding and Engagement in Politics," *Journal of Politics* 76 (2014): 1017–1031.

73. Delli Carpini and Keeter, *What Americans Know*, Chap. 6.

74. Ibid., 265.

75. Kuklinski et al., "Misinformation"; Kull, Ramsay, and Lewis, "Misperceptions, the Media, and the Iraq War."

76. Martin Gilens, "Political Ignorance and Collective Policy Preferences," *American Political Science Review* 95 (2001): 379–396.

77. Larry M. Bartels, "Uninformed Votes: Information Effects in Presidential Elections," *American Journal of Political Science* 40 (1996): 194–230.

78. Stephen Earl Bennett and Linda L. M. Bennett, "Out of Sight, Out of Mind: Americans' Knowledge of Party Control of the House of Representatives, 1960–1984," *Political Research Quarterly* 46 (1993): 67–80; Stephen Earl Bennett, Staci L. Rhine, and Richard S. Flickinger, "The Things They Cared About: Change and Continuity in Americans' Attention to Different News Stories, 1989–2002," *Harvard International Journal of Press/Politics* 9 (2004): 75–99; Delli Carpini and Keeter, *What Americans Know*.

79. The American National Election Studies (ANES; www.electionstudies.org), The ANES 2012 Time Series Study, Stanford University and the University of Michigan.

80. The American National Election Studies (www.electionstudies.org), *The ANES Guide to Public Opinion and Electoral Behavior* (Ann Arbor: University of Michigan, Center for Political Studies, producer and distributor).

81. The American National Election Studies (ANES; www.electionstudies.org), The ANES 2012 Time Series Study, Stanford University and the University of Michigan.

82. The American National Election Studies (www.electionstudies.org), *The ANES Guide to Public Opinion and Electoral Behavior* (Ann Arbor: University of Michigan, Center for Political Studies, producer and distributor).

83. Ibid.

84. Ibid; The American National Election Studies (ANES; www.electionstudies.org), The ANES 2012 Time Series Study, Stanford University and the University of Michigan.

85. Burns, Schlozman, and Verba, *Private Roots of Public Action*.

86. Lonna Rae Atkeson, "Not All Cues Are Created Equal: The Conditional Impact of Female Candidates on Political Engagement," *Journal of Politics* 65 (2003): 1040–1061.

87. David E. Campbell and Christina Wolbrecht, "See Jane Run: Women Politicians as Role Models for Adolescents," *Journal of Politics* 68 (2006): 233–247.

88. "2014 Political Polarization and Typology Survey," Pew Research Center, Washington, DC, June 26, 2014, http://www.people-press.org/files/2014/06/APPENDIX-4-Typology-Topline-for-Release.pdf (accessed August 3, 2015).

89. "1-in-10 Americans Don't Give a Hoot about Politics," Pew Research Center, Washington, DC, July 7, 2014, http://www.pewresearch.org/fact-tank/2014/07/07/1-in-10-americans-dont-give-a-hoot-about-politics (accessed July 10, 2015).

90. Ibid.

Chapter 9

1. David G. Barnum, "Decision Making in a Constitutional Democracy: Policy Formation in the Skokie Free Speech Controversy," *Journal of Politics* 44 (1982): 493.

2. James L. Gibson and Richard D. Bingham, "Skokie, Nazis, and the Elitist Theory of Democracy," *Western Political Quarterly* 37 (1984): 34.

3. John L. Sullivan, James Piereson, and George E. Marcus, "An Alternative Conceptualization of Political Tolerance: Illusory Increases 1950s–1970s," *American Political Science Review* 73 (1979): 784.

4. Samuel A. Stouffer, *Communism, Conformity, and Civil Liberties: A Cross-Section of the Nation Speaks Its Mind* (Garden City, NY: Doubleday, 1955), 54.

5. See, in particular, Alexander Hamilton, James Madison, and John Jay, *Federalist* Nos. 10 and 51, in *The Federalist Papers*, ed. Clinton Rossiter (New York: Penguin, [1787] 1961).

6. Hazel Erskine, "The Polls: Freedom of Speech," *Public Opinion Quarterly* 34 (1970): 485, 486.

7. Respectively, James W. Prothro and Charles M. Grigg, "Fundamental Principles of Democracy: Bases of Agreement and Disagreement," *Journal of Politics* 22 (1960): 282; John L. Sullivan, James Piereson, and George E. Marcus, *Political Tolerance and American Democracy* (Chicago: University of Chicago Press, 1982), 203; analysis of 1998–1999 Multi-Investigator Study, http://sda.berkeley.edu/sdaweb/analysis/?dataset=multi2.

8. Prothro and Grigg, "Fundamental Principles of Democracy"; Herbert McClosky, "Consensus and Ideology in American Politics," *American Political Science Review* 58 (1964): 361–382.

9. Erskine, "Polls," 482.

10. David G. Lawrence, "Procedural Norms and Tolerance: A Reassessment," *American Political Science Review* 70 (1976): 80–100; James L. Gibson and Richard D. Bingham, "On the Conceptualization and Measurement of Political Tolerance," *American Political Science Review* 76 (1982): 603–620.

11. Stouffer, *Communism, Conformity, and Civil Liberties*.

12. For a more detailed description of the General Social Survey, visit http://www.norc.uchicago.edu/GSS+Website.

13. Others finding increases in tolerance since the 1950s include James A. Davis, "Communism, Conformity, Cohorts, and Categories: American Tolerance in 1954 and 1972–73," *American Journal of Sociology* 81 (1975): 491–513; Lawrence, "Procedural Norms and Tolerance"; J. Allen Williams Jr., Clyde Z. Nunn, and Louis St. Peter, "Origins of Tolerance: Findings from a Replication of Stouffer's Communism, Conformity, and Civil Liberties," *Social Forces* 55 (1976): 394–408; John Mueller, "Trends in Political Tolerance," *Public Opinion Quarterly* 52 (1988): 1–25.

14. For similar conclusions regarding trends in public tolerance over time, see Thomas C. Wilson, "Trends in Tolerance toward Rightist and Leftist Groups, 1976–1988: Effects of Attitude Change and Cohort Succession," *Public Opinion Quarterly* 58 (1994): 539–556; Chelsea E. Schaffer and Greg M. Shaw, "Tolerance in the United States," *Public Opinion Quarterly* 73 (2009): 404–431.

15. See also James L. Gibson, "Measuring Political Tolerance and General Support for Pro-Civil Liberties Policies: Notes, Evidence, and Cautions," *Public Opinion Quarterly* 77 (2013 Special Issue): 45–68.

16. Sullivan, Piereson, and Marcus, "Alternative Conceptualization of Political Tolerance"; Sullivan, Piereson, and Marcus, *Political Tolerance and American Democracy*. See also John L. Sullivan and George E. Marcus, "A Note on 'Trends in Tolerance,'" *Public Opinion Quarterly* 52 (1988): 26–32; Michal Shamir and John Sullivan, "The Political Context of Tolerance: The United States and Israel," *American Political Science Review* 77 (1983): 911–928.

17. Sullivan, Piereson, and Marcus, "Alternative Conceptualization of Political Tolerance," 793.

18. James L. Gibson, "Intolerance and Political Repression in the United States: A Half Century after McCarthyism," *American Journal of Political Science* 52 (2008): 96–108.

19. See Gibson, "Measuring Political Tolerance," for a similar conclusion.

20. Sullivan, Piereson, and Marcus, *Political Tolerance and American Democracy*, 257.

21. Gibson, "Intolerance and Political Repression," 107.

22. Stouffer, *Communism, Conformity, and Civil Liberties*, Chap. 4; Prothro and Grigg, "Fundamental Principles of Democracy"; Davis, "Communism, Conformity, Cohorts"; Clyde Z. Nunn, Harry J. Crockett Jr., and J. Allen Williams Jr., *Tolerance for Nonconformity* (San Francisco: Jossey-Bass, 1978); James L. Gibson, "Alternative Measures of Political Tolerance: Must Tolerance Be 'Least-Liked'?" *American Journal of Political Science* 36 (1992): 560–577; Wilson, "Trends in Tolerance"; Ewa A. Golebiowska, "Individual Value Priorities, Education, and Political Tolerance," *Political Behavior* 17 (1995): 23–48.

23. Prothro and Grigg, "Fundamental Principles of Democracy"; Lawrence Bobo and Frederick C. Licari, "Education and Political Tolerance: Testing the Effects of Cognitive Sophistication and Target Group Affect," *Public Opinion Quarterly* 53 (1989): 285–308.

24. John L. Sullivan, George E. Marcus, Stanley Feldman, and James E. Piereson, "The Sources of Political Tolerance: A Multivariate Analysis," *American Political Science Review* 75 (1981): 92–106.

25. Prothro and Grigg, "Fundamental Principles of Democracy," 291. For a similar argument, see Lawrence, "Procedural Norms and Tolerance."

26. Nunn, Crockett, and Williams, *Tolerance for Nonconformity*, 170.

27. Bobo and Licari, "Education and Political Tolerance."

28. Stouffer, *Communism, Conformity, and Civil Liberties*; Golebiowska, "Individual Value Priorities."

29. Williams, Nunn, and St. Peter, "Origins of Tolerance."

30. Diana C. Mutz, *Hearing the Other Side: Deliberative versus Participatory Democracy* (Cambridge, UK: Cambridge University Press, 2006), Chap. 3.

31. Sullivan et al., "Sources of Political Tolerance," 103. See also Bobo and Licari, "Education and Political Tolerance"; Gibson, "Alternative Measures of Political Tolerance"; and Gibson, "Measuring Political Tolerance."

32. Gibson, "Alternative Measures of Political Tolerance"; Sullivan et al., "Sources of Political Tolerance"; Gibson, "Measuring Political Tolerance"; James L. Gibson, "Homosexuals and the Ku Klux Klan: A Contextual Analysis of Political Tolerance," *Western Political Quarterly* 40 (1987): 427–448; George Marcus, John L. Sullivan, Elizabeth Theiss-Morse, and Sandra L. Wood, *With Malice toward Some: How People Make Civil Liberties Judgments* (Cambridge, UK: Cambridge University Press, 1995); George Marcus, John L. Sullivan, Elizabeth Theiss-Morse, and Daniel Stevens, "The Emotional Foundation of Political Cognition: The Impact of Extrinsic Anxiety on the Formation of Political Tolerance Judgments," *Political Psychology* 26 (2005): 949–963.

33. Gibson, "Homosexuals and the Ku Klux Klan"; Marcus et al., *With Malice toward Some*.

34. Stouffer, *Communism, Conformity, and Civil Liberties*; Sullivan et al., "Sources of Political Tolerance"; Gibson, "Homosexuals and the Ku Klux Klan"; Gibson, "Alternative Measures of Political Tolerance"; Marcus et al., *With Malice toward Some*.

35. Ewa A. Golebiowska, "Gender Gap in Political Tolerance," *Political Behavior* 21 (1999): 43–66.

36. Mueller, "Trends in Political Tolerance."

37. Marcus et al., *With Malice toward Some*.

38. Ibid., 81.

39. Gibson, "Homosexuals and the Ku Klux Klan."

40. Patricia G. Avery, Karen Bird, John L. Sullivan, and Sandra Johnstone, "Exploring Political Tolerance with Adolescents," *Theory and Research in Social Education* 20 (1992): 386–420.

41. Ibid.; Donald P. Green et al., "Does Knowledge of Constitutional Principles Increase Support for Civil Liberties? Results from a Randomized Field Experiment," *Journal of Politics* 73 (2011): 463–476.

42. Marcus et al., *With Malice toward Some,* 123–124.

43. Ibid., 127.

44. For a complete list of types of leaders analyzed, refer to Stouffer, *Communism, Conformity, and Civil Liberties,* 17.

45. Ibid., Chap. 2.

46. Nunn, Crockett, and Williams, *Tolerance for Nonconformity*; McClosky, "Consensus and Ideology in American Politics"; David G. Barnum and John L. Sullivan, "The Elusive Foundations of Political Freedom in Britain and the United States," *Journal of Politics* 52 (1990): 719–739.

47. Robert W. Jackman, "Political Elites, Mass Publics, and Support for Democratic Principles," *Journal of Politics* 34 (1972): 753–773. For a similar conclusion, see Nunn, Crockett, and Williams, *Tolerance for Nonconformity.*

48. V. O. Key Jr., *Public Opinion and American Democracy* (New York: Alfred A. Knopf, 1961); Robert A. Dahl, *Who Governs? Democracy and Power in an American City* (New Haven, CT: Yale University Press, 1961); McClosky, "Consensus and Ideology in American Politics."

49. John L. Sullivan et al., "Why Politicians Are More Tolerant: Selective Recruitment and Socialization among Political Elites in Britain, Israel, New Zealand and the United States," *British Journal of Political Science* 23 (1993): 53.

50. Darren W. Davis, "Public Opinion, Civil Liberties, and Security in the Post-9/11 Context," in *Understanding Public Opinion,* 3rd ed., ed. Barbara Norrander and Clyde Wilcox (Washington, DC: CQ Press, 2010), 83; emphasis in original.

51. For similar conclusions, see Adam J. Berinsky, *In Time of War: Understanding American Public Opinion from World War II to Iraq* (Chicago: University of Chicago Press, 2009), Chap. 7; Brigitte L. Nacos, Yaeli Bloch-Elkon, and Robert Y. Shapiro, *Selling Fear: Counterterrorism, the Media, and Public Opinion* (Chicago: University of Chicago Press, 2011), Chap. 3; Leonie Huddy, Stanley Feldman, Charles Taber, and Gallya Lahav, "Threat, Anxiety, and Support of Antiterrorism Policies," *American Journal of Political Science* 49 (2005): 593–608.

52. Lynn M. Kuzma, "The Polls—Trends: Terrorism in the United States," *Public Opinion Quarterly* 64 (2000): 90–105.

53. Darren W. Davis and Brian D. Silver, "Civil Liberties vs. Security: Public Opinion in the Context of the Terrorist Attacks on America," *American Journal of Political Science* 48 (2004): 30.

54. Ibid., 31.

55. Clem Brooks and Jeff Manza, *Whose Rights? Counterterrorism and the Dark Side of Public Opinion* (New York: Russell Sage Foundation, 2013).

56. For other examinations of public attitudes since 9/11, see Yaeli Bloch-Elkon, "The Polls—Trends: Preventing Terrorism after the 9/11 Attacks," *Public Opinion Quarterly* 71 (2007): 142–163; Darren W. Davis, *Negative Liberty: Public Opinion and the Terrorist Attacks on America* (New York: Russell Sage Foundation, 2007); Jennifer L. Merolla and Elizabeth J. Zechmeister, *Democracy at Risk: How Terrorist Threats Affect the Public* (Chicago: University of Chicago Press, 2009).

57. Brooks and Manza, *Whose Rights,* 8.

58. Ibid., 146.

59. Ibid., 114; emphasis added.

60. See also Nacos, Bloch-Elkon, and Shapiro, *Selling Fear,* Chap. 3.

61. Brooks and Manza, *Whose Rights,* 132.

62. Randal C. Archibold, "Immigrants in Arizona May Face New Curbs," *New York Times,* April 15, 2010, sec. A.

63. Adam Liptak, "Blocking Parts of Arizona Law, Justices Allow Its Centerpiece," *New York Times,* June 25, 2012, sec. A.

64. McClosky, "Consensus and Ideology in American Politics," 376; emphasis in original.

65. Avery et al., "Exploring Political Tolerance with Adolescents," 411.

66. Garrett Epps, "What Makes Indiana's Religious-Freedom Law Different?" *The Atlantic*, March 30, 2015, http://www.theatlantic.com/politics/archive/2015/03/what-makes-indianas-religious-freedom-law-different/388997 (accessed July 20, 2015); Erik Eckholm, "Context for the Debate on 'Religious Freedom' Measures in Indiana and Arkansas," *New York Times*, March 31, 2015, http://www.nytimes.com/2015/04/01/us/politics/context-for-the-debate-on-religious-freedom-measures-in-indiana-and-arkansas.html (accessed July 20, 2015).

67. Barnum, "Decision Making in a Constitutional Democracy," 497.

68. Sullivan, Piereson, and Marcus, *Political Tolerance and American Democracy*, 9.

CHAPTER 10

1. "Women in the U.S. Congress 2015," Center for American Women and Politics, Eagleton Institute of Politics, Rutgers University, New Brunswick, NJ, 2015, http://www.cawp.rutgers.edu/women-us-congress-2015 (accessed September 6, 2015).

2. "Women in National Parliaments," Inter-Parliamentary Union, Geneva, Switzerland, 2015, http://www.ipu.org/wmn-e/classif.htm (accessed August 14, 2015).

3. Carole Kennedy, "Is the United States Ready for a Woman President? Is the Pope Protestant?" in *Anticipating Madam President*, ed. Robert P. Watson and Ann Gordon (Boulder, CO: Lynne Rienner, 2003), 133; "2004 Presidential Election," http://www.archives.gov/federal-register/electoral-college/2004/popular_vote.html (accessed July 1, 2011); "2008 Official Presidential General Election Results," http://www.fec.gov/pubrec/fe2008/2008presgeresults.pdf (accessed July 1, 2011); "Official 2012 Presidential General Election Results," http://www.fec.gov/pubrec/fe2012/2012presgeresults.pdf (accessed August 14, 2015).

4. Edward S. Greenberg and Benjamin I. Page, *America's Democratic Republic*, 2nd ed. (New York: Pearson Education, 2007), 101.

5. Lydia Saad, "Support for Nontraditional Candidates Varies by Religion," Gallup, June 24, 2015, http://www.gallup.com/poll/183791/support-nontraditional-candidates-varies-religion.aspx (accessed September 7, 2015).

6. Mariana Servín-González and Oscar Torres-Reyna, "Trends: Religion and Politics," *Public Opinion Quarterly* 63 (1999): 592–621.

7. Justin McCarthy, "In U.S., Socialist Presidential Candidates Least Appealing," Gallup, June 22, 2015, http://www.gallup.com/poll/183713/socialist-presidential-candidates-least-appealing.aspx?utm_source=Politics&utm_medium=newsfeed&utm_campaign=tiles (accessed September 7, 2015).

8. "Voters Remain in Neutral as Presidential Campaign Moves into High Gear," Pew Research Center, February 23, 2007, http://people-press.org/2007/02/23/voters-remain-in-neutral-as-presidential-campaign-moves-into-high-gear (accessed July 1, 2011).

9. B. Keith Payne et al., "Implicit and Explicit Prejudice in the 2008 American Presidential Election," *Journal of Experimental Social Psychology* 46 (2010): 367.

10. Spencer Piston, "How Explicit Racial Prejudice Hurt Obama in the 2008 Election," *Political Behavior* 32 (2010): 437.

11. Brian A. Nosek et al., "Pervasiveness and Correlates of Implicit Attitudes and Stereotypes," *European Review of Social Psychology* 18 (2007): 36–88.

12. Payne et al., "Implicit and Explicit Prejudice," 367.

13. Herbert Asher, *Polling and the Public*, 8th ed. (Washington, DC: CQ Press, 2012), 197–198.

14. Daniel J. Hopkins, "No More Wilder Effect, Never a Whitman Effect: When and Why Polls Mislead about Black and Female Candidates," *Journal of Politics* 71 (2009): 769–781.

15. Piston, "How Explicit Racial Prejudice."

16. Ibid., 444–446.

17. Gary M. Segura and Ali A. Valenzuela, "Hope, Tropes, and Dopes: Hispanic and White Racial Animus in the 2008 Election," *Presidential Studies Quarterly* 40 (2010): 497–514.

18. Payne et al., "Implicit and Explicit Prejudice."

19. Ibid.; Nathan P. Kalmoe and Spencer Piston, "Is Implicit Prejudice Against Blacks Politically Consequential? Evidence from the AMP," *Public Opinion Quarterly* 77 (2013): 305–322; Josh Pasek, Tobias H. Stark, Jon A. Krosnick, Trevor Tompson, and B. Keith Payne, "Attitudes toward Blacks in the Obama Era: Changing Distributions and Impacts on Job Approval and Electoral Choice, 2008–2012," *Public Opinion Quarterly* 78 (2014): 276–302; Tessa M. Ditonto, Richard R. Lau, and David O. Sears, "AMPing Racial Attitudes: Comparing the Power of Explicit and Implicit Measures in 2008," *Political Psychology* 34 (2013): 487–510.

20. Payne et al., "Implicit and Explicit Prejudice," 227.

21. American National Election Studies, "2008–2009 ANES Panel Study Questionnaires," August 2010, 224, http://www.electionstudies.org/studypages/2008_2009panel/anes2008_2009panel_qnaire.pdf (accessed July 5, 2011).

22. B. Keith Payne, Clara Michelle Cheng, Olesya Govorun, and Brandon D. Stewart, "An Inkblot for Attitudes: Affect Misattribution as Implicit Measurement," *Journal of Personality and Social Psychology* 89 (2005): 277–293.

23. American National Election Studies, 222–227.

24. Payne et al., "Implicit and Explicit Prejudice."

25. Pasek et al., "Attitudes toward Blacks"; Kalmoe and Piston, "Is Implicit Prejudice"; Ditonto, Lau, and Sears, "AMPing Racial Attitudes."

26. Michael S. Lewis-Beck, Charles Tien, and Richard Nadeau, "Obama's Missed Landslide: A Racial Cost?" *PS: Political Science and Politics* 43 (2010): 69–76. See also David P. Redlawsk, Caroline J. Tolbert, and William Franko, "Voters, Emotions, and Race in 2008: Obama as the First Black President," *Political Research Quarterly* 63 (2010): 875–889.

27. Pasek et al., "Attitudes toward Blacks."

28. Jennifer L. Lawless, "Women, War, and Winning Elections: Gender Stereotyping in the Post–September 11th Era," *Political Research Quarterly* 57 (2004): 479–490.

29. Kathleen Dolan, *When Does Gender Matter? Women Candidates and Gender Stereotypes in American Elections* (Oxford: Oxford University Press, 2014), Chap. 3.

30. Lawless, "Women, War, and Winning Elections," 483–487.

31. Dolan, *When Does Gender Matter?*, Chaps. 4–5.

32. Matthew J. Streb, Barbara Burrell, Brian Frederick, and Michael A. Genovese, "Social Desirability Effects and Support for a Female American President," *Public Opinion Quarterly* 72 (2008): 76–89.

33. On this distinction between principles of equality and implementation, see Howard Schuman, Charlotte Steeh, Lawrence Bobo, and Maria Krysan, *Racial Attitudes in America*, rev. ed. (Cambridge, MA: Harvard University Press, 1997).

34. Ibid., 108.

35. *Parents Involved in Community Schools v. Seattle School District No. 1 et al.,* 551 U.S. 701 (2007).

36. Gary Orfield and Chungmei Lee, "Historical Reversals, Accelerating Resegregation, and the Need for New Integration Strategies," Civil Rights Project/Proyecto Derechos Civiles, UCLA, August 2007, http://civilrightsproject.ucla.edu/research/k-12-education/integration-and-diversity/historic-reversals-accelerating-resegregation-and-the-need-for-new-integration-strategies-1/orfield-historic-reversals-accelerating.pdf (accessed July 2, 2011).

37. Ibid., 11.

38. See the research by Bobo and Kluegel, which makes a distinction between opportunity-enhancing policies and equal-outcome policies; Lawrence Bobo and James R. Kluegel, "Opposition to Race-Targeting: Self-Interest, Stratification Ideology, or Racial Attitudes?" *American Sociological Review* 58 (1993): 443–464.

39. "Trends in Political Values and Core Attitudes: 1987–2007," Pew Research Center, Washington, DC, March 22, 2007, 40, 70, http://people-press.org/2007/03/22/trends-in-political-values-and-core-attitudes-1987-2007 (accessed August 11, 2011). The question wording and context have varied over time. In 2007, the wording was the following: "As I read some programs and proposals that are being discussed in the country today, please tell me whether you strongly favor, favor, oppose, or strongly oppose each. . . . Affirmative action programs designed to help blacks, women and other minorities get better jobs and education." In 1995,

the question opened with "In order to overcome past discrimination . . ." and was not part of a list of items.

40. James Sidanius, Pam Singh, John J. Hetts, and C. Chris Federico, "It's Not the Affirmative Action, It's the African-Americans: The Continuing Relevance of Race in Attitudes toward Race-Targeted Policies," in *Racialized Politics: Values, Ideology, and Prejudice in American Public Opinion*, ed. David Sears, James Sidanius, and Lawrence Bobo (Chicago: University of Chicago Press, 2000). See also David C. Wilson, David W. Moore, Patrick F. McKay, and Derek R. Avery, "Affirmative Action Programs for Women and Minorities: Expressed Support Affected by Question Order," *Public Opinion Quarterly* 72 (2008): 514–522.

41. Bruce Drake, "Public Strongly Backs Affirmative Action Programs on Campus," Pew Research Center, April 22, 2014, http://www.pewresearch.org/fact-tank/2014/04/22/public-strongly-backs-affirmative-action-programs-on-campus (accessed September 7, 2015).

42. Analysis of American National Election Study 2012 Time Series.

43. Ta-Nehisi Coates, "The Case for Reparations," *The Atlantic*, June 2014, http://www.theatlantic.com/magazine/archive/2014/06/the-case-for-reparations/361631 (accessed September 2, 2015).

44. Philip J. Mazzocco et al., "The Cost of Being Black: White Americans' Perceptions and the Question of Reparations," *Du Bois Review: Social Science Research on Race* 3 (2006): 261–297.

45. Ibid., 286.

46. For additional research on support for gay rights, see Gary R. Hicks and Tien-tsung Lee, "Public Attitudes toward Gays and Lesbians: Trends and Predictors," *Journal of Homosexuality* 51 (2006): 57–77; Gregory M. Herek, "Gender Gaps in Public Opinion about Lesbians and Gay Men," *Public Opinion Quarterly* 66 (2002): 40–66; Gregory B. Lewis, "Black-White Differences in Attitudes toward Homosexuality and Gay Rights," *Public Opinion Quarterly* 67 (2003): 59–78; Donald P. Haider-Markel and Mark R. Joslyn, "Beliefs about the Origins of Homosexuality and Support for Gay Rights: An Empirical Test of Attribution Theory," *Public Opinion Quarterly* 72 (2008): 291–310.

47. This saying originally comes from Barry Goldwater, but it was popularized during the 2008 presidential election when then-senator Hillary Rodham Clinton used it to call for the end of the "Don't Ask, Don't Tell" policy; see Robin Toner, "For 'Don't Ask, Don't Tell,' Split on Party Lines," *New York Times*, June 8, 2007, A1.

48. *Bowers v. Hardwick*, 478 U.S. 186 (1986).

49. *Lawrence and Garner v. Texas*, 539 U.S. 558 (2003).

50. For additional data, see Paul R. Brewer and Clyde Wilcox, "Trends: Same-Sex Marriage and Civil Unions," *Public Opinion Quarterly* 69 (2005): 599–616.

51. Dawn Michelle Baunach, "Changing Same-Sex Marriage Attitudes in America from 1988 through 2010," *Public Opinion Quarterly* 76 (2012): 364–378.

52. Thomas R. Marshall, *Public Opinion and the Supreme Court* (London: Unwin Hyman, 1988).

53. Justin McCarthy, "Same-Sex Marriage Support Reaches New High at 55%," Pew Research Center, Washington, DC, May 21, 2014, http://www.gallup.com/poll/169640/sex-marriage-support-reaches-new-high.aspx (accessed August 14, 2015).

Chapter 11

1. James Bennet, "Executive Dysfunction," *The Atlantic*, January/February 2015, 12.

2. The Declaration of Independence, July 4, 1776, http://www.ushistory.org/declaration/document/index.htm (accessed August 10, 2011).

3. David Easton, *A Systems Analysis of Political Life*, with a new preface (Chicago: University of Chicago Press, 1979); Joseph S. Nye Jr., "Introduction: The Decline of Confidence in Government," in *Why People Don't Trust Government*, ed. Joseph S. Nye Jr., Philip D. Zelikow, and David C. King (Cambridge, MA: Harvard University Press, 1997); Arthur H. Miller, "Rejoinder to 'Comment' by Jack Citrin: Political Discontent or Ritualism?" *American Political Science Review* 68 (1974): 989–1001.

4. Easton, *Systems Analysis of Political Life*.

5. Ibid., 274.

6. Arthur H. Miller, Edie N. Goldenberg, and Lutz Erbring, "Type-Set Politics: Impact of Newspapers on Public Confidence," *American Political Science Review* 73 (1979): 67.
7. Miller, "Rejoinder to 'Comment' by Jack Citrin," 989.
8. Marc J. Hetherington, *Why Trust Matters: Declining Political Trust and the Demise of American Liberalism* (Princeton, NJ: Princeton University Press, 2005), 9.
9. Jack Citrin, "The Political Relevance of Trust in Government," *American Political Science Review* 68 (1974): 973–988; Marc J. Hetherington, "The Political Relevance of Political Trust," *American Political Science Review* 92 (1998): 791–808.
10. Miller, Goldenberg, and Erbring, "Type-Set Politics," 67.
11. Mark E. Warren, "Democratic Theory and Trust," in *Democracy and Trust*, ed. Mark E. Warren (Cambridge, UK: Cambridge University Press, 1999).
12. Hetherington, *Why Trust Matters*.
13. Warren, "Democratic Theory and Trust," 341.
14. Russell Hardin, "Do We Want Trust in Government?" in *Democracy and Trust*, ed. Mark E. Warren (Cambridge, UK: Cambridge University Press, 1999).
15. Hetherington, *Why Trust Matters*.
16. Originally, five questions were created; the fifth asked whether respondents believed that politicians are smart. This item is generally not analyzed by scholars examining public trust because it does not correlate very well with the other four trust items. Perhaps for this reason, the question has not appeared on an ANES survey since 1980.
17. Donald E. Stokes, "Popular Evaluations of Government: An Empirical Assessment," in *Ethics and Bigness: Scientific, Academic, Religious, Political, and Military*, ed. Harlan Cleveland and Harold D. Lasswell (New York: Harper, 1962), 64.
18. Citrin, "Political Relevance," 974.
19. M. Stephen Weatherford, "Economic 'Stagflation' and Public Support for the Political System," *British Journal of Political Science* 14 (1984): 187–205; Paul R. Abramson and Ada W. Finifter, "On the Meaning of Political Trust: New Evidence from Items Introduced in 1978," *American Journal of Political Science* 25 (1981): 297–307.
20. Hetherington, *Why Trust Matters*; Luke Keele, "Social Capital and the Dynamics of Trust in Government," *American Journal of Political Science* 51 (2007): 241–254; Marc J. Hetherington and Thomas J. Rudolph, "Priming, Performance, and the Dynamics of Political Trust," *Journal of Politics* 70 (2008): 498–512.
21. John R. Zaller, "Monica Lewinsky's Contribution to Political Science," *PS: Political Science & Politics* 31 (1998): 182–189.
22. Jane Mansbridge, "Social and Cultural Causes of Dissatisfaction with U.S. Government," in *Why People Don't Trust Government*, ed. Joseph S. Nye Jr., Philip D. Zelikow, and David C. King (Cambridge, MA: Harvard University Press, 1997).
23. Jack Citrin and Donald Philip Green, "Presidential Leadership and the Resurgence of Trust in Government," *British Journal of Political Science* 16 (1986): 450.
24. Citrin and Green, "Presidential Leadership."
25. Weatherford, "Economic 'Stagflation'"; M. Stephen Weatherford, "How Does Government Performance Influence Political Support?" *Political Behavior* 9 (1987): 5–28; Hetherington, *Why Trust Matters*. For a counterargument, see the essays in Joseph S. Nye Jr., Philip D. Zelikow, and David C. King, eds., *Why People Don't Trust Government* (Cambridge, MA: Harvard University Press, 1997).
26. Hetherington and Rudolph, "Priming, Performance," 510.
27. Hetherington, *Why Trust Matters*, Chap. 2.
28. Hetherington and Rudolph, "Priming, Performance."
29. "Distrust, Discontent, Anger and Partisan Rancor," Pew Research Center, Washington, DC, April 18, 2010, http://people-press.org/2010/04/18/distrust-discontent-anger-and-partisan-rancor (accessed August 11, 2011).
30. See, for example, Lonna Rae Atkeson and Cherie D. Maestas, *Catastrophic Politics: How Extraordinary Events Redefine Perceptions of Government* (Cambridge, UK: Cambridge University Press, 2012), Chap. 6.

31. "Trust in Government Nears Record Low, but Most Federal Agencies Are Viewed Favorably," Pew Research Center, Washington, DC, October 18, 2013, http://www.people-press .org/2013/10/18/trust-in-government-nears-record-low-but-most-federal-agencies-are-viewed-favorably (accessed July 23, 2015).

32. Ibid.

33. Vanessa Williamson, Theda Skocpol, and John Coggin, "The Tea Party and the Remaking of Republican Conservatism," *Perspectives on Politics* 9 (2011): 25–43.

34. Ibid.; "Tea Party's Image Turns More Negative," Pew Research Center, Washington, DC, October 16, 2013, http://www.people-press.org/2013/10/16/tea-partys-image-turns-more-negative (accessed July 23, 2015); Kevin Arceneaux and Stephen P. Nicholson, "Who Wants to Have a Tea Party? The Who, What, and Why of the Tea Party Movement," *PS: Political Science and Politics* 45 (2012): 700–710; Kate Zernike and Megan Thee-Brenan, "Poll Finds Tea Party Backers Wealthier and More Educated," *New York Times*, April 14, 2010, http://www.nytimes .com/2010/04/15/us/politics/15poll.html?adxnnl=1&ref=teapartymovement&adxn nlx=1313157108-np8Vr3GKFct46 xrrRpcKgA (accessed August 12, 2011).

35. Arceneaux and Nicholson, "Who Wants to Have a Tea Party?"; Brian Rathbun, "Steeped in International Affairs? The Foreign Policy Views of the Tea Party," *Foreign Policy Analysis* 9 (2013): 21–37; Daniel Tope, Justin T. Pickett, and Ted Chiricos, "Anti-Minority Attitudes and Tea Party Movement Membership," *Social Science Research* 51 (2015): 322–337.

36. Williamson, Skocpol, and Coggin, "Tea Party"; Arceneaux and Nicholson, "Who Wants to Have a Tea Party?"

37. Zernike and Thee-Brenan, "Poll Finds Tea Party Backers."

38. Arthur H. Miller, "Political Issues and Trust in Government: 1964–1970," *American Political Science Review* 68 (1974): 951–972.

39. David C. King, "The Polarization of American Parties and Mistrust of Government," in *Why People Don't Trust Government*, ed. Joseph S. Nye Jr., Philip D. Zelikow, and David C. King (Cambridge, MA: Harvard University Press, 1997).

40. Thomas E. Patterson, *Out of Order* (New York: Knopf, 1993); Joseph N. Cappella and Kathleen Hall Jamieson, *Spiral of Cynicism: The Press and the Public Good* (Oxford: Oxford University Press, 1997).

41. Miller, Goldenberg, and Erbring, "Type-Set Politics."

42. Diana C. Mutz and Byron Reeves, "The New Videomalaise: Effects of Televised Incivility on Political Trust," *American Political Science Review* 99 (2005): 1.

43. See also Diana C. Mutz, *In-Your-Face Politics: The Consequences of Uncivil Media* (Princeton, NJ: Princeton University Press, 2015), Chap. 4; Richard Forgette and Jonathan S. Morris, "High-Conflict Television News and Public Opinion," *Political Research Quarterly* 59 (2006): 447–456.

44. Jody Baumgartner and Jonathan S. Morris, "*The Daily Show* Effect: Candidate Evaluations, Efficacy, and American Youth," *American Politics Research* 34 (2006): 341–367.

45. Ibid., 348.

46. Scott Walker for America, http://scottwalker.com (accessed August 7, 2015).

47. Gary Orren, "Fall from Grace: The Public's Loss of Faith in Government," in *Why People Don't Trust Government*, ed. Joseph S. Nye Jr., Philip D. Zelikow, and David C. King (Cambridge, MA: Harvard University Press, 1997), 95.

48. Shmuel T. Lock, Robert Y. Shapiro, and Lawrence R. Jacobs, "The Impact of Political Debate on Government Trust: Reminding the Public What the Federal Government Does," *Political Behavior* 21 (1999): 244.

49. Fay Lomax Cook, Lawrence R. Jacobs, and Dukhong Kim, "Trusting What You Know: Information, Knowledge, and Confidence in Social Security," *Journal of Politics* 72 (2010): 397–412.

50. Vesla M. Weaver and Amy E. Lerman, "Political Consequences of the Carceral State," *American Political Science Review* 104 (2010): 817–833.

51. Ibid., 818.

52. Stokes, "Popular Evaluations of Government"; Orren, "Fall from Grace"; Hetherington, *Why Trust Matters*; Timothy E. Cook and Paul Gronke, "The Skeptical American: Revisiting the

Meanings of Trust in Government and Confidence in Institutions," *Journal of Politics* 67 (2005): 784–803.

53. For similar conclusions, see "Trust in Government Nears Record Low."
54. Marisa A. Abrajano and R. Michael Alvarez, "Assessing the Causes and Effects of Political Trust among U.S. Latinos," *American Politics Research* 38 (2010): 110–141.
55. Miller, "Political Issues and Trust in Government"; Weaver and Lerman, "Political Consequences of the Carceral State"; Abrajano and Alvarez, "Assessing the Causes"; Susan E. Howell and Deborah Fagan, "Race and Trust in Government: Testing the Political Reality Model," *Public Opinion Quarterly* 52 (1988): 343–350; James M. Avery, "Race, Partisanship, and Political Trust Following *Bush versus Gore* (2000)," *Political Behavior* 29 (2007): 327–342.
56. Paul R. Abramson, *Political Attitudes in America* (New York: Freeman, 1983); Shayla C. Nunnally, *Trust in Black America: Race, Discrimination, and Politics* (New York: New York University Press, 2012); Gina Yannitell Reinhardt, "Race, Trust, and Return Migration: The Political Drivers of Post-Disaster Resettlement," *Political Research Quarterly* 68 (2015): 350–362.
57. Howell and Fagan, "Race and Trust in Government"; but see Melissa Marschall and Paru R. Shah, "The Attitudinal Effects of Minority Incorporation: Examining the Racial Dimensions of Trust in Urban America," *Urban Affairs Review* 42 (2007): 629–658.
58. Nunnally, *Trust in Black America*, Chap. 7.
59. "A Year After Obama's Election: Blacks Upbeat about Black Progress, Prospects," Pew Research Center, Washington, DC, January 12, 2010, http://pewsocialtrends.org/files/2010/10/blacks-upbeat-about-black-progress-prospects.pdf (accessed July 27, 2015).
60. Jeffrey M. Jones, "In U.S., Confidence in Police Lowest in 22 Years," Gallup, June 19, 2015, http://www.gallup.com/poll/183704/confidence-police-lowest-years.aspx?utm_source=position3&utm_medium=related&utm_campaign=tiles (accessed July 27, 2015).
61. Miller, "Political Issues and Trust in Government"; Miller, "Rejoinder to 'Comment' by Jack Citrin." For similar arguments, see Stokes, "Popular Evaluations of Government"; William A. Gamson, *Power and Discontent* (Homewood, IL: Dorsey Press, 1968); Orren, "Fall from Grace."
62. Citrin, "Political Relevance," 978.
63. "Trust in Government Nears Record Low."
64. Hetherington, "Political Relevance of Political Trust." For similar conclusions, see Weatherford, "How Does Government Performance"; Orren, "Fall from Grace."
65. Hetherington, *Why Trust Matters*; Marc J. Hetherington and Jason A. Husser, "How Trust Matters: The Changing Political Relevance of Political Trust," *American Journal of Political Science* 56 (2012): 312–325.
66. Hetherington, *Why Trust Matters*, 139.
67. Hardin, "Do We Want Trust in Government?"
68. Russell J. Dalton, *Democratic Challenges, Democratic Choices: The Erosion of Political Support in Advanced Industrial Democracies* (Oxford: Oxford University Press, 2004).
69. Mark E. Warren, "Introduction," in *Democracy and Trust*, ed. Mark E. Warren (Cambridge, UK: Cambridge University Press, 1999), 8.
70. Rosalee A. Clawson, Elizabeth R. Kegler, and Eric N. Waltenburg, "The Legitimacy-Conferring Authority of the U.S. Supreme Court: An Experimental Design," *American Politics Research* 29 (2001): 566–591.
71. "General Social Surveys, 1972–2014: Cumulative Codebook," National Opinion Research Center, Chicago, March 2015, http://publicdata.norc.org:41000/gss/documents//BOOK/GSS_Codebook.pdf (accessed July 25, 2015).
72. James L. Gibson, Gregory A. Caldeira, and Lester Kenyatta Spence, "Measuring Attitudes toward the United States Supreme Court," *American Journal of Political Science* 47 (2003): 354–367.
73. John R. Hibbing and Elizabeth Theiss-Morse, *Congress as Public Enemy* (Cambridge, UK: Cambridge University Press, 1995).
74. Ibid., 45.
75. Also see Gibson, Caldeira, and Spence, "Measuring Attitudes."
76. Hibbing and Theiss-Morse, *Congress as Public Enemy*, 104.
77. "Trust in Government Nears Record Low."

78. "As Midterms Near, GOP Leads on Key Issues, Democrats Have a More Positive Image," Pew Research Center, Washington, DC, October 23, 2014, http://www.people-press.org/2014/10/23/as-midterms-near-gop-leads-on-key-issues-democrats-have-a-more-positive-image (accessed July 25, 2015).
79. Hibbing and Theiss-Morse, *Congress as Public Enemy*, 171–173.
80. Ibid., 149.
81. For more on how partisan conflict lowers public approval of Congress, see Mark D. Ramirez, "The Dynamics of Partisan Conflict on Congressional Approval," *American Journal of Political Science* 53 (2009): 681–694.
82. Hibbing and Theiss-Morse, *Congress as Public Enemy*, Chap. 5.
83. James L. Gibson and Gregory A. Caldeira, "Knowing the Supreme Court? A Reconsideration of Public Ignorance of the High Court," *Journal of Politics* 71 (2009): 429–441.
84. Jeffery J. Mondak and Shannon Ishiyama Smithey, "The Dynamics of Public Support for the Supreme Court," *Journal of Politics* 59 (1997): 1114–1142; Vanessa A. Baird and Amy Gangl, "Shattering the Myth of Legality: The Impact of the Media's Framing of Supreme Court Procedures on Perceptions of Fairness," *Political Psychology* 27 (2006): 597–614.
85. James L. Gibson and Gregory A. Caldeira, "Has Legal Realism Damaged the Legitimacy of the U.S. Supreme Court?," *Law and Society Review* 45 (2011): 195–219; Brandon L. Bartels and Christopher D. Johnston, "Political Justice? Perceptions of Politicization and Public Preferences Toward the Supreme Court Appointment Process," *Public Opinion Quarterly* 76 (2012): 105–116; Stephen P. Nicholson and Thomas G. Hansford, "Partisans in Robes: Party Cues and Public Acceptance of Supreme Court Decisions," *American Journal of Political Science* 58 (2014): 620–636.
86. Hibbing and Theiss-Morse, *Congress as Public Enemy*, 162.
87. On this point, see also John R. Hibbing and Elizabeth Theiss-Morse, *Stealth Democracy* (Cambridge, UK: Cambridge University Press, 2002).
88. Hibbing and Theiss-Morse, *Congress as Public Enemy*, 147.
89. Lyda Hanifan, "The Rural School Community Center," *Annals of the American Academy of Political and Social Science*, 67 (1916): 130, quoted in Robert D. Putnam, *Bowling Alone: The Collapse and Revival of American Community* (New York: Simon and Schuster, 2000), 19.
90. Putnam, *Bowling Alone*, 19.
91. Keele, "Social Capital," 241.
92. Kenneth Newton, "Trust, Social Capital, Civil Society, and Democracy," *International Political Science Review* 22 (2001): 201–214.
93. Emily M. Farris and Mirya R. Holman, "Social Capital and Solving the Puzzle of Black Women's Political Participation," *Politics, Groups, and Identities* 2 (2014): 331–349.
94. Putnam, *Bowling Alone*, Chaps. 16–20; Amy Caiazza and Robert D. Putnam, "Women's Status and Social Capital in the United States," *Journal of Women, Politics & Policy* 27 (2005): 69–84. For related arguments, see Sharon D. Wright Austin, *The Transformation of Plantation Politics: Black Politics, Concentrated Poverty, and Social Capital in the Mississippi Delta* (Albany, NY: SUNY Press, 2006); Marion Orr, *Black Social Capital: The Politics of School Reform in Baltimore, 1986–1998* (Lawrence: University Press of Kansas, 1999).
95. Daniel P. Aldrich, *Building Resilience: Social Capital in Post-Disaster Recovery* (Chicago: University of Chicago Press, 2012); Daniel P. Aldrich and Michelle A. Meyer, "Social Capital and Community Resilience," *American Behavioral Scientist* 59 (2015): 254–269.
96. David A. Schultz, "The Phenomenology of Democracy: Putnam, Pluralism, and Voluntary Associations," in *Social Capital: Critical Perspectives on Community and "Bowling Alone,"* ed. Scott L. McLean, David A. Schultz, and Manfred B. Steger (New York: New York University Press, 2002).
97. Putnam, *Bowling Alone*, 111–113.
98. Ibid., Chap. 9.
99. Ibid., 50–52; Robert D. Putnam, "Bowling Alone: America's Declining Social Capital," *Journal of Democracy* 6 (1995): 65–78.
100. Putnam, *Bowling Alone*, 71.
101. Ibid., 115.

102. Maryann Barakso, "Civic Engagement and Voluntary Associations: Reconsidering the Role of the Governance Structures of Advocacy Groups," *Polity* 3 (2005): 315–334.

103. Robert Wuthnow, *Sharing the Journey: Support Groups and America's New Quest for Community* (New York: Free Press, 1994); Kenneth Newton, "Social Capital and Democracy," *American Behavioral Scientist* 40 (1997): 575–586; Carl Boggs, "Social Capital as Political Fantasy," in *Social Capital: Critical Perspectives on Community and "Bowling Alone,"* ed. Scott L. McLean, David A. Schultz, and Manfred B. Steger (New York: New York University Press, 2002).

104. Putnam, *Bowling Alone*, 148–152.

105. Brian D. Mc Kenzie, "Reconsidering the Effects of Bonding Social Capital: A Closer Look at Black Civil Society Institutions in America," *Political Behavior* 30 (2008): 25–45.

106. Michael J. Shapiro, "Post-Liberal Civil Society and the Worlds of Neo-Tocquevillean Social Theory," in *Social Capital: Critical Perspectives on Community and "Bowling Alone,"* ed. Scott L. McLean, David A. Schultz, and Manfred B. Steger (New York: New York University Press, 2002), 115.

107. Thomas H. Sander and Robert D. Putnam, "Still Bowling Alone? The Post-9/11 Split," *Journal of Democracy* 21 (2010): 9–16.

108. Miki Caul Kittilson and Russell J. Dalton, "Virtual Civil Society: The New Frontier of Social Capital?," *Political Behavior* 33 (2011): 625–644.

109. Javier Sajuria et al., "Tweeting Alone? An Analysis of Bridging and Bonding Social Capital in Online Networks," *American Politics Research* 43 (2015): 708–738.

110. Putnam, *Bowling Alone*, Chap. 13; Robert Putnam, "Tuning In, Tuning Out: The Strange Disappearance of Social Capital in America," *PS: Political Science and Politics* 28 (December 1995): 664–683. See also Pippa Norris, "Does Television Erode Social Capital? A Reply to Putnam," *PS: Political Science and Politics* 29 (1996): 474–480; John Brehm and Wendy Rahn, "Individual-Level Evidence for the Causes and Consequences of Social Capital," *American Journal of Political Science* 41 (1997): 1002–1003.

111. Putnam, *Bowling Alone*, Chap. 13; Norris, "Does Television Erode Social Capital?"

112. Boggs, "Social Capital as Political Fantasy."

113. R. Claire Snyder, "Social Capital: The Politics of Race and Gender," in *Social Capital: Critical Perspectives on Community and "Bowling Alone,"* ed. Scott L. McLean, David A. Schultz, and Manfred B. Steger (New York: New York University Press, 2002).

114. Manfred B. Steger, "Robert Putnam, Social Capital and a Suspect Named Globalization," in *Social Capital: Critical Perspectives on Community and "Bowling Alone,"* ed. Scott L. McLean, David A. Schultz, and Manfred B. Steger (New York: New York University Press, 2002), 267–268.

115. Schultz, "Phenomenology of Democracy," 91.

116. Michael S. James et al., "Standard & Poor's Downgrades US Credit Rating from AAA to AA+," ABC News, August 5, 2011, http://abcnews.go.com/Business/standard-poors-downgrades-us-credit-rating-aaa-aa/story?id=14220820 (accessed August 15, 2011).

CHAPTER 12

1. "Different Faiths, Different Messages," Pew Research Center, Washington, DC, March 19, 2003, http://people-press.org/2003/03/19/different-faiths-different-messages (accessed July 20, 2011).

2. Ole R. Holsti, *Public Opinion and American Foreign Policy*, rev. ed. (Ann Arbor: University of Michigan Press, 2004), 278.

3. "President Bush Addresses the Nation," March 19, 2003, http://georgewbush-whitehouse.archives.gov/news/releases/2003/03/20030319-17.html (accessed July 20, 2011).

4. "Independents Oppose Party in Power … Again," Pew Research Center, Washington, DC, September 23, 2010, http://people-press.org/2010/09/23/independents-oppose-party-in-power-again (accessed July 20, 2011).

5. "Growing Doubts about McCain's Judgment, Age and Campaign Conduct," Pew Research Center, Washington, DC, October 21, 2008, http://people-press.org/2008/10/21/growing-doubts-about-mccains-judgment-age-and-campaign-conduct (accessed July 20, 2011).

6. "President's Address to the Nation," January 10, 2007, http://georgewbush-whitehouse .archives.gov/news/releases/2007/01/20070110-7.html (accessed July 20, 2011).

7. "Broad Opposition to Bush's Iraq Plan," Pew Research Center, Washington, DC, January 16, 2007, http://people-press.org/2007/01/16/broad-opposition-to-bushs-iraq-plan (accessed July 20, 2011).

8. "Remarks of President Barack Obama—Responsibly Ending the War in Iraq," February 27, 2009, http://www.whitehouse.gov/the-press-office/remarks-president-barack-obama-ndash-responsibly-ending-war-iraq (accessed July 21, 2011).

9. AP-GfK Poll, http://pollingreport.com/iraq.htm (accessed July 21, 2011).

10. "Iran Nuclear Agreement Meets with Public Skepticism," Pew Research Center, July 21, 2015, http://www.people-press.org/2015/07/21/iran-nuclear-agreement-meets-with-public-skepticism (accessed August 9, 2015).

11. Ibid.

12. CNN-ORC poll, http://www.pollingreport.com/iran.htm (accessed August 9, 2015).

13. Benjamin I. Page with Marshall M. Bouton, *The Foreign Policy Disconnect: What Americans Want from Our Leaders but Don't Get* (Chicago: University of Chicago Press, 2006), Chap. 4.

14. "Remarks by the President on the Iran Nuclear Deal," August 5, 2015, https://www.whitehouse .gov/the-press-office/2015/08/05/remarks-president-iran-nuclear-deal (accessed August 9, 2015).

15. For a description of this and other mechanisms linking opinion and policy, see Alan D. Monroe and Paul J. Gardner Jr., "Public Policy Linkages," in *Research in Micropolitics*, Vol. 2, ed. Samuel Long (Greenwich, CT: JAI Press, 1987).

16. David S. Broder, "A Mob-Rule Moment," *Washington Post*, July 5, 2007.

17. Paul Burstein, "The Impact of Public Opinion on Public Policy: A Review and an Agenda," *Political Research Quarterly* 56 (2003): 29.

18. See, for example, Frank R. Baumgartner, Suzanna L. De Boef, and Amber E. Boydstun, *The Decline of the Death Penalty and the Discovery of Innocence* (Cambridge, UK: Cambridge University Press, 2008); Jeffrey R. Lax and Justin H. Phillips, "Gay Rights in the States: Public Opinion and Policy Responsiveness," *American Political Science Review* 103 (2009): 367–386; Bruce Russett, *Controlling the Sword: The Democratic Governance of National Security* (Cambridge, MA: Harvard University Press, 1990).

19. Benjamin I. Page and Robert Y. Shapiro, "Effects of Public Opinion on Policy," *American Political Science Review* 77 (1983): 175–190.

20. Alan D. Monroe, "Consistency between Public Preferences and National Policy Decisions," *American Politics Quarterly* 7 (1979): 3–18; Alan D. Monroe, "Public Opinion and Public Policy, 1980–1993," *Public Opinion Quarterly* 62 (1998): 6–28.

21. See also Martin Gilens, "Inequality and Democratic Responsiveness," *Public Opinion Quarterly* 69 (2005): 778–796.

22. James A. Stimson, Michael B. MacKuen, and Robert S. Erikson, "Opinion and Policy: A Global View," *PS: Political Science and Politics* 27 (1994): 29–35.

23. James A. Stimson, *Public Opinion in America: Moods, Cycles, and Swings* (Boulder, CO: Westview Press, 1991); Robert H. Durr, "What Moves Policy Sentiment?" *American Political Science Review* 87 (1993): 158–170.

24. James A. Stimson, Michael B. MacKuen, and Robert S. Erikson, "Dynamic Representation," *American Political Science Review* 89 (1995): 548.

25. Robert S. Erikson, Michael B. MacKuen, and James A. Stimson, *The Macro Polity* (Cambridge, UK: Cambridge University Press, 2002), Chap. 9; Stimson, MacKuen, and Erikson, "Dynamic Representation."

26. Stuart N. Soroka and Christopher Wlezien, *Degrees of Democracy: Politics, Public Opinion, and Policy* (Cambridge, UK: Cambridge University Press, 2010), Chap. 7.

27. See also Burstein, "Impact of Public Opinion"; Robert Y. Shapiro, "Public Opinion and American Democracy," *Public Opinion Quarterly* 75 (2011): 982–1017.

28. Robert S. Erikson, Gerald C. Wright, and John P. McIver, *Statehouse Democracy: Public Opinion and Policy in the American States* (Cambridge, UK: Cambridge University Press, 1993); Elizabeth Rigby and Robert S. Erikson, "Whose Statehouse Democracy? Policy Responsiveness to Poor versus Rich Constituents in Poor versus Rich States," in *Who Gets Represented?*,

ed. Peter K. Enns and Christopher Wlezien (New York: Russell Sage Foundation, 2011). For a more qualified assessment, see Jeffrey R. Lax and Justin H. Phillips, "The Democratic Deficit in the States," *American Journal of Political Science* 56 (2012): 148–166.

29. Page and Shapiro, "Effects of Public Opinion on Policy"; Soroka and Wlezien, *Degrees of Democracy*; Monroe, "Consistency"; Burstein, "Impact of Public Opinion"; Paul Burstein, "Why Estimates of the Impact of Public Opinion on Public Policy Are Too High: Empirical and Theoretical Implications," *Social Forces* 84 (2006): 2273–2289.

30. Donald J. Devine, *The Attentive Public: Polyarchical Democracy* (Chicago: Rand McNally, 1970).

31. Vincent L. Hutchings, *Public Opinion and Democratic Accountability* (Princeton, NJ: Princeton University Press, 2003).

32. V. O. Key Jr., *Public Opinion and American Democracy* (New York: Alfred A. Knopf, 1961), Chap. 21; R. Douglas Arnold, *The Logic of Congressional Action* (New Haven, CT: Yale University Press, 1990); John R. Zaller, "Coming to Grips with V. O. Key's Concept of Latent Opinion," in *Electoral Democracy*, ed. Michael B. MacKuen and George Rabinowitz (Ann Arbor: University of Michigan Press, 2003).

33. Paul Burstein, *American Public Opinion, Advocacy, and Policy in Congress: What the Public Wants and What It Gets* (Cambridge, UK: Cambridge University Press, 2014).

34. Ibid., Chap. 3.

35. For a similar argument, see Benjamin I. Page, "The Semi-Sovereign Public," in *Navigating Public Opinion: Polls, Policy, and the Future of American Democracy*, ed. Jeff Manza, Fay Lomax Cook, and Benjamin I. Page (Oxford: Oxford University Press, 2002).

36. Martin Gilens, *Affluence and Influence: Economic Inequality and Political Power in America* (Princeton, NJ: Princeton University Press, 2012); Martin Gilens, "Policy Consequences of Representational Inequality," in *Who Gets Represented?* ed. Peter K. Enns and Christopher Wlezien (New York: Russell Sage Foundation, 2011); Larry Bartels, *Unequal Democracy: The Political Economy of the New Gilded Age* (Princeton, NJ: Princeton University Press, 2008); James N. Druckman and Lawrence R. Jacobs, "Segmented Representation: The Reagan White House and Disproportionate Responsiveness," in *Who Gets Represented?* ed. Peter K. Enns and Christopher Wlezien (New York: Russell Sage Foundation, 2011).

37. Rigby and Erikson, "Whose Statehouse Democracy?" See also Elizabeth Rigby and Gerald C. Wright, "Political Parties and Representation of the Poor in the American States," *American Journal of Political Science* 57 (2013): 552–565.

38. Gilens, *Affluence and Influence*, Chap. 2.

39. Ibid., Chap. 3.

40. Ibid., 83.

41. Martin Gilens and Benjamin I. Page, "Testing Theories of American Politics: Elites, Interest Groups, and Average Citizens," *Perspectives on Politics* 12 (2014): 564–581.

42. Page with Bouton, *Foreign Policy Disconnect*, 223.

43. John G. Geer, *From Tea Leaves to Opinion Polls: A Theory of Democratic Leadership* (New York: Columbia University Press, 1996), Chap. 2; Robert M. Eisinger, *The Evolution of Presidential Polling* (New York: Cambridge University Press, 2003).

44. Eisinger, *Evolution of Presidential Polling*; Lawrence R. Jacobs, "The Recoil Effect: Public Opinion and Policymaking in the U.S. and Britain," *Comparative Politics* 24 (1992): 199–217.

45. Jacobs, "Recoil Effect," 210.

46. Geer, *From Tea Leaves to Opinion Polls*, Chap. 2.

47. Eisinger, *Evolution of Presidential Polling*; Lawrence R. Jacobs and Robert Y. Shapiro, "The Rise of Presidential Polling: The Nixon White House in Historical Perspective," *Public Opinion Quarterly* 59 (1995): 163–195.

48. Kathryn Dunn Tenpas and James A. McCann, "Testing the Permanence of the Permanent Campaign: An Analysis of Presidential Polling Expenditures, 1977–2002," *Public Opinion Quarterly* 71 (2007): 349–366.

49. Ibid.; Shoon Kathleen Murray and Peter Howard, "Variation in White House Polling Operations: Carter to Clinton," *Public Opinion Quarterly* 66 (2002): 527–558.

50. Tenpas and McCann, "Testing the Permanence"; Murray and Howard, "Variation in White House Polling Operations." For a comparison of polling in the Reagan, Clinton, and George

W. Bush White Houses, see Diane Heith, *Polling to Govern: Public Opinion and Presidential Leadership* (Palo Alto, CA: Stanford University Press, 2003), Chap. 8.

51. Heith, *Polling to Govern*, Chap. 3.

52. James N. Druckman and Lawrence R. Jacobs, "Lumpers and Splitters: The Public Opinion Information That Politicians Collect and Use," *Public Opinion Quarterly* 70 (2006): 453–476.

53. Heith, *Polling to Govern*, 44–45.

54. Druckman and Jacobs, "Segmented Representation."

55. Susan Herbst, *Reading Public Opinion: How Political Actors View the Democratic Process* (Chicago: University of Chicago Press, 1998), Chap. 2.

56. Eisinger, *Evolution of Presidential Polling*, 188–190.

57. Herbst, *Reading Public Opinion*, Chap. 2.

58. Ibid., 53, 54.

59. James N. Druckman and Lawrence R. Jacobs, *Who Governs? Presidents, Public Opinion, and Manipulation* (Chicago: University of Chicago Press, 2015).

60. Ibid., Chaps. 5–6.

61. Ibid., 101.

62. Quoted in ibid., 78.

63. Ibid., 119, emphasis in original.

64. Lawrence R. Jacobs and Robert Y. Shapiro, *Politicians Don't Pander: Political Manipulation and the Loss of Democratic Responsiveness* (Chicago: University of Chicago Press, 2000).

65. Ibid., 48.

66. Ibid., Chap. 3.

67. Ibid., 108; emphasis in original.

68. Ibid., 106–112.

69. Ibid., Chap. 4.

70. Hilary Stout, "Many Don't Realize It's Clinton's Plan They Like," *Wall Street Journal*, March 10, 1994.

71. Druckman and Jacobs, *Who Governs?*, 127, emphasis in original.

72. Robert Y. Shapiro and Lawrence Jacobs, "Simulating Representation: Elite Mobilization and Political Power in Health Care Reform," *The Forum* 8, no. 1 (2010): Article 4.

73. Ibid., 9.

74. Shoon Kathleen Murray, "Private Polls and Presidential Policymaking: Reagan as a Facilitator of Change," *Public Opinion Quarterly* 70 (2006): 477–498; Druckman and Jacobs, "Lumpers and Splitters"; Druckman and Jacobs, "Segmented Representation."

75. Jacobs, "Recoil Effect"; Geer, *From Tea Leaves to Opinion Polls*; Heith, *Polling to Govern*.

76. Jacobs and Shapiro, *Politicians Don't Pander*, 147–148.

77. Brandice Canes-Wrone, *Who Leads Whom? Presidents, Policy, and the Public* (Chicago: University of Chicago Press, 2006); Jacobs and Shapiro, *Politicians Don't Pander*, Chap. 9.

78. For overviews of this topic, see Holsti, *Public Opinion and American Foreign Policy*, Chap. 1; Page with Bouton, *Foreign Policy Disconnect*, 219–223.

79. Page, "Semi-Sovereign Public," 337.

80. "Iraq Trip Sways Congressman against Pullout," *All Things Considered*, National Public Radio, August 21, 2007.

81. Page and Shapiro, "Effects of Public Opinion on Policy"; Burstein, "Impact of Public Opinion."

82. Monroe, "Consistency"; Monroe, "Public Opinion and Public Policy."

83. Larry M. Bartels, "Constituency Opinion and Congressional Policy Making: The Reagan Defense Buildup," *American Political Science Review* 85 (1991): 457–474; Thomas Hartley and Bruce Russett, "Public Opinion and the Common Defense: Who Governs Military Spending in the United States?" *American Political Science Review* 86 (1992): 905–915; Richard Sobel, *The Impact of Public Opinion on U.S. Foreign Policy since Vietnam: Constraining the Colossus* (New York: Oxford University Press, 2001); Holsti, *Public Opinion and American Foreign Policy*.

84. Robert Y. Shapiro and Lawrence R. Jacobs, "Public Opinion, Foreign Policy, and Democracy: How Presidents Use Public Opinion," in *Navigating Public Opinion: Polls, Policy, and the*

Future of American Democracy, ed. Jeff Manza, Fay Lomax Cook, and Benjamin I. Page (Oxford: Oxford University Press, 2002).

85. Brandon Rottinghaus, "Following the 'Mail Hawks': Alternative Measures of Public Opinion on Vietnam in the Johnson White House," *Public Opinion Quarterly* 71 (2007): 367–391.

86. The original finding was presented in Page and Shapiro, "Effects of Public Opinion on Policy."

87. Lawrence R. Jacobs and Benjamin I. Page, "Who Influences U.S. Foreign Policy?" *American Political Science Review* 99 (2005): 107–123.

88. Ibid., 110.

89. Ibid., 120. For a similar conclusion, see G. William Domhoff, "The Power Elite, Public Policy, and Public Opinion," in *Navigating Public Opinion: Polls, Policy, and the Future of American Democracy*, ed. Jeff Manza, Fay Lomax Cook, and Benjamin I. Page (Oxford: Oxford University Press, 2002).

90. Page with Bouton, *Foreign Policy Disconnect*.

91. Ibid., Chap. 2.

92. "United in Goals, Divided on Means: Opinion Leaders Chicago Council Survey Results 2014," Chicago Council on Global Affairs, June 2, 2015, http://www.thechicagocouncil.org/publication/united-goals-divided-means (accessed August 9, 2015).

93. Page with Bouton, *Foreign Policy Disconnect*, Chaps. 4–5.

94. Ibid., 109.

95. Ibid., Chap. 7.

96. "Public Sees U.S. Power Declining as Support for Global Engagement Slips," Pew Research Center, December 3, 2013, http://www.people-press.org/2013/12/03/public-sees-u-s-power-declining-as-support-for-global-engagement-slips (accessed August 9, 2015).

97. Page with Bouton, *Foreign Policy Disconnect*, 215.

98. E. E. Schattschneider, *The Semi-Sovereign People: A Realist's View of Democracy in America* (New York: Holt, Rinehart and Winston, 1960); Page, "Semi-Sovereign Public."

CHAPTER 13

1. Dennis Chong and James N. Druckman, "Framing Theory," *Annual Review of Political Science* 10 (2007): 120.

Glossary

Acceptance. Stage in the political persuasion process during which people decide they agree with the content of a persuasive argument. (Chapter 4)

Accessibility model. Model of opinion formation that says that easily accessible concepts (due, for example, to media coverage) influence people's political judgments. (Chapter 3)

Accuracy. A news norm that calls for journalists to provide correct information, often achieved by relying on official sources. (Chapter 3)

Activated mass opinion. Beliefs that are salient to citizens and lead them to be politically active. (Chapter 6)

Activation effect. Effect that occurs when political communication encourages citizens to support presidential candidates who share their preexisting values and predispositions. (Chapter 3)

Adolescent socialization. Development of political attitudes during the teenage years. (Chapter 2)

Adult socialization. Development of political attitudes during adulthood. (Chapter 2)

Advocacy journalism. A form of journalism that is committed to only some of the news norms because it is also concerned with providing news from a particular perspective. (Chapter 3)

Affect misattribution procedure. Research technique used to determine whether people mistakenly apply their affective reactions to one object (such as a black or white face) to a different object; an assessment of implicit prejudice. (Chapter 10)

Affective polarization. Negative feelings or hostility toward political opponents coupled with warm feelings toward political allies. (Chapter 5)

Agenda-setting effects. Effects that occur when the media influence which issues citizens view as important. (Chapter 3)

Aggregate studies. Examinations of more than one political event or topic, such as analyzing policymaking in many issue domains across multiple years. (Chapter 12)

Archival research. A type of research method that entails reading and interpreting documents from historical collections. (Chapter 12)

Atheists. People who oppose churches or formal religion. (Chapter 9)

Attention to politics. The degree to which citizens follow politics and political events. (Chapter 8)

Attitude. Positive or negative evaluation of an object (such as a person or issue). (Chapter 1)

Attitude change. Degree to which political opinions fluctuate over time. (Chapter 4)

Attitude constraint. Situation that exists when political opinions are related to one another; degree to which researchers can predict a person's opinion toward a political object when knowing his or her opinions toward other objects. (Chapter 5)

Attitude importance. Degree to which a specific attitude is personally meaningful or relevant. (Chapter 1)

Attitude instability. Degree to which political opinions change over time. (Chapter 4)

Attitude stability. Degree to which political opinions remain the same over time. (Chapters 2, 4, 5)

Attitudes toward affirmative action. Opinions regarding a variety of policies that ensure equal treatment of minorities and whites in education and employment. (Chapter 10)

Attitudes toward gay and lesbian rights. Opinions regarding rights (such as employment policies and intimate relationships) for gays and lesbians. (Chapter 10)

Attitudes toward groups. Opinions toward important social and political groups that shape political attitudes. (Chapter 7)

Attitudes toward institutional members. Attitudes toward members of Congress, the president, and Supreme Court justices. (Chapter 11)

Attitudes toward the institutions of government. Attitudes toward the Congress, presidency, and Supreme Court. (Chapter 11)

Attitudes toward reparations. Opinions regarding remedial policies that would address the harmful effects of slavery on Americans living today. (Chapter 10)

Attitudes toward same-sex marriage. Opinions regarding same-sex marriage. (Chapter 10)

Attitudes toward school integration. Opinions regarding black and white students attending the same schools. (Chapter 10)

Attrition. Drop-off in the number of respondents in a panel study. (Appendix)

Authoritarians. People who have a predisposition to value sameness and conformity to group norms; people who prefer order and rely on authorities to provide that order. (Chapter 6)

Balanced question. Survey question that provides two points of view (such as support and opposition). (Appendix)

Belief system. Set of related, coherent political attitudes; attitudes are related because they derive from overarching worldview (such as political ideology). (Chapter 5)

Beliefs. Thoughts or information regarding an attitude object, often concerning what a person thinks is true about the object. (Chapter 1)

Benevolent leader imagery. Viewing political leaders in very positive terms, believing that leaders do good deeds. (Chapter 2)

Big Five. The core personality traits of openness to experience, conscientiousness, agreeableness, extraversion, and emotional stability. (Chapter 6)

Bill of Rights. The first ten amendments to the U.S. Constitution. (Chapter 9)

Black nationalism. An identity or ideology based on support for black self-determination, support for black economic and social independence, distance from whites and white supremacy, and support for a global black community. (Chapter 7)

Black political ideology. Political belief system present among African Americans; specific views often include group-based perspectives, such as beliefs regarding the status of blacks in society. (Chapter 5)

Black utility heuristic. Among black citizens, use of racial group interests as a cue to determine an individual's own issue opinions and party preferences. (Chapter 7)

Bradley effect. Tendency in the past for black candidates to receive more support in preelection polls than on Election Day; named for Tom Bradley, black candidate for California's governor in 1982. (Chapter 10)

Bystanders. Citizens who are not registered to vote and who essentially pay no attention to politics. (Chapter 8)

Case study. An in-depth analysis of a specific political event or arena, such as the passage of a piece of legislation or policymaking surrounding one issue. (Chapter 12)

Central route to persuasion. Process by which attitudes can change when a person is motivated and able to carefully consider persuasive communication; any resulting attitude change is likely to endure. (Chapter 4)

Changes in public expectations of government. Changes in what people think the government should do when new problems that the government is ill equipped to handle are forced onto the government's agenda. (Chapter 11)

Chapter-based civic associations. Community-based organizations whose members meet regularly, such as parent-teacher associations, the American Legion, and the Jaycees. (Chapter 11)

Childhood socialization. Development of political attitudes that happens before adolescence. (Chapter 2)

Citizen apathy. Lack of interest or involvement in political matters. (Chapter 1)

Civic education. Education about government and politics in schools. (Chapter 8)

Civic engagement. Actions by individuals and collectives to identify and address public issues. (Chapter 11)

Civil liberties. Rights granted to citizens that are protected from government suppression, such as freedom of speech or freedom of religion. (Chapter 9)

Civil rights. Government guarantees of political equality for people. (Chapter 10)

Classical models of democracy. Theories based on ancient Athenian democracy; key characteristics include active citizen participation in political debates and decisions. (Chapter 1)

Closed-ended questions. Survey questions with a limited set of response options. (Appendix)

Cognitive dissonance theory. Approach to understanding attitudes that posits that people prefer to maintain consistency across their beliefs, attitudes, and attitude-relevant behaviors and that, when inconsistencies arise, people will work to regain consistency. (Chapter 4)

Collective public opinion. Political attitudes of an aggregation of people, such as all citizens of a nation. (Chapter 4)

Communists. People who favor communism as a system of government, particularly wanting a society without the evils of capitalism so that people can fully benefit from their own labor. (Chapter 9)

Compassion issues. Social welfare policies that help others, such as programs that aid children, the elderly, or the poor. (Chapter 7)

Concentrated. The quality of the U.S. mass media that a few large companies own the majority of the media. (Chapter 3)

Confidence in Congress. Faith in the people running Congress. (Chapter 11)

Confidence in the executive branch. Faith in the people running the executive branch of the federal government. (Chapter 11)

Confidence in the Supreme Court. Faith in the people running the Supreme Court. (Chapter 11)

Conglomerate. The quality of the U.S. mass media that large corporations own several media companies as well as nonmedia companies. (Chapter 3)

Consensual politics. Context during which disagreements between the major political parties are relatively minor and the political environment is not dominated by discussion of conflictual issues. (Chapter 5)

Conservatives. People whose political ideology emphasizes order, tradition, individual responsibility, and minimal government intervention in economic matters. (Chapter 5)

Considerations. Pieces of information or reasons held by individuals that cause them to support or oppose a political issue. (Chapter 4)

Constitutional framework. Formal system of government, as enshrined in the Constitution. (Chapter 9)

Content analysis. Research technique used to examine the content of communication. (Appendix)

Context. Broader environment, potentially including the features of a person's community or nation, or events occurring in other nations. (Chapter 9)

Convenience sample. A sample whose respondents are selected in a way that is easy for the researcher, such as by asking for volunteers. (Appendix)

Conversion effect. Effect that occurs when political communication leads citizens to change from one candidate to another. (Chapter 3)

Corporate. The quality of the U.S. mass media that most media outlets have the primary goal of making money. (Chapter 3)

Counterterrorism policies. Government actions that are intended to combat terrorism. (Chapter 9)

Crafted talk. Rhetoric and messages that officials communicate to the citizenry in an attempt to influence public opinion. (Chapter 12)

Cross-sectional study. Method for assessing political opinions by examining a sample of individuals at one time. (Chapter 4)

Cynicism. A lack of trust in government that stems from the belief that government is not functioning well. (Chapter 11)

Democratic elitists. Democratic theorists who view competitive elections as the primary mechanism by which citizen preferences are expressed and who also believe that governmental decisions are better made by political elites than the public. (Chapter 1)

Democratic responsiveness. Result that occurs when political leaders enact public policy that coincides with the genuine opinions of the public. (Chapter 12)

Democratic theory. Field of study that focuses on defining the proper characteristics, often normative, of a democracy. (Chapter 1)

Diffuse support. Public opinions about the political system, such as contentment with the form of government and attachment to the norms and structure of the regime. (Chapter 11)

Direct democracy. Governmental system whereby citizens meet, discuss, and decide on the content of the laws. (Chapter 1)

Economic inequalities. Differences in economic status among groups of citizens, such as those earning high versus low incomes. (Chapter 12)

Efficacy. Belief that citizens can influence the decisions of government officials and that officials are responsive to the public. (Chapter 2)

Egalitarianism. Belief that people are equal and should be treated the same regardless of their personal characteristics. (Chapters 6, 7)

Ego defense. Theory that people have specific attitudes because the attitudes protect their egos or images of themselves from outside threats. (Chapter 4)

Elaboration likelihood. Approach for understanding persuasion that focuses on the degree to which people generate cognitive responses to persuasive communication. (Chapter 4)

Elite discourse. Discussion of political topics (such as issues or candidates) by leaders that is communicated to the public. (Chapter 4)

Emotions. Feelings about or affect regarding an attitude object. (Chapter 1)

Empirical analyses. Examinations that focus on accurately describing and/or explaining real-life phenomena. (Chapter 1)

Enemy combatants. Government designation used to classify those people suspected of threatening national security or waging war against the nation. (Chapter 9)

Ethnographic research. Method for assessing political attitudes and behaviors in which researchers immerse themselves in a setting or community, observing individuals, asking them questions, and more generally interacting with them. (Chapter 5)

Expectations gap. The difference between what the public expects the president to accomplish and how the president actually performs in office. (Chapter 4)

Experiment. A type of research design that has two key characteristics: (1) the experimenter manipulates a feature of the study, and (2) subjects are randomly assigned to experimental conditions. (Appendix)

Explicit prejudice. Consciously expressed prejudice. (Chapter 10)

Exposure to diversity. Degree to which individuals are in contact with people who are different, particularly people who hold different political views from their own. (Chapter 9)

External validity. The characteristic of a study that the findings can be generalized beyond the sample and context used in that study. (Appendix)

Extremity. Degree to which support or opposition toward an attitude object is strong or slight. (Chapter 1)

Factions. Groups of citizens who pursue their self-interest rather than advocating for the common good of the community or nation. (Chapter 1)

Family politicization. Degree to which parents participate in politics and family members discuss politics with each other. (Chapter 2)

Financial costs of war. Monetary expenses of engaging in a war. (Chapter 4)

Focus groups. A type of research method for assessing political attitudes in which citizens are brought together in a group and asked what they think about political topics using open-ended questions. (Appendix, Chapter 8)

Formal education. Years of educational attainment in an institution (such as a school or university). (Chapter 9)

Forum for diverse views. Place where a range of political opinions is provided. (Chapter 3)

Framing effects. Effects that occur when media frames influence public opinion on an issue. (Chapter 3)

Functional theories. Approach for understanding the development of attitudes by focusing on the motivations people have for holding specific attitudes; examples of these motivations include knowledge and ego defense. (Chapter 4)

Gender gap in party identification. Differences between men and women in party identification; studies show there is a tendency for women to be more likely than men to identify with the Democratic Party. (Chapter 7)

Gender gap in political knowledge. Differences between men and women in knowledge of politics; studies commonly show that men are more knowledgeable about politics than women. (Chapter 8)

Gender stereotypes. Beliefs about males as a group and females as a group that citizens apply to individual men or individual women. (Chapter 10)

Generalist. Someone who is knowledgeable about all political topics. (Chapter 8)

Generational effect. Changes in political attitudes to an entire age cohort, caused by events or features of the political context. (Chapter 2)

Genetic inheritance. Transmission of traits, opinions, and so forth from parents to offspring via genes. (Chapter 2)

Group consciousness. An awareness of how membership in a particular group shapes the life chances of individuals. (Chapter 7)

Group membership. Using personal characteristics to assign a person to a social or demographic group, such as one based on gender or race. (Chapter 7)

Hard news. News regarding political leaders, important issues, and significant events. (Chapter 3)

Heuristics. Mental shortcuts used for processing and understanding information; for example, a person relying on the ideology of the sponsor of a new policy to determine his or her own opinion toward the policy. (Chapter 8)

Historical events. Important political events that shape public opinion. (Chapter 6)

Homosexuals. Individuals who have intimate relationships with people of their same sex. (Chapter 9)

Honeymoon period. Time early in a president's term when public approval tends to be higher. (Chapter 4)

Horse race. Discussing political campaigns in terms of which candidates are leading, gaining momentum, or falling behind. (Chapter 3)

Hypodermic model. Perspective that views the media as quite persuasive and citizens as unable to resist media messages. (Chapter 3)

Ideologically contentious. Quality of politics characterized by salient political actors (such as members of political parties) disagreeing over the key issues of the day, particularly when the disagreements fall along ideological lines. (Chapter 5)

Ideology. Conservatism or liberalism; overarching set of beliefs regarding the proper role of government in society, in regulating the economy, and in individuals' lives. (Chapters 2, 5)

Implementation. Translating abstract policies into practice. (Chapter 10)

Implicit prejudice. Unintentional, nonconscious prejudice. (Chapter 10)

Importance model. Model of opinion formation that says that important concepts are weighted more heavily in citizens' minds (for example, due to media coverage) and then influence people's political judgments. (Chapter 3)

Impressionable years model. Perspective that views political attitudes as changing during late adolescence and early adulthood and then remaining more stable throughout the rest of the life span. (Chapter 2)

In-depth interviewing. A type of research method for assessing political attitudes by asking respondents open-ended questions and allowing respondents to answer however they wish and in as much detail as they want to provide. (Appendix, Chapter 5)

Individualism. Belief that people should get ahead on the basis of their own efforts. (Chapter 6)

Informal social interaction. Casual interaction among neighbors or friends. (Chapter 11)

Information environment. The amount of information about politics that is present in the media. (Chapter 8)

Informed. Quality of citizens who hold accurate factual beliefs about politics. (Chapter 8)

Interest groups. Organizations or collections of individuals who attempt to influence governmental decision makers regarding specific issues. (Chapter 1)

Interest in politics. Degree to which people find politics appealing or are curious about politics. (Chapter 8)

Intermediary. Link between citizens and political elites. (Chapter 3)

Internal validity. A characteristic of a study that allows a researcher to conclude that one factor causes another. (Appendix)

Interpersonal trust. The degree to which people think others can be trusted, are fair, and are helpful. (Chapter 11)

Issue salience. Level of public concern for a political issue. (Chapter 12)

Knowledge function. Theory that people have specific attitudes because the attitudes help them to understand the world around them. (Chapter 4)

Leaners. Individuals who describe themselves as partisan independents but who do feel close to one of the political parties. (Chapter 1)

Learning theory. Approach for understanding the development of attitudes whose basic premise is that attitudes are obtained much like habits; that is, people grow to like or dislike attitude objects after repeated exposure to the object. (Chapter 4)

Least liked group. Group whose political views or behaviors a person loathes the most; survey research method for assessing public tolerance of those holding unpopular political views. (Chapter 9)

Legacy media outlets. Media organizations that existed before the Internet. These include broadcast and cable television, print newspapers, radio, magazines, and books. (Chapter 3)

Liberals. People whose political ideology favors government intervention in the economy when necessary to combat features of the free market (such as discrimination and low wages); also, individuals who value equality and openness to dissenting views. (Chapter 5)

Libertarians. People who have a predisposition to favor minimal government involvement in the economy or society; also value diversity and individual freedom. (Chapters 5, 6)

Life cycle effects. Effects that occur when people's political attitudes are strongly influenced by their age rather than, for example, developing only when they are young. (Chapter 2)

Limited information processors. Description of people that emphasizes that humans do not have the cognitive abilities to systematically process complex political information and thus use heuristics. (Chapter 8)

Linked fate. Belief that a person's life chances are tied to the fate of demographic group(s) to which he or she belongs. (Chapter 7)

Longitudinal study/survey. *See* Panel or longitudinal study/survey.

Low-information rationality. The result of citizens using heuristics, such as party identification or cues from trusted groups, to figure out their own political stances. (Chapter 8)

Mainstream effect. The effect that, when political elites agree on an issue, the more politically aware a person is, the more likely he or she will hold the same opinion as the elites. (Chapter 4)

Malevolent leader imagery. Viewing political leaders quite negatively; believing that leaders are not good people. (Chapter 2)

Manipulation. The act of researchers varying access to information, events, or whatever is the focus of the research among the experimental participants. (Appendix)

Marketplace of ideas. Many different political views being available in the public arena. (Chapter 9)

Militarists. People who believe that military leaders rather than elected officials should rule a nation. (Chapter 9)

Millennials. Generation of Americans born after 1980. (Chapter 2)

Minimal effects model. Perspective that views citizens as resistant to media messages because they filter media content through their preexisting attitudes. (Chapter 3)

Misinformed. Quality of citizens who hold inaccurate factual beliefs about politics. (Chapter 8)

Mixed-mode approach. Using more than one method to collect survey data; for example, a researcher could conduct the same survey with some respondents interviewed via phone and other respondents completing the survey on the Internet. (Appendix)

Moral issues. Issues that address matters related to the family or morality, such as pornography, gay marriage, and school prayer. (Chapter 7)

Moral traditionalism. Belief that traditional family and societal organization is best. (Chapter 6)

Multilateralism. Foreign policy goals that emphasize working with other nations and international bodies such as the United Nations. (Chapter 12)

Multiple-choice questions. Questions that provide several possible answers from which a respondent can select. (Chapter 8)

Muslim extremists. Members of the Muslim faith who hold extreme political views, such as advocating terrorism. (Chapter 9)

National mass membership organizations. Organizations that are not community based; individuals participate by paying dues but rarely by working with other citizens to solve problems. (Chapter 11)

National probability sample. Subset of people who have been chosen randomly to accurately represent a larger population; generally used for selecting individuals for opinion polls. (Chapter 2)

Neutrality. A news norm that calls for journalists to not inject their personal opinions into news coverage. (Chapter 3)

News norms. Standards and customs that shape the behavior of journalists. (Chapter 3)

Newsbeats. A news norm that calls for journalists to be assigned to cover specific institutions or topic areas, called beats. (Chapter 3)

Newsworthiness. A news norm that calls for journalists to cover conflict. (Chapter 3)

Nonattitudes. Political opinions that are fleeting, not well considered, or lacking meaning for people who hold them. (Chapter 4)

Normative. Conclusions or statements that focus on how the world should operate; in the realm of democratic theory, views regarding how government and society ought to be structured, including what ought to be the role of the citizenry. (Chapter 1)

Normative threats. Situations in which core values are called into question. (Chapter 6)

Objective measures of economic well-being. Statistics such as the inflation rate or the unemployment rate that indicate the state of the economy. (Chapter 4)

Objectivity. A news norm that calls for journalists to provide both sides of an issue. (Chapter 3)

Official sources. News sources that primarily include government officials but also other powerful people in society. (Chapter 3)

Old-fashioned racism. A set of beliefs about the innate inferiority of black Americans. (Chapter 7)

Open-ended questions. Survey items that allow respondents to answer however they see fit; these items do not present respondents with predetermined response options. (Appendix, Chapter 5)

Operational ideology. Individual's views toward specific public policy issues. (Chapter 5)

Opinion. Expression of a preference toward an object; verbal or written expression of an attitude. (Chapter 1)

Opinion leadership. Act of political elites educating or shaping the attitudes of the citizenry, such as by describing policy proposals and reasons for supporting them. (Chapter 12)

Opinion-policy congruence. Degree to which citizen preferences and governmental decisions are the same. (Chapter 12)

Opinion trends. General direction of aggregate public preferences, such as liberal or conservative swings. (Chapter 12)

Pack journalism. When journalists assigned to the same newsbeats all cover the same stories (and don't cover other stories). (Chapter 3)

Pan-ethnic identity. Identification with a broad ethnic group (such as Latino) regardless of one's country of origin or descent (for example, Mexico or Cuba). (Chapter 7)

Panel or longitudinal study/survey. Assessing the political opinions of the same people at two or more times. (Appendix, Chapter 2)

Participatory democracy. Theory of democracy that emphasizes the importance of political participation by the public and believes the public to be capable of meaningful participation. (Chapter 1)

Partisan independence. Viewing oneself as not identifying with a political party. (Chapter 1)

Partisan motivated reasoning. Processing information so that it conforms with one's preexisting party identification. (Chapter 5)

Partisan news. Media outlets that cover and present the news from a specific political point of view. (Chapter 5)

Partisans. People who identify with a political party. (Chapter 1)

Party identification. Allegiance with or attachment to a political party (typically the Democratic Party or the Republican Party); a self-classification rather than a description of a person's behavior. (Chapters 1, 2, 5)

People and players. A type of political knowledge; knowledge about key people and groups. (Chapter 8)

Perceptions of the state of the economy. Public assessments about economic conditions. (Chapter 4)

Period effect. Change in the political attitudes of many people, regardless of their ages, caused by events or features of the political context. (Chapter 2)

Peripheral route to persuasion. Process by which attitudes can change when a person is not motivated or able to carefully consider persuasive communication; any resulting attitude change is likely to be only temporary. (Chapter 4)

Personality traits. Stable personal characteristics (such as dogmatism, conscientiousness, and empathy). (Chapters 6, 9)

Pluralistic intolerance. The result when the public does not support the free expression rights of many different political groups. (Chapter 9)

Pluralistic roots. Perspective that public opinion is shaped by several factors, not just ideology. (Chapter 6)

Pluralists. Democratic theorists who believe that groups perform an essential role as intermediaries between the public and political elites. (Chapter 1)

Pocketbook issues. Issues that affect people's personal economic circumstances. (Chapter 6)

Polarization effect. The effect that occurs when political elites disagree on an issue; the attitudes of more politically aware citizens will coincide with their existing predispositions, especially when the elite disagreement falls along party or ideological lines. (Chapter 4)

Policy mood. Broad measure of aggregate public opinion; generally captures whether the public feels that the government is too active or not active enough. (Chapter 12)

Policy sentiment. Broad measure of aggregate public opinion; synonym of policy mood. (Chapter 12)

Political awareness. Degree to which people follow political matters closely. (Chapter 4)

Political expertise. Degree to which people are knowledgeable about and interested in political matters. (Chapter 9)

Political generation. An age cohort that has distinctive political attitudes, likely because of the political experiences encountered during their impressionable years. (Chapter 2)

Political knowledge. Facts about politics stored in citizens' long-term memories. (Chapter 8)

Political opinionation. Degree to which people have attitudes on political matters. (Chapter 2)

Political polarization. Divide in the political preferences of the public; commonly understood as opinions clustered at the extremes. (Chapter 5)

Political predispositions. People's existing political orientations, including core values and enduring beliefs. (Chapter 4)

Political reality explanation/model. Perspective that political attitudes are based on real political phenomena; for example, lower levels of trust among blacks are due to the fact that they have less political power than whites. (Chapters 2, 11)

Political socialization. Process by which people learn about politics and develop political opinions. (Chapter 2)

Political structure. Institutional features of a political system. (Chapter 8)

Political times. Features of the broader environment during a particular era that can shape public opinion toward specific issues or people. (Chapter 9)

Political tolerance. Public support for civil liberties, particularly support for the rights of individuals or groups whose views people oppose. (Chapter 9)

Popular sovereignty. Principle that the power in a democratic society ultimately rests with the citizenry. (Chapters 1, 12)

Population. All the elements of interest. (Appendix)

Prejudice. Negative affect that is felt toward a specific societal group. (Chapter 1)

Presidential approval. Public's level of approval or disapproval of the president's job performance. (Chapter 4)

Priming. Effect that occurs when the media or politicians emphasize particular issues or personal characteristics and then citizens rely on those issues or characteristics as they evaluate political leaders. (Chapters 3, 12)

Principles of equality. Abstract beliefs that blacks and whites should be treated equally. (Chapter 10)

Private polls. Opinion surveys that are conducted for political leaders (most notably the president) to assess public opinion. (Chapter 12)

Public attentiveness. Following politics and political news closely. (Chapter 12)

Public judgment. Opinions that result once people have thoroughly considered a political issue and the consequences of their views. (Chapter 1)

Public opinion. The preferences of people toward governmental and policy matters; generally considered as the aggregation of individuals' views. (Chapter 1)

Public opinion poll. A type of research method for assessing political attitudes in which a large sample of citizens (typically randomly selected from the population) are each asked the same list of questions. (Appendix)

Question order effects. Effects that occur when the order of survey questions influences respondents' answers to those questions. (Appendix)

Question wording effects. Effects that occur when the wording of survey questions influences respondents' answers to those questions. (Appendix)

Race-coded policies. Policies that are race-neutral yet have become linked with racial minorities in the minds of white citizens. (Chapter 7)

Race-neutral policies. Policies that affect citizens regardless of race. (Chapter 7)

Race-targeted policies. Policies designed to specifically aid racial minorities, such as affirmative action and the government taking steps to ensure fair treatment in employment. (Chapter 7)

Racial gap in political knowledge. Differences between whites and racial minorities in political knowledge; in general, studies find that whites are more knowledgeable about politics than racial minorities but that the gap disappears for knowledge of issues particularly important to minorities. (Chapter 8)

Racial identity. Belief that a person's fate is tied to the fate of his or her racial group. (Chapter 7)

Racial profiling. Selecting someone for questioning or extra scrutiny on the basis of race or ethnicity. (Chapter 9)

Racial resentment. A form of prejudice that focuses on the moral character of blacks and contends that blacks do not work hard enough and that they take what they have not earned (similar to symbolic racism). (Chapter 7)

Racialization of poverty. Tendency to overrepresent racial minorities, particularly blacks, in images of poor people. (Chapter 7)

Racists. People who believe members of their own race are superior to members of other racial groups. (Chapter 9)

Rally round the flag. Heightened support for the president during time of national crisis. (Chapter 4)

Random assignment. Process of assigning subjects to experimental conditions such that chance alone determines which subject gets which condition. (Appendix)

Random digit dial. A procedure for selecting phone numbers by chance alone. It ensures that all phone numbers are included in the population rather than only those numbers that are available through a phone listing. (Appendix)

Random sample. A sample in which chance alone determines which elements of the population make it into the sample. (Appendix)

Receive-accept-sample model. Framework for understanding political persuasion; whether attitude change results will depend on exposure to and agreement with persuasive communication as well as what considerations are at the top of a person's head at a given point in time. (Chapter 4)

Reception. Stage in the political persuasion process during which people are exposed to, attend to, and understand persuasive communication. (Chapter 4)

Reinforcement effect. Effect that occurs when political communication reinforces people's existing political preferences. (Chapter 3)

Representative democracy. Governmental system whereby citizens elect officials to represent their views and make decisions. (Chapter 1)

Resistance. Processes by which people ensure that persuasive communication does not change their attitudes; also, motivations people hold to withstand attitude change. (Chapter 4)

Response order effects. Effects that occur when the order of response options to a survey question influences respondents' answers to those questions. (Appendix)

Rules of the game. A type of political knowledge; knowledge about the institutions and processes of politics. (Chapter 8)

Sample. A subset of the elements of interest (that is, a subset of the population). (Appendix)

Sampling bias. Selecting cases to study that do not accurately represent the broader population from which they are drawn. (Chapter 12)

Selective exposure. Choosing news outlets based on the political content of the news; more specifically, consuming news that coincides with one's existing political views. (Chapter 5)

Self-interest. A person's narrow, economic interests. (Chapter 6)

Self-perception theory. Approach to understanding attitude formation and change; key premise is that people infer their attitudes from their own behaviors. (Chapter 4)

Shared environment. Experiences and upbringing that are the same between individuals; particularly relevant when examining twins. (Chapter 2)

Short-answer questions. Open-ended questions that require respondents to answer without providing any answer options. (Chapter 8)

Simulated responsiveness. When public policy corresponds with the opinions of the public but only after citizen views have been cultivated by leaders to reflect the policy goals of the leaders; in other words, public policy does not necessarily reflect the genuine wishes of the public. (Chapter 12)

Social adjustment. Theory that people have specific attitudes because the attitudes conform to those of peers in their social network. (Chapter 4)

Social capital. Degree to which people connect with and trust other citizens and engage in civic activities in their communities. (Chapter 11)

Social desirability. Pressure to not express true attitudes that might be perceived as politically incorrect, especially when asked survey questions on sensitive topics, such as race or religion. (Chapter 10)

Social media. Communication technologies and devices that allow for virtual social interaction. (Chapters 3, 11)

Social movements. Citizens organizing and working together to influence politics. (Chapter 6)

Social network. The collection of individuals with whom a person discusses politics regularly. (Chapter 4)

Socialists. People who favor socialism or, more specifically, government or communal ownership of the means of production. (Chapter 9)

Socialization agents. Sources of political learning or political opinions; individuals or institutions that foster learning or development of opinions. (Chapter 2)

Sociotropic concerns. General concerns about society. (Chapter 6)

Soft news. News that has nothing to do with public policy. (Chapter 3)

Soft news media. Media outlets that cover politics in a primarily entertainment-oriented format. (Chapter 3)

Specialist. Someone who has knowledge on some topics but not others. (Chapter 8)

Specific support. Attitudes toward the performance of political leaders and governmental outputs, such as public policies. (Chapter 11)

Status quo bias. The likelihood that public policy will remain the same when the public does not desire a policy change is higher than the likelihood that policy will change when the public desires change. (Chapter 12)

Stereotypes. Beliefs about the characteristics of members of social groups; the beliefs can be positive or negative. (Chapter 1)

Subjects. Participants in an experiment. (Appendix)

Substance of politics. A type of political knowledge about political issues. (Chapter 8)

Subtle effects model. Perspective that views the media as having influence over citizens via agenda setting, priming, and framing. (Chapter 3)

Support for democratic norms. Support for key principles of democratic governance, such as majority rule. (Chapter 9)

Survey. A type of research method for assessing political attitudes in which a large sample of citizens (typically randomly selected from the population) are each asked the same list of questions. (Appendix)

Survey-based experiment. An experiment embedded in a survey whereby subjects are randomly assigned to experimental conditions. (Appendix, Chapter 9)

Survey mode. Method used to collect survey data. Examples include surveys conducted over the phone, via the Internet, through the mail, or face-to-face. (Appendix)

Symbolic ideology. Ideological self-identification (as conservative, moderate, liberal, or something else). (Chapter 5)

Symbolic racism. The belief that blacks do not work hard enough and that black disadvantage cannot be explained by discrimination (similar to racial resentment). (Chapter 7)

Tabloid journalism. A form of journalism that is much less committed, if at all, to news norms. (Chapter 3)

Tea Party movement. Movement that emerged in 2009; loosely connected local groups whose members possess conservative political views and low trust in government. (Chapter 11)

Threat perceptions. Beliefs that a person or a group endangers an individual's personal security, his or her way of life, or the security of the nation. (Chapter 9)

Timebound. Characteristic of a study whereby it only applies to a limited time period. (Chapter 8)

Tolerance curriculum. Educational lessons and activities designed to increase public support for civil liberties, particularly for groups holding unpopular political views. (Chapter 9)

Tracking polls. Survey questions that are asked every day, using a different sample of respondents each day, and for which the results are averaged across a set number of days (usually three). (Chapter 4)

Traditional journalism. A form of journalism that exhibits a strong commitment to news norms. (Chapter 3)

Transfer of affect. Application of emotions held toward one attitude object to a related object, thus influencing attitudes toward the second object. (Chapter 4)

Trust. Degree to which people agree that political leaders are honest and act in the public's interests. (Chapter 2)

Trust in government. A positive evaluation of the government in Washington; particularly having faith in the performance of government and in political leaders. (Chapter 11)

Trust in government scale. Four survey questions used by the American National Election Studies to measure the public's trust in government. (Chapter 11)

Two-step flow of communication. Flow of political information first from the media to attentive citizens, called opinion leaders, and then from these attentive citizens to their friends and family who are not as engaged in politics. (Chapter 3)

Unilateral foreign policies. Governmental actions that feature one nation "going it alone" rather than working together with other nations or international organizations. (Chapter 12)

Uninformed. Quality of citizens who do not hold factual beliefs about politics. (Chapter 8)

Unshared environment. Experiences and upbringing that differ between individuals; particularly relevant when examining twins. (Chapter 2)

USA Patriot Act. National legislation granting certain powers to government officials with the goal of fighting terrorism. (Chapter 9)

Use-of-force issues. Issues that deal with military force or violent acts (such as the death penalty and the use of handguns). (Chapter 7)

Utilitarian function. Theory that people have specific attitudes toward an object because of the benefits provided by or the punishment inflicted by the attitude object. (Chapter 4)

Value-expressive function. Theory that people have specific attitudes because these attitudes allow them to express their core beliefs and values. (Chapter 4)

Value of free expression. Importance of people discussing and debating a wide range of political views in public. (Chapter 9)

Values. Abstract enduring beliefs regarding how the world should work. (Chapters 1, 6)

War casualties. Number of soldiers killed during wartime. (Chapter 4)

Watchdog. The role of the media in scrutinizing and investigating the actions of public officials. (Chapter 3)

Women's issues. Issues that are presumed to be of particular interest to women, such as abortion and the role of women in the workforce. (Chapter 7)

Index